special indexes

Library

DATE DUE		
DEC X X X X	APR 3 0 1980	
X X X X X 73	SEP 1 4 1981	
X XAUG X 9 1973		
X X X X X MAR 1 0 1974		
X X X X X NOV 9 1975		
X DEC X X 1975 X		
DEC 2 X 8 1976 X X X		
AUG X X X 78		
MAR 3 0 1979		
X MAY 1 0 1979		
X X X X 1986 X X X		

AMERICAN
FINANCIAL
INSTITUTIONS

CONTRIBUTING AUTHORS

DOUGLAS H. BELLEMORE · *Chairman, Economics Department, College of Business Administration, Boston University, and Investment Economist, American Institute of Finance*

FRANCIS J. CALKINS · *Professor of Finance, Marquette University*

CARL F. DISTELHORST · *Vice President and Director of Education, American Savings and Loan Institute*

ELVIN F. DONALDSON · *Professor of Finance, Ohio State University*

EDWARD E. EDWARDS · *Professor of Finance, Indiana University*

WALTER B. FRENCH · *Deputy Manager, American Bankers Association*

KERMIT O. HANSON · *Assistant Professor, College of Business Administration, University of Washington*

NORRIS O. JOHNSON · *Assistant Vice President, The National City Bank of New York; formerly Manager, Research Department, Federal Reserve Bank of New York; Treasurer-General, Government of Iran*

DONALD L. KEMMERER · *Professor of Economics, University of Illinois*

F. W. MUELLER, JR. · *Dean, College of Commerce, De Paul University*

J. MARVIN PETERSON · *Director of Research, Federal Reserve Bank of Minneapolis*

LEONARD RALL · *Associate Professor of Economics, Michigan State College*

RAYMOND RODGERS · *Professor of Banking, Graduate School of Business Administration and School of Commerce, Accounts and Finance, New York University*

JOSEPH J. SCHROEDER · *Executive Secretary, Chicago Chapter, American Institute of Banking; Secretary, Association of Reserve City Bankers*

FAYETTE B. SHAW · *Associate Professor of Economics, College of Commerce, De Paul University*

HERBERT SPERO · *Associate Professor of Economics, The City College of New York*

AUDLEY H. F. STEPHAN · *Chairman, Department of Economics, Rutgers University*

HAROLD W. STONIER · *Executive Manager, The American Bankers Association*

JOHN A. STOVEL · *Assistant Professor of Economics, School of Business Administration, University of Minnesota*

NORMAN STRUNK · *Executive Vice President, United States Savings and Loan League, Chicago*

VICTOR V. SWEENEY · *Associate Professor of Insurance, University of Florida*

JAMES B. TRANT · *Dean, College of Commerce, Louisiana State University and Agricultural and Mechanical College*

ARTHUR R. UPGREN · *Professor of Economics, School of Business Administration, University of Minnesota*

ROGER W. VALENTINE · *Halsey, Stuart & Company Inc.*

MERWIN H. WATERMAN · *Professor of Finance, University of Michigan*

EDITOR

Herbert V. Prochnow

AMERICAN
FINANCIAL
INSTITUTIONS

Essay Index Reprint Series

BOOKS FOR LIBRARIES PRESS
FREEPORT, NEW YORK

INTERNATIONAL STANDARD BOOK NUMBER:
0-8369-2017-1

LIBRARY OF CONGRESS CATALOG CARD NUMBER:
76-128290

PRINTED IN THE UNITED STATES OF AMERICA

Preface

A PRACTICAL need has existed for some time for a new integrated study in one volume of the entire American financial structure. Competent and capable studies have been made of individual institutions, but the value of having one book which would present the complete financial organization of the United States has long been apparent. The changes in this field of economic activity in recent years have been far-reaching and important.

It is believed that students of finance, money, banking, investments, and related subjects in our colleges and universities would benefit from a text which would give them an understanding of all the major American financial institutions, their functions, relationship, methods of operation, and the distinct services each one provides in our economy.

It is also felt that bankers, businessmen, industrialists, attorneys, accountants, and others would find in a comprehensive discussion of our financial institutions not only much informative material of value but also the broad perspective needed to understand how the American financial structure is organized and operates.

In view of the highly specialized nature of many types of financial institutions, it seemed especially desirable to ask members of the faculties of a number of universities and others associated in positions of responsibility with financial organizations to undertake the preparation of this study. Students in these fields will recognize in the names of the contributing authors many who have spent years studying the particular financial institutions they discuss. Consequently, it is believed the book describes our financial institutions in a far more competent manner than would be possible if one author or a small number of authors undertook a discussion of all the many types of organizations.

Each contributing author has been encouraged to describe the relationship of the particular financial institution he has discussed to other institutions, with the thought that opposing viewpoints might be not only interesting but also especially informative to the reader.

Each author is necessarily responsible only for the portion of the book he has written.

Extensive additional suggested readings are included in the book so that those who desire to study some of our financial institutions at greater length will be assisted in their work.

The editor invites readers, particularly members of the faculties of colleges and universities, to make suggestions to him and to the contributing authors relative to the material to be included in succeeding editions of the book so that it may reflect the best thinking of an increasing group of students of these institutions.

To the extent that this book provides a better understanding of how our principal financial institutions function and how they serve the entire American economy, it will have accomplished its objective.

HERBERT V. PROCHNOW

Table of Contents

AMERICAN
FINANCIAL
INSTITUTIONS

History of Commercial Banks

by FAYETTE B. SHAW

Associate Professor of Economics, College of Commerce
De Paul University

THE MODERN industrial nation of any importance has a wonderful and almost bewildering array of financial institutions which facilitate the trading of goods and services and the flow of capital. Though some of these were known in ancient and medieval times, most of them have arisen in the era which began with the Industrial Revolution in the latter part of the eighteenth century. The earliest and most important financial institution is the commercial bank; in financing the day-to-day transactions of the business world, it enables all of the other financial institutions to function, and it contributes directly to their activities.[1]

The Function of the Commercial Bank

Though commercial banking becomes very complex as it grows larger, in its fundamental processes it is simple. It could be carried on by a private individual or a partnership; but modern times require that the bank be a corporation with a charter, stockholders, a board of directors, officers appointed by the board, and staff. It receives from the people in the community the money which they do not wish to keep at home or on their persons and holds it for them, promising to pay back what it owes them or to pay to others, on demand. Because the banker knows from experience that not all of his depositors are going to want all of their money at the same time, he can safely lend out a substantial portion of it to those

---

[1] This chapter draws heavily upon two main sources: F. W. Mueller, Jr., *Money and Banking*. New York: McGraw-Hill Book Co., Inc., 1951. C. W. Wright, *Economic History of the United States*. New York: McGraw-Hill Book Co., Inc., 1949.

who can convince him of their financial competence, keeping on hand only sufficient funds to meet day-to-day transactions and a reserve to meet unforeseen demands. Not only does he lend the deposits which the community leaves with him, but he can actually increase the purchasing power in the hands of the population by extending bank credit. He does this by having a borrower sign a note promising to pay a fixed sum at a given time, accompanied by interest at a designated rate. This note becomes an asset on the account books of the bank. The proceeds of the loan may be taken in one or more of three ways. The borrower may take out currency issued by the sovereign government under which he lives. Or, if the bank has the confidence of all, it may issue bank notes which the borrower is willing to receive because he knows that they will be generally accepted in business deals. (A bank note is a promise to pay on demand the sum of legal tender currency stated on the face of the note. Although all banks at one time issued bank notes, this practice has almost completely fallen into disuse for commercial banks, and only the central banks, the Federal Reserve Banks in the United States, may issue bank notes.) The third and most common way in which the loan is handled is by the use of the bank deposit. The banker credits the account of the borrower, a liability account for the bank, and the borrower spends the proceeds by writing one or more checks which the bank honors when they are presented. Into this account the borrower can deposit funds which he receives, to pay them out later, as his needs dictate. The bank can continue to increase bank credit by making loans and crediting deposits, as long as it has reserves which are adequate either in the judgment of the manager or according to the regulations established by the authorities. This bank credit can be decreased as loans are repaid and not renewed, and as new loans are lesser in total amount. Thus do the banks increase and decrease the purchasing power at the command of the business world. It will be seen at once that the bank is a potent force in the distribution of the capital of the community and of the nation, for it can direct funds into what seem to be the most profitable channels and away from the less desirable ones; by the contacts which the officers have in the business world, the bank can exert powerful influences upon that world.

Whereas the chief functions of the banking system are the receipt of deposits and the making of loans, these do not constitute its only activities. Banks effect the transfer of funds from place to place, exchange dollars for the currencies of other countries and vice versa, buy and sell stocks and bonds for their customers, invest surplus bank funds in approved bonds, receive the savings of the community, collect funds for customers, and finance the issuance of new securities. All these activities

center about the furnishing of bank credit and the facilitating of payments.

The Colonial Period and the Confederation to 1789

Commercial banking in the United States began in a crude way during the colonial period of American history.[2] One phase of the excessive issues of bills of credit by colonial governments took the form of notes issued as loans in limited amounts to individuals, bearing 5 per cent interest, repayable over a period of years, and secured by land or other property. This practice began early in the eighteenth century in South Carolina and was soon taken up in succession by other colonies. Here only the loan feature was present. This was not true banking, for the deposit function was absent. But it was a slight beginning.

In the decade from 1730 to 1740, businessmen sought to alleviate the lack of capital by the establishment of land banks. Not many were established, but one of these, the Land Bank of 1740, may be regarded as typical. Under the conditions of its establishment, it was to furnish currency secured by real estate, redeemable in the future in commodities; its capital was to be £150,000 (but in reality the underwriters merely agreed to borrow that much). Each subscriber as a borrower was to furnish a satisfactory mortgage to be paid in twenty annual installments, the payments to be made in manufacturing notes or certain enumerated commodities such as flax, cordage, and bar-iron. The defects in this arrangement were that the notes had no agreement to redeem, the bank actually had no capital, and the mortgage could be paid off entirely in commodities, leaving bills still in circulation. In opposition to this Land Bank was the Silver Bank, whose notes were put in circulation in 1740. This bank was to receive notes on a silver basis, and it was mutually agreed by subscribers to refuse to receive the bills of other governments not redeemable in gold and silver except at a discount to be fixed by the company. The Silver Bank was not to receive the Land Bank bills under any conditions. The Silver Bank's notes were to be issued for fifteen years (due in 1755) and were to be redeemable in silver at designated rates in which the value of silver changed by an equal amount annually. Such were the valuations of the notes of the Land Bank and the Silver Bank that concurrent circulation was impossible. The issues put out by these land banks, of which there were several, were never large in amount, and their existence was short-lived. In 1741, Parliament amended the Bubble Act of 1720 to include colonial schemes. This was clearly *ex post facto* legislation and was an added cause of disaffection

---

[2] Mueller, *op. cit.*, Ch. XII.

between the colonies and the home land. Both of the two mentioned banks went into liquidation amid litigation, the Silver Bank to be terminated much more quickly than the Land Bank. The last entry of the affairs of the Land Bank was made in 1768. However unfortunate this action of Parliament appeared, it is true that the banks of that period represented only large batches of paper money with inadequate security for the note holders and an unsound basis of operation.

With the formation of the United States of America, banking took another step forward. In 1781, when the Continental currency became valueless, Robert Morris organized the Bank of North America (it had been preceded by the Bank of Pennsylvania, a private bank), to help feed the soldiers. The charter was approved by Congress. The stock sold slowly, but incoming specie helped, and when the Government of the Confederation subscribed to $250,000, some wealthy individuals then bought shares. When doubts arose as to the Confederation's right to charter, Morris obtained a charter from the Pennsylvania legislature. But complaints were made that the bank was guilty of favoritism, extortion, and harshness to debtors; and Pennsylvania repealed the charter in 1785. Morris continued to operate without it, however, taking steps meanwhile to obtain a Delaware charter, and in 1787 Pennsylvania rechartered the bank.

This institution rendered important services. It discounted commercial paper. It supplied a circulating medium to replace the depreciated Continental currency, and made loans to the government to provide food and clothing to the troops. It set a good example for successful banking, rendering patriotic service to the government, redeeming notes in specie on demand, and—with minor omissions—paying dividends regularly.

Then in 1784 Massachusetts chartered the Bank of Massachusetts, with no restrictions except that the legislature was given the right to examine its affairs. No mention was made of notes, for the prerogative of bank note issue was taken for granted. In 1792, the legislature added a few restrictions: no notes smaller than five dollars were to be issued; notes and loans were never to total more than double the stock actually paid in; directors were made liable for violations (but dissent or absence would exonerate them); a statement of affairs was to be reported semi-annually to the government (but no form was required); and the bank was prohibited from dealing in its own or other bank shares and in merchandise.

The Bank of New York opened without a charter in 1784 under the sponsorship of Alexander Hamilton. A charter was applied for in 1785 and another in 1789, but both were refused. Finally a charter granted in 1791 provided that debts of the bank should not exceed three times

the capital actually paid in; that the bank should not hold real estate, except what was necessary to conduct business or for security for loans already contracted; and that it could not deal in stocks of any kind, or any kind of merchandise, except that it might sell stocks pledged as collateral for loans. Loans were to run for thirty days only, and no loan was to be repaid by a new note. Payments to the bank were to be made in its own notes or in specie. Overdrafts were not allowed. Gold coins were to be received by weight only. As a result of the state's emission of bills, the bank divided itself into two parts: a specie bank which kept its accounts in dollars, and a paper bank which kept its accounts in pounds sterling. The limitations on the bank, the earliest in the nation, made it unpopular; and the regulation of notes and loans was a conservative measure to guard against expansion. The prohibition against the bank's stock purchases was good, for its own stock provided a cushion for the benefit of its creditors; if the bank bought its own stock, it would ultimately possess no capital. The limitations on real estate purchases were good, but those on the purchase of government securities were of debatable value. It is obvious that the Bank of New York was a specie bank in contrast to the land banks heretofore popular in the colonial period.

The Bank of New York owed its start to Alexander Hamilton, but his interest in banking neither started nor ended with it. As early as 1779, he was writing Robert Morris about a proposed land bank, and in 1780 and 1781, as the Continental currency became more demoralized, his plans took more concrete form. Hamilton's plans, however, were not limited by state lines, and he soon dismissed the idea of the land bank. In 1790, in response to a request by the House of Representatives of the new Congress of the United States, he submitted his report on public credit, commerce, and finance. This report listed the advantages of a national bank: first, it would augment the active or productive capital; second, it would afford greater facility to government in obtaining pecuniary aid, especially in sudden emergencies; third, it would facilitate the payment of taxes. And there were disadvantages: first, it would seem to increase money; second, it would tend to prevent other kinds of lending; third, it would furnish temptation to overtrading; fourth, it would offer aid to ignorant adventurers; fifth, it would give bankrupt and fraudulent traders a fictitious credit; and sixth, it would have a tendency to banish gold and silver from the country. Hamilton then refuted these objections: first, a country without mines must buy its money (gold or silver) with its products; second, it is necessary, therefore, to have an active agriculture, industry, and labor system; third, money aids in the establishment of these; and fourth, therefore, since good industry can evolve with a bank, a bank will insure a sufficient

supply of gold and silver. Out of this report came the first Bank of the United States.[3]

The First Bank of the United States, 1791–1811, and the Aftermath

After much debate, President Washington in 1791 signed the bill creating the first Bank of the United States.[4] It had a capital of $10,000,-000, consisting of 25,000 shares at $400 each, one-quarter to be paid in specie and three-quarters in government bonds bearing 6 per cent. The government's subscription to stock worth $2,000,000 was accomplished by a feat of financial prestidigitation: the government gave to the bank $2,000,000 in bills of exchange on Amsterdam; it then borrowed the bills and gave the bank its note for $2,000,000.

The headquarters of the bank was at Philadelphia, but although branches were not originally planned, several were established from Boston to New Orleans, each to be autonomous. Bank notes were issued, but the total never exceeded $6,000,000. Counterfeiting became prevalent, and the center of this activity was believed to be Winchester, Virginia. The charter did not stipulate that the government was to deposit its funds in the bank, but owing to working arrangements between the bank and the Treasury, government funds on deposit by 1806 amounted to $5,400,000, and the average balance was estimated to be somewhere between $3,500,000 and $4,200,000. The bank claimed that government deposits were unprofitable and paid no interest on them, but its critics maintained that other banks would rejoice in such a monopoly.

In the course of its commercial duties, the bank aided importers, especially in their arrangements for paying import duties. With the organization of the bank, the methods of collecting revenue in the United States changed. Heretofore, collectors had kept the funds, giving bond for faithful performance. In 1800 the bank became the collector, a change that resulted in increased speed and economy in that service. At this time the tariff duties were the chief source of revenue, and any merchant who failed to pay such duties lost all credit at the customs house, was denied further accommodation at the bank, and was refused the privilege of renewing his loans. Opponents of the bank, however, claimed that collections were no better than before.

In other ways, the bank aided private business and the nation, for though state banks increased rapidly in those years, few were so soundly managed as the big bank; its notes, unlike those of most state banks, cir-

---

[3] For further information on these three banks, cf. Mueller, *op. cit.*, Ch. XII.
[4] *Ibid.*

culated freely and were generally acceptable throughout the country, providing a sound currency. More than this, the bank helped to maintain the soundness of all bank currency by presenting the notes of some poorly managed state-chartered banks for prompt redemption, thus embarrassing any bank which failed to honor its notes promptly.

The charter of the bank was to expire in 1811, twenty years from date of issue. In 1808 and in 1810 application for a new charter was duly made to Congress and refused. The issue created strong partisanship. Stockholders were in favor of rechartering, citing the service of the bank to the government. Albert Gallatin, Secretary of the Treasury, likewise was in favor, stressing the transmission and safekeeping of government funds and the economical collection of revenues. Some banks, including the Bank of New York, and many Philadelphia citizens were in favor of rechartering, for they feared losses and prostration of credit and confidence if the bank were not continued. Among the opponents, one of the strongest objections to the bank was the large amount of stock held abroad, even though foreign stockholders had no vote and no voice in the management. There were many who questioned the constitutionality of the chartering of a bank by the federal government. Then there were some who were opposed on the grounds of expediency. The bank had become a government bank, not a merchants' bank. Specie had disappeared and only paper money was in circulation, and there were those who denied that the notes formed a universal exchange medium throughout the country. The utility of the bank in revenue collection was denied, and it was said that the bank was not impartial in granting loans. Not the least important objection was Jefferson's solid opposition on the ground that the monopoly of a single bank was certainly an evil. A temporary extension was refused, a state charter was denied, and the Bank of the United States closed its doors on March 3, 1811, and proceeded to wind up its affairs.

In appraisal, it may be said that the bank was conservative and that it had few competitors. It had a system of permanent loans, a universal practice which was pernicious because of the shortage of loanable funds: permanent loans to the Government cut down its capacity to service merchants. The charge of partiality was not sustained, though there was some evidence that large importers and traders were accommodated while other would-be borrowers who were acceptable to other banks were refused. In the main the bank seems to have furnished accommodation to all reasonable borrowers at reasonable rates and to have helped drive out usurers. And it influenced smaller banks to operate within the limits of conservative practice.

Prior to 1790 there were only three banks in operation: the Bank of North America, the Bank of Massachusetts, and the Bank of New York,

all chartered after 1780. Now banking began to increase rapidly, with eight banks being organized in 1791. In 1801 there were 30 state-chartered banks with total capital of $12,000,000; in 1805, 75 with capital of $30,000,000; and by 1811, 88, with capital totaling about $43,000,000. The largest number of banks was in New England, along the seaboard. By 1811 they were spreading into the West and South. By 1816, the number had increased to 246 with a capital of $125,700,000. These banks were state-chartered, but sometimes the state governments subscribed to the capital stock, hoping to facilitate the handling of government funds and the increase of capital so urgently desired. These banks were liberal in their granting of credit. Their bank notes issued in large quantities to fill the void left by the withdrawal of the notes of the Bank of the United States, increased to the large sum of $110,000,000 by 1816. Loans made by them to the government were meager, and with the lack of a universally accepted paper money such as the Bank of the United States had provided, the problems of fiscal management and war costs were increased. Banking practices were lax. Loans were made on inadequate and improper security, the cash reserves were not sufficient, and the overissue of bank notes resulted in their depreciation: that is, those who accepted payments in bank notes did so only at a discount, lacking confidence in the issuing banks. Merchants had to have bank note "listings" to consult, and as the depreciation of individual issues changed, these were soon out of date. Bank reserves were inadequate, for specie flowed abroad to meet necessary payments, or to New England banks which were soundly managed, thus stripping Western and Southern banks of what little gold they might have had. Then in 1814 the city of Washington was captured by British troops, whereupon the gold standard was suspended and controls over the issue of bank notes were removed. On a gold standard, a person presenting a bank note to the bank for payment in gold as promised on the face of the note is supposed to receive the stated amount in gold coins. In spite of the gold standard existing prior to 1814, however, bank notes circulated at less than their face value because of the difficulty of presenting a note for redemption at the bank of its origin. With the requirement of redeeming notes in gold suspended, the notes depreciated even further. Bank notes were no sounder than the banks issuing them, and most banks were not sound. One result of such a situation is that "good notes" are hoarded, since, if a man owes another a debt, he will pay with the poorer note and keep the higher-quality note for himself. The poorer note is said to be overvalued. Meanwhile the Treasury of the United States was required to accept depreciated notes at par, but it had to make payments in depreciated notes. This double standard increased the cost of

the War of 1812. But these problems were soon to be corrected with the coming of the Second Bank of the United States in 1816.[5]

The Second Bank of the United States, 1816–36

In 1814, a petition from a New York group asked Congress to establish a new bank, and a bill for the purpose was introduced but did not pass. When Dallas became Secretary of the Treasury in 1814, he too favored a bank, but it was not until 1816 that Congress finally acted. In most respects the second Bank of the United States was like the first, except that it was over three times as large: its capital was $35,000,000, of which the United States Government subscribed one-fifth and individuals four-fifths. One-quarter of the stock was to be paid for in specie (gold or silver) and three-quarters in specie or funded debt of the United States. The individual subscriptions could be paid for in installments: 30 per cent on subscribing, 35 per cent in six months, and the remaining 35 per cent in twelve months. The beginning of the bank was scandalous. In spite of the requirement concerning specie, little was actually paid in. In 1816, the bank announced that loans would be made for the exclusive accommodation of stockholders, who put up their stock as collateral of the same value as the loan; they then received bank notes, which they could present for specie to the bank. But this lending on the bank's own stock drained the bank of specie and practically nullified the requirements, though not entirely so; it reached a maximum amount of $11,245,000 in 1818. The headquarters of the bank was to be at Philadelphia, with an office to be opened in Washington when Congress should require it, and other offices to be opened in any state in which 2,000 shares had been subscribed, upon application of the legislature or of Congress. By 1817, nineteen branches had been opened, and by 1831, eight more. Of all the banks, the Baltimore branch was the worst offender against sound banking. The home office in Philadelphia had loans outstanding of $10,800,000; at the same time the total at the Baltimore bank, owing to the speculation of its officers, stood at $9,200,000. As if this were not enough, the Baltimore office was defrauded of $1,600,000 by its president and cashier. In 1818 this office failed.

However, from 1819 to 1823 Langdon Cheves was president of the Bank of the United States, to be followed by Nicholas Biddle from 1823 to the end of his life. Under Cheves, the loans were decreased, and note circulation was cut in half; better control of the branches introduced sound business methods. Biddle continued the good work, seeking to make the bank's notes a truly national currency by increasing their amount in a proper way, and by holding the state banks to strict ac-

5 Mueller, op. cit., Ch. XII; Wright, op. cit., pp. 367-370.

countability for their notes. The Bank of the United States would receive the notes of state banks in payments made to it, but would pay
out only its own notes. Then when it had a certain amount of notes
issued by a state bank, it would present them for payment, as a bank
note is a promise to pay legal tender currency or specie. To maintain its
standing, the state bank would make every effort to redeem its notes.
Thus the standard of banking practice was raised. This helped to check
excessive issues of state bank notes, and the circulating medium of the
nation was markedly improved, though not all bank notes could be
kept at par without depreciation, and even the notes of a branch of the
Bank of the United States remote from Philadelphia sometimes were
slightly depreciated, but never by more than 1 per cent. After 1826,
Biddle began to extend the dealings in foreign and domestic exchange.
Just as a person may have an account in a bank from which he can
take funds as he needs and to which he can add funds he receives, so
can a bank have an account in another bank to which it can add funds
and from which it can make payments. If a person wishes to make a payment in a distant part of the country, he can ask his bank to write a
cashier's check on its account in the distant area, and he can send this
check to the creditor. This cashier's check is known as a domestic bill
of exchange. If, however, the bank has an account in a foreign bank,
this account will be expressed in terms of the currency of the nation
in which the foreign bank is located—if in London, for example, in
pounds, shillings, and pence. Then if an American wishes to make a
payment in England, he presents dollars to his bank and asks the cashier
to write a cashier's check on the London bank for the equivalent in
English currency. He then uses this cashier's check to make his payment.
This is called a foreign bill of exchange, foreign exchange, or in this case,
a bill on London or sterling exchange. Thus is trade facilitated between
different parts of a nation and between one nation and another, and thus
did Biddle extend the services of the big bank to its customers.

Further, the bank came to be the holder of most of the specie reserves
of the country. As the state banks kept relatively little reserve, they
tended to fall back on the big bank in time of need. In time of stringency,
the bank could extend loans to state banks. Such loans were successful in
1825, but not so in 1828 and 1831–32, when the bank was itself too
heavily involved in excessive loans in the South and West. But there
much of its business was done, there was the most extravagant banking
done, and there was the greatest control of state banks exercised by the
Bank of the United States. In New England, banking was fairly sound,
and it was much improved in the Middle Atlantic states. Elsewhere the
standards were low, though not as low as they would have been without
the controlling influence of the big bank.

The charter of the second Bank of the United States was to expire in 1836, and renewal became a matter of moment in 1829 when Jackson expressed doubts about its constitutionality and its success in establishing a sound currency. In the ensuing years, the "Bank War" involved much that was irrelevant and exaggerated. The bank became a political football when Henry Clay made it the issue in the election of 1832. With Clay's defeat, Jackson, whose hatred of the bank had become violent, vetoed the bill which Congress passed in 1832, and Biddle accepted the defeat as final. The government began to deposit its funds in selected state banks, and the Bank of the United States began to wind up its affairs. In some states, state charters were taken out to continue branches in business, and Pennsylvania issued a charter for the Philadelphia bank. The sum of $2,000,000 in cash was paid, and $100,000 per year for twenty years was promised for the franchise. New stock was sold, and the old stockholders were paid off, with the government receiving $115.58 per share. The capital, which remained at $35,000,000, was too large to be profitably employed, but the new bank subscribed to the stocks of railroads, canals, and turnpikes, until by March 1836 it had $20,000,000 invested in such stocks. This investment continued, and the bank became a leading speculator in the panic of 1837. Becoming too involved, it suspended specie payments in 1837, 1838, and 1841, the last being its final year, after which it went into liquidation, a process lasting fifteen years. The creditors were paid in full, the shareholders lost everything, and Biddle went bankrupt, a penniless and broken man. He died in 1844.

The Inter-Bank Period, 1836–63: Conditions and Regional Reforms

The period from 1836, when the charter of the second Bank of the United States expired, to 1863, when Congress passed the first of many acts which defined the National Banking System, is often called the inter-bank period.[6] With the removal of the restraints of the second Bank of the United States on a national basis, and with state laws lax and banking practices commonly more lax, this period was characterized by excessive issues of bank notes, inadequate reserves, flagrant abuses in the making and repayment of loans, evasion of what laws were passed to safeguard banking, and frequent failures. It was called a period of "wildcat banking" because many banks were located in backwoods regions where wildcats lived; such locations made it difficult for noteholders to present their notes for redemption in specie, and if anyone had so ventured, he probably would have found only an empty shack, for many banks were truly "wildcat" in nature. But this period witnessed also the

[6] Mueller, *op. cit.*, Ch. XIII.

beginnings of sound commercial banking practices both on a limited regional basis and in the case of individual banks, as well as the beginnings of adequate legislative regulation.

One of the earliest attempts to improve the quality of bank notes, the Suffolk plan, which followed the system introduced by the New England Bank in 1814,[7] was made in New England. Country banks needing funds on short notice used to come to Boston to make loans at reduced rates payable at three to five days' notice. The notes of Boston banks circulated at par, but those of country banks were at a discount of from 1 to 5 per cent because of the expense of shipping them back to their respective origins and because of doubts about their redeemability. This discount had an effect which plagued the Boston banks. According to Gresham's Law, bad money drives out good, and here the law was working out. The Boston banks, trying to make profits by lending their notes, found their notes repeatedly presented for redemption while people used the depreciated bank currency in payment of bills. So the Suffolk plan was adopted. Each country bank was required to make a $2,000 interest-free deposit in the Suffolk Bank in Boston, if the capital of the country bank was $100,000 or less, and a greater deposit if the capital was more. Then when a country bank's notes were presented, the Suffolk Bank would redeem them, and the country bank had to keep its deposit in the Suffolk sufficiently above the permanent deposit to meet note redemptions. The notes were then packaged to await instructions. Any New England bank in good standing which made appropriate arrangements with the Suffolk Bank could enjoy this service. The Suffolk Bank (founded in 1818) had adopted the policy of sending country bank notes which it received in payment to the issuing banks for redemption, and failure to redeem could mean failure of the bank. Other Boston banks joined in the practice. But the maintenance of country banks' deposits in the Suffolk centralized and simplified this process and made it possible for all banks' notes to circulate at par value. This plan, begun in 1825, was recognized by law in 1845, when Massachusetts passed a law which forbade any bank to pay out any notes but its own. This law compelled banks to send country notes to the Suffolk. By 1857, five hundred banks were embraced in the system, and the Suffolk Bank in reality controlled the New England currency until the advent of the National Banking System in 1863. Thus good banking came to New England.

The next important step in the attempts to safeguard the currency came in New York State.[8] The Bank Recharter Act of 1829 contained the "bank fund" principle. Each bank chartered or rechartered was to pay into the fund an amount equal to 1 per cent of its capital each year until

---

[7] Mueller, *op. cit.*, Ch. XIII.
[8] *Ibid.*

3 per cent had been paid in. This fund was to be applied to bank debts (not including capital) of failed banks, but the fund was not to be used until the assets of the failed bank had been exhausted and the deficiency established which the fund was to pay. When the fund was so reduced, the comptroller was to call on banks for new contributions at the old rate. All went well until 1837, when three Buffalo banks failed. The act of 1837 was passed to pay immediately the notes of failed banks; its purpose was to prevent depreciation. In 1840 eleven banks failed, and the first three in the order of failure exhausted the fund. The bank commissioner said that the law provided for the payment of all creditors, which would include depositors as well as noteholders, but the law of 1842 amended the original to provide that noteholders had an original and prior lien on the assets. The charges against the fund prior to 1842 were sufficient to absorb all contributions for years to come, and it was not until 1866 that the last charter of the safety fund banks expired. In that year, after the last contribution had been made by the banks, there remained a surplus of $88,048, and claims had been paid to creditors of banks failing prior to 1842. It was proposed to pay notes of banks failing since 1842, but only a few were presented, since most notes had been lost or destroyed in the belief that they were worthless. The fund was finally wound up when $13,144.19 was paid into the state treasury. This was the first of several attempts by states to introduce the principle of insurance into banking, but all of them failed; it was not until the 1930's that the insurance of bank deposits on a national scale was tried by the federal government. By that time the safety of bank notes had been assured, and as their importance declined, deposits became the chief form of bank credit.

The "bank fund" was an experiment that failed, though it did reimburse the holders of notes of some banks. The free-banking system was an innovation which was successful, at least in part.[9] Up until this time, banking was a monopoly, and each bank required a charter passed by the state legislature. Favoritism and wire-pulling were inevitable, and the group with the most political pull won out in a controversy. In 1838, New York passed the Free Banking Law of 1838 which gave adequate protection to noteholders. In those days the debts of the United States and of the states were commonly referred to as "stocks," but the word did not convey the same meaning as that of stocks of corporations today. Under the Free Banking Law of 1838, in order to issue notes, the bank was required to deposit with the comptroller of New York "stocks" of the United States, of the State of New York, and/or of any other state approved by the comptroller, and/or bonds and mortgages on improved, productive, and unencumbered real estate on which the value of the

---

[9] Mueller, op. cit., Ch. XIII.

property must be double the amount of the mortgage, with interest at 6 per cent. Notes could then be issued in the amount of the deposited securities, but the notes were to specify whether they were secured by stocks or bonds. In case of default in redemption of notes, the securities were to be sold and the proceeds paid to the noteholders. The state was in no way responsible for the notes, except in the administration of the deposited securities. A special charter was no longer required. Any group conforming to the general requirements of the law could organize a bank: this was what was meant by calling the law the Free Banking Act. This Act stimulated incorporation, and by the end of 1839, 133 new banks had been organized, of which 76 were actually started. But the mortality was high. From 1839 to 1850, 32 banks failed with a circulation of $1,468,243, of which the notes were redeemed at rates varying from par to 30 cents on the dollar, with aggregate losses of $325,487. From 1851 to 1861, there were 25 failures with a circulation of $1,648,000 and losses of only $72,849. The diminished loss indicates increasing perfection of the system. It was discovered that bonds and mortgages were not "quick" collateral. That is, they could not be readily sold at par and sometimes had to be sold at less than par. Further, the "stocks" of some of the states suffered depreciation and proved faulty as security. From these defects stemmed the losses incurred. Accordingly the legislature provided that the securities accepted by the comptroller were to be limited to those of the United States and of the State of New York.

The constitution of 1846 contained significant provisions. It made noteholders preferred creditors. Both noteholders and depositors were creditors of the bank. The depositor usually lived in the same town and was presumed to know the condition and reputation of the bank. The noteholder, however, did not necessarily have such acquaintanceship, as notes often circulated far from home. Hence the provision to make noteholders preferred creditors protected the noteholders. Another clause made stockholders liable for debts of the bank to an amount equal to their shares. This provision was double liability. Not only could a stockholder lose his investment in the stock of the bank, but he could be assessed an amount equal to the par value of the stock if necessary to pay off the creditors. It is obvious that this could work serious hardship on stockholders. Another clause provided that no special charter for banking should be granted or extended. Thus the constitution of 1846 embodied the free banking principle already enunciated in the act of 1838.

Other legislative changes in 1842 provided that all country banks redeem their notes in New York City or Albany at not more than one-half of 1 per cent discount, but as this did not prove entirely satisfactory, it was provided in 1844 that no one was to transact business except at the place of his actual residence. This too was not wholly satisfactory. In

sum, it may be said that the two great contributions to banking made by New York were the general incorporation law which removed the monopoly from banking, and the bond deposit system. By 1860, sixteen states had adopted the plan of requiring the deposit of bonds at the state capital as security for notes, though the poor credit of many states nullified the benefits many times. Nevertheless, the principle was adopted when the National Banking System was brought into existence.

This does not exhaust by any means the catalogue of defects and abuses in financial management, but it does indicate some major problems. Among other abuses was the one in which a subscriber to bank stock might borrow perhaps the full amount required to pay for his stock; and as the charter usually required some specie to be paid in, this specie was often borrowed temporarily for the purpose. It is evident that some banks began business practically without capital. Then too, loans were made on real estate; such loans have the disadvantage that deposits must be paid on demand and notes redeemed on demand, whereas real estate and real estate mortgages are unliquid, not easily sold, and sometimes nonsalable. Loans on real estate are not to be deplored if not excessive; but in this period, all banking abuses were likely to be excessive if indulged in at all. The same may be said of loans on securities. Especially dangerous was the common practice of lending on the bank's own stock. The banks' investing of funds in stocks of companies could be carried to excess, especially in those days when securities markets scarcely existed or were of recent development. To the disadvantage of sound banking, merchandise loans often prompted speculation to excess. And state ownership of stock, in whole or in part, sometimes led to the financing of unsound state projects. Slowly laws were passed to control these practices.

Among the notable banks of the inter-bank period was the State Bank of Indiana established in 1834, started after the veto of the bill to recharter the second Bank of the United States. One-half of the stock was to be owned by individuals, the other half by the state; and its capital was to be $1,600,000, all paid in specie—mostly Mexican and Spanish dollars. After the individual subscribers had advanced $37\frac{1}{2}$ per cent of their subscription, the state advanced the other $62\frac{1}{2}$ per cent, floating "bank bonds" in New York for this purpose. The home office was in Indianapolis, and there were ten branches, each of which was liable for the debts of the others. No branch could lend on the security of bank stock. Each branch had to receive notes of any other branch at par. The total for the system reached its maximum ($4,000,000) in 1851. The sagacity and fidelity of the State Bank of Indiana's management made this institution outstanding. The president himself usually made the semiannual inspection of the branches at odd times and with thoroughness. When the charter expired in 1859, the State of Indiana realized

a profit of $3,500,000, and shareholders received $153.70 per share. During liquidation, a bill to charter the Bank of the State of Indiana was passed to succeed the old bank. The state had no share in this institution, which continued until 1865, when the tax of 10 per cent on bank notes curtailed its operations, and it liquidated.[10]

Another outstanding institution was the Wisconsin Marine and Fire Insurance Company founded by a Scotsman by the name of George Smith in 1839.[11] The Wisconsin legislature granted him a charter providing for business of marine, fire, and life insurance only, and specifically excluding "banking privileges." "Banking privileges" then meant the issuance of notes, for the custom of having deposits had scarcely begun in the West. However, the charter did grant the right to "receive money on deposit and loan same." Nevertheless, Smith began to issue certificates of deposit very similar to bank notes, payable to bearer as "George Smith money." At first he redeemed in specie only at Milwaukee, but later he established six paying agencies, one as far east as New York and one as far south as St. Louis. Smith was "wildcatting" in such a barefaced manner that the legislature undertook an investigation, during which it was recommended that the charter be repealed. But Smith claimed the question to be a judicial problem, not a legislative one, and nothing more was done. He provided amazing elasticity of bank notes. There was no limit to his issues, since he alone was the sole judge. He lent largely on transactions in grain on time loans. Then he substituted his demand notes for time notes, and when time notes were paid, he redeemed his demand notes. In 1853, under the Wisconsin "free bank act" Smith disposed of his interest and the bank became a "free" bank under new management. In spite of the "wildcat" nature of his operations, he remained solvent, and he seems to have supplied badly needed banking capital in the West.

A serious and successful effort to bring order and soundness to chaotic conditions is found in the Louisiana Bank Act of 1842,[12] which was strictly enforced until 20 years later when the Civil War overwhelmed the nation. This was the first law requiring a definite proportional specie reserve against deposits. This reserve was to equal one-third of all liabilities due the public. The other two-thirds was to be made up of commercial paper (loans based upon short-term transactions) having not more than 90 days to run to maturity. All commercial paper was to be paid at maturity; if the borrower should default on his loan, his accounts were closed, and his name was sent to all other banks as a delinquent. All banks were to be examined quarterly or more often, and bank direc-

---

[10] Mueller, op. cit., Ch. XIII.
[11] Ibid.
[12] Ibid.

tors were to be made individually liable for loans made in violation of the law unless they voted against the illegal procedure. No bank was to have less than 50 shareholders, each to own at least 30 shares. If a director left the state for more than 30 days or failed to attend five successive meetings of the board of directors, he was to resign and the vacancy was to be filled immediately. No bank was to pay out any notes but its own, and all banks were required to pay balances to each other in specie every Saturday or be liquidated. Such strictness assured sound banking of a high order and was as an oasis in the desert.

With the passing of the second Bank of the United States, the federal government again had the problem of managing its own receipts and disbursements, and it turned to the privately owned state-chartered banks. In 1836, the requirements were passed which guided officials in the selection of banks as government depositories. There was to be not less than one in each state and territory. These banks were required to redeem their own notes properly, and banks which could not pay specie were to be dropped from the list. All banks had to make regular statements of condition. In consequence, depositories increased steadily in number. Political influence was so strong that the Secretary of the Treasury had a hard time following the law, for more money was sometimes left on deposit in some banks than the law permitted, while there was delay often in honoring drafts. Violations of the law were known, as when a bank issued notes for less than five dollars, contrary to the laws and regulations. Meanwhile the nation was experiencing an inflation, with speculation rampant and signs of apparent prosperity: increased imports, higher prices owing largely to note issues, and increased sale of public lands. Meanwhile, to make the situation all the worse, the Treasury had a surplus deposited in state banks. Then in 1836 a Specie Circular was issued which required that public lands be paid for in gold and silver. This pricked the bubble of inflation, for specie was nearly impossible to obtain in the scramble for it. Congress had to meet, for government officials could receive and pay out the notes of specie paying banks only, and since no banks were paying specie on demand, the fiscal machinery of the government stopped. Congress considered three relief plans: the revival of a national bank, the continuation of the system of 1836 (that of the use of state banks), and the keeping of money by public officials. Up until 1840 money was kept by both the public officials and the banks.[13]

The Independent Treasury System

In 1840, the Independent Treasury was established, with the intention of having all funds due the government paid in specie eventually by

---

[13] Mueller, *op. cit.*, Ch. XIII.

the beginning of the fifth year thereafter. However, this proved unsatisfactory, and in 1841 the law was repealed. Later, President Polk in a message to Congress urged the re-establishment of the Independent Treasury, and discussion was renewed. Proponents argued that the union of government and banks was unconstitutional, for the Constitution says that "no money shall be drawn from the Treasury but in consequence of appropriations made by law." The first Congress had decreed that "it shall be the duty of the Treasurer to receive and keep the moneys of the United States," which meant a "substantive" Treasury and a "real" Treasurer. The whole argument was one of states' rights. In favor of the banks were the arguments that by them the government could have safer keeping and freer transmission of funds, easier and more inexpensive collection of revenues, greater facility of obtaining loans, and interest on government deposits. In 1846 the law was passed, and the Independent Treasury again came into existence to stay until the Federal Reserve System took over the handling of the funds.

The Independent Treasury may have solved the problem of taking care of government funds safely, but it was far from satisfactory in its influence upon the banking system. When payments were being made into the Treasury, this involved the withdrawal of gold from circulation and from the bank reserves, which in turn influenced business and the price level by tending to depress prices. The disbursements of funds had the opposite effect. Receipt and disbursement took place at irregular intervals which had no relation to the needs of business. Accordingly the operations of the Treasury sometimes disturbed the money market and business generally. Only from 1846 to 1863 did the government keep its own money exclusively in its own vaults. After 1863, when the National Banking System was established with improvements in banking, the successive Secretaries of the Treasury and Congress gradually abandoned the "divorce of Bank and State." The Secretary was allowed to deposit funds in selected national banks; this kept the money in circulation and prevented the government's hoarding of funds that reduced bank reserves, circulation, and prices, and subsequent disbursements that increased them. This move gave a great deal of power to one man who, if he used bad judgment, could make matters worse than before, and whose interference, high-minded and well planned as it might be, was bound to be arbitrary.[14] Nevertheless it was not until the Federal Reserve System was established that this particular phase of fiscal problems was settled.

---

[14] Mueller, *op. cit.*, Ch. XIII.

The National Banking System

The year 1863 saw the beginnings of the National Banking System.[15] One of its origins lay in the unhappy state of the finances of the Union Government during the Civil War. Secretary of the Treasury Chase was going to follow the example of his predecessor in office, Gallatin, in the War of 1812, of financing the war costs on borrowed funds and increasing taxes only to cover the increased cost of the interest on the debt. It is not necessary to discuss here the government's fiscal problems during the war, except to show how they were related to the banks. In this connection, Congress passed a revenue act in 1862 intended to raise money by taxation, but this failed substantially. Then it was planned to issue $150,000,000 worth of 7.3 per cent bonds, which the banks proposed to sell to the public. This failed too, and while the public subscribed to a portion of the issue, the banks had to assume most of it and carry the bonds as investments in their portfolios. Here was a serious problem. Chase wanted the banks to pay the Treasury in specie, which he could then hoard, paying out small denomination demand notes where he could. The banks protested and refused to redeem these demand notes in specie or their own notes. Then the Trent affair (concerning the Confederate emissaries Mason and Slidell) shook public confidence, specie paid out by the Treasury in payment of bills went into hoarding, the stock market crashed, gold was drained out of the United States as payment for imports, and on December 30, 1861, New York banks suspended specie payments, to be followed by Philadelphia and Boston concurrently. To suspend specie payments means that when a person holding a bank note asks the bank to redeem it in gold as required, the bank refuses; and when this became general, it meant that the nation was no longer on a specie standard, but on a paper money standard.

When suspension occurred, the condition of the currency throughout the nation varied widely. In New York, the regulations of the "free banking" system were rigidly enforced and notes were received in payment beyond the locality of issue. In Massachusetts the bank note circulation was in good condition because of the successful operation of the Suffolk System which kept notes at par. But in the West the situation was chaotic. There was a mixture of both good and bad notes—mostly bad. Notes on banks in other states were accepted only at discounts; these discounts varied so that only a professional money changer or "note broker" could tell good from bad. The federal government avoided losses by refusing to accept paper of any kind. The laws of all the states, each legis-

---

[15] On the National Banking System, cf. Mueller, *op. cit.*, Ch. XIV and Wright, *op. cit.*, pp. 444-445, 671-676.

lating for its own banks, were not uniform, and within each state the quality of the banks varied. Variations in the totals of circulation were due to occasional suppression acts by individual states; failures in years of depression, which operated to reduce the number of banks; and the price situation, which induced new emissions or reduced those outstanding. If this were not enough, the number and variety of banks and their outstanding note issues made counterfeiting rife.

In 1861, Secretary Chase suggested the preparation of bank notes under federal direction to be delivered to banks and to be secured by the pledge of United States bonds. This was the essential feature of the bond-deposit requirement of New York State. Chase claimed the advantages of uniformity of currency, uniformity of security behind the notes, a safeguard against depreciation of notes, protection from exchange charges, and a large demand for government securities. Thus Chase thought to accomplish two purposes: the improvement of the currency and the sale of government bonds to raise money in time of the great war then beginning. However, it was not until 1863 that the first act was passed. Hugh McCulloch came from Indiana to be the first Comptroller of the Currency. So many amendments were suggested that a complete revision was made which resulted in the act of 1864.

The National Banking Act of 1864 took particular pains to remedy the evils of unsound note issues, the plague of banking. It provided first for federal incorporation of the banks. In cities of not over 6,000 in population, the minimum capital allowed was $50,000, in cities of 50,000 or less, $100,000, and in cities of more than 50,000, $200,000. Shares were to be of the par value of $100, and double liability was imposed on stockholders—that is, stockholders were made liable for the debts of the bank to the amount they had invested and to the amount of their stock to the par value thereof if necessary to liquidate the debts. There was provision also for the building up of surplus until it equaled not less than 20 per cent of the capital. An amendment in 1900 provided that in cities of not more than 3,000, the minimum capital might be $25,000. This was to encourage banking in smaller communities, with the safeguards of the system.

Then the act provided that the bank must deposit with the Treasurer of the United States registered bonds in the amount of not less than $30,000, or one-third of the capital stock; and if the capital of the bank were increased, so must be the bonds increased, always to be at least one-third of the capital. After delivery of the bonds the banking association was to be allowed to receive notes equal to 90 per cent of the current market value of the bonds, but not to exceed 90 per cent of the par value. At no time was the note issue to exceed the amount of capital actually paid in. Congress fixed the maximum total of notes to be issued

by the system at $300,000,000, to be issued in denominations of 1, 2, 3, 5, 10, 20, 50, 100, 500, and 1,000 dollars. Not more than one-sixth of the notes furnished any bank should be in denominations of less than five dollars, and then only until gold redemption was resumed; after the gold redemption no notes were to be issued for less than five dollars. It was further provided that notes were to be received at par in all parts of the United States for taxes, excises, public lands, and other dues to the United States except import duties, and were to be payable by the United States for all debts except interest on the public debt and in redemption of the national currency. The bonds were to be held exclusively as security for the notes, and if their value fell in the market below the limit required to support the circulation, the Comptroller could require the deficiency to be made up. The notes could not be used to procure money to be paid in for capital stock; thus the National Banking Act of 1864 prohibited a once common abuse by which wildcat banks had started practically without paid-in capital. Nor could the notes be used to increase the capital stock. A bank could not pay out for loans, discounts, bills, or for deposits the notes of any bank which were not at such time receivable by the paying bank at par. Nor should one bank knowingly pay out the notes of any other bank which was not at the time redeeming its notes in United States lawful money.

In lieu of other taxes to the United States, a bank should pay the government 1 per cent on its average circulation, one-half of 1 per cent on its average deposits, and one-half of 1 per cent on its capital beyond the amount invested in government bonds. It was further provided that when a bank refused or was unable to redeem its notes in lawful money, the Comptroller of the Currency, who was and is the head of the National Banking System, was to appoint a special agent to take charge. The securities were to be forfeited and to be cancelled by the Treasury at current market prices, while holders of notes were to present them to the Treasury for payment. The United States was to have a prior lien upon all the assets of the failed bank to pay any deficiency not covered by the bonds for the notes paid.

In 1866, the law was amended twice to provide that any national bank or any state bank paying out notes of a state bank after July 1, 1866, should pay a tax of 10 per cent thereon, and that any person using the notes of state banks should likewise pay a tax of 10 per cent, effective August 1, 1866. This effectively taxed away the profits to be realized in the lending of bank notes and resulted in the disappearance of state bank notes from the circulation. Then in 1870, Congress raised the maximum amount of national bank notes from $300,000,000 to $354,000,000; in 1875 this limitation was repealed, and no other limit on the total was set. In 1900 another amendment provided for a note issue equal to the par

value of the bonds deposited and for the limited issue of notes of less than five-dollar denomination. In 1874 the Treasury was made the sole redeeming agency for the bank notes, and a fund of 5 per cent of the amount issued was to be kept with the Treasury for redemption thereof.

But depositors also came in for some protection. Three classes were distinguished. Central reserve cities were New York, later Chicago, and for a while, St. Louis. Banks in these cities had to keep a reserve of 25 per cent against their deposits. This reserve was to be made up of "lawful money" and was to be kept in each bank's own vaults, except for the redemption fund in Washington, which might be counted as a part of the 25 per cent. Banks in reserve cities, which eventually included about two dozen other large cities, were to keep a reserve of 25 per cent against deposits, but half of this might be kept on deposit in banks in central reserve cities. All others came into the category of country banks which were to keep a reserve against deposits of 15 per cent, of which three-fifths could be on deposit in either class of reserve cities. These requirements for reserves became more important because, as time passed, there was marked growth in the making of loans in the form of deposit credit, while loans by means of bank notes declined. This arrangement of deposits is known as pyramiding, and it had its dangers. New York City was the focal point of the system, and this city was always subject to withdrawal of funds by out-of-town banks. The danger of sudden and heavy withdrawals compelled the New York banks (which paid interest on out-of-town deposits) to keep a large proportion of liquid assets. New York banks had no other resources to which they might turn. Accordingly they invested in the call loan market, in which loans were made on stock market collateral, subject to repayment on demand of the lenders. Thus were reserves concentrated in New York, a convenient practice most of the time, but dangerous in times of stress in the money market.

Congress also laid down limitations on lending policies. No bank could loan more than 10 per cent of its capital to any one borrower. No bank could be indebted at any time for an amount exceeding its capital stock except for its bank notes, its deposits, liability for bills of exchange drawn against money actually deposited, and liability to stockholders for dividends and reserved profits. Loans on real estate were forbidden, but under certain circumstances the banks were allowed to hold such property. A bank might own real estate in which to carry on its business. It could make no loan with real estate as security, but it could take over property mortgaged in good faith by way of necessity for debts previously contracted; that real estate conveyed to it in satisfaction of debts previously contracted in the course of its dealings, and that purchased under judgment to secure debts owed to the bank was acceptable. No

other real estate might be owned; real estate acquired as a result of the loaning process was not to be held longer than five years. Unhappy experience had shown that real estate loans were unliquid in the face of depositors' insistent withdrawals, since real estate cannot be sold readily. The purpose of these restrictions was to keep the bank in the commercial banking business—that is, making loans and discounts, receiving deposits, and handling other related transactions—and to prevent it from becoming a non-banking business of any sort. To remedy an old abuse of wildcat days, no bank was allowed to make a loan on its own capital stock.

To remedy the defects of the independent treasury and to interweave the fiscal policies of government and business, the Secretary of the Treasury could designate selected national banks as depositories of public funds, except customs receipts, and use them as agents of the government. The Treasury might require United States bonds as a guaranty of faithful performances, and every such depository was to receive at par the notes of all banking associations incorporated under the act. Finally, among the provisions which activated the system were those which enabled state banks to become national banks. Last but not least in this enumeration, the Comptroller of the Currency could compel the banks to make reports in the form prescribed, and publication of the reports was provided for that the public might know of the banks' condition.

It was hoped that most state banks would choose to become national banks, and at first this hope was nearly realized. By 1865, there were over 1,500 national banks, a number almost equal to the number of state banks in 1860; and by 1868, there were only about 250 state banks in the nation. The national banks thus were early established in a dominating position. After 1865 there was fairly steady growth, until in 1900 there were 3,700 banks, and in 1914, 7,500. But a significant change was in the making. The bank notes increased at first, then decreased, then increased again; when the amendment of 1900 was passed (which sought to make the issuance of notes more profitable), the total bank notes increased further. Yet a much greater increase took place in the loans and discounts and deposits, reflecting the increasing importance of bank deposits and the declining relative importance of bank notes. The chief defect of the national bank notes lay in their inelasticity.[16] It is desirable to have the purchasing power ebb and flow with the changes in business. National bank notes did not do this. The change in their amount was due to the changes in the prices of government bonds which were deposited at Washington for security. High bond prices encouraged the sale of bonds to enjoy the profits thereon, while low bond prices had the opposite effect; if the needs of business corresponded, it was largely accidental. But as businesses and individuals became accustomed to the use of the

---

[16] Wright, op. cit., pp. 674-676.

deposit account with the accompanying check book, this form of bank credit took the ascendancy, and the bank note became less important. The banking legislation of the administration of President Franklin D. Roosevelt included provisions that meant the eventual retirement of all national bank notes, for the Federal Reserve notes took the place of bank notes and deposits became the most important of all media.

The state banks meanwhile, which were approaching extinction in 1868, took a new lease on life and grew in numbers; by 1893, the state commercial banks outnumbered the national banks, though their resources were much smaller, and their number continued to exceed that of the national banks. As bank notes became less important, there were three chief reasons why many bankers could still prefer state charters. One was the greater freedom of choice which state banks were allowed in making loans, especially the right to make loans on real estate, which was obviously important in rural areas. Another was the lower reserve requirements permitted by state laws, especially against time and savings deposits. And a third was that among state institutions there developed a specialization of functions that led to three important kinds of banking: the commercial bank, the trust company, and the savings bank which might be either stock or mutual. There were no sharp dividing lines which set off one against the others, for commercial banks and trust companies often performed the same services, and commercial banks usually had savings departments. Perhaps the savings bank was the most clearly defined of all.[17]

Nor did the use of the national banks necessarily mean safety for the depositors. It came to be acknowledged that bank notes were entirely safe, since they were redeemed by the Treasury if the bank failed. But reserve requirements did not always protect the depositors. Poor loans could still be made, and bad judgment of the banker could and did lead to disaster, as the record of failures in the twentieth century shows. Federal legislation in the 1930's brought about many changes, supposedly reforms, but none perhaps instilled greater confidence in depositors at the time than did the insurance of deposits to a limited amount in the Federal Deposit Insurance Corporation. Another reform was the separation of commercial banking from investment banking. Little by little, commercial banks had made loans to facilitate the issuance of new stocks and bonds. Sometimes these loans proved unliquid, as had excessively large amounts of real estate loans long ago. In them, many a bank found its downfall.[18]

This then is our commercial banking structure: The state chartered banks and the national banks divided into the same three categories of

17 Wright, *op. cit.*, pp. 676-679.
18 *Ibid.*, pp. 687-689.

central reserve, reserve, and country banks. These facilitate the commerce of the nation.

Suggested Readings

Allen, A. M., et al., Commercial Banking Legislation and Control. London: Macmillan and Company, Ltd., 1938.

Anderson, T. J., Jr., Federal and State Control of Banking. New York: The Bankers Publishing Company, 1934, Chapters I, II, III, IX.

Bremer, C. D., American Bank Failures. New York: Columbia University Press, 1935.

Catteral, Ralph C. H., The Second Bank of the United States. Chicago: The University of Chicago Press, 1903.

Chandler, Lester V., The Economics of Money and Banking. New York: Harper & Bros., 1948, Chapter 11.

Chapman, John M., Concentration of Banking; The Changing Structure and Control of Banking in the United States. New York: Columbia University Press, 1934.

Dewey, D. R., and Holdsworth, J. T., The First and Second Banks of the United States. Washington: National Monetary Commission, Government Printing Office, 1910.

Foster, M. B., and Rodgers, Raymond, (Editors), Money and Banking. New York: Prentice-Hall, Inc., Third Edition, 1947, Chapters 4, 5, 29, 30, 31, 32. Chapters 29-32 deal with foreign banking systems, and involve some history.

Mueller, F. W., Money and Banking. New York: McGraw-Hill Book Company, 1951, Cf. footnotes.

Peterson, J. M., and Cawthorne, D. R., Money and Banking. New York: The Macmillan Company, 1949, Chapter V.

Prather, C. L., Money and Banking, Chicago: Richard D. Irwin, Inc., 1946, Chapters XVI. XVII.

Sprague, O. M. W., Banking Reforms in the United States. Cambridge: Harvard University Press, 1913.

Sprague, O. M. W., History of Crises under the National Banking Act. Washington: National Monetary Commission, Government Printing Office, 1911, 1912.

Thomas, R. G., Our Modern Banking and Monetary System. New York: Prentice-Hall, Inc., Second Edition, 1950, Chapters XVIII, XIX.

Westerfield, R. B., Money, Credit and Banking. New York: The Ronald Press Company, Revised Edition, 1947.

Wright, C. W., Economic History of the United States. New York: McGraw-Hill Book Company, Inc., New Second Edition, 1949, Chapters IX, XV, XXIV, XXXIX. Cf. footnotes.

2

Structure and Functions of Commercial Banking

by F. W. MUELLER, JR.

Dean, College of Commerce
De Paul University

IT IS CLEAR from the preceding chapter that banking has had a long and, for the most part, an honorable history. The system which we have today has evolved over several centuries. There has grown up a variety of customs and usages, some quite indispensable and others that continue only because of inertia. Nor are the systems in all countries alike. In Great Britain, for example, the negotiable bill has always exercised a powerful influence over English banking practices and legislation. In this country, however, preference early was shown for the "open account," which influenced our own banking development. It is necessary, therefore, to determine what banking system is going to be subjected to study; this chapter is limited chiefly to an investigation of the structure and functions of the American banking system.

Significance of Commercial Banks

The commercial banking structure is the core of modern financial systems. Every commercially and industrially advanced nation today has its commercial banking system adapted to its own needs. There is no phase of the economy in such nations, whether it be personal, corporate, or government economic activity which is not touched directly or indirectly by the commercial banking system.

All financial institutions are important, and any differences are largely of degree and not in kind. What is the hub of a wheel without spokes? But what are spokes without the hub! Each completes the other and neither is more important than the other. In conjunction, however, they

serve a most useful function for man: they have been one of the principal means whereby man's energies have been multiplied many times, and they have relieved him of innumerable physical burdens. So it is with the banking system. It has been a means in conjunction with other specialized financial institutions to shape, and to be shaped by, the resulting economic system of which it is a part.

Similarities and Differences

The commercial banking system is similar in many respects to other financial institutions. Commercial banks deal primarily in money or rights to receive money. They also perform a service which cannot easily be objectified but to which great value is attached. Commercial banks simultaneously become creditor and debtor, and not infrequently to the same person at the same time. In making loans, for instance, the commercial bank becomes a creditor of its borrowers from whom a future payment is due. But as a depository it becomes a debtor to the depositor, to the extent of the latter's deposit. Frequently a depositor also borrows from his bank of deposit. In such a case the bank becomes both debtor and creditor, while the depositor also assumes the dual role of creditor and debtor. Furthermore, the commercial banks—in addition to making loans of a short term nature for a matter of months—will buy long-term investments running for a period up to 20 or 30 years. But what has been said is equally applicable to the New York Life Insurance Company, the Reconstruction Finance Corporation or a savings and loan association. Thus all financial institutions stand on a common foundation. In succeeding chapters this will become increasingly clear. But also it will become clear that each institution, including commercial banking, also has its unique function to fulfil.

The student is cautioned to distinguish commercial banks and commercial banking from industrial banks and investment banking. There are other institutions which may also use the term "banks" or "banking," but this terminology only indicates that such organizations are normally of the same genus: that is, they deal in money or rights to receive money. This chapter is concerned with commercial banks or the correlative activity, commercial banking—a distinct and unique specie of the genus banking. Care in studying the next section should reduce any misconceptions.

Unique Aspects of Commercial Banking

Several factors differentiate commercial banking from other financial institutions. First, it has a longer continuous history than any other

financial mechanism, with the exception of money; its evolution, therefore, provides it with a continuity which cannot be matched. Second, through its operations it has largely supplanted specie (gold and silver) as exchange media, and it has supplemented currency (bank notes) to the extent that the latter is today merely the small change for business. Third, it supports and is supported by every other financial institution and financial market. Investment banking and the stock market, and even the government itself, would be unable to sustain themselves except with the cooperation of the commercial banking system. Nor, it must be added, could banks be the kind of institutions they are without the aid of the specialized financial institutions. Fourth, because the banking system provides the bulk of the exchange media, it has become the keystone of domestic exchange. Fifth, for a number of reasons which cannot be considered here, the commercial banking system—at least in normal times—is the center of the foreign exchange market, that delicate mechanism which provides for the exchange of one currency such as the dollar into another currency such as the pound sterling. By this process it becomes the permissive factor in international trade.

The last unique factor which differentiates commercial banking from other types of financial institutions is the capacity to expand bank credit. This capacity is really the heart of the commercial banking functions. As an illustration, suppose a savings and loan association to have received share deposits of $1,000,000. With these funds presume it buys $1,000,000 in mortgages. Having performed these operations, it may acquire no more mortgages until it receives more share deposits. The commercial banking system, however, it quite different. Within limitations not stated here, if the banking system has $1,000,000 in deposits, it may buy from $4,000,000 to $9,000,000 in mortgages. That is to say, the commercial banking system has an expansive quality—its most unique feature—not possessed by other financial institutions.

The expansion of bank credit will be alluded to later. The student, however, is asked to take this significant aspect on faith, since a proper understanding requires a wider theoretical background.[1] It is here that difficult theoretical as well as practical problems are encountered. Of all the unique aspects of commercial banking, however, the expansion of bank credit is the most significant; it serves as the most important differentiating characteristic between the commercial banking system and all other financial institutions.

---

[1] This problem has received wide treatment. See Raymond P. Kent, *Money and Banking*. New York: Rinehart & Co., Inc., 1947, Ch. 15. Also F. W. Mueller, Jr., *Money and Banking*. New York: McGraw-Hill Book Co., Inc., 1951; Ch. 22.

Analysis of the System

Several approaches may be resorted to in order to survey the field of commercial banking. In this chapter it is proposed to analyze first the organization of a bank and the organization of the system of banks. Second, it is proposed to examine the operations involved in the commercial banking complex, and finally attention will be turned to some functional aspects of the banking process. In this manner the student may gain a foundation for matters to be considered later in greater detail. In this way it is hoped that the warp and woof of the institutional financial pattern will be made clear to the student. At this point let us turn to bank organizational problems.

The first thing to notice about the banking system of the United States is its duality. Banks are special types of corporations, and the right to bring into being a corporate entity is a sovereign power of the individual states. We then have forty-eight distinct state sources from which such banks can derive their authority. Banks which derive their authority in this manner are known as state banks.

But we also have another authority from which bank charters may be derived, namely the federal government. Since the latter is sovereign only in such matters as have been delegated to it by the states, and since there was no delegation of authority specifically authorizing the establishment of banks, any exercise of this power must of necessity rest upon some implied constitutional power. This power was found to exist by the Supreme Court,[2] and has been upheld subsequently [3] on numerous occasions. Banks organized under this authority are known as national banks.

But this dual source of authority also brings with it many problems. First, it means that we really have two banking systems working side by side. Second, it means that there are in reality 49 sources from which bank charters may•be obtained and that each source is free to determine the conditions upon which its own offspring may be allowed to operate. Finally, it means that the regulation of banking, if banking is to be regulated at all, can originate from 49 sources. To be most effective, all regulating agencies should have reasonably common objectives and agree upon common limitations. Such unanimity however does not exist and as a consequence, clarity of procedure is not present. Add to this confusion in regulation such agencies as the Federal Deposit Insurance Corporation and the Reconstruction Finance Corporation, both of which cut across the lines of charter sources, and it becomes clear that the dual

---

[2] See McCulloch v. Maryland. 4 Wheaton 316.

[3] See Osborne v. U. S. 9 Wheaton 738 (1824); Farmers and Mechanics National Bank v. Dearing. 91 U. S. 29 (1895); Davis v. Elmira Savings Bank. 161 U. S. 275 (1896).

nature of our banking system has given rise to many unique and distressing problems. So important are these problems and their solutions that a later chapter will deal with them in detail.

Let us examine now some of the major provisions relating to the organization of a national bank.[4] We shall examine in order the application, capital, surplus, earnings, and liability. This list is by no means exhaustive, but each step is significant in bringing a national bank into existence.

To establish a national bank, an organization certificate must be filed with the Comptroller of the Currency in Washington. Among other things the certificate must be filed by not less than five natural persons and must state (1) the name to be assumed, subject to the approval of the Comptroller, (2) the anticipated place of business, (3) the amount of capital stock together with the number of shares, (4) the names and places of residence of the original shareholders, and (5) that the certificate is filed to enable the incorporators to take advantage of the title in pursuance of banking functions as permitted by the laws relating thereto. This certificate or application must be notorized, and upon filing with the Comptroller the association becomes a body corporate.

This certificate is examined by the Comptroller, and if all the requirements of the statute have been met, he will issue to the association a certificate of permission under seal, which is the permission granted to the incorporators to commence business. This permission certificate must be published for at least 60 days, during or after which, the association may commence business.

Some of what appear above to be routine statements are, however, carefully circumscribed. One of the limitations applies to the capital account. The amount of capital required is based upon the population of the community in which the proposed bank will function. Where the population is 6,000 or less, no less than $50,000 capital is permitted. If the population is over 6,000 but does not exceed 50,000 the minimum capital must be $100,000. Where the population is over 50,000, the minimum capital must be $200,000. Whereas at one time the shares were required to be $100 par, the statute has been revised so that such shares may be $100 or any "less amount as may be provided in the articles of association." The minimum amount of capital therefore is determined by the population of the community where the bank will function.

Before the commencement of business, however, not less than 50 per cent of the capital must be paid in. Furthermore the balance of the capital must be paid in in installments of 10 per cent and not less frequently

---

[4] This material may be found in *Federal Laws Affecting National Banks as of January 1, 1950,* published for the Comptroller of the Currency of the U. S. by the Government Printing Office.

than once a month. With certain exceptions, no association may commence business "until it shall have a paid-in capital surplus equal to 20 per centum of its capital." This particular provision regarding capital and surplus was motivated by the scandalous practices that grew up during the period from 1836 to 1863, which was reviewed in the preceding chapter.

Prior to March 9, 1933, national banks were permitted to have only one class of capital stock; but on the above date the Emergency Banking Act was passed, and by one of its provisions national banks were permitted to issue preferred stock and/or capital debentures. The stock was limited to a 6 per cent cumulative dividend, and suitable provisions for retirement of both the stock and/or debentures were written into the law. Since the great bulk of such funds was obtained from the Reconstruction Finance Corporation, it is in this manner that the latter came to have a very real interest in the regulation of banking. While there still remain a few such commitments, the bulk of such liabilities has been paid off.

We now come to the dual problems of earned surplus and dividends. Since capital and surplus are the principal financial cushions protecting depositors from loss, it is important from a social point of view that minimum safeguards for the benefit of the depositors, and for the indirect exclusion of irresponsible opportunists, be established. In addition to the provision for minimum capital, the national banking statute provides that from earnings, not less than 10 per cent be added regularly to surplus until the latter equals the capital account. After these two accounts are equal, earnings are available for dividends at the discretion of the directors.

Finally we come to the question of the liability of the stockholder. In the original National Bank Act it was provided that stockholders would be liable for an amount equal to the par value of their stock, in addition to their original investment. To illustrate, suppose you bought a share of $100 par stock from a new bank at $120 a share (the $20 being your proportionate contribution to the required paid-in capital surplus), and that later the bank's losses wiped out both the capital and surplus. Suppose you were still a stockholder and a deficit capital account existed: you would be liable to pay in an additional $100. This principle designed in particular to protect depositors was known as "double liability."

It was never particularly serviceable, however, for three reasons. First, there was the problem of determining who really was liable—the holder of stock at the time the bank was closed, or a preceding holder at the time the loans were made which later resulted in closure. Second, the financial responsibility of the stockholder was not infrequently based

upon the very stock for which he was being assessed, and that stock having no value, his own financial responsibility was thereby wiped out. Third, in any general banking difficulties, the financial value of all other assets was likewise reduced if not eliminated, and thus bank stockholders had little if any resources from which to meet the assessment.

Consequently, under the Emergency Banking Act mentioned above, supplemented by the provisions of the Banking Act of 1935, it was provided that "such additional liability shall cease on July 1, 1937. . . ." This provision was passed for two reasons. One of the reasons was examined in the paragraph above, and the second reason was a matter of policy. Since the capital accounts of all banks had been greatly impaired during the early '30's, it was presumed that the issuance of non-assessable stock would be more attractive to prospective investors, and that the hesitancy of those with funds to buy bank stock could be greatly reduced by such a move. Consequently the double liability on national bank stock is no longer effective.

It should be clear by now that the organization of a national bank is far from simple, and that many safeguards have been erected principally as a protection for the public. Public interest plays a much more significant part in the field of finance in general and in banking in particular than in other types of businesses. Banking is looked upon as being akin to a public utility; that is, it is conceived to be vested with a public interest. Furthermore most (if not all) of the statutory banking limitations have been based upon what appeared in retrospect to be abuses of the kind which could be eliminated or at least reduced by the legislative process. Most of the legislation, therefore, is the product of bitter experience.

We cannot leave this aspect of organization without touching upon the other side of the problem—namely, state banks. It is obvious to the student that we are unable to examine even in cursory fashion as has been done above for national banks, all of the remaining legislation bearing upon the banks in each of the forty-eight states.[5] We will attempt, therefore, to summarize briefly some of the major differences to be found between national and state banks.

Let us look first at the variability of capital requirements for state banks. Minimum capital varies from a low of $10,000 in many states to as high as $500,000. In Iowa, Nebraska and other states a minimum of $10,000 is all that is needed to open a bank. In Michigan, however, in communities of 300,000 population or more there is a minimum requirement of $500,000. Under state statutes the minimum may be lower and the maximum may be higher in certain instances than is true under the National Bank Act. These examples are extremes, and the median

---

[5] For a survey see the *Federal Reserve Bulletin* for December, 1940, pp. 1267-74.

minimum appears to be $25,000. This is half the minimum required by the National Bank Act.

There is just as little uniformity in state double liability. Whereas double liability was originated in state statutes which the National Bank Act took over in 1863, a large number of states have followed Congress in removing double liability. The solution is still confused. Some states have had no double liability at any time, and have thus been relieved of making up their minds as to what to do. Other states have suspended double liability if the bank concerned was a member of the Federal Deposit Insurance Corporation. In many states the provision for double liability is a constitutional provision, and any repeal could only be accomplished by revising the constitution. Revising the basic law is always a difficult process, as it should be. It is therefore not surprising that in this category some states were successful in their attempts at repeal while others were not. In Indiana, Utah and some other states, the constitutional provision for double liability was successfully deleted from the basic law. Illinois and Oregon were unsuccessful in their attempts to revise their constitutions, and both states still have double liability. There is thus no single descriptive statement which can be made concerning the double liability of state bank stocks.

In general it can be said that state statutes relating to banking are more liberal and less restrictive than comparable sections of the National Bank Act. There is generated, therefore, a form of competitive advantage, sometimes in favor of banks organized under the National Bank Act but more frequently in favor of banks organized under state statutes. Because of this latter characteristic, more state charters are currently in use than national bank charters. On June 30, 1950, there were about 14,600 banks in operation. Of this number about 4,900 were national banks. On the basis of these figures about one-third of the total number of banks were national, while about two-thirds were state banks, including a few proprietary banks. From the standpoint of deposit liability, out of a total of $163.7 billion of deposits in all classes, national banks held $82.4 billion, or slightly more than 50 per cent.[6] That is to say, while the number of national banks is smaller than the number of state banks, the importance of the former in terms of deposits outweighs the latter.

The organization of the individual bank which we have been discussing (whether it derives its charter by the authority of the state in which it is organized or through the federal government) brings us to another significant characteristic of American banking: unit banking. Generally speaking, in this country we have a large number of technically independent banks which are individually organized and man-

---

[6] These figures taken from the *Federal Reserve Bulletin*, November 1950, pp. 1493-95.

aged.[7] This is in contrast to other countries (notably Canada and England) where a few banks have hundreds or thousands of branches. Unanimity of action is thus much simpler in these latter cases than in the United States. Nevertheless this point must be made clear: whereas United States banks are technically independent, each is greatly influenced by the system of banks; that is, functionally each bank in the system must for a variety of reasons "keep step" with all of the other banks. This influence of the system upon each individual bank reduces the freedom of action which is normally supposed to be available to each bank. The individual bank is one thing and the system of banks is quite another thing.

Internal Organization of a Commercial Bank

Now that we have given a brief description of the statutory organization of a commercial bank, let us turn our attention to the internal organization of a modern commercial bank. Because we cannot trace the development of each banking function, let us suppose that the bank is fully developed.

Modern commercial banking has often been described as department store banking. That is, the bank is equipped to perform practically any financial service which its customers require. The modern bank has become highly departmentalized; in the typical, large urban institution, the bank will commonly be found to have a savings department, trust department, foreign exchange department, real estate department, bond department, and loan department. It is not difficult to add to these departments in large banks where a more refined subdivision may be required by the volume or nature of the business transacted. On the other hand, a small bank in an agricultural area may well have all of the functions which are performed by specialized departments in a large bank carried on, if at all, by a single individual. This differentiation will occur only up to that point which is economically justifiable and will thus vary widely from bank to bank.

To keep such an organization functioning smoothly, it is necessary that some management hierarchy be charged with administration. At the top, of course, is the board of directors elected by the stockholders. Within this group is usually one denoted as chairman of the board, sometimes functional, but not infrequently honorary. The next in line is the president, who is usually the chief executive officer and who is followed by a vice-president. Larger institutions may have several vice

---

[7] For the sake of brevity, branch banking is not discussed here, though its importance in some states such as California should not be minimized.

presidents; depending upon the size of the institution, these officials may be followed by second vice-presidents and assistant vice-presidents.

The next member of the hierarchy is the cashier, who forms a very important cog in the management of the bank. In reality he is ordinarily responsible for the detailed multiple activities carried on by the bank. He is generally the secretary and treasurer of the organization, attending directors meetings and keeping minutes thereof as well as being responsible for signing all official reports and having authority to issue cashier's checks. He is the one upon whom legal process is served and who enters into both the operational and financial management of the bank. It devolves upon the cashier to see that all operations of the bank mesh according to both law and usage.

Now every bank is not organized in this fashion. A small bank may have one person occupy the positions of president and cashier, dispensing with both the chairman of the board as well as with the position of vice-president. Between these extremes each bank will adjust its management hierarchy to perform the functions required by its clientele.

Operational Management

There are two broad problems which any bank must solve satisfactorily. One of these problems involves operations, and the other involves financial management. Let us look first at operational management, which has to do chiefly with those operations through which direct contact with the customer results. This division in turn can be broken down conveniently into the operational management of the commercial banking department and the trust department.

Most large banks have three types of tellers: the receiving teller, the paying teller and the savings teller. It is the receiving teller who takes in currency, checks, and matured negotiable instruments for collection from the depositor; he credits the latter, conditionally in the case of checks, with the sum deposited. The paying teller provides for the withdrawals, as his title indicates. Both of these tellers continually have customer contacts, and both of these operations apply to the commercial side of the banking operation.

In the savings department there are also tellers, but these tellers usually perform both functions, that is receiving and paying. This division of tellers indicates at once to us that there are two principal types of deposits received by the commercial bank. These deposits may be called commercial or demand deposits and time or savings deposits. This point is worth a moment's digression.

Demand deposits are those deposits which are subject to transfer by check or are convertible into currency without notice, at the option of

the depositor. Traditionally the original and only type of deposit which the early commercial banks received, these deposits are functionally the exchange media which have supplanted specie and currency; individuals and businessmen of all classifications use such deposits for current payments.

Time or savings deposits normally take on the characteristic indicated; that is, these funds are current surpluses of the depositors, which presumably will not be used for current payments, and to which the depositors will attempt to add gradually. In addition, these deposits technically require notice of withdrawal on the part of the depositor. That they are assumed to be somewhat more permanent than demand deposits is reflected in the use to which the bank puts them. While these distinctions have become somewhat blurred in recent years, nevertheless, the banks are required to account for each category separately. We shall meet deposits in another connection later.

In addition to the tellers already mentioned, there are usually exchange tellers, collection tellers, and note tellers. These men carry out the operations indicated. Exchange tellers handle drafts which are purchased and drawn on out of town banks. Depending upon the size of the bank, they may also arrange for the purchase and sale of foreign exchange. Collection tellers are those who accept from customers negotiable paper which is payable at distant points; they also handle the paper for collection for the customer. The usual procedure is for the customer to leave the note for collection, and when the funds are available to have it deposited to the credit of his account. The note teller is the teller who handles notes upon which the bank is the payee. In other words the note teller receives and preserves the evidence of the borrowing and lending process carried out by the customer as debtor and the bank as creditor. These operations are very carefully organized and meticulously balanced out each day, for no teller can have other than one answer at closing time—namely, the right one!

Trust department operational management is organized similarly to the commercial department, but the management is adapted to the trust department's own peculiar needs. Trust departments carry on their activities to provide a particular kind of service to the financial community. They perform an outstanding service in that they act as bailees for hire. This is not an all-inclusive description of their activities, but it does emphasize a very significant aspect of the service performed.

The various trust operations may be broken down into significant categories. First, there are personal trusts, which may be subdivided into court and living trusts. In such cases the trust department (acting as trustee) possesses the legal title to the property (through court order or by voluntary agreement), but the beneficiary receives the income under

the conditions stipulated. In corporate trusts the trust company may act as trustee under a mortgage or as trustee under an agency account (such as transfer agent or registrar) for a public issue of stock. Again there are any number of agency accounts under which the trustee may act either for corporate or personal beneficiaries. Finally, the trust company acts as custodian of securities under a wide variety of circumstances. Trust departments of commercial banks thus operate in an extremely wide field. This aspect of the financial institution is taken up in detail at a later point. It is important to understand that the billions of dollars worth of property over which trust departments of commercial banks exercise varying degrees of control require that management be exceptionally careful in organizing its activities so that it may stand up to strict accountability. This strict accountability is applicable to all phases of commercial banking. It behooves bank management to so organize its administration that responsibility is clearly centered in all of its many phases of activity.

Financial Management

As important as operational management is, it is secondary to financial management. It is fair to say that the whole of the organization of a bank has as its major objective the successful financial operations of the institution. Even with poor or inadequate operational management, it is possible to have successful financial management; without the latter nothing can compensate, no matter how well operations are managed. Financial management is the testing ground for the sagacity of management, and here the success of the bank will be determined. Let us examine the financial management from the standpoint of both the commercial department and the trust department.

There are two principal areas in which financial management is brought into play. The first of these is in lending operations which deal with so-called customer loans and short-term open-market paper. Under normal circumstances there are always corporations, partnerships, individuals, trusts, estates and others which are in the market for funds. Some of these corporations, trusts, and so on will be depositors, while some may not be. It is immaterial to the lending bank so long as the intended borrowing operation gives rise to "bankable paper." Bankable paper is the note of the borrower which meets both the quantitative and qualitative requirements of the leading bank. Since each loan is unique insofar as it possesses a risk factor different from that of all other loans, the same type of loan to two different borrowers may well (and probably will) carry different interest or discount rates. That is why

customer loans are so named, for personal factors enter to determine both the amount of and the rate on the loan.

What the prospective borrower wants to do is to borrow, say, $10,000 today and to repay it in six months. Assuming that the bank is able to lend, the question is raised as to whether it is willing to do so. Whether it is willing to do so will depend upon a great variety of factors: the prospective borrower's record on his previous borrowings, the financial condition of his business, the kinds of customers to whom he sells, the state of general business conditions, and his record of integrity. It is the business of the credit department of the bank to assemble and analyze the quantitative data which are directly related to the business itself. The principal means are through the balance sheets and profit and loss statements for a series of years. This material is analyzed, and in conjunction with other material, it is made available to the lending officers.

Lending operations are the heart of the modern commercial bank. In a small bank without the elaborate paraphernalia of the large organization, one man will probably take care of all loans. But the small banker probably has a great advantage in having had long and continuous associations with the prospective borrower; what the banker may lack in terms of supplementary assistance, such as a credit department offers, he gains by long personal acquaintanceship.

In a large bank, the banker and prospective borrower will of course be acquainted, but their association may be sporadic. In addition, the large metropolitan bank can make much larger loans than can the small bank. It is essential, therefore, that the banker bring all pertinent information to bear upon each lending operation. Some banks organize their lending into elaborate classifications, so that each lending officer may become completely familiar with the peculiarities of particular types of businesses. The figure opposite indicates the organization of the lending division of The First National Bank of Chicago in its commercial banking department. Each department has anywhere from five to eight lending officers. These men review the analysis and information provided by the credit department and in conjunction with their knowledge of the particular business and of economic conditions, they may commit the bank's funds to a borrower.

There is a wide variety of ways in which the resulting loans may be classified. They may be classified according to the type of borrower, the type of business, by maturity, by security, or in any other meaningful manner. Let us examine for illustrative purposes the possible, though not exhaustive, classification of loans by security.

The banker is anxious to lend, but quite reasonably he is also anxious to be repaid. If he can obtain security he will take it, and modern banks take a wide variety of security. A banker may make a loan if the

THE FIRST NATIONAL BANK OF CHICAGO

Divisional Classification

DIVISION A

Meat Products   Grain, Flour and Feed   Coal
        Live Stock Commission   Wool
    Doctors and Lawyers   Bankruptcy

DIVISION B

Textiles, Clothing, Dry Goods, Millinery   Department Stores
    Mail Order Houses   Merchandising Sundries   Furs
                            Jewelers

WOMEN'S BANKING DEPARTMENT

DIVISION C

Iron and Steel   Electrical Products   Automobiles
        Agricultural Implements   Machinery   Radio
                    Manufacturing Sundries

DIVISION D

Insurance   Publishing   Advertising   Printing
        Paper and Paper Products   Installment Financing
                            Miscellaneous

DIVISION E

Groceries, Drugs, Dairy Products   Produce and Cold Storage
    Distillers, Brewers   Sugar   Confectionery, Tobacco
                Beverages, Restaurants, Bakers, Hotels
    Collection and Commercial Agencies   Schools, Churches, Cemeteries
        Hospitals, Undertakers   Laundries, Lodges, Charities

DIVISION F

Banks and Bankers

DIVISION G

Public Officials   Real Estate   Mortgage Bankers
    Hides, Shoes and Leather Products   Tires and Rubber
        Musical Instruments   Building and Loan Associations
                    Title and Guarantee Companies

DIVISION H

Amusements   Estates, Capitalists   Stocks and Bonds
    Public Utilities   Transportation   Custom House Brokers
Bankers   Tank Cars, Dry Docks, Warehouses and Forwarders

DIVISION I

Petroleum   Contractors   Cement, Stone, Brick, Paints, Glass
    Plumbing and Heating Supplies   Hardware   Lumber
        Furniture   Accountants, Engineers, Architects

DIVISION J

Intermediate and Serial Loans

FIGURE 1

borrower obtains a satisfactory endorser or co-signer who acts as security for the principal obligor. The banker may require inventory or security such as warehouse receipts or field warehouse receipts. He may require the assignment of title to new equipment purchased or, if this is impractical, a chattel mortgage. One of the simplest means of securing a loan is by such negotiable securities as federal government or state bonds and listed or unlisted securities. Not infrequently accounts receivable are pledged or the cash value of life insurance policies carried by the borrowing company on the life of an executive of the company. The list of property or rights to property which can be and customarily are used is a long one; it adds to the banker's assurance that the loan will be repaid when due, in default of which the pledged property itself can be used to extinguish the debt.[8]

It must not be supposed that all loans are secured. A large variety of loans cannot be secured. If a shoe store buys new shoes for the Easter trade, it cannot both keep them in stock and physically pledge them at the bank. As a consequence (presuming the proprietor to have no other assets for collateral), if a loan is made at all it must be made on an unsecured basis. That this is by no mean uncommon is indicated by a recent study [9] which shows that of all the loans outstanding by member banks on November 20, 1946, 35.6 per cent were unsecured while 61.1 per cent were secured. That is to say, about one-third of the number of loans were unsecured while about two-thirds were secured. In terms of dollar value, more than half were unsecured while less than half were secured. Unsecured loans therefore loom large as a means for bank accommodation.

It was mentioned earlier that banks also engaged in short-term open-market loans. Here it is that the rate is determined by market forces in an impersonal way, as contrasted to customer loans. This type of paper (government bills and certificates, high-grade short-term bonds, acceptances, and commercial paper) is acquired for one of two reasons. First, there may not be sufficient customer-loan demand to use all of the available funds which the bank desires to employ. Second, banks (like anyone else) cannot afford to carry all of their eggs in one basket; they desire to diversify their lending operations and thus their assets. If a bank buys a 180 day note of the United States Steel Corporation in the open market, it has effectively made a loan to the corporation just as much as if it had made a loan in the same amount to one of its own customers. There are major differences between the two operations, the most significant being that the open market provides a means for

---

[8] For a study of loan distribution by security see Tynan Smith, *Security Pledged on Member Bank Loans to Business; Federal Reserve Bulletin,* June, 1947, pp. 665.
[9] *Ibid.*

diversifying the bank's assets which would not otherwise be available. The officer in charge of such open-market operations thus has just as heavy responsibility as any other lending officer.

We now come to the second area of financial management, the purchase of investments. Before World War I, investments did not figure significantly in commercial banking operations. After World War I and especially during the decade of the '20's, such securities found much favor for a variety of reasons. Unfortunately the indiscriminate purchase of investment securities was, at least in part, the Waterloo of many banks. Since the early '30's there has been an augmentation of security purchases by banks, chiefly this time in the field of federal obligations. There is not space here to trace this financial metamorphosis, but it has left a decided impression on the banking system. Thus on June 30, 1950, all banks in the country had total loans of $44 billion and investments amounting to $76 billion.[10] Thus banks owned one and two-thirds as many investments on this date as they held loans. But of the investments, $65 billion were United States government obligations while only $11 billion were non-government securities. That is, for every dollar of non-government securities, the banking system held six dollars of federal government securities.

Without going into detail, we may say that there are two excellent reasons why this condition has come about, but there is also one very significant hazard. First, as in the case of short-term open-market paper, it permits a wide diversification of maturities. Second, since these investments are largely freely marketable securities, any single bank may sell almost any amount at will without appreciably affecting the market prices. The great hazard is that if there was any concerted move on the part of all banks to sell, the market could be demoralized, not only forcing down the price of these securities but also tending to increase generally the open-market rate of interest (which would adversely affect the whole of the banks' portfolio). This is one of the major problems with which the Federal Reserve System and the Treasury have been wrestling since the end of World War II. Whatever answer may eventuate, it is clear that investment operations of the commercial banks are massive today, and investments are used as lending media to a greater extent than might be expected.

So far we have considered loans and investments as a means for banks to accommodate various types of borrowers. The sum of these evidences is commonly referred to as the earning asset portfolio, so-called because these loans and investments make up the principal means whereby the banks derive a money income. Other things being equal, the earning assets determine the strength of a bank. If the assets accumulated in the

[10] *Federal Reserve Bulletin*, November, 1950, p. 1495.

lending process are "good," the bank is "strong," but if these assets are "weak," so is the bank weak.

In this section on financial management, a brief examination should be made of the trust department's operations. Trust departments as a rule make no customer loans such as we have been considering; rather they confine their activities to the purchase and sale of investments with the specific objective of preserving the funds entrusted to them consistent with the income derived. These activities may be carried out for either personal or corporate beneficiaries.

In carrying out their activities, the trust department may act only as an agent, or it may have discretionary authority. As an agent it may act for a corporation in the purchase of the latter's outstanding bonds to fulfill sinking-fund requirements. Under nearly every corporate trust agreement the trust department acts only as agent; that is, it performs only the specific functions delegated to it in the trust deed. Where a trust department has discretionary authority, its responsibility is multiplied. Suppose a man sets up a trust fund of $500,000 for the benefit of his wife and two children, with the stipulation that the income be distributed to the beneficiaries, but that the principal be reinvested (as bonds mature or are called) at the discretion of the trustee. If bonds in an amount of $10,000 mature, the trustee must reinvest the funds. But suppose the bonds default? Is the trustee liable? That will depend upon a variety of factors. Suffice it to say here that care and extreme prudence are essential in such financial management. Since the value of trusts runs into the billions much of the financial management of trusts is on a discretionary basis, it is obvious that except for the use of extreme care, trust departments could easily engage themselves in disastrous liability.

Both the financial management of a bank and its operational management are normally aided by a special staff or by service departments. Larger banks will thus have departments of business development, internal audit, internal analysis of operations, planning and systems, personnel, equipment and supplies, and building management. Additional departments may be established where required. Smaller banks will dispense with most of these departments if not all of them. But whether departmentalized or not, every bank should have available some means of preserving internal efficiency, if only on a very informal basis.

We have now examined both the operational and financial management of a commercial bank. These activities have sprung up because there is a need for them which can be economically justified. Banking is a very intricate affair, and whereas some aspects of it may run themselves once they are established, the important aspects upon which everything else hinges require decisions. This is the obligation of man-

agement. Management will make its decisions in terms of the functions which are to be performed, and it is to the functions of banking that we next turn.

Functional Aspects of Commercial Banking

Banking viewed as a system is a huge credit mechanism through which the allocation of scarce resources is accomplished. This allocation is achieved through the combination of the deposit function and lending function. Having built up a background of bank organization and management, we are now ready to turn our attention to these functions.

Credit

Of all of the banking concepts, that of credit is probably the most elusive. It is commonly said that a man "has credit," that a bank "extends credit" or that "credit is based upon the three C's of capital, character and capacity." Nothing in any of these notions tells us anything about what credit is or what the function of credit is. It is these notions we shall investigate.

We might first ask, "What does credit do?" To this there are two answers: first, credit provides the mechanism whereby a person may acquire real goods without giving an equivalent value of goods in exchange; second,—as an indirect consequence—there is a redirection of the flow of real goods, different from what would otherwise take place.

Let us look at the first idea. The object of man economically, under the modern roundabout process of production, is to use goods which he does have to obtain goods which he does not have. Each individual is faced with the need of exchanging the result of his productivity for the productivity of others. In early days this was done by barter, but this method was clumsy to say the least, and any refined system of multiple exchanges was impossible. In barter the exchanges were concurrent: the economic contribution made by one person was immediately compensated by the receipt of goods of equivalent value. There was no overhanging debt due to or from anyone.

Under modern productive methods the procedure is quite different. Most productive processes take at least weeks to complete, and many take years. Even if the end products were bartered, only a small proportion of those who contribute to the completion of the products could afford to wait for their share of the bartered goods. If they did wait, they would during that waiting period be creditors to the extent of their efforts.

But this is the bridge which money has provided. By custom as well

as by necessity, individuals are compensated at stipulated periods for their economic contribution; this compensation measures the extent to which men may share in the products produced by others. Money merely measures the proportionate share to which the recipient is entitled. So long as he holds the money he is still a social creditor, since he has not completed the economic process. Only when he "spends" the money and receives goods has he completed the process of exchanging goods which he has for goods which he does not have.

If the recipient prefers for the sake of safety not to carry all of his money on his person, he can easily nowadays deposit it in a bank. By so doing he still maintains his status as a social creditor, and the bank, to the extent of his deposit, becomes his debtor. Since almost everyone attempts to anticipate the rainy day, the depositor too will attempt to increase his deposit account gradually in order to establish a financial "backlog." If everyone does this, there will result a fund of deposits which in reality represents unredeemed claims on the real social income. If deposits in the aggregate tend to stay at about the same volume, banks are thus provided with a means whereby they can lend the unexercised claims, so long as the original depositors do not need them. This lending process permits the borrowers to obtain goods without giving concurrent value in exchange. The borrower is in effect substituting the past productive efforts of society for his own future productivity, the source out of which the original status quo will be restored. Thus we have established a means whereby one of the functions of credit (the acquisition of goods without the concurrent exchange of an equivalent value in real goods by the borrower) can be accomplished.

There naturally flows from this another consequence: the direction of goods' distribution takes on a pattern different from that which would exist if credit were not available. Thus if both A and B desire a particular product (though neither is in a position to pay "cash" for it) and if A can borrow and does so, while B is unable to borrow, A will be able to direct the goods to himself. Thus it is that when millions of these credit transactions are continually being consummated in every conceivable field, the pattern of real income distribution may be at considerable variance from what would otherwise be the case.

If this is what credit does, what may we say it is? We can say that credit is that capacity of the borrower to acquire current goods in anticipation of his future productivity. At the heart of credit is the prospect of the future production of goods and services which it is estimated can be traded in the open market at competitive prices in return for exchange media. The determination of this future capacity is very troublesome. If a prospective borrower is known to be without this capacity, no credit activity will ensue. But sometimes when credit is presumed, it

does not eventuate. It is this risk which must be assumed by the lender. What the credit system (and the banking system in particular) attempts to do is to evaluate risks and to make current goods available to those risks which are the most promising. In this way the current real resources are allotted among the various would-be claimants, the aggregate activities of which go to make up the economy of "business."

Bank Credit

When the earned claims to goods in the form of money are deposited in a bank, the depositor becomes a bank creditor. The volume of bank credit will increase or decrease as money is deposited or withdrawn.

Bank loans are another and more important way in which bank credit is emitted. We have already discussed several types of bank loans: customer paper, open-market paper, and investments. When a bank buys or discounts such paper from a previous holder, a strange thing occurs. Almost no one desires to receive money or currency; rather, a man would prefer to take bank credit, i.e., have his own deposit account credited. This is due to several reasons, two important ones being convenience and safety. The result is that when a bank discounts a note for $1,000, at say 5 per cent, the deposits of that bank go up by $1,000 less the discount. In a roundabout way that is what happens when open-market paper or investments are purchased. That is where most of the "deposits" come from rather than from the deposit of "money."

The process sketched above is what is known as the *expansion of bank credit*. It is clear from this process that total deposits of a bank and a banking system may go substantially beyond the earned but unredeemed claims of the depositors of money. Since a deposit of an unredeemed claim and a deposit arising from a loan are indistinguishable, it appears that more claims in the form of bank deposits can be generated than there are current goods to satisfy the claimants, at a given price level. This introduces us to one of the most vexatious problems in banking theory: what influence does the volume of bank credit have upon the price structure? We shall not examine that question here, but suffice it to say that (under normal circumstances) repayments of loans and the contraction of bank credit are offset by the extension of loans and the expansion of bank credit by the banking system, in approximately equal amounts. This process—the expansion and contraction of bank credit—is the unique function fulfilled by the banking system; the process is of such significance that the student must exercise criticism of our financial system with the utmost caution until he is thoroughly familiar with this procedure.

Reserves

A natural conclusion to what has been said above might well be that if a little expansion of bank credit is good, more would be better; and if banks can thus expand their own deposits, there must be no limit. This conclusion is not valid, however, because the banks are faced with the limitation of legal reserves. These reserves are defined by law as to the quantity, quality, and domicile. Let us examine these notions.

Minimum legal reserves, which normally differ for time and demand deposits, are set by 47 states (all except Illinois) and also by the National Bank Act for national banks. Using the latter for illustration, the original National Bank Act set a minimum of 25 per cent or 15 per cent as the proportion of all deposits which must be carried as a reserve, depending upon the location of the bank. Since the inception of the Federal Reserve Act in 1913, these proportions have undergone many changes, and today reserves against demand deposits of national banks vary from a minimum of 7 per cent to 13 per cent, up to 14 per cent to 26 per cent, depending upon the location of the bank. For time deposits in any national bank regardless of location, the reserve varies from 3 per cent to 6 per cent.

To simplify matters let us look only at demand deposits and presume that the bank under consideration has $1,000,000, originally deposited in the form of specie and currency, and is required to keep a 20 per cent legal reserve. This bank will obviously have "cash" and deposits of equivalent amounts. Presuming the bank is anxious to acquire earning assets and thus to expand its deposits, it may acquire $4,000,000 in earning assets to give it a total deposit of $5,000,000. Beyond this it may not expand, for its reserve of $1,000,000 is just 20 per cent of its deposit liabilities. No bank will work this close to the limit of its capacity, and to simplify the situation further we have cut through many qualifications. This indicates that the legal reserve under which a bank operates is a limiting device for the expansion of bank credit.

Under the National Banking System, and insofar as all member banks of the Federal Reserve System are concerned, all legal reserves must be kept on deposit with the Federal Reserve Bank of the district in which the member is located. That is to say, all such banks may keep their legal reserves only in central bank credit. This was a provision ultimately put into the Federal Act to overcome some acute difficulties under which the National Banking System labored before 1913.

Whereas the principle of expansion and the limitations imposed by legal reserves operate upon state banks in similar fashion, two differences should be stressed. Non-member state banks as a rule are subject

to lower reserve requirements by their state banking authorities than are national and state member banks; this means non-member state banks may expand to a higher degree. Secondly, non-member state banks may deposit their reserves in "approved depositories," which means, by and large, in some other larger commercial bank. Thus the quantity, quality and domicile of reserves of non-member state banks varies from the similar qualifications for national and state-member banks. It is clear that the duality of our system raises some problems peculiar to American banking.

Summary

Let us take a quick survey now, and see the ground we have traversed by using some simple examples. First, in organizing a bank we accounted for the capital structure; assuming (for the sake of simplicity) that these funds are committed to a building and its furniture and fixtures, and that as a national bank it must subscribe to Federal Reserve Bank stock,[11] the accounts would be shown as in Schedule A below:

SCHEDULE A

Assets		Liabilities	
Federal Reserve Bank Stock	$ 18,000	Capital	$500,000
Building, Furniture and Fixtures	582,000	Surplus	100,000

Suppose now that the bank is open for business and that corporations, partnerships, and individuals come in and make deposits in currency in the amount of $500,000 (as shown in Schedule B) of which $400,000 is in demand deposits and $100,000 in time deposits. Presuming this national bank to have a required reserve of 20 per cent against demand deposits and 5 per cent against time deposits, these amounts will then have to be deposited in the Federal Reserve Bank of the district.

SCHEDULE B

Assets		Liabilities	
Cash in Vault	$415,000	Deposits:	
Reserve Deposit at Federal Reserve Bank	85,000	Demand	$400,000
		Time	100,000
Federal Reserve Bank Stock	18,000	Capital	500,000
Building, Furniture, and Fixtures	582,000	Surplus	100,000

Next let us assume that over a period of time this bank expands its credit by making loans and by buying investments; the results of these operations show up as an increase in the bank's deposit liabilities. But as the liabilities increase, so must the legal reserves at the Federal Reserve

---

[11] As explained in the following chapter.

Bank. Schedule C below indicates these changes after completion of these operations.

SCHEDULE C

Assets		*Liabilities*	
Cash in Vault	$ 50,000	Deposits:	
Reserve Deposit at Federal Re-		Demand	$2,225,000
serve Bank	450,000	Time	100,000
Loans and Discounts	1,300.000	Capital	500,000
Investments	525,000	Surplus	100,000
Federal Reserve Bank Stock ...	18,000		
Building, Furniture, and Fixtures	582,000		
Total	$2,925,000		$2,925,000

From this simple statement three important consequences may be observed. First, this bank does not lend all that it can theoretically lend, since it still has $50,000 remaining in its vault. This procedure is in accord with good practice, for every bank must retain some funds to pay out to depositors who wish to convert their deposits into currency. Second, by hypothesis, the reserve required against time deposits (5 per cent) is $5,000, and the reserve against demand deposits (20 per cent) is $445,000, the sum of the two equaling $450,000—the amount which the bank has on deposit at the Federal Reserve Bank. Normally reserves will not run so close to the legal minimum, but these figures will serve to illustrate the point. Finally, of total deposits of $2,325,000, a total of $1,825,000 is derived from the expansion of bank credit; this amount is the sum of the obligations in the earning asset portfolio. Again, such close correlation will not be found in practice, but if the point of bank credit expansion is made clear, the purpose is well served.

The student should understand that the illustrations above are greatly simplified for the sake of isolating the significant factors in which we have been interested. Nevertheless, a resemblance between the illustration and the bank statement of a modern fully developed commercial bank will be clear by an examination of Figure 2. While the items in Figure 2 are more numerous and the amounts significantly larger, this bank itself had the same kind of humble beginning as did the bank indicated in our illustrations. But more significantly the principles in each case are identical.

It should be clear by now why, at the beginning of the chapter, it was said that the commercial banking system is the core of modern financial institutions. That statement will be increasingly meaningful as progress is made in succeeding chapters, for these chapters will repeatedly show the relationship of specialized financial institutions to commercial banking and the indispensability of the latter in an age of highly specialized, roundabout processes of production.

THE FIRST NATIONAL BANK OF CHICAGO

STATEMENT OF CONDITION DECEMBER 31, 1950

Assets

Cash and Due from Banks		$ 612,756,801.04
United States Obligations—		
Direct and Guaranteed Unpledged	$ 615,680,362.54	
Pledged—To Secure Public Deposits and Deposits Subject to Federal Court Order	180,564,014.22	
To Secure Trust Deposits	84,398,667.34	
Under Trust Act of Illinois	512,000.00	881,155,044.10
Other Bonds and Securities		133,425,165.27
Loans and Discounts		953,329,881.10
Real Estate (Bank Building)		2,204,723.08
Federal Reserve Bank Stock		4,800,000.00
Customers' Liability Account of Acceptances		3,946,772.95
Interest Earned, Not Collected		6,128,632.29
Other Assets		1,162,650.31
		$2,598,909,760.14

Liabilities

Capital Stock		$ 75,000,000.00
Surplus		85,000,000.00
Other Undivided Profits		4,023,283.46
Discount Collected, But Not Earned		1,478,134.05
Dividends Declared, But Unpaid		1,500,000.00
Reserve for Taxes, etc.		22,593,921.71
Liability Account of Acceptances		4,526,949.75
Time Deposits	$ 449,418,887.22	
Demand Deposits	1,757,522,519.27	
Deposits of Public Funds	197,845,527.53	2,404,786,934.02
Liabilities Other Than Those Above Stated		537.15
		$2,598,909,760.14

FIGURE 2

Suggested Readings

Cleveland, Frederick Albert, *Funds and Their Uses.* New York: D. Appleton-Century Co., Inc., 1922, (Rev.), Chapters 2 and 12.

Horbett, John E., *Banking Structure in the United States, in Banking Studies, Board of Governors of the Federal Reserve System.* Washington, 1941, pp. 87-113.

Madden, John T.; Nadler, Marcus and Heller, Sipa, *Money Market Primer.* New York: The Ronald Press Co., 1948.

Moulton, Harold G., *Financial Organization and the Economic System.* New York: McGraw-Hill Book Co., Inc., 1938, Chapters 8 and 17.

Phillips, Chester Arthur, *Readings in Money and Banking.* New York: The Macmillan Co., 1916, Chapters 9 and 10.

Willis, H. Parker, and Edwards, Geary W., *Banking and Business.* New York Harper & Brothers, 1925, (Rev.), Chapters 2, 4, 5 and 6.

3

The Federal Reserve System

by DONALD L. KEMMERER

Professor of Economics, University of Illinois

Central Banking

THE Federal Reserve System is a central banking system. A central bank is the banks' bank. It performs for banks the same functions that banks perform for their customers. A central bank holds deposits for commercial banks: these are called the commercial bank's legal reserves. A central bank lends money to a commercial bank provided that the commercial bank has adequate collateral or good credit. A central bank creates credit and lends it to commercial banks. This created credit takes two forms: central bank notes or created deposits. The latter are added to the commercial bank's legal reserve account. Like any other bank, the central bank itself must have legal reserves against its bank notes and against the deposits that it holds. And the central bank has nearly all the other basic characteristics of a commercial bank—stockholders, board of directors, a president and other officers. It differs from commercial banks in three primary respects, however. As mentioned above, it deals with banks, not with individuals. It does not have to make a profit. It will accept losses if that is necessary to regulate the supply of bank credit. Regulating the nation's supply of bank credit is one of the main responsibilities of a central bank.

The United States was one of the last major nations to acquire a central banking system. True, twice we had had a combination central bank-commercial bank-investment bank when the First Bank of the United States (1791–1811) and the Second Bank of the United States (1816–36) flourished. The Independent Treasury System (1846–1921)— despite its requirements that all receipts and disbursements be in specie —hardly qualified as a central banking system. For one thing it never

pretended to make loans or to accept deposits. Finally, the National Banking System, founded in 1863, was in no sense a central banking system, for it lacked a head bank and a policy making board. Indeed, its omissions in this respect dramatically pointed to the need for a central banking system.

The National Banking System

Yet the National Banking System was a tremendous improvement in its time. After its founding only national banks might issue bank notes, and for the first time the country had reliable bank notes. But the requirements for national bank charters were so strict that many state banks began to encourage their customers to use checking accounts to get around the need for bank notes.[1] The use of checks increased immensely after this. In general, national banks were dependable banks and relatively few of them failed. But the National Banking System developed serious faults, and these eventually had to be remedied. The most glaring of these faults were: (1) inelastic bank-notes, (2) decentralized reserves, (3) inadequate methods of handling foreign exchange, (4) too much dependence on the Treasury, (5) insufficient provision for loans to farmers, (6) a cumbersome system for clearing and collecting checks, and (7) no central bank. When these faults became unbearable, the American banking system was overhauled and rebuilt; that reconstruction gave us the Federal Reserve System. But first the faults themselves deserve closer examination.

The national bank notes were inelastic. That means that the supply of notes did not expand and contract automatically with the needs of business: their expansion and contraction depended on other economic forces. National bank notes were, by law, backed at least 100 per cent by certain United States government bonds. The notes were supposed to earn double interest for the banks, i.e., interest from the government on the bonds and interest from the loans to the customers; but these earnings were actually meager. The bonds paid only low interest rates, and the notes were subject to some additional expenses like taxes. Consequently when the price of government bonds rose, the banks were inclined to sell the bonds for a profit even though such sales meant that banks had to retire the bank notes. Likewise when the price of bonds was low, banks were inclined to buy bonds and then obtain bank notes and try to lend them. Unfortunately there was little relationship between bond prices and business needs; for example, bond prices sometimes rose when business was undergoing a healthy expansion; this

---

[1] So did the national banks, for legal reserve requirements against demand deposits were considerably smaller than those against national bank notes.

caused banks to sell their bonds, and then they had less to lend.[2] True, banks could lend bank deposits, but their loans in that department were generally at a maximum, and so there was little elasticity there either. The nation needed bank credit that would expand and contract with the needs of business.

National bank reserves were too decentralized. Under the National Banking System there were three kinds of banks; they varied according to the size of the city where they were located. Most banks were "country" banks; some situated in a few dozen middle-sized cities were "reserve city" banks; and a select few located in two or three large cities, chiefly New York and Chicago, were "central reserve city" banks.[3] "Country" banks were permitted to keep 60 per cent of their reserves against deposits in banks in the bigger cities; and the medium-sized city banks were permitted to keep 50 per cent of their reserves against deposits in the banks in the large cities. The banks received interest on these redeposited reserves. Most of these deposits went to New York. The New York National Banks were able to pay interest because they loaned these funds on the call money market. That market supplied stock market speculators with funds for their operations. Call loans were well secured, were callable on 24 hours' notice, and the interest rate was subject to change daily. This somewhat complicated system of bank reserves worked well in normal times, but in panic times and occasionally in the fall of the year it was inclined to break down. If a "tight" money situation threatened, some small and medium city banks demanded their reserves, rates on the call market rose sharply, speculators slackened their operations, stock prices fell, uncertainty spread, more banks demanded their reserves, and the circle of unrest widened. If individuals in a town doubted the solvency of their bank and a "run" on the bank developed, the bank stood only as long as its cash reserves lasted. Other banks were not inclined to help it for fear a "run" might hit them next. There was no central bank to turn to for help. Thus in time of distress, substantial as well as weak banks sometimes failed. After three major experiences of this sort (in 1873, 1893, and 1907), and numerous minor ones, it was obvious that reforms were in order.

The other five faults of the National Banking System may be described simply. Because foreign exchange transactions had to be financed through London, the process was expensive, and it tended to give away our business secrets to English competitors.

By 1914 the federal government was keeping its funds in nine subtreasuries and in 1,584 national bank depositaries. The Treasury

---

[2] See Alexander D. Noyes, *History of the National Bank Currency,* a National Monetary Commission Report, Washington, 1910.

[3] For a time St. Louis was a third central reserve city.

hoarded its funds at certain times of the year and thus created a scarcity of money and credit. Also some depositary banks depended unduly on the Treasury for extra deposits to help them keep their houses in order.

Farmers were dissatisfied with the National Banking System because national banks were forbidden to make loans on real estate security. That was the chief security farmers had to offer.

Clearing houses in the nation charged varying amounts for clearing checks. Some cities were even "free cities" in this respect. Banks tended to route their checks through the free or inexpensive cities and to avoid the costly ones. The amount of checks in transit, the "float," as it was called, was large. It was socially wasteful to route checks in this cumbersome manner, and it was economically dangerous, for checks in collection were counted as reserve and yet might prove in the end to be worthless.

But the fault of the National Banking System that led, more than any other, to a demand for reform was the lack of a central bank. A total of 243 banks failed in the 1907–08 panic, 31 of them national banks. Worse records had been compiled in the 1890's, but this—on top of the experiences of the past—made people especially impatient.

Fear of a "Money Trust"

Congress in 1908 passed the Aldrich-Vreeland Act, a law designed to do two things: first, to provide an emergency currency in the event of another serious panic and thus help solvent but illiquid banks; and second, to establish a National Monetary Commission to study our own experiences and needs, to investigate foreign central banking systems, and to recommend necessary reforms. This Commission, consisting of 18 senators and representatives, was headed by Nelson Aldrich, a prominent and able Republican senator from Rhode Island. The Commission employed a number of academic men to make the necessary studies of American and foreign banking experiences and their 40 or more reports have become classic studies in the field of financial history. Aldrich himself went abroad to study foreign systems, and he read extensively to acquaint himself with the fundamentals of the problem. The Commission finally proposed a single central banking system to be known as the National Reserve Association. This central bank was to be controlled largely by directors elected by the country's large banks. That feature was fatal to a plan which otherwise was good.

It must be remembered that these reforms were being advanced in an era when "trust busting" was very much in the headlines. A transcontinental railroad trust had been broken in 1904, a meat packers' trust

had been under fire, and in 1911 both the oil and tobacco trusts had been found guilty and ordered dissolved. For some time there had also been rumors of a "money trust." It was well known that J. P. Morgan, the investment banker, had in the Panic of 1907 been the final arbiter as to which distressed financial houses deserved a life-saving loan and which ones would have to perish. He had been a one-man Federal Reserve System and Reconstruction Finance Corporation, to use the parlance of a later generation. It did not matter that he had executed this responsibility with considerable wisdom; people said that one man should not have so much power in a democracy. He and his colleagues were alleged to control over $20 billion in banks, insurance companies, and industries. There were stories to the effect that if one displeased Morgan, the offender would find it hard to obtain a loan even with the best of security. In 1912 an investigation of this "money trust" was demanded and authorized by Congress. Representative Arsène Pujo of Louisiana headed the investigating committee. Morgan and his partners and colleagues were called in to testify and hundreds of pages of evidence were gathered. Morgan insisted that it was impossible to obtain a trust in money; skillfully side-stepping all leading questions, he denied that he had any power. The committee nevertheless reported that there was evidence of "a vast and growing concentration of money and credit in the hands of a comparatively few men." [4]

This then was the atmosphere in which the public was asked to accept Nelson Aldrich's plan for a central bank controlled by the big bankers. The plan would have been vigorously opposed had the Republicans remained in power. That party split in 1912, however, when the Progressive or Bull Moose faction bolted and nominated ex-President Teddy Roosevelt. The regulars chose President William Howard Taft, and the Democrats picked an ex-college president and recent reform governor of New Jersey, Woodrow Wilson. Wilson won and appointed one of his staunch supporters in the Democratic party, William Jennings Bryan, to a cabinet post. Bryan was influential in Wilson's first administration. When Bryan had been a presidential candidate himself, he had declaimed against the selfish and corrupt power of the moneyed men of Wall Street. And by tradition, up to that time anyway, the Democratic party favored states' rights and decentralization of power. All this had an important bearing on the character of the structure of the new central banking system. Carter Glass, a congressman from Virginia, assumed responsibility for the framing of a more acceptable law. He kept many of the fine features of Aldrich's proposal but endeavored to distribute the authority and control.

---

[4] *Report of the Pujo Committee* (Feb. 28, 1913), p. 129.

Structure of the Federal Reserve System

The Federal Reserve System was a central banking system superimposed on the National Banking System. All national banks were obliged to join the Federal Reserve System. That requirement meant that every national bank had to buy capital stock in the new system equal to three per cent of its own capital and surplus: i.e., an Indianapolis National Bank with a capital and surplus of $1,200,000 had to buy $36,000 of capital stock of the Federal Reserve System.[5] Nonnational banks were also encouraged to join the new system if they would conform to certain minimum standards, but at first only a few large ones saw fit to join. Thus the owners of the Federal Reserve System were the "member banks," chiefly national banks. Their owners, in turn, were tens of thousands of investors scattered over the country. But in this case, as shall be seen, control did not go with ownership.

To avoid concentration of central banking power in the East the country was divided into twelve districts of presumably equal financial needs (see Figure 1, p. 56). Each district had its own Federal Reserve Bank. Thus New York and Atlanta, Chicago and Minneapolis, Boston and San Francisco were put on an equal footing, or so it might seem. Actually the New York Federal Reserve Bank, since it does more business than any other, has wielded more influence than the others. At the head of each of these twelve regional central banks there was a board of directors of nine men. The boards consisted of three types of directors. The three Class A directors were bankers, and the three Class B directors were businessmen and farmers. These six, representing lenders and borrowers, were elected by the member banks on a basis of "one bank, one vote." A third group of three, the Class C directors, were appointed by the Federal Reserve authorities in Washington; they represented the public and the government, and two of them held the chairmanship and vice-chairmanship, respectively, of the boards. Observe that no single group—borrowers, lenders, or public alias government—has a majority on these boards. A majority of at least two groups must agree to enact any policy or to pass any motion. This arrangement was of course carefully planned to avoid dominance by any economic interest, especially dominance by the banker interest. It was a fine system of checks and balances which some critics have since wished had also been used on the more important top Board heading the whole system.

The Federal Reserve System was headed at this time by a Board of seven. The Secretary of the Treasury and the Comptroller of the Cur-

---

[5] It might later have to buy another three per cent. This requirement has never been invoked.

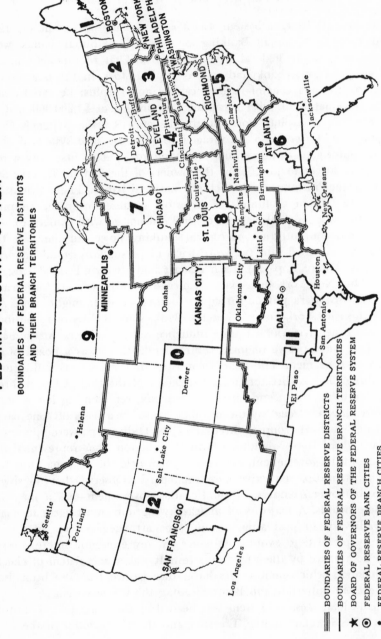

FEDERAL RESERVE SYSTEM

BOUNDARIES OF FEDERAL RESERVE DISTRICTS
AND THEIR BRANCH TERRITORIES

BOSTON

NEW YORK
PHILADELPHIA
WASHINGTON

Buffalo
Detroit
CLEVELAND
Pittsburg
Cincinnati
Baltimore
RICHMOND
Charlotte

Jacksonville

Nashville
Birmingham ATLANTA
Memphis
Louisville
CHICAGO
ST. LOUIS
Little Rock
New Orleans

MINNEAPOLIS
Omaha
KANSAS CITY
Oklahoma City
Houston
DALLAS
San Antonio

Helena
Denver

El Paso

Salt Lake City

Seattle
Portland
SAN FRANCISCO

Los Angeles

BOUNDARIES OF FEDERAL RESERVE DISTRICTS
BOUNDARIES OF FEDERAL RESERVE BRANCH TERRITORIES
BOARD OF GOVERNORS OF THE FEDERAL RESERVE SYSTEM
★ FEDERAL RESERVE BANK CITIES
● FEDERAL RESERVE BRANCH CITIES

FIGURE 1

Federal Reserve Bulletin

rency were members ex officio. Five others were appointed by the President with advice and consent of the Senate, but no more than one was to come from any Federal Reserve district. The President also designates which men are to be the chairman and vice-chairman of this Board. Notice that the owners of the system have no voice in the choice of the top Board members. The theory is that the Federal Reserve System is a non-profit-making institution operated for the good of the country as a whole. Thus the policy making Board crowning the Federal Reserve System is politically appointed. But since such a Board might at times need expert advice, a Federal Advisory Council of 12 bankers is provided. They are to be chosen by the 12 Federal Reserve Bank Boards and to meet with the Federal Reserve Board at least four times a year and more often if necessary. This Council has often given good advice, but the Board is not compelled to accept the Council's advice.

The Federal Reserve Board has many responsibilities, small and large. They range from passing on the admission of state banks to membership and removing officers and directors of member banks for violations of law or for unsound banking practices to altering rediscount rates and making use of other credit control devices. The Board is the most important decision-making body in the system. Once appointed, it was originally supposed to be free of political pressure; to ensure this, the members enjoyed long tenure and good salaries as measured by government standards. It is still a matter of debate whether this "freedom from political pressure" is an impossible ideal.

Faults of the National Banking System Remedied

The Federal Reserve System successfully corrected most of the faults of the banking system preceding it. Let us see how it did so.

The inelastic national bank note, backed by government bonds, was supplemented by a new elastic bank note, the Federal Reserve note.[6] After some preliminary experimentation, that note was backed at least 40 per cent by gold and the remaining 60 per cent or less by commercial paper—that is, promissory notes and drafts. These were expected to be short-term and self-liquidating in character. (Self-liquidating loans are for projects that will pay for themselves during the term of the loan; an example is a loan of $1000 for 90 days to a toy store to stock up for the Christmas trade; presumably this would be paid off within a month after the holiday season.) Thus the amount of new bank notes outstanding expanded in busy seasons or in prosperous periods as businesses borrowed more from the banks and the banks in turn borrowed from the Federal

---

[6] A Federal Reserve Bank note was also devised and used on four separate occasions for different purposes but it was never well received and was abolished in 1945.

Reserve Banks; likewise, the supply of these notes contracted in dull seasons or in poor times as businesses paid off their debts to the banks and the banks did the same to the Federal Reserve Banks.

Member banks were required (after 1917) to keep all their legal reserves against deposits in the Federal Reserve Bank in their district. The amount of legal reserve required still varied depending on the size of the city in which the member bank was located. The requirement for New York and Chicago banks was 13 per cent; for 50 or so middle-sized cities' banks it was 10 per cent; and for other member banks, it was 7 per cent. For time deposits in all member banks it was 3 per cent. The concentration of these legal reserves in the Federal Reserve Banks served several purposes. For one thing, it took legal reserves out of a speculative money market; for another, it provided the regional central bank with a nucleus of funds to lend to any solvent but illiquid bank in need of help. Such a bank might now rediscount eligible paper at its Federal Reserve Bank or even secure an advance (loan) on its own signature accompanied by satisfactory collateral. No longer was rediscounting or seeking loans from another bank a sign of weakness.

Under the new Federal Reserve System a market was created in which bills of exchange (drawn in dollars on American banks and business houses) could be rediscounted or sold. America became less dependent on the London money market. This became especially important as World War I progressed and American funds played an ever more active role in financing that war and the reconstruction period afterward.

With the Federal Reserve Banks available to help, banks no longer felt so dependent on the Treasury. And, as will be seen shortly, the government itself made great use of the new central banking system during the war. As a consequence, the old sub-treasury system was liquidated in 1921.

Probably the fault which the Federal Reserve System did the least to remedy was the virtual prohibition of loans on real estate which made it so difficult for farmers to obtain long-term loans from national banks. This, however, was partially remedied in 1916 when an agricultural Federal Reserve System was set up in the form of Federal Land Banks to assist joint stock land banks to handle long-term loans. Similarly a Federal Intermediate Credit System was established in 1923 to assist farmers' cooperatives in the handling of loans of three to five years. Eventually these and other agricultural credit institutions were gathered up in 1933 under one agency, the Farm Credit Administration. Likewise the laws and regulations governing real estate loans were successively relaxed in 1916, 1927, 1933 and 1935.

The clearing and collecting of checks was greatly improved by the

Federal Reserve System. Each Federal Reserve Bank served as a clearing house for all the member banks in its district and also for some other banks (known as "non-member clearing banks") which wished to make use of the System's clearing privileges. The method of operation is simple. Member banks' legal reserves served also as their clearing accounts. A check by John Doe drawn on Bank A payable to Richard Roe who endorsed it for deposit in Bank B would be deducted from Bank A's legal reserve and added to Bank B's. The banks would of course make the proper entries in their own houses on their customers' accounts. This new system greatly reduced the size of the "float" and the length of time it took to collect a check. It did not, however, eliminate local clearing houses: they were still more efficient than the Federal Reserve Banks for purely local clearing operations. To handle payments between Federal Reserve districts, an Interdistrict Settlement Fund [7] was established in Washington with special telegraphic communication to all Federal Reserve Banks. Thus today it is the exceptional check that is not cleared in about two days' time.

Finally, the new system gave the nation a central bank whose primary interest at first was to soften the impact of depressions by helping worthy but distressed banks. Federal Reserve Banks stood ready to rediscount eligible paper of such banks or to make them advances. Profits were supposedly a minor consideration of the Federal Reserve Banks, although they have generally made handsome profits. Later the authorities at the head of the new system began to think in terms of not merely softening depressions, but of preventing them. But the first major task that the Federal Reserve System had to face, upon opening its doors in November 1914, was the financial dislocation caused by the outbreak of World War I in August. Somewhat later the System played an active financial role in our participation in that great war.

Financing World War I

The total direct American expenditures attributable to World War I were $32.8 billion. This is more than we had spent in the century preceding World War I; in other words it was a stupendous amount for that time. Fortunately, we had just renovated our tax structure in 1913 and our banking system in 1914; we had a good money system; and thanks to no major wars for two generations, we had a light public debt. The improved banking system was to play an important role in financing the war. For one thing, the five war-bond campaigns which raised a total of $21.4 billion were handled very largely by the Federal Reserve System. The enormous detail involved in this may be judged

[7] Until 1933 it was called the Gold Settlement Fund.

from the fact that about 22,000,000 persons subscribed for Liberty Bonds in the Fourth Loan.

To appreciate the part played by the Federal Reserve System in financing the great emergencies of the last generation, especially the two world wars, we should first recall some simple but fundamental facts about war financing. There are three basic ways of financing a war: by taxation, by borrowing, and by creating money; and they are desirable in that order. Unfortunately, they are also immediately painful in the same order. In other words, taxation is the best but most painful way; creating money is the worst but at first the least painful way. Borrowing stands in between, and borrowing was what the new banking system was expected to facilitate in an emergency. Patriotic citizens were encouraged not only to lend their savings to their government by buying war bonds, but they were also urged to borrow from their banks to buy additional bonds and to pay for them with future savings. The banks were willing to hold the bonds as collateral for the loans, and the Federal Reserve Banks in turn were willing to advance the banks any credit they might need to accomplish the transaction. Such war loans were not self-liquidating and were not always soon paid off. Occasionally banks had to take over the bonds themselves.

An even more important feature af war financing, however, was the fact that banks themselves bought many billions of dollars of short-term government obligations, paying for them with credit of the banks' own creation, or if necessary, with credit based on reserves borrowed from the Federal Reserve Banks. Between June 1914 and June 1920, total loans and investments of all commercial banks more than doubled. The largest item in the increase was bank loans. The second largest was U.S. government obligations, which grew from $1 billion to $4 billion. The point of all this is that during these six years, as a result of indirect and direct purchases of government obligations, the total supply of currency outside banks and of demand deposits doubled. The price level somewhat more than doubled. The primary concern of the Federal Reserve Banks during most of this period was seeing to it that the government and the war industries had all the funds they needed when they were needed. Just as steel companies manufactured steel for the war effort, the Federal Reserve System produced credit for the war effort. To the extent that this could be done by efficient handling of tax receipts or by drawing on the past savings of citizens, the Reserve System was glad to assist. Its main aim, however, was to provide the credit somehow, and much of it had to be created more or less indirectly. It might appear that all of the credit was borrowed, but actually some of it was created in a subtle but roundabout fashion. Yet the Federal Reserve System could hardly have done otherwise. And it un-

doubtedly did the job better, with less strain on the economy's finances and with less inflation, than the archaic pre-war banking system possibly could have done it.

The Post-War Depression

Although World War I fighting ended with the Armistice of November 11, 1918, the costs of hostilities and demobilization continued high for another year. Furthermore, prices continued to rise. There was speculation in numerous basic raw materials that seemed in short supply; merchants ordered more goods than they needed because they knew from experience that only part of those orders would be filled; manufacturers planned further expansion of their plants; bank loans increased, interest rates rose, and businessmen found the prosperity enjoyable. Yet an economist with experience could see that a "boom and bust" was in the making. That was just the sort of thing which the Federal Reserve System was created to alleviate. But it was the System's first real experience, and some ineptness was to be expected.

The chief credit control device at this time was the rediscount rate. It was not a powerful tool. The Federal Reserve Board should have made vigorous use of it in mid-1919 to discourage further borrowing from the Federal Reserve Banks by the member banks to finance business loans. Such a rediscount rate increase would have raised interest rates and raised the costs of speculation and of business expansion. The Federal Advisory Council urged this step in the summer of 1919, but the Board denied that business was overexpanded. Already the Board was facing a problem that was to plague it many times again. The Treasury was dictating policy to it. The Treasury had a large short-term debt of $6.5 billion which it wanted to convert into longer-term obligations and wanted to get into the hands of the public. Low interest rates kept bond prices attractively high and kept costs of financing down. To the Treasury it was a secondary consideration that low interest rates stimulated speculative activity.

Finally, late in 1919, with virtually no warning, the Board reversed its stand and raised rediscount rates. The stock market slumped and a cry of anguish from Wall Street was followed by a demand for Congressional investigation of the Board. But speculative activity revived, and despite another raise in the rediscount rate in January, the boom continued until late spring. By that time prices were so far ahead of wages that many people had to watch their buying habits, and a "buyers' strike" was said to be under way. Merchants began cancelling their inflated orders to manufacturers, raw material speculators saw the markets for their hoards dry up, and all began cutting prices to save

what they could. Between May 1920 and May 1921, wholesale prices fell 40 per cent and the index of industrial production dropped about 25 per cent. Once this panic and depression began, the Federal Reserve Banks performed yeoman service in helping solvent distressed banks. Borrowing at Federal Reserve Banks actually increased during the critical second half of 1920. The Federal Reserve System lived up to every reasonable expectation after the panic struck, but the System had not done well in preventing the panic from developing. More effective preventive action was to be the next goal.

The Discovery of Open-Market Operations

About 1922 the Federal Reserve authorities accidentally discovered a new and powerful credit control device known as the open-market operation. The open markets through which the operations took place were the markets for bankers' acceptances and for Treasury certificates, especially the latter. These were the markets in which banks and big corporations invested their surplus funds, hence the markets where marginal interest rates were determined. By buying or selling in these markets, the Federal Reserve authorities were able to exert considerable leverage on interest rates. Even more important, Federal Reserve operations in these markets affected member banks' legal reserves and hence the banks' ability and their willingness to lend to customers. Let us see more specifically what the mechanics of an open-market operation are.

If the Federal Reserve authorities believe that business is expanding too rapidly, they may engage in open-market *selling* operations to curb the expansion. Let us assume that the Open Market Committee orders the sale of $100,000,000 of Treasury certificates owned by the Federal Reserve Banks. All 12 Banks are expected to participate in these operations. The offer of so many Treasury certificates necessarily forces down the quotations on them. Purchasers—whether they be individuals, corporations, or banks—usually pay for the certificates with checks on their bank accounts. These checks are directly or indirectly payable to the Federal Reserve Banks offering the certificates, and the Banks cash them simply by deducting the amount of the checks from the accounts of the commercial banks on which they are drawn. Those accounts of course are the banks' legal reserve accounts. A reduction in those accounts curtails, perhaps several fold, the ability of those banks to make business loans. This condition tightens the credit supply and tends to result in higher interest rates that raise the cost of business expansion and so discourage it. Open-market selling operations were sometimes accompanied by raising rediscount rates to accomplish the same purpose in two ways at once.

Contrariwise, if the Federal Reserve authorities believe that business conditions are unduly dull and need stimulating, they may engage in open-market *buying* operations. The mechanics are similar but in reverse. The Federal Reserve Banks might agree to buy $100,000,000 of Treasury certificates on the open market from anyone (individuals, corporations or banks) who will sell them. The Federal Reserve Banks pay for the certificates with their own checks which are deposited in the buyers' banks and are promptly added by those banks to their accounts in the Federal Reserve Banks. Those accounts are their legal reserve accounts. Increasing those accounts enables the banks to make more business loans by reducing the interest rates or otherwise encouraging customers to borrow. The Federal Reserve authorities sometimes accompany open-market buying operations with a reduction in rediscount rates. On the whole, open-market buying operations are less effective than open-market selling operations, and the explanation is found in the old adage, "You can lead a horse to water, but you cannot make him drink." In other words, if businessmen foresee an unprofitable future, a mere reduction in interest rates will probably be insufficient to change their minds.

Open-market operations were the great financial discovery of the 1920's. The Federal Reserve authorities came to believe that they could now do more than soften the impact of depressions: they could virtually prevent them. The experience of the years from 1922 to 1928 seemed to bear out that belief. Boomlets were pricked in 1922, 1925 and late 1927, and the country was lifted out of threatened recessions in 1924, early 1927 and 1928. Open-market operations were also used to assist Great Britain and other neighbors to return to the gold standard. When the nations were ready to resume specie payments, the Federal Reserve authorities engaged in open-market buying operations to reduce interest rates here and to make this country a less attractive place to send funds (some of them in gold) for investment.

The 1925–29 Boom and Crash

Unfortunately, open-market buying operations in the 1920's came in an era when the ardor for business expansion and speculation needed dampening more than it needed stimulating. Bank reserves and deposits had already been expanded by World War I. Between 1922 and 1928, Federal Reserve Credit (that is, bills bought, bills rediscounted, and U.S. Government obligations) increased from $1.32 billion to $1.76 billion or by about 33 per cent. All banks expanded their loans and investments from $39.8 billion to $58.6 billion between 1922 and the end of 1929, or by about 50 per cent. To what extent there is a causal

relationship here, it is hard to say. The Chase National Bank's able economist, the late B. M. Anderson, blamed the 1929 boom and panic largely on the additional reserves created by open-market buying operations.[8] In any event mounting reserves were hardly calculated to discourage loans, investments, business expansion and a growth of speculation. Banks made loans to customers on real estate collateral; and loans were made to finance purchases of securities and of agricultural commodities. Banks invested in many securities other than U.S. government obligations; some of these were good, some were poor, but most of them were inflated, for stock averages more than doubled between 1925 and 1929. An important reason for these investments was the simple fact that there was not nearly enough eligible paper (short-term self-liquidating notes and drafts) for banks to put their funds in. The expansion of bank reserves caused by the war and by the open-market buying operations mentioned above made the banks all the more anxious to find new outlets for their funds. The purchase of stocks stimulated the stock market and made stocks seem that much more attractive and sound.

Of course there were experts to rationalize and justify this new development. It was pointed out that one share of Ford stock of $100 (if bought in 1903) would have been worth $1,000,000, in 1928. If our stupendous industrial growth could increase security values that way, of course there was nothing unhealthy, or so it was argued by many who pointed to the stock values of thriving companies doubling every two years. It was also contended that although securities were not self-liquidating, they could always be disposed of, when necessary, on our well-organized stock markets. Many believed (or seemed to believe) that major depressions could be prevented by the new credit control device, open-market operations. These illusions were all tragically smashed in October 1929.

The speculative mania of 1925–29 saw the prices of stocks rise sharply. General Motors tripled in price, Radio Corporation of America rose six fold, and General Electric went up eight fold. The situation attracted thousands of new "investors" many of whom were speculating with their meager savings, hoping to double their money by buying on a margin. No wonder the volume of shares traded more than doubled, and no wonder the bubble burst when enough people finally came to believe that stock prices could go no higher. Speculations are built on optimism; prices must not stand still. Prices must rise to satisfy the optimism, or disillusionment sets in on a wide scale: the "bust" has arrived. It arrived in October 1929, on one day of which 16 million shares were sold (one million shares sold is a busy day), and some stocks fell over 10 per cent.

By 1932 stocks had fallen, on the average, to a quarter of their 1929 values.

Bank Failures and the 1933 Bank Holiday

The decline in stocks and also in real estate and in agricultural commodities (for the prices of all these were linked together), was bound to affect American banks. Even during the prosperous 1920's an average of over 600 banks failed each year. Banks in some communities were largely dependent on the success of local crops, on local business conditions, and on the judgment of the banks' local managers, who often showed more optimism and aggressiveness than they did foresight and a feeling of responsibility for the banks' stockholders. The mounting number of bank failures, shown by the accompanying table, and the declining prestige of the banking profession (not to mention worsening economic conditions

TABLE 1

BANK FAILURES, 1921–34

1921 (*previous worst depression year*)	505
1922 (*low year, 1922–29*)	366
1926 (*high year, 1922–29*)	976
1922–29 average	651
1929	659
1930	1,350
1931	2,293
1932	1,453
1933 (*bank moratorium year*)	4,000
1934 (*F.D.I.C. in operation*)	57

at home and abroad as the depression deepened) reached a climax in the fall and winter of 1932–33. As more banks failed, more people withdrew their deposits for safekeeping, or at least held more cash. Various measures were taken to provide the banks with the extra bank notes they needed to remain liquid. One important step was the Glass-Steagall Act of 1932, which permitted banks temporarily to back requests for Federal Reserve notes with U.S. government bonds instead of with gold or eligible commercial paper only.[9] The Federal Reserve System assisted with open-market buying operations, and the Hoover Administration created the Reconstruction Finance Corporation. But all these efforts, and others too, were not enough.

The 1933 banking crisis began in Nevada in November 1932; it reached serious proportions in Michigan by February; and it culminated in all the other major states and in the nation as a whole in early

---

[9] This became permanent in 1945. Most Federal Reserve notes are backed by gold certificates and United States government securities today.

March. President Franklin D. Roosevelt was being inaugurated at this time, and he declared a nation-wide banking holiday lasting several days. As a result of the holiday, all banks were closed and investigated; some 2,000 never opened their doors again. Financial aid was extended to others by letting them sell preferred stock to the Reconstruction Finance Corporation.

Banking Reforms of 1933–35

Congress began to think seriously of remedying the defects in our banking system which this last great panic and depression had revealed. Since the standing and the prestige of bankers and former financial giants were at very low ebb, their influence in determining the nature of the reforms was less than it ordinarily would have been. Indeed, new economic philosophies that were distasteful to them were brought forward. Government was given a larger hand in determining monetary policies, and financiers a smaller one. Policies were decided more and more in terms of collective concepts such as the national income, total investment, and consumer spending. A revolution in economic theology took place with John M. Keynes supplanting Alfred Marshall as the "prophet on the mount." Deficit spending became acceptable, and thrift was sometimes considered evil. Those who espoused these new theories and helped put them into law and into effect achieved great prestige.

As far as the Federal Reserve System is concerned, there were four laws in particular, enacted between 1933 and 1935, that changed the framework of the System and redirected the viewpoints of its policy makers. These were the Banking Acts of 1933 and of 1935, and to a lesser degree the Securities Act of 1933 and the Securities and Exchange Act of 1934. What did these four pieces of legislation accomplish? The banking legislation of 1933–35 may be analyzed under four headings: (1) what it did to restore confidence in banks; (2) what it did to strengthen banks; (3) what it did to remove the bankers' temptation to speculate; and the most important (4), what it did to increase the power of the Federal Reserve System.

The action of the government in closing all banks in March 1933 and only reopening those which passed inspection helped to restore confidence in banks. But it was felt that something also had to be done to reduce the nation's large number of bank failures and to prevent the "runs" which were so dramatically tragic and fatal in every panic. The 1933 law established a temporary Federal Deposit Insurance Corporation, and the 1935 law made it permanent. The F.D.I.C. is an organization separate from the Federal Reserve System. Depositors in all banks

belonging to it had their deposits insured up to $5,000 until 1950. Since then their deposits have been insured up to $10,000. All members of the Federal Reserve System have to belong to the F.D.I.C. and other banks may do so by meeting its requirements. The majority of banks promptly joined the new system, with the result that most depositors were protected, cautious people became willing to put their savings in banks again, and bank failures fell off encouragingly. These results came about because the F.D.I.C. examined its member banks, because it took steps to correct bad practices, and because it liquidated weak banks before failure took place. The F.D.I.C. has had success in protecting depositors, and today it has $1 billion of assets. It could not unaided withstand a 1929–33 depression, but it may do a great deal toward preventing one.

Several steps were taken with a view to strengthening banks. Restrictions on the formation of branch banks were eased. National banks might have branches in states where state banks were permitted to have them. The greatest number of failures had been among small single banks, and this fact had often been contrasted, perhaps unfairly, with the Canadian branch banking system's record of only one failure in many years. Another step was the loosening of restrictions on real estate loans. This was done partly to attract state banks with such business into the Federal Reserve System. And partly it was effected because believers in the new economic philosophy stressed the need for more capital investment to pull the country out of the depression. To encourage more banks to join the Federal Reserve System, capital requirements were eased, too, and the old double liability feature on national bank stock was removed. Not only state banks but also mutual savings banks and Morris Plan banks were encouraged to join. Finally, in times of emergency, member banks were permitted to borrow from the Federal Reserve System on their own notes secured to the satisfaction of the Federal Reserve Bank. No longer was it necessary to have eligible paper. All this was intended to encourage banks to lend, to stimulate capital formation in the nation, and to provide bankers with a feeling of greater security. But the new methods marked a sharp departure from the theory of the Federal Reserve System's founders that self-liquidating paper should be the basis for credit expansion.[10]

Member banks were henceforth forbidden to make interest payment on demand deposits, and they were forbidden to borrow from Federal Reserve Banks for speculative purposes. The elimination of the payment of interest on demand deposits was done partly to offset the cost to the banks of federal deposit insurance. The Federal Reserve Banks were ex-

[10] After 1932 Federal Reserve notes could be backed by United States government bonds up to 60 per cent, by special permission, which was readily obtained. Since 1945 they may be backed 75 per cent; permission is no longer required.

pected to keep themselves informed of the nature of the loans made by member banks in their district. Also the Banking Act of 1933 required that commercial banks and investment banks should no longer be combined as they had been with rather disastrous results in the 1920's. In addition, the two Securities Acts of 1933 and 1934 were themselves "a pure food and drug law for securities:" the seller had to state the nature of the ingredients. If the investment banker withheld pertinent information and the buyer could later claim that he would not have bought the securities had he been given such information, the seller was subject to severe penalties. This restriction may have tended to improve the quality of securities, especially of those listed on the stock exchanges.

Perhaps the most important feature of the new legislation was the endeavor to enlarge the powers of the Federal Reserve Board over the 12 Federal Reserve Banks and over the member banks. This was accomplished in several ways. The name of the Board was altered to "Board of Governors of the Federal Reserve System." Thus each of the seven members had the title of governor during his tenure of 14 years. The Secretary of the Treasury and Comptroller General were no longer ex officio Board members. The President still appointed the chairman and vice-chairman, but they held these offices for only four years at a time. President Roosevelt chose a Board in 1935 that was largely new; he appointed Marriner Eccles, a Utah banker of 22 years' experience, as the new chairman. Not only did the President have more power over the Board, but the Board had more authority over the Federal Reserve Banks. The boards of the Federal Reserve Banks now appointed the presidents and vice-presidents of their Banks subject to the approval of the Board of Governors in Washington. The Bank president selected the Bank officers. Thus the officers were responsible to the Bank president and the president to the Board of Governors. The Board might remove any member bank officer if he continued "unsafe and unsound practices" after having been warned.

The seven members of the Board of Governors, together with five representatives of the Federal Reserve Banks, constitute the Federal Open Market Committee which exercises open-market powers of credit control. Since 12 is a somewhat unwieldy number for prompt action, the duties of this group are sometimes delegated to an executive committee of five, or even of two (the Board chairman and the New York Federal Reserve Bank president). The decisions of this group are binding on all Federal Reserve Banks. The Board also reviews rediscount rates every two weeks. Finally the Board obtained two important new credit controls. Under the Securities and Exchange Act of 1934, it was given the power to fix margin requirements on stock exchanges. Because the Federal Reserve Board was unable to control the amount of credit available for specula-

tion in 1925–29, it now got power to dictate the rules of speculation.[11] An even more important control was given the Board under the Banking Act of 1935. This was the authority to increase the legal reserves against deposits required of member banks as much as 100 per cent above the pre-1935 figure. In other words, the Board might raise or lower legal reserves anywhere between minima of 7, 10 and 13 per cent, the old reserve rates for demand deposits, and 14, 20 and 26 per cent, the maximum rates. This was regarded as a tremendously powerful credit control device. Some experts feared that even the threat of using it might have a disrupting influence on the economy. At the same time that more control was given the Board over member banks' deposits, the national banks were deprived of their former privilege of issuing national bank notes, and arrangements were made to retire gradually the notes in circulation.

The Federal Reserve System now had new top personnel, new powers, and some new credit controls; but it also had greater responsibilities than ever before. Would the new problems be similar to the old ones, or at least recognizably similar? The first problem turned out to be not at all similar.

The Problem of Excess Reserves

A major financial problem in the latter 1930's was the excess reserves of member banks. Back in the 1920's excess reserves of $50 million were large; in 1932 the figure of $120 million was regarded as distinctly abnormal. By the end of 1935 excess reserves amounted to about $3,000 million. These growing excess reserves were the result of open-market buying operations in the early 1930's and of the inflow of gold from abroad after devaluation in 1933–34. The total of excess reserves was well above the $2,400 million of Federal Reserve Bank holdings of bills and U.S. government obligations. In other words, if the Federal Reserve System had engaged in open-market selling operations on a scale grand enough to dispose of all their bills and government securities, the member banks would still have had large excess reserves ($3,000 million less $2,400 million leaves $600 million). What was the meaning of that? It simply meant that in case another business boom developed, the Federal Reserve Banks could not control it with open-market selling operations.

The new credit control of changeable legal reserve requirements had been created partly to meet such a situation. When the index of industrial production showed a rapid return toward prosperity in 1936, the Board decided to make use of the new reserve controls. Reserve require-

---

[11] At times in 1929 half the funds on the call-money market came from sources other than banks, i.e., from persons or corporations with surplus cash to lend temporarily.

ments were doubled between August 1936 and May 1937 (see Table 2), and also margin requirements were imposed for the first time. In addition, the Treasury created a new device to offset the continued inflow of gold from abroad. This was gold sterilization. Fundamentally the government bought gold with bonds instead of with new money [12] and thus prevented gold from becoming a reserve for multiple credit expansion. Momentarily the combination of these controls brought excess reserves to a figure below the Federal Reserve Banks' supply of bills and government securities. Although that condition lasted less than a year, the fear of uncontrollable credit expansion disappeared for a longer time. In its place the Federal Reserve System now faced another but more familiar problem.

TABLE 2

MEMBER BANK RESERVE REQUIREMENTS AT SELECTED DATES

Period in Effect	Central Res. City Banks	Reserve City Banks	Country Banks	Time Deposits, All Member Banks
June 21, 1917–Aug. 15, 1936	13	10	7	3
Aug. 16, 1936–Feb. 28, 1937	19.5	15	10.5	4.5
Mar. 1, 1937–Apr. 30, 1937	22.75	17.5	12.25	5.25
May 1, 1937–Apr. 15, 1938	26	20	14	6
Apr. 16, 1938–Oct. 31, 1941	22.75	17.5	12	5
Nov. 1, 1941–Sept. 15, 1948	20-26*	20	14	6
Sept. 16, 1949–May 4, 1949 †	26	22	16	7.5
May 5, 1949–June 30, 1949 †	24	21	15	7
June 30, 1949–Aug. 31, 1949	24	20	14	6
As of Jan. 1951	24	20	14	6

* Changed five times, ranging between 20 and 26 per cent.
† Period of temporarily high requirements.
Source: *Federal Reserve Bulletin*, March, 1951, p. 282.

The 1937–39 Depression

The Federal Reserve authorities had been accused, after the 1920 and 1929 debacles, of using their controls in a "too little and too late" manner. Yet some critics contended that the changeable reserve-requirement control given the Board in 1935 was too heavy an instrument for the delicate financial operations the Board must engage in. As we have seen, the Board chose not to repeat the limited use of its controls as in 1920 and 1929. The boom collapsed and became a depression of some consequence. This took place immediately after reserve requirements were set at their maximum. There were many opinions on "What caused the depression?" For obvious reasons of timing, some said it was the drastic

[12] That is, instead of with gold certificates. Federal Reserve Banks had to hold them as their legal reserves against deposits and Federal Reserve notes.

imposition of higher reserve requirements. Others pointed to the sharp decline in deficit spending by the government about this time. Still others contended that the boom collapsed because businessmen had become more pessimistic over the opportunities for profits.[13] The latter explanation merely raised the further question of why businessmen had become more pessimistic. This was the era of the sitdown strike in Detroit and of the mounting strength of the new industrial labor union, the C. I. O. This organization won several notable victories, thereby raising labor costs, and reducing probable profit margins.

Regardless of the causes of the new depression, something had to be done to cure it. The Board engaged in minor open-market buying operations and lowered rediscount rates during the summer of 1937. In the fall some gold was desterilized, margin requirements were reduced, and easier requirements for loans were announced. Still the depression grew. In the spring all sterilized gold was reactivated and reserve requirements were reduced. By the summer of 1938 the depression was still worse; the Board had been unable to stop it from growing. Incidentally, the excess reserves were as great as they had been in 1936 and were destined to become still larger, although no one was worrying about them any more. The Board was finding that the control of depressions was a very difficult undertaking indeed. The country was flooded with panaceas. The Board issued a statement to the effect that there were many phases of economic life that could not be controlled through monetary means alone. Still such means were important, and the Federal Reserve System asked to be entrusted with greater money controls. It was said that the powers of the Treasury over money out-weighed those of the Federal Reserve System. This opinion was to be heard more and more frequently in the 1940's.

Financing World War II

World War II broke out in Europe in September 1939; in December 1941, this country was drawn in. This war was fought on a much grander scale than World War I; for one thing, we were engaging major military powers on two fronts at the same time; for another, the war lasted over twice as long; and for a third, our cash outlay was about 12 times as great. We put some 12 million men under arms and supplied them and millions more of our allies' troops with food, munitions and other military necessities. World War II cost us nearly $350,000,000,000 between 1940 and 1945. What part did the Federal Reserve System play in all this?

---

13 B. M. Anderson's explanation.

It was pointed out in connection with the discussion of World War I that there are three basic ways of financing a war: by taxation, by borrowing (selling bonds), and by creating money. Modern governments do not create more money simply by printing it; that is too crude. Selling bonds either directly or indirectly *to banks* is a more subtle way of creating money. In World War I the nation's supply of demand deposits and currency in circulation doubled, and so did the price level. In World War II demand deposits and currency in circulation tripled but the price level was kept under better control. This great increase in demand deposits and currency was an important consequence of the way that Congress and the Treasury financed the war. About 40 per cent of the cost of the war was paid for out of taxes, although in the early years taxes contributed a smaller part than that. About 33 per cent of the cost of the war was paid for out of borrowings from non-bank sources, but this too was smaller in the early war years. The remaining 27 per cent of the cost of the war came from banks, some of it being created money and some not.

How did the banks create money and credit? There were several ways. In the early days of the war the banks bought half the war bonds; but after 1942 banks were not allowed to buy bonds directly. At all times, however, they were encouraged to invest in Treasury bills (which mature in three months) and Treasury certificates (which mature in a year). Soon most of their excess reserves were converted into such short-term government obligations.

Banks were forbidden to hold bonds with maturities longer than 10 years away and could not buy bonds directly from the Treasury. Yet banks preferred bonds to bills, certificates, or notes, because the bonds carried a higher rate of interest. This higher rate would normally be the compensation for the lender's accepting a longer maturity, but that was changed about 1942. The Treasury asked the Federal Reserve Banks to redeem all government obligations at par or better on demand. This request was to eliminate any fear by bond buyers that bonds would fall sharply in price just when the owners might want to cash them. World War I Liberty bonds had fallen to 82 in 1920, and some potential bond buyers, remembering their losses, hesitated to buy World War II bonds, especially at low rates. In order for the banks to get possession of bonds of 10 years or less maturity that they might hold, they had to buy them, generally at a premium, from private owners. To get the funds for this, the banks sold their Treasury bills and certificates to the Federal Reserve Banks. This shifting from short term to long term securities, especially prevalent during bond drives, was called a "roll-over operation." This process amounted to an open-market buying operation of Federal Reserve Banks, and it increased the banks' legal reserves. In the

course of the war the Federal Reserve Banks thus accumulatd $24 billion of government obligations, many of them being Treasury bills and certificates. By 1945, the banks of the nation held about 40 per cent of the national debt, and the Federal Reserve Banks had repurchased 9 per cent more. All this, of course, helped to increase the supply of demand deposits and to feed the war-time flames of inflation.

During the course of the war the Board received a new credit control which it designated as Regulation W. This control was intended to regulate the conditions of installment buying of consumers' goods. Basically it required that all charge accounts be paid within 60 days, that installment credit be limited to one year, and that customers pay one-third of the purchase price at the outset. There were numerous variations in these rules for different goods, and the number of goods regulated was changed from time to time. This control was in operation during most of the period from 1941 to 1949 and probably helped somewhat to soften the impact of inflation.

The Federal Reserve System helped tremendously in the enormous mechanical job of marketing government securities and in maintaining an even flow of credit. In 1943 alone the Federal Reserve Banks handled 267,000,000,000 government checks. They managed eight mammoth bond drives raising $157 billion dollars. In 1942, 40 per cent of their personnel were engaged in government service of some kind. They arranged to have nearly 11,000 banks serve as government depositaries so that funds raised in any area would, insofar as possible, be spent in that area; thus some areas would not periodically be flooded with funds and others drained of them. Also, as during World War I, they helped see to it that funds were regularly supplied the government by the sale to banks of Treasury bills and Treasury certificates. These bills and certificates could then be retired with the proceeds of periodic bond drives. All this mechanical assistance was extremely important.

The Post-War Situation

When the war ended in mid-1945, member banks no longer had large excess reserves in the same free form that they had them in the 1930's; they possessed enormous quantities of government securities, and these were all convertible on demand into cash or were suitable for backing Federal Reserve notes. Thus if member banks desired, they could expand their loans greatly. Open-market selling operations and higher rediscount rates were virtually forbidden by the Treasury. For one thing, the Treasury wanted to maintain low interest rates to keep down the cost of servicing a $260 billion national debt; a one per cent rise in interest rates would add $2.6 billion to the tax burden. Open-market sell-

ing operations, if successful in curbing credit expansion, would lower bond prices, increase bond yields, and thereby necessitate higher interest rates when the next refunding took place. But such open-market operations were unlikely to be unsuccessful in curbing credit expansion. They were more likely to result in the sale of government securities to the Federal Reserve Banks by banks whose reserves were curtailed. In other words, any such open-market selling operation would probably be offset by an equivalent open-market buying operation.

Combating Post-War Inflation

The Board had several weapons which in normal times could be used to meet the post-war inflation, but they were not available when they were needed. Legal reserve requirements were already at their maximum except for central reserve city banks, which were not trouble spots. The Board made use of Regulation W, but that control was due to expire shortly. Margin requirements were increased to 100 per cent in February 1946. But using open-market selling operations was out of the question because of the Treasury's opposition.

The Board persuaded the Treasury to increase interest rates on Treasury bills and certificates, but no substantial changes were made in note and bond rates. When the Treasury had a cash surplus right after the war, that was used to retire some of the public debt. Likewise when a surplus developed in 1947 and 1948, it also was used to retire some of the public debt. The most effective place to apply this surplus was against government securities held by the Federal Reserve Banks, for that procedure amounted to an open-market selling operation. The Treasury bought up these securities by writing checks against their depositary accounts in commercial banks and by giving them to Federal Reserve Banks. In 1946 and 1947 the Treasury bought over $6 billion of government securities from the Federal Reserve Banks in this way. But many member banks simply sold more government securities to the Federal Reserve Banks to replenish their reserves. Federal Reserve Bank net holdings of government securities accordingly dropped only $2 billion in this period.

The Board next went to Congress and asked for new powers. They wanted higher reserve requirements, a renewal of Regulation W (now expired), and a new legal reserve provision requiring banks to keep, say, 10 per cent additional legal reserves in government securities. The first two requests were granted in August 1948 for less than a year's period, but the third was denied. The Board made partial use of the power to raise reserve requirements in September 1948 (see Table 2, p. 70).

Dealing with a Depression

In the spring of 1949 a recession seemed to threaten. The depression weapons were brought out and swung into action. Margin requirements were cut, and reserve requirements were reduced three times in six months. Regulation W was relaxed even before it expired in June, and the Board announced that it was abandoning its policy of maintaining "a relatively fixed pattern of rates." This last statement simply meant that the Federal Reserve Banks were selling bonds less freely than before. Sometime late in 1949, fear of the recession evaporated and good times resumed.

War Threatens Again

With the outbreak of war in Korea in June 1950, a new boom materialized and the Board was again face to face with the threat of inflation. The Board took stronger action than it had in some time. First rediscount rates were raised from $1\frac{1}{2}$ per cent to $1\frac{3}{4}$ per cent. Despite the Treasury's opposition, yields on government securities were allowed to drift a little higher. In September, Regulation W was revived in a moderate form and in October it was stiffened. Also a new credit control, Regulation X was initiated. This regulation was to discourage the mounting expansion of long-term credit for building homes. Other credit restrictions like maximum reserve requirements and the creation of an additional special bond reserve for banks were discussed in financial circles and to some extent in the press. Bank loans increased about 25 per cent during 1950 and the cost of living rose 7 per cent. In January 1951 the Board raised both reserve requirements and margin requirements.

Suggested Readings

For fuller but easy-to-read accounts of the Federal Reserve System, the following books are especially recommended.

Bach, George L., *Federal Reserve Policy Making.* New York: Alfred A. Knopf, Inc., 1950.

Goldenweiser, E. A., *Monetary Management.* New York: McGraw-Hill Book Co., Inc., 1949.

Kemmerer, E. W., and Kemmerer, D. L., *ABC of the Federal Reserve System.* New York: Harper & Brothers, 1950. 12th ed.

For discussions of current problems affecting the Federal Reserve System and for up-to-date financial statistics consult

The Federal Reserve Bulletin, monthly, Washington,

The Federal Reserve Chart Book, monthly, Washington, and

The Annual Report of the Board of Governors, Washington.

4

The Development of Our Monetary Institutions

by J. MARVIN PETERSON

Director of Research
Federal Reserve Bank of Minneapolis

ON MAY 31, 1950, the quantity of money owned by the public of the United States was $169.5 billion. This great volume of money consisted of $85.3 billion of demand deposits, $59.5 billion of time deposits, and $24.7 billion of currency outside banks.

These figures compare with those indicating money supply[1] in the following amounts for selected years since 1860:*

1860	...............$ .07 billion		1929	..............$ 54.8 billion
1870	.... 1.4 "		1933	.... 40.8 "
1880	.... 2.9 "		1939	.... 60.2 "
1890	.... 5.5 "		1941	.... 73.4 "
1900	.... 8.8 "		1945	.... 138.4 "
1905	.... 13.2 "		1946	.... 157.8 "
1910	.... 16.9 "		1947	.... 164.1 "
1915	.... 20.6 "		1948	.... 165.7 "
1920	.... 39.6 "		1949	.... 165.6 "
1925	.... 48.1 "			

* Sources: 1860–1910, *Statistical Abstract;* 1915–40, *Banking and Monetary Statistics,* Board of Governors of the Federal Reserve System; 1945–50, *Federal Reserve Bulletin.*

Numerous questions might be asked concerning the growth of our money supply. The following questions which might be considered the most important, furnish an outline for the treatment of our monetary institutions in this chapter and the next one:

1. What changes in our monetary institutions are responsible for the growth in the money supply?

2. Have our monetary institutions operated to produce stability or instability in our economy?

---

[1] Demand deposits adjusted, time deposits and currency outside banks.

3. What are the processes by which money might be created or destroyed?

4. What are the objectives of monetary policy?

Partial answers to the first and second questions make up the subject matter of this chapter. The third and fourth questions furnish subject matter for the next chapter.

Development of U.S. Monetary System

The money supply under bimetallism. In the early years of the history of our government, the bimetallic standard was adopted under which gold and silver coins could be minted in unlimited quantities; that is, any person was free to present for coinage any amount of either metal. Hence we had "free coinage" under this system.

Although provision for the coinage of silver and gold under bimetallism gave assurance of a safe currency, few coins were minted in the early years of our nation and the economy suffered from the lack of adequate media of exchange. This deficiency was partly overcome for a time by the note issues of the first Bank of the United States, which represented the initial attempt at a form of central banking in this country. This bank issued bank notes which were not legal tender but which were, nevertheless, receivable by the federal government as long as they were redeemable in specie at par value. They helped considerably in supplying a much needed currency at a time when coins were scarce.

In practice, however, the first Bank of the United States did not possess exclusive note-issuing powers. State banks, organized under state charters, were also given this power. Thus the federal government did not take full advantage of the constitutional provision that forbids any state to coin money or emit bills of credit. Congress alone, according to this clause in the Constitution, has the power to "coin Money" and "to regulate the Value thereof."

In an attempt to prevent the overissue of notes by state banks, the first Bank of the United States frequently sent back such notes to the issuing banks for redemption in specie. This practice forced the state banks to maintain specie redemption.

When the charter of the first Bank of the United States expired in 1811, Congress refused to renew it. State banks thereupon began to issue bank notes in abundance, and new banks were organized with the primary purpose of issuing bank-note currency. The result was the suspension of specie payments for all but a few of the most conservative banks in New England.

The controversy over the second Bank of the United States. Partly as a result of a period of confusion in monetary matters, and partly as a

result of the country's having become involved in a second war with England, another attempt at central banking was made when, in 1816, the second Bank of the United States was established.

The record of this new federal bank presents a mixture of good and bad management. Its management, however, was not the most important consideration. More important is the fact that the second Bank of the United States precipitated a controversy over the constitutionality and practicability of a central banking institution in an environment wherein sentiment favored freedom from control. A central banking institution, which likely would operate on the theory that the money supply should be subject to quantitative and qualitative controls, was unpopular among adherents of states' rights. Free banking and cheap money were the popular demands of the day. An impediment to the satisfaction of those demands was removed when President Andrew Jackson brought about the liquidation of the second Bank of the United States beginning in 1833.

Wildcat banking, 1836–63. For a period of 27 years—1836–63—state banking expanded without the interference of the federal government and without competition with federally-chartered banking institutions. Several states established state-owned banks which issued bank notes; state-chartered banks were organized in large numbers and were given note-issuing powers; and non-chartered private banks accepted deposits and issued bills of exchange which circulated as money.

The term "wildcat banking" was applied to practices of the institutions which were established primarily for the purpose of monetizing private credit. Very little capital was required to set up these "money factories" which issued bank notes in the hope that the notes would circulate in distant places and not come home for redemption. In some cases no reserve was maintained for the redemption of notes.

Many of the malpractices of these banking institutions were inexcusable. Yet, the country was expanding and some sort of money and credit was needed to finance that expansion. Particularly on the frontier, new money was needed for the building of canals, railroads, wholesale and retail trade establishments, and the opening of new areas for farming, manufacturing, and mining.

Although free banking was not the best possible answer to the pleas of the frontier for more money, it, nevertheless, provided a source of funds not available elsewhere. It should be observed that:

> ... Many large and thriving business firms of today can trace the beginnings of their success to the time when they needed and obtained bank loans for working capital purposes. These firms at the time had no credit rating, no favorable balance-sheet ratios; they had little to recommend them as being

credit-worthy except a "faith in America" which was shared by the banker who extended credit to them.[2]

Nevertheless, if everyone had taken advantage of the privilege under free banking to set up his own money printing press irrespective of his contribution to production, the newly created money would have greatly depreciated in value. That restraint must somehow be placed on the creation of money; that the economy should at the same time be supplied with an adequate quantity of a good money is the lesson to be learned from our period of "wildcat banking."

The National Banking System. The federal government reentered the field of banking with the passage of the National Banking Act in the midst of the Civil War. Under this Act federally chartered banks were permitted to issue bank notes, the once-familiar national bank notes which were secured by government bonds. These notes were far superior to the state bank notes in two respects—uniformity and security. Their uniformity was attributable to the fact that all such notes, irrespective of the issuing bank were the same in quality. They were secure or safe because they were backed by government securities and a redemption fund.

Greatly contributing to uniformity in the nation's supply of currency was the act of Congress in 1866 which taxed state bank notes issues out of existence.

Although the National Banking System gave the economy a high quality currency, it cannot be said that the national bank acts by any means solved the money problem. These acts did not do so mainly because under them the nation was not provided a currency which would expand proportionately with the growth of the economy. Yet deposit banking was developing in the post-Civil War period which promised to provide the economy an adequate amount of media of exchange.

The Growth of Deposit Currency

For almost a century after the establishment of our federal government, bank notes and Treasury currency (gold and silver coins and certificates) made up the great bulk of our nation's money supply. Deposit banking, however, was growing in importance, especially after 1866 when state banks were in effect prohibited from issuing notes. By 1895 bank deposits had grown to an amount almost twice the total of bank notes and Treasury currency combined. In 1950 deposit money reached six times the amount of total currency in the hands of the public.

---

[2] J. Marvin Peterson and D. R. Cawthorne, *Money and Banking*, rev. ed. New York: The Macmillan Company, 1949, p. 83.

Thus we entered a new period in the history of our monetary institutions—the period of the pre-eminence of checkbook money. In the meantime, reliance on the mechanisms of the bimetallic standard was fading into oblivion. Although bimetallism was left on the statute books for a long time, a series of coinage acts whittled away at its foundations. Under these acts, coinage of silver money was regulated by Congress and was not "free" in the sense that anyone could present any quantity of silver to the mints for coinage.

While bimetallism was by gradual steps abandoned, gold remained on a free coinage basis until 1933. Until that time anyone was free to create money by digging gold from "them thar hills" to present to the mints for coinage. This procedure, being costly, presented no great danger that the economy would be flooded by cheap money. In fact, its shortcoming was that not enough money could be created by this method.

Businessmen wanted and needed—and were willing to pay for—a greater amount of money than could be obtained from savers of gold coins or gold bullion. Businessmen got a large part of the money they needed for business expansion from commercial banks which extended credit to them. In this process of bank credit expansion an ever growing quantity (yet not a steadily growing quantity), of deposit currency was created.

Finally—in 1933—by act of Congress, gold ceased to serve as a medium of exchange. It did not thereupon lose value, because the Government of the United States has offered to purchase at a fixed price any quantity of gold that might be presented. Instead of bank notes and bank deposits being redeemable in gold, gold became redeemable in bank deposits or bank notes. (The procedures by which gold is today exchanged for deposit money are described in the next chapter.)

Deposit money, having relegated bank notes and Treasury currency to a lowlier position, quantitatively, in our monetary system, has posed a new problem in monetary management. How can the quantity of deposit money be adjusted to the needs of the economy so that it might be neither too scarce nor too plentiful in relation to the supply of goods and services?

An answer which was once widely accepted as an altogether satisfactory one was provided by the commercial loan theory of bank credit.

The Commercial Loan Theory of Bank Credit

In view of the fact that deposit money had relegated Treasury currency and bank notes to a minor role (quantitatively) in the total money supply, statesmen and monetary theorists sought a method for the control of the quantity of that form of money in order that it should not

become excessive in relation to the quantity of goods. The answer or solution was simple: tie the quantity of this money to the production of goods. If this were done, it was thought, there could be no overissue of money; neither could money be too scarce.

The application of this theory to banking operations required that bank credit should not be used to finance additions to fixed plant and equipment; these should be financed from the savings of individuals and business firms. Only loans for commercial purposes (as distinguished from investment, consumption, and speculative purposes) should be made by commercial banks. More specifically, only goods-in-process should be financed by bank credit. Such financing would mean that deposit money created by bank credit expansion could not outgrow production. It also would mean that a decline in the money supply would always accompany a decline in the volume of transactions involving goods-in-process.

Possibly the best illustration of the desirable and proper functioning of this theory is furnished by bank credit extended to a manufacturer to finance a purchase of raw materials. The manufacturer would convert the raw materials into finished products, sell those products, and use a part of the proceeds of such sales to repay the bank loan.

Bank loans extended for such commercial, productive purposes were described as self-liquidating since they could be repaid in a short period of time from the proceeds of the sales of goods. Each of these transactions would create new money when the loan was made and contract the money supply when it was repaid. This process would, when repeated, result in the creation and retirement of money, as before.

The supply of money, according to the commercial loan theory, would change proportionately with changes in the volume of production, both in the course of the business cycle and in the course of the secular trend. In the prosperity phase of the cycle, the demand for commercial loans and the money supply would, it was argued, increase proportionately to the increase in production—not at a greater rate—and in periods of depression, the decline in demand for new commercial loans would cause a contraction in the money supply proportionate to the decline in production.

In the course of a rising secular trend in production, wherein greater need for fixed capital has been met by savings from past incomes of individuals and businesses, the greater volume of production induces greater demand for commercial loans; such loans, when granted, increase the money supply.

Thus the ratio of money to the flow of goods in the production process, it was believed, would remain unchanged in both the short run and the long run, if strict adherence to the commercial loan theory of bank credit were maintained at all times.

Shortcomings of the commercial loan theory. Although the commercial loan theory may present a commendable guide to the individual commercial banker, it has shortcomings as a guide to monetary management. Surely, good short-term commercial loans are a most desirable type of asset for commercial banks. Yet, it cannot be denied that these loans—rising in prosperity and falling promptly in recession—might accentuate rather than mitigate the business cycle.

In the prosperity phase of the business cycle—whatever the forces that might have initiated the upturn in business activity—a rise in bank loans, whether those loans are for investment, consumption, or commercial purposes, increases the money supply. Although commercial loans quite quickly increase the supply of goods, whereas investment loans do so more slowly, both types of bank loans increase the demand for goods. The net effect is inflationary, especially when the economy is operating at capacity or near-capacity levels.

In most periods of upturn in business activity, an increase in commercial loans accompanies an accumulation of business inventories. This development may be partially speculative in character, rather than purely commercial. It also is to be noted that inventory accumulation financed by bank credit not only increases the money supply, but it also increases the business demand for goods while the supply available to the public has not increased proportionately. While retailers' shelves and manufacturers' stockpiles of raw materials and semi-finished goods are rising, money is paid into the pockets of industrial employees, miners, farmers, *et al.*, which is new money to the extent that commercial bank credit is involved. Also, the greater velocity of the existing money supply induced in the process is equivalent to an increase in its quantity. Thus inventory accumulation based on commercial loans can set in motion a chain of cause and effect that increases the public's money supply at more than a one-to-one relationship to the supply of finished goods available to the public.

In the recession phase of the business cycle—whatever may have been the forces which initiated the downturn in business activity—a fall in bank loans, whether those loans were originally made for investment, consumption, or commercial purposes, decreases the money supply.

In most periods of downturn in business activity and falling prices, a decline in inventories takes place. This development makes possible the liquidation of bank loans originally made for commercial purposes. The decline in inventories is thereby accompanied by a drop in the money supply, and a factor which accentuates the business cycle is produced.

While it cannot be denied that factors other than changes in the volume of commercial loans may be more important, especially as forces

initiating the different phases of the business cycle, changes in the volume of commercial credit do, in fact, accentuate the cycle. If adherence to the commercial loan theory provides the business world with the desired amount of bank credit, it should not be assumed that such an amount of bank credit—or any other form of credit affecting the money supply and money expenditures—is the most desirable from the point of view of monetary stability in the economy as a whole.

Commercial Loan Theory under the Federal Reserve System. In the language of the Federal Reserve Act of 1913 one finds an implied adherence to the commercial loan theory of bank credit. It is stated in this Act that discount rates shall be fixed "with a view to accommodating commerce and business."

Under this injunction, standards of eligibility of paper for rediscounting by member banks were established. In general, loans made for short-term, commercial, productive purposes would give rise to eligible paper, whereas paper created in the process of extending funds for consumption, investment, and speculative purposes would not be eligible.

As a result of the establishment of the Federal Reserve System, the member commercial banks were given access to a central banking institution with power to convert customers' paper into currency (Federal Reserve notes) or reserve balances. Should member banks choose the latter alternative—the conversion of eligible assets into reserve balances—the money-creating potentialities of bank loans would be magnified several times.

In its practical application, the injunction that the Federal Reserve Banks should accommodate commerce and business meant that Federal Reserve credit would flow most freely in periods of prosperity and much less freely in periods of recession. This must necessarily be the case, because only in periods of prosperity would the volume of commercial paper be rising, whereas the volume of such credit falls abruptly in the early stages of recession.

The changing character of commercial banking. The foregoing discourse on the commercial loan theory was undertaken in order that developments in money and banking from the beginning of the Federal Reserve System to the present time might better be described. We now take up again the story of the development of our monetary system.

The Federal Reserve System was put into operation at the outbreak of World War I. It, therefore, became necessary for the new central banking system to devote greatest attention to its fiscal functions. Doubtless, the new System gave invaluable service to the Treasury in its war-financing program and helped bring the war to a successful conclusion. Immediately after the end of the war, the Federal Reserve Board was anxious to develop a monetary policy suitable to peace time conditions.

The formulation of this policy was, however, deferred until the Victory Bond Drive in 1919 might successfully be completed.

In the meantime, a sharp inflation as measured by commodity and real estate prices had set in. This inflation was characterized by great inventory accumulation as prices advanced and by a boom psychology related to farm lands and other real estate. In the subsequent sudden break in commodity and real estate markets, the Federal Reserve Board became the target of sharp criticism, especially from the farm bloc in Congress, because the Board failed to stem the tide of widespread liquidation. (The Board had drastically raised the rediscount rate in May 1920 and did not support government bond prices which declined sharply in 1920–21.)

The recovery from the post-war recession was rapid, especially in the industrial sector of the economy, and a period of stability in the price level was experienced.

During this short period of stability in the price level, economic changes with important repercussions on commercial banking took place. Owing to numerous consolidations and mergers, big business firms grew much faster than the smaller ones. These large business units were in most cases less dependent on bank credit for the purchase of raw materials than was the case when the units were smaller. Thus the growth in size of business units was one cause of the decline in commercial loans.

In the 1920's conditions were favorable to the financing of business expansion through the issuance of equity securities. Commercial banks became involved in this type of financing by loans on securities. Some of them organized security affiliates for the underwriting and marketing of stocks and bonds. Commercial banks also invested heavily in long-term corporate bonds.

The character of bank assets thereupon changed. A smaller proportion of bank funds was invested in short-term commercial loans and a larger proportion in long-term assets.

The Federal Reserve Board, lacking such selective controls as the determination of margin requirements on security loans, felt helpless to cope effectively with the situation in 1928–29. The use of over-all controls such as open-market operations and the discount rate, it was felt, would hurt productive pursuits and would do little to dampen speculation.

After the stock market crash in October 1929, the small volume of commercial paper in the possession of commercial banks was reduced by the repayment of loans. Little eligible paper was available for rediscount when widespread fears by depositors over the safety of their funds developed. In a frantic effort to convert assets into cash, banks dumped securities on the open market. This effort to gain cash was futile. Al-

though an individual bank might gain cash by selling bonds to depositors of other banks, the whole banking system, obviously, could not gain cash by these actions. Only by the conversion of assets into cash by a currency-issuing authority (such as the Federal Reserve Banks) can the banking system gain cash in a period of widespread liquidation and hoarding. This is the lesson to be learned from our bitter experiences in the years of recession and depression of the early 1930's.

In less than two years from mid-1931, over 7,000 banks had disappeared and we had suffered a decline of $15 billion of our money supply. Thus it was demonstrated that the monetary factor can turn an already sufficiently serious normal recession following the collapse of a speculative boom into a devastating depression.

There followed a program of reform known as the "New Deal," in which monetary policy played only a minor role, except that it contributed to the maintenance of extremely low interest rates. Fiscal policies built upon the beneficence of deficit spending by the federal government overshadowed monetary policy. Some restraint, however, was attempted in 1936 when an increase in reserve requirements was ordered as a means of curbing an upturn in business activity that appeared to possess some inflationary characteristics. Business activity declined in 1937–38 and later revived with the outbreak of war in Europe.

The financing of United States' participation in World War II is doubtless familiar to all readers. It is sufficient to state that commercial banks at the outbreak of the war had very large excess reserves which enabled them to purchase government securities in large amounts. As the war progressed the Treasury put forth continuously greater efforts to sell bonds to the public. Nevertheless, it was necessary to sell great amounts of securities to the banking system. As a consequence, bank deposits (adjusted) increased from $65.2 billion on June 30, 1941, to $124.3 billion on December 31, 1945. At the same time, currency outside the banks increased from $8.2 billion to $26.5 billion in the same period. The commercial banks were enabled to furnish this greater amount of currency to the public and to maintain higher reserve balances against their greater deposit liabilities by reason of the Federal Reserve's ability to convert government securities into currency or member banks' reserve balances. Federal Reserve bank credit expanded from $2.2 billion on June 30, 1941, to $24.3 billion on December 31, 1945, thereby creating approximately the same amount of currency and member bank reserve balances.

In the period following World War II (1945–50), the great monetary issues centered around open-market operations of the Federal Reserve System, the fiscal policies of the U.S. Treasury, and the interrelationships between them. Open-market purchases by the Federal Reserve

System's Open Market Committee were designed during periods of weakness in the market to maintain prices on government securities above par. Although short-term securities were sold while the long-terms were being purchased, and vice-versa, the net effect was that monetary policy was not as effective as it might have been in the absence of the government security support purchases by the Federal Reserve System.

In this same period (1945–50), the United States Treasury's accounts reveal a cash surplus at times and a cash deficit at others. On the whole, the high levels of government expenditures (whether the budget was balanced or unbalanced) and the easy money policies of such government agencies as those operating in the residential housing field were inflationary in effect.

Monetary Institutions and Economic Instability

An erratic price level indicates instability. "We have sixty-cent dollars" is an expression frequently heard these days. What does it mean? The implication in this utterance sometimes is that the government has deliberately and foolishly debased the currency of the land—that the dollar was once a good dollar and that now it is a bad dollar. If this implication is correctly stated, another is present—that the dollar at an earlier date had an absolute quality that was excellent and that no change should have been made concerning it.

Although it is true that governments or other authorities can unwisely tamper with the money of the land by altering the metallic content of coins and the collateral security of paper currency, it is not necessarily true that a higher value of money in one period of time indicates good money and that a lower value of money in another period signifies bad money. Money that has rapidly risen in value is probably just as bad as money that has rapidly fallen in value.

Usually, a falling value of money indicates inflation; a rising value of money indicates deflation. Both situations, especially when sharp changes take place, are bad, whether the primary cause is monetary in character or non-monetary.

Figure 1, a chart of the price level in the United States, 1800–50, clearly reveals how difficult it is to select a period of time which can aptly and correctly be described as a period wherein "good money" was circulated. Obviously, the most pronounced changes in the value of money have accompanied wars. Although changes have been less spectacular in periods of peace, they, nevertheless, have been substantial. This is true even if the sharp declines in the price level which have characterized the periods immediately following wars are ignored.

The table on page 88 shows changes in the purchasing power of the dollar in selected periods, 1808–1949.

The rise in the price level which has taken place in wartime is quite easily explained. During wars the flow of money increases at a faster rate than the flow of goods available to the public for which money may be exchanged. The money supply may be increased during wars by the issuance of government notes or by purchases of government securities by the banking system. The supply of goods available to the public is at the same time greatly restricted by the diversion of productive resources to military purposes.

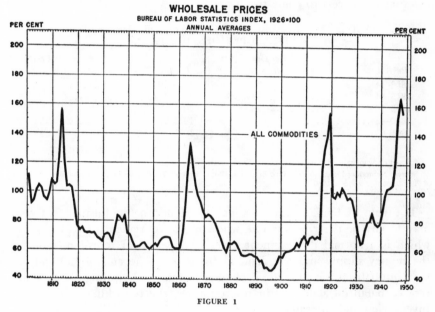

WHOLESALE PRICES
BUREAU OF LABOR STATISTICS INDEX, 1926=100
ANNUAL AVERAGES

FIGURE 1

Changes in the price level in peacetime are not as easily explained, because the flow of money and the flow of goods, instead of being readily identifiable with government operations, become a function of intricate cost-price relationships which influence capital expenditures, the volume of bank credit, and other business decisions.

Bank credit has been a factor causing instability. In most business cycles bank credit doubtless has been a factor causing instability, although it must also be observed that bank credit expansion has, in some periods of our monetary history, given the economy a much-needed larger money supply when other monetary mechanisms have failed to do so.

Both an expansion and a contraction in the money supply, insofar as bank credit is the cause of either of these developments, tend to be cumu-

lative. A rise in business activity likely induces an increase in bank loans and purchases of securities by banks. The result is a corresponding increase in the money supply, which, in turn, induces greater expenditures on goods and services. The continuation of these sequences of more money and more goods leads eventually to a condition of full employment. At this stage the price level is likely to rise. Higher prices may then cause speculative buying and a greater demand for bank credit to finance such purchases. Finally, the exhaustion of bank reserves, the overstocking of inventories, a reduction of consumer demand, a break in speculative markets, or some other combination of factors, causes the cumulative process to come to an end.

CHANGES IN THE PURCHASING POWER OF THE DOLLAR—
SELECTED PERIODS, 1808–1949 *

Period	Per Cent Change	Period	Per Cent Change
1808–14	− 39	1866–79	+ 84
1815–34	+ 134	1897–1910	− 40
1835–36	− 23	1915–20	− 73
1840–43	+ 32	1921–22	+ 58
1861–65	− 70	1929–32	+ 43
		1940–48	− 71

* Based on wholesale price index. Bureau of Labor Statistics.

Source: Reproduced from "Money Can Easily Get Out of Hand," *The Business Review*, Federal Reserve Bank of Philadelphia, February, 1950.

The role of bank credit in a period of decline in business activity may briefly be described as one whereby the retirement of bank loans, which is a normal development early in a period of recession, reduces the money supply and the demand for goods. The end of liquidation may result from a combination of such factors as the piling up of bank reserve balances, a decline in interest rates, the restocking of depleted inventories, and increased exports.

As previously stated, no inference should be drawn from this exposition on the role of bank credit that it is always the primary cause of the change from one phase of the business cycle to another. On the contrary, some other factor or combination of factors is more likely to induce recovery or recession. The foregoing analysis serves only to support the contention that bank credit may accentuate either phase of the cycle.

Lessened importance of short-term commercial debt. In the past two decades, commercial loans of banks have declined in importance relative to other bank assets. This development resulted from a low demand for loans during the depression of the 1930's and the lack of need for bank loans during World War II, while at the same time the deficit financing by the United States Treasury provided an abundant supply of government securities available for the investment of bank funds.

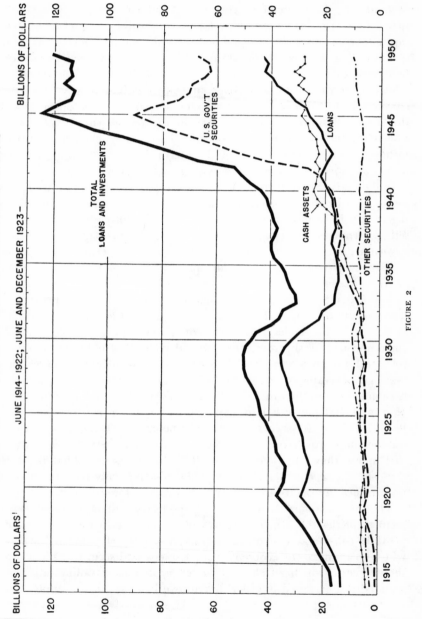

PRINCIPAL ASSETS OF ALL COMMERCIAL BANKS

JUNE 1914-1922; JUNE AND DECEMBER 1923-

BILLIONS OF DOLLARS

TOTAL LOANS AND INVESTMENTS

U. S. GOV'T SECURITIES

CASH ASSETS

LOANS

OTHER SECURITIES

FIGURE 2

The composition of principal commercial bank assets, 1915–49, is depicted in Figure 2. Attention is called to the fact that not all loans of banks are commercial in character. In the recent post-war years a spectacular rise has occurred in long-term loans to business firms for capital investment purposes, real estate loans, and consumer loans. More spectacular is the rise to pre-eminence of government securities among bank assets.

The significance of the increase in bank holdings of government securities since 1933 is that short-term commercial loans no longer provide the principal source for an increase in the money supply as was the case in earlier years. The monetization of federal government securities, rather than the monetization of short-term debt, has become the chief means of providing the economy with greater money supply.

Individuals can convert government securities into money by following either of two courses of action: (1) they can redeem unmatured savings bonds in cash or present matured securities for cash, or (2) they can sell government securities to the banking system. Banks can convert government securities into reserve balances which permit an expansion of loans and deposits, or they can draw upon excess reserve balances to obtain currency.

The Federal Reserve Banks, under an amendment to the Federal Reserve Act adopted in 1931, are permitted to deposit government securities as collateral for Federal Reserve notes. Prior to the passage of this amendment, only short-term commercial paper and gold could serve as collateral for such currency. It seems very unlikely that hereafter a shortage of available collateral for Federal Reserve notes will be experienced, as was the case in 1930–31. In those years the declining supply of commercial paper led to impounding a greater proportion of gold behind Federal Reserve notes. Shortly before the Federal Reserve Act was amended to permit government securities to serve as security for such notes, they had become virtually gold certificates. That being the case, short-term commercial paper did not adequately perform its function to meet automatically the public's demand for currency.

The revolutionary change in the monetary system making government securities the principal source of an increase in the money supply provides considerable assurance against a scarcity of money. Whether it will help to make the economy more stable would seem to depend upon the degree to which an effective monetary and fiscal policy can be formulated and executed in order that an overly great money supply should not be created.

The optimum condition concerning the flow of money. The conclusion that our monetary system, during most of its history, has contributed to instability rather than stability in the economy seems inescapable. A

valid generalization is that our monetary system has gone into high-gear to create new money in periods of prosperity and that it has operated to destroy money in periods of depression.

Greater stability in the money supply would have contributed to greater stability in the economy. It does not follow, however, that a static money supply would induce the greatest possible stability. Two reasons may be advanced in support of this latter observation. The first of these is that the rate of money use—its turnover or velocity of circulation—may change appreciably, whereby a lower velocity of money in a depression might more than offset the influence of a larger money supply, and a smaller supply might circulate with greater rapidity in a period of prosperity. Thus the absolute quantity of money is not the only condition to be watched if the greatest possible monetary stability is to be achieved.

The other consideration is that the secular growth of the economy requires that the money supply should increase in close relationship with the growth in the volume of production and trade.

The optimum condition—the best and most desirable state—is that wherein the flow of money payments relative to the flow of goods contributes to the maintenance of business stability at high levels of production and employment and to steady growth of the economy. Surely, our monetary institutions should not operate—automatically or through monetary management—to accentuate that degree of instability which may be assigned to non-monetary factors.

The Commercial Banking Process

Before an attempt is made in the following chapter to explain the functioning of our present-day monetary mechanism, it is appropriate to undertake a brief treatment of the essential characteristics of the commercial banking process. The approach which seems most elucidating may be called the accounting approach which employs a hypothetical bank balance sheet.

Major bank balance-sheet items. The major items on the balance sheet of any commercial bank are two liability items and three asset items. The chief liability items are (1) capital stock, and (2) deposits. The principal asset items are (1) loans, (2) investments, and (3) reserve balances.

Capital stock of a commercial bank. In the United States, the federal government imposes requirements setting forth the minimum amount of capital stock that must be subscribed before a new national bank may be established, whereas each state imposes such requirements for the formation of state banks. One purpose served by the imposition of these requirements is to discourage or prevent the establishment of

banking institutions by persons with inadequate financial resources. Another is to prevent the formation of banks with such small amounts of capital that the total amount of business they can transact forbids a proper diversification of the banks' assets. Both state and federal authorities also are authorized to refuse charters to proposed banking institutions which seek to locate at places where banking facilities are already adequate.

Let us assume that the promoters of a new commercial banking venture have been granted a charter to establish a bank with capital stock of $100 thousand and that they have proposed to begin business with a paid-in surplus of $20 thousand. At the beginning, the balance sheet of the bank might appear as follows:

Assets		*Liabilities*	
Cash	$120,000	Capital Stock	$100,000
		Surplus	20,000
	$120,000		$120,000

Hypothetical balance sheet of a commercial bank. When the new bank is ready to invite business from the public, it may announce its willingness to make loans and receive deposits. Presumably, its owners withdraw deposits from other banks and place them in the new institution. Others are induced to do likewise. Some loans are made and the borrowers receive credit for the amount of the proceeds of the loans on newly-established checking accounts. Thus deposit accounts are attracted to the new bank. This development requires that reserves against deposit liabilities be deposited by the bank with duly recognized reserve depositaries.

Shortly after its opening, the new bank might reveal a financial statement as follows:

Assets		*Liabilities*	
Loans	$ 75,000	Capital stock	$100,000
Investments	150,000	Surplus	20,000
Due from other banks	40,000	Undivided profits	2,000
Cash in vault	10,000	Deposits	200,000
Other assets	47,000		
	$322,000		$322,000

It is noticeable that the new bank has reduced its cash from the first statement to the amount needed in daily banking transactions; that it has attracted new deposits; that it has made loans and has purchased investments on which it has earned interest; that it has set up a reserve account with a reserve depositary; and that it has put current earnings into an undivided profits account.

After a time, the growth of the bank is reflected in a financial state-

ment which may be similar to those of many other commercial banks, as follows:

Assets		Liabilities	
Loans	$1,000,000	Capital stock	$ 100,000
Investments	1,650,000	Surplus	100,000
Reserves and deposits with		Undivided profits	30,000
other banks	650,000	Reserves for contingencies	10,000
Cash in vault	130,000	Deposits	3,260,000
Bank building	50,000		
Other assets	20,000		
	$3,500,000		$3,500,000

It will be observed that the deposits (demand and time deposits combined) are about 13½ times its capital accounts (capital stock, surplus, undivided profits and reserves for contingencies). Its loans are slightly more than 30 per cent of its deposits, while investments are about 50 per cent of deposits. Reserves may be about 15 per cent of demand deposits and 5 per cent of time deposits, depending on reserve requirements and the amount of excess reserves the bank might choose to hold. Balances with other banks may be kept in financial centers for convenience in settling clearing balances and for other purposes. The amount of cash in vault would, of course, vary from time to time as experience with seasonal factors and other considerations might determine. It will also be noted that the bank has built up its surplus account in order to strengthen it to withstand a period of adversity which it might experience.

The nature of bank deposits. Attention is called to the fact that our hypothetical bank has built up both its earning assets and its deposits simultaneously. No suggestion has been offered in the description of the growth of this bank that the accumulation of deposits either preceded or followed the growth of its earning assets. Such implication has been avoided because it is unrealistic to assume that a bank incurs liabilities and subsequently invests them, as is the case when it is said that a bank invests its deposits.

The consideration most essential to an understanding of the nature of bank deposits is that they are liabilities of banks. They are debts owed by banks, whereas earning assets are debts owed to banks. Thus banks are dealers in two sets of debts. An increase in them reflects an increase in money transactions, whereas a decrease in them reflects a decrease in money transactions in the economy. Another apt description of the banking process is that banks "create and destroy money." This is true because writing off debts owed to banks (earning assets) and bank deposits (debts owed by banks) is a destruction of money, whereas a rise in the earning assets of banks and their deposits means the creation of money.

Bank loans and investments. Since it has been necessary to explain that the accumulation of earning assets of banks, mostly loans and investments, results in the creation of bank deposits, it is unnecessary now to deal further with this subject.

The nature of reserve balances and requirements. It is often assumed that banks maintain reserve balances in order to preserve the banks' liquidity. This is a misconception if it is thought that reserve balances are accounts from which withdrawals can readily be made to meet the demands of the banks' depositors. Only the excess reserves of a "going" bank are available to meet the claims of its creditors.

Since banks' reserve balances (to the extent that such balances are required to be held by a reserve depositary) are not available to meet depositors' withdrawals, it is necessary to explain the purpose of reserve requirements. Their purpose is to place limits on bank credit expansion. If no requirements were imposed concerning minimum reserve balances, there would be no limit on bank credit expansion, except the good judgment of bankers concerning the desirable degree to which it should be carried. Placing discretion in the hands of banking authorities to raise or lower reserve requirements gives them power to curb or to encourage credit expansion of the commercial banking system. In a period of general expansion, a drastic raising of reserve requirements might prohibit banks from further credit expansion, whereas in a recession a lowering of such requirements will free reserve balances so that banks might be encouraged to grant more loans.

Bank executives know that the reserve balances are affected by the degree of bank credit expansion or contraction in the banking system. If the rate of bank credit expansion in the banking system is greater than that of the individual bank, the individual bank quite likely will gain excess reserve balances. If, on the other hand, in a period of general expansion the individual bank expands credit at a faster rate than the rate of expansion in the banking system, the bank quite likely will lose reserves.

If, in a period of general contraction, the individual bank fails to contract credit at as fast a rate as that which is taking place in the banking system, it will lose reserves. If it contracts credit at a faster rate, it likely will gain reserve balances.

Although it is beyond the scope of this chapter to explain the instruments of credit control, it is appropriate to point out that the reserve-requirements instrument is unselective in its application to banks. It affects all banks alike in relation to their deposits, irrespective of the nature of their assets or the credit policies they are pursuing.

In summary, the banking process involves the creation and destruction of money. Banks gain earning assets by giving in exchange claims

against themselves. In this exchange new money is created. Debtors of banks retire those debts by giving claims against banks in exchange. In this exchange, money is destroyed. When the claims of banks and the claims against banks both rise, the money supply of the economy—other things being equal—rises. When the claims of banks and the claims against banks both fall, the money supply of the economy—other things being equal—falls.

Suggested Readings

Board of Governors of the Federal Reserve System, *Banking Studies*. Washington, 1941.

Board of Governors of the Federal Reserve System, *The Federal Reserve System —Its Purposes and Functions*. Washington, 1947.

Chandler, Lester V., *An Introduction to Monetary Theory*. New York: Harper & Brothers, 1940.

———. *The Economics of Money and Banking*. New York: Harper & Brothers, 1948.

Conant, C. A., *A History of Modern Banks of Issue*. New York: G. P. Putnam's Sons, 1927, Chapters XIII, XIV, XV.

Dewey, D. R., *State Banking Before the Civil War*. (National Monetary Commission), Washington, 1910.

———. *Financial History of the United States*. New York: Longmans, Green and Co., 1934.

Goldenweiser, E. A., *The Federal Reserve System in Operation*. New York: McGraw-Hill Book Company, 1925.

Hansen, Alvin H., *Monetary Theory and Fiscal Policies*. New York: McGraw-Hill Book Company, 1949.

Harding, W. P. G., *The Formative Period of the Federal Reserve System*. Boston: Houghton, Mifflin Company, 1925.

Harris, S. E., *Twenty Years of Federal Reserve Policy*. Cambridge: Harvard University Press, 1933.

Hepburn, A. B., *A History of Currency in the United States*. New York: The Macmillan Co., 1924, Chapters XVII-XIX.

Holdsworth, J. T. and Dewey, D. R., *The First and Second Banks of the United States*. (National Monetary Commission), Washington, 1910.

Kemmerer, E. W. and Kemmerer, Donald L., *The ABC of the Federal Reserve System*, 12th Edition. New York: Harper & Brothers, 1950.

Mints, Lloyd W., *A History of Banking Theory*. Chicago: University of Chicago Press, 1948.

Mitchell, W. C., *A History of the Greenbacks*. Chicago: University of Chicago Press, 1903.

Noyes, A. D., *Forty Years of American Finance, 1865–1907*. New York: G. P. Putnam's Sons, 1909.

Peterson, J. Marvin and Cawthorne, D. R., *Money and Banking*. New York: The Macmillan Company, 1949, Chapter V.

Phillips, C. A., *Bank Credit*. New York: The Macmillan Company, 1920.

Reifler, W. W., *Money Rates and Money Markets in the United States*. New York: Harper & Brothers, 1930.

Sprague, O. M. W., *History of Crisis Under the National Banking System.* (National Monetary Commission), Washington, 1910.

Sumner, W. G., *History of Banking in the United States.* New York: Bradford Rhodes and Company, 1896.

Warburg, P. M., *The Federal Reserve System.* New York: The Macmillan Company, 1930, Vols. I, II.

Willis, H. P., *The Theory and Practice of Central Banking.* New York: Harper & Brothers, 1926.

5

The Functioning of Our Present-Day Monetary Mechanism

by J. MARVIN PETERSON

Director of Research
Federal Reserve Bank of Minneapolis

THE MAIN thesis of the previous chapter is that the monetary mechanism of the United States has not supplied the economy in any state of its development with the "right" amount of money. To be sure, no one can say that a certain absolute quantity of money is the right amount for a specified period of time. One can only say, looking backward, that the money flow in certain periods was excessive and that at other times it was deficient relative to the flow of goods.

Under our present-day monetary mechanism, the money supply might rise in prosperity periods and decline in times of depression as much as in the past. We have no automatic regulator that governs either its rate of increase or decrease. Instead, we rely more than ever before upon management of the money supply.

Before one can understand the issues involved in monetary management and entertain intelligent opinions concerning it, one must, of course, know the mechanics of our monetary system. We, therefore, next turn attention to operating parts of our monetary mechanism. Thereafter, the objectives of monetary policy are briefly stated.

The Monetary Mechanism

The monetary mechanism defined. The monetary mechanism consists of the instrumentalities and organizations by which money is supplied the economy and through which money expenditures are made.

The money supply in the hands of the public, as has been stated in

97

the previous chapter, consists of coins, currency outside banks, and bank deposits. One classification of the types of money in circulation in the United States divides the total into two kinds: (1) currency (coins, bank notes, and Treasury certificates) and (2) deposits (checkbook money). Another classification also divides the total into two parts: (1) bank money (Federal Reserve notes and bank deposits) and (2) Treasury money (coins, silver certificates, and other Treasury currency). Either one is a satisfactory classification of the money supply.

The significance of money expenditures. It will be observed that the definition of the monetary mechanism given above states that the monetary mechanism provides means whereby money expenditures are effected. The significance of money expenditures is that they constitute the effective demand for goods. The level of these expenditures determines the level of business activity, whether business is good or bad. The level of these expenditures also determines whether the economy shall suffer inflation or deflation. If the money expenditures are excessive, relative to the available volume of goods, an inflationary situation exists; a low or insufficient volume of money expenditures means deflation.

Thus the effect of changes in the money supply works itself out through money expenditures. Holders of a large amount of money—larger than they previously held—might withhold expenditures. At other times, holders of money might be eager to exchange it for goods or property, despite the fact that the volume of money has remained constant or diminished. Usually, however, money expenditures increase when the money supply increases and they decline when the money supply falls.

It is difficult to determine which is cause and which is effect—whether the money supply has increased because people have called forth a greater money supply by their eagerness to spend, or whether the eagerness to spend has been induced by a greater money supply. The eagerness of business enterprisers to borrow and spend money on capital goods provides a good case wherein appraisals of the business outlook have much to do with the rate of money flows and the level of the money supply. If the most common appraisal among them is that the business outlook is good, much money may be called into existence by their borrowing short-term or long-term funds from the banking system. If their general appraisal is that the business outlook is bad, they will make net repayments of debt to the banking system and thereby destroy a part of the total money supply.

To spend or not to spend—that's the question which the public (consumers, investors, and enterprisers) must answer. And there are more things in the public's behavior than are ever dreamed of in the monetary economist's philosophy or formulae.

Whether his theory is complete or incomplete, accurate or inaccurate, the monetary economist must take account of both the level and pattern of money expenditures, the volume of the money supply, and the interrelationships of the two.

Component parts of total money expenditures. During the year from December 31, 1947, to December 31, 1948, the money supply (deposits and currency outside banks) declined almost $900 million. In this same period "Gross National Product or Expenditure" increased $26.7 billion.

The accompanying table serves to point out the pattern of money expenditures in this year and to reveal the components into which total money expenditures may be divided.

GROSS NATIONAL PRODUCT OR EXPENDITURE

(In billions of dollars)

	1947	1948
Gross national product	235.7	262.4
Personal consumption expenditures	166.9	178.8
Durable goods	22.0	23.5
Nondurable goods	96.2	102.2
Services	48.8	53.1
Gross private domestic investment	31.1	45.0
New construction	13.8	17.9
Producers durable equipment	17.2	20.7
Changes in business inventories	0.1	6.5
Net foreign investment	8.9	1.9
Government purchases of goods and services	28.8	36.7
Federal	15.7	20.9
State and local	13.1	15.8

Source: *Federal Reserve Bulletin,* June, 1950, p. 735.

There may be considerable variation from one period to another in the pattern of money expenditures. For example, personal consumption expenditures may increase or decrease at a faster rate than gross private domestic investment. If so, business activity in some fields will be favorably affected while other fields will be less favored by the turn of events. Thus not only changes in total money expenditures should be studied by the careful student, but the composition of that total as well.

Major Factors Affecting the Money Supply

Consolidated condition statements for banks and the monetary system. One of the most convenient sources of information on the monetary system is provided by a table entitled "Consolidated Condition Statements for Banks and the Monetary System" which is carried in each issue of the *Federal Reserve Bulletin.* This table, taken from a recent issue of the *Bulletin,* is reproduced here.

TABLE 1

CONSOLIDATED CONDITION STATEMENTS FOR BANKS AND THE MONETARY SYSTEM

All Commercial and Savings Banks, Federal Reserve Banks, Postal Savings System, and Treasury Currency Funds

(In millions of dollars)

Date	Gold	Treasury Currency	Total	Loans, Net	Total	Commercial and Savings Banks	Federal Reserve Banks	Other	Other Securities	Total Assets, Net—Total Liabilities and Capital, Net	Total Deposits and Currency	Capital and Misc. Accounts, Net
						U. S. Government Obligations						
1929–June 29	4,037	2,019	58,642	41,082	5,741	5,499	216	26	11,819	64,698	55,776	8,922
1941–June 30	22,624	3,149	61,387	25,305	26,984	23,539	2,184	1,261	9,098	87,160	79,357	7,803
1945–Dec. 31	20,065	4,339	167,381	30,387	128,417	101,288	24,262	2,867	8,577	191,785	180,806	10,979
1946–Dec. 31	20,529	4,562	158,366	35,765	113,110	86,558	23,350	3,202	9,491	183,457	171,657	11,800
1947–Dec. 31	22,754	4,562	160,832	43,023	107,086	81,199	22,559	3,328	10,723	188,148	175,348	12,800
1948–Dec. 31	24,244	4,589	160,457	48,341	100,694	74,097	23,333	3,264	11,422	189,290	176,121	13,168
1949–June 30	24,466	4,597	156,491	47,148	97,428	74,877	19,343	3,208	11,915	185,554	171,602	13,952
1949–Dec. 31	24,427	4,598	162,681	49,604	100,456	78,433	18,885	3,138	12,621	191,706	177,313	14,392
1950–June 30												
1950–Dec. 31												

Source: *Federal Reserve Bulletin*, June 1950, p. 696.

TABLE 1—Continued

CONSOLIDATED CONDITION STATEMENTS FOR BANKS AND THE MONETARY SYSTEM

(In millions of dollars)

| Date | Total | Foreign Bank Deposits Net | U. S. Government Balances | | | Deposits Adjusted and Currency | | | | | | |
| | | | Treasury Cash | At Commercial and Savings Banks | At Federal Reserve Banks | Total | Demand Deposits | Time Deposits | | | | Currency Outside Banks |
								Total	Commercial Banks	Mutual Savings Banks	Postal Savings System	
1929–June 29	55,776	365	204	381	36	54,790	22,540	28,611	19,557	8,905	149	3,639
1941–June 30	79,357	1,949	2,275	753	980	73,400	37,317	27,879	15,928	10,648	1,303	8,204
1945–Dec. 31	180,806	2,141	2,287	24,608	977	150,793	75,851	48,452	30,135	15,385	2,932	26,490
1946–Dec. 31	171,657	1,885	2,272	3,103	393	164,004	83,314	53,960	33,808	16,869	3,283	26,730
1947–Dec. 31	175,348	1,682	1,336	1,452	870	170,008	87,121	56,411	35,249	17,746	3,416	26,476
1948–Dec. 31	176,121	2,103	1,325	2,451	1,123	169,119	85,520	57,520	35,804	18,387	3,329	26,079
1949–June 30	171,602	1,927	1,307	2,304	438	165,626	81,877	58,483	36,292	18,932	3,259	25,266
1949–Dec. 31	177,313	2,150	1,312	3,249	821	169,781	85,750	58,616	36,146	19,273	3,197	25,415
1950–June 30												
1950–Dec. 31												

Source: *Federal Reserve Bulletin*, June 1950, p. 696.

The table may be reconstructed in outline form as follows: (Figures are those for December 31, 1949, in billions of dollars).

Assets of our Monetary System—total	191,706
Gold	24.427
Treasury currency	4,598
Bank credit—total	162,681
Loans, net	49,604
U.S. Government obligations—total	100,456
Commercial and savings banks	78,433
Federal Reserve Banks	18,885
Other	3,318
Other securities	12,621
Liabilities and Capital—total	191,706
Capital and miscellaneous accounts	14,392
Total deposits and currency	177,313
Foreign deposits, net	2,150
U.S. Government balances	
Treasury cash	1,312
At commercial and savings banks	3,249
At Federal Reserve Banks	821
Deposits adjusted and currency total	169,781
Demand deposits	85,750
Time deposits—total	58,616
Currency outside banks	25,415

Total deposits adjusted plus currency outside banks as set forth in this Consolidated Statement correspond to the public's money supply as defined elsewhere in this chapter and in the previous chapter. "Total currency and deposit liabilities of the banking system can only increase or decrease to the extent that there are corresponding changes in gold or earning assets, or less importantly, corresponding changes in Treasury currency or offsetting changes in capital and miscellaneous accounts, net." [1] In other words, the public's money supply changes in volume corresponding with net changes in the volume of all other items in the Consolidated Condition Statement.

Numerous factors affect the volume of deposits and currency, each of which is reflected in one way or another in the Consolidated Condition Statement. Some of these are explained by the use of the familiar "T" accounts, which are simplified statements of condition representing the balance sheets of commercial banks, the Federal Reserve Banks, and the United States Treasury. Following this demonstration, the major factors affecting deposits and currency during a recent period will be considered in detail.

The major methods by which the money supply may be increased are: (1) United States Treasury purchases of gold and silver; (2) an increase

---

[1] Morris Copeland and Daniel H. Brill, "Banking Assets and the Money Supply Since 1929," *Federal Reserve Bulletin*, January, 1948, p. 24.

in commercial bank loans; (3) an increase in commercial bank holdings of outstanding U.S. government obligations and other securities: (4) Federal Reserve Bank purchases of securities from non-bank investors; and (5) direct purchases by commercial banks of U.S. government securities which are issued to finance a Treasury deficit.

Reductions in the money supply are effected by (1) a decline in bank loans; (2) net sales of securities by commercial banks to non-bank investors; (3) net sales by the Federal Reserve Banks to non-bank investors; (4) the use of a Treasury cash surplus, built up by an excess of tax receipts over expenditures, to retire securities held by the banking system.

Some of the major factors affecting the volume of bank deposits and currency are briefly explained in following paragraphs.[2]

Gold stock and the money supply. In the evolution of our monetary system, gold has been removed from use as a medium of exchange in domestic markets. Whereas gold was once readily convertible into coins by the presentment of gold bullion at the mints for coinage, gold is now purchased by the Treasury; in exchange, the seller of gold gets checks which may be presented at banks in exchange for a bank deposit or currency. The currency so obtained is not in gold certificates—most likely it is in bank notes, namely, Federal Reserve notes. Usually the option chosen by the seller of gold is to take a bank deposit in exchange.

For illustrative purposes, let us take the case of U.S. Treasury purchases of gold from a foreign nation and trace step-by-step this gold's conversion into bank deposits.

In *Step 1*, the Treasury buys gold from a foreign nation and pays for it by drawing on its deposits with the Federal Reserve Banks. In *Step 2*, the Treasury issues gold certificates to the Federal Reserve Banks, thereby building up Treasury deposits to their former level. In *Step 3*, the foreign nation spends funds in the United States by issuing checks drawn against the Reserve Banks in favor of individuals and businesses that deposit them in commercial banks.

These steps result in entries on the books of the U.S. Treasury, the Federal Reserve Banks, and the commercial banks as follows:

United States Treasury

	(1)	(2)	(3)			(1)	(2)	(3)
Gold	+			Gold certificates		+		
Treasury deposits at Federal Reserve Banks	−	+						

---

[2] For a complete explanation of the derivation of the Consolidated Condition Statement for Banks and the Monetary System see "Banking Assets and the Money Supply Since 1929," by Morris A. Copeland and Daniel H. Brill, *Federal Reserve Bulletin*, January, 1948, pp. 24-32.

Federal Reserve Banks

	(1)	(2)	(3)		(1)	(2)	(3)
Gold certificates		+		Treasury deposits	−	+	
				Foreign deposits	+		−
				Member-bank deposits			+

Commercial Banks

	(1)	(2)	(3)		(1)	(2)	(3)
Reserve balances			+	Deposits			+

The net effect of the gold inflow is to increase:

1. the gold holdings of the U.S. Treasury and its gold certificate liability;
2. the gold certificate holdings of the Reserve Banks and member-bank deposits;
3. the reserve balances and the deposits of the commercial banks.

By tracing these steps it can be seen that gold purchases of the U.S. Treasury increase the deposits of commercial banks which are a part of the public's money supply. Additions to the gold supply also increase bank reserve balances which form the base for an expansion in bank loans, and, consequently, a further expansion in the money supply.

Bank loans and the money supply. A concept of the banking process entertained by most bankers and other citizens is that banks accumulate money from depositors and then lend those deposits.

The monetary economist is dissatisfied with any explanation of the banking process which does not explain the money-creating and money-destroying nature of changes in the volume of commercial bank loans. That an increase in the volume of the loans of all commercial banks does in fact create money and that a decrease in the loans of all commercial banks destroys money should be clearly understood by all students of our economic institutions. This fact can best be demonstrated by bookkeeping entries as follows:

First Commercial Bank

	(1)	(2)		(1)	(2)
Loans	+ 1		Deposits	+ 1	− 1
Reserves		− 1			

Second Commercial Bank

	(1)	(2)	(3)	(4)		(1)	(2)	(3)	(4)
Loans			+ .8		Deposits	+ 1	+ .8	− .8	
Reserves		+ 1		− .8					

In *Step 1*, the First Commercial Bank makes loans of $1 million to its customers based on excess reserves of the same or larger amount. As a result, its customers are given deposit credits in the amount of $1 million. In *Step 2*, the borrowers draw on their newly-created deposit credits in order to put the funds to the uses for which those funds were borrowed. The Second Commercial Bank, let us assume, receives checks for $1 million from the borrower-depositors of the First Commercial Bank. The Second Commercial Bank thereupon gains $1 million of reserve balances. (It is admittedly unrealistic to assume that the deposits created by the loans of the First Commercial Bank are completely withdrawn from it. Frequently, of course, the borrower writes checks in favor of other depositors of the same bank.) In *Step 3*, the Second Commercial Bank makes loans of $0.8 million, which is the amount of the excess reserves gained in *Step 2*, assuming a 20 per cent reserve requirement. In *Step 4*, borrowers from the Second Commercial Bank draw checks against their newly-created deposit credits in favor of depositors of the Third Commercial Bank. Thus far, bank deposits of the first two banks have increased by $1 million, but the Third Commercial Bank is now in a position to increase its loans and deposits.

This demonstration of the effect of commercial bank credit on the money supply might be extended to a long series of commercial banks. It can then readily be seen that the whole system of commercial banks might, on the basis of $1 million of excess reserves, expand credit and deposits as much as $5 million.

Conversely, a decline in reserve balances diminishes the base upon which bank credit is founded. Such diminution of reserve balances—caused by a decline in gold stock, an increase in currency in circulation, or a tying-up of reserve balances in higher reserve requirements—might set in motion a cumulative decline in bank credit and a consequent decline in the public's money supply which far exceeds the volume of the transactions giving impetus to the movement.

A decline in the free reserve balances of banks causes bankers to be wary in granting new loans, and it causes bankers to refuse extensions of old loans; if the decline in reserve balances involves deficiencies in their reserve accounts, bankers may also be forced to sell other assets such as government securities to the Reserve Banks or the open market. In other words, a stricter rationing of bank credit likely follows a decline in reserve balances, especially if the trend toward a diminution of such balances is persistent.

A decline in bank loans and a corresponding reduction in the money supply might also be induced by the unwillingness of individuals and businesses to apply for new loans.

Commercial bank investments and the money supply. Banks may

change the volume of money by actions other than alterations in the volume of loans to customers. One such action involves the variations in the volume of security transactions with non-bank investors. When commercial banks buy securities from non-bank investors, bank deposits rise, since banks give deposit credit in return for the purchased securities. Conversely, sales of securities from the portfolios of commercial banks to non-bank investors reduce bank deposits because those investors draw on deposit credits to pay for their investments. The securities so traded may be federal government obligations or other securities.

These transactions, the first being the case of securities purchased by banks and the second, sales of securities to non-bank investors, may be depicted as follows:

Commercial Bank

Investments	+	Deposits	+

Commercial Bank

Investments	−	Deposits	−

Federal Reserve credit and the money supply. The Federal Reserve Banks may alter the money supply either on the initiative of the member banks, or on their own initiative. An example of the former is the rediscounting operations of the Reserve Banks, while open-market operations furnish an example of the latter procedure.

A member bank may rediscount customers' paper with a Reserve Bank or obtain advances from that source on its own note secured by government-security collateral. In either case, property is exchanged for Reserve Bank credit, i.e., reserve balances or Federal Reserve notes.

In the case of rediscounts and advances which are exchanged for reserve balances, the commercial banks have enlarged the bank credit-expansion potential. This type of transaction may be shown as follows:

Commercial Bank

	(1)	(2)		(1)	(2)
Reserve balances	+		Notes payable	+	
Loans		+	Deposits		+

Federal Reserve Bank

	(1)		(1)
Discounts and ad- vances	+	Member bank de- posits	+

In *Step 1,* the member bank has borrowed funds from the Reserve Bank and receives credit on its reserve balance (member bank deposits). In

Step 2, the commercial bank expands the money supply by making loans based on its enlarged reserve balance.

On its own initiative, the Federal Reserve System may, through the operations of its Open Market Account, expand or contract the money supply. If purchases of government securities are made from non-bank investors, the Reserve Banks draw checks on themselves in favor of the sellers of those securities. These checks, when deposited in banks, increase the volume of this form of money, namely, bank deposits.

Sales of securities by the Reserve Banks to non-bank investors diminish bank deposits because the purchasers ordinarily pay for their purchases by drawing on their deposit credits at banks.

Open-market purchases by the Reserve Banks from non-bank investors may be shown as follows:

Federal Reserve Bank

Government securities	+	Member bank reserve balances	+

Commercial Bank

Reserve balances	+	Deposits	+

Open-market sales to non-bank investors may be shown as follows:

Federal Reserve Bank

Government securities	—	Member bank reserve balances	—

Commercial Bank

Reserve balances	—	Deposits	—

Purchases of government securities by the Reserve Banks from commercial banks increase the reserve balances of the commercial banks at the expense of their security holdings, whereas sales of government securities by the Reserve Banks to the commercial banks increase the latters' security holdings and reduce their reserve balances.

Thus it should carefully be noted that additions to the security holdings of the Reserve Banks increase the public's money supply and bank credit expansion potential; decreases in the assets of the Reserve Banks have the opposite effect.

A common error on the part of bankers and students of money and banking is found in the idea that the Reserve Banks in the act of buying securities "use up" a part of the monies deposited with them by the

member banks. That this is an error is clearly seen in the bookkeeping entries shown. Purchases by the Reserve Banks do not "use up" reserve balances; instead such purchases augment those reserve balances.

Government balances and the money supply. An increase in U.S. government deposits with the Federal Reserve Banks or the commercial banks diminishes the public's money supply because such balances represent money extracted from the public by tax collections or sales of securities to the public. Conversely, a decline in U.S. Treasury deposits reflects expenditures in excess of receipts.

Treasury transactions and the money supply. Sales of new U.S. government securities to the banking system in order to meet a Treasury deficit have an expansive effect on the public's money; the retirement of maturing securities held by the banking system contracts the money supply.

The effect of sales of new securities to the commercial banks may be demonstrated as follows:

Commercial Bank

	(1)	(2)	(3)		(1)	(2)	(3)
Government securities	+			Treasury tax and loan account	+	−	
Reserve balances		−	+	Deposits			+

Federal Reserve Banks

	(1)	(2)	(3)
Member bank deposits		−	+
Treasury deposits		+	−

In *Step 1,* the commercial banks buy new government securities from the Treasury and give credit to the Treasury's accounts with them, namely, the "Treasury Tax and Loan Accounts." In *Step 2,* the Treasury transfers funds from its accounts with commercial banks to the Federal Reserve Banks. In *Step 3,* the Treasury spends the money by drawing checks on the Reserve Banks which are deposited in commercial banks.

The net effect of these transactions is to increase the government security holdings and the deposit liabilties of commercial banks. All other entries cancel out. Thus the public's money supply is increased.

The retirement of maturing government securities held by the banking system is a factor of decrease in the money supply. This is true because taxes paid into the Treasury decrease people's holdings of deposits and currency; and such receipts when used to retire government securities held by the banking system cancel banks' liabilities and are not returned directly to the public.

The effect of the retirement of maturing government securities on the money supply can be seen in the following bookkeeping entries. In *Step 1,* the Treasury collects taxes and deposits the receipts to its Treasury Tax and Loan Accounts. In *Step 2,* the Treasury transfers funds from the commercial banks to the Federal Reserve Banks. In *Step 3,* the Treasury retires securities held by commercial banks.

Commercial Banks

	(1)	(2)	(3)		(1)	(2)	(3)
Government securities				Deposits	—		
Reserve balance		—	+	Treasury Tax and Loan Account	+	—	

Federal Reserve Bank

	(1)	(2)	(3)
Treasury deposits		+	—
Member bank deposits		—	+

The net effect of these transactions is to decrease bank holdings of government securities and bank deposits. Later, however, bank loans can be expanded, on the basis of reserves released by the lowered deposits.

Effect of Federal Reserve purchases of government securities on the Consolidated Condition Statement. Let us next take two situations which may be used to show the effect of typical monetary transactions on the Consolidated Condition Statement. The first of these, let us say, is the purchase of government securities from non-bank investors by the Federal Reserve Open Market Account. In *Step 1,* these purchases are made by means of a check issued by the Reserve Bank to the seller of the securities. In *Step 2,* the seller presents the check for deposit credit at his bank. In *Step 3,* the bank obtaining reserve balances resulting from *Step 1* expands its loans. These transactions may be depicted as follows:

	(1)	(2)	(3)
Assets:			
Bank credit			
U.S. government securities held by Federal Reserve Banks	+		
Loans, net			+
Liabilities:			
Demand deposits		+	+

This illustration is a double one in the sense that two transactions, each of which involves a net addition to bank deposits, are involved in

it. Their net effect on the Consolidated Condition Statement is an increase in bank deposits, an increase in Federal Reserve holdings of U.S. government securities, and an increase in bank loans. The effect of such transactions on bank reserve balances will be set forth later in this chapter.

The second illustration shows changes in the Consolidated Condition Statement caused by gold inflow as follows. In *Step 1,* the Treasury buys gold from a foreign nation and pays for it by drawing on its deposits at Federal Reserve Banks. In *Step 2,* the Treasury issues gold certificates to the Federal Reserve Banks. In *Step 3,* the foreign nation spends funds in the United States.

	(1)	(2)	(3)	Net effects
Assets:				
Gold	+			+
Liabilities:				
Treasury cash	+	−		0
Foreign deposits	+		−	0
Deposits and currency				
Demand deposits adjusted			+	+
Treasury deposits	−	+		0

The net effect on the Consolidated Condition Statement is an increase in gold holdings and bank deposits. Treasury cash, Treasury deposits, and foreign deposits go up at one stage and down at another, leaving the level of each of these items on the Consolidated Condition Statement the same as before.

Major factors affecting deposits and currency, July 1, 1949 to June 30, 1950. In recent years the Board of Governors of the Federal Reserve System in its *Federal Reserve Bulletin* has published semiannually articles on monetary conditions which contain explanations of the major factors affecting deposits and currency in a recent period.[3] Students of financial institutions find these articles to be valuable supplements to the monthly computations of the Consolidated Condition Statement since they reveal, by quarterly periods, the effect on deposits and currency of Treasury transactions and market transactions of the banking system in U.S. government securities, as well as the effect of gold flows and changes in bank loans and investments. The latest available report at the time this is being written is the one built around Table 2.

It should be noted from Table 2 that Treasury transactions and market transactions of the banking system in U.S. government securities may, over a period of a year, have a minor effect on deposits and cur-

---

[3] See the *Federal Reserve Bulletins* for July 1950, December 1949, and May 1949.

TABLE 2

MAJOR FACTORS AFFECTING DEPOSITS AND CURRENCY
JULY 1949–JUNE 1950

(In billions of dollars, partly estimated)

Item	1949		1950		Total, July 1949– June 1950
	July-Sept.	Oct.-Dec.	Jan.-Mar.	Apr.-June	
Factors affecting deposits and currency [a]					
Gold outflow	+0.1	−0.2	−0.2	b	−0.2
Loans to private borrowers and securities of State and local governments and of corporations held by commercial and mutual savings banks	+1.6	+1.6	+1.7	+1.7	+6.6
Treasury transactions [c]	−1.3	+0.7	−1.4	+1.6	−0.5
Market transactions of banking system in U. S. Gov't securities [d]	+1.2	+1.3	−2.2	+0.4	+0.6
Other factors, net	−0.9	+0.1	−0.6	−0.5	−1.8
Changes in deposits and currency held by individuals and businesses, total	+0.7	+3.5	−2.7	+3.2	+4.7
Demand deposits adjusted	+1.2	+2.7	−2.5	+2.7	+4.1
Time deposits [e]	−0.1	+0.2	+0.7	+0.4	+1.2
Currency outside banks	−0.4	+0.5	−0.8	b	−0.7

[a] Signs before figures indicate effect on deposits and currency. Changes are net.
[b] Less than 50 million dollars.
[c] Treasury deposits, decrease (+) or increase (−), and Treasury sale (+) of new U. S. Government securities to, or retirement (−) of maturing securities held by the banking system which includes commercial banks, mutual savings banks and Federal Reserve Banks. Figures include an 800 million dollar increase in Treasury bills in July-September 1949 and a 1.1 billion increase in April-June 1950.
[d] Excludes sales of new bills by the Treasury as indicated in note above.
[e] Includes changes in deposits at commercial banks, mutual savings banks, and the Postal Savings System.
NOTE.—Changes are based on figures for June 30, Sept. 28, and Dec. 31, 1949, and Mar. 29 and June 28, 1950· All data for June 28, 1950 are estimated. Figures may not add to totals because of rounding.
Source: *Federal Reserve Bulletin*, July 1950, p. 776.

rency and yet have a substantial influence in quarterly periods during that year.

Factors Affecting Reserve Balances

The foregoing illustrations of changes in the Consolidated Condition Statement caused by different types of monetary transactions reveal that such transactions affect bank reserve balances. These and other transactions affecting reserve balances may be consolidated into an analytical statement relating to the level of reserve balances. Such a statement for the period (December 31, 1941, to December 31, 1945) is appended as Table 3.[4]

---

[4] For explanations of the construction of the statement of the supply and use of reserve balances, see John K. Langum, *Review of Economic Statistics*, August 1939, and "Member Bank Reserves, Reserve Bank Credit, and Related Items," *Banking and Monetary Statistics*, Board of Governors of the Federal Reserve System, pp. 360-366.

TABLE 3

MEMBER BANK RESERVE, RESERVE BANK CREDIT, AND RELATED ITEMS
DECEMBER 31, 1941 TO DECEMBER 31, 1945

(In millions of dollars)

Changes in the following factors
tended to increase member bank
reserve balances:

1. An increase in discounts and advances of the Federal Reserve Banks	246	
2. An increase in Reserve Banks' holdings of U.S. government securities	22,008	
3. An increase in other Reserve Bank credit	476	
4. An increase in Treasury currency outstanding....	1,092	
5. A decrease in nonmember deposits	52	
Total factors of increase		23,874

Changes in the following factors
tended to decrease member bank
reserve balances:

1. A decrease in gold stock	2,672	
2. An increase in money in circulation	17,355	
3. An increase in Treasury cash holdings	72	
4. An increase in Treasury deposits with Federal Reserve Banks	110	
5. An increase in other Federal Reserve accounts....	204	
Total factors of decrease		20,413
		3,461*
Increase in member bank reserve balances		3,465*

* Difference in figures due to rounding.
Source: *Federal Reserve Bulletin*, June 1950, p. 686.

This demonstration reveals that an increase in the following items
increases member bank reserve balances:

Federal Reserve credit outstanding
    Discounts and advances
    U.S. government securities
    All other Reserve Bank credit
Gold stock
Treasury currency

Increases in the following items tend to reduce member bank reserve
balances:

Money in circulation
Treasury cash holdings
Treasury deposits with Federal Reserve Banks
Nonmember deposits
Other Federal Reserve accounts

A study of Table 3 shows that in the period covered, increases in Federal Reserve Banks' holdings of U.S. government securities and an increase in Treasury currency outstanding were the largest items among factors tending to increase member bank reserve balances, the first of these being much larger than the second. The decrease in gold stock and the increase in money in circulation were the most important factors tending to decrease member banks' reserve balances. The second of these was much larger than the first.

It is thus made obvious that Federal Reserve Banks' purchases of government securities enabled the commercial banks to meet the great increase in the public's demand for currency and at the same time to meet the greater reserve balances required against greater deposit liabilities.

Let us next construct a table showing factors affecting member bank reserve balances for a more recent period (July 1, 1949, to June 30, 1950), when required reserve balances declined, an effect attributed mostly to a decline in reserve requirements. The computations appear in Table 4.

TABLE 4

MAJOR FACTORS AFFECTING MEMBER BANK RESERVES
JULY 1949–JUNE 1950

(In billions of dollars)

Item	July 1– Nov. 23, 1949	Nov. 24– Dec. 31, 1949	Jan. 1– June 30, 1950	Total, July 1, 1949– June 30, 1950
Factors affecting bank reserves:[1]				
Gold stock...	+0.1	−0.1	−0.2	−0.2
Money in circulation..............................	[2]	−0.1	+0.4	+0.3
Treasury deposits at the Reserve Banks.................	[2]	−0.4	−0.1	−0.5
Federal Reserve holdings of U. S. Gov't securities:				
Restricted bonds...............................	[2]	[2]	−1.4	−1.4
Other securities...............................	−1.6	+1.2	+0.7	+0.3
Other factors.......................................	−0.4	[2]	[2]	−0.4
Changes in member bank reserves, total.................	−1.9	+0.6	−0.6	−1.9
Excess reserves.....................................	−0.3	+0.4	−0.6	−0.5
Required reserves, total.............................	−1.6	+0.2	[2]	−1.4
Effect of:				
Reduction in reserve requirement percentages........	−2.2	....	....	−2.2
Change in deposits.............................	+0.6	+0.2	[2]	+0.8

[1] Signs before figures indicate effect on bank reserves.
[2] Less than 50 million dollars.
Source: *Federal Reserve Bulletin*, July 1950, p. 778.

Changes in excess reserve balances are caused by two sets of factors: (1) those affecting the deposit liabilities of banks which raise or lower required reserve balances, and (2) changes in reserve requirements. In

the period July 1 to November 23, 1949, a reduction in reserve requirements released $2.2 billion from required reserve balances to make that amount of funds available for investment in loans or securities. The significance of such a release of required reserve balances is that the public's money supply may be increased through an increase in bank loans and bank purchases of securities from non-bank investors. Such use of free reserve balances will, as has been explained earlier, raise the volume of deposits and currency. It might also tend to lower the prevailing level of interest rates and thereby give the economy the stimulus associated with "easy money."

A graphic presentation of "Member Bank Reserves and Related Items" reproduced from *Federal Reserve Charts* is presented as Figure 1.

Elements of Fiscal and Monetary Policies

Broadly stated, the objective of monetary and fiscal policies is to promote stability in the economy at high levels of production and employment. The primary responsibility for formulating these policies lies with government, particularly the federal government, and the Board of Governors of the Federal Reserve System. This is true although individuals and groups of individuals who make decisions to spend, save, produce, or invest might wish to modify those decisions in such manner as to promote greater stability in the economy. In periods of great inflation or deflation, however, the individuals and groups of individuals who are most conscious of the stabilization problem manifestly have not achieved the desired result by their acts and forbearances. Unless it is true that under all circumstances actions of governments do more harm than good, government stabilization policies might mitigate developing tendencies toward instability in private business.

The greatest fear, widely held, concerning the role of government in formulating and executing economic policies is that government is likely to have a bias in favor of inflation. In periods of prosperity, when good policy dictates that government spending should decline and that tax revenues should increase, political considerations might dictate that government expenditures should increase and that tax revenues should decline. In depression periods, declining tax revenues might, contrary to good policy, lead to increased tax rates and a cut in government expenditures. If such is the make-up of government operations, such shortsighted policies would accentuate rather than mitigate economic instability.

Whether stabilization policies formulated and executed by government or by such public bodies as the Board of Governors of the Federal Reserve System can alter the general economic climate in such manner

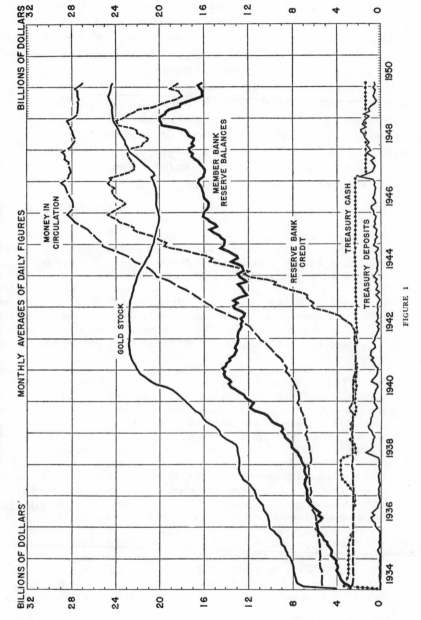

MEMBER BANK RESERVES AND RELATED ITEMS

MONTHLY AVERAGES OF DAILY FIGURES

BILLIONS OF DOLLARS

MONEY IN CIRCULATION

MEMBER BANK RESERVE BALANCES

GOLD STOCK

RESERVE BANK CREDIT

TREASURY CASH

TREASURY DEPOSITS

FIGURE 1

as to promote stability is being tested at the present time in the United States. The objective in the minds of most people who favor some sort of stabilization policy is that such policy should not operate by directives from government which would endanger free private enterprise. Decisions concerning what to consume and produce, where to work, and how to employ resources would be left to the free choices of individuals, as is the case under an economy of free enterprise.

Most economists and many businessmen think that using monetary and fiscal policies for stabilization purposes is compatible with our democratic, free-enterprise system. This view was expressed by J. Cameron Thomson, president of the Northwest Bancorporation, and Chairman of the monetary and fiscal policy committee of the Committee for Economic Development in testimony before the subcommittee on monetary, credit, and fiscal policies, as follows: [5]

> I want to draw a sharp distinction between fiscal, monetary, and debt-management policies on the one hand and direct controls on the other hand. By direct controls, I mean such measures as Government price controls, wage controls, rationing, allocations, and controls over the direction of investment. Failure to distinguish between these two kinds of measures is responsible for much confusion in public discussion and could lead to serious error in public policy. Two kinds of confusion are common. One is to reject the attempt to achieve greater stability by fiscal, monetary, and debt-management policies by putting these policies in the same class with direct controls over the details of private economic activity. The other is to accept and justify all manner of direct controls by putting them in the same class with indirect financial measures for stability.
>
> Fiscal, monetary, and debt policies are appropriate means for attacking the problem of instability in a free society. The problem of instability is essentially a problem of broad forces affecting the over-all magnitudes of the economy. The problem arises when millions of workers are simultaneously unempolyed, or when there is a general, although probably uneven, rise of most prices. The advantage of fiscal, monetary, and debt policies is that they allow the Government to influence the over-all forces—especially the level of aggregate demand—that determine the stability of the economy without necessarily involving the Government in detailed control of the particulars of the economy. These over-all measures will, of course, affect different individuals and businesses differently. But the differences are determined by the market process, not by Government decisions. The Government does not have to make decisions that are with rare exceptions better left to the market—the price of shoes relative to the price of automobiles, whether the ABC company or the XYZ company should prosper, what kind of a job John Jones or Robert Smith should have.
>
> Direct controls do involve Government decisions about the particular interrelationships of the parts of the economy. One virtue claimed for them

---

[5] "Monetary, Credit, and Fiscal Policies," *Report of the Subcommittee on Monetary, Credit, and Fiscal Policies of the Joint Committee on the Economic Report*, Senate Document No. 129, Washington, 1950, p. 10.

by their advocates is that they are "selective." But adding together a very large number of selective controls is surely a clumsy, expensive, inefficient, and politically dangerous way to get the over-all effect needed to deal with the stability problem. While the market process is not perfect, any general substitution of Government decisions for it would result in serious loss of efficiency, progress, and stability.

But more than efficiency, progress, and stability are at stake. Freedom is also at stake. Any widespread system of direct controls would necessarily involve widespread power of Government to affect the economic fortunes of particular individuals, businesses, industries, and regions "selectively"; that is discriminatingly. This power would have to be exercised by the Executive subject to only the most general statutory limitations. It would be the power to reward or punish, to coerce, by administrative action. The existence of such a power would ominously threaten the survival of our free society, for so long as the free society might endure.

We hear the concepts of "freedom" and "statism" used so much and so loosely that we become callous and impatient with them. But, on the specific problem of this subcommittee, I am convinced that the importance of fiscal, monetary and debt policy will not be sufficiently appreciated until we learn to make the distinction between power to coerce individuals and power to affect the general behavior of the economy. A precise line cannot be drawn between appropriate and inappropriate powers; yet, we must recognize that there is a direction in which we should not move except in cases of clearest necessity and even then only with utmost caution.

Importance of fiscal policies. In recent years expenditures by federal, state, and local governments have occupied an increasingly important position in the economy. In 1949 such expenditures were approximately $60 billion, compared with a national income of a little more than $200 billion. Clearly, government expenditures exert a major influence on production, employment, and prices in the economy as a whole.

That being the case, changes in the financing of government expenditures and changes in their magnitude, timing, and composition furnish the "stuff" from which fiscal policy is made. Whether government expenditures are financed wholly from tax revenues or in part from tax revenues and in part by borrowing profoundly affects total money supply and money expenditures. When financed wholly by tax revenues, taxes collected by one method have different effects from those attending taxes collected by another method. When financed partly by borrowing, whether the receipts of borrowing are collected from one group or another—whether from the banking system or the public—makes a great difference on money supply and velocity. And changes in the terms of borrowing—the interest rates and maturities of securities—induce different decisions among prospective lenders, depending on alternative choices for lending at the time.

The same magnitude of government expenditures has different effects at different times. At one time a certain amount of government ex-

penditures may be highly inflationary and at another the same amount may have effects which may be described as counter-deflationary. Not only is the magnitude of government expenditures important with reference to the *time* element; the size of such expenditures also determines importantly the kind of economy we have. An economy in which 30 per cent of total money expenditures are made by government is quite different from an economy in which government expenditures are 5 per cent or 10 per cent of the total.

The composition, as well as the magnitude and time of government expenditures, is an important consideration in any appraisal of their effects on the economy. The effects of government expenditures depend on who receives them. Payments for one purpose may discourage private investment, whereas payment for another purpose may stimulate private investment. Government payments may transfer funds from one geographical area to another, from one group in the economy to another, or from one nation to another.

Irrespective of one's views concerning the role of government in the economy, it must be recognized that the government's power to tax and spend is a great power.

Elements of fiscal policy. A basic consideration in the formulation of fiscal policy is that government tax revenues should be higher relative to government expenditures in periods of high employment than in periods when the trend in unemployment is upward. Most economists would agree that this proposition is a basic element in fiscal policy. Some of them would re-enforce it with another: that the absolute level of government expenditures should be lower in periods of high employment than in periods of substantial unemployment.

The propositions stated in the previous paragraph would reject the annually balanced federal budget, because a budget that is balanced each year would necessitate a decrease rather than an increase in government expenditures in a period of high unemployment and falling tax revenues. The annually balanced budget would also require increased government expenditures in a period of high employment and rising tax revenues. As far as tax rates are concerned, the annually balanced budget would require in periods of prosperity a very great reduction, unless government expenditures are drastically raised, while in periods of depression it would call for great increases in tax rates or drastic reductions in government expenditures.

Politicians and economists are probably not far apart in periods of depression, because both groups would probably agree that tax rates should not be raised to exceptionally high levels or that government expenditures should drastically be cut in that phase of the business cycle. In the prosperity phase of the cycle, however, most politicians

would probably back away from the accumulation of a great treasury cash surplus through high tax revenues and a simultaneous reduction in government expenditures.

It has been estimated that with every rise of $1 billion in national income, tax receipts will increase about $0.3 billion. Similarly, tax receipts will fall about $0.3 billion with every drop of $1 billion in national income. (These estimates are based on the federal tax system of 1949). If these estimates are no more than approximately correct, it is clear that an annually balanced budget would call for severe cuts in tax rates or great increases in government expenditures in periods of rising national income, and for severe cuts in government expenditures or great increases in tax rates in periods of falling national income.

Substitutes for the annually balanced budget. Almost all economists agree that the annually balanced budget must be abandoned if we wish to adopt a stabilizing fiscal policy. They are not, however, agreed on a substitute for the annually balanced budget.

Some of them contend that the budget should be balanced over a business cycle rather than annually. Budget deficits in some years would be covered by budget surpluses of other years. Hence government spending, whatever the amount may be, would be paid for by an equal amount of revenue, but probably not revenue collected wholly in the same year in which the expenditures are made. The demerit of this proposal is that legislative bodies likely would not find and adopt a guide to the determination of changes in the phase of the cycle to which adjustments in tax rates and expenditures could be made.

Another proposal is that tax revenues and such expenditures as those for unemployment benefits and relief should be budgeted each year at the same amount as in a year of high employment without inflation. If, under this plan, the Congress increased expenditures in a year of high employment and rising national income, those expenditures would be met by increased taxes and not out of revenues derived from a higher national income than that of a base or "normal" year. In a year when employment and tax revenues would fall because of a slump in business activity, increased taxes would not be ordered. In other words, tax rates would be set to balance the budget in a normal year and would not be lowered in periods when those rates are abnormally productive due to inflation (they would then yield a treasury cash surplus), nor would they be raised (and expenditures cut) in a period of falling national income.

Still another plan for inducing stability through fiscal policy is the enactment by Congress of statutes providing for an automatic rise in tax rates on personal incomes when an index of prices or production or employment rises by a specified amount, and a drop in such tax rates when the chosen index reflects falling prices or business activity.

Economists disagree on the degree of reliance that should be placed on automatic or "built-in" stabilizers involving fiscal policy. Some of them admit the "logic" or "theory" behind one or another of these proposals for a stabilizing fiscal policy, but they see obstacles in the way of their consistent application. Almost all of them hope that if automatic stabilizers, other than those such as the progressive personal income tax, the corporation income tax, and unemployment compensation already in effect, are not adopted that discretionary stabilizing actions will be taken by the Congress.

Elements of monetary policy. The most elemental proposition concerning monetary policy upon which there is general agreement is that money and credit should be relatively "tight" in periods of rising prices, production, and employment and relatively "easy" in periods of falling prices, production, and employment.

There might, however, be some disagreement over the extent to which central banking authorities ought to interfere with "natural" market prices concerning interest rates. Presumably, market rates would, without interference from anyone, tend to rise in periods of strong demand for funds, which is likely to be a period of prosperity, and fall in a period of low demand, which is likely to be a period of recession. Traditional economic theory would proclaim this to be true. Some skeptics, however, would assert that money rates and availability of funds may be tight at the beginning of recession or depression and that central banking operations might beneficially make easier the availability and cost of loanable funds. The skeptics also doubt that money rates and money supply will, by reason of market forces, effectively tighten in prosperity periods short of a boom and a crash. They, therefore, would allow monetary authorities promptly to nudge the general interest rate upward in periods of prosperity and downward in periods of recession. To do so would be action consistent with traditional central banking policy, if not consistent with pure *laissez faire* economics.

During the deep depression, following the stock market crash of 1929, many economists who previously had placed considerable reliance on the stabilizing effects of traditional monetary policy in the hands of central banking authorities began to entertain grave doubts regarding the efficacy of such policy as an instrument for maintaining economic stability. Many of them turned to fiscal policy as a better means for achieving stability. Most of them, however, agree that tight money conditions can turn a mild recession into a deep depression and that easy money can accentuate a recovery movement and perhaps turn it into a dangerous boom.

The Report of the Subcommittee on Monetary, Credit, and Fiscal Policies (familiarly known as the Douglas Committee) of the Joint Com-

mittee on the Economic Report rejected the idea that for stabilization purposes little or no reliance should be placed on monetary policy. A part of this report follows: [6]

> As indicated earlier, we believe that an appropriate, flexible, and vigorous monetary policy, employed in coordination with fiscal and other policies, should be one of our principal instruments for achieving and maintaining economic stability. For several reasons we reject the idea, held by a few economists and others, that for stabilization purposes little or no reliance should be placed on monetary policy and that we should rely exclusively on other measures, such as fiscal policies. (1) It is highly doubtful that fiscal policy would be powerful enough to maintain stability in the face of strong destabilizing forces even if monetary policy were neutral, and a conflicting monetary policy could lessen still further the effectiveness of fiscal policy. (2) Monetary policy is strong precisely where fiscal policy is weakest; it is capable of being highly flexible. It can be altered with changes in economic conditions on a monthly, daily, or even hourly basis. (3) It is a familiar instrument of control and thoroughly consistent with the maintenance of our democratic government and our competitive free-enterprise system. It is certainly much to be preferred over a harness of direct controls. (4) Our monetary history gives little indication as to how effectively we can expect appropriate and vigorous monetary policies to promote stability, for we have never really tried them.
>
> For example, the effectiveness of these policies during the late 1920's was seriously reduced by the Federal Reserve's lack of powers for the selective control of security loans. After 1929, a vigorous easy-money policy was not adopted until bank reserves had been allowed to shrink for more than 2 years, thousands of banks had failed, and general business confidence had dwindled; and after World War II its use as a restrictive measure with which to combat inflation was very seriously hampered by considerations relating to the management of the Federal debt. With our improved banking structure and the benefit of our past experience, we should be able to look forward to more effective monetary management characterized by timely, vigorous, and flexible actions.

Quantitative controls. The traditional instrument of central banks, evolved for use in tightening or easing money rates as monetary policy might dictate, is the discount rate. Raising this rate, which is the rate at which banks or other borrowers might obtain funds from the central bank, would tend to discourage marginal borrowers from applying for loans. To the extent that potential borrowers might refrain from borrowing, a brake would be placed on further credit expansion. Conversely, lowering the rate might in periods of recession discourage further credit contraction.

The Federal Reserve System, in its earlier years, placed great reliance on the efficacy of the discount rate. Later, greater reliance was placed on open-market operations, a tool of monetary policy that has come to

---

[6] *Ibid.*, pp. 18-19.

be recognized as the most powerful in the kit of instruments of the Federal Reserve System.

Open-market operations are classified as a quantative instrument of money policy because they affect the supply of funds in the market. This tool is not selective because it does not specifically withhold funds for certain uses, as is the case with qualitative controls. As has been demonstrated earlier in this chapter, purchases of securities by the Federal Reserve System from non-bank investors result in a rise in bank deposits and reserve balances of banks, whereas sales of securities by the Federal Reserve System have the opposite effect.

A third quantitative instrument of credit control is the power vested in the Board of Governors of the Federal Reserve System to change, within the limits fixed by statute, the minimum ratio of reserves to deposits that the member banks in the System are required to hold. Raising the reserve requirements reduces the loan-expansion potential of banks, because the banks' ability to make loans depends on their "free" reserve balances. If any bank would expand credit it must have excess reserves or ways of procuring additional reserve balances, such as selling securities or discounting assets at the Federal Reserve Banks. Lowering reserve requirements frees reserve balances, previously required, for use as a base for bank credit expansion.

Thus, actions by the Federal Reserve System (1) lowering the discount rate, (2) purchasing securities in open-market operations, and (3) lowering reserve requirements, encourage bank credit expansion, because such actions invite the use of Federal Reserve credit or make reserves available for bank loans. Actions which reduce free reserve balances or discourage the use of Federal Reserve credit are (1) sales of securities by the Federal Reserve System, (2) raising the reserve requirements, and (3) raising the discount rate.

Qualitative controls. In recent years the Federal Reserve System has been vested with new powers which have become known as *selective* or *qualitative* controls. Examples are (1) controls over stock-exchange margins, and (2) controls over down payments and maturity provisions in installment sales contracts. These controls are selective in character because they single out certain types of credit extensions to the exclusion of others. Controls over stock-exchange margins were given to the Federal Reserve System following the stock market crash of 1929, because it was felt that easy credit for speculative purposes had damaged the economy. Power of control over the terms of installment sales contracts was given to the Federal Reserve System during World War II, because it was felt that easy credit for consumption purposes would burden the economy with an unnecessarily large volume of production for civilian use at a

time when great efforts were being made to divert production resources to military purposes.

The area of agreement on monetary and fiscal policies. Monetary economists agree on the broad outlines of good monetary and fiscal policy: that new money should not be injected into the market places when boom conditions threaten the economy, and that money should not be destroyed by restrictive monetary and fiscal policies in a period of depression. That policies running counter to this proposition have been pursued in the past can hardly be doubted. That monetary and fiscal policies which accentuate booms and busts are not to be followed in the future might well be the demand of all citizens interested in the maintenance of our cherished political and economic institutions, since booms and busts threaten the stability of these institutions.

Despite its limitations, monetary policy deserves the support of persons fearful of direct controls. Quite often the alternative to monetary actions to achieve greater stability in the economy, assuming greater stability to be desirable and possible, is direct control over production, prices, and employment. Control over the money supply may rightly be regarded as the least undesirable of all types of controls and as the most consistent with an economic system of free enterprise.

It is appropriate to end this section on the elements of monetary policy with excerpts from "Monetary, Credit, and Fiscal Policies," a report of the subcommittee of the Joint Committee on the Economic Report, as follows: [7]

> We recommend not only that appropriate, vigorous, and coordinated monetary, credit, and fiscal policies be employed to promote the purposes of the Employment Act, but also that such policies constitute the Government's primary and principal method of promoting those purposes.
>
> . . . .
>
> Those who would oppose using monetary, credit, and fiscal policies for stabilization purposes, either by refusing to give the Government adequate powers or by obstructing its use of these powers, must therefore either oppose the purposes of the Employment Act or find other methods of equal effectiveness and of equal compatibility with our democratic free-enterprise system.
>
> We do not know precisely how much effectiveness as a stabilizing device we can expect from appropriate, vigorous, and coordinated monetary, credit, and fiscal policies. Our past experience is of little help in making such an estimate, for a timely, vigorous, and coordinated use of all these policies for stabilization purposes has never been seriously attempted in this country. Fortunately, however, the validity of our recommendations does not need such a precise estimate; it is enough to know that these methods can be very powerful and that they are preferable to other methods for promoting general economic stability.

---

[7] Document No. 129, 81st Congress, 2nd Session, United States Government Printing Office, Washington 1950, pp. 5 and 11.

Suggested Readings

Beckhart, B. H., *The New York Money Market*. New York: Columbia University Press, 1931.

Blough, Roy, "Political and Administrative Requisites for Achieving Economic Stability," *American Economic Review, Proceedings*, May 1950, pp. 165-178.

Board of Governors of the Federal Reserve System, "Member Bank Reserves, Reserve Bank Credit, and Related Items," *Banking and Monetary Statistics*. Washington, D.C.: Government Printing Office, 1941, pp. 360-366.

Board of Governors of the Federal Reserve System, *The Federal Reserve System —Its Purposes and Functions*. Washington, D.C.: Government Printing Office, 1947.

Bopp, Karl R., "Central Banking at the Crossroads," *American Economic Review, Supplement*, March 1944, pp. 276-277.

Burgess, W. R., *The Reserve Banks and the Money Market* (revised edition). New York: Harper & Brothers, 1946.

Copeland, Morris A. and Brill, Daniel H., "Banking Assets and the Money Supply Since 1929," *Federal Reserve Bulletin*, January 1948, pp. 24-32.

Committee for Economic Development, *The Stabilizing Budget Policy*. New York: The Committee, 1950.

———, *Monetary and Fiscal Policy for Greater Economic Stability*. New York: The Committee, 1948.

Ellis, Howard S., "Central and Commercial Banking in Postwar Finance," from *Economic Reconstruction*, edited by Seymour E. Harris. New York: McGraw-Hill Book Co., 1946.

Federal Reserve Bank of Philadelphia, *The Quest for Stability*. Philadelphia: The Bank, 1950.

Goldenweiser, E. A., *Monetary Management*. New York: McGraw-Hill Book Co., 1949.

Hansen, Alvin H., *Fiscal Policy and Business Cycles*. New York: W. W. Norton and Company, Inc., 1941.

———, *Monetary Theory and Fiscal Policies*. New York: McGraw-Hill Book Co., 1949.

Hardy, C. O., *Credit Policies of the Federal Reserve System*. Washington: The Brookings Institution, 1932.

Keynes, J. M., *A Treatise on Money*. New York: Harcourt, Brace and Company, 1930.

Langum, John K., "Federal Reserve Open Market Policy, 1934–1939," *Financial and Investment Review* (Minneapolis), 1939.

———, "Supply and Use of Reserve Balances," *Review of Economic Statistics*, August 1939.

McCracken, Paul W., "The Present Status of Monetary and Fiscal Policy," *The Journal of Finance*, March 1950, pp. 24-48.

Mints, Hansen, Ellis, Lerner, and Kalecki, "A Symposium on Fiscal and Monetary Policy," *The Review of Economic Statistics*, May 1946, p. 76.

Mints, Lloyd W., *A History of Banking Theory*. Chicago: University of Chicago Press, 1948.

Peterson, J. Marvin, and Cawthorne, D. R., *Money and Banking*. New York: The Macmillan Company, 1949, Chapters XIX-XXI.

Phillips, C. A., *Bank Credit*. New York: The Macmillan Company, 1920.

Phillips, C. A., *Readings in Money and Banking.* New York: The Macmillan Company, 1921.

Prochnow, Herbert V., *Term Loans and Theories of Bank Liquidity.* New York: Prentice-Hall, Inc., 1949.

———, "Bank Liquidity and the New Doctrine of Anticipated Income," *The Journal of Finance,* December 1949, pp. 298-314.

Reifler, W. W., *Money Rates and Money Markets in the United States.* New York: Harper & Brothers, 1930.

Senate Document No. 129, 81st Congress, 2d Session, "Monetary, Credit, and Fiscal Policies," *Report of the Subcommittee on Monetary, Credit, and Fiscal Policies.* Washington, 1950.

Sweezy, Alan R., "Fiscal and Monetary Policy," *The American Economic Review,* Supplement, May 1946.

Szymczak, M. S., "Development of Federal Reserve Banking," *Federal Reserve Bulletin,* December 1940.

———, "Monetary Policy in a Free Economy," *Federal Reserve Bulletin,* September 1950.

Whittlesey, Charles R., "Federal Reserve Policy in Transition," *Quarterly Journal of Economics,* May 1946.

Williams, John H., *Postwar Monetary Plans and Other Essays.* New York: A. A. Knopf, 1944.

Willis, H. P., *The Federal Reserve System.* New York: The Ronald Press Company, 1923.

——— and Steiner, W. H., *Federal Reserve Banking Practice.* New York: D. Appleton and Company, 1926.

6

Savings and Loan Associations
and Mutual Savings Banks

_by_ CARL F. DISTELHORST

Vice President and Director of Education
American Savings and Loan Institute

THE TWO principal types of supervised financial institutions which specialize in the promotion of individual thrift and in the management of savings funds are savings and loan associations and mutual savings banks. Each of these systems of savings institutions has been established for more than a century and, on the whole, has been conducted for the benefit of persons of small or modest means who aspire to buy or build a house of their own; to provide for their own security; or through savings, to acquire some stake in our system of free enterprise.

In the words of Calvin Coolidge: "It is not too much to say that almost the whole of what we call civilization today is the difference between saving what we make today for use on the morrow and exhausting it at the time we receive it." The more than 32,000,000 savings accounts totaling $34,000,000,000 in savings and loan associations and mutual savings banks testify to the important role of these local savings institutions in the economic progress of our nation. The investment of these savings funds by these savings institutions has contributed in no small way toward making our country a nation of home owners and toward the financing of America's public utilities, railroads, and other industries.

Savings and Loan Associations

At the beginning of 1951 there were some 5,900 savings and loan associations serving nearly every trading area of the nation. They had total resources of $16,500,000,000 and over 11,500,000 savings accounts with

total balances exceeding $14,000,000,000. Although several savings and loan associations have passed the $100,000,000 mark, the typical associations located in metropolitan areas range in size from $5,000,000 to $25,-000,000. Those located in outlying communities, neighborhood areas of large cities, or in the smaller towns, often are around $1,000,000 or smaller in size.

Savings and loan associations are locally owned and managed savings and home financing institutions. They offer their savings account facilities to the public and reinvest these funds primarily in amortized first mortgage loans on the security of residential dwellings. A portion of the savings funds are also invested in obligations of the United States Government to provide an immediate source of funds if necessary to meet requests for the withdrawal of savings. With few exceptions, savings and loan associations are mutual or cooperative organizations. This means that they have no capital stock, and the ownership and power of control rests with the holders of savings and other types of accounts. All earnings of a mutual savings and loan association are distributed, pro rata, among the savings and investment accounts after deductions for expenses of operation and after transferring to reserves and undivided profits a portion of the earnings to provide for possible future losses on loans and investments.

Historical background. The Oxford Provident Building Association was the first savings and loan association in this country. It was organized at Frankford (now a part of Philadelphia), Pennsylvania in 1831. Among the organizers were two pioneer manufacturers who, as natives of England, were familiar with the work of the English building societies in encouraging workmen to save systematically. The home on which the first amortized loan was made in this country still stands occupied, and in 1947 it was purchased by the federal savings and loan associations of Philadelphia.

The America of 1831 was a growing and expanding nation. Although largely agricultural, manufacturing and commerce were rapidly becoming important. In the cities there was emerging a wage-earning class of men who were not generally property owners and for whom there were no home financing facilities. A few mutual savings banks had been established but they did not grant home loans to the wage-earning class. Commercial banks did not accept savings accounts, and their main business was that of discounting commercial paper or making business loans. The time was ripe for a cooperative movement which would provide home financing on suitable terms not then available to the working class. The early leadership for this movement came largely from tradespeople, workers, and professional men of moderate means but of excel-

lent repute in their communities. Many, if not most of them, served without remuneration.

The early savings and loan associations were voluntarily formed neighborhood groups responding to this type of leadership. The Oxford Provident Building Association, for example, had about 40 members. Each agreed to save a specified amount each week. As large enough sums were thus accumulated, they would be loaned to one of the members of the group. But as the funds available to lend were thus limited, some of the members of the group had to postpone their home ownership plans while wating for sufficient funds to accumulate. It soon became apparent that to provide a steady supply of home financing funds it would be necessary to invite others to open savings accounts. Experience showed that half a dozen savings accounts were required to supply the funds necessary to finance the purchase of one home.

Hence, it was but a few years after the first savings and loan association was founded that these home financing institutions, of necessity, also became savings institutions. By the 1850's these associations began to place increased emphasis on their savings function in order to meet the demand for home loans.

As it was carried from city to city by a migrating population, the savings and loan idea spread gradually to other parts of the country. By 1851 a savings and loan association had been established in Chicago; by 1865 there was one in San Francisco; and by 1890 they were in operation in every state and territory in the nation.

In the absence of any unified organizing force these associations came to be known by a wide variety of names, and they developed many different plans of operation. In New England, for example, they came to be known as "cooperative banks," and in Louisiana and other scattered areas as "homestead associations." Their most common corporate title in their earlier days was that of "building and loan association" or "building association," but as their savings function came into greater prominence, more of them began to adopt the "savings and loan" title, or its abbreviated form, "savings association." "Savings association" appeared in the corporate titles of some of the charters issued prior to the close of the nineteenth century and is now coming into greater usage.

Organization, supervision, and management. The early savings and loan associations were voluntary associations in the nature of a partnership. Subsequently, they took on the corporate form securing their charters, in many instances, under the general corporate laws. This explains how certain corporate terminology such as "shares" (for savings accounts) came into early use. In time, the various states developed special laws or codes for savings and loan operations, and in some states such laws are now a part of the banking or general financial institutions' laws.

As in the case of commercial banks, the charter under which an association operates may be issued by a state or federal authority. This dual system of savings associations arose in 1933 when authority for issuing charters was granted by Congress in the Home Owners' Loan Act. Federal associations may be established either by the granting of new charters or by the conversion of existing state chartered associations to a federal charter. The purposes of creating a federal system were to meet a need that existed in many communities for adequate thrift and home financing facilities and to provide a more uniform plan of operations, incorporating the best practices of savings and loan associations up to that time. There is little doubt but that the dual system has contributed greatly toward uniformity and in extending savings and home financing facilities into areas previously not served. It bears emphasizing that regardless of source of charter or of the diversity of their laws or corporate names, the state and federally chartered associations operate as a single and unified system of thrift and home financing institutions.

An application for permission to organize a new savings and loan association may be made by a small group of responsible citizens of a community, usually five or more. Basic requirements are that applicants must be of good character and responsibility; that there must be a need for such an institution in the community; that there must be reasonable probability of the association's usefulness and success; and that it must be demonstrated that the association can be established without undue injury to properly conducted existing local thrift and home financing institutions. It is generally required that a specified minimum number of persons must subscribe to a minimum amount of capital in the form of savings and investment accounts. All federally chartered associations must be members of the Federal Home Loan Bank System and the Federal Savings and Loan Insurance Corporation.

Federal charters are granted by the Home Loan Bank Board, an agency of the federal government. The petition to organize a state-chartered association is generally filed with the state's savings and loan commissioner, who may be the head of a separate state department or of a subdivision of the state banking department. In many of the states membership in the Federal Home Loan Bank System and in the Federal Savings and Loan Insurance Corporation is required by the authorities issuing new charters.

In the several state or federal chartering authorities also rests the responsibility for supervising the operations of savings and loan associations in the public interest. In addition to submitting at least annual reports to their respective state or federal supervisory authorities, savings and loan associations are subject to periodic examinations, generally once each year. The purpose of such examinations is to determine compliance

with the laws, charter and by-laws under which they operate; solvency or insolvency and the trend with respect thereto; and the integrity of the management and personnel.

Because of the mutuality of savings association operations, and reflecting their early history when they operated as closely knit neighborhood groups, both their savings and borrowing customers are known as members, and it is generally so provided in their laws. All members have a right to vote, and the usual provision is that each borrower-member shall have one vote while savings members usually are allowed one vote for each $100 balance or fraction thereof in their account, with a maximum limit of 50 votes per member. In some states where the law provides that savers subscribe to share accounts, wherein shares with a maturity value (usually $100) are purchased through installment savings, the saver has one vote for each share subscribed.

The right to vote carries with it the privilege of electing the directors as well as the right to vote on other general corporate matters at annual or properly called special meetings of the members. Voting may be by proxy, and it is common practice for either a proxy committee or the management to receive proxies from the members. Proxies, however, are revocable, and occasionally the members not satisfied with the present management have been known to exercise their right in the selection of other directors.

In electing directors, the members of savings associations delegate to them the full responsibility for the proper conduct of the business. Since the directors are generally leading citizens engaged in various other businesses and professions, it is inexpedient for them to manage the details of daily operations. These responsibilities are delegated by the directors to a full-time executive officer who assembles the necessary additional personnel for the daily conduct of the business. The directors determine the broad general policies, and the top executive officer is responsible for their execution.

The laws governing savings associations generally relate to their savings functions; provisions for paying withdrawals on savings; liquidity requirements; the lending of money on the security of first mortgage loans on real estate; other investment powers; the right to borrow money; distribution of earnings; requirements for the accumulation of reserves for possible losses; and other miscellaneous and general corporate requirements.

Permanent capital stock companies. In Ohio and in a few of the western states, principally in California, it is permissible to organize savings and loan associations which issue permanent capital stock, or guarantee stock. Such stock is transferable but not withdrawable. The owners of the permanent stock are the owners of the association, and their stock

may be charged with losses to the full extent of such investment, should reserves and undivided profits prove to be insufficient. By law, the permanent capital stock type of savings and loan associations is required to maintain at least a minimum capital structure in relation to total resources or savings accounts of all types. The development of capital stock companies was originally motivated by the desire to provide the savers with an additional safety factor and also to make possible a guaranteed rate of interest on the savings accounts. As a result of adverse experiences in the 1930's, interest on savings deposits in guarantee or permanent stock companies is no longer guaranteed.

Savings account operations. By law, a savings account in a savings and loan association is not called a deposit. Through the years, many different types of accounts were developed. Some state laws still adhere to the term "share account," which is reminiscent of the early days of these financial institutions when they operated under general corporate laws. The trend, however, is distinctly in the direction of simplification. The federal charter and a few of the state charters provide for a single type of account called a savings account. In many other instances the only additional type of account is an investment account. A savings account can be opened with a nominal amount, and savings can be added or withdrawn at the saver's will. For this type of account a pass book is issued. Dividends, as declared by the association, are added to the saver's ledger account and entered in the pass book, when next presented, after a dividend has been declared. Some of the state laws refer to this type of account as an optional savings account.

The investment account was devised for the individual, or other investors of lump sums, who preferred to receive their dividends periodically in cash and for whom a savings account was not especially suitable. Certificates are issued for investment accounts in $100 units or in multiples thereof. Periodically, as dividends are declared, the holders of investment certificates receive dividend checks. For purposes of simplicity in operations, some associations now issue pass books for these lump sum investments and arrange to pay out the semiannual or quarterly dividends in cash.

Another type of account generally identified with what is known as the "serial plan" of savings and loan operation is the installment share account. Though the serial plan associations are no longer common in most sections of the country and though their number is steadily declining, a brief description of their plan of operation is in order. The serial plan association does not open new savings accounts at all times throughout the day or week. Rather, a specific time is designated, usually at the beginning of each annual, semiannual, or quarterly period at which new accounts will be opened. Those who wish to open accounts at

that time subscribe to a number of installment share accounts in accordance with the amount the subscriber plans to save every month. For each share subscribed, a typical requirement is that 50¢ per month must be paid thereon until the share matures—that is, until the total of the monthly savings plus the dividends credited equals the share's maturity value of $100.00. To illustrate, a person wishing to commit himself to saving $10 per month would subscribe to 20 installment shares. All of the shares subscribed by all who "join the series" at a given time are carried along to maturity in the same group called a "series." Dividends are generally allocated to the series as a block and not on each individual account.

The installment share account in a serial plan association contemplates that the saver will save regularly every month. At one time, failure to save regularly as agreed resulted in imposing a fine on the saver. If the account is not carried on to maturity as agreed, some associations also allow a lower rate of dividend upon withdrawal. In this manner failure to save regularly is penalized. Although this type of account and plan of operation had merit in its disciplinary approach to saving, it was not considered flexible enough to attract a steady flow of savings. The more flexible savings account operation of today was developed alongside the serial plan as far back as the 1860's. Many of the serial associations now also offer both the optional savings account and the investment account. Most of the savings and loan associations and cooperative banks still operating on the serial plan are located in the East.

The modern approach to encourage regular savings is the bonus account. Under this plan the saver opens the usual type of savings account but also agrees to save a stated amount each month for a specified period of time. If the plan is continued to the end as agreed, an additional bonus dividend is added to the regular dividends as a reward for regular savings. The bonus provisions vary with the state and federal laws, but the additional return may be as much as 1 per cent more and the required periods to qualify for the bonus range from five to 15 years.

The permanent capital stock companies in Ohio offer certificates of deposit and savings deposit accounts which are creditor obligations of these associations. The California stock companies offer full-paid certificates, installment certificates, accumulative certificates, and prepaid certificates. While they do not bear a fixed rate of return, it is common for such certificates to specify a maximum rate of return that can be paid thereon, if declared.

Other variations or classes of savings accounts are also offered in some states, but these plans do not figure prominently in the aggregate of savings association operations.

With few exceptions, savings associations are not limited by law in

the maximum size of accounts that can be accepted, although some associations as a matter of operating policy, do fix such limits.

Safety of savings. The principal concern of most savers is the safety of their savings and their availability when needed. The rate of return is secondary to these other considerations.

Factors affecting the safety of savings in savings associations include the quality of management, the mortgage lending policies and administration, the accumulation of reserves for losses, insurance of accounts, and supervision.

Lending powers are restricted by law, as discussed later, but laws in themselves do not assure freedom from risk. Sound appraisals, careful review of the personal risk, monthly amortization of the loans, provisions for the monthly payment of taxes and insurance, careful collection procedures, guarantee and insurance of loans to veterans by the Veterans Administration and insurance of loans as provided by the Federal Housing Administration—all have contributed substantially to the reduction of risks in mortgage lending. In addition to these safeguards in the selection of servicing of mortgages, all savings associations are required by law to accumulate reserves against which losses may be charged as they arise. In general, the requirement is that a certain minimum percentage of annual net income must be transferred to reserves for losses until such reserves (including undivided profits or unallocated reserves) are the equivalent of 10 or 15 per cent of assets, depending upon the law under which the association operates. The typical savings association, in recent years, has transferred 25 to 35 per cent of its annual income to reserves and undivided profits. In the aggregate their total reserves and undivided profits approximate 8 per cent of their assets. Supervisory authorities, in their periodic examinations of the associations, also afford the saver a certain amount of protection in their review of operating and lending practices of savings associations.

The final source of protection to the savers, if all else fails, is the insurance of accounts as provided by the Federal Savings and Loan Insurance Corporation.

Withdrawal of savings. The laws under which savings associations operate specify the manner in which withdrawal requests shall be handled. As savings institutions the associations are not required to pay out on demand, although it is customary to do so. Most of the laws provide that a 30- or 60-day written notice of withdrawal may be required.

When the notice requirement is invoked, withdrawal notices are numbered and paid out in the order of filing. In times of general financial emergency when it may not be feasible to pay all withdrawals within the notice period, the laws generally prescribe the procedure to be followed.

While the laws are not uniform in this respect, a typical provision is that one-third of all receipts must be applied to paying withdrawals until all requests have been honored. In order to alleviate hardship cases among savers, it is also frequently provided that the directors may authorize withdrawal payments up to $100 to any one account holder in any one month without regard to the order of filing notice. It is also sometimes provided that not more than $1,000 shall be paid on account of any one withdrawal request in the order filed and that upon the payment of such an amount, any balance on notice will be renumbered and returned to the end of the list.

For federal associations operating under the new Charter "N," the charter empowers the Home Loan Bank Board to prescribe withdrawal procedures by regulation. This is in keeping with practice among mutual savings banks and provides for more flexibility in meeting conditions as they arise.

The provisions permitting an orderly plan for meeting withdrawal requests are realistic and often prevent needless closing of financial institutions when general economic conditions do not permit normal operations. Realists are aware that the credit and financial structure of our economy is such that it is impossible at any one time, good or bad, to liquidate it entirely in cash, except with printing press money.

Liquidity of savings. Adequate liquidity to meet withdrawal requests without delay is provided in several ways: by maintaining adequate working cash balances; by investment of a portion of the resources in government bonds; from amortization and interest payments on mortgage loans; and by borrowing from the Federal Home Loan Bank, the reserve credit system for savings, and home financing institutions. Most savings associations hold at least 15 per cent of their resources in cash and obligations of the United States Government. For many this ratio is as high as 25 per cent or more. Savings associations which are members of the Federal Home Loan Bank System may be required by regulation to maintain a liquidity reserve of cash and United States government bonds up to 8 per cent of their total savings accounts. A few of the state laws also establish minimum liquidity reserves. Not to be overlooked as another source of funds are the regular payments made on amortized mortgages. A study of mortgage loan payments in the 1930's for savings and loan associations in one of the large eastern states showed that even in the worst year, 1933, loan payments received were equal to 12.4 per cent of the total savings and investment accounts at the beginning of that year. In addition, there are some who look to the marketability of FHA and veterans' loans, although many are skeptical of this source in a period when cash is scarce. Beyond their own resources, savings associations which are members of the Federal Home

Loan Bank System in most instances have legal authority to borrow an amount equal to 50 per cent of their total savings accounts. All these sources of funds combined should adequately fortify savings associations to meet withdrawals in as great a volume as the continued functioning of our economy will permit. It is anticipated that by reason of the confidence created by insurance of accounts, future withdrawal pressures will fall short of the extremities of the 1933 banking crisis.

Dividends. The return paid on savings by savings and loan associations is called dividends, not interest. Dividend rates of 2 or $2\frac{1}{2}$ per cent per annum are most common. A few associations pay dividends at the rate of 3 per cent or higher. The rate of dividend that can be paid on savings depends on the rate of interest available on mortgages, yields on other investments, expenses of operation, and the amount of earnings transferred to reserves. Mortgage lending rates are influenced to a great extent by the 4 per cent maximum interest that may be charged on guaranteed or insured loans to veterans and the maximum $4\frac{1}{4}$ per cent rate permitted on FHA loans. Yields on obligations of the United States Government range from slightly more than 1 to $2\frac{3}{4}$ per cent. Expenses of operation vary with locality and management objectives and policies and range from 1 to $1\frac{1}{2}$ per cent of the savings account. Dividends are calculated on the basis of the amount in the account and for the time it was there in a manner similar to interest. All federal associations calculate dividends under the same prescribed method, and the methods of dividend calculation by the state chartered associations are reasonably uniform.

Home financing facilities. The balance sheet of a typical savings association would show approximately 80 per cent of its resources invested in first mortgage loans secured by residential real estate; approximately 15 per cent in cash and obligations of the United States Government; and the remainder in miscellaneous assets, including office building and equipment. Though in many states savings associations have long had broad investment powers comparable to those of mutual savings banks, the associations have always been conducted primarily as home financing institutions. Their great contribution to the American way of life was to develop and popularize a plan of home financing that brought home-ownership within the reach of the low- and middle-income families. They pioneered the low-downpayment, long-term, monthly amortized loan more than a century ago. It was not until the advent of the Federal Housing Administration, created by Congress in 1934, that the amortized home loan came into general use by other types of financial institutions. With few exceptions, the home mortgage lending activities of savings associations are confined to the communities in which they are located and in their immediate vicinity.

As a safeguard to the many small savers whose funds are being managed, the manner in which savings associations may invest their savings funds is prescribed by laws, rules, and regulations. With respect to their power to invest in first mortgages on the security of real estate, the laws generally prescribe the types of real estate by which mortgage loans may be secured; the maximum amount that may be loaned in relation to the appraised value of the security; the maximum size of any one loan regardless of the value of the security; provisions for repayment of loans, including the maximum term for which a loan may be granted; and the lending area within which an association may grant mortgage loans. The various state and federal laws are not uniform.

Most of the state laws grant the associations broad powers to invest in first liens secured by almost any type of real estate; some require that it be improved real estate, prohibiting loans on vacant land; a few permit first mortgage loans only on the security of residential real estate or limit the amount that can be loaned on other types of real property. In spite of these broad provisions, however, approximately 90 per cent of all mortgage loans held by savings associations are first liens on single family dwelling units (generally owner occupied); loans on two to four family dwelling units rank next in volume. In rural areas some associations will grant mortgage loans on farms, and in the larger urban centers some associations engage in limited financing of multi-family dwellings. Seldom do they extend mortgage credit on business, industrial, or other types of property.

The maximum loan permitted in relation to the appraised value of the property is generally established by the various state laws, although in some states the law is silent. Where the maximum is established, the most frequent figure is 80 per cent of appraised value. For the most part these lending ratios apply to one- to four-family dwellings and lower percentages are frequently established for mortgages secured by other types of property.

The amount which a savings association will actually lend on the security of a given piece of property, within the limits established by law or regulation, depends on a number of factors including the age, condition, location and marketability of the property; the borrower's character and credit standing; and the judgment of the directors and management regarding the general economic outlook as it applies to real estate price trends.

Many of the state laws also fix the maximum amount of any one loan, with $20,000 being the most common limitation; other states set $15,000 to $25,000 maximums. Some state laws relate the maximum loan permitted to the size of the association.

Except for loans insured by the Federal Housing Administration or

guaranteed or insured by the Veterans Administration, the state laws often prohibit savings associations from writing mortgage contracts for a term of more than 20 years. Most states, however, specify no maximum terms, and in a few instances the term is either 15 years or 25 years. Shorter terms are sometimes required on mortgage loans secured by other than residential property. Loans not amortized monthly are often restricted to shorter terms such as three or five years. Ten, twelve, fifteen, and twenty years are the most common terms for which home mortgage loans are written by savings associations.

Except for an amount equal to 15 per cent of their total resources, federally chartered savings associations may lend only upon the security of first liens on new homes or combination home and business properties within 50 miles of the association's home office. They may lend up to 80 per cent of the appraised value of the property but not more than $20,000 for terms up to 20 years on a monthly amortized basis. Lower percentage straight loans are permitted for terms not to exceed five years. Federally chartered savings associations are also authorized to grant loans insured by the Federal Housing Administration or guaranteed or insured by the Veterans Administration in accordance with the regulations and procedures as established by these federal agencies. They may invest up to 15 per cent of their resources in first liens secured by other types of real estate (such as multi-family apartments and business properties) without regard to the 50 mile lending radius and the $20,000 maximum. The percentage of loan to appraised value permitted on the security of such other real estate is established by regulation and generally ranges from 50 to 66⅔ per cent of the appraised value, depending on the type of property and the terms of repayment.

Many, though not all, savings associations finance builders, both large and small, in the construction of new homes. In recent peacetime years this type of financing has represented nearly one-third of their annual mortgage lending volume. Several states have granted savings associations limited powers to purchase land for the purpose of building thereon residential units for rent or for sale. This arrangement permits the association to assemble larger sums of capital in a more efficient manner than is available in some areas for residential construction purposes.

Other investment powers. In addition to their primary investment function of financing home ownership, savings associations are authorized by both the federal and the various state laws to make loans on the security of savings account pass books, to invest in direct and guaranteed obligations of the United States Government, and to make unsecured property improvement loans insured by the Federal Housing Administration.

Investments in obligations of the United States are primarily to provide a source of funds which can be readily converted into cash in the event of heavy withdrawals of savings. Government bond holdings of savings associations will range from 5 to 25 per cent or more of their total resources.

Unsecured property improvement loans are closely related to the basic home financing function. It is appropriate that the financial institutions which specialize in financing home ownership should also provide adequate credit facilities to assist in keeping such homes modern and in a good state of repair. Although the authority to grant such loans is generally limited to loans insured by the Federal Housing Administration or by the Veterans Administration, the federally chartered associations and some state chartered associations have limited powers to make unsecured property improvement loans; and in some states loans may be made for other purposes, even though the loans are not guaranteed or insured by a federal agency.

About three-fourths of the states permit savings associations to invest in obligations of their respective states, and nearly as many authorize investments in municipal bonds. Several states grant savings and loan associations essentially the same broad investment powers as the savings banks in their states.

Although the investment powers of savings associations are quite broad, it is significant that these associations have continued to confine their investment operations almost wholly to first liens on single-family residential property. Experience has demonstrated that the value of residential real estate for security purposes is more durable and more apt to survive the rigors of our fluctuating economy than are business or industrial properties or debt obligations of corporations.

Other financial services. Many savings associations offer financial services to their customers or to the general public in addition to the basic savings and home financing services. Included among these additional services are: Christmas saving and vacation club accounts, school savings, payroll deduction savings plans, sale of money orders and traveler's checks, safety deposit boxes, and general counsel and advice on home construction and family financial matters.

Not all savings associations offer every one of these services, and in some states the services may be limited by state laws. Special services are generally offered to customers who prefer to complete as many as possible of their financial transactions at the same place. The offering of these services also brings in others who may become customers.

Federal Home Loan Bank System. The Federal Home Loan Bank System was established by Congress in 1932 to provide a central reserve credit system for savings institutions engaged in home mortgage finance.

Membership in this system is required of all federal savings and loan associations and is open to state chartered savings and loan associations, mutual savings banks, and life insurance companies which meet the requirements of membership. As of December 31, 1950, membership in the system consisted of 3,894 savings and loan associations representing over 90 per cent of the assets of all such financial institutions, 29 mutual savings banks, and seven life insurance companies.

Consideration was first given to the establishment of a reserve system for home financing institutions when the Federal Reserve System was established in 1913. It required a financial crisis to crystallize the need. Early in December, 1931, President Herbert Hoover called a Conference on Home Building and Home Ownership. This Conference, following President Hoover's recommendation, unanimously approved the creation of what is now the Federal Home Loan Bank System. A bill was promptly introduced in Congress and passed in the summer of 1932. It provided the first vehicle by which savings and home financing institutions could develop a central reserve credit system of their own.

The principal purposes of the Federal Home Loan Bank System are to assist in providing ample funds on reasonable terms for the purchase of homes; to provide means by which surplus funds of member institutions in one part of the country may be available to members of the System in another part of the country; and to provide a source of funds to savings institutions in periods of heavy withdrawal of savings. The economic environment of the early and middle 1930's provided an immediate opportunity to the Federal Home Loan Bank System to demonstrate its usefulness. The heavy withdrawals of savings in that period had all but dried up the supply of home mortgage funds. By advancing funds to its member savings and home financing institutions, this reserve credit system did more than make new funds available for home loans. It made funds available to meet withdrawals of savings promptly, thereby helping to restore confidence in its member savings institutions and attracting a new flow of savings.

The Federal Home Loan System functions through 11 regional banks, each serving its member institutions in its established area. District I, for example, is comprised of the New England states, and the Home Loan Bank for that district is located in Boston, Massachusetts. The Home Loan Bank Act provides for no more than 12 nor less than eight regions, each served by a regional bank. The system is supervised by a Home Loan Bank Board of three appointees of the President of the United States, by and with the advice and consent of the Senate. This Board also directs the operations of the Federal Savings and Loan Insurance Corporation and is charged with the chartering, supervision, and rules and regulations governing federal savings and loan associations. The Home

Loan Bank Board is now one of the constituent agencies of the Housing and Home Finance Agency. The other agencies are the Federal Housing Administration and the Public Housing Administration.

The management of each of the regional banks of the system is vested in a board of 12 directors, residents of the district in which the bank is located. Four of the directors are appointed by the Home Loan Bank Board and are known as public interest directors. The remaining eight are elected by the member institutions.

The Federal Home Loan Bank System has three principal sources of funds: capital stock owned by its members, deposits of members, and the sale of its obligations in the open market. When the System was established, the United States Treasury provided the original capital for the regional banks in the aggregate amount of approximately $125,000,-000, with provision for its redemption as adequate stock was purchased by the member institutions. Substantially all of the government's stock has now been retired. Members of the system are required to own stock equivalent to at least 2 per cent of the aggregate of the unpaid balances of their home mortgage loans.

Members of the System are also encouraged to maintain deposit balances with their respective regional banks. Both demand deposit and interest-bearing time deposit facilities are available. These deposit facilities offer the means of making a surplus of funds in the possession of some members available to other members in areas where funds are in demand.

The third source of funds is through the sale of the joint obligations of the regional banks comprising the system. The sale of these obligations to banks, insurance companies, savings and loan associations, and other investors has provided a substantial source of funds to the Federal Home Loan Banks to advance to their member institutions. The total amount of these obligations outstanding exceeds half a billion dollars. As a safeguard in the event of an emergency when the open money markets may not be receptive, the Secretary of the Treasury of the United States is authorized to purchase obligations of the Federal Home Loan Bank System in an amount not to exceed one billion dollars.

Member institutions having need for funds may secure advances from their respective regional banks. These advances are in the form of loans, which may be written for a period as long as 10 years. The Home Loan Banks do not discount paper, as does the Federal Reserve System. Rather, advances generally are secured by home mortgage loans. The advances may be repaid in quarterly installments extending over a period of 10 years, a term which is consistent with the long term use of funds by the member institutions. To meet seasonal requirements short-term advances are also extended, often without security. The borrowing powers

of the member institutions are set forth in their respective state and federal laws.

The System has functioned largely as it was conceived. It has provided billions of dollars of home financing funds to meet peak seasonal requirements of its members as well as meeting much of the need for funds in growing areas where the local supply of savings fell short of the demand for home financing funds. On several occasions, such as a brief period following Pearl Harbor, the member savings and loan associations secured advances for the purpose of paying withdrawals promptly. The System has thus demonstrated that there is also a need for its reserve credit facilities in helping to keep savings accounts liquid when savers either need their funds or fear that they cannot be withdrawn. In this function the Home Loan Bank System helps to sustain public confidence in its member savings institutions, an important factor in attracting a steady flow of savings for home financing.

Federal Savings and Loan Insurance Corporation. The Banking Act of 1933 provided for the creation of the Federal Deposit Insurance Corporation as a means of restoring the public's confidence in commercial banks through the insurance of bank deposits. Less than a year before, Congress had established the Federal Home Loan Bank System to provide, among other things, greater liquidity for savings accounts in savings and loan associations in order to strengthen public confidence in these thrift and home financing institutions. This reserve credit system was proving to be of considerable benefit, but it became evident that the added assurance provided by insurance of savings accounts was as essential to the complete restoration of public confidence in savings and loan associations as it had been to commercial banking. Accordingly, in 1934, Congress added Title IV to the National Housing Act and provided for the establishment of a Federal Savings and Loan Insurance Corporation to insure the safety of savings in savings and loan associations.

The Federal Savings and Loan Insurance Corporation insures savings accounts in savings associations up to $10,000. It insures neither liquidity of savings accounts nor the rate of return thereon. Its sole function is to protect the safety of savings. The insurance becomes operative when an insured institution is declared in default by the proper public supervisory authority or by a court of competent jurisdiction, depending upon the source of the association's charter. Besides its function of paying off savings account holders in the event an insured association is declared in default and ordered liquidated, the Federal Savings and Loan Insurance Corporation possesses broad preventive powers to come to the assistance of an association in the early stages of any difficulty. For example, in order to prevent a default or to restore an insured association

in default to normal operations, the Insurance Corporation may make a cash contribution or loan to such institution or purchase its assets.

The procedure by which the Insurance Corporation pays out on insured accounts in the event of default and liquidation of an insured association is provided for in the law. When the proper state or federal supervisory authority takes charge of an insured savings association declared in default, the Insurance Corporation immediately determines who the holders of insured savings accounts are, notifies them, and proceeds to return funds up to the $10,000 amount insured. The settlement provisions as amended by Congress in 1950 are substantially the same as apply for the Federal Deposit Insurance Corporation and Section 5, subsection (b) of section 405 of Title IV of the National Housing Act, as amended, and read as follows:

> In the event of a default by any insured institution, payment of each insured account in such insured institution which is surrendered and transferred to the Corporation shall be made by the Corporation as soon as possible either (1) by cash or (2) by making available to each insured member a transferred account in a new insured institution in the same community or in another insured institution in an amount equal to the insured account of such insured member: PROVIDED, That the Corporation, in its discretion, may require proof of claims to be filed before paying the insured accounts, and that in any case where the Corporation is not satisfied as to the validity of a claim for an insured account, it may require the final determination of a court of competent jurisdiction before paying such claim." (Approved September 21, 1950.)

The initial capital of the Federal Savings and Loan Insurance Corporation, in the amount of $100,000,000, was paid in by the Home Owners' Loan Corporation, and ownership was subsequently transferred to the United States Treasury. This capital, plus the accumulated annual insurance premiums paid in by the member insured associations, constitutes the reserve fund for the protection of insured savings accounts. Premiums were originally assessed at the rate of $1/8$ of 1 per cent per annum on the total amount of all insured accounts plus all creditor obligations of the insured associations. In 1950 the premium rate was reduced to $1/12$ of 1 per cent. The Insurance Corporation may make an additional assessment at the same rate as the premium, if losses so require. The reserves accumulated through payment of insurance premiums and the net earnings on invested funds of the Insurance Corporation were approximately equal to the $100,000,000 capital stock at the close of 1950. During 1950, Congress authorized the gradual redemption of the capital stock. Half of the Corporation's annual income is to be applied to the redemption of the stock, and it is estimated that by 1960 the Federal Savings and Loan Insurance Corporation will be wholly owned by its member savings associations, at which time it will function

as a privately owned insurance operation but subject to the supervision, rules, and regulations of the Home Loan Bank Board.

At the close of 1950, 2,860 savings associations (with 81 per cent of the total resources of that business) had their accounts insured by the Federal Savings and Loan Insurance Corporation. Insurance of accounts is required of all federally chartered savings and loan associations and is available to all state chartered associations which apply and qualify.

Insured associations are subject to the periodic supervision of the Insurance Corporation, which also requires each insured institution to make annual additions to a special reserve for losses until such reserve equals 5 per cent of the total savings accounts.

In March, 1934, four months before the Federal Savings and Loan Insurance Corporation was authorized by Congress, the state of Massachusetts enacted legislation establishing its own fund for the insurance of share accounts in cooperative banks (savings and loan associations). This is a compulsory program for all cooperative banks in that state, and under an assessment arrangement all accounts are fully insured.

Though insurance of accounts has been an important factor in the recent development of the savings and loan business, the primary strength of the business rests in its management, its assets (which consist primarily of monthly payment home mortgage loans and obligations of the United States Government), and the reserves which are accumulated against which future losses may be charged.

Mutual Savings Banks

Historical background. The first mutual savings bank in this country was organized by a wealthy businessman and philanthropist, Condy Raquet. Though it was not formally incorporated by the Pennsylvania Legislature until February 25, 1819, it opened its doors and received its first deposits on December 2, 1816. Recognizing the need for the encouragement of thrift among the working class and the absence of any other media through which these people could save, he invited other prominent men of his city to join in founding The Philadelphia Savings Fund Society. Standing as a symbol of the wisdom of that idea and of the strength and stability of mutual savings banking, this first of the American savings banks is still in operation. Indeed, its resources have grown to beyond $700,000,000, and it is one of the nation's largest.

The chief function which this Society performed was to provide a safe place to deposit and accumulate savings. Prior to that time, such small amounts as the average person could afford to save were usually entrusted to a shopkeeper or other business proprietor who happened to own a strong box. Besides being cumbersome and risky, this system did not

provide for capital accumulation through the investment of savings funds. To quote the language of some of the early charters, savings banks were organized "to receive and safely invest the savings of mechanics, laborers, servants, minors and others, thus affording to such persons the advantages of security and interest for their money, and in this way ameliorating the condition of the poor and laboring classes by engendering habits of industry and frugality."

At about the time that The Philadelphia Savings Fund Society was being formed, a similar group of enterprising citizens in Massachusetts were organizing The Provident Institution for Savings in the Town of Boston. They received a charter from the Commonwealth of Massachusetts on December 13, 1816, and began business on February 19, 1817. The savings bank idea spread rapidly into Maryland, New York, Connecticut, and Rhode Island.

Not all of these early savings institutions incorporated the term "Savings Bank" in their titles, and today some still go under the titles of "Institution for Saving," and "Saving Fund Society." The inclusion of "Five Cents" and "Dime" in the corporate names of some also is suggestive of their interest in those of modest savings ability.

The founders of savings banks were all leading citizens with benevolent and philanthropic interests. They often gave of their time without compensation and, in some instances, paid expenses of operation out of their own pockets so that all earnings on their invested savings were distributed.

Savings banking today. As of the beginning of 1951 there were 529 mutual savings banks with $20,050,000,000 of all types of deposits held by more than 15,000,000 regular depositors, plus nearly 5,000,000 special accounts representing school savings, Christmas savings, and others.

With few exceptions, mutual savings banking has confined itself to the New England states and other eastern states including Delaware, Maryland, New Jersey, New York, and Pennsylvania. Beyond these states a few savings banks may be found in Indiana, Minnesota, Ohio, Oregon, Washington, and Wisconsin. In all, mutual savings banks are found in only 17 states, and their greatest concentration of savings deposits is found in the following four states:

State	Savings Bank Deposits, Jan. 1, 1950	Per Cent to Total
New York	$11,102,124,122	57.5%
Massachusetts	3,249,364,968	16.8
Connecticut	1,321,379,428	6.9
Pennsylvania	1,061,615,989	5.5
Other 13 savings bank states	2,552,826,759	13.3
	$19,287,311,266	100.0%

Though not constituting a nationwide system of savings institutions, in the communities where mutual savings banks do operate they are generally a substantial element among the other financial institutions. There are nearly 50 mutual savings banks with resources exceeding $100,000,000, and 80 or more of them have celebrated their one hundredth anniversaries.

The reasons why savings banking did not develop into a nationwide system of savings institutions are a matter of conjecture. Some plausible explanations have been given. The big expansion in savings bank charters took place from the 1850's through the 1870's, with the greatest period of expansion being the period following the Civil War up to the panic of 1873. During that period only half a dozen mutual savings banks were formed in Indiana, Minnesota, and Ohio. Nearly all of the economic development west of the Alleghenies at that time was agricultural. The farmer, it is reasoned, had little need for savings banks and was more inclined to plow his savings back into more land and live stock which he understood and in which he had faith.

Meanwhile changes had occurred in commercial banking and, along with other developments, the commercial banks began to welcome savings accounts. Though national banks had no specific authority to establish savings departments until the Federal Reserve Act of 1913, liberal interpretation of the law by the Comptroller of the Currency resulted in their offering savings account services along with many of the state chartered banks. Meanwhile, too, savings and loan associations had expanded rapidly throughout the Midwest and Far West and had established themselves as savings institutions in thousands of communities, both large and small. Operating largely as small neighborhood thrift and home financing institutions, they served most of the wage earners' savings needs.

Except for the conversion of a savings and loan association to a savings bank in 1949 in the State of Washington, there have been no new savings banks chartered since 1934.

Mutual savings banks defined. The United States Supreme Court (96 U.S. 388) has defined a mutual savings bank as:

> An institution in the hands of disinterested persons, the profits of which, after deducting the necessary expenses of conducting the business, inure wholly to the benefit of the depositors, in dividends, or in a reserved surplus for their greater security.

Mutual savings banks are organized for the purpose of receiving small savings to be invested by the bank to best advantage for the savers, not so much with an objective of earning a high rate of return but with greater consideration for the savings' safety and availability to the

savers when needed. Mutual savings banks have no capital stock. Rather, the holders of savings accounts are the co-owners, and to them belong all earnings whether distributed as dividends or set aside in surplus to the extent considered expedient to provide for possible investment losses. The savers, as owners, would also share pro rata in any distribution of assets except to the extent of prior claims represented by borrowed funds. Holders of savings accounts in mutual savings banks, though co-owners, are generally referred to as depositors.

While their primary function is to accept and manage the accumulation of small savings funds, in three states (namely, Indiana, New Jersey, and Ohio) mutual savings banks may accept checking accounts. The extent to which they may offer other than savings deposit services and the manner in which they may invest such funds, as well as many of the other details of operation, are governed by their charter and by-laws and by the laws of the state in which they are chartered.

Organization, management, and supervision. The laws governing the organization, management, and supervision of mutual savings banks are generally found in a special code known as the banking law in the states in which they operate. It should be pointed out that there is no provision for granting savings bank charters by an agency of the federal government as there is in the case of commercial banks and savings and loan associations.

A savings bank may be organized, usually on petition by the organizing group (or incorporators) filed with the superintendent of banks of the state. When the character, responsibility, and general fitness of the incorporators have been satisfactorily determined and the need and prospects for future success of the proposed savings bank have been established a charter may be issued. Some state superintendents of banks will not approve a new charter unless the Federal Deposit Insurance Corporation will insure its deposits.

The co-owners or depositors in mutual savings banks do not possess any rights in management. This power is usually vested in a board of trustees (also known as board of managers or board of directors) which often is a self-perpetuating body. While generally the trustees serve indefinitely, the Massachusetts law prescribes fixed terms, but vacancies are filled or successors elected by the trustees. Savings bankers believe that this system of self-perpetuating trustees has attracted the highest type of citizens to savings bank trusteeships.

The trustees are generally prominent business and professional men, not necessarily acquainted with the details of savings banking. Accordingly, the responsibilities of daily operations are delegated to the active officers and staff. The trustees serve as a policy-making body.

All savings banks are under the supervision of their respective state

banking departments. Such supervision is conducted in the public's interest to determine the soundness of each bank, its compliance with the laws, and the integrity of its management and personnel.

A savings bank has all the powers which are expressed in its charter as well as those which may be reasonably implied in the ordinary operations of its business. Following are some of the typical powers of mutual savings banks:

1. To receive and repay deposits.
2. To invest depositors' funds in property, securities, and other loans, as prescribed by the laws of the state.
3. To declare dividends.
4. To borrow money for the purpose of repaying depositors.
5. To become a member of the Federal Reserve System.
6. To become a member of the Federal Home Loan Bank System.
7. To become a member of the Federal Deposit Insurance Corporation.
8. To rent to its depositors and other persons safe deposit boxes.
9. To collect promissory notes or bills of exchange.

In addition, mutual savings banks are authorized to perform a variety of other financial services as discussed later in this chapter.

Savings accounts. The typical depositor in a savings bank is an individual of small means who saves a portion of his or her regular earnings. The average size of the accounts, exclusive of special club accounts and school savings, is approximately $1,300. Some states place a limit on the maximum amount which any one person or organization may have on deposit in any one savings bank as follows: Connecticut, $20,000; Massachusetts, $4,000 (plus an additional amount in accrued dividends not to exceed $4,000); Minnesota, $5,000; New Jersey, $25,000; New York, $7,500; Oregon, $5,000; and, Wisconsin, $5,000.

In a strict sense of the word mutual savings bank deposits are long-term deposits and, accordingly, their laws provide that a savings bank may require notice from its depositors before paying withdrawals. Such notice, typically, is 60 or 90 days, although some banks retain the privilege of requiring a longer notice. The withdrawal provisions are usually printed in the savings account pass book. Failure to pay a depositor's withdrawal request upon the expiration of the notice period may constitute a default on the part of the bank. However, in New York the banking board has power to regulate withdrawals of deposits or share accounts from any banking institution, if necessary, because of the existence of unusual and extraordinary circumstances. Such a regulation, for example, could provide for limited payments on withdrawals similar to those typically prescribed by laws governing savings and loan associa-

tions. Some savings banks retain flexible powers for their trustees to extend the notice period in the event of an emergency.

Withdrawals. While the notice requirement has been relied upon to educate the public about the differences between a savings institution and a commercial bank, as a practical matter the public has become accustomed to expect that under ordinary circumstances it can withdraw its savings from a supervised financial institution without delay. Most savings banks, under ordinary circumstances, pay out on savings accounts without requiring notice.

The real problem this condition presents is that of preparing for large and sudden withdrawals or long periods of withdrawal. Fortunately, in the past 75 years, those periods have been few and of relatively short duration for the mutual savings banks. In the public interest, most savings bank laws require a minimum percentage of liquid assets ranging from 3 to 10 per cent of deposits, and the laws prescribe that such liquidity be in the form of cash on hand, on deposit, or in obligations of the United States Government.

The typical savings bank financial statement will show around 4 to 5 per cent in cash and commercial bank deposits plus an additional 40 or 50 per cent of its deposits in United States government securities. The high ratio of government obligations reflects, in part, the dearth of other investment opportunities in relation to the bulge in savings experienced during World War II. In the mid-1930's, cash and government obligations held by savings banks ranged around 15 to 20 per cent of deposits.

In more recent years, however, habits in the use of savings accounts have changed considerably. Savings accounts show increasing turnover as savers apparently set up shorter-term savings goals and use savings accounts in lieu of checking accounts (on which service fees are levied). Studies show that total annual withdrawals from savings accounts in mutual savings banks now approximate 25 to 30 per cent of the average deposit balances, a figure considerably above the turnover of a generation ago. The turnover of savings accounts in savings and loan associations approximates the same ratio. The higher savings account turnover suggests a need for higher liquidity ratios than was once customary.

Dividends. The earnings of mutual savings banks are primarily derived from interest earned by the investment of the savings funds. Quarterly or semiannually, after allowing for operating expenses and setting aside a proper amount in surplus to provide for possible future losses, the trustees determine the rate of dividend which can be paid. The distribution is called dividends because it is dependent wholly on the net earnings of the savings bank and is not a fixed rate of return which savings banks are obligated to pay. Accounts with a fixed or guaranteed rate of return are not permitted as in the case of commercial banks. Because

dividends are calculated on the basis of the amount deposited and the period of time the amount has been on deposit, some savings banks have adopted the term "interest-dividend," which means dividends calculated as interest. As dividends are declared they are entered on the depositor's ledger card in the bank and added to the account balance. Subsequently, as the depositors bring in their pass books, the dividends are also recorded therein. Dividends generally are not paid on amounts withdrawn between dividend distribution dates; but dividends do accrue on deposits made during the period.

The exact formula for computing dividends is generally not regulated by the savings bank laws, and there are in excess of 20 basic methods of dividend calculation. Most of the differences in dividend calculations center around account activity. With few exceptions, the rate of dividends paid on savings deposits by mutual savings banks has ranged from $1\frac{1}{2}$ to $2\frac{1}{2}$ per cent in recent years. The over-all average rate of dividends is approximately 2 per cent; this rate is paid by about two out of every three savings banks.

Safety. The factors in savings bank management which have a bearing on the safety of deposits are, prudent investment policy, effective collection procedures for amortized mortgage loans, continued supervision of the portfolio of securities, and the accumulation of a surplus to meet unforeseeable losses. In addition, these banks are supervised by their respective state banking departments; most of them are also members of the Federal Deposit Insurance Corporation, which insures deposits up to $10,000. However, Massachusetts provides its own Mutual Savings Central Fund which insures in full all savings bank accounts in the state; and Connecticut has its own Savings Banks' Deposit Guaranty Fund which guarantees all deposits in full in most of the savings banks of that state. The savings banks of New Hampshire maintain a mutual protection organization for the protection of their depositors.

While all of the savings bank laws provide for the accumulation of a surplus account against which losses can be charged, the specific requirements of the several states vary. In the aggregate, the surplus of all mutual savings banks approximates 10 per cent of their total resources. Most of the savings banks in the East report somewhat greater surplus ratios than those operating elsewhere in the country.

Investment of savings funds. The investment of deposits to the best advantage of the saver is one of the most important functions of savings bank officers and trustees. The manner in which such funds are invested has a direct bearing on the safety of the depositors' funds, their availability when needed, and the rate of dividends which can be paid as a reward for savings. It is understandable, therefore, that the investment powers of savings banks are carefully prescribed by law and subject to

the rules and regulations of the supervisory authorities. In general, these laws and regulations indicate the types of securities eligible for investment, restrict the amount which may be invested in any one issue or category, and state the conditions under which real estate loans and collateral loans can be made. Some of the state banking commissioners or banking boards issue so-called legal lists of securities which meet the prescribed qualifications and are considered to be legal investments. In Maryland and Delaware the selection of investments is left to the savings bank officers, although the selection is subject to severe examination by their banking departments. The "prudent man" rule for savings bank investments is coming into greater favor.

All savings banks are authorized to invest in direct and guaranteed obligations of the United States Government, state, county and municipal bonds, real estate bonds and mortgages, gas, electric and water bonds, collateral loans secured by bank pass books on legal securities, and unsecured property repair and improvement loans insured under Title I of the Federal Housing Act. All but one or two states permit investments in railroad bonds, equipment obligations, and telephone bonds. In addition, the majority of savings bank laws authorize investments in loans secured by life insurance policies, Canadian bonds, obligations of the International Bank for Reconstruction and Development, acceptances and bills of exchange, bonds of industrial corporations, bank and trust company stocks, loans without collateral but with two or three endorsers, and stock in a Federal Reserve Bank and in a Federal Home Loan Bank as necessary to qualify for membership. A few of the states also permit investments in street railway bonds, obligations of foreign governments, guaranteed mortgage bonds, small personal loans on a monthly amortization basis, farm loan bonds, federal, state and joint stock land bank bonds, corporate stocks, participation certificates, and ground rent certificates.

The following summary of the distribution of savings bank resources as of January 1, 1951, shows, however, that savings bank deposits are primarily invested in government bonds and real estate mortgages:

DISTRIBUTION OF MUTUAL SAVINGS BANK ASSETS
JANUARY 1, 1951

Cash	3.5%
United States Government Obligations....	48.5
Mortgage Loans	35.8
Other Securities	11.0
Other Loans and Assets	1.2
Total	100.0%

Twenty years ago, real estate mortgages constituted slightly more than 50 per cent of total savings bank assets; railroad, state and municipal

and public utility bonds about 30 per cent; and cash and United States government obligations, 10 per cent. State and municipal bonds were considered among the liquid assets available for heavier than usual withdrawals. During the depression and recovery years of the 1930's, real estate mortgage holdings declined steadily (as did all types of corporate and municipal bonds), and by the time of Pearl Harbor, cash and United States government obligations represented over 42 per cent of all mutual savings bank assets; real estate mortgages, barely 40 per cent; and municipal, railroad and utility bonds, about 11 per cent.

During World War II and the first two postwar years, substantially all of the net increase in savings bank deposits was invested in United States government obligations; in 1947 government obligations reached nearly 65 per cent of savings banks' total assets. At the peak, savings bank holdings of these obligations of our federal government exceeded $12 billion.

Since then there has been a shift in savings bank investment policy. Considerable emphasis has again been placed on real estate mortgages, largely in reliance upon the FHA insured and veterans' guaranteed loans. They yield a higher return than other available types of investments and, consequently, not only are the bulk of new savings deposits being invested in mortgage loans, but holdings of United States government securities are also being liquidated and reinvested in mortgage loans. From June 30, 1947, through December 31, 1950, real estate mortgage loan balances of the savings banks increased from $4.6 billion to $8 billion, with nearly half of that increase occurring in 1950 alone.

In contrast with 20 years ago, when the monthly amortized mortgage was either unknown or unrecognized in savings bank circles, the bulk of the currently held mortgage loans are on an amortized basis. The typical savings bank straight mortgage loan proved to be very unsatisfactory during the depression of the 1930's, and a very high percentage of them had to be foreclosed. The savings bank mortgage loan portfolio of today also is secured by fewer commercial and business properties and a much higher proportion of residential real estate, including many single family dwellings.

While there is some variance among the state laws regulating investments in mortgage loans, the trend is in the direction of expanding the savings banks' powers along lines similar to those of savings and loan associations and beyond that to permit home financing operations on a nationwide scale. About one-third of the savings bank states place no limit on the amount of deposits which may be invested in real estate mortgages, but the remaining states limit real estate mortgage investments to 50 to 75 per cent of savings bank deposits. (Seventy per cent of deposits is the more typical figure.)

In the largest savings bank states of New York and Massachusetts, limited power has recently been granted the savings banks to invest in mortgage loans insured by the Federal Housing Administration and secured by residential property located anywhere in the United States. For the Massachusetts savings banks the same also applies to combination loans insured by the Federal Housing Administration, the secondary portion of which is guaranteed by the Veterans Administration. This extension of the real estate mortgage lending limits beyond state lines reflects the pressure of excess funds which savings banks have in New York and Massachusetts; and these banks prefer not to invest their excess funds in more government bonds or bonds of private corporations, because of their relatively low yield. Savings banks have come to regard amortized mortgage loans secured by residential real estate as quite desirable for the investment of savings funds.

Savings banks in New York may also own and operate multi-family housing projects in which three or more savings banks must participate. In some instances savings banks may also acquire title to land to facilitate the development and financing of large housing projects.

Also, pressed by the desire to improve earnings and to diversify further their higher yield investments, savings bankers are seeking greater authority to invest in common stocks under the "prudent man" rule.

For the most part, shifts in savings bank investment policies are contingent upon the rate of return available on the different types of legal investment, changes in risk characteristics (for example, the adoption of the monthly payment mortgage plan and the insurance or guarantee of mortgages by federal agencies contributed heavily to the renewed interest in real estate mortgages), and the relative supplies of the different types of legal investments. Each economic era brings with it certain investment fashions and preferences.

Other financial services. Though originally established primarily to manage the savings of the wage earner, mutual savings banks have offered, from time to time, new and extended services. Such additional services are generally offered as a matter of convenience to their depositors and to attract new savings customers. The list of such additional services is a long one, and not all services are available from all savings banks; many services are subject to the provisions of the various state laws.

Additional services closely related to the savings account operations are school savings programs and a variety of short-term, specific purpose, or club accounts such as Christmas clubs, vacation, and travel clubs. Savings banks were among the first to cooperate in school savings accounts, and approximately two out of every three of these banks offer this service to nearly 2,000,000 participating children with about $50,-

000,000 on deposit. Nearly 2,500,000 persons have one or another of the various club accounts.

In a majority of the 17 mutual savings bank states, the savings banks also offer safe deposit facilities, sell travelers' checks, issue treasurers' checks, and maintain collection departments. In a minority of these states they also issue money orders and register checks, perform trust functions, offer life insurance to mortgagors to cover the balance of the mortgage, and sell life insurance over-the-counter. The latter service is a far-reaching development which merits further comment.

Savings bank life insurance. Savings bank life insurance is regular, legal reserve life insurance provided by and sold by savings banks in Massachusetts, New York and Connecticut under the authority of specific legislation for that purpose. In these states 81 savings banks have each organized what amount to small life insurance companies as separate departments of the banks and under the same laws which apply to life insurance companies but with certain special safeguards. The funds of the life insurance departments are kept separate from the funds of the savings departments, and each pays its own direct expenses and shares pro rata in the general overhead expenses. Through a central state fund in each of the three states, a unification of mortality is provided to achieve a greater spread of risks.

The life insurance is sold "over-the-counter" to reduce the sales costs involved when insurance is sold by individual salesmen. Standard forms of ordinary-life, straight-life, limited payment-life, endowment, and five-year renewable term policies on a participating basis, as well as group life insurance to employers and labor unions, are offered. In Massachusetts, $1,000 is the maximum amount of insurance which any one bank may issue on any one life; in Connecticut, the limit is $3,000 for any person; and in New York state, $5,000 for any person.

The earliest authority for savings banks to sell life insurance was granted in Massachusetts in 1907. Similar legislation was enacted by the New York State Legislature in 1938 and by Connecticut in 1941. Until the late 1920's, the Massachusetts savings banks showed only nominal interest in the plan. In recent years the idea has taken hold, and considerable interest in "over-the-counter" life insurance has developed not alone among savings bankers outside the three states in which it is now offered, but also among leaders in the savings and loan business.

There are now more than 500,000 savings bank life insurance policies in force amounting to $500,000,000.

Although savings bank life insurance was developed to make such protection available at the lowest possible cost and within the reach of the working man, adherents to the plan recognize that a substantial

number of people need competent, professional counsel with respect to their insurance programs, which is the function of life insurance salesmen.

Summary. It will be observed that though each of these two types of savings institutions had its origin at about the same time in history and in the same city, their roots were somewhat different. Savings banking originated largely as a philanthropy and was sponsored by wealthy business and professional men with the paternalistic objective of managing "the savings of mechanics, laborers, servants and others." On the other hand, savings and loan associations were both sponsored and operated by the workers themselves and as cooperative organizations for their mutual benefits. For savings banks, investments in home mortgage loans were but an alternative type of investment of savings funds. Savings and loan associations, on the other hand, have always considered the promotion of home ownership as one of their primary functions along with the promotion of thrift. The associations developed the monthly amortized home loan plan and used it almost exclusively for more than a century before its adoption by other types of financial institutions.

As time passed, other types of financial institutions offered savings account services (including the merging of savings programs with life insurance contracts), and extended credit for the purchase of homes. A review of the principal sources of home financing funds will reveal that they flow primarily from the accumulated small savings of the people in savings and loan associations, in savings accounts in commercial banks, in savings bank deposits, and in savings funds combined with life insurance contracts. However, savings and loan associations have always been the dominant home financing institutions, financing annually the purchase of nearly as many homes as the commercial and savings banks and life insurance companies combined. In recent years they have also shown the exceptional growth indicated in the following tabulation:

	Total Savings Accounts (in millions)	Annual Net Increases in Savings Account Balances (in millions)		
	Dec. 31, 1950 *	1950	1949	1948
Savings and Loan Associations	$14,030	$1,570	$1,496	$1,211
Mutual Savings Banks	20,050	780	885	641
Commercial Banks	35,460	360	130	276
Totals	$69,540	$2,710	$2,511	$2,128

*Preliminary estimates.

Though at the close of 1950 the total savings account balances in savings and loan associations were not as great as for either the commercial or mutual savings banks, the trend in the flow of savings into

these financial institutions was somewhat different. In each of the past three years the net flow of savings into savings and loan associations was greater than the combined flow of savings into the commercial and mutual savings banks.

While each of the principal financial institutions offers both savings and home financing services, the close relationship between the two suggests that a single specialized savings and home financing system has a real place in the American economy alongside such other specialized financial systems as commercial banking and life insurance. This is the role of the savings and loan system which for more than a century has specialized in both of these services. At present it does not, appear probable that the mutual savings banks, with their limited number of institutions located outside of the eastern states, will develop into a nationwide system.

Suggested Readings

Bodfish, Morton, and Theobald, A. D., *Savings and Loan Principles.* New York: Prentice-Hall, Inc., 1938.

Bodfish, Morton (Editor), *History of Building and Loan in the United States.* Chicago: United States Savings and Loan League, 1931.

Lintner, John, *Mutual Savings Banks in the Savings and Mortgage Markets.* Andover, Mass.: The Andover Press, Ltd., 1948.

Savings Banking. New York: American Institute of Banking, 1946.

Sutcliffe, William G., and Bond, Lindley A., *Savings Banks and Savings Department Management.* New York: Harper & Brothers, 1930.

Welfling, Weldon, *Savings Banking in New York State,* Durham, North Carolina: Duke University Press, 1939.

7

Urban Real Estate Financing

by NORMAN STRUNK

Executive Vice President
United States Savings and Loan League
Chicago, Illinois

Nature of Real Estate Credit

LIKE ANY commodity that has economic value, real estate provides a basis for credit. It has served as security for debts since ancient times, and the whole modern industrial system is based in great part upon real estate credit. Real estate is durable: it cannot be carried away, it cannot be hidden. It is relatively easy to make certain that real estate can be taken by the lender in repayment of debt if the borrower defaults.

Real estate credit is usually long-term credit. Loans secured by real estate typically extend at least 10 years and sometimes as long as 40 years. In the case of most debts secured by real estate, the purpose of the debt is to buy land and build on it or to pay for an existing building. The rental income of the property—or in the case of an owner-occupied home, the portion of the borrower's income that is normally set aside for housing costs—is not sufficient to repay the loan over a period shorter than from 10 to 15 years.

Because of the long period of time over which the real estate loan is to be repaid and because the nature of the security, the personal credit of the borrower and his income capacity frequently assume less importance in the transaction than the value of the property pledged as security for the loan. For this reason an analysis of the neighborhood in which the property is located, the appraised value of the property itself, and the income potentialities of the property assume great importance in the study of mortgage loan applications by the mortgage loan officers of banks, savings and loan associations, insurance companies and other mortgage lending institutions.

Today, practically all real estate loans are "amortized" loans; that is to

say, the debt is gradually repaid over the period of years for which the debt extends. Usually the borrower agrees to make monthly, quarterly, or semiannual payments. A portion of each payment is a repayment of the principal of the loan, and the remainder is interest on the outstanding loan balance for the period covered by the payment. In the case of most monthly payment amortized loans, the borrower pays the same dollar amount each month during the life of the loan. The payments on a typical monthly amortized mortgage loan are illustrated in Table 1.

TABLE 1

ILLUSTRATION OF MONTHLY AMORTIZED LOAN PAYMENTS

Amount Borrowed: $10,000; Interest Rate; 4½%; Term of Loan: 16 Years

Time			Monthly Payment		Balance
Years	Months	Total	Interest Portion	Principal Repayment	Due on Loan At End of Month
0	1	$73.20	$37.50	$35.70	$9,964.30
0	2	73.20	37.40	35.80	9,928.50
0	3	73.20	37.20	36.00	9,892.50
3	1	73.20	32.40	40.80	8,586.20
3	2	73.20	32.20	41.00	8,545.20
3	3	73.20	32.00	41.20	8,504.00
7	1	73.20	24.30	48.90	6,434.30
7	2	73.20	24.10	49.10	6,385.20
14	1	73.20	6.20	67.00	1,599.60
15	10	73.20	.80	72.40	134.10
15	11	73.20	.50	72.70	61.40
Final Payment		61.60	.20	61.40	0

The exact monthly payment on amortized loans depends upon a combination of the interest charged on the loan and the number of years within which the loan is to be completely repaid, and, of course, the amount borrowed. The monthly payments required to amortize a $10,000 loan at various interest rates and various maturities are shown in Table 2:

TABLE 2

MONTHLY PAYMENTS REQUIRED TO REPAY AN
AMORTIZED MORTGAGE LOAN OF $10,000

Maturity	Annual Interest Rate				
	4%	4½%	5%	5½%	6%
10 years...........	$101.25	$103.64	$106.07	$108.53	$111.02
12 years...........	87.55	90.00	92.49	95.02	97.58
15 years...........	73.97	76.50	79.08	81.71	84.39
20 years...........	60.60	63.26	66.00	68.79	71.64
25 years...........	52.78	55.58	58.46	61.41	64.43

For several reasons, a mortgage lending operation is an expensive business to conduct when it is compared to the extension of unsecured credit to business firms and corporate bond financing. Most mortgage loans are made to individuals on the security of their individual homes or business properties. These transactions involve dealing with applications from individuals for loans for comparatively small amounts; most loans on homes range from $5,000 to $10,000. Making a mortgage loan involves an appraisal of the value of the property, a process that takes from 30 minutes to several hours of the time of one or more individuals. Lending involves securing careful credit reports and legally complicated title services and loan-closing services. It usually involves monthly collections of payments on the loan. The lender must make certain that real estate taxes on the property securing the loan are kept up-to-date by the borrower and that the borrower carries at least enough fire insurance on the property to cover the amount of the mortgage loan. Frequently the lender will have the borrower pay to him in regular monthly installments an amount sufficient to permit the lender to pay the real estate taxes and insurance premiums on behalf of the borrower. In this way the lender is certain that the taxes are kept current and that the property is fully insured. Occasionally properties must be re-appraised and, of course, at times loans must be foreclosed, in which case the property must be "bought in" at a foreclosure sale and improved, managed and re-sold in satisfaction of the debt. In addition, reserves against losses must be provided.

The cost of operating a typical home mortgage business is estimated at a minimum of 1 per cent of the amount invested. It is larger if the investor is dealing with a portfolio of mortgage loans aggregating less than $500,000 or if he is making loans in a number of cities. In addition, at least $\frac{1}{2}$ of 1 per cent of the amount invested should be set aside annually to loss reserves. The costs of making mortgage loans secured by commercial or industrial properties or large apartment buildings are somewhat smaller as a percentage of the total amount invested, since fewer transactions must be made in order to invest the same amount profitably. In a portfolio of loans on commercial, industrial and multi-family residential properties, however, risks are somewhat greater than in a portfolio of loans on owner-occupied homes.

Real estate loans require the use of savings funds which cost the lender 2 per cent or more. In addition, provision for losses must be set aside totaling at least $\frac{1}{2}$ per cent of the aggregate amount invested. With these basic expenses, it is difficult for mortgage lenders to invest funds profitably at less than 4 per cent. In many cases, due to the costs involved in making a loan and the risks in the transaction, an interest

rate in excess of 5 per cent and sometimes in excess of 5½ per cent is required.

Interest rates on mortgage loans naturally reflect the availability of funds for investment in real estate mortgages. During periods of excess funds in the hands of savings and loan associations, banks, and insurance companies, mortgage loan interest rates tend to decline. The reverse, of course, is true when funds come to these institutions in lower volume relative to the demand for loans and when banks, savings and loan associations, and insurance companies have an ample amount invested in mortgage loans. In the past decade, interest rates on mortgage loans have moved up and down within a range of about 1 per cent.

Within the last 15 years, home mortgage finance has come to be endowed with a substantial amount of broad public interest. This has been occasioned by shortages of housing during World War II, by the difficulty of war veterans in finding suitable living accommodations upon their return to civilian life, and by the existence of large slum areas in most of our cities. As a result, the United States Congress has provided a broad program of federal government participation in the housing and home financing field. This program will be described later in this chapter. Federal legislation in the field of home mortgage finance has generally driven interest rates on mortgage loans downward. The return to the savers and investors in institutions that make home mortgage loans likewise has been reduced.

Countless proposals for federal government participation in housing and home finance have been and will continue to be presented before Congress. Most of the proposals involve subsidies of one type or another for housing for families of low-income or other groups. Many of these proposals involve forms of socialized credit, direct loans by federal agencies, and schemes to subsidize mortgage interest rates.

Legal Aspects

The buying and selling of real estate is more complicated legally than the buying and selling of other types of property. Possession does not indicate ownership of real estate as is the case of most personal property. The ownership of real estate is not transferred by transfer of the possession of the property but by the execution and delivery of a legal document called a "deed." Furthermore, because relatively large sums of money are involved in the ownership and transfer of real estate, many legal precautions not typically found in dealings with other commodities are taken. A real estate mortgage is legally complicated because it involves questions of the title to real estate, which in turn involves abstracts and title searches, or title insurance policies.

Before anyone can safely loan money on the security of real estate, he must make certain that the ownership of the property is actually in the name of the borrower and that the borrower can actually give a "first mortgage" to the property. The lender must make certain that there are no "clouds" on the title which would make it inadvisable to rely upon the real estate as security for the loan, such as existing long-term leases, previous mortgage debts still unpaid, and dower claims against the property. For a person to prove a valid title to real estate under the laws in this country, he must "record"—usually in the County Recorder's Office—a "deed" to the property signed by the previous owner. Determining the ownership of property involves a search of the public records; this search, in theory, requires tracing the ownership of property—the "chain of title"—back to the original government or sovereign authority which first owned and sold the property. Breaks in the chain of title cast doubt upon the validity of anyone's ownership. Deaths, divorces, inheritance disputes and the like all complicate the problem of tracing ownership of property from the original owner to present owners.

There are a number of systems employed in this country to determine the validity of a person's title to real estate, the most common of which is to have a lawyer examine an "abstract," which is nothing more or less than a digest of every document in the public records affecting the title to the real estate, such as deeds, mortgages, and Probate Court actions. In some areas in the country abstracts are not commonly made, and in these areas attorneys make a search of the actual records in the county offices. In most of the larger cities and in many of the smaller cities, there are title companies which insure the owner of real estate against the risk that title to the property is actually not in his name by promising to compensate him against loss if some other person later proves to have title to the property. In most cases, title companies will, in addition to insuring the title to the owner, also issue a "Mortgagee's Insurance Policy" that assures a mortgage lender that he has a first mortgage on the property. Before issuing a title insurance policy, the title company will itself make a search of the public records and trace the chain of title. In a few areas the county government will issue a certificate of title known as "Torrens" certificate which definitely places the ownership of the property in a certain person.

The two basic documents required in a real estate mortgage transaction are a *note* and a *mortgage*. The *note* is not unlike notes used in other credit transactions except that it makes specific reference to the mortgage which is drawn at the same time. The *mortgage* is drawn to secure the note. In some states a *trust deed* is used as a substitute for the ordinary mortgage but its function is the same.

A mortgage is essentially a "conveyance" (a transfer) of the title of land

given by the borrower to the lender as security for the payment of a debt, with the provision that the conveyance is not actually in effect so long as the debt is paid as promised in the note and that such conveyance is completely void upon the complete repayment of the debt. Thus, in effect, when a person or corporation borrows money and gives a mortgage as security, the borrower transfers the title of the property to the lender, with the provision that the borrower can remain in possession of the property and use it just as though he had not made this transfer so long as he makes the required interest and principal payments on the loan. In the early days of the use of the mortgage instrument, a lender could immediately take possession of the property if the borrower failed to make his payments on the exact due date under the transfer of title given in the mortgage. In some instances the lender took actual possession of the property at the time the loan was made and kept the property until the loan had been repaid. Present-day laws greatly modify stringent interpretations of the transfer of title made in the mortgage instrument and now go so far as to provide that borrowers have rights to "redeem" the property within a reasonable time if the borrower defaults and the property is forfeited to the lender as a result.

In most states today if a borrower defaults on his debt, the lender files in the court a suit to foreclose the property under the terms of the mortgage. The court then typically arranges for the property to be sold at public auction. If bidders at this auction pay more for the property than the unpaid balance on the debt secured by the mortgage, the balance above the mortgage debt goes to the owner of the property. Frequently, however, there is no bidder at the foreclosure sale except the mortgage holder who typically will bid only the amount of his mortgage; in this case the lender then acquires title to the property for eventual resale, and the borrower loses his entire interest in the property. Sometimes there are holders of second and third mortgages or other secured creditors. In such cases the second mortgage holder receives money from the foreclosure sale only after the first mortgage holder has been satisfied in full. Sale of property at a foreclosure sale when there is a first and second mortgage against the property is illustrated below:

Original Value of Property	$10,000
First Mortgage	6,000
Second Mortgage	2,000
Property Sold at Foreclosure Sale for	$7,000
First Mortgage Holder Receives	6,000
Second Mortgage Holder Receives	1,000
Original Owner Receives	0

For a typical home mortgage loan the mortgage instrument is usually a single sheet of paper 8½ by 15 inches, printed on both sides. In addi-

THIS INDENTURE WITNESSETH: That the undersigned _____

_____

_____

of _____, County of _____, State
of _____, hereinafter referred to as the Mortgagor, does hereby
Mortgage and Warrant to

FIRST SAVINGS ASSOCIATION OF BLANKVILLE

a corporation organized and existing under the laws of the _____
_____, hereinafter referred to as the Mortgagee, the follow-
ing real estate, situated in the County of _____, in the
State of Illinois, to-wit:

TOGETHER with all buildings, improvements, fixtures or appurtenances
now or hereafter erected thereon, including all apparatus, equipment, fixtures or articles, whether in single units or centrally controlled, used to
supply heat, gas, air conditioning, water, light, power, refrigeration, ventila-
tion or otherwise and any other thing now or hereafter therein or thereon
the furnishing of which by lessors to lessees is customary or appropriate,
including screens, window shades, storm doors and windows, attached floor
coverings, screen doors, venetian blinds, in-a-door beds, awnings, stoves and
water heaters (all of which are declared to be a part of said real estate
whether physically attached thereto or not): and also together with all ease-
ments and the rents, issues and profits of said premises which are hereby
pledged, assigned, transferred and set over unto the Mortgagee.

TO HAVE AND TO HOLD all of said property unto said Mortgagee for-
ever, for the uses herein set forth, free from all rights and benefits under
the Homestead Exemption Laws of the State of Illinois, which said rights
and benefits said Mortgagor does hereby release and waive.

TO SECURE:

1. The payment of a note and the performance of the obligation therein
contained executed and delivered concurrently herewith by the Mortgagor
to the Mortgagee in the sum of _____
($_____) Dollars, which is payable as provided in said note, to be
applied, first, to interest, and the balance to principal until said indebtedness
is paid in full.

2. Any additional advances made by the Mortgagee to the Mortgagor, or
his successors in title, prior to the cancellation of this mortgage, provided
that this mortgage shall not at any time secure more than _____
_____ ($_____) Dollars, plus
any advances necessary for the protection of the security, interest and costs;
and

3. All of the covenants and agreements in said note (which is made a part
of this mortgage contract) and this mortgage.

A. THE MORTGAGOR COVENANTS:

(1 To pay immediately when due and payable all general taxes, special
taxes, special assessments, water charges, sewer service charges and other
taxes and charges against said property, including those heretofore due (the
monthly payment provided by said note in anticipation of such taxes and
charges to be applied thereto), and to furnish the Mortgagee, upon request,
with the original or duplicate receipts therefor.

(2) To keep the improvements now or hereafter situated upon said prem-

ises insured against loss or damage by fire, lightning, windstorm and such other hazards, including liability under laws relating to intoxicating liquors and including hazards not now contemplated, as the Mortgagee may reasonably require to be insured against, under policies providing for payment by the insurance companies of moneys sufficient either to pay the cost of replacing or repairing the same or to pay in full the indebtedness secured hereby, in such companies, through such agents or brokers, and in such form as shall be satisfactory to the Mortgagee. Such insurance policies, including additional and renewal policies shall be delivered to and kept by the Mortgagee, and shall contain a clause satisfactory to the Mortgagee making them payable to the Mortgagee as its interest may appear.

(3) To promptly repair, restore or rebuild any buildings or improvements now or hereafter on the premises which may become damaged or destroyed; to keep said premises in good condition and repair, and free from any mechanic's or other lien or claim of lien not expressly subordinated to the lien hereof; not to suffer or permit any unlawful use of or any nuisance to exist on said property nor to diminish nor impair its value by any act or omission to act; to comply with all requirements of law with respect to the mortgaged premises and the use thereof;

(4) That if the Mortgagor shall procure contracts of insurance upon his life and disability insurance for loss of time by accidental injury or sickness, or either such contract, making the Mortgagee assignee thereunder, the Mortgagee may pay the premiums for such insurance and add said payments to the principal indebtedness secured by this mortgage, to be repaid in the same manner and without changing the amount of the monthly payments, unless such change is by mutual consent.

B. THE MORTGAGOR FURTHER COVENANTS:

(1) That in the case of failure to perform any of the covenants herein, the Mortgagee may do on the Mortgagor's behalf everything so covenanted; that the Mortgagee may also do any act it may deem necessary to protect the lien hereof; that the Mortgagor will repay upon demand any moneys paid or disbursed by the Mortgagee for any of the above purposes and such moneys together with interest thereon at the rate provided in said note shall become so much additional indebtedness hereby secured and may be included in any decree foreclosing this mortgage and be paid out of the rents or proceeds of sale of said premises if not otherwise paid; that it shall not be obligatory upon the Mortgagee to inquire into the validity of any lien, encumbrance, or claim in advancing moneys as above authorized, but nothing herein contained shall be construed as requiring the Mortgagee to advance any moneys for any purpose nor to do any act hereunder; and that Mortgagee shall not incur any personal liability because of anything it may do or omit to do hereunder;

(2) That upon the commencement of any foreclosure proceeding hereunder, the court in which such bill is filed may at any time, and without notice to the Mortgagor, or any party claiming under him, appoint a Receiver with power to manage and rent and to collect the rents, issues and profits of said premises during the pendency of such foreclosure suit and the statutory period of redemption, and such rents, issues and profits, when collected, may be applied before as well as after the Master's sale, towards the payment of the indebtedness, costs, taxes, insurance or other items necessary for the protection and preservation of the property, including the expenses of such receivership, or on any deficiency decree whether there be a decree therefor in personam or not, such Receiver may elect to terminate any lease junior to the lien hereof; and upon foreclosure of said premises, there shall be allowed and included as an additional indebtedness in the decree of sale all

MORTGAGE—(*Continued*)

expenditures and expenses together with interest thereon at the rate specified in said note, which may be paid or incurred by or on behalf of the Mortgagee and deemed by the Mortgagee to be reasonably necessary either to prosecute such suit or to evidence to bidders at any sale held pursuant to such decree the true title to or value of said premises; all of which aforesaid amounts together with interest as herein provided shall be immediately due and payable by the Mortgagor in connection with (a) any proceeding, including probate or bankruptcy proceedings to which either party hereto shall be a party by reason of this mortgage or the note hereby secured; or (b) preparations for the commencement of any suit for the foreclosure hereof after the accrual of the right to foreclose, whether or not actually commenced; or (c) preparations for the defense of or intervention in any suit or proceeding or any threatened or contemplated suit or proceeding which might affect the premises or the security hereof, whether or not actually commenced. In the event of a foreclosure sale of said premises there shall first be paid out of the proceeds thereof all of the aforesaid items.

In this instrument the singular includes the plural and the masculine includes the feminine and the neuter and this instrument shall be binding upon the undersigned and his heirs, personal representatives, successors and assigns.

IN WITNESS WHEREOF, we have hereunto set our hands and seals, this _____ day of _____, A. D. 19___.

_____ (SEAL) _____ (SEAL)

_____ (SEAL) _____ (SEAL)

STATE OF   } SS.:
COUNTY OF

I, _____, a Notary Public in and for said County, in the State aforesaid, DO HEREBY CERTIFY that _____ _____, personally known to me to be the same person(s) whose name(s) (is) (are) subscribed to the foregoing Instrument, appeared before me this day in person and acknowledged that _____ signed, sealed and delivered the said Instrument as _____ free and voluntary act, for the uses and purposes therein set forth, including the release and waiver of the right of homestead.

GIVEN under my hand and Notarial Seal, this _____ day of _____, A. D. 19___.

_____
NOTARY PUBLIC

My Commission expires: _____

tion to the date, the names of the borrower and lender, an exact "legal description" of the property and a brief statement of the amount of the debt and the terms of repayment, the mortgage includes these promises or "covenants" which the borrower makes in addition to his promise to pay the debt as scheduled: (1) to pay all taxes, special assessments and other charges levied by the local government upon the property;

(2) to keep the property in good repair and not to permit any "waste" of the property; (3) to keep the property fully insured against fire, windstorm and other hazards as the lender may require; (4) not to permit the property to be used for any unlawful purpose; (5) to allow, except with the permission of the lender, no substantial changes, alterations or additions to the property. A sample mortgage form is shown on pages 162-64.

Financing Residential Property

Of the approximately $55,000,000,000 non-corporate urban mortgage debts outstanding at the end of 1949, $37,181,000,000 was secured by one- to four-family non-farm homes.[1] The financing of urban residential property thus is the most important single sector of the urban real estate mortgage field.

In 1949, 67 per cent of all mortgage loans of $20,000 or less (chiefly on single-family homes and small apartment buildings) were made directly by institutional lenders—by savings and loan associations, commercial banks, mutual savings banks, or insurance companies. The balance were made by individuals or by mortgage brokerage firms which in turn usually sell the loans to individual investors or institutional investors such as life insurance companies and banks situated in other cities. The following table shows the total dollar amount and the percentage of the total of mortgage loans under $20,000 made by various types of lenders:

TABLE 3

ESTIMATED DOLLAR VOLUME OF NON-FARM MORTGAGE
RECORDINGS OF $20,000 OR LESS

(Thousands of dollars)

Type of Lender	1940	1945	1949
Savings and Loan Associations	$1,283,628	$2,017,066	$ 5,059,612
Insurance Companies	333,724	249,849	1,618,020
Commercial Banks	1,005,893	1,097,039	3,364,889
Mutual Savings Banks	169,907	216,981	1,064,138
Individuals	640,350	1,402,487	2,298,962
All other Mortgagees	597,866	666,397	2,773,572
Total	$4,031,368	$5,649,819	$16,179,193

Source: Home Loan Bank Board.

Home mortgage loans being made today are of three basic types: (1) mortgage loans insured by the Federal Housing Administration; (2) mortgage loans guaranteed or insured by the Veterans Administration ("GI loans" to veterans of World War II) and; (3) loans made without either

---

[1] Source: Home Loan Bank Board.

FHA or VA insurance or guarantee and known in the parlance of the mortgage business as "conventional" mortgage loans. As will be described later, FHA insured and VA guaranteed or insured loans are made by private mortgage lending institutions just as any other loans. The FHA and Veterans Administration insure or guarantee the lender against all or part of the loss that might be incurred by the lender if the borrower defaults.

As indicated in the following table, most residential real estate loans are conventional loans; i.e., they are not insured or guaranteed by either the Federal Housing Administration or the Veterans Administration.

TABLE 4

TYPE OF MORTGAGE LOANS MADE

(Amounts in thousands)

Year	Estimated Non-farm Mortgage Recordings of $20,000 or less	FHA Insured Home Loans	VA Insured or Guaranteed Home Loans	"Conventional Loans"—Non-FHA or VA
1940	$ 4,031,368	$ 762,084	....	$3,269,284
1942	3,942,613	973,271	....	2,969,342
1944	4,605,931	707,437	....	3,898,494
1946	10,589,168	422,009	$2,302,307	7,864,852
1947	11,728,677	894,747	3,286,165	7,547,765
1948	11,882,114	2,117,927	1,880,966	7,883,221
1949	11,828,001	2,213,202	1,423,591	8,191,208

Source: Home Loan Bank Board, Federal Housing Administration and Veterans Administration.

The maximum interest rate on FHA loans is limited by law and regulation of the FHA to 4¼ per cent. An additional ½ of 1 per cent insurance charge is paid monthly by the borrower to the lender who passes it on to the FHA. This makes an effective interest charge to the borrower of 4¾ per cent. The interest rate on all loans guaranteed or insured by the Veterans Administration is limited by law to 4 per cent, without any additional recurring charges or costs to the borrower. The interest rates on conventional home mortgage loans in the period since 1937 have ranged with very few exceptions from 4 per cent to 6 per cent with the exact interest rate depending upon several factors as follows:

A. The risk of the loan which is dependent upon the nature of the property securing the loan; the relation of the amount of the loan to the value of the property; the percentage of the borrower's monthly income required to meet the loan payments; the neighborhood in which the property is located; and the personal credit history of the borrower.

B. The community in which the property is located, with interest rates generally lower in the large metropolitan areas where usually there

is more capital available for home loans than in the small rural communities.

C. The customary practice of the particular institution making the loan. Some lending institutions consistently follow the practice of making no loans below a certain minimum interest rate and rely upon personal service to the borrowers to offset competition of lenders charging a lower interest rate.

As a result of the outbreak of war in Korea on June 25, 1950, in which the military forces of the United States have actively participated, and the subsequent passage of the Defense Production Act in September, 1950, the federal government through the Board of Governors of the Federal Reserve System and the Housing and Home Finance Agency now regulates the down payments (or maximum loan as a percentage of the sales price) and maximum maturity of most home mortgage credit.

Under the authority given in the Defense Production Act, the Board of Governors of the Federal Reserve System on October 12th issued Regulation X which sets maximums on the amount and maturities for all loans which are not guaranteed or insured by any government agency (non-FHA and non-GI loans) for the purchase of houses, the construction of which was started after August 3, 1950. Concurrently the FHA and the VA issued new regulations relative to loans which these agencies insure or guarantee that substantially reduces the maximum loan as a percentage of purchase price of the house which the FHA and VA will insure. The maximum loan maturity requirements for FHA and GI loans apply to existing houses as well as new houses started after August 3, 1950. The Defense Production Act of 1950 prohibited the government from controlling "conventional" financing on any houses on which construction was started prior to August 3, 1950.

A schedule of the maximum amount for various loans according to the purchase price of the home under Regulation X as issued on October 12, 1950, and the regulations of the same date of the Veterans Administration and the FHA is reproduced as Table V. The maximum maturity for all FHA, all GI, and conventional loans on houses started after August 3, 1950, is limited by current regulations to 20 years, except in the case of loans of $7,000 or less which may have a maturity of not more than 25 years. The regulations also provide that all such loans must meet the requirements of the regulations relative to amortization.

It is probable that the maximum loan amounts and the maximum maturities for home loans of all types will be varied by the Board of Governors of the Federal Reserve System, the Veterans Administration, and the Housing and Home Finance Agency from time to time depending on the progress of the nation's military program. Government control of

mortgage credit provides an indirect means for controlling the volume of house production throughout the country and reduces inflationary pressures in the real estate market. When people can no longer buy houses with 5 per cent or 10 per cent cash payments (as many could with FHA and GI loans prior to October 12) but must pay 20 per cent or 30 per cent down for the same house, the number of buyers, of course, is substantially reduced. With fewer buyers there will be fewer new houses built, and more materials and manpower will be made available for armament production.

TABLE 5

SCHEDULE OF MAXIMUM LOAN AMOUNTS FOR CONVENTIONAL, FHA AND "GI" LOANS UNDER REGULATIONS ISSUED PURSUANT TO DEFENSE PRODUCTION ACT OF 1950

(Terms in Effect on January 2, 1950)

Purchase Price of Home	Conventional Loans *	FHA Loans †	"GI" Loans †
$ 5,000	$ 4,500	$ 4,500	$ 4,750
6,000	5,150	5,150	5,750
7,000	5,800	5,800	6,500
8,000	6,450	6,450	7,250
9,000	7,100	7,100	8,000
10,000	7,700	7,700	8,700
11,000	8,300	8,300	9,400
12,000	8,900	8,900	10,100
13,000	9,500	9,500	10,550
14,000	10,100	10,100	11,000
15,000	10,700	10,700	11,450
16,000	10,900	10,900	11,700
17,000	11,100	11,100	11,950
18,000	11,300	11,300	12,200
19,000	11,500	11,500	12,450
20,000	11,700	11,700	12,700
21,000	11,800	11,800	12,850
22,000	11,900	11,900	13,000
23,000	12,000	12,000	13,150
24,000	12,100	12,100	13,300
24,250	12,125	12,125	13,337.50
Over 24,250	50% of price	50% of price	45% of price

* Applies only to houses the construction of which was started after August 3, 1950.
† Applies to all houses except where commitments to guarantee or insure the loan had been made prior to October 12, 1950.

Hereafter in this chapter, references will be made to the maximum loan amounts and maturities as set forth in the basic laws under which loans are insured or guaranteed by the Veterans Administration or the FHA or made by lending institutions without FHA or VA guarantees. These maximums applied before the effective date of regulations issued under the authority of the Defense Production Act which supersede the provisions of the basic law under which loans are made or guaranteed.

For example, most savings and loan associations are authorized by the law and their charter to make loans up to 80 per cent of the value of property. The FHA is authorized to insure in some cases loans up to 95 per cent of the value of property with maturities in some cases up to 30 years. The regulations issued under the Defense Production Act restrict and reduce those terms to the maximum stated in Regulation X and those issued under the Defense Production Act by the VA and the FHA.

Today, practically all home mortgage loans are amortized monthly, with monthly payments being a fixed amount throughout the life of the loan. Prior to the passage of the Defense Production Act by Congress, the loan term on most FHA mortgage loans ran from 20 to 25 years. Some FHA loans were amortized over 30 years. Loans guaranteed or insured by the Veterans Administration have a maximum maturity under the provisions of the Servicemen's Readjustment Act of 30 years, but in actual practice few extend beyond 25 years, and most have a maturity of 18 to 20 years. The loan term on conventional home loans rarely is in excess of 20 years and is more typically 15 to 20 years on new houses and 12 to 15 years on existing and older houses.

In the case of all FHA and VA loans and most conventional home loans, the borrower is required to add an amount to each monthly payment equal to one-twelfth of the annual fire insurance premium and real estate tax bill. Depending, of course, on the type of property and the city in which the house is located, the additional payment for taxes and insurance will range from $12.00 to $25.00 per month on a house valued at $10,000 to $15,000.

Loans on homes are typically made by mortgage lending institutions for a higher percentage of the market value of the property than loans on other types of urban real estate. The amount that any lending institution will loan on a home depends upon many factors, particularly the type and size of the home and its location, the credit standing of the borrower, and whether the loan is insured or guaranteed by the FHA or the VA. The policy of lending institutions relative to the amount they will lend as related to the market value of the property also depends upon the period of the business and real estate cycle and the general outlook for real estate prices. On conventional loans in a period when the outlook for real estate is generally favorable and when there is no great housing shortage which causes houses to sell greatly in excess of their appraised value, savings and loan associations will make loans from 70 per cent to 75 per cent and sometimes 80 per cent of the value of the property securing the loan, except where the provisions of Regulation X now limit the loan to a lower percentage. Because of the regulations under which they operate, banks and insurance companies typically lend a somewhat smaller percentage of the value of property on non-govern-

ment insured loans. In periods of great housing shortages and rapidly rising real estate prices such as were experienced in the immediate post-war years, practically all lending institutions limited their conventional loans to 65 per cent (or less) of the market value of the homes securing the loans. During the first months of 1950, most savings and loan associations, for example, limited their loans to 70 per cent of the market value on loans secured by houses newly constructed and to 60 per cent of market value of existing houses.

Because of the protection offered the lender by the FHA and the VA, loans guaranteed or insured by these government agencies have typically been much higher as a percentage of the value of property. Some types of FHA loans have been made for as much as 95 per cent of the value of the property and typically run from 80 per cent to 85 per cent of the value of the property. During the first two years of the guaranteed loan program of the Veterans Administration and again in the first few months of 1950, approximately half of all the GI loans made were without any down payment or (were made for 100 per cent of the price of the property). More typically loans guaranteed by the Veterans Administration have been for 85 per cent to 90 per cent of the value of property.

Many individuals buying a house or arranging with a contractor to have one built, either know of the various sources of home mortgage loans in the community or find out from their friends where a home loan can be secured. Individuals then arrange their own mortgage financing by direct contact with the savings and loan association, bank or insurance company representative. Frequently, when the individual purchases a house through a real estate broker, the broker will assist the individual purchaser-borrower in contacting a lending institution. The broker may arrange the details of the loan on behalf of the buyer with the institution lending the money, and may collect a commission from the lender for bringing the borrower to him.

In the case of houses being built for an individual owner by a contractor, the owner should arrange his mortgage financing before he signs a contract with the builder. Certainly it is wise in all instances for the person buying or building a house to have some general information as to the availability of mortgage funds before signing a contract to purchase a home or to have one built. In the case of a person's buying a new house from a builder, as is the situation in most of the larger communities today where builders are usually concerned with housing developments, the builder himself will arrange the mortgage financing before the house is started; the ultimate purchaser of the home then usually assumes the mortgage loan arranged by the builder.

Where a new house is to be built or is under construction, the contractor usually is able to arrange for the lending institution to disburse

funds to him periodically as the house is being built. A portion of the total amount of the loan will be paid to the builder, for example, when the foundation is in; another portion will be paid when the house is under roof and the plumbing and heating roughed in; a third portion will be paid to the builder when the plastering or all interior finishing is completed, and the balance of the loan will be paid at the time the house is finished and occupied.

The typical procedure in securing a home mortgage loan is for the borrower to have an interview with an officer of a lending institution and sign a loan application which gives data about the house and credit information about himself. The lender then investigates the borrower's credit and makes an appraisal of the property which is to secure the loan. The loan application is then reviewed by the officers of the lending institution or by a loan committee, and the borrower is notified that his loan has been approved subject to an examination of the "title." Lending institutions in some areas frequently are able to notify borrowers within 24 or 48 hours after submission of an application for a home mortgage loan that the loan will be made as requested or on some other basis, subject only to the title examination, or rejected entirely. If the title examination made by the title company or an attorney is satisfactory, the borrower is called in to "close the loan." This involves having the borrower sign a note and mortgage, at which time the lending institution will disburse the funds to him or to some other person designated by him.

In the case of a loan to finance the construction of a new house, the lender, of course, secures the plans and specifications of the proposed new house together with an estimate of the cost to build it prepared by the builder. The lender investigates the credit and reliability of the builder in addition to that of the borrower. An appraisal is made of the lot and of the proposed house on the basis of the blueprints and specifications. After the usual title search, the loan is usually "closed" before the house is started. The note and mortgage, the building contract, construction loan agreement and other papers required by the laws of the particular state for the full protection of the lending institution are signed at the "loan closing." The borrower's down payment is frequently paid to the lending institution; this institution may disburse the money on behalf of the borrower to the contractor or to the material men, the carpenters, plasterers, and subcontractors. Advances are made to the borrower or builder as construction proceeds. When the house is finished, a final inspection is made of the property and the balance remaining in the mortgage loan account is disbursed.

Financing Commercial Property

Very frequently mortgage loans are needed by individuals or business firms desiring to buy or build retail store buildings, office buildings, hotels, and other commercial properties purchased, not for owner occupancy, but as investments or for business purposes. The financing of commercial property is a specialized phase of the real estate mortgage field, and most such loans are made by banks and insurance companies or by local mortgage firms for insurance companies. Small commercial properties are sometimes financed by savings and loan associations, but in the main these institutions confine their real estate mortgage loans to loans secured by residential properties. There is no arrangement for government guarantee or insurance of loans on commercial buildings, as for residential properties, except that the construction of apartment buildings can be financed with FHA-insured loans.

Life insurance companies and banks are generally limited by law in their loans on commercial property to from 50 per cent to 66⅔ per cent of the value of the property. The making of loans on commercial real estate involves primarily an analysis of the property pledged to secure the payment of the loan. Those who make such loans must be familiar with the rental income of similar properties, the costs of owning and operating the property, the appropriate capitalization rates for the net income of such buildings, and the alternative uses for the structure if the person buying the building does not make a success in his venture or for other reasons is unable to repay the loan. Particularly important in loans of this type is the location of the property. If the property is to be rented under a long-term lease to a tenant of unquestioned credit (such as a large drug company or national grocery chain), a larger loan can be granted than if the property is rented to a new business unit whose credit is not well established.

Practically all commercial loans are amortized, just as are loans on residential property; however, more payments on commercial loans are made quarterly or semiannually than is the case with payments of loans on homes. Loan terms run from five to thirty years depending upon the nature and location of the property, the credit of the borrower, and the intended use of the property.

There are a great variety of terms and arrangements for loans on commercial properties. Frequently the borrower may be required to pay a greater amount monthly or quarterly in the early years than in the later years of the loan. Sometimes the amortization schedule will not require complete liquidation of the loan during the period of the loan but rather requires a lump sum to be due at maturity. This amount can either be

paid off in cash or it can be refinanced. The borrower may be required to make large payments on the principal of the loan during periods when the income from the building is larger than anticipated; thus the loan can be retired more promptly. There may be requirements that prevent the borrower from paying any dividend or from limiting the dividends on the capital stock of the firm buying and operating the property, so long as the mortgage is outstanding on the property or until the loan is paid off to a certain specified amount.

In the past few years insurance companies have been using a new arrangement in the financing of commercial properties. Insurance companies frequently finance such buildings by purchasing them outright and giving a long-term lease to the retail store, garage or other commercial concern which is to occupy the building. As far as the organization which will operate the building is concerned, this has about the same effect as a long-term mortgage loan; rent payments on the lease usually approximate what the firm would pay if it borrowed the money to buy the building itself and made regular payments on a mortgage loan.

In the 1920's and through some of the 1930's, large buildings were commonly financed by a mortgage bond issue, similar in most respects to the mortgage bond issues of utility companies and railroads. Mortgage bond issues on office buildings, hotels and large apartments, however, have generally disappeared since the large institutional investors (such as life insurance companies and mutual savings banks) have had substantial increases in their investment funds; these investors typically make the entire loan to finance the purchase or construction of a large building (just as a savings and loan association will loan money to an individual to buy or build a house) instead of buying a part of a bond issue secured by a mortgage on the building. Likewise, the individual investor in real estate mortgages has tended to disappear except in the smaller communities where there is no active institutional investor such as a savings and loan association, bank or mortgage company.

Financing Industrial Properties

The traditional system of financing the purchase or construction of a factory building or other industrial property has been for the industrial firm to sell common or preferred stock or a bond issue and to purchase or build the needed plant with the proceeds from the sale of these securities. More and more, however, small industrial concerns (and in some cases, large nation-wide manufacturing firms) are financing the building of a factory, warehouse, or office building with an ordinary real estate mortgage loan from a bank or insurance company; or such small con-

cerns may have a life insurance company purchase the building outright and lease it back to the firm under a long-term lease. Most mortgage financing of such industrial properties is done by life insurance companies. This area of the field of real estate finance is particularly complicated and requires men highly trained in the valuation of industrial sites and plants. The interest rates on industrial real estate loans are typically lower than on home loans because of the large amount of money involved and because there is less cost in servicing these loans per dollar invested than in a typical home mortgage loan. Most industrial loans are written to be amortized in 10 years, frequently with 50 per cent and sometimes 60 per cent amortization required in the first five years of the loan. Usually there are arrangements prohibiting payments of dividends in excess of a certain amount and payments of salaries to officers of the business firm over certain amounts so long as the mortgage loan is above a certain per cent of the value of the property. There may be arrangements requiring the firm to keep minimum balances in working capital and other requirements designed to protect the lender against loss such as maintenance of full insurance on the building and payment of real estate taxes.

Most mortgage bond issues of the corporations of the country are designed to finance the purchase of plants or industrial sites. These are highly complicated legal instruments; they differ essentially from an ordinary mortgage loan on an industrial plant in that in a bond issue, individual bonds, usually in $1,000 denominations, are sold to individual investors; all the bonds are secured by a single mortgage instrument, and the bond holders are represented by trustees. In the case of an ordinary mortgage loan, only one person or lender is involved. There is no basic difference in the mortgage instrument or in the terms of the loan.

Sources of Real Estate Credit

As mentioned previously, the most important sources of real estate loans are savings and loan associations, commercial banks, savings banks, insurance companies, and mortgage companies.

Savings and loan associations as savings institutions have been described in the previous chapter. These institutions are limited by law in their investment of funds to government bonds and first mortgage loans on real estate, usually improved urban real estate. At the close of 1949, savings and loan associations held $11,750,482,000 worth of mortgage loans, at least 95 per cent of which were secured by residential property and which amounted to 80.5 per cent of the assets of these institutions. Federal savings and loan associations are prohibited, with certain limited exceptions, from investing more than 15 per cent of their assets in mort-

gage loans on properties located more than 50 miles from the association office or on properties other than one- to four-family residences. They may invest another 15 per cent of their assets in unsecured (without a mortgage) loans made for the improvement or repair of property, such as FHA Title I loans. All other loans of the association must be loans secured by a first mortgage on one- to four-family residences. State-chartered associations in most states have similar legal limitations, or by policy and practice they limit their loans to first mortgage loans on homes in the area in which the association is located.

Federal savings and loan associations and most state-chartered associations are authorized by their charter to make loans up to 80 per cent of the value of residential property securing the debt and can make conventional home mortgage loans for a maximum of 20 years. Since the issuance of Regulation X under the Defense Production Act, loans in many instances are limited to lower percentages of the value of properties than 80 per cent. Associations also have authority to make FHA insured home loans or loans guaranteed or insured by the Veterans Administration up to the maximum percentage of value permitted and for the full term permitted by these agencies for loans which they will insure or guarantee. To the extent savings and loan associations are permitted to invest in mortgage loans secured by property other than one- to four-family residential property, the maximum percentage of value and the maximum maturity is frequently less. For example, federally chartered associations are limited on loans secured by non-residential property to 60 per cent of value and a 15-year maturity.

Savings and loan associations are specialists in home mortgage financing. As local institutions they are usually able to give as quick or quicker service on loan applications than other lenders, many of which must check details with their home office in some other city. Typically, savings and loan associations make mortgage loans for their own investment and not to sell to others.

As shown in the table on page 176, savings and loan associations make most of their loans as "conventional" loans. In recent years, 20 per cent or less of all mortgage loans made by savings and loan associations were insured or guaranteed by the FHA or VA compared with 40 per cent and 50 per cent for other types of lenders.

The preference of savings and loan associations for conventional loans is explained by the fact that these institutions, being local institutions and more familiar with the community and their borrowers, do not feel the need to shift all or part of the risk in the loan to a government agency. Typically they prefer to keep all of the reserves accumulated to safeguard their mortgage portfolio in their own hands, rather than have a part of it maintained for them by a government agency as in the case

TABLE 6

TYPES OF HOME MORTGAGE LOANS MADE BY VARIOUS
LENDING INSTITUTIONS, YEAR 1949

	Total	"Conventional" Non-FHA or VA	FHA Insured	VA Insured or Guaranteed
Savings and Loan Associations...	100%	84.3%	6.5%	9.2%
Commercial Banks	100	58.4	27.5	14.1
Mutual Savings Banks	100	59.6	14.3	26.1
Life Insurance Companies	100	45.4	48.5	6.1
Mortgage Companies	100	42.8	31.8	25.4

Source: U. S. Savings and Loan League.

of FHA loans. Furthermore, savings and loan associations are permitted by law to make loans to a higher percentage of the value of the real estate on a conventional loan basis than are banks or insurance companies. Use of the FHA and the VA to make 70 per cent and 80 per cent loans is not required by associations as in the case of loans by banks and insurance companies which are limited by law to 60 per cent or 66⅔ per cent of the value of the property on conventional loans.

Commercial banks typically have a real estate loan department which handles these loans with specialized personnel familiar with all the legal and technical aspects of real estate finance. Commercial banks will usually make all types of real estate loans—on apartments, retail store properties, office buildings, and small factory buildings, as well as loans on homes. At the close of 1949, commercial banks and trust companies held approximately $10,420,000,000 of real estate loans of which $8,520,000,000 was secured by residential properties.[2] Banks typically make loans only on properties in the communities in which the bank is located and in the surrounding communities, although they may buy FHA loans from banks and mortgage companies secured by properties in other localities. Except for loans insured or guaranteed by the FHA or the VA, banks are generally limited by law to 60 per cent of the value of the property securing the loan and to a maturity of ten years.

The mutual savings banks, located primarily in eastern cities, at the close of 1949 had $6,479,000,000 or 30.1 per cent of their assets invested in real estate loans, primarily mortgage loans on homes and residential properties.[3] These institutions make but 6 per cent of the total of all mortgages under $20,000, but in New York State, mutual savings banks account for about 30 per cent and in Massachusetts about 40 per cent.

[2] Estimates based upon holdings of banks insured by the FDIC. Data for Insured Banks from *Report of Assets and Liabilities of Insured Banks as of December 31, 1949,* published by the Federal Deposit Insurance Corporation, Washington, D.C.
[3] Source: The National Association of Mutual Savings Banks.

Lending practices of mutual savings banks are very similar to those of savings and loan associations in that most loans made by these institutions are secured by properties located in the home city of the bank, are amortized, and are primarily for the purchase or construction of single-family homes. Mutual savings banks typically are limited by the law under which they operate to loans of 70 per cent or 75 per cent of the value of the property securing a loan and to loans of 20-year maturities. These institutions, of course, are subject to the maximum loans authorized by Regulation X. They can also make FHA and VA loans to the maximums permitted by these agencies.

Recently, savings banks in the states of New York and Massachusetts have been authorized to make FHA loans secured by properties located in other states. Except for FHA loans, savings banks in most cases are limited to loans secured by properties located in the state which the bank has its office. To a very limited extent these banks are financing large rental projects and slum clearance projects in the eastern cities. Because these banks dominate the savings business in the eastern states, and because the long-term savings placed with them may appropriately be placed in mortgage loans, these institutions will doubtless remain a major source of mortgage money in the eastern states.

Life insurance companies at the end of June 1949 had approximately $11,757,000,000 invested in urban real estate mortgage loans of which $7,454,000,000 was invested in mortgage loans secured by homes and apartments. Non-farm mortgage loan investments amounted to 19.4 per cent of their total assets.[4] Life insurance companies find mortgage loans a highly desirable type of investment, since such loans typically have a higher yield than bond investments of equivalent safety; and further, the life insurance reserve funds may be invested safely in long-term obligations. As evidence of the tremendous capacity of life insurance companies to make home mortgage loans, the combined policy reserves of all life insurance companies totaled $51,456,000,000, compared to the $19,287,000,000 of savings accounts in mutual savings banks and $37,-000,000,000 in the time deposits of commercial banks.

Insurance companies typically make real estate loans at a lower interest rate than do other types of lenders, but at the same time insurance companies limit the properties on which they will make loans to the newer and better located buildings; and they show a definite preference for larger loans. The rate at which life insurance companies can afford to make mortgage loans depends on the interest rates of other forms of investment, mainly corporate bonds.

Life insurance companies make real estate loans on the entire range of urban land improvements from large office buildings and factories

[4] *Life Insurance Fact Book. 1950,* published by the Institute of Life Insurance.

to single-family homes. Because they are typically limited by law to loans of not more than 66⅔ per cent of the value of the property except for FHA and VA loans, and because most of their loans are by necessity secured by properties in cities other than where their home offices are located, in the residential mortgage field these institutions have shown a definite preference for FHA-insured or VA loans.

Some life insurance companies make real estate loans direct, with their own salaried staffs located in branch offices in the major cities around the country; these are mainly loans secured by commercial and industrial properties. But most life insurance companies' lending is arranged through so-called "mortgage correspondents," which are either local mortgage firms or the mortgage departments of the larger real estate brokerage offices which make loans for sale to others. Life insurance companies use mortgage correspondents, because it is impossible to originate mortgage loans and "service" loans scattered throughout the country direct from their home offices.

Usually, a reputable real estate or mortgage firm will be appointed as the loan correspondent for a particular city by a life insurance company which makes loans in the area served by that mortgage company. One mortgage firm may represent several life insurance companies and other investors. It will solicit mortgage loans and will make the loans with the firm's own funds. After a loan has been made and the funds disbursed to the borrower, the mortgage firm will "sell" the loan to one of the lenders it represents. In the case of large loans the correspondent will usually secure a commitment from one of its life insurance company outlets to purchase the loan before the loan is actually made. After the funds are disbursed and the loan sold to the insurance company, the correspondent is required to collect the interest and principal payments due on the loan, to see that the borrower keeps the property in good repair, and to see that the taxes and insurance payments are kept up-to-date. If the borrower becomes delinquent on his loan payments, the correspondent is expected to make appropriate collection efforts; if the loan has to be foreclosed, that too is handled by the loan correspondent.

The correspondent is typically compensated for his services by selling the loan to the life insurance company at a premium. For example, a $15,000 loan might be sold to an insurance company for $15,300. This premium over the face amount of the loan would cover part of the cost to the correspondent for making the loan (at least that part of the origination cost not paid by the borrower) plus some profit to the correspondent. In addition, the life insurance company would pay its correspondent a certain amount for servicing the loan, collecting monthly payments, and seeing that the taxes and insurance payments are made.

Typically, the payment to the correspondent for servicing the loan is ½ of 1 per cent of the loan balance annually.

Insurance companies usually will not make construction loans as will local institutions such as banks and savings and loan associations. If a builder is financing a project by a mortgage loan from an insurance company, the mortgage correspondent must usually make the construction loan and make the payouts to the builder during the course of construction with its own funds. After a house has been finished and sold to an occupant, the loan would then be ready for delivery to the insurance company. This requires that the mortgage correspondent have substantial funds so that he can "warehouse" the loans until they can be sold. Mortgage correspondents frequently augment their own capital funds for this type of lending operation by borrowing from commercial banks.

Most new houses financed by insurance companies are under FHA-insured loans. By use of the FHA, the mortgage broker can secure a commitment from the FHA to insure the loan upon the completion of the house in accordance with previously approved plans and specifications. Insurance companies usually have no hesitation in buying any loan that is FHA-insured, and the mortgage broker is thus protected in being able to sell his loan upon the completion of the house.

In recent years, a number of the large eastern life insurance companies have financed the building of large apartment developments such as Parkchester and Stuyvesant Town in New York and Parkfairfax in Virginia. In these cases the insurance companies own the apartment building and land outright under special laws which permit direct investment in residential properties.

Federal Agencies

At the close of 1949, the federal government had approximately an $18,000,000,000 stake in home mortgage finance. This has arisen through the operations of the Federal Home Loan Bank System, the Federal Savings and Loan Insurance Corporation, the Federal Housing Administration, the Loan Guarantee Division of the Veterans Administration, the Home Owners Loan Corporation and the Federal National Mortgage Association.

The operations of the Federal Home Loan Bank System and the Federal Savings and Loan Insurance Corporation have been described in a previous chapter. The Home Owners Loan Corporation was established by act of Congress in 1933. Its primary purpose was to make loans on a long-term, amortized basis to home owners in danger of losing their properties through foreclosure and to prevent continued liquidation of

PROVISIONS FOR FHA INSURANCE

Authorized by the National Housing Act as Amended and by Administrative Rules and Regulations as of May 2, 1950

(Rents, values, mortgage limits, etc., subject to underwriting considerations)

FEDERAL HOUSING ADMINISTRATION

(1) Title and Section of the Act	(2) Purpose of Authorization	(3) Type of Constr. (Urban or Rural Non-farm Unless Specified Otherwise)	(4) Min. No. Fam. Units per Ins. Contract	(5) † Amount Insurable	(6) † Loan-Value Ratio	(7) Term of Loan	(8) Interest Rate
				MAXIMUM LIMITS			
Class 1(a)	Finance repair, alteration or improvement of existing structure	All Types (farm and non-farm)	None	$2,500 Max. net proceeds each loan	None (except as required by lender)	3 yrs., 32 days	$5.00 discount per $100 face amt. per year
Class 1(b)	Finance alteration, repair, improvement, or conversion of existing structures	2-family or more intended use (farm and non-farm)	2	$10,000 Max. net proceeds each loan	As for Class 1(a)	7 yrs., 32 days	$5.00 discount per $100 face amt. per yr. if $2500 or less $4.00 discount per $100 face amt. per yr. if in excess of $2500
Class 2(a)	Finance new construction for other than residential or agricultural use	Non-residential and non-farm	None	$3,000 Max. net proceeds each loan	As for Class 1(a)	3 yrs., 32 days	$5.00 discount per $100 face amount per year
Class 2(b)	Finance new non-residential farm constr.	Non-residential farm	None	$3,000 Max. net proceeds each loan	As for Class 1(a)	7 yrs., 32 days; or if secured by first lien 15 yrs., 32 days	$5.00 discount per $100 face amt. per $3.50 discount per $100 face amt. per yr. if maturity is over 7 yrs., 32 days

TITLE I

	Finance new construction, owner-occupancy, or sale	1-family	1	$4750. Owner occupant $4250. Operative Builder	95%—Owner Occupant 85%—Operative Builder	30 years from date of insurance	4½%
Sec. 8ff **	Finance proposed or existing dwellings	1-4 family	1	$16,000—1 or 2 family $20,500—3 family $25,000—4 family	80%	25 years, if originally approved prior to start of construction. Otherwise, 20 years	4½%
Sec. 203b2(A)	Finance dwellings for owner-occupant borrowers only	1-family	1	$9,450	95% of 1st $7000 plus. 70% of next $4000	25 years	4½%
Sec. 203b2(C) **	Finance dwellings for owner-occupants and operative builders	1-family	1	Owner—occupant borrower $6650—1 or 2 bdrm. $7600—3 bedroom $8550—4 bedroom Operative—builder borrower $5950—1 or 2 bdrm. $6800—3 bedroom $7650—4 bedroom	95% for Owner—Occupant borrower 85% for Operative Builder borrower	30 years	4½%
Sec. 203b2(D) †† **	Finance farm property; 15% of loan to be used for constr. of new improvements, alteration or repair	1-4 family	1 proposed or existing	As for Sec. 203b 2(A). (C), or (D)	As for 203b2(A), (C), or (D)	As for 203b2(A), (C), or (D)	4½%
Sec. 203d **	Finance Proposed or Rehabilitation Rental Housing (a) Private Corp. (b) Public Bodies	Detached, semi-detached, row or multi-family	12	$5,000,000 Private Corp. $50,000,000 Public Bodies $8100 per unit of 4½ or more rooms av. or $7200 per unit of less than 4½ rooms av.	90% of first $7000 plus 60% of next $3000	Satisfactory to Commissioner; 2½% min. level Prin. payment	4%
Sec. 207	Finance proposed const. of non-profit cooperatives. Occupancy restricted to members	Detached, semi-detached, row, or multi-family	12	$5,000,000 $8,100 per family unit $1,800 per room Higher limits to veterans	90% of replacement cost Higher limits to veterans	40 years	4%
Sec. 213 Project Management Type							

TITLE II

181

PROVISIONS FOR FHA INSURANCE (*Continued*)

Authorized by the National Housing Act as Amended and by Administrative Rules and Regulations as of May 2, 1950

(*Rents, values, mortgage limits, etc., subject to underwriting considerations*)

FEDERAL HOUSING ADMINISTRATION (*Continued*)

TITLE II (*Continued*)

(1) Title and Section of the Act	(2) Purpose of Authorization	(3) Type of Constr. (Urban or Rural Non-farm Unless Specified Otherwise)	(4) Min. No. Fam. Units per Ins. Contract	(5) MAXIMUM LIMITS † Amount Insurable	(6) MAXIMUM LIMITS † Loan-Value Ratio	(7) MAXIMUM LIMITS Term of Loan	(8) Interest Rate
Sec. 213 Project Sales Type	Finance proposed const. of non-profit cooperatives for sale to members	Single family detached, semi-detached or row	12	Not to exceed greater of (a) a sum computed on separate mtge. for each dwelling equal to total of max. mtge. amounts meeting requirements of Para. (A), (C), or (D) of Sec. 203 or (b) amount computed as under Management Type project	90% of Replacement Cost Higher limits to veterans	40 years	4%
Sec. 213 Individual Sales Type	Finance individual mortgage on property released from Project Sales Type Mortgage	1-family	1	Unpaid balance of project mtge. allocable to the individual prop.	Unpaid balance of project mtge. allocable to the individual prop.	Not to exceed unexpired term of project mtge. at time of release	4%
Sec. 609 Type A	Finance manufacture of housing for which binding contracts to purchase are assigned as security; security substitution permitted	All types residential	None established	According to needs of individual manufacturers	90% of necessary current cost of manufacture (exclusive of profit)	1 yr. from date of note (may be refinanced and extended 1 yr.)	4%
Sec. 609 Type B	Short-term financing to purchasers for part payment of deliveries; Avail. with Type A only	All types residential	None established	80% of purchase price	80% of purchase price	180 days from date of delivery	4%

Title	Section	Purpose	Type	No.	Maximum Mortgage	Loan Ratio	Term	Amortization	Interest
TITLE VI	Sec. 610 (Under Sec. 603)	Finance sale by U. S. Gov't, of housing acquired or constructed under Public Laws 9, 73, 353, 781, and 849, as amended, so-called "Greenbelt Towns", TVA villages, and first resales.	1 to 7 family	1	None	90%	25 years		4½%
	Sec. 610 (Under Sec. 608)	As for 610 under 603 (Release clause provisions pursuant to Commissioner consent)	8 Units or more	8	$5,000,000	90%	25 years		4%
	Sec. 611 Project Mortgage	Finance operative builders construction for sale; blanket mortgage covers cost of fabrication or erection (release clause provisions)	1-family	25	$5950—1 or 2 bedroom $6800—3 bedroom $7650—4 bedroom	85%	25 years	2% initial prin. curtail on level annuity	4%
	Sec. 611 Individual Mortgage	Finance the sale on individual dwelling upon release from the project mortgage	1-family	1	To owner—occupant Same as Sec. 203b2-(D). To builder—unpaid balance of project mortgage allocable to individual property	Owner—occupant Same as Sec. 203b2-(D). Builder—unpaid balance of project mortgage allocable to individual property	Owner—occupant Same as Sec. 203b2-(D). Or if to builder mortgagor unexpired term of blanket mtge. or 30 yrs. whichever is less		Same as Sec. 203b2-(D) for owner—occupant If builder—mortgagor 4%
TITLE VII		Insure yield on total equity investment in rental housing for families of moderate income—rents limited to $100 average and $120 max. per unit	Rental units plus such other stores, offices, community buildings, etc. satisfactory to the Commissioner as a necessary part of the project	25	(a) Minimum annual amortization charge of 2% on estab. investment. (b) An insured annual return of 2½% on the outstanding investment.	No mortgage liens permitted on developments covered by contract	Until the outstanding investment amounts to not more than 10% of the established investment		No interest Min. annual return 3½%(Insured annual return 2½) of outstanding invest. plus 2% min. amortization of estab. investment.
TITLE VIII	**	Finance production of rental housing for military personnel upon certification of need by Secretary of Defense	Detached, semi-detached, row or multi-family	8	$5,000,000; $8,100 per unit ($9,000 when single-family detached)	90% of replacement cost	Satisfactory to the Commissioner 2½% min. level prin. payment or 1½% initial curtail on level annuity		4%

* Note: "None" does not exclude restrictions of the Housing Expeditor's Office.
** FNMA will purchase Sec. 8 loans, all Sec. 203 loans and Title VIII loans (military housing) on an over-the-counter basis *only* provided the insurance became fully effective on or after March 1, 1950 and *also provided* the loan has been in the association's portfolio at least two months after effective date of the insurance.

† Colums 5 and 6 are higher for Alaska.
†† Commissioner is authorized to increase maximum mortgage amounts in any geographical area where he finds cost levels so require.

real estate credits by banks, savings and loan associations, and insurance companies. The HOLC refinanced home loans which were in default to savings and loan associations, banks, and other institutions. At the peak of its operation, it had loans outstanding of $3,093,000,000. At the present time (1951) the corporation is rapidly being liquidated and loans on its books at the end of 1950 amounted to only $230,661,000.

The government agency which has received the most publicity in home mortgage operations is the Federal Housing Administration, created by act of Congress in 1934. The FHA is an insuring agency. It does not loan money. It insures loans made by private lending institutions on single-family homes and rental properties. It insures the lender against loss on the loans he makes which are insured by the FHA.

The theory behind the creation of the FHA was that by providing government insurance against loss on home mortgage loans, more private funds would be made available for the financing of homes; it would thus be possible to reduce the interest rates and other costs of home financing and make possible higher percentage loans amortized over a greater number of years, all of which would enable more people to buy or build homes. In its 16 years the program of the Federal Housing Administration has undergone many revisions and has been greatly expanded from that originally envisioned by Congressional leaders. During the war years, 1941–45, the FHA insurance was used to encourage the construction of homes in areas which suffered a critical housing shortage because of the concentration of war industries. Its wartime program terminated on July 1, 1946. In the immediate postwar period, the FHA insurance was used to encourage the financing of new homes built for purchase by veterans of World War II. This last phase of the program reached its termination date on April 1, 1950.

At the present time the Federal Housing Administration, through various sections of the Act, insures loans under 21 different programs. A summary of the FHA programs and the type of loans it insured including the maximum mortgage amounts and the maximum maturities on May 2, 1950, is given in the chart on pages 180-183. These were the terms permitted by the National Housing Act of 1934 as amended. Since then, as a result of the passage of the Defense Production Act of 1950, these terms have been changed substantially under regulations of the FHA effective October 12, 1950.

The primary program of Title I of the National Housing Act (FHA Title I loans) is that which falls under Section 3, providing for the insurance of loans for the repair and modernization of homes. Under this section, lending institutions are insured against loss on loans made for the repair, improvement or modernization of property (i.e., repairing a roof, installing a modern heating and plumbing system, building a

garage, and painting and redecorating a house). These loans are limited to $2,500 and are secured by a mortgage. The maximum term is 37 months. They are discount loans with a maximum discount of $5.00 per $100.00 of loan per year, which means a maximum effective interest rate of 9.72 per cent. From the beginning of this program in 1934 to March 1950, 10,252,000 of these repair and improvement loans had been made, totaling $3,970,461,000. These have been made chiefly by commercial banks and finance companies.

Most FHA Title I property improvement loans originate with contractors and building supply firms, such as lumber yards, roofing companies and the like. In the typical case, a home owner will secure from a firm doing repair or improvement work an estimate of the amount required to make the desired improvement. This firm—as a lumber yard or roofing company—will make the estimate and assist the owner of the house desiring to make the improvement in securing an FHA Title I loan to finance the job. The borrower then is asked to sign a Title I application and a note made payable to the firm making the improvements. That firm then will check, usually by telephone, with a local Title I lender, usually a bank or savings and loan association, to see if that lender will make the desired loan. If the lender agrees to do so, the work will then be done as agreed upon. After it has been completed, the borrower and contractor sign statements indicating that the work has been completed. The firm which did the work then takes the loan application and the signed completion certificate to the lender who then buys the loan as it had previously agreed to do. The firm thereby receives payment for the work done. The lender then owns the note, and the borrower makes his payments on the note to the lending institution. Usually in the case of these loans, the lending institution does not see the property on which the improvements are being made, nor does it see the borrower. The whole transaction is handled by mail or by telephone, the lending institution relying upon the good faith and reputation of the firm doing the work and upon the insurance of the FHA. Lenders have been almost completely protected against loss on such loans by the FHA.

The operation of the FHA in making loans for the purchase or construction of new homes is currently done primarily under Title II, Section 203 of the National Housing Act. The FHA insurance is handled through a mutual mortgage insurance fund, which operates very much like the reserve fund of any insurance company. This insurance fund was created with capital initially subscribed by the RFC and is built up by premiums paid to the FHA by borrowers on insured mortgages. The premiums currently are $\frac{1}{2}$ of 1 per cent of the outstanding loan balance. Losses by a lending institution on an FHA-insured defaulted loan are met out of the fund, with the lender in effect trading the defaulted

loan (or the property which secured the loan after the loan had been foreclosed by the lender) for a debenture of the FHA, which is fully guaranteed as to principal and interest by the United States government. The debentures are issued for an amount covering the unpaid principal amount of the loan plus the payments made by the lender for taxes, special assessments, and insurance premiums plus foreclosure costs to a maximum of $75. Debentures issued on loans insured by the FHA after May 15, 1950, bear interest at the rate of $2\frac{1}{2}$ per cent.

To be eligible for insurance under Section 203 of the Act, a loan must meet certain detailed requirements. It must be secured by a first mortgage on a property designed principally for residential use for not more than four-family occupancy, bear interest at a rate not greater than $4\frac{1}{4}$ per cent (reduced from $4\frac{1}{2}$ per cent on April 24, 1950, and originally 5 per cent), and be located in sections of a city meeting certain standards of desirable residential neighborhoods. The maximum mortgage that may be insured on houses of various costs and the maximum maturity are given in the foregoing chart. It should be noted that in certain cases it is possible for a loan up to 95 per cent of the value of the property and of 30-year term to be eligible for insurance by the FHA. All FHA loans must be amortized, direct reduction loans with the borrower making monthly payments of principal and interest on the loan plus $\frac{1}{12}$ of the annual insurance premium which is in turn passed on to the FHA mutual mortgage insurance fund. The FHA also requires that all borrowers on FHA-insured loans pay monthly installments to the lender to cover the tax and insurance charges.

The mechanics of handling an FHA-insured mortgage loan application work somewhat as follows: An individual borrower applies for a mortgage loan at a bank, savings and loan association or other FHA-approved lending institution. If it appears to the loan officer that the proposed loan will meet the requirements of the FHA and the lender wishes to have the loan insured by the FHA, or the borrower requests an FHA loan, the necessary loan application is prepared and sent by the officer of the lending institution to the local FHA office for approval. The FHA staff examines the credit of the borrower and has the house that is to secure the loan appraised by an FHA staff appraiser. If the loan is approved by the FHA, the lending institution is notified by the FHA that it will insure a loan made on the property in question under the terms and conditions outlined in the application or as required by the FHA in its notification to the lender. The lending institution then proceeds to draw up the necessary note, mortgage papers and other necessary documents, and the loan is handled as any other loan. After the loan has been closed and necessary papers have been forwarded to the FHA office, the lender receives an FHA insurance certificate covering that loan.

If an insured loan is in default, the lender must notify the FHA and start foreclosure proceedings according to FHA regulations or otherwise acquire title and possession to the property. Having foreclosed on a defaulted FHA-insured loan and taken title to the property, the lender transfers title and possession of the property to the FHA and obtains in exchange debentures of the mutual mortgage insurance fund.

In the case of newly constructed houses and with the exception of the FHA program under Section 613, the FHA will not insure the construction loan (i.e., will not insure the lender against loss on advances made to builders during the course of construction), but will insure the loan only upon completion of the house. The FHA, however, will give a commitment to insure the loan once the house is completed, provided the house is completed in accordance with plans and specifications previously approved by the FHA.

The aggregate insuring operations of the FHA under its various sections and titles are summarized in Table 7.

TABLE 7

SUMMARY OF INSURING OPERATIONS OF FEDERAL HOUSING
ADMINISTRATION

From Beginning of Program through 1949

Type of Program	Number of Dwelling Units	Amount of Loans Insured
Title I, Classes		
1, 2 and 3	9,985,158	$ 3,945,474,208
Title II		
Home Mortgages	1,662,687	8,482,629,185
Rental Projects	43,388	168,285,004
Title VI		
Home Mortgages	624,478	3,638,231,842
Rental Projects	295,538	2,143,747,041
Manufactured Housing	1,150	3,338,280
Site-fabricated Homes	275	1,650,000
Title VII		
Yield Insurance	......	......
Title VIII		
Military Housing	1,540	12,070,800
TOTAL	12,614,214	$18,395,426,360

Veterans Administration

The foremost measure enacted to provide home mortgage loans to veterans of World War II was Title III of the Servicemen's Readjustment Act of 1944, commonly known as the "GI Bill of Rights." This Act, and subsequent amendments, provided that the Veterans Admin-

istration would guarantee or insure loans to veterans of World War II made by private lending institutions. To March 31, 1950, a total of 1,736,706 "GI" loans had been made to veterans of World War II under the act totaling $9,700,000,000. This compares with 495,507 loans in the amount of $2,082,000,000 insured by the FHA in the first five and one-half years of its program. This GI loan program is scheduled to continue until July 1957, unless further extended by Congress. The present law offers a guarantee for real estate loans to qualified veterans to $7,500 or 60 per cent of the total loan, whichever is less. Up until April 20, 1950, the guarantee was the lesser of $4,000 or 50 per cent and the higher guarantee limits apply only to veterans who had not previously availed themselves of the benefits of this program. This guarantee is unusual in that the Veterans Administration does not guarantee the lender against loss on the entire loan; but the VA assumes the "first risk" on the loan. The guarantee is designed to take the place, up to the amount of the guarantee, of the usual cash down payment ordinarily associated with mortgage lending; the guarantee acts as the borrower's equity in the property would act in an ordinary loan. The nature of the VA guarantee can be most easily understood by reference to what might happen in a typical foreclosure as outlined below.

	Ordinary Loan	GI Loan
Purchase price of home	$12,000	$12,000
Amount lending institution would be willing to lend *at its own* risk	$7,000	$7,000
Amount actually loaned	$7,000	$11,500
Amount of down payment	$5,000 in cash	$500 in cash and $4,500 in VA guaranty
Assuming loan defaulted immediately after being made and property was sold for	$9,000	$9,000
Loss to lending institution	None, since only $7,000 was loaned	$2,500, but lender is reimbursed in full for loss since VA guaranty exceeded this amount
Loss on down payment or guaranty	$3,000 loss to borrower	$500 loss to borrower and $2,000 loss to VA unless it can later collect this amount from veteran
Actual loss to lender	None	None

As seen from this illustration, lenders can make larger loans to veterans than they can to non-veterans on the same house. It is important to understand that the Veterans Administration loans no money. It merely endorses the veteran borrower's credit up to the amount of the

guarantee, and the program is designed generally to permit a lending institution to make a loan to a veteran equal to the amount it would loan on the same house to a non-veteran plus an amount equal to the guarantee. For a loan to be eligible for guarantee or insurance by the Veterans Administration, it must be made by a veteran of World War II for the construction or purchase of a home which the veteran himself will occupy. The interest rate on the loan may not exceed 4 per cent and the sales price of the home to the veteran may not exceed its "reasonable value" as determined by an appraisal of the property. There is no limit on the amount that can be borrowed by a veteran by this plan except that the amount of the guarantee is limited and he can use his full guarantee only once.

A nominal amount of GI loans is made under an insurance plan as distinguished from the guarantee plan just described. Under this insurance plan, lending institutions are reimbursed for all losses on loans to qualified veterans up to 15 per cent of the aggregate amount of such veterans' loans made under the "insured plan."

In many respects the veterans' loan program is almost completely a "no red tape" program. The law provides that "any loan . . . made in compliance with the provisions expressed in this title is automatically guaranteed by the government." Under the usual procedure any qualified lending institution can follow the simple requirements for GI loans set forth in the Act and the regulations. The only part that the Veterans Administration office plays in the loans made under the automatic guarantee procedure is to have the property appraised. As a result, if the loan officer of a lending institution is certain that the veteran borrower is eligible and that the purchase price of the house does not exceed the value as determined by the VA appraiser, he can make the loan just as he would to a non-veteran. After the loan has been made and the funds disbursed, the lending institution then notifies the Veterans Administration that the loan has been made. The Veterans Administration is then bound by its regulations to issue a certificate of guarantee. There is also a procedure whereby the lending institution can ask for prior approval on the loan from the Veterans Administration if there is some doubt as to the eligibility of the veteran or the loan. There are no restrictions as to the nature of the mortgage instrument, no prescribed loan forms except an appraisal form and a form used by the lender to notify the VA of the loan, no restrictions on the type or location of the property, nor any of the other restrictions and time-taking procedures frequently associated with government programs. The GI loan program was designed to make home ownership possible on the part of veterans who ordinarily would be good borrowers but who, because of several years of military service, did not have the same opportunity to save for

a cash down payment on a home as did those who enjoyed wartime civilian earnings. It is important to understand, of course, that not all veterans are able to get a GI loan even when they meet the technical requirements of the law, since many do not have sufficient income to undertake the costs of home ownership; still other veterans are not able to demonstrate a good credit standing.

Veterans' or "GI" loans, being limited to a maximum of 4 per cent interest, have been made in volume varying according to the availability of funds in the hands of lending institutions for mortgage loans and the ability of lending institutions to loan money at 4 per cent interest. In the early years of the program, when lending institutions were faced with the problem of idle money, a tremendous volume of GI loans was made. Beginning about November 1947, when interest rates generally began to rise, lending institutions did not have sufficient funds to make the higher interest loans available to them and these institutions reduced their volume of 4 per cent loans to veterans and others. The GI loan program has also varied in volume since the government has provided (through the Federal National Mortgage Association) a so-called secondary market, which permitted lenders to sell certain of their GI and FHA loans to this government agency.

During the spring of 1950, GI loans were being made in increasing volume as interest rates again tended to go to lower levels and as the maximum rate on FHA loans was cut to 4 and one-quarter per cent. Many lenders felt that after the reduction in the FHA rate to $4\frac{1}{4}$ per cent, the $\frac{1}{4}$ of 1 per cent differential between the rate on GI loans and FHA loans was not sufficient to compensate the lender for the added time required to make FHA loans; most lenders feel that they are better protected under the guarantee of the Veterans Administration than under the insurance of the FHA.

Federal National Mortgage Association

The Federal National Mortgage Association was chartered in 1938 by the Federal Housing Administrator (head of the FHA) pursuant to the authority given him in the National Housing Act. The Federal National Mortgage Association has been wholly owned by and a part of the Reconstruction Finance Corporation; but by the terms of Reorganization Plan #22, the FNMA was transferred in September 1950, to the Housing and Home Finance Agency from the RFC. All of the funds for the operation of the FNMA will continue to come from the United States Treasury. The purpose of this government operation is to provide a "secondary market" for home mortgages insured or guaranteed by government agencies (FHA- or VA-insured or guaranteed mortgages) through

the purchasing of such mortgages from private lenders or mortgage companies. It is essentially a device for the channeling of government funds into the home mortgage market. At the end of March 1950, the FNMA's total holdings of mortgages were approximately $1 billion, and it had at that time outstanding commitments to purchase an additional $1,400,-000. The FNMA (popularly known in mortgage circles as the "Fanny May") buys loans and either sells them or holds the loans for an indefinite period, very much as an insurance company buys and holds mortgage loans purchased from others around the country. The exact terms and types of mortgages which the FNMA can purchase has varied from time to time, as its funds have been increased by Congress and the restrictions on the types of loans it may buy have been altered by Congressional acts. At the present time, the FNMA will buy only FHA or VA loans, the original principal amount of which was $10,000 or less, insured or guaranteed under Section 501 or 502 of the Servicemen's Readjustment Act (certain GI loans) or Sections 8, 203, 603, or 803 of the National Housing Act (certain FHA loans). It will buy only loans which have been insured or guaranteed after March 1, 1950, and which have been in existence for at least two months.

Since the outbreak of the military action in Korea, the program of the Federal National Mortgage Association has been substantially reduced. The FNMA now is buying generally only those loans it had made commitments to buy prior to the passage of the Defense Production Act of 1950. On the other hand, the FNMA is actively engaged in selling as many of the loans it holds in its portfolio as possible—the sales being made to private buyers such as banks, insurance companies and savings and loan associations. The FNMA is generally a device for increasing the availability of easy credit into the mortgage market. After July 1950, the intention of the government has been to reduce the amount of credit available for home mortgage loans; the activities of the FNMA have, as a result, been substantially altered.

Conclusion

The federal government has a more direct and controlling voice in the rates and terms under which mortgage loans, particularly for the purchase and construction of residential property, are made than in most other fields of finance. There have been great political pressures for the federal government to take many steps toward liberalizing mortgage lending terms and decreasing the interest rate on home mortgage loans. These pressures have resulted in great part from the housing shortage (an effect of the dearth of house building during the depression years and during World War II, and of the increasing desire of young families to

own a home of their own) and from the whole trend toward more government activity in recent years in the attempted solutions of personal and economic problems. As the rates and terms on home mortgage loans have been liberalized and interest rates on home mortgage loans have been decreased, there naturally has been a similar indirect effect on the arrangements for financing commercial and industrial property, because both types of property compete in the same mortgage market.

The future of the mortgage market is a clouded one, particularly at this time when the extent of the military involvements of the forces of this country during the next decade are considerably in doubt. The announced program of the federal government at this point is so to restrict the terms and rates of residential financing that the construction of homes in the year 1951 will be reduced to 800,000 or 850,000 units compared to construction at the rate of 1,300,000 homes during 1950. If there is a need for further reduction of home construction in order to save critical materials and manpower for armament production, the credit restrictions imposed by the federal government as authorized by the Defense Production Act may be revised. There is little doubt but that through the adjustment of the maximum credit terms, the government can be quite successful in encouraging or discouraging private home building. In addition, of course, the federal government has power under various acts of Congress to restrict home construction by such direct means as limiting orders, putting materials required in the construction of houses under a priority system, and requiring permits to build a home.

Suggested Readings

Benson, P. A. and North, N. L., *Real Estate Principles and Practices,* Third Edition. New York: Prentice-Hall, Inc., 1947.
Bodfish, Morton and Theobald, A. D., *Savings and Loan Principles.* New York: Prentice-Hall, Inc., 1938.
Colean, Miles, *American Housing.* New York: Twentieth Century Fund, 1944, Chapter 9.
Colean, Miles, *Impact of Government on Real Estate Finance in the United States.* New York: National Bureau of Economic Research, 1950.
Edwards, E. E., *Urban Real Estate Financing by Savings and Loan Associations.* New York: National Bureau of Economic Research, 1951.
Grange, W. J., *Real Estate,* Revised edition. New York: The Ronald Press Company, 1940, Chapters 10, 11, 12, 13.
McMichael, S. L., *How to Finance Real Estate.* New York: Prentice-Hall, Inc., 1949.
Ratcliff, R. U., *Urban Land Economics.* New York: Prentice-Hall, Inc., 1950.
Saulnier, R. J., *Urban Mortgage Lending by Life Insurance Companies.* New York: National Bureau of Economic Research, 1950.
Weimer, A. M. and Hoyt, Homer, *Principles of Urban Real Estate,* Revised edition. New York: The Ronald Press Company, 1948, Chapters 15 and 16.

8

Factors
Bank Financing of Accounts Receivable
Commercial Paper

by RAYMOND RODGERS

*Professor of Banking, Graduate School of Business Administration
and School of Commerce, Accounts and Finance
New York University*

Factors

Early origin of factoring. The factor is one of our oldest financial institutions, yet it is one of the least known. The traditional dictionary definition of a factor is "one who acts or transacts business for another." The word comes directly from the Latin verb *facio,* which means in everyday language "he who does things." This derivation, with its reference to the Roman practice of entrusting the management of property or business to others, indicates the early origin of factoring.

Blackwell Hall in London, which was dedicated to the wool industry in 1397, is generally considered the birthplace of the *commercial* factor, the institution which played such an important part in the textile industry in the ensuing centuries.

From England, factoring came to the United States through the English textile mills' practice of appointing a selling agent in this country and holding the agent responsible for the credit risk on the sales that were made. A little later, the English mills began to turn to the agent for advances on the merchandise in his possession and on the outstanding accounts. The developing American textile manufacturers, who needed financing even more than the English mills, naturally turned to these agents for such assistance. The need for the services rendered is indicated

by the fact that some of our present-day factoring organizations had their origin as early as 1808.

This long historical evolution of factoring is particularly interesting as it puts the factor in a category different from most of our specialized institutions, which arose because the commercial banker was too conservative to meet a pressing economic need. (The most outstanding example of this, of course, is the sales-finance company!) Thus, factoring developed along *with* banking; it stands on its own feet, and it should be studied as a separate and distinct financial institution.

More recent developments. Traditionally, the factor was a full-fledged businessman. As a commission agent of the manufacturer, he received goods on consignment, stored them, and sold them. As he had possession of the goods, he could safely make loans to the manufacturer on the security the goods afforded. In addition, since he guaranteed the credit standing of the purchasers, he could safely make advances up to a high percentage of the uncollected accounts.

In the first quarter of the present century, this traditional broad scope of activities was greatly narrowed. In line with the specialization of the times, the merchandising activities were abandoned in favor of concentration on the financial functions. Competition forced the mills to carry larger inventories and to devote more effort to selling. Selling methods became more direct; sales departments were organized by the manufacturers; or agents devoted exclusively to selling were appointed. This divorce of the merchandising and financial functions left the factor a financial institution in the strictest sense of the term.

The depression of the 1930's forced widespread consolidations and changes in financial organization of the factors themselves. The low level of textile sales reduced factoring income, and the high level of business failures caused abnormally high credit losses. Consolidations to secure greater financial strength and increased diversification in the type, quality, and size of accounts financed were inevitable under such circumstances. Also, control of several of the larger factors was bought by sales-finance companies in an effort to use profitably their own idle funds and the low cost funds thrust on them by the commercial banks.

Current status of factoring. Exact figures on total factoring volume are not available. Estimates run from $2½ billion to $3½ billion of accounts receivable acquired during a 12-month period. Figures are available, however, which show that the seven largest factors have a yearly accounts receivable volume of more than $1½ billion, so an over-all estimate of more than $3 billion would seem reasonable. Factoring is thus an important part of the broad service of credit which is so indispensable to modern business.

Likewise, there are no reliable figures on the number of factors. The

National Conference of Commercial Receivable Companies Inc.,[1] the national trade association in the receivables field, however, has only 60 members of which only 10 are "old line" factors, so the total is quite small.

Current legal basis of factoring. In 1904 a New York court, in disregard of the divorce of merchandising and selling from financing and credit checking, refused to accord a security position to a factor who did not sell, on the ground that his financing activities were separate and apart from either actual or constructive possession of the goods. This decision so undermined the very foundation of factoring that the problem was taken to the New York State Legislature, which, in 1911, passed the New York Factors Act. This act, with subsequent amendments, provides a means whereby factors and commission agents can establish a lien on goods and on their proceeds when sold, whether in actual or constructive possession. The statutory lien created by this legislation even extends to future goods! Nearly half of the other states, particularly those with important textile interests, now have similar statutes, so that factors who operate along traditional lines have proper protection in such states.

Functions of factoring. Because of the close relationship between the factor and his clients, he performs many important advisory functions, such as aiding in the choice of selling agents and in the determination of selling policies, in addition to the following conventional factoring functions:

1. The most important service of the factor is the assumption of credit and collection risks.
2. The next most important function is the discounting of sales through the purchase of accounts receivable.
3. Loans on other than accounts receivable constitute an important part of the financing service rendered the client. Loans are made on the security of inventory on hand or in process of manufacture. Even mortgage loans on fixed assets are made at times.

Basically, the factor furnishes credit guaranty service and finances working capital requirements on the security of accounts receivable and inventory.

Industries served by factors. While factoring has played its most important role in the huge textile industry, it is equally serviceable in any other industry made up of a large number of small or medium-size manufacturers. Concerns in such industries have a real need for the credit protection which the factor alone, of all our financial institutions, can give them. Also, industries frequently need the working capital

[1] New York City.

which can be realized through the sale of their accounts receivable to the factor.

The present-day furniture and shoe industries are good examples of industries with conditions favorable to the development of factoring; and, as might be expected, factoring is growing in both. Factoring is also being used in a score of other fields ranging from floor coverings through plastics to toys.

As a matter of fact, any company which desires to make all sales equivalent to cash sales, or needs to turn a large part of inventory into cash, fits the factoring pattern and should present its problem to the factor to see if suitable arrangements cannot be made.

The factoring agreement. If discussion develops a mutually satisfactory basis of operations, a factoring agreement assigning the accounts to the factor is entered into by the simple method of sending the client a letter-form of agreement in duplicate, which he signs and returns the original to the factor. This agreement governs the future relationship between factor and client. As the factoring agreement is in sufficient detail to give a good idea of the factoring operation, a typical agreement [2] is included for the information of the reader on pages 197-9. Close study of this form will be helpful to anyone with a serious interest in factoring.

Putting the agreement into operation. Considerable detailed work is necessary in starting the factoring operation. The credit standing of the customers' accounts which are to be taken over must be checked by the factor. And there must be a physical transfer of the accounts.

On the information side, since there is so little public knowledge of factoring, announcement of the new arrangement is made in the trade journals. Also, letters of explanation are sent to all of the customers whose accounts are taken over. Special meetings are held with the client's sales force and office workers, so that they can answer favorably any question which may be asked by customers. In addition, a contact officer is assigned by the factor to handle the special questions which will arise from time to time. This transition (or "take-over" period) usually occupies the week before the contract goes into effect. After the special arrangements have been completed, the factoring relationship is on an operating basis and the client begins to submit his orders to the factor's credit department for approval.

Special features of the credit department. Orders are submitted by telephone, teletype, messenger, telegram or mail. Regardless of the method of communication, orders are handled by a unit of the factor known as the Order Board. Clerks, usually women, in this group place the transactions on which the client desires approval on order sheets

[2] Courtesy of William Iselin Co., Inc., New York.

WILLIAM ISELIN & CO., Inc.
357 FOURTH AVENUE
New York 10, N.Y.

CABLES GREENCANAL N Y

[Date]

[Name of company]
[Address]

Gentlemen:

We are pleased to confirm the terms on which we are to act as your factor for all sales of your merchandise. These sales are to be made by you in your name.

1. All orders obtained by you from customers will be submitted to our Credit Department and we will assume the entire credit risk on the shipments it approves. On approved shipments, we will bear the credit loss on the uncollected invoice if a customer, after receiving and accepting delivery, fails to pay in full because of his financial inability to pay, but we are not to be responsible where non-payment results from any other cause. Credit approvals may be withdrawn prior to but not after shipment.

2. We will, on your request, remit to you at once the net amount of sales after goods are shipped and the invoice and shipping documents are submitted to us, subject to a reasonable reserve. This reserve will vary with our experience with your account and is to provide for possible returns, claims or defenses of customers or any sums owing by you to us, and for possible credit losses on any shipments made without our credit approval. If not so requested, your credit balance less reserves will be remitted to you at reasonable intervals.

3. Should any disputes with customers arise, we will cooperate in their adjustment, but we reserve the right at any time to charge back to your account the amount involved if an alleged claim, defense or offset is asserted. You agree to notify us promptly of all disputes and to issue credits immediately (with duplicates to us) upon the acceptance of returns or granting of allowances.

FIGURE 1. *Specimen Contract*

and take them to the credit man responsible for the accounts of that client. The approval, disapproval, or modified approval of the credit man is then communicated to the client. Exact record is kept of the time involved, usually a matter of only a few minutes.

Questions of allowances, adjustments, and requests for additional time to make payment are also submitted to the credit department of the factor for disposition.

WILLIAM INKLIN & Co., Inc.

4. You hereby assign to us in absolute ownership all accounts receivable created by your sales while this agreement is in effect. We hereby agree to purchase all of your accounts receivable in accordance with the terms of this agreement and, in payment, to remit to you the net amount of sales as herein provided or to apply such net amount against any indebtedness on your part to us or advances we may have made to you prior to the date of shipment. Should a debit exist in your account, you agree to pay the amount involved at any time that we so request.

5. The "net amount of sales" means gross sales less our commission and discounting, after deducting all credits and discounts granted to customers on the shortest terms indicated in each sale. Our commission will be charged to your account as of the fifteenth of the month, and the net amount of sales will be credited as of the end of the month. Our discounting is computed at the rate of six per cent per annum from the end of the month to the average due date of all sales billed during the month, adding ten days for collection and clearance of checks. Interest in your account is debited and credited at the rate of six per cent per annum.

6. In assigning your accounts receivable to us you represent and warrant that each account is based on an actual sale and delivery of merchandise, that the customer is liable for the payment of the amount stated in the invoice according to its terms without offset, defense or counterclaim, and that the original invoice bears notice of assignment to us. As owners of the accounts, we shall have the right of bringing suit, and of endorsing customers' remittances for collection, in your name or ours. The assignments of accounts include the rights of replevin, reclamation and stopping in transit, and your rights to the merchandise which, if returned by customers, you agree to sell on our behalf with the proceeds payable to us unless otherwise directed.

7. This agreement, together with all assignments of accounts hereunder, is to be construed according to the laws of the State of New York. Termination of this agreement shall not affect any of your obligations with respect to accounts receivable purchased by us, any advances made by us, or any other indebtedness to us, incurred prior to the effective date of such termination, and pending final accounting, we may withhold payment of any credit balance in your account unless supplied with an adequate indemnity. Should either party be in default hereunder, become insolvent, fail to meet its debts as they mature, or commit an act of bankruptcy, this agreement will be terminable by the other at any time; otherwise, this agreement goes into effect as of the date hereof and will continue until terminated by either party on ninety (90) days' prior notice in writing.

FIGURE 1 (continued)

The credit man is the key to success in factoring. Quick, in fact, almost instantaneous decisions must be made on large amounts if the client is to get the service to which he is entitled. Although conventional credit methods are employed, the high degree of specialization involved permits the development of exceptional credit skill. In addition to superior credit ability, the credit man, as indicated above, must also have the executive ability to settle merchandise disputes, to supervise collection

WILLIAM ISELIN & CO., INC.   PAGE 3

8. For our services as described herein, we shall be entitled to a commission of [rate written out] per cent (%) on the net sales.

If the foregoing is in accordance with your understanding, will you please sign and return both copies to us, after which we will return the original to you with signatures completed for your files.

Very truly yours,

WILLIAM ISELIN & CO., INC.

By

President

Read and agreed to:

[NAME OF ACCOUNT]

By

FIGURE 1 *(continued)*

problems, to grant extensions of time, to adjust terms, and otherwise make decisions on questions involving the accounts of the clients assigned to him.

Operating procedure.[3] At the end of each day, two copies of the in-

---

[3] The Weller thesis listed at the end of this chapter gives a splendid description of factoring techniques, operating methods and services.

voices covering the day's shipments are forwarded to the factor by each client. Documentary evidence that delivery has actually been made—postal, transportation, or delivery receipts—accompanies each invoice. One copy of this invoice is forwarded to the Accounts Receivable book-keeper where it is posted to the account card of the customer (the account debtor, not the client). The other copy of the invoice is used to prepare the Account of Sales report (showing the value of the sales for the month) and the Account Current report (showing the client's balance with the factor), which are furnished to each client monthly. After posting to these reports, this invoice is forwarded to the credit man, as a further safeguard against a shipment's being made without the credit approval of the factor.

The Account of Sales is the record of gross sales less all deductions for any reason. The factor's commission is then deducted and the balance is given a future value-date, based on the average due date of the invoices plus the 10-day (or other) period authorized in the factoring agreement for collection time. Interest for the period between this value-date and the current date (end of the month involved) is then deducted. In this connection it should be noted that the proceeds are then credited to the Account Current and *immediately begin to draw interest at the same rate.*

The Account Current is the medium through which a record of withdrawals by the client and relevant interest computations are made. On the first day of each month, this account is customarily credited with interest at the rate of 6 per cent (or whatever rate is agreed upon) on the balance carried forward from the previous month. Likewise, interest is debited at the same rate on all withdrawals by the client from the day they are made until the end of the month; again, it should be noted that this procedure merely offsets, for the days involved, the interest credit made at the beginning of the month (for the entire month).

The right to inspect the pertinent books and records of the client is accorded the factor in the factoring agreement. While such a visitorial privilege is unique in business relationships, experience has shown that it is highly necessary in this method of financing to keep fraud and other dishonesty to a minimum. If one periodic (but not *regular*) examination reveals excessive withdrawals of money by the principal, numerous exchanges, unusual credits to the personal account of the principal, or transactions with check-cashing agencies, the factor is able to take remedial action before it is too late. Incidentally, one of the most damning things in such an examination is for the books to be behind the date of the examination. The factor will insist that they be brought up-to-date, even if he has to use his own employees to do it.

Notification of the change of ownership (as opposed to non-notification) has long been a point of bitter contention in the field of accounts receivable financing. The old line factors generally (unless there is some special reason for an exception) insist on notification. A stamped or printed notice similar to the following is put on each invoice:

> This bill is assigned to and payable only to our factors, the ___ ___ ___ ___ ___,
> to whom notice must be given of any merchandise returns or claims for shortage, nondelivery, or other reasons.

Method of making advances on inventory. The operating procedure in making advances against the inventory of finished goods or against raw materials (preferably basic raw materials which are readily salable) is so important that it warrants separate consideration.

Customarily, the factor will advance up to 80 to 90 per cent (or whatever percentage is specified in the factoring agreement) of the credit balance in the client's *Account Current*. If this amount does not cover the client's requirements, the factor *may* also make an advance on the security of the inventory or even on an unsecured basis in exceptional cases. The total of such advances rarely exceeds 5 to 10 per cent of the factor's volume since the advances are made only to *supplement* the traditional accounts receivable method of financing the client, and are, consequently, kept to a minimum. In contrast with the factored accounts receivable, which are purchased outright, the goods against which an advance is made are only consigned to the factor. While he does not acquire title, he does arrange to secure legal possession, and thus he gets into position to protect his lien against other creditors.

The method whereby possession is arranged is quite interesting. The part of the client's warehouse or other premises where the consigned merchandise is stored is leased by the factor. A notice is then posted at this section to warn all and sundry that the merchandise is on consignment to the factor. To make "reassurance doubly sure," the factor may put an employee of the client on his own payroll at a *nominal* salary as custodian, and specify that only this employee can have access to the consigned goods. In this fashion, defects that might be found in his lien in the various states are largely avoided; and, in any event, the factor has possession! This method of securing possession is analogous to the "field warehousing" which commercial bankers use at times, except that the factor does not engage an outside organization to do the work. Field warehousing could be, and sometimes is, used in exactly the same way to gain possession for purposes of protection.

Although the factor has physical possession, he does not *own* the goods; they belong to the client. It follows that it is the responsibility of the client to bear the costs of insurance, storage, handling and ship-

ping. Special clauses are inserted in the insurance making it payable, either partially or completely to the factor, "as his interests may appear." In connection with all of this, it should be kept in mind that a basic legal requirement obliges the consignee or holder of the lien to be able to identify the merchandise at all times to make his claim "stick."

In the normal course of events, the consigned inventory turns into accounts receivable and, as the accounts are later paid, cash. In fact, so far as bookkeeping procedure is concerned, the loans are liquidated when the sales are billed, as the factor credits the net proceeds of the billing to the loan account, since he has taken over the accounts receivable. Thus, there is a very close connection between lending on inventory and lending on accounts receivable.

Factors also make some loans on mortgage and other security; some factors even make unsecured loans at times. Such loans, although made by factors, have no special characteristics, so they need not be discussed here.

Typical departments in a factoring organization. Most factors today are organized as corporations, although several of the well-known old line organizations are still partnerships in the tradition of private banking. Whatever their legal form of organization, their internal organization—disregarding nomenclature—is fairly uniform. In addition to the conventional departments that all business organizations have (such as new business, treasurer's, accounts receivable, collection, mail, stenographic, and building operation departments), the factor has several specialized departments, a description of which will give a better idea of the business of factoring.

The *Credit Department* should head any such list of specialized departments. Although credit departments are common in American business, in no other line are they so highly specialized or so important— not even in commercial banks. The *Order Board*, previously described, is an important service unit of this department.

The *"Account Sales" Department* (although it may not have this exact name) is responsible for the preparation of the previously described *Account of Sales* and the *Account Current* reports for clients.

The *"Advance" Department,* as it is ordinarily called, is responsible for turning the actual funds over to the client as requested. It corresponds to the loan department in a commercial bank. Employees in this department check up on the physical aspects of the security offered. For example, they see that the merchandise is actually consigned to the factor and that it is taken care of, with due regard to the legal technicalities and pitfalls.

It is interesting to note, at this point, that if the client desires to bor-

row against inventory, he must submit a budget showing estimated future sales and the cash needed for purchases, payrolls and other expenses to realize those sales. This budget is worked out by the client with the cooperation and guidance of the "Advance" department. After such a budget is agreed upon, it controls the amount and time of the advances.

The "Advance" department, upon request, will furnish the client a memorandum account showing his balance and its derivation, as of any day during the month. Thus the client is able to ascertain exactly how he stands at any time.

Charges made for services. Charges made for factoring, like those made for everything else, vary with the services rendered; competition operates here just as in other lines. The factoring charge varies from a fraction of 1 per cent to 2 per cent, and even more, of the total volume of sales. It should be noted that this charge is *flat* and not per annum; also, it is a service charge and not *interest,* contrary to public impression.

The factoring charge covers the assumption of all credit losses, all credit and collection work, and the advisory and other services rendered. Factors maintain that the economies a business can effect by utilizing their services more than cover the factoring fee. The client no longer has the expense of maintaining a credit department—and he gets a higher grade of credit service than if he did! His bookkeeping expense is considerably reduced, as the accounts receivable bookkeeping is done by the factor. Collection expense is also shifted to the factor. And, above all, the client no longer has to worry about or carry the financial burden of credit losses. (These offsets should be included in any weighing of the fees charged.)

An understanding of the basis used in determining the precise rate of charge will be helpful in ascertaining whether factoring services are economically feasible for a particular business. In view of this, the principal items influencing the amount of charge will now be outlined.

The *volume of sales* is, naturally, a basic consideration. Factors generally do not actively solicit accounts with sales volume of less than $250,000 a year. Possibilities of growth, however, are not overlooked, and for this and other special reasons, much smaller accounts may be taken over.

The *average size of invoice* is a closely allied consideration that obviously has a direct effect on the factor's costs. The clerical detail on a $10,000 invoice is the same as on a $10 one.

The *nature of the business* has a great effect on the costs and credit risks borne. A toy manufacturer, for example, with a line in which retail sales are made only during the Christmas shopping season, is conducting his business on a basis entirely different from that of a cotton

goods manufacturer with staple lines. Likewise, a manufacturer of beach wear has different merchandising, credit, and financing problems from those of a manufacturer concentrating on the production of working men's overalls.

The *type of trade* of a client is another important consideration. A manufacturer selling to the "cloak and suit" trade, for example, faces hazards peculiar to that line. Style factors, intense competition, and the typically small capital of those engaged in this business create risks which must be covered in the factoring rate.

The *terms of sale* have a controlling bearing on the credit risk assumed by the factor. The longer the terms of sale, the greater is the credit exposure in any line: this works in both directions in factoring— the risk that the purchaser may not pay is greater, and the risk that the client may get into difficulties is also greater. As credit terms vary widely, particularly in the textile industry, the necessity of adjusting the factoring rate to fit the actual conditions is apparent.

Any *special services* rendered will likewise have to be included in the factor's rate of charge. For example, the so-called house accounts (those occupying space on the factor's premises), pay a higher factoring fee to cover the additional cost of the space, light, and telephone usage, and the *billing* of their customers.

On the other hand, a smaller charge can be made when the factor does not bear the credit risk. This situation arises when the factor refuses to approve the credit risk on an order from a purchaser, and the client insists that the sale go through. Such a transaction is known as "department risk," and if the purchaser does not pay, the loss is the client's. Of course, the factor is entitled to payment for bookkeeping and collection services on such transactions.

Interest, usually at the rate of 6 per cent (per annum), is credited by the factor from the average due date (value-date) of the accounts receivable. A charge at the same rate is made for the remaining days of the month on all withdrawals by the client from his balance in the *Account Current.* However, since the client's balance was credited with 6 per cent interest at the *beginning* of the month, this charge is merely an offset, unless he withdraws enough to have the use of some of the factor's funds; in the latter case the client has a net debit of 6 per cent.

Interest at agreed rates is also charged on all advances on inventory and mortgage and other loans.

Financial operations of the factor. Factors have not achieved the preferred borrowing position of the sales-finance companies, which have literally had funds thrust on them by the banks and insurance companies. The sales-finance company installment paper, signed by consumers, is preferred as ultimate security to the accounts receivable (open

book accounts) due from dealers, upon which the factor chiefly relies. There is also a tendency on the part of the banks to view factors as competitors who should be kept in bounds! In reality the factor is in far less direct competition with banks than many other agencies, especially the sales-finance companies. But, whether soundly based or not, the banks' attitudes and views have affected the financing of the factor.

Equity capital has been largely supplied to factors from private sources. This is especially true of those factors organized as partnerships. In the case of those factors using the corporate form of organization, considerable amounts have come latterly via parent organizations in the sales-finance field. These parent finance companies took advantage of their own current financial popularity by selling securities to the public, or by borrowing from the banks and insurance companies at very low rates and passing the funds on to the subsidiary. Some factors have also sold issues of securities to the public, but this practice has been rare.

Bank loans to factors, as indicated before, have not reached the absolute or the relative proportions of bank loans made to finance companies. In contrast to the sales-finance companies, which borrow from three to five times their net worth, the total loans payable (to all sources) by factors range from year to year only from one-half to one and a half times net worth; similarly, related to assets, the average range of total loans payable by the factor is from 15 to 30 per cent of his total assets. Thus, a much smaller proportion of borrowed capital from banks and other outside sources is employed by factors than is generally thought.

In recent years, the most important capital source has been the credit balances in the *Accounts Current*. Whereas these balances accounted for less than 10 per cent of total liabilities in the 1920's, and varied from 20 to 30 per cent in the 1930's, in recent years they have been around 50 per cent. Throughout the 1940's, the amount of capital from the credit balances not only exceeded the capital raised from all other sources, but in some years the amount was more than twice as great. This development further emphasizes the previous observation that the chief function of the factor is *factoring,* and not the lending of money.

While an enormous increase in clients' funds left with the factor has been caused, to a considerable extent, by the great wartime and postwar prosperity of the textile industry, there are other considerations involved. Some clients have always made it a practice to finance themselves and use a factor only for the basic factoring services of credit information, credit guaranty, collections and relevant accounting and clerical services. The high interest rate paid by the factor on collected balances left undrawn has also undoubtedly been an important cause of this develop-

ment, as the return has been three or four times what the client could get elsewhere with comparable safety.

Capital requirements. The amount of capital required for a given volume of business depends primarily on the exact nature of the factor's loans and advances, and on the rapidity and the extent to which the clients draw down their balances. As seen in the preceding paragraph, in times of prosperity and easy money, obtaining capital is not much of a problem. By the same token, with different conditions, the opposite may be true. Therefore, the factor must view his balances as the commercial banker views his demand deposits.

The amount of advances and the overdrafts on the accounts receivable purchased and the loans on inventory and other security, also directly affect capital requirements.

The turnover or average length of time the receivables are outstanding is another matter that directly affects the capital requirements of the factor. For example, in World War II, the average length of time for payment of factored accounts dropped from 48 days in 1941 to 27 days in 1944, with a corresponding increase in liquidity. After the end of the war, the trend, as would be expected, was in the opposite direction; the average number of turnover days, however, is not expected to reach prewar proportions so long as business continues at a high level. This high business level contributes to an easier capital position for the factor.

Bad debt losses constitute few problems in factoring. One company publicly announced that the net credit losses of its subsidiaries for the 10-year period ending December 31, 1948, were only $\frac{4}{100}$ of 1 per cent. While this period was one of continuous and unprecedented expansion in business, and therefore not typical, the losses in other past periods have also been very small. In fact, in recent years, the reserves set aside for losses have been more than adequate and have thus served as another source of capital.

While figures on profits are scarce, the fact that several of the leading organizations have survived more than a century of economic stress and strain is proof that earnings have been satisfactory. Moreover, the increasing competition in factoring demonstrates that present profits compare favorably with those in other lines.

From an investment standpoint, factoring has several attractive features. Its capital is very small in relation to volume. It has a relatively small labor force. It requires no machinery and but little in the way of equipment. It has no problems of obsolescence or retooling. It is, thus, in an especially favorable position to adapt its operations to new conditions. This flexibility and the inherent advantages of this type of busi-

ness should attract an increased flow of capital to this field in the years ahead.

Competition is growing. Competition in factoring is keen and growing. This competition comes from other factors and, latterly, from finance companies and commercial banks. In a strict sense, neither the finance companies nor the banks are competitors of the factors, as they do not render the basic factoring services of credit guaranty, accounts receivable bookkeeping, and collections. Banks and finance companies do, however, lend on accounts receivable and thus take potential customers of the factors out of the market.

Finance companies may either buy or discount accounts receivable. In either event, the finance companies insist on recourse to the manufacturer; that is, the manufacturer must guarantee the accounts they finance. Finance companies will, ordinarily, advance a smaller amount than the factor, say, 70 to 80 per cent of the face amount of the receivables. While their charges vary as to method of determination and amount, the charges are definitely higher than those of the banks and are higher than the interest component in the factoring charges. In fact, the finance company charge is usually $\frac{1}{25}$ to $\frac{1}{30}$ of 1 per cent *flat* for each day the money is advanced. As this charge is calculated on the face amount of the accounts, the effective rate for the money actually received ranges from 10 to 14 per cent. In addition, a minimum annual volume of $100,000 in accounts receivable financed is usually required.

While not all banks will make loans on the security of accounts receivable, their number is growing and such banks will undoubtedly be much more important competitively in the future. As mentioned before, banks, in common with the finance companies, only lend money. They do not render the unique specialized services characteristic of the factor.

Problems of factoring. The greatest problem in the field of factoring is the lack of public understanding of the functions performed and services rendered. This lack of knowledge of factoring operation has caused the general public to view the factors' activities with suspicion. Even today, there is still entirely too much secrecy for the good of the factor, as well as the good of the public. A more enlightened public relations and information policy would not only lead to great public appreciation of the value of factoring, but it would also lead to increased business. It is to be hoped that factors, particularly the leading ones, will stop being so old-fashioned!

Another problem of recent years has been the foreign accounts receivable. While factors will not handle the sales of an exporter, they more or less have to take the foreign credits that may constitute a part of the accounts receivable of a domestic client. As the foreign accounts taken by factors are estimated at less than 2 per cent of total volume, even for

the New York factors, quantitatively the problem is not very great. Nevertheless, the unsettled international conditions, the foreign exchange restrictions, the manipulated exchange rates, and the basic difficulties of collecting from foreign debtors have made even this small amount of business a real "headache." In consequence, although the factoring charge is four or five times as high as on domestic sales, foreign billings are accepted with great reluctance—and no solution to the difficulties in this field is in sight.

Another problem, although it is not generally appreciated, is that there has been no testing of credit since 1937. Ever higher prices and easy salability of inventories through more than a decade of boom has undoubtedly caused some "softness" to develop in credit extension. The return of seasonal buying to the same extent as before the war (or the sales difficulties of even a minor depression) would undoubtedly disclose that some weaknesses have developed and would necessitate a general tightening up in operations and credit policy.

Place of the factor in our economy. History accords factoring an important role in the development of our huge textile industry. It has been said that without the credit and financing services extended by factors, our textile industry could not have reached the great size and diversity of products which characterize it today. Even if factoring had done nothing else, this accomplishment alone would warrant the conclusion of one of the leaders in the field, who said: "Factoring is an institution of honorable tradition and long experience. Its increasing volume and scope and its many benefits to industry are its economic justification." [4]

In recent years, factoring has more than held its position relative to other financial institutions. Also, it has grown faster than the textile industry with which it has been closely identified. Specifically, in the last 20 years, while textile production was doubling, factoring increased sixfold.

Looking to the future, factoring has great opportunity for increased service to business. Since the 1930's, it has shown a willingness to adapt itself to new conditions and to do the necessary pioneering and experimentation without which any human institution atrophies. This expansion into fields other than textiles is a good augury for the future; it is also an indication that competition will be keen.

Basically, factoring means that a company is selling for cash, and this should prove especially attractive to small and medium-size companies which find the capital markets closed to them because of regulations and other developments. In addition, as business becomes increasingly

---

[4] Herbert R. Silverman, "Factoring as a Financing Device," *Harvard Business Review*, Volume XXVII, Number 5, September 1949, p. 608.

complex, the specialized credit service of the factor should become of even greater value to more and more industries and organizations.

Bank Financing of Accounts Receivable

Commercial banks newcomers in field. One of the very newest lending developments is the financing of accounts receivable by commercial banks. The depression of the early 1930's literally forced commercial banks into starting this type of financing. "Rescue parties" organized by the banks frequently could only look to the accounts receivable for security because of the depleted capital structure of borrowers. Banks thereby entered the field which had formerly been the exclusive domain of the factor and the *commercial* finance company (not to be confused with the sales-finance company, which many of them later became), reluctantly and gingerly, to remedy desperate situations. But other economic pressures that soon materialized caused many commercial banks to view the financing of accounts receivable as something which might be developed as a normal outlet for bank funds.

Of the many developments since 1933 which have influenced commercial banks to begin this method of financing, the following are worthy of note:

1. Difficulty in getting good commercial loans of conventional character.
2. Chronic surplus loanable funds.
3. Declining interest rates on other earnings assets, particularly government bonds.
4. Growing "respectability" of this type of financing because of the success and relatively high profits of the agencies specializing in it.
5. Increased safety because of improved legal position afforded by court decisions and laws in the various states, further establishing the validity of the lender's lien on assigned accounts.

It is indeed surprising that banks did not start this type of lending much sooner. Bankers had always regarded accounts receivable as the most liquid asset, other than cash, on a borrower's balance sheet; and bankers had relied very heavily on accounts receivable in making loans. Paradoxically, however, bankers refused to take the preferred position which a specific lien on assigned accounts would have given them. Whether from orthodoxy, inherent conservatism, or less charitable reasons, the fact is that banks did not willingly enter this field; many of them still refuse to have anything to do with accounts receivable lending.

The reluctance of the banks to develop this method of lending is, in

many respects, unfortunate. Under present conditions, there is a need for such credit extension; other agencies will supply this need to the extent that the commercial banks refuse to do so. The banks are well equipped to handle this business, and they can probably do so at less social cost than any other agency. Certainly, they have the "inside track" in obtaining the business, for the potential borrowers have to maintain a deposit account with a bank and, thus, are already customers! Moreover, banking offices are located conveniently to the borrowers; the proximity of the borrower makes it easier for the bank to give loans the special servicing they require. Branch banking, in particular, lends itself to this type of financing.

Despite the manifest competitive advantages which they have in the field, commercial banks do not yet actively seek accounts receivable loans. There are a few exceptions to this generalization, and their number will undoubtedly grow; but the fact remains that at present the great majority of banks reserve this method of financing to meet special situations which may develop in the operations of conventional borrowers.

Function of accounts receivable financing by banks. The basic function of all credit extension by banks is to place purchasing power in the hands of those who can use it most productively. Accounts receivable lending definitely falls within this orthodox category, for it is used to bridge the gap between high productive and sales capacities and inadequate capital. From the standpoint of economic and banking theory, accounts receivable lending is one of the soundest of all loans, for it is definitely and specifically confined to working capital purposes.

One of the best ways to get an idea of the functions of an institution is to review the services rendered. Organizations which seek accounts receivable financing (whether at a bank, finance company or factor) do so for the following reasons:

1. Depleted working capital resulting from over-investment in fixed assets; financial drain of a strike; withdrawal of capital from the business because of death, or other controlling reason without adverse credit implications;
2. Inadequate working capital because of rapid expansion or defective initial promotion;
3. To take quick advantage of a profitable opportunity to expand or to change methods of operation;
4. Extremely seasonal business which requires borrowing to the absolute maximum to carry the peak load;
5. Prevention of dilution of ownership or loss of control when additional capital becomes imperative; and, finally,

6. Financial condition so poor that credit facilities are not available on any other basis. (Banks will not make accounts receivable loans to such an organization unless they are already lending to it when the unsatisfactory situation develops.)

The revolving credit facilities afforded by accounts receivable financing are particularly suitable for any of the above needs, because the credit risk of the lender and the costs of the borrower are closely geared to the business actually transacted.[5]

Lending operations. Superficially, accounts receivable lending by banks resembles the operation of factors, since both are concerned with accounts receivable; but the similarity is more apparent than real. Strictly speaking, the bank does not render any of the basic *factoring* services. It does not physically maintain the accounts receivable; that is, it does no accounts receivable bookkeeping. It does not give any collection service. Moreover, contrary to the factor's practice of placing notification of assignment on each bill, the bank in nearly all cases keeps its connection with the accounts receivable as secret as possible.

The credit man of the bank cannot specialize in one line, nor can he acquire the daily intimate contact with one customer's operations that characterizes the credit men of the factor. Consequently, the bank's credit service, to the extent that it is made available to the borrower, cannot be as valuable as the service of the credit men of the factor.

The non-notification method of financing accounts receivable is generally followed by banks. In this type of financing, the accounts are assigned to the bank without any notice, either to trade debtors or the borrower's creditors, that an assignment has been made. Banks, as a matter of protection, however, include in the contract the right to put any of the accounts on a notification basis, if circumstances warrant. Such action is ordinarily taken in cases when the bank suspects fraud and wants to authenticate the shipments and the amounts due. Such action is also taken when the bank suspects that the borrower's financial condition has deteriorated to the point where bankruptcy threatens. It is also necessary for the bank to give proper notification to establish a valid lien on the assignment of receivables under government contracts in excess of $1,000.

Banks advance from 75 to 90 per cent of the net amount of the valid [6] accounts receivable assigned to them. The exact percentage loaned is

---

[5] For a comprehensive discussion of the procedures involved in handling bank loans on assigned accounts, see Chapter 17 of *Practical Bank Credit,* 2nd ed., by Herbert V. Prochnow and Roy A. Foulke, published by Prentice-Hall Inc., New York, 1950. This chapter was written by John W. Kearns, Counsel, The First National Bank of Chicago.

[6] After elimination of all memorandum, consignment, contra, intra-company, officers' and employees' accounts.

determined by a careful consideration of the credit rating of the underlying trade debtors, the hazards of the borrower's line of business, the past collection experience and debt record, the selling terms, the selling costs, the number of accounts sold, and the profit margin. The typical loan is for 80 per cent and, ordinarily, none is for less than 70 per cent, for it is felt that when conditions require a larger margin, it is too risky for a commercial bank to hazard its demand funds.

Audit and verification of the borrower's accounts. An essential feature of all accounts receivable financing is the contractual right of the lender to audit the pertinent accounts of the borrower. In the case of banks making such loans, this feature pertains chiefly to the accounts receivable ledger, the cash receipts journal and the accounts payable ledger. Examinations should be made by a trained auditor at least every other month on an unannounced basis. The practical aspect of these examinations, particularly under the non-notification method of lending followed by the banks, is obvious. The examinations also have a legal effect. To establish its lien on the assigned receivables, the bank must exercise some *dominion* over the accounts. This method of policing the accounts by periodic examination aids in establishing dominion and avoids the danger of a plea of estoppel based on failure to assert the rights acquired under the assignment.

If a situation develops in which the bank deems it necessary to verify the outstanding balances on the accounts receivable directly with the trade debtors, a firm of public accountants is utilized for the purpose. The bank may either arrange for its own clerks to use the account verification form and return envelope of the accounting firm, or it may engage the firm to do the entire job. In either case, the reply envelope is coded so that it can be quickly separated from the accountant's mail and forwarded to the bank.

Select receivables plan or lending. Banks have two basic plans of lending on accounts receivable. The *Select Receivables Plan,* which is the one generally used by the banks, is preferable where the number of trade debtors is small but where the dollar value of each account is relatively large. It is also best where borrowers have a large number of accounts but can secure all the financial assistance they need by assigning their larger receivables.

Under the Select Receivables Plan, generally, only the choicest accounts are assigned, and their number is such that the clerks in the bank can, in a sense, give them individual attention. Under this plan, the borrower may, or may not, be required to sign a promissory note. If he does sign a note, it is merely an acknowledgment of the debt and is not on a demand basis. As remittances are received by the bank, they are applied against the oldest outstanding note, until it is retired, and so on.

Under this plan, copies of all invoices on the assigned accounts must be sent to the bank. In addition, all the receivables assigned to the bank must be clearly marked on the accounts receivable ledger. This is called bookmarking, and even though the laws of a state may not require it, the practice aids in establishing and defending the lien. All remittances received on assigned accounts must be forwarded to the bank in the form in which they were received; they must not be commingled with the other funds of the borrower. Finally, the bank must be informed of all returns and allowances on the assigned accounts and must be reimbursed for such adjustments by check of the borrower.

If one of these receivables is not paid within 31 days after its net due date, it becomes ineligible as a basis for loans and is charged back to the borrower on a 100 per cent basis. While this is more than was loaned on the overdue receivable, the charge is in accordance with the principle of assignment, and it tests the borrower's ability to cover a delinquency.

A typical Select Receivables loan agreement [7] is inserted below for the information of those who desire to know the details of the contractual basis of this financing.

	THE
ASSIGNMENT OF ACCOUNTS	CHASE
	NATIONAL
	BANK

KNOW ALL MEN BY THESE PRESENTS, that the Undersigned, for value received, hereby assigns to The Chase National Bank of the City of New York (hereinafter referred to as the "Bank") all of the accounts listed and set forth in the schedule, marked "SCHEDULE   ", hereto annexed, and all right, title and interest of the Undersigned in and to the same and all the right, title and interest of the Undersigned in and to all accounts heretofore assigned to the Bank by the Undersigned, and all the proceeds thereof, together with any and all security pertaining thereto.

I. The Undersigned hereby authorizes the Bank, in the name of the Bank or otherwise, to demand, sue for, collect and give acquittance for any and all moneys due and/or to become due upon or by virtue of said accounts and the said security, and to compromise, prosecute or defend any action, claim or proceeding with respect thereto, to sell, assign, pledge or make any agreement regarding or otherwise deal with the same and also, with respect to said accounts and the said security, to exercise all the rights and remedies which the Undersigned might exercise but for the execution of this instrument.

II. The Undersigned hereby warrants to the Bank that (1) the Undersigned is the owner of said accounts and every part thereof and that none of said accounts is in any respect encumbered; (2) each of said accounts is a true statement of a *bona fide* indebtedness incurred by the debtor named therein, now owing to the Undersigned, and that there are no defenses or counterclaims to the same.

III. The Undersigned covenants and agrees with the Bank as follows:

(1) To execute and deliver to the Bank at any time or times a supplemental assignment or supplemental assignments of any of said accounts and such other and further instruments of assurance as the Bank may request and deem necessary to rectify

---

[7] Courtesy of The Chase National Bank of New York.

any mistake or to carry into effect the full intent and purposes hereof and otherwise to do any and all things and acts whatsoever, which the Bank may request, to perfect the assignment of said accounts to the Bank.

(2) To account to the Bank for the full amounts of the accounts hereby assigned and not to retain or to attempt to retain any dominion or control over any of said accounts hereby assigned to the Bank or the proceeds thereof or the merchandise represented thereby.

(3) To notify the Bank, immediately upon receipt, of all information received by the Undersigned which may in any way affect the value of said accounts or the rights or remedies of the Bank in respect thereto.

(4) To furnish to the Bank such statements and information with respect to the business of the Undersigned as the Bank may request.

(5) To allow the Bank, by its agents, at any time during business hours, so long as the Undersigned shall be directly or indirectly indebted to the Bank in any amount whatsoever, to examine and make extracts from the books of account and other records of the Undersigned.

(6) To reimburse the Bank for any and all legal and other expenses incurred in and about the checking, handling and collection of the accounts hereby assigned to the Bank and the preparation and enforcement of any agreement relating thereto.

(7) To deliver to the Bank, immediately upon receipt, all checks and other negotiable paper, endorsed in blank or to the order of the Bank, and all cash, received by the Undersigned either as payment of or as security for the payment of any of the said accounts.

(8) All sums of money, which are proceeds of said accounts of said security, collected or otherwise received by the Undersigned or the Bank, shall be deposited in a special account in the Bank in the name of the Undersigned and shall be held by the Bank as collateral security for the payment of the indebtedness of the Undersigned to the Bank. The Undersigned shall not have the right to withdraw by check or otherwise any part of said special account. The Bank may from time to time, in its sole discretion, apply any part of the credit balance in said special account to the payment of any of the obligations of the Undersigned to the Bank, whether or not the same be due.

(9) If, at any time, the Bank shall not, for any reason, be satisfied with any of said accounts hereby assigned, the Undersigned will, upon the request of the Bank, in lieu thereof, pay to the Bank the face amount thereof or assign to the Bank another account or other accounts in amount and otherwise satisfactory to the Bank.

(10) The Bank shall be liable to account only for said accounts and the said security and the proceeds thereof actually received by it.

(11) The rights and remedies of the Bank hereunder are cumulative and are not in lieu of, but are in addition to, any other rights and remedies which the Bank may have under the provisions of any promissory note or agreement of the Undersigned, or otherwise.

IV. The covenants and warranties of the Undersigned herein set forth shall enure to the benefit not only of the Bank but also of its successors and assigns.

IN WITNESS WHEREOF, the Undersigned has duly executed this instrument this

_____ day of _____, 19____.

(SEAL)

BY_____

Aggregate Receivables Plan of lending. The other basic plan of lending on accounts receivable by banks is the *Aggregate Receivables Plan.* This method is most practical when the borrower has many small accounts and the dollar value of each is relatively small.

The Aggregate Plan is, essentially, a streamlined method of handling the assigned accounts. While, legally, it is substantially the same as the Select Plan, from a technical and operating standpoint, it is quite different. One basic difference is that copies of invoices are not sent to the bank; they are retained by the borrower. Also, as the bank is not concerned with specific accounts, there are no chargebacks for ineligibility, as under the Select Plan.

Under the Aggregate Plan, the usual practice is for the borrower to make a weekly assignment of all new accounts receivable. This is done by sending the bank a Schedule of Accounts Receivable, showing date, number, name of buyer and net amount of each invoice. An assignment accompanies each Schedule so that the total of these invoices (less the accounts excluded for one reason or another) can be immediately added to the loan base.

In contrast to the Select Receivables Plan, under which a note is not considered essential by some banks, this plan requires a promissory note to cover each advance. After each weekly assignment, the borrower is notified of the additional amount he can borrow. This is usually 80 per cent of the net assigned accounts (less the amounts excluded and the amounts pledged as security for previous borrowing).

Banks require a note under this plan because *all* the accounts are assigned, and there is no additional margin, as under the Select Receivables Plan. Moreover, the note cannot be reduced by counterclaim, discount, or return of the merchandise, as in the case of the open book account.[8] Probably most important of all, the bank can liquidate the borrowing at any time after the note is due, without waiting to collect on the assigned accounts receivable of the trade debtors.

The heart of the Aggregate Receivables Plan is the Monthly Aging Report on the accounts receivable. A typical report shows, for each account, the balance at the end of the month involved; the report contains columns for the amounts due in each of the three immediately preceding months and a final column for all amounts due prior to those months. In this way, the accounts which have not been paid within the limits of the overdue period stipulated in the loan agreement are indicated as delinquent and eliminated from the loan base. The period of time allowed before classifying an item as delinquent is determined by a study of the previous collection experience of the borrower and comparable companies in the same or similar lines. It varies from 30 to 90 days past the due date, depending on the line of business of the borrower.

---

[8] As the receivables are not purchased outright but are taken on an assignment basis, with full recourse to the assignor (the borrower), this would not adversely affect the position of the bank on its loan unless the borrower was in financial difficulties.

Under this plan, more receivables can be handled with less work. Therefore, banks may be expected to turn to it in increasing numbers in the future.

Rates on accounts receivable loans. Bank rates on this type of lending are still in flux. They vary widely, depending on the bank's appraisal of the risk involved (which includes the financial standing of the borrower), the terms of sale of the borrower, the financial standing of the borrower's trade debtors, the size of the accounts, and, of course, the competition. Six per cent on the amounts actually outstanding plus a service fee on each item seems to be the goal of most banks. Parenthetically, this service charge reaches substantial proportions on a percentage basis in cases where the average size of the assigned invoice is small. Summarizing, it is not a cheap way for the bank to lend and, consequently, is not a cheap way to borrow. Each potential user of this credit service should study his own situation to see if he has more attractive alternatives and, if not, to see if this type of credit accommodation would be worth its costs to him.

Problems of this type of lending. The opposition of the banks to notification of assignment is a little hard to understand. They have always been in the forefront of all movements to raise credit standards, to increase available credit information, and to disseminate it more widely. Their insistence on non-notification is thus "not in character." This secrecy surrounding non-notification lending gives the public the impression that it is unsound. It might be well to come to grips with this attitude as a social, economic and public relations problem.

Another problem, inherent in this type of lending, is the temptation to fraud. Although it has been largely quiescent in recent years, the problem will once more become pressing when competition increases, inventory balloons, and collections freeze.

The greatest problem in this field is whether accounts receivable lending will be developed by the banks as a normal and desirable method of credit extension, or whether it will continue to be treated as something a little less than desirable, if not positively abnormal. As was stated earlier in this chapter, there is a need for this kind of financing. This need will be met. The only question is: will the banks meet it?

The entry of some of the leading banks into this field in recent years, and the time and money they have spent in developing internal operating methods [9] to handle this business, seem a good augury for the future.

---

[9] The 225-page Hess thesis listed in the bibliography gives the entire system, operating methods, and forms used by a large New York bank.

The Commercial Paper Market

Early development. As early as the 1790's, the practice of selling bills of exchange and promissory notes through intermediaries seems to have been fairly common. These intermediaries (known as "note *brokers*" or "bill *brokers*") apparently did not purchase the paper themselves. This is confirmed by Henry Clews in his autobiography, *Twenty Eight Years in Wall Street,* in which he says that in 1857 he "inaugurated the system . . . of buying merchants' acceptances and receivables out and out, the rate being governed by the prevailing ruling rate for money, with the usual commission added."

The commissions charged borrowers by these early bill brokers for their services covered a wide range, but the great majority probably fell between ⅛ of 1 per cent and 1 per cent.

While there were many individuals and concerns that would place notes sporadically, as opportunity presented, there were very few that developed enough regularity and size to be recognized as "commercial paper houses." There were never more than 50 organizations in the field, and, of these, less than 25 were large organizations; of the latter, 10 to 15 ordinarily handled 90 per cent of the total business. In particular, from 1921 onward, the number of organizations warranting the use of the term "commercial paper house" steadily declined because of mergers and withdrawals from the business; in 1950 there were less than 10 houses specializing in commercial paper in the entire country.

In the early days, and even as late as 1912, credit abuses were so common in the commercial paper market, that they might be said to have been characteristic of it. Concerns with such poor credit standing that they could borrow little elsewhere could often find some dealer willing to "push" excessive amounts of their obligations. Concerns too small to be widely known, and thus with little demand for their notes, could, likewise, often get access to the commercial paper market. Inadequate credit investigation, excessive borrowing and low standards of a few participants sometimes culminated in spectacular losses in times of financial strain. In particular, overissue became so serious that there was a widespread demand that all commercial paper be registered in one central place.

As a result of the unsatisfactory standards which developed, lenders more and more viewed the commercial paper market with criticial eyes. Lenders became very selective in their choice of paper, and the character of the market gradually changed until, today, only companies with unquestionable credit standing and a net worth of at least $250,000 sell their paper through commercial paper houses.

The commercial paper market today. Through the use of audited financial statements, independent credit investigations, and considerable control over the borrowing and business policies of borrowers, the commercial paper dealers in recent years have raised the standards until the commercial paper market compares very favorably with the other divisions of the money market. In fact, its record on losses in the dark days of the early 1930's is almost unbelievable. For example, in the 10-year period, 1929–38, which included the most depressed years in recent history, the losses were only $4/100$ of 1 per cent of the average outstandings; furthermore, since 1936, there have been no open-market losses and only five financial embarrassments. This record is better than that of banker's acceptances during the same period; and it is surpassed only by that of the short-term government issues, on which the yield is lower. In short, since 1929, commercial paper has proved to be one of the safest, most liquid, and most remunerative obligations in the entire money market.

Recent rates reflect the high standards in the commercial paper market. Thus, during the first seven months of 1950, the rate on prime four to six months' paper ruled at $1\frac{1}{4}$ to $1\frac{3}{8}$ per cent, or an average of 1.31 per cent during each month. In fact, today's rates are so low that many observers feel the market has become too selective and too exclusive to render the full service of which it is capable.

From the standpoint of volume, today's (June 1950) open market with reported [10] outstandings of around $250,000,000, compares unfavorably with the peak of $1,296,000,000 reached in February 1920. In short, from a quantitative standpoint, the commercial paper market is not very important. This is further indicated by the maximum open market outstandings in recent years of $388,000,000 in February 1942, and the minimum of only $60,000,000 in May 1933. (These figures do not include the General Motors Acceptance, Commercial Investment Trust, and Commercial Credit Company paper sold *direct* to purchasers.)

Measured by the companies selling their paper in the market, the comparison with 1920 is even more unfavorable, for the number has declined from 4,395 in that year, to less than 400 in 1950.

In the same fashion, as pointed out before, there has been a marked decline in the number of commercial paper houses active in the field, until today there are less than 10.

Summarizing, the commercial paper market is made up of a large group of lenders, a comparatively small group of borrowers, and an extremely small group of dealers. It is an open market, nationwide in scope and entirely impersonal.

Method of operation. Nowadays, operations are confined almost ex-

---

[10] Compiled by the Federal Reserve Bank of New York.

clusively to "straight" single name promissory notes bearing the blank endorsement of the issuing concern. More than 95 per cent of the paper is unsecured. The most common denomination is $5,000, but $10,000, $25,000, and higher denominations, even as high as $1,000,000, may be issued. Also, smaller units, such as $2,500, called "splits," are sometimes issued, especially in the Midwest. Maturity ranges from 90 days to six months, which, of course, directly affects the total annual commission paid the commercial paper house by the borrower.

Borrowers cover a wide range, but textile and dry goods concerns constitute the most important group; this group is followed by those engaged in the processing of foodstuffs, particularly the flour millers; this, in turn, is followed by borrowers in the metals and hardware field. Less than 1 per cent of all business enterprises are large enough and have good enough credit standing to sell their paper advantageously in this market.

Lenders are largely, in fact almost exclusively, commercial banks. Nowadays, banks are not as hostile to the issuance of commercial paper as they were in the past. There are two reasons for this: first, banks need the paper; second, commercial paper dealers now insist that borrowers maintain lines of credit, adequate balances, and satisfactory banking relationships as a prerequisite to handling their paper.

The usual charge or "commission" is $\frac{1}{4}$ of 1 per cent *flat*, that is, on the face amount of the note, regardless of maturity. In addition, the notes are always sold on a discount basis at the going market rate. They are sold by personal solicitation of salesmen, by mail and by telephone. The purchaser is ordinarily given a 10-day option period, during which he can return the paper subject to interest adjustment for the period held.

Dealers secure a substantial part of their capital requirements by borrowing from the commercial banks on the collateral of their purchased paper. They operate through branches, correspondents, reciprocal arrangements, and variously. Also, nearly all dealers engage in such other financial activities as investment dealing, brokerage, and acceptances.

Services of the commercial paper market. From a broad economic point of view, the commercial paper market brings about a more effective utilization of the country's productive resources. It permits pooling of loanable funds and demands for funds on a nationwide basis, and thus reduces seasonal, geographic and other tendencies toward diversity. This advantage is particularly needed in the United States, because we do not have nationwide branch banking systems as in other countries. (By the same token, no other country has the exact counterpart of the American commercial paper house.)

When a local bank, because of legal limitations or its own diversi-

fication policies, cannot meet the requirements of a borrower, the credit burden can be shifted to a national basis if the concern meets the minimum standards of the open market. (Of course, the same object can be accomplished by the local bank inviting its city correspondent or correspondents to participate in the loan.)

Generally, it is considerably cheaper for the borrower to sell paper through dealers than to borrow over-the-counter. Also, the ability to sell paper in the open market gives a borrower definitive bargaining power at his bank.

Sales-finance companies have utilized direct sale of commercial paper as a method of securing permanent working capital. Obviously, the liquidity of such paper depends largely on the ability of the purchaser to shift it to another holder!

This market furnishes the commercial banks a highly satisfactory short-term investment in which they can fit the maturity to their exact needs. Moreover, at maturity they deal with the issuer at arm's length; there is no pressure to renew to keep a large depositor friendly. This is a real advantage in times of financial stress. A further advantage to the bank is that such paper (when it gets within 90 days of maturity) is eligible for rediscount at the Federal Reserve Bank.

Shortcomings of this method of financing. Small business, the backbone of America, is precluded from using this market.

There is an ever-present temptation to "rotate" borrowing between this market and the banks in such way that long-term capital will be supplied by agencies with short-term liabilities. This is sometimes listed as an advantage, but it certainly is a dubious one.

Despite protestations to the contrary, this market is liable to prove a "fair weather friend." This is because it is basically a market for surplus funds; when the surplus funds dry up, or when purchasers become prejudiced regarding a particular type of borrower, there is little that can be done about it. Only the commercial banks have the loan expansion power which enables an emergency to be met. And although those utilizing the commercial paper market are now required by their dealers to maintain proper banking relationships, it seems reasonable to expect that in times of financial emergency, a bank will give preference in accommodation to the concern which gave them all of its business in boom times, rather than to the one which placed part of its business in the open market!

For the great majority of organizations, it is much safer and much better to develop closer relations with a good commercial banker.

Future place of the commercial paper market in the economy. Competition by the commercial banks for direct loans has greatly reduced the temptation for borrowers to use the commercial paper market. It is

too easy and too convenient to borrow at the banks. Organizations which meet the high standards of the commercial paper market also qualify for very low rates and advantageous terms at the commercial banks. Continuation of easy money rates in the foreseeable future will intensify this competition for loans to the detriment of the commercial paper market.

Recently devised methods of borrowing, particularly term loans, offer increasingly serious competition to commercial paper financing. To be specific, most borrowers prefer the longer periods and the definite due dates offered by term lenders. For the average borrower, the term loan gives greater peace of mind than open-market borrowing with its short maturities and the ever present possibility that changing economic, industrial, or internal conditions may make continued borrowing difficult.

All in all, under present economic conditions and outlook, the prospect for long-range growth of the commercial paper market is considerably less encouraging than that for most other financial institutions.

Suggested Readings

FACTORS AND ACCOUNTS RECEIVABLE FINANCING

Bank Management Commission, *Loans on Accounts Receivable* (Booklet No. 25). New York: American Bankers Association, 1942.

Hess, Arthur Henry, *Accounts Receivable Financing by Banks,* an unpublished M.B.A. thesis submitted to the faculty of the Graduate School of Business Administration, New York University, New York, 1948.

Proceedings (of various annual conventions). New York: National Conference of Commercial Receivable Companies, Inc.

Prochnow, Herbert V. and Foulke, Roy A., *Practical Bank Credit,* Second Edition. New York: Prentice-Hall, Inc., 1950, Chapter 17.

Saulnier, Raymond J. and Jacoby, Neil H., *Accounts Receivable Financing.* New York: National Bureau of Economic Research, 1943.

Silverman, Herbert R., "Factoring as a Financing Device," *Harvard Business Review,* XXVII, Number 5, September 1949.

Weller, Robert T., *The Role of the Factor in Modern Finance,* an unpublished M.B.A. thesis submitted to the Faculty of the Graduate School of Business Administration, New York University, New York, 1948.

COMMERCIAL PAPER

Foster, Major B. and Rodgers, Raymond, *Money and Banking,* Third ed. New York: Prentice-Hall, Inc., 1947.

Greef, Albert O., *The Commercial Paper House in the United States.* Cambridge: Harvard University Press, 1938.

9

Agricultural Financing Institutions

---

by KERMIT O. HANSON

Assistant Professor, College of Business Administration
University of Washington

Nature of Agricultural Credit

THE PROBLEMS encountered in financing agriculture differ in several respects from those of industry and commerce. One of the most obvious differences is the fact that a farm is a home as well as a business: consequently, many loans to farmers are in the nature of both consumption and production loans. Among other major differences are the small size of farms, the location of farms, and the risks peculiar to agriculture. Because of the relatively small size of their units, farmers cannot avail themselves of funds through the sale of bonds or stock; rather, farmers are dependent upon sources of credit where loans can be obtained. The location factor is significant because our vast agricultural areas are at considerable distances from the large metropolitan centers where surplus funds are normally available. Credit institutions are needed to channel funds from the money markets to the small farms which characterize our agriculture.

In addition to risks experienced by business generally, agriculture is subject to serious risks due to weather, disease, insect pests and other natural hazards. Not to be overlooked, in the absence of government price guarantees, is the risk of highly fluctuating prices. Since the demand for many farm products is quite inelastic, the farmer is faced with low unit prices in years of abundant crops; high unit prices prevail only in years of relative scarcity. Furthermore, agricultural prices are sensitive to changes in general business conditions. Agricultural land values tend to fluctuate directly with changes in the prices of agricultural commodities. Speculation has fostered optimistic capitalization of agricultural earnings in prosperous times, with the result that purchasers in

such periods have become saddled with heavy debt loads which all too often lead to foreclosure.

The above factors have caused funds to be more scarce and more costly to agriculture than to urban enterprises which financial institutions were originally developed to serve. Although this differential has prevailed since colonial times, it has become increasingly serious as agriculture has undergone the transition from a subsistence to a commercial stage. The dire need for capital by agriculture, together with the favorable political position of agriculture, resulted in the Federal Farm Loan Act of 1916 which authorized the Federal Land Bank System and the joint stock land banks. Since that time, the federal government has established numerous lending agencies to serve the varied credit requirements of a changing agriculture. During this same period, private sources of credit have improved their services to agriculture. The relationship between governmental and private credit agencies has been both complementary and competitive. One of the functions of this chapter is to highlight some of the issues involved in the question of public and semipublic versus private credit institutions serving agriculture.

Classification of Lenders

Farmers require long-term credit to finance the procurement of land and permanent improvements, and they require intermediate and short-term credit to finance their current productive operations. Farmers also require credit to finance their cooperative organizations. These various credit needs of agriculture are quite distinct and separate. Therefore, in discussing agricultural financing institutions it is convenient to classify them in accordance with the type of credit which they provide, that is (1) long-term, (2) intermediate and short-term, and (3) credit for farmers' cooperatives. Institutions providing (1) long-term and (2) intermediate and short-term credit will be further classified according to whether they are (1) private or (2) public and semipublic. It should be noted that some institutions, such as commercial banks, provide more than one type of agricultural credit and will therefore be treated under each appropriate classification. Further, it should be observed that the Farm Credit Administration now supervises several public and semipublic agencies which provide varied facilities to farmers. Although each of these agencies will be discussed under its proper classification, it may be helpful to consider first the structure of the Farm Credit Administration.

Farm Credit Administration

Origin and development. In 1933 the existing federally-sponsored farm credit facilities were consolidated under the Farm Credit Administration. Major institutions at that time were the federal land banks and the federal intermediate credit banks which had been authorized in 1916 and 1923, respectively. The production credit system and the banks for cooperatives, established in 1933, and the Federal Farm Mortgage Corporation, created in 1934, were also placed under the supervision of the Farm Credit Administration. Although it was originally planned that all federal sources of agricultural credit would be under the Farm Credit Administration, the government has subsequently established such independent agencies as the Commodity Credit Corporation, the Farmers' Home Administration and the Rural Electrification Administration. Nevertheless, the Farm Credit Administration remains the largest federal agricultural credit organization. In 1939 the Farm Credit Administration became a part of the Department of Agriculture.

Organizational structure. Figure 1 shows the organizational structure of the Farm Credit Administration at the central office, district offices, and local level. The central office is located at Washington, D.C. The Secretary of Agriculture is responsible for the general supervision and direction of the Farm Credit Administration, but executive authority is exercised by the governor; he is assisted by deputy governors and by four commissioners who are designated as Land Bank Commissioner, Production Credit Commissioner, Intermediate Credit Commissioner, and Cooperative Bank Commissioner. The governor and the four commissioners are appointed by the President of the United States by and with the advice and consent of the United States Senate. Each of the commissioners supervises the activities of his respective institutions in the 12 districts.

The 12 district boundaries and office locations are shown in Figure 2. It will be noted that district boundaries follow state lines and that districts have been so formed that they include areas of diversified agriculture in order that risk within each district may be minimized. At each district office of the Farm Credit Administration is located a federal land bank, a federal intermediate credit bank, a production credit corporation, and a bank for cooperatives. The activities of these banks are under the direction of a district farm credit board consisting of seven members. Three of these members are appointed by the governor of the Farm Credit Administration and one each is elected by the local national farm loan associations, the local production credit associations, and the farmers' cooperatives borrowing from the banks for cooperatives; the

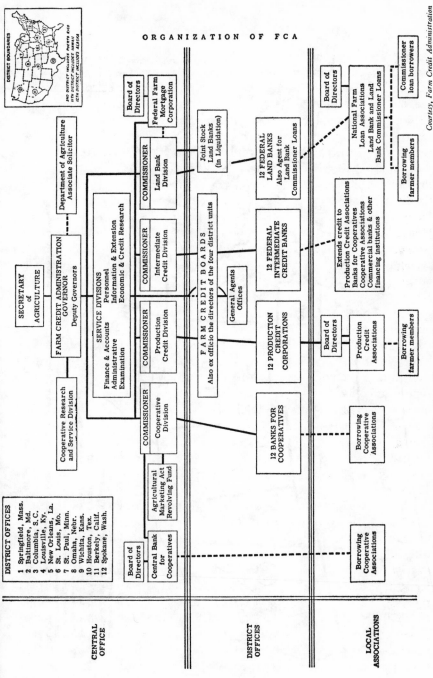

FIGURE 1. *Organization Chart of the Farm Credit Administration*

Courtesy, Farm Credit Administration

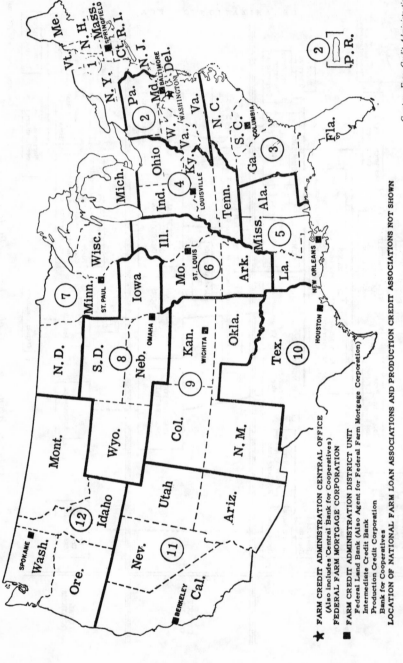

Courtesy, Farm Credit Administration

FIGURE 2. *Farm Credit Administration District Boundaries and Location of District Units*

★ FARM CREDIT ADMINISTRATION CENTRAL OFFICE
(Also includes Central Bank for Cooperatives)
FEDERAL FARM MORTGAGE CORPORATION

■ FARM CREDIT ADMINISTRATION DISTRICT UNIT
Federal Land Bank (Also Agent for Federal Farm Mortgage Corporation)
Intermediate Credit Bank
Production Credit Corporation
Bank for Cooperatives

LOCATION OF NATIONAL FARM LOAN ASSOCIATIONS AND PRODUCTION CREDIT ASSOCIATIONS NOT SHOWN

seventh member is appointed by the governor from three nominees selected by ballot by the national farm loan associations. The board elects
or appoints officers and employees in each of the district agencies; officers
and personnel may be jointly employed by more than one institution.

In each district the activities of the several institutions are coordinated
by a general agent, who acts as representative of the governor. The
general agent is supported by a small staff of specialists and serves on a
district advisory committee together with the presidents of the four
major agencies. Although the four units are coordinated by the general
agent's office and are under the same board of directors, each unit is
independent of the others and is responsible for its designated credit
operations.

Within each district, farmers have organized cooperative associations
in order to obtain credit from Farm Credit Administration agencies.
Farmers desiring long-term loans from federal land banks must become
members of national farm loan associations. Farmers wishing to secure
short-term loans from the production credit system must become members of production credit associations. Farmers' marketing, purchasing,
and service cooperatives may obtain credit from banks for cooperatives.
The federal intermediate credit banks do not make loans directly to
farmers; these institutions are banks of discount which are a source of
funds for public and private institutions making intermediate and short-
term loans to farmers.

Long-Term Credit Sources

PRIVATE

Commercial banks, private mortgage companies, insurance companies,
and miscellaneous lenders are among the oldest institutions which have
provided farm mortgage credit to agriculture. The phrase "long-term
credit" is almost inappropriate when discussing farm real estate loans in
the early periods. Prior to the creation of the Federal Land Bank System
in 1916, most loans secured by mortgages on farm real estate were for
periods of five years or less, thereby necessitating numerous costly re-
newals. In fact, it was the short term of such loans, together with high
interest and commission charges and lack of credit facilities in some
areas, which led to agitation for the establishment of the federal land
banks. However, these institutions have since tailored their lending
policies more to the requirements of agriculture and have retained important positions in the long-term agricultural credit field. Table 1 and
Figure 3 show the farm mortgage holdings of the more important
lenders.

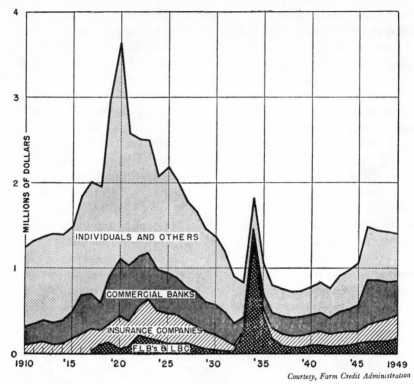

Courtesy, Farm Credit Administration

FIGURE 3. Farm Loans Made and Mortgages Recorded by Principal Lenders, 1910–1949

TABLE 1

FARM MORTGAGE DEBT OUTSTANDING BY PRINCIPAL LENDERS, UNITED STATES, JULY 1, 1950

(Millions of dollars)

Private institutions and others:		
Life insurance companies	$1,281	
Commercial banks	919	
Individuals and others	2,202*	
Total private		$4,402
Public and semipublic institutions:		
Farm Credit Administration		
Federal land banks	$ 935	
Federal Farm Mortgage Corporation.	51	
Farmers' Home Administration	190	
Total public and semipublic		1,176
Total by all lenders		$5,578

*January 1, 1950
Source: *Agricultural Finance Review*, Vol. 13 (November 1950), p. 87.

Commercial banks. These institutions hold an important position in the farm credit field because of their large number and also their volume of business. Since a large majority of the commercial banks in the United States are in towns with less than 10,000 population, they are ideally situated to serve agriculture. In addition to their loan services, they provide such services as checking accounts, savings accounts, safe deposit boxes, and financial counsel. However, as will be brought out more fully in a later section, commercial banks are better able to serve the short-term than the long-term credit requirements of agriculture. Since deposits of their customers constitute their major source of funds, their primary obligation is to their depositors. Consequently, they must maintain a liquid position in order to meet deposit withdrawals of their customers. To protect the interest of depositors, lending is limited in relation to deposits, capital, and other factors including special limitations imposed by boards of directors. Nevertheless, commercial banks in agricultural areas are active in investing a portion of their funds in high grade farm mortgage loans. Many banks have extended their services to farmers by making arrangements to sell or assign farm mortgage loans to life insurance companies, thereby enabling the banks to secure funds quickly if necessary.

Private mortgage companies. For the most part private mortgage companies have served as middlemen between the investors and farmers requiring long-term credit. The importance of these local institutions, which were quite numerous in early periods, is not reflected by data such as presented in Table 1 and Figure 3 because the activities of the private mortgage companies have been primarily to assist insurance companies and banks in distant centers to invest in farm mortgages. Loans made by these private mortgage companies from their own funds have been included in the classification "individuals and others." Some farm mortgage companies acted as local agents for distant investors, and other companies issued debentures backed by farm mortgages. These debentures were sold to investors, and the funds thus obtained were used for additional farm mortgage financing. Some companies issued certificates which represented fractional shares of specific mortgages.

Farm mortgage companies and other middlemen (including local bank officials, lawyers, insurance agents, and others) frequently collected high brokerage fees from both borrowers and lenders. Nevertheless, these companies were very important in the agricultural field during the westward advance of agriculture across the nation. In recent years they have dwindled both as to number and significance because several large insurance companies and the federal land banks have local offices which provide low-cost, long-term farm mortgage credit.

Life insurance companies. Life insurance companies, through various

brokers, were lending money on farm mortgages prior to the Civil War and are today among the largest holders of farm mortgages. However, it must be noted that the major function of life insurance companies is not to provide farm credit; their interest in the agricultural credit field is prompted by a desire to invest their funds safely and for as high a rate of return as possible.[1] Consequently, insurance companies restrict their lending activities to only the best agricultural areas where they compete strongly with the other lenders. During the depression of the early 1930's, insurance companies sharply curtailed their volume of lending; a substantial number of mortgages held by them were refinanced by the federal land banks and the Federal Farm Mortgage Corporation. This temporary withdrawal from the farm mortgage field no doubt reflected concern over the large number of farms which were acquired because of the inability of farmers to meet payments on mortgages. However, with the subsequent recovery of agriculture, insurance companies have shown renewed interest in farm lending and are again highly competitive with other lenders. Many companies have acquired trained personnel to supervise their farm lending activities, and some companies have established branch office systems. Companies also contact farmers through local loan agents who may be institutions or individuals employed on a commission basis. During recent years several companies have made agreements to purchase qualified loans from local banks. This arrangement appears to be beneficial to both parties in that it provides an outlet for investment funds of insurance companies and also improves the liquidity position of local banks. It is likely that insurance companies will continue to be an important source of long-term credit in the better farming areas.

Individuals and others. As shown in Table 1, individuals and others hold the largest volume of farm mortgage loans. Included in this classification are former farm owners who have accepted mortgages from the purchasers, and private investors who purchase farm mortgages from lending agencies. Also included are farm mortgage holdings of various institutions such as schools, fraternal orders, and religious organizations. In a great many cases, borrowers from this group of lenders would be unable to obtain the required amount of funds from a formal lending institution. In some cases lenders extend very favorable terms to borrowers, and, of course, in other cases lenders dictate rather severe terms. Although the availability of credit from these lenders varies with economic conditions, it is probable that they will continue to provide a large portion of the long-term agricultural credit.

---

[1] Life insurance companies have less than 2 per cent of their assets invested in farm mortgages. *Life Insurance Fact Book*, Institute of Life Insurance, 1950, p. 64.

Long-Term Credit Sources

PUBLIC AND SEMIPUBLIC

Private institutions providing long-term agricultural credit have not been designed, adapted, or interested in providing credit in all agricultural areas or in periods of depression. High interest rates, excessive fees, short terms, and lack of adequate credit resulted in a mounting pressure for federal action. Commencing in 1908, under President Theodore Roosevelt, various public and private groups were formed to study the problem. In 1913, both a public and a private commission studied cooperative credit organizations in Europe.[2] In 1916, Congress passed the Federal Farm Loan Act which authorized both the Federal Land Bank System and a system of joint stock land banks. This provision for two competing systems, the one cooperative and the other private, was the result of a compromise between those favoring a federally supervised cooperative system and those desiring a private system with some federal sponsorship. Each of these systems will be discussed in the following sections.

The Federal Land Bank System. Until the Farm Credit Administration was established in 1933, the federal land banks were under the jurisdiction of the Federal Farm Loan Board, which, in turn, was under the Treasury Department. The present organization is shown in Figure 1. The Federal Land Bank System now consists of the Land Bank Division of the central office of the Farm Credit Administration, the 12 district Federal Land Banks, and, within each district, a large number of national farm loans associations whose membership is comprised of farmers who are both the borrowers from and the owners of the system.

The Secretary of the Treasury originally subscribed for most of the capital stock of the 12 Federal Land Banks. Additional capital was provided during the depression in the 1930's. However, the last of this capital was repaid in 1947, and the farmer-borrowers now own the system. In case of an emergency, a $125,000,000 capital fund is available in the U.S. Treasury.

The Federal Land Banks secure funds through the sale of consolidated farm loan bonds. These bonds are the joint and several obligations of the 12 banks and are issued against collateral security of an equal amount of first mortgage farm loans, or United States government obligations owned by the Federal Land Banks. The United States does not guarantee these bonds either as to principal or interest. The vast majority of these bonds are held by commercial banks.

---

[2] The United States Commission was authorized by the United States Congress and the American Commission was delegated by the Southern Commercial Congress.

In addition to providing funds for lending purposes, the Federal Land Banks supervise the operations of the national farm loan associations within their respective districts. National farm loan associations are cooperative organizations formed by 10 or more borrowers and are chartered by the Farm Credit Administration; these associations operate as local lending offices for the Federal Land Banks. Membership can be held only by farmer-borrowers who must buy stock in the association in an amount equal to 5 per cent of their respective loans; the association, in turn, buys an equal amount of stock in the district Federal Land Bank. Each association is managed by a board of directors elected from and by its own members. This board selects the association officers and hires the employees, including the secretary-treasurer who is in charge of the association office and who cannot be a director. The major functions of the associations are to accept and pass upon applications for loans, endorse loans if made, disburse loan funds, make collections, and service all loans. Associations are liable for all loans endorsed and they are required to maintain certain reserves. During the depression of the 1930's, a great many associations became impaired or insolvent. The Federal Land Banks instituted programs of rehabilitation, reorganization, and consolidation of associations. Of the approximately 5,000 associations which had been chartered, over 1,200 were operating in 1949, all of which were solvent and unimpaired.[3]

Federal Land Bank loans may be made only to applicants who are, or will soon be, engaged in agriculture. Major purposes for which loans may be made are to purchase land for agricultural uses, to provide buildings and farm improvements, to liquidate debts incurred in farming operations, and to provide funds for general long-term agricultural uses. Most Federal Land Bank loans have been made for the purpose of refinancing other loans and indebtedness. All loans must be secured by first mortgages. The term of loans may range from five to 40 years; terms of around 33 years have been most common. The size of loans was originally limited to $10,000, but in 1923 the limit was increased to $25,000; in 1933 the Land Bank Commissioner was authorized to grant special approval for loans up to $50,000, and this ceiling was raised to $100,000 in 1949. Initially, loans could not exceed 50 per cent of the appraised value of the land plus 20 per cent of the appraised value of permanent, insured improvements; in 1933 appraisals were placed on the basis of normal values rather than current values, and in 1945 loans were permitted up to 65 per cent of the normal agricultural value of the

---

[3] For statistics pertaining to the organization and operation of Farm Credit Administration institutions, the reader is referred to Farm Credit Administration *Annual Reports;* the *Agricultural Finance Review,* published by the Bureau of Agricultural Economics, USDA, includes data pertaining to both public and private lenders.

farm. Appraisals are made by land bank appraisers who are appointed by the Farm Credit Administration and, as public officials, are not under the jurisdiction of the Federal Land Banks. This arrangement serves to protect the interest of the borrowers and bondholders as well as the Federal Land Bank System.

Interest rates to borrowers, which are influenced by the interest rates the Federal Land Banks must pay on their consolidated bonds, cannot exceed 6 per cent. Since 1935, the prevailing interest rate on new loans has been 4 per cent, and in 1944 the Federal Land Banks reduced the rate on all outstanding loans to 4 per cent. A few of the banks have very recently raised their interest rates on new loans to 4½ per cent. From 1933 to 1944 Congress granted an interest subsidy to Federal Land Bank borrowers; that is, the borrowers were authorized to pay a rate less than the contract rate of interest. Since the Federal Land Banks are dependent upon their earnings to meet their expenses (including interest payments to bondholders at a fixed rate), the government reimbursed the banks for the amount of interest reduction granted the borrowers.

All loans are repayable on an amortized plan providing for regular annual or semiannual installments. However, during the depression of the 1930's the farmer-borrowers were greatly benefited by a liberal land bank policy of granting reamortizations, extensions, and deferments on loans. This policy was made possible by U.S. Treasury subscriptions of paid-in surplus equal to the amount of loan payments extended or deferred. Also developed were variable and suspended payment plans geared to the borrowers' income patterns. Many private lenders have followed the lead of the Federal Land Banks in providing long-term amortized loans.

The number and volume of loans made by the Federal Land Banks has fluctuated considerably. After the first bank was chartered in 1917, there was a spurt of lending activity, particularly in those areas where interest rates were high. In 1920 the banks virtually ceased operations pending a Supreme Court test of their constitutionality.[4] Lending activities were resumed in 1921 and loans outstanding continued to increase until 1930, when new loans were exceeded by payments and foreclosures. Lack of funds and lack of authority to make second mortgage loans severely handicapped the ability of the banks to serve agriculture in the early 1930's. However, Congress appropriated additional capital funds in 1932, and in 1933 Congress authorized Land Bank Commissioner loans which could be made on second mortgages; these loans will be discussed in the section on the Federal Farm Mortgage Cor-

---

[4] Howard H. Preston has given the issue of constitutionality thorough treatment in his article "The Federal Farm Loan Case," *Journal of Political Economy*, Vol. XXIX, No. 6, June 1921, pp. 433-454.

poration. As a result of this action, the Federal Land Banks undertook a huge program of refinancing agricultural debt during the period from 1933 to 1935. A peak of $2,702,000,000 of loans outstanding was reached in 1935. This amount has declined substantially since that time primarily because of the improved agricultural conditions, the higher prices of agricultural land, and the increased competition from private lenders. Currently, the banks' policy of lending on normal values is under considerable discussion. Normal values, based on 1909–14 farm prices, have been used to counteract the tendency in depression periods to lend amounts insufficient for agriculture's needs and in prosperous periods to lend amounts in excess of agriculture's ability to repay. This policy, initiated by the Federal Land Banks, has been adopted in various forms by many private lenders. However, in the current period of prosperity, many private lenders, feeling that values based on 1909–14 prices are no longer realistic even for a long-run period, have shifted their concept of normal upward.

Joint stock land banks. These institutions, authorized along with the Federal Land Banks by the Federal Farm Loan Act in 1916, were placed in liquidation in 1933.[5] The Federal Farm Loan Board was empowered to charter as joint stock land banks those private mortgage companies which had a minimum of $250,000 capital stock; each joint stock land bank was authorized to obtain funds through the sale of bonds which were tax exempt but were in no way guaranteed by the government. In contrast with Federal Land Banks, the joint stock land banks were liable only for their own bonds. The joint stock land banks had several advantages over the Federal Land Banks; borrowers faced no stock requirements and less delay in negotiating loans; the banks could select their own territory and could make larger loans; the banks could lend to all farm owners rather than only to owner-operators.[6] However, the boom period in which the joint stock land banks operated, combined with their small capital reserve requirements, led to extreme financial difficulties in the early 1930's. During the period from 1917 to 1933, 88 joint stock land banks had been incorporated, but only 44 were in existence when Congress ordered liquidation in 1933; liquidation was completed in 1950.

Federal Farm Mortgage Corporation. In 1933, the urgent need for agricultural credit resulting from low farm prices, the financial distress of private sources of agricultural credit, and the inability of the Federal

---

[5] William G. Murray has an excellent discussion on joint stock land banks in his book, *Agricultural Finance*. Ames, Iowa: Iowa State College Press, 1947, Chapter 21.

[6] A joint stock land bank could operate in the state in which it was organized plus any one adjoining state; it could lend as much as $50,000 to one borrower, and total loan volume was limited to 15 times the amount of its capital and surplus.

Land Banks to meet farmers' long-term credit requirements, prompted Congress to pass the Emergency Farm Mortgage Act authorizing Land Bank Commissioner loans. Initially the Treasury provided emergency funds of $200,000,000. In 1934 Congress established the Federal Farm Mortgage Corporation, which could issue bonds guaranteed by the government as a means of obtaining additional funds for loans. The Federal Farm Mortgage Corporation was also authorized to buy Federal Land Bank bonds and to make direct loans to Federal Land Banks.

Loans to individual farmers were limited to $7,500 (originally $5,000), and together with any first mortgage loan, could equal 75 per cent of the normal value of the farm property. Loans were secured by first or second mortgages on real or personal farm property. Although the loans were direct loans from the Land Bank Commissioner and required no purchase of stock by the borrowers, the Federal Land Banks acted as agents for the Land Bank Commissioner.

Designed as a depression measure, the bulk of Land Bank Commissioner loans were made in the first few years following authorization. With the passing of the need for this source of credit, Congress allowed the authority to make these loans expire on July 1, 1947. However, the Federal Farm Mortgage Corporation still exists; it still has loans outstanding; and it is available to resume lending operations if authorized by Congress.

The Farmers' Home Administration. Established in 1946, the Farmers' Home Administration is essentially a consolidation of various welfare and rehabilitation programs initiated by the government as far back as 1933. Since this institution provides both long-term and short-term credit, some of its functions will be discussed in the section which treats short-term credit sources.

The Bankhead-Jones Act of July, 1937, authorized the Secretary of Agriculture to use appropriated government funds to aid farm tenants and a few other eligible persons to purchase farms. This program was to be administered by the Farm Security Administration, which became a part of the Farmers' Home Administration in 1946. The organizational structure of the Farm Security Administration consisted of county, district, state, and 12 regional offices; the latter offices were eliminated when the Farmers' Home Administration was established.

Loans are made only to applicants who are unable to obtain credit from other public or private sources. Loans may be obtained to enlarge undersized farms as well as to purchase efficient family-size farms. Since 1946 veterans have been given preference. The loans, which cannot exceed $12,000, are to be repaid over a term of 40 years at 4 per cent interest. The Farmers' Home Administration is also authorized to insure mortgages on loans by private lenders which are similar to its own loans.

The Farmers' Home Administration is a welfare agency which supplements but does not compete with the institutions discussed in the previous sections.

Intermediate and Short-Term Credit Sources

PRIVATE

Agriculture requires intermediate and short-term credit for production purposes, that is, for working capital. Although intermediate credit generally refers to loans having terms from nine months to three years, whereas short-term credit refers to loans with terms of less than nine months, it is extremely difficult to draw a sharp line between these two types of credit. Furthermore, since both types of loans are used to provide operating capital, it is convenient to consider them jointly. Credit advances of the more important lenders in this field are shown in Table 2.

TABLE 2

INTERMEDIATE AND SHORT-TERM CREDIT OUTSTANDING BY
PRINCIPAL LENDERS, UNITED STATES, JULY 1, 1950

(Millions of dollars)

Private institutions:		
Commercial banks		$2,898
Public and semipublic institutions:		
Farm Credit Administration		
Federal intermediate credit banks	$ 58	
Production credit associations	527	
Farmers' Home Administration		
Production and subsistence loans	279	
Disaster loans	37	
Emergency crop and feed loans	61	
Commodity Credit Corporation	340	
Total public and semipublic		1,302
Total by all lending institutions		$4,200

Source: *Agricultural Finance Review*, Vol. 13 (November 1950), p. 96.

Commercial banks. Commercial banks lead all other lenders in providing agriculture with intermediate and short-term credit. Located in communities throughout the nation, commercial banks are ideally situated to serve the farmers with a minimum of red tape. Because banks must retain a relatively high degree of liquidity in order to meet depositors' withdrawals, they are better able to provide short-term credit than long-term credit secured by real estate mortgages. Loans are usually granted for periods of a year or less and are made on both a secured and

an unsecured basis, depending upon the borrower's credit standing in the community. However, the commercial banks have not always been in a position to provide intermediate and short-term credit where and when it was required. During periods of depressed farm prices, farmers not only have been unable to repay their old production loans, but also they have required additional credit for working capital. This situation, which became widespread in the early 1920's and again in the 1930's, was a contributing factor leading to the establishment of the Federal Intermediate Credit Bank system in 1923 and the production credit system in 1933. Commercial bank short-term credit has been deficient in areas (1) where risk is high, (2) where loans are too small to be profitable, (3) where farmers' individual loan requirements are too large for small country banks to handle, and (4) where bank deposits are inadequate for loans needed. Nevertheless, it is likely that commercial banks will continue to be the most important single source of intermediate and short-term agricultural credit.

Merchants and dealers. Short-term credit is frequently extended by merchants and dealers in connection with their sales of machinery and supplies to farmers. Inasmuch as merchants are primarily interested in sales, their credit advances are usually costly and are not tailored to the individual farmer's needs. Also, this type of credit has proven hazardous on occasion to the merchants. Although this source of credit was very important in early periods, it has declined with the development of institutions which can better serve agriculture's short-term credit requirements.

Cattle loan companies. These organizations came into prominence in the early years of the twentieth century.[7] Local banks were unable to provide the increasing amount of intermediate and short-term credit required by the expanding cattle industry in the West. Cattle loan companies served as middlemen between eastern sources of capital and the western ranchers. Some companies were independent corporations, but the larger companies were usually affiliated with a large bank in a livestock marketing center. This latter arrangement enabled banks to circumvent the limitations on bank loans and to make unlimited advances through the medium of cattle loan companies. Packing houses also found it profitable to control cattle loan companies.

In the prosperous years during and immediately following World War I, cattle loan companies increased in numbers and in amount of credit advanced. Much of this activity was speculative and unsound, and a great many of the companies failed when prices collapsed in the early 1920's. Agitation for improved intermediate credit financing led to the

---

[7] Forest M. Larmer has presented a very complete account of livestock financing in his book *Financing the Livestock Industry*. New York: The Macmillan Co., 1926.

establishment of the Federal Intermediate Credit Bank System in 1923. Although this system provided an outlet for loan paper held by cattle loan companies, the unsound financial structure of many of the companies, together with the improvement of other sources of credit, has led to the dissolution of all but a very few companies.

Intermediate and Short-Term Credit Sources

PUBLIC AND SEMIPUBLIC

Federal Intermediate Credit Bank system. As indicated in the preceding sections, private sources of intermediate and short-term credit were placed under severe financial stress following the price depression of 1921 and were unable to provide the credit required by agriculture. In 1923, 12 Federal Intermediate Credit Banks were created at the same locations as the 12 Federal Land Banks. These Federal Intermediate Credit Banks do not make direct loans to farmers; they purchase or discount agricultural loan paper held by direct lending institutions.

Unlike the Federal Land Banks, which are now borrower-owned, the Federal Intermediate Credit Banks are entirely owned by the government and are required to pay a franchise tax on annual earnings to the United States. Funds for lending operations are obtained from the sale of consolidated debenture bonds, which are the joint and several obligations of the 12 banks and which are supported by the agricultural paper purchased or discounted from direct lenders. The government does not guarantee these bonds. A Federal Intermediate Credit Bank may also obtain funds by borrowing from other Federal Intermediate Credit Banks or from any other source.

These banks may discount or loan on notes which mature in three years or less from the date discounted or accepted. The discount rate may not exceed the interest rate on the most recent issue of debentures by more than 1 per cent, except by special approval of the governor of the Farm Credit Administration.

The Federal Intermediate Credit Banks did not develop as anticipated. Some of the reasons why private institutions did not avail themselves of this source of credit were (1) the inacceptability of their loans for discounting; (2) the narrow margin of 1½ per cent (later raised to 4 per cent) by which the rate charged farmers was allowed to exceed the rate charged by the Federal Intermediate Credit Banks; and (3) the ability of sound private banks to discount acceptable paper with other private banks.

The depression of the 1930's brought increased activity to the Federal Intermediate Credit Banks. However, the widespread failures of com-

mercial banks deprived the Federal Intermediate Credit Banks of the outlets needed in order to provide agriculture with required credit. It was as a consequence of this that such institutions as the regional agricultural credit corporations and the production credit system were established. Since 1933, the Federal Intermediate Credit Banks have principally served the production credit associations and the banks for cooperatives. These services will be discussed in subsequent sections.

Regional agricultural credit corporations. The Emergency Relief and Construction Act of 1932 authorized the Reconstruction Finance Corporation to establish a regional agricultural credit corporation in any farm credit district. Accordingly, 12 corporations were created, with all capital stock being held by the Reconstruction Finance Corporation; most of this capital was repaid in the 1930's.

In 1933 the supervision of the corporations was transferred to the Farm Credit Administration, and in 1934 the corporations were retired from active lending because of the provision of a permanent short-term credit source in the newly established production credit system. The district corporations were merged into the Regional Agricultural Credit Corporation of Washington, D.C., and, although lending activities were not regularly engaged in, some emergency livestock loans and fruit loans were made in 1937 and 1941, respectively.

To aid production for war effort, lending activities were resumed in 1943. In 1949, the corporation was abolished and its assets, liabilities, and records were transferred to the Secretary of Agriculture, who delegated administration to the Farmers' Home Administration. The functions of the corporation can be revived as an emergency measure when required credit is not available from other sources.

The production credit system. Established by the Farm Credit Act of 1933, this system consists of the Production Credit Division in the central office of the Farm Credit Administration, 12 district production credit corporations, and over 500 production credit associations comprised of farmer-borrowers. These institutions were established to provide outlets for Federal Intermediate Credit Bank funds which were sorely needed by agriculture. As mentioned in earlier sections, it was the financial distress and inadequacy of private sources of credit which contributed to this situation.

The 12 production credit corporations, which Congress capitalized with appropriated funds, were made responsible for promoting the organization of the local production credit associations, for providing part of the capitalization, and for supervising the activities of the associations when in operation.

Production credit associations are formed by 10 or more borrowers and have two classes of stock. Class A stock is issued for capital advanced

by a production credit corporation and is non-voting; class B stock is purchased by borrowers in an amount equal to 5 per cent of the loans; each stockholder has only one vote. The two classes of stock share alike in dividends, but Class A is preferred in case of liquidation. Unlike national farm loan associations, which must buy stock in the Federal Land Banks, the production credit associations do not buy stock in the production credit corporations. Associations are now more than two-thirds borrower-owned. Each association is managed by a board of directors elected from and by its members. Many associations now have offices which are joint or adjacent to national farm loan association offices.

Associations provide loans used by farmers as working capital, that is, for financing crops and livestock programs, for procurement and maintenance of equipment, and for refinancing short-term obligations. Ordinarily, first liens on livestock, equipment, or crops are required as security for loans. The term of loans is usually one year or less, although it may be renewed. Loans are budgeted; funds are advanced to borrowers as they are needed and the borrowers pay interest only on the amounts outstanding. The rate of interest may not exceed by more than 4 per cent the rediscount rate charged by the Federal Intermediate Credit Banks. Production credit associations obtain funds by endorsing borrowers' notes and rediscounting these notes, accompanied by related loan papers, with the district Federal Intermediate Credit Bank.

Production credit associations have experienced substantial financial growth, particularly in the West and South; in this connection it may be observed that loans to ranchers in the West are frequently too large for local banks to carry, whereas many loans in the South are too small to be attractive to private sources of credit.

In recent prosperous years, commercial banks with adequate funds in good agricultural areas, such as the Midwest corn belt, have strongly resented the competition of production credit associations. However, it is likely that commercial bankers in these areas will continue to provide the bulk of the short-term credit during good times; commercial banks provide numerous services for customers, in addition to granting loans with a minimum of red tape, and the locations of commercial banks are more accessible than are the relatively few production credit associations, which are usually located at considerable distances from many farmers.

Production credit associations have been significant because of their interest rate competition, their availability in periods of financial distress, their emphasis upon borrowers' ability to pay rather than upon mere chattel security, and also because of their cooperative character.

Farmers' Home Administration. As stated previously, in connection

with long-term agricultural credit, the creation of the Farmers' Home Administration in 1946 was essentially a consolidation of various existing short-term and long-term credit programs of a welfare nature. Loans under this authority can be made, subject to various limitations, only to those borrowers who are unable to obtain needed credit from other private or public sources. Loans are made from appropriated funds.

Loans with maturities up to five years may be made to finance operating equipment and supplies, including family living expenses and medical care. An individual borrower may obtain advances of not more than $3,500 in any one year and he is limited to a total loan of $5,000. The rate of interest is 5 per cent on the unpaid principal. Liens are usually placed on the property purchased with the loan, but the main security is the borrower's honesty and ability.

Commodity Credit Corporation. In 1933 this agency was created by executive order to make loans to farmers who stored commodities under the provisions of the government's crop and price control program. It is not a lending institution in the same sense as are commercial banks or production credit associations. The Commodity Credit Corporation was originally an independent agency capitalized by the Treasury and the Reconstruction Finance Corporation; in 1939 it was placed under the Department of Agriculture.

As a means of supporting farm prices, the Corporation establishes a loan value on commodities (corn, cotton, wheat, tobacco, rice, and so on) covered by the current control program; then it makes loans based on this value to producers who are operating under the control program. Actually, most loans are made by private lending institutions under an agreement whereby the Corporation agrees to purchase the note when it comes due.

Under this program, farmers are granted non-recourse loans at 3 per cent interest in exchange for a chattel mortgage on the security. Principal advances have been on corn, cotton, and wheat. If the market price is below the loan "price," the borrower may liquidate his obligation by delivering the commodity—and with no interest charge; the Corporation absorbs the loss. If the market price happens to be above the loan "price," the farmer sells his commodity, repays his loan and interest charge, and retains the differential. In 1948, this plan was modified to permit the farmer to obtain an option to deliver a stated maximum amount of a commodity within a certain period, thereby eliminating much of the paper work involved in making a formal loan.

Instituted as a temporary depression measure, the Commodity Credit Corporation's life has been extended through the last several years of prosperity. Some observers feel strongly that its existence and the extent

of its activities are dependent more upon political than financial exigencies.

Credit Sources for Farmers' Cooperatives

Farmers have extended their activities to include ownership of a wide variety of marketing, purchasing, and service cooperatives. Farmer members provide a portion of the capital required by their cooperatives, but additional funds must frequently be borrowed to finance buildings, equipment, operating costs, and storage of commodities. Farmers' cooperatives, as a whole, have experienced difficulty in obtaining required funds. After considerable agitation, the government has adopted a policy of fostering the development of farmers' cooperatives and has provided credit facilities to supplement private sources.

Commercial banks. These institutions have been active in providing credit to farmers' cooperatives, particularly to the larger and stronger cooperatives. In lending to cooperatives, as in lending to individual farmers, commercial banks have advantages over government institutions in that they are located in the communities which they serve; they can negotiate loans more rapidly; and in some cases they have been able to charge lower rates of interest to well-established cooperatives. For the most part, a harmonious relationship exists between the commercial banks and the federally sponsored banks for cooperatives; in fact, the commercial banks are an important source of funds for the banks for cooperatives.

Agricultural Marketing Act, 1929. Although the Federal Intermediate Credit Banks were authorized to make loans for limited purposes to farmers' cooperatives, this means of providing funds was inadequate. In 1929 the Agricultural Marketing Act created the Federal Farm Board, whose functions included lending to farmers' cooperatives and to stabilization corporations. Congress provided a revolving fund of $500,000,000. The Federal Farm Board made numerous advances, especially on cotton, but its price stabilization activities were pronounced failures. In May 1933, by executive order, the outstanding loans and the balance of the revolving fund were placed under the administration of the Farm Credit Administration.

Banks for cooperatives. The Farm Credit Act of June 1933 authorized the governor of the Farm Credit Administration to charter a Central Bank for Cooperatives and 12 district banks for cooperatives.

The original capital consisted of the revolving fund balances transferred from the Federal Farm Board. Capital stock must be purchased by cooperatives which obtain loans. Banks for cooperatives may obtain funds for lending activities from Federal Intermediate Credit Banks,

other banks for cooperatives, and commercial banks. The Central Bank for Cooperatives may also issue debentures; however, it was not until January 1950 that the first issue of these debentures was offered to investors.

Banks for cooperatives are authorized to make three types of loans: (1) commodity loans, with terms usually from three to nine months, secured by approved commodities in storage; (2) short-term operating capital loans, usually secured by liens on equipment, real estate, or inventories; and (3) facility loans for acquisition or development of physical facilities. Facility loans are secured by first liens on physical property and usually mature in less than 10 years, although this period may extend up to 20 years. Interest rates may not exceed 6 per cent per year, and interest is charged only on the unpaid principal balances. The governor of the Farm Credit Administration determines the interest rates; in July 1950, rates were $2\frac{1}{4}$ per cent for commodity loans, 3 per cent for operating loans, and 4 per cent for facility loans.

To be eligible for a loan, a cooperative must meet these requirements: (1) it must be operated for the mutual benefit of its members and must do more business with members than nonmembers; (2) no member may have more than one vote, regardless of the amount of stock he may own; and (3) the association must limit its dividends to not more than 8 per cent per year. Cooperatives which are granted loans must buy stock in the bank for cooperatives equal to 1 per cent of the amount of a commodity loan and 5 per cent of the amount of an operating or facility loan. Loans to cooperatives operating in more than one farm credit district (or loans which are too large to be handled by a district bank for cooperatives) are made by the Central Bank for Cooperatives; the Central Bank may also participate with district banks in making large loans. Banks for cooperatives are in a position to provide more supervision and technical advice to borrowers than are most private lenders.

The banks for cooperatives did not progress as rapidly as anticipated prior to World War II; either cooperatives were not eligible, did not require financing, or they could obtain required credit from commercial banks. However, a substantial increase in loans occurred commencing in 1940. Although some of this increase was due to wartime conditions, it appears that farmers' cooperatives will continue to require large amounts of credit because of the growth and integration of individual cooperatives which are serving an agriculture that is becoming more and more commercialized.

The Rural Electrification Administration. This administration was established with independent status in 1935, but, together with the Farm Credit Administration and Commodity Credit Corporation, it was placed under the Department of Agriculture in 1939. The purpose of the agency

was to facilitate much needed electrification of rural areas by making loans available to private or public utilities, cooperative groups, municipalities, individuals, or others.

Although it was originally anticipated that most loans would be made to existing utility companies, such has not been the case; the program did not gain momentum until farmers were assisted in forming cooperative associations. These associations have obtained the bulk of all loans made. As some evidence of the progress of this program, it may be noted that farms in the United States receiving central station service increased from slightly over 10 per cent in 1935 to almost 80 per cent in 1949.

Loans may be made for the entire cost of plant and line construction. Loans are amortized over a period of 35 years at a rate of 2 per cent interest. Funds for the program are appropriated annually by Congress. In 1949, Congress amended the original act to provide a similar program for rural telephone systems, which are sadly lacking in certain rural areas.

Appraisal of Agricultural Financing Institutions

The past 35 years have witnessed a marked improvement in credit facilities available to agriculture. In the long-term credit field, farmers had been plagued with high interest rates, high loan fees, short loan terms, and almost complete lack of credit in some areas all of the time and in most areas during depressions. The Federal Land Banks, which began active operations in 1917, have pioneered long-term amortized loans at low uniform interest rates, and the use of the normal agricultural value concept in making appraisals. These and other modifications beneficial to agriculture have been adopted in large part by private lending institutions providing long-term credit to farmers. Commercial banks, with their primary responsibility to depositors, probably will continue to make some funds available to better risks in good areas. Life insurance companies, whose primary interests also are in other fields, are likely to continue their strong competition for long-term loans in the best agricultural areas, especially during periods of prosperity. The Federal Land Banks and their national farm loan associations, which are cooperatives now wholly owned by their borrower-members, are a competitive stabilizing influence in those areas served by other lenders and are important sources of credit in high-risk areas and during depression periods.

In the intermediate and short-term credit field, it is likely that commercial banks will continue to be the most important source of credit. However, commercial banks in the past have not been an adequate source of short-term credit during periods of financial strain. This situa-

tion has been considerably alleviated by the production credit associations whose funds are obtained by discounting borrowers' notes with the Federal Intermediate Credit Banks. Production credit associations have introduced better loan budgeting, more limitation of advances to productive purposes, and lower interest charges. Opponents of these institutions, particularly in areas where private lenders have a good supply of available funds, argue that a subsidized production credit system constitutes an unwarranted infringement upon their operations. It has been suggested that this argument would not be valid if production credit associations charged interest rates which would make the associations self-supporting if their loan volume was maintained comparable to that of similar private institutions.[8] In this connection, it should be noted that the loan volume of production credit associations declines relative to that of commercial banks during prosperous periods. Production credit associations are serving a real need in some areas in periods of prosperity as well as in depression, and it appears that farmers in all areas may desire to have the production credit system available for emergency periods.

Credit requirements of farmers' cooperatives appear to be quite adequately met by commercial banks and the banks for cooperatives. During times when funds are abundant, much of the credit for the larger cooperatives is provided by commercial banks at very low interest rates. In fostering the development of farmers' cooperative organizations, the banks for cooperatives provide much technical information and service not ordinarily available at commercial banks; and the banks for cooperatives provide considerable credit to smaller cooperatives which are unable to obtain low-cost commercial bank loans. Some private businesses in competition with farmers' cooperatives regard the financial and technical aid extended by the banks for cooperatives as undesirable subsidization. Discussions of this issue involve social and economic objectives as well as financial considerations.

The Rural Electrification Administration has provided a large amount of credit in a field not served by private lending institutions. The program has unquestionably improved living standards in rural areas. The economic soundness of the program will be determined in years to come by the ability of the local cooperatives to repay the loans.

The Farmers' Home Administration and the Commodity Credit Corporation are not competitive institutions financing agriculture. These agencies must be appraised more on the basis of their welfare and political merits than on their financial soundness.

---

[8] Murray R. Benedict, "The Relation of Public to Private Lending Agencies (in Agriculture) and Recent Trends in Their Development," *Journal of Farm Economics,* Vol. XXVII, No. 1, Feb. 1945, pp. 100-101.

In summary, it may be noted that agricultural financing institutions supervised or operated by the federal government tend to fall into two classifications: those institutions which are operated on sound financial principles (such as the Federal Land Banks) and those agencies which make loans on above-normal risks in the pursuit of welfare objectives. This distinction should always be recognized when evaluating the merits of the several institutions.

Suggested Readings

Agricultural Finance Review published annually by the Bureau of Agricultural Economics, United States Department of Agriculture.

Annual Reports, Bulletins, and *Circulars* published by the Farm Credit Administration, United States Department of Agriculture.

Baird, F. and Benner, C. L., *Ten Years of Federal Intermediate Credits.* Washington, D.C.: The Brookings Institution, 1933.

Butz, Earl L., *The Production Credit System for Farmers.* Washington, D.C.: The Brookings Institution, 1944.

Duggan, I. W. and Battles, Ralph U., *Financing the Farm Business.* New York: John Wiley and Sons, Inc., 1950.

Galloway, George B. and Associates, *Major Government Lending Agencies.* The Library of Congress Legislative Reference Service, Public Affairs Bulletin No. 57. Washington, D.C., June 1947, pp. 1-117.

Larmer, Forrest M., *Financing the Livestock Industry.* New York: The Macmillan Co., 1926.

Murray, William G., *Agricultural Finance,* Second Edition, revised. Ames, Iowa: The Iowa State College Press, 1947.

Norton, L. J., *Financing Agriculture,* Revised. Danville, Illinois: The Interstate, 1948.

Sparks, E. S., *History and Theory of Agricultural Credit in the United States.* New York: Thomas Y. Crowell Co., 1932.

10

The Commodity Exchange

by HERBERT SPERO

Associate Professor of Economics, the City College of New York

Functions and Predecessors

A COMMODITY EXCHANGE is an organized market whose members trade in contracts requiring delivery of a stated amount of specified goods at fixed future dates. These exchanges, originating just prior to the Revolutionary War, have played a significant and important role in world trade markets. The first American exchange, organized in 1752, was located in lower New York City and dealt in domestic produce. Although the Board of Trade of the City of Chicago was officially established in 1848, it first resembled an organized commodity exchange in 1865. Future trading in wheat, corn, oats, rye, barley, soybeans, cotton, cottonseed oil, lard, and other pork products is now the regular order of business of the Chicago Board of Trade, currently the outstanding commodity exchange in the world.

The commodity market, termed an exchange in Great Britain and a bourse on the Continent, preceded the modern commodity exchange. These markets, successors to and more effective than the medieval fair, originally handled a variety of commodities. Subsequently the markets were divided into specialized trading centers, each functioning under an individualized set of rules, although the centers did not manifest the characteristics of the modern commodity exchange.

Commodity or Physical Markets

Commodity markets are physical markets located in major production and transportation centers through which commodities move on their way to market. Rail and water terminal points from which a commodity

is sent to the big trading centers of the world like New York, Chicago, Kansas City, Memphis, Winnipeg, Cairo, and Liverpool, are the *primary physical markets*. Large urban trading centers like the aforementioned cities are the *central markets*.

The earliest commodity markets in the United States dealt in the country's major farm products—tobacco, cotton, and grains. Today, innumerable local physical markets dot the economic landscape and ship their products on to central physical markets which, in turn, distribute the products throughout the nation and the world.

Two types of transactions are effected in the physical markets: *spot* and *forward* commodity purchases and sales. A spot purchase or sale is an actual or cash deal for a commodity *identical to a sample shown the buyer*. A buyer can accumulate a small or a large quantity of goods as his needs dictate; he may buy only a few bags of corn to feed his chickens, or he may buy several thousand bushels of wheat for conversion into flour. When a farmer sells a physical quantity of wheat to a grain elevator or warehouse, he is selling cash wheat. A forward transaction requires delivery of certain quantities of specified or standard grades at some future date at an agreed upon price. Buying and selling for forward delivery originated in the United State before the Civil War:

> Back before the War between the States each individual who at any time had to own wheat bore the full risk while it was in his hands. Because the farmer was the original holder, he bore the risk up to the minute he sold his grain. Because farmers brought their wheat to market in a very short period, the market was glutted during the harvest season and prices took a beating. When the year's crop was about used up supplies often became short and prices high. Millers either had more wheat offered to them at harvest time than they could use, or they had to pay premium prices to stay in business toward the end of the crop year.
>
> To protect themselves from these violent seasonal swings, the practice grew up of buying and selling for "forward delivery." This simply means that a miller would, for example, agree on May 1 to buy 5,000 bushels of wheat for 90 cents a bushel to be delivered by August 1. In other words, the buyer and seller both agreed on a price today for a sale that would not be finally completed until three months from now.
>
> Though this was far from an ideal solution of the price problem, it did make it possible for the miller to do some planning ahead with reasonable assurance that skyrocketing prices would not wreck his business. The seller, however, was still faced with the possibility that prices would rise and that he would be forced to deliver wheat worth a lot more than he had agreed to sell it for. For example, if he sold 5,000 bushels "forward" at 90 cents a bushel and then had to deliver three months later when wheat was worth, say $1.10 a bushel he would have lost a possible profit of $1,000.
>
> The seller did not like it. Consequently, the practice grew up of buying and selling these "forward" contracts so that the holder of a contract who did not want to stand the risk could transfer it to someone who was willing to carry it. (Remember that back in the 19th Century, just as today, some-

body, willy-nilly, was forced to carry the risk. Dealings in "forward" contracts were a partial and crude means of shifting part of the risk from someone who did not want to carry it to someone who was willing to.) [1]

The Role of the Broker and Dealer

The major traders in the physical markets are brokers and dealers. The qualified brokers are familiar with all phases of commodity trade and market activities; these men are the agents or representatives for producers and local dealers in the primary markets or for dealers and converters in the central markets. Assuming no financial risk, the brokers receive a commission for marketing produce to dealers or converters who examine the spot samples that the brokers have on hand. Commission agents perform functions similar to those of the brokers. Dealers, basing their operations on price forecasts, are the risk takers in commodity markets. In the physical markets dealers help to minimize the chance of loss to both the raw material producer and the manufacturer. Local dealers buy from producers for forward delivery and assume the risk of a loss if the market for the purchased commodity drops. Local dealers sell to central market and export dealers who, in turn, sell to converters. The latter is thus assured of a supply of goods of a definite quality at a definite price. The converter is thus relieved of the risk of an advance in raw material prices.

Dealers are vital if producers are to be encouraged to produce and yet to avoid the risks of the market, of weather and soil influences, of foreign exchange fluctuations, and of turns in the wheel of business fortune. (A producer may not turn out the exact quality and quantity of goods he agreed to deliver; the purchaser may be bankrupt by the date of payment for the commodities; shifts in the values of foreign currencies and in the credit standings of foreign customers may threaten the advisability of foreign commitments.) Similarly, dealers protect manufacturers against risks peculiar to the manufacturers' calling. (What if the demand for a commodity purchased in a primary or central trading area improves, and the seller shifts deliveries to contractors willing to pay more? What if the seller does not deliver the quality of goods agreed upon?)

Since dealers usually finance both producers and their buying customers, the dealers assume a credit risk if defaults on their credit extensions occur. Credit risks grow out of a forward seller's default on his contract with a dealer-buyer who then must cover his sale to a converter at a higher market price. From a manufacturer's default on a purchase contract, a loss may result that forces the dealer to liquidate inventory on a declining market.

---

[1] *How to Buy and Sell Commodities*, a Merrill Lynch, Pierce, Fenner & Beane publication, March 1949, p. 5.

Besides the assumption of the credit risk and the loss which may be caused by an unforeseen price change, the dealer has to contend with still another speculative risk. He may buy up small amounts of a commodity for delivery to large buyers, or he may purchase commodities from large central market dealers for delivery in small parcels to small buyers. What if prices go against the dealer by rising while the dealer buys for large purchasers who contracted to pay a fixed price, and falling below the agreed price on forward purchases by small buyers?

Need for Commodity Exchanges

The assumption of the price and credit risk requires a large amount of capital to be wielded by a large number of risk-taking dealers. The lack of adequately capitalized dealers penalizes producers, converters, and consumers. Uncertain future prices necessitate a greater profit margin for the producer and converter and a higher price to the consumer. The constant overhanging threat of fluctuating prices hampers production and plagues the buying public. The weaknesses of the commodity markets have been clearly stated:

> . . . in the physical markets there is no continuous market sufficiently large to absorb all potential transactions for forward deliveries without sharp disruption of prevailing prices. There is no assurance that such transactions can ever be made in any large volume when they are needed. There is no certainty that the contract, if made, will be consummated at contract time. Default by either buyer or seller is possible without protection to the other against default and heavy losses. Finally, in the physical market, except in rare cases when operating through an agent without disclosure of the principals, the buyer or seller must always disclose himself as such and 'show his hand' at least through brokers, when it may not be to his advantage to do so.[2]

A group of dealers is needed with enough capital to assure a broad and continuous market for production at a price stimulating or stabilizing output. The net result of these physical market defects was the organization of commodity exchanges to supplement the work of physical commodity markets. The services of these exchanges led to a greater inflow of risk-taking capital into the commodity dealers' hands and to the entrance of a larger number of risk-taking dealers into the commodity trading business. Speculative capital and speculator activity thus became a part of commodity exchange operation.

---

[2] Julius B. Baer and Olin Glenn Saxon, *Commodity Exchanges and Futures Trading*. New York: Harper & Brothers, 1949, p. 129.

Services of the Commodity Exchange

People who buy and sell on commodity exchanges desire speedy marketability and the capacity to buy quickly the items sold for future delivery. Ready marketability is provided in part by the development of standardized contracts whose individual terms vary only as to price and delivery date. These contracts pass readily from hand to hand in the course of trading, for buyers and sellers are familiar with their provisions.

The confidence developed by the standardized contract is strengthened by exchange sponsored grading and inspection systems. Market traders are certain that the contracts bought and sold cover standardized grades established by federal or state law (in the case of grains and cotton) or by commodity exchange rulings or decisions by commodity trade associations (in the case of sugar, coffee, rubber, and hides, to mention only a few). When cotton is inspected and graded, it is first sampled and weighed by the Cotton Exchange's inspection bureau; subsequently the United States Department of Agriculture grades and certifies the weight and type of all deliveries in accordance with the provisions of the Cotton Futures Act of 1916. This legislation incorporated into law the grading standards previously used by the cotton trade. The Commodity Exchange, Inc., where hides are traded has developed precise descriptions of grades accepted in the trade. Its future contract permits delivery of 18 different grades of domestic hides and four grades of frozen South American hides.

Commodity marketability is further encouraged by a warehousing system allowing ready sale of negotiable warehouse receipts representing stored goods certified as to quality by an accompanying certificate. Banks readily lend against these receipts to increase the borrowers' working capital and business volume and thus reduce operating costs.

The wealth of commodity information broadcast by wire, cable, radio, newspaper, and ticker stimulates exchange activity. Such guides as price movements, production figures, and international trade statistics determine spot and forward prices. Producers, converters, and merchants can better decide on the advisability of spot, forward, and hedging operations. International price maladjustments may call for arbitrage operations to correct the maladjustments. The effects of commodity exchange statistical services are manifold:

(1) It makes possible the discounting of the future; that is, it enables dealers and speculators to exercise their best judgment at once in the form of actual transactions, and thus to reflect this current information in the quotations long before it would otherwise be impressed upon the general public. Thus, the effect of a short or bumper crop upon prices is reflected, that is, discounted, weeks in advance. . . . (2) It steadies prices. The daily discounting of current events makes unnecessary . . . a sudden decline or rise

in price upon the wide publication of events which have been slowly developing. . . . (3) It helps to regulate the rate at which the year's crop is consumed. . . . It is a well-recognized fact that the exchange quotations for contracts which call for delivery in the new crop months depend not entirely upon the prospects of the new crop, but are vitally influenced by the smallness or largeness, as compared with previous years, of the old crop yet unsold, as reflected by the "visible supply" or by statistics relating to holdings which have not yet left the producer's hands. (4) It serves to "level" prices between different markets.[3]

Hedging

How do producers, merchants, or converters insure themselves against the risk of speculative losses? How do they protect their financial positions against the major dangers of commodity price variations? What if a forward seller or buyer defaults on his contract to his dealer? How is the dealer to protect his financial position? Price and credit risks are the major hazards confronting risk takers in commodity markets. The hedge is the technique of protection.

Assume that a flour miller agrees in May to deliver in December at an agreed upon price 10,000 barrels of a specified grade of flour to a baking concern. The quoted selling price is based on the going exchange rate for December wheat. The flour miller wants assurance of a reasonable profit and must protect himself against an upward speculative movement in December wheat prices. Any advance in the latter will reduce his normal profit. He could eliminate the price risk by buying spot wheat in the physical market and store it in a warehouse for eventual conversion into flour in December; or he could purchase the wheat in the physical market for forward delivery; again the miller may purchase and store types of wheat other than that which the contract with the baking organization called for. (This substitute grain could be later exchanged for the type needed to comply with the contract.) But such procedures to avoid the price risk would be economically undesirable. Purchasing in May would tie up a good part of the miller's working capital and reduce his capacity for additional business until the baking concern paid for the flour in December. The miller would also lose interest on his tied up capital and be burdened with storage charges on the spot wheat, thus curtailing his profit on the deal. Again, how certain could he be that wheat of the desired grade would be available on the spot market? The purchase and storage of types of wheat other than stipulated in the contract (with the intention of later exchanging it for the type specified in the contract) would also be unattractive. The wheat would again freeze

---

[3] *The Functions of Produce Exchanges, American Produce Exchange Markets*. Philadelphia: American Academy of Political and Social Science, 1911, pp. 17-21.

the flour merchant's capital, involve carrying charges, and absorb the miller's limited time in a search for wheat of the necessary type. The purchase of wheat in the physical market for forward delivery is not accompanied by any of these risks to the flour miller; but the danger of adverse price changes and losses is still present, although the risk is shifted to the dealer who agrees to comply with the miller's forward delivery of the wheat. Since none of these procedures would prove satisfactory to the miller, how can he insure the price risk?

The commodity exchange offers the miller a solution; the large volume of transactions conducted thereon creates a broad market, reduces the dealer's risk, and permits his retention of the order to deliver flour of a specified variety to the baking concern. The miller buys contracts for the required amount of December wheat in May, when the flour contract is drawn up. Then, in November the miller purchases the necessary amount of the desired quality of wheat in the spot or physical market, liquidating his future contracts at the same time. Any price advance or decline in the futures market is offset by a corresponding price movement in the spot market. The price risk is insured, for a hedge is provided against an advance in December wheat by the miller's purchasing a quantity of the grain when spot wheat of the needed amount and quality must be bought to fulfill the contract with the baker buyer.

> A hedge . . . is merely a sale of any commodity for future delivery which is offset by the ownership or purchase of a like quantity of the cash commodity—the actual physical product as distinguished from "futures contracts"; conversely, a purchase of any commodity for future delivery which is offset by the sale of a like quantity of the cash commodity. In a "nutshell" the theory of hedging is that all purchases or sales of a commodity are offset by sales or purchases of an equivalent quantity of futures contracts in the same commodity.[4]

The credit risk is the other major risk confronting commodity producers, dealers, and converters. A producer negotiates a futures sales contract with a dealer. Will that dealer be solvent and pay his debt on the due date? Months will elapse between the day of sale in the physical market and the time of delivery and payment. How can the producer protect himself against a default and the likelihood of liquidating piled up inventory at a heavy loss? The hedge offers him a solution. He sells the futures contract on the commodity exchange. When the producer's inventory is on hand, he sells it on the spot market and offsets his future sales by repurchasing the future contracts. How about the manufacturer who buys working capital from a dealer for future delivery? He can escape the risk of nondelivery by the purchase of a forward contract for

---

[4] Hedging, An Insurance Medium in Marketing Agricultural Commodities. Chicago: Chicago Board of Trade Centennial, 1948, p. 4.

a variety of grades, some of which are not desired. Subsequently he sells out the miscellaneous variety and purchases the commodities he needs in the spot market.

Relation Between Spot and Future Prices

Why are price movements in the physical market usually paralleled by price changes in the exchange market? For the simple reason that the spread between the spot and forward price of the same grade of goods hinges on the charges for carrying commodities in storage over a period of time. These charges include such costs as loss of interest on the money tied up in the items, insurance, and loss of weight of the goods stored. If these costs total one cent from May to December, then December futures on both the exchange and physical markets ordinarily are one cent above the spot price in May. If at any time December futures exceed May spot prices by more than one cent, both speculative and nonspeculative traders will buy May spot and hedge by selling at prices above the cost plus all carrying charges for the period of the futures contract. Such transactions are significant when a heavy crop is harvested and marketed (thus depressing spot prices and offering excellent profit opportunities to traders in futures). Eventually the market situation will be corrected as spot goods become scarce. If December futures were to slump below the one cent differential, then hedgers would lose, since they would sell their future contracts at a lower figure than they would buy up spot wheat. While hedging is not always a perfect insurance against a price risk, it minimizes the danger of heavy losses.

The Futures Contract

The first trading in futures occurred in 1859 on the Chicago Board of Trade. The expansion of America's grain area had piled up in grain elevators or warehouses huge quantities of wheat which could not be sold as rapidly as they were received. The elevators issued warehouse receipts showing the amount and grade of grain stored. Trading in these receipts developed as they passed from hand to hand by endorsement. The original wheat shipper was not necessarily its ultimate owner. Whereas early warehouse receipts represented specific lots of grain, eventually they became claims on wheat of a specific grade without reference to specific lots. All shipments of a type of grain were combined, and part of the combination was available in exchange for grain elevator receipts. This general claim on a bulk of grain facilitated forward trading in wheat coming a great distance to Chicago. It was traded on the physical market on a "to arrive at some future date" basis.

Cotton future dealings developed out of the difference in time arrival between the news affecting cotton prices and cotton. The steamships carrying news always preceded the cotton loaded on slow moving sailing ships. Therefore cotton was sold on a sample basis in New York "to arrive" in Liverpool. If sales could not be made in New York on a sample basis, the sample was sent to Liverpool by steamer. The commodity was again offered on a "to arrive" basis in this trading center as the cotton carrying sailing vessel left its southern port. The cable led to selling by description of the cotton grade. Trading in contracts requiring shipping in a specific month developed in New York, and the New York Cotton Exchange, incorporated in 1871, was the first commodity market designed expressly for the purpose of dealing in contracts for future delivery. Today the Exchange is the world's principal futures market.

While physical markets afford future trading accommodations, they offer no assurance that sellers will always be able to find buyers for specific quantities of goods of a definite quality at desired monthly delivery dates. Nor are buyers certain that they will be able to purchase definite amounts of goods of a certain quality for delivery at specific monthly times. The commodity exchanges offer a constant market for futures contracts. They provide trading facilities capable of handling large offerings and heavy bids. The risk-taking dealer and speculator is prepared to buy up the offerings or to supply a volume of future contracts adequate to satisfy the bidders. A division of the futures market, the clearing association, protects traders against the other great commodity trading threat, the credit risk. This association assures the buyer and seller that there will be no default, and it guarantees fulfillment of contracts.

The business practices and rules of a commodity exchange govern the terms of the future contract. Each contract is a basis contract permitting commodity deliveries of the contract grade or some other grade at the discretion of the seller but at a price above or below the contract price. The contract calls for delivery during a specified calendar month. Performance of the contract is guaranteed by a proviso that a margin shall be deposited with a third party by the contracting parties. Thus the buyer is shielded against a default on the seller's part if the price of the commodity rises, and the seller is assured of payment in event of a price decline. Delivery of the goods stored in approved warehouses in the city in which the exchange is located is made by delivery of warehouse receipts for the commodity.

A typical contract, coffee futures contract "D," (described Santos No. 4), provides the coffee industry with the means of handling and distributing a most important world commodity with the maximum protection against fluctuating prices.

CONTRACT "D"

(Described Santos No. 4 Contract)

Office of

New York, ...19....

Sold for M.

To M.

32,500 lbs., in about 250 bags, of SANTOS Coffee grading from No. 2 to
No. 6 inclusive, provided the average grade shall not be above No. 3 nor below No. 5. Nothing in this contract however shall be construed as prohibiting a delivery averaging above No. 3 at the No. 3 grade.

Deliverable from licensed warehouse in the Port of New York between the
first and last days of .... inclusive.

At the rate of .... cents per pound for No. 4 with additions or
deductions for other grades according to the rate of the New York Coffee
and Sugar Exchange, Inc., existing on the afternoon of the day previous to
the date of the notice of delivery.

The Coffee to be Fair to Good Roast, Soft.

Either party to have the right to call for margins as the variations of the
market for like deliveries may warrant, which margins shall be kept good.

This contract is made in view of, and in all respects subject to the rules
and conditions established by the New York Coffee and Sugar Exchange,
Inc., and in full accordance with Section 102 of the By-Laws.

....

(Brokers.)

(Across the face is the following):

For and in consideration of one dollar to..............in hand paid, receipt whereof is hereby acknowledged, ... accept this contract with all
its obligations and conditions.

Source: *History and Operation of the New York Coffee and Sugar Exchange, Inc.* New York Commodity Exchange,
Inc., 1947, p. 20.

Like all future contracts, it clearly sets down the conditions to which
buyers and sellers subscribe. The unit of trading is specified to facilitate
hedging and avoid speculation by shoestring operators hampered by a
large enough minimum trading unit. All trades are in multiples of that
unit at a rate of so much per pound for the standard or basis grade (No. 4
Santos coffee). If other grades are delivered, additions to or deductions
from the price are made according to the rates of the New York Coffee
and Sugar Exchange, Inc., on the day prior to the date of delivery notice.

The futures basis contract offers various advantages. Since it lists the

grades deliverable, dumping on the Exchange of commodity types not marketable in the physical markets is prevented. The standard grade, traded actively on the physical and hedged markets, assures producers, dealers, and converters of a ready commodity trading medium. Speculators are protected against corners and squeezes, for an adequate volume of goods is available to cover future contracts. A corner is a manipulation permitting discharge of outstanding contracts only at prices dictated by the operators of the corner. A squeeze also results from the inability to discharge contracts, but only because goods do not arrive from foreign shores in time to allow deliveries in the month or grade stipulated. The merchants who purchase the postponed deliveries enter the physical spot or exchange markets to buy the commodities and to comply with their contracts. The rush to purchase specific grades in due time squeezes the position of the commodity hunters whose unhappy situation is known in the trade.

Delivery on a futures contract may take place during any one of 12 or even 18 months, although trading is confined to certain months because of cultivation, warehousing, and transportation conditions. The seller can deliver at any time during the month specified in the future contract. He is free of the danger of slow transportation which might postpone the arrival of his goods and force commodity purchases at a high price to satisfy buyer claims. The seller transfers his title to the goods by transfer of a warehouse receipt and an exchange certificate of quality and weight to the buyer.

A summary of fundamental facts about commodity futures involving minimum price variations, actively traded months, high and low seasonal price points, and economic determinants affecting prices is presented on page 258. A brief explanation of commodity price future quotations is offered on page 259.

Organization of a Commodity Exchange

The organization of the Chicago Board of Trade is typical of commodity exchanges dealing in cash and future contracts. Whereas its formation depended on a special act of the Illinois legislature, today general incorporation procedures govern exchange organizations. The Commodity Exchange Inc., established in 1933, is a New York state corporation, a merger of the New York Hide Exchange, the National Metal Exchange, The Rubber Exchange of New York, and The National Raw Silk Exchange.

The Board membership (1,420 individuals) represents all phases of the grain business; farmers' elevators and cooperatives, country and terminal elevators, flour millers, soybean crushers, corn processors, brewers, meat

BASIC FACTS ABOUT IMPORTANT COMMODITY FUTURES

Commodity	Contract Size; Minimum Price Variation	Most Actively Traded Months	Crop Year	Normal Seasonal Price Pattern High	Low	Important Economic Factors Affecting Prices
BUTTER	20,000 lbs. $10.00	April, May, June Nov., Dec., Jan.	None	Dec.	June	Storage stocks, supplies during Nov., Dec. & Jan., production during May.
COCOA	30,000 lbs. $3.00	Mar., May, July, Sept., Dec.	None	Jan.	June	World crop reports, political conditions, rate of imports and allocations, storage stocks, domestic disappearance.
COFFEE	32,500 lbs. $3.25	Mar., May, July, Sept., Dec.	None	None	None	World crop reports, internal political conditions, rate of imports, domestic disappearance and stocks.
CORN	5,000 bu. $6.25	May, July, Sept., Dec.	Oct. 1 to Sept. 30	Aug.	Nov. Dec.	Crop estimates, visible supplies, disappearance, exports, loan figures, carryover, also weather.
COTTON	100 bales $5.00	Mar., May, July, Oct., Dec.	Aug. 1 to July 31	July	Dec	Crop estimates, general conditions in cotton textile business, exports, loan figures, carryover, also weather.
COTTONSEED OIL (N. Y.)	60,000 lbs. $6.00	Jan., Mar., May, July, Sept., Oct., Dec.	None	Jan. Feb.	Aug.	Cotton production, rate of disappearance, competition from other fats and oils, cottonseed stocks.
EGGS	14,400 doz. $7.20	Oct., Nov., Dec., Jan.	None	Nov.	April	Number of layers on farms, storage stocks, government support, production.
HIDES	40,000 lbs. $4.00	Mar., June, Sept., Dec.	None	None	None	Cattle slaughter, cattle population trends, general conditions in shoe and leather business, imports, exports.
LARD	40,000 lbs. $10.00	Mar., May, July, Sept., Oct., Dec.	None	Sept.	April May	Hog runs, rate of consumption, U. S. cold storage stocks, competition from other fats and oils.
OATS	5,000 bu. $6.25	May, July, Sept., Dec.	July 1 to June 30	May	Aug.	Crop estimates, visible supplies, disappearance, exports, loan figures, carryover, also weather.
ONIONS	30,000 lbs. $6.00	Nov., Jan., Feb., Mar.	No Standard	None	None	Crop production, planted acreage, also weather, rate of consumption, storage stocks and quality.
SOYBEANS	5,000 bu. $6.25	May, July, Oct., Dec.	Oct. 1 to Sept. 30	May	Oct.	Crop estimates, visible supplies, disappearance, exports, loans, vegetable oil consumption, weather.
SUGAR (Domestic)	112,000 lbs. $11.20	Mar., May, July, Sept.	Quota— calendar year	None	None	National income, consumption, U. S. Sugar Act, supplies, quotas.
WHEAT	5,000 bu. $6.25	May, July, Sept., Dec.	July 1 to June 30	May	Aug.	Crop estimates, visible supplies, disappearance, exports, loan figures, carryover, also weather.
WOOL	Tops 5,000 lbs. $5.00 Wool 6,000 lbs. $6.00 (clean)	Mar., May, July, Oct., Dec.	None	Dec.	May June	Production, general conditions in wool textile business, imports, world production, sheep population trends.

FIGURE 1

Source: *How to Buy and Sell Commodities.* New York: Merrill Lynch, Pierce, Fenner & Beane, 1949.

packers, brokerage houses, exporters, and transportation companies. When a candidate is accepted and buys a seat on the Exchange, he must abide by all its rules of fair business conduct, uniform trade practices, and contracts; and he must agree to arbitrate disputes in addition to providing trade information to Exchange members. The privileges of member-

• Commodity Futures Trading in Detail •

READING THE QUOTATIONS

GRAINS are all quoted in dollars and cents and fractions of a cent per bushel. The smallest variation is ⅛ of a cent per bushel.

"Open" means the price at which the first transaction of the day took place. The "High" and "Low" are the highest and lowest price at which transactions were made during the day.

"Close" is often given as two prices. Unless these are definitely marked as "bid" and "asked" it means that trading was taking place at both prices or a range between those prices as the closing bell sounded. This type of close is often reported in an active market and is called a "split close." The clipping we have reproduced also shows the prices at the close of the previous trading day.

The last columns show the highest and lowest price at which contracts have been made since the first trading day in the contract.

COTTON is quoted in cents and fractions of a cent per pound. As you will note there are two digits to the right of the decimal, so the smallest variation is 1/100 of a cent. In the cotton trade this is called a "point."

You will note that March, for example, is quoted twice, once without any year given and once under 1950. A year is mentioned only if two contracts are being traded for the same month a year apart.

LARD is quoted in cents and hundredths of a cent per pound, but the minimum fluctuation is 2½ hundredths of 1¢ per pound.

EGGS are quoted in cents and hundredths of a cent per dozen, but the minimum fluctuation is 5 hundredths of 1¢.

COFFEE is quoted in cents and hundredths of a cent per pound.

BUTTER is quoted in cents and hundredths of a cent per pound, but the minimum fluctuation is 5 hundredths of 1¢.

SUGAR is quoted in cents and hundredths of a cent per pound or $11.20 on each contract for 112,000 pounds. The #5 is for sugar to be delivered duty paid, in the United States.

WOOL tops and grease wool are both quoted in cents and tenths of a cent per pound.

COTTONSEED OIL quoted in cents and hundredths of a cent per pound, equal to $6 on the New York contract for 60,000 pounds, or $3 on the New Orleans contract for 30,000 pounds.

HIDES are quoted in cents and 1/100 of a cent per pound.

POTATOES are quoted in dollars and cents per 100 pound bag.

ONIONS are quoted in dollars and cents per 50 pound sack.

COCOA is quoted in cents and 1/100 of a cent per pound.

FOOTNOTES – "Nominal" means that no trades were made at this figure. The price is determined for settlements by the clearing house.

A "bid" means the price at which buyers were willing to buy.

The "asked" or "offering" price are both the same thing—the price that sellers are asking or the price at which they are offering the commodity.

To prevent temporary panic conditions from demoralizing markets or temporary periods of elation from boosting prices through the roof, exchanges restrict the daily price range to some maximum figure. If price fluctuations reach the daily trading limit it is generally stated in a footnote to the table of quotations.

FIGURE 2

Source: *How to Buy and Sell Commodities*, New York: Merrill Lynch, Pierce, Fenner & Beane, 1949.

ship are available to partnerships if one of the partners is an Exchange member. These privileges are also granted to a corporation if an executive officer is an Exchange member. Applicants for membership can be rejected if their personal or financial records appear undesirable to the

membership committee. Exchange members are expected to provide relevant information during the period when the candidate's name is known to them. Membership recommendations are passed on to the governing board, which elects by a majority vote or as its rules provide. The number of seats is fixed and can be changed only by charter modification. The price of a seat varies directly with the volume of business, the financial strength of the Exchange, and the number of existing seats.

The Chicago Board of Trade points out:

> . . . three basic advantages to membership in an exchange. (1) Numerous buying and selling interests from many sections of the country are concentrated there. This means great quantities of grain move into the terminal market. Representatives of large companies can thus do volume buying. (2) Buyers who must have special types and grades of grain can fill their needs, and sellers know that all types and grades can find a market. (3) The cost of doing business is less for a member than a nonmember. For example: brokerage-house commission charges for buying and selling a 5,000 bu. grain futures contract are $15.00 for a nonmember, and $7.50 for a member not on the trading floor.[5]

As in other commodity exchanges, a secretary and an executive vice-president discharge the Board of Trade's administrative work, while its government is vested in 15 directors, a president, and two vice-presidents. The Exchange's functions are facilitated through committees composed of members skilled in the activities germane to the committees' work. Prominent among these committees are the following: (1) An arbitration and appeals committee for the settlement of disputes ordinarily growing out of customer transactions. Exchange members may resort to this committee or any one of the parties to a dispute can lodge a complaint and force arbitration upon an opposing interest. Forceful arbitration is typical of most exchanges. The Chicago Board of Trade encourages but does not force arbitration. The arbitration committee ruling can be reviewed by an appeals committee whose decision is binding and final. If a member refuses to comply with this committee's suggestions, the mere threat of expulsion from the Exchange is usually enough to force compliance. Exchange members held responsible by arbitration rulings have comparable claims on the customers for whom they were acting in the disputed transaction. Disputes as to grade rarely arise, for the commodities offered in settlement of a contract are supported by a certificate of quality. (2) A business conduct committee receives complaints of unethical and unprofessional practices, investigates, and reports its findings to the board of governors. The matters are then considered by (3), a supervisory committee that looks into the disputes and turns over its findings

---

[5] *Marketing Grain through a Grain Exchange.* The University of Illinois, College of Agriculture—Vocational Agriculture Service, in cooperation with The Chicago Board of Trade, pp. 1-2.

to the board of governors, which is empowered to penalize the accused if found guilty. (4) A quotation committee is authorized to settle all disagreements over price quotations established by outcry across the ring or pit, the trading area on the floor of commodity exchanges. It enforces the rule requiring an immediate report on the time and price of every trade; it records price quotations, established daily closing bid and asked prices, and nominal quotations for inactive months as guides to traders and the clearing house. (5) A floor committee seeks to establish and maintain a calm trading atmosphere; committee members present on the floor are authorized to settle price disputes on the spot. (6) A committee on information and statistics (whose name indicates its duties) and a committee on grading and warehousing that oversees the work of the exchange's inspection bureau are also important.

Spot Trading on the Chicago Board of Trade

While the chief function of a commodity exchange is the maintenance of a market place for futures trading, some organized exchanges (including grain exchanges) spot deal. The Chicago Board of Trade's procedure in a wheat spot trade calls for the wheat's inspection and grading upon arrival at a terminal point to determine whether it meets the United States Government's official standard. Inspectors from the Illinois State Grain Inspection Bureau take samples from each car of grain arriving overnight. Five or more samples are taken with an instrument called a trier to determine if the wheat in the car is of uniform grade. Each sample is emptied into a separate bag and inspected by licenced grain experts of the State of Illinois. These experts work under the supervision of the United States Department of Agriculture by authority of the United States Grain Standards Act of 1916. A part of the inspected wheat is put in a paper bag and forwarded to the commission merchant to whom it was consigned. The Board of Trade also operates a sampling department using the same grading procedures as the state. If the quality of wheat is disputed, the commission merchant or shipper can request a new sampling test; and if the merchant is still dissatisfied, he can appeal to the federal government. Assuming that there is satisfaction with the sampling and grading process, each freight car of wheat is then sold for spot delivery on the basis of the sample.

Cash trading is effected on a long row of tables lining one wall of the trading area:

> On each market day buyers for elevators, exporters, millers and processors circulate among the cash grain tables, making their competitive bids on the grain offered for sale. Prices on cash or "spot" grain are quoted at so much over or under the current or near futures contract. When the commission

merchant has fully canvassed the market and is satisfied that he has obtained the best bid, he then follows the instructions of the shipper. If he has been instructed to sell at the highest price possible he does so. The shipper may, however, wish to be advised as to the grade of grain and the bid price. In this case, the commission merchant will wire or telephone the shipper this information, and the shipper, in turn, will instruct the receiver as to the price to accept. The shipper may, however, give instructions to carry the car over in hope of obtaining a better price the next day.[6]

Futures Trading on the Chicago Board of Trade

Futures trading takes place in the pits or rings on the Exchange floor. A pit is octagonal and consists of a series of steps on which brokers trading in futures contracts stand facing one another.

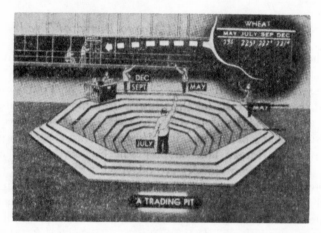

FIGURE 3

Brokers occupying particular positions in a pit are dealing in futures for different delivery months. They trade in either standard or round lots of 5,000 bushels of grain or in job lots of 1,000 bushels. (In the case of oats a job lot consists of at least 2,000 bushels.) Those brokers trading in job lots are concentrated in one section of the pit.

Brokers in the ring are either floor brokers executing customer orders or operating for their own account. These latter middlemen help stabilize wheat prices by closing out their holdings when they advance too much in price and acquiring futures contracts when the price is unduly depressed in their opinion. These brokers' offerings and bids help make a market, for bids and offers are brought together quickly. The trading brokers are not overly desirous of heavy profits on a single operation;

---

[6] Robert H. Moulton, *A Manual of Trading in Grain Futures and in Cash Grains on the Chicago Board of Trade.* Chicago Board of Trade, 1942, p. 6.

rather they are interested in small profits and avoidance of severe losses on individual transactions.

While each type of grain is traded in an individual ring or pit, the method of trading is similar for all. When a commission house receives a flash order to buy or sell futures at the market price, it immediately contacts its telephone man on the trading floor who signals the order to the firm's floor broker in the pit. As soon as the flash order is executed, the customer is advised. All other orders including limited orders directing brokers to carry them out at stated prices and perhaps limiting the time during which they may be executed (if no time limit is given a broker, such an order is good only for the day) and stop loss orders are forwarded in writing to pit brokers. When these orders are executed, the pit brokers indicate on the orders the prices at which they were bought or sold; after this has been done, the commission house customers are notified. Brokers trade by open outcry and also use hand signals to indicate their bids or offers over the noise. The shouting and gesticulation give an appearance of confusion belied by the general understanding at the pit of either the shouts or the hand signals. A typical futures transaction affords a clear picture of the method of trading on the Board of Trade:

> The prompt and elaborate collection of trade information disseminated by the grain trade is valuable for a number of reasons. In the first place, it makes possible the discounting of the future—that is, it enables dealers, investors, and the speculative trade to exercise their best judgment at once in the form of actual transactions, and thus to reflect this current information long before it would otherwise be impressed upon the public; it steadies prices, the daily discounting or price measuring of current events making unnecessary a sudden rise or decline in price upon the wide publication of events which have been slowly developing; and it enables the individual farmer to know the price of his grain from day to day, because transactions, if private, would not be recorded, or might be designed to mislead, and certainly would not be representative of the general judgment.

How One May Trade

Only members of the Chicago Board of Trade are permitted to buy and sell grain on the floor of the exchange. Therefore, the nonmember who wishes to trade must do business through some commission house holding a membership on the Board. For this privilege, the nonmember pays a commission of $15.00 for each 5,000 bushels traded in, each trade including both a purchase and a sale. The unit of trading in grain futures is a contract calling for five thousand bushels. There is a lesser unit of one thousand bushels, known as a "job lot"—except in the case of oats, where two thousand bushels is the minimum job lot contract—roughly representing a carload of grain. Nonmember commissions or job lot trades are proportionately higher than the commission on regular contracts. A regular contract of five thousand bushels of grain cannot be closed out in the pit against an equal volume of job lot contracts—each being a separate contract.

The first step necessary to trade is for one to open an account with a commission house. This means making a deposit of a sum commensurate with the probable volume of one's trading. The practice of leaving a deposit of money to bind a bargain, and as security for faithful performance of a contract, is so common in all kinds of business as scarcely to need comment. In real estate transactions, the value which a property has over and above any mortgage is called an "equity." When chattels or other property are bought, partly for cash, partly on time, the cash payment is called in book language "earnest money."

In the parlance of the exchanges, when a trader buys partly for cash, partly on time, the amount of money which he puts up is called a "margin." The name is all that differentiates it from a similar deposit in numerous forms of transactions entered into in all kinds of outside business every day. There is no difference in principle between margin trading and those other forms of business transactions, but, upon the exchanges, the margin method is much more general, and the margins necessary are much smaller than are required in other commodities that are not dealt in on grain exchanges.

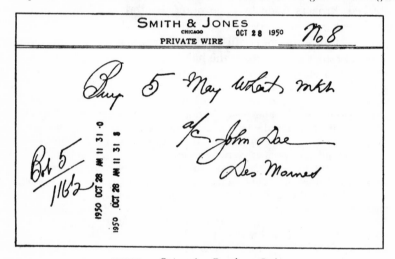

FIGURE 4. *Copy of a Purchase Order*

The minimum margins required in grain trading are fixed by regulation, but it is left to individual houses to determine what they consider a safe rate above the minimums according to the type of market prevailing. A margin is kept good by being maintained at the same distance from the market level. Thus, if one buys wheat at $1.05 a bushel and the price later declines to $1.02, then an additional 3 cents a bushel is deposited.

A Typical Futures Transaction

. . . The following transactions show how one large wire house in Chicago, here designated as "Smith & Jones," handles customers' orders transmitted through the firm's branch office at Des Moines, Iowa.

On October 28, 19—, a customer, who will be referred to as "John Doe," gave an order through the Des Moines office of Smith & Jones to buy 5,000

bushels of May wheat. The order was what is known as a "market order" as distinguished from a "limited order" which always carries a stated price, and this means that the order was to be executed at once at whatever the market price might be.

John Doe's order to buy 5,000 bushels of May wheat was instantly transmitted from the Des Moines office to Smith & Jones by the firm's private

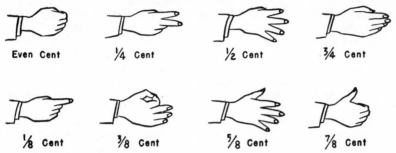

Even Cent   ¼ Cent   ½ Cent   ¾ Cent

⅛ Cent   ⅜ Cent   ⅝ Cent   ⅞ Cent

FIGURE 5. *Price Signs Used in Pit Trading on the Chicago Board of Trade*

wire to Chicago. In the Chicago office of the firm, the order was received over what is known as the Des Moines wire by a telegraph operator in a room with many other operators on additional wires all busy like him taking hundreds of orders coming in from the dozens of branch offices in various parts of the country. At the moment this particular order arrived from

W. B. MARTIN				W. B. MARTIN			
BOUGHT Chicago, 10/28 1941				SOLD Chicago, 19			
✓ May W 116⅝ ⅞							
Barrel & Co.							

FIGURE 6. *Trading Card* *

* Source: Robert H. Monetors, *A Manual of Trading in Grain Futures and in Cash Grains on the Chicago Board o, Trade.* Chicago: Chicago Board of Trade, 1942, pp. 12–14.

Des Moines it appeared on the following specially prepared order form marked "private wire," and simultaneously was given an individual number. The order in this instance was No. 8, and thereafter until executed with lightning-like rapidity in the pit and reported back was known by that number.

From the receiving operator, the telegram passed swiftly under a time-clock stamp and to one of a corps of telephone operators communicating verbally to other operators on the trading floor of the Board of Trade who are within a few feet of the wheat pit, and in a position to signal visually the firm's brokers in the pit. The telephone operators on the floor, when working on what is known as "flash orders," merely make a note of the number of an order and then by the usual finger and hand code (see Figure 5 on page 265) direct a broker for their firm to "buy 5 May wheat" or whatever the order may be. Just the moment the broker in the pit can get the attention of a seller, which usually is a matter of seconds, the trade is made and noted on the broker's trading card below. Quantities are indicated on one finger of the hand held vertically for each unit of five thousand bushels. The unit of price change is usually one-eighth of a cent a bushel. The fractions are indicated by the fingers of the hand held horizontally, as shown in the price code illustrated above. It is assumed that everyone trading knows or can see from the blackboards the full cent at which trading is taking place. The palm of the hand extended and held inward is a bid to buy, and the palm outward is an offer to sell.

If clients operate with borrowed funds, they must establish margins to protect their positions. The Exchange fixes minimum margin requirements subject to individual broker adjustment and varying 10 to 33 per cent of the market value of the commodity lot purchased or sold. If prices advance or decline, the customer must maintain the required margin. Failure to preserve such a margin results in the closing out of his contracts. Some exchanges do not call for margins on hedging operations. Commodity margins are smaller than security market margins. Unlike security price fluctuations, commodity price changes in any one trading day are limited. The Chicago Board of Trade restricts price changes during any one day to 10 cents per bushel of wheat. If price fluctuations exceed this limit, trading is barred except within the price limit. This prohibition is expected to afford commodity operators an opportunity to judge the forces responsible for the severe price change, offer the operators a breathing spell to prevent panic, and allow the readjustment of variation margin requirements by commission houses, the clearing house, and traders. Other reasons for lower customer margins are the constantly active commodities market (virtually assuring the saleability of futures contracts as against the inactivity of some securities), and the ordinary procedure of closing out commodity contracts for delivery, whereas securities in a margin transaction are usually acquired for a favorable price change which may not occur.

Commission rates on the Chicago Grain Exchange are $15 for each 5,000 bushels traded; the brokerage fee for handling job lots is higher. Members not on the trading floor are charged only $7.50 for the purchase or sale of 5,000 bushels of wheat. Membership in the Exchange always

offers a commission advantage. Foreigners invariably pay higher rates for brokerage services.

The record or trading cards of buying and selling brokers provide the information for contract trading slips. At the end of each day, buyers and sellers sign each others' slips carrying their names, prices, number, and delivery months of the contracts. The buyer and seller have recognized their mutual obligations through these contract slips which supply information for daily reports to the clearing house by Exchange members. Enforced by high standards of business conduct on the Chicago Board of Trade, disputes are infrequent and settled by the Commodity Exchange's arbitration committee.

While trades are being consummated, they are closely observed by trained employees located in the "pulpit." This position offers a clear view of every section of the pit. The observers make a written record of all deals effected in all pits at prices 1/8 of one cent above or below the last quoted price as well as the hour, minute, and 10 second interval when the new price was noted. This information is sent to a central transmitting office, which advises the entire world by wire, radio, and cable of changing price quotations on the Chicago Board of Trade. The central office helps keep floor brokers and traders informed of changing price situations. It telegraphs the new quotations back to the "pulpit," and blackboard markets record the current prices for different delivery months.

The Commodity Clearing House

Contract slips are the basis of the commodity clearing house's chief task: the reduction of the number of settlements among commodity brokers. House A, acting for a customer sells contracts for delivery to a client of brokerage house B, which has also sold contracts of the same delivery month to House A. Only the difference in the contracts bought from and sold to each house is settled or washed out.

The clearing house arranges delivery of a commodity sold under a futures contract. When the date of delivery arrives, a transfer notice is prepared and issued for submission at the clearing house at the price of the preceding day. The clearing house turns the notice over to an exchange member who requires the goods for settlement of a long contract. If he does not wish the commodity, he sells a contract of the same month and delivers the transfer notice to the buyer. Any receiver of the notice holding it longer than half an hour "stops the notice" and must accept delivery of the goods; the notice may not circulate more than one day. The buyer makes payment and receives the warehouse receipt.

The clearing house also assumes the uncleared contracts of every mem-

ber against all other members. It guarantees performance of these contracts, assuring buyers of their commodities and sellers of contract prices. The financial strength of the clearing house is built up in several ways to carry out its purposes. Commodity exchanges establish member firm margin requirements to guard against defaults to the clearing house. They build up protective funds as exemplified by the arrangement of the New York Coffee and Sugar Exchange, Inc.

> Each clearing member must advance to the Clearing Association an amount of funds (presently $15,000) which collectively (together with such surplus as the Clearing Association may devote to the same purpose) constitutes a Guaranty Fund. These funds may be used for payment of any loss or damage to the Clearing Association resulting from the default of any clearing member, thus providing protection for the Clearing Association, the Clearing Member and the customer.
> This Association accepts contracts offered to it by Clearing Members for clearance, and by such acceptance assumes the obligations imposed and succeeds to all the rights and benefits accruing therefrom, becoming thereby the seller to the buyer, or the buyer to the seller, as the case may be.[7]

The surplus backing up a commodity exchange's guaranty fund is obtained from contract clearance fees. Commodity exchange assessments on member firms restore impaired guaranty funds.

Member firms must initially deposit with the clearing house association minimum original margins, which can be increased by the association's board of managers or directors. The margin on a member firm's straddle position—where there are long contracts for delivery in one month and short contracts for delivery in another month—is smaller than the margin required for a balanced position in any one month. An adequate margin is assured through the variation margin. If a member firm's contracts for clearance fluctuate in value and show a loss between contract and settlement prices, the commodity house is called (if necessary, hourly) to put up an added market difference or variation margin. The pledge of additional margin on the Commodity Exchange in New York is facilitated by its requirement that each clearing member's office be located within one-half mile of the Clearing Association's office. When a member suffering heavy market losses does not reenforce its margin position by certified check within an hour after notification of the growing discrepancy between contract and settlement prices, the Clearing House must close out the firm's contracts by buying up or selling on the Exchange floor the contracts necessary to settle the firm's position. Losses of the Exchange will be covered by the margins and other firm resources with the commodity market. If a profit is shown, the clearing firm can withdraw the surplus in its contract position. While clearing house mem-

---

[7] *History and Operation of The New York Coffee and Sugar Exchange, Inc.*, New York, 1947, p. 6.

bers have failed occasionally, their assumed obligations have been well protected by their established margins.

The Commodity Exchange Act

The general purpose of the Grain Futures Act of 1922, amended in 1936, is insurance of fair practices and honest dealings in specified major farm products on commodity exchanges. Futures commission merchants and floor brokers must register with the Secretary of Agriculture before they can solicit or execute orders for commodities (like grain, cotton, butter, eggs, rice, and potatoes) listed in the Act. All futures contracts on or subject to the rules of a board of trade in the United States must be made by or through a member of a board of trade designated as a contract market. Speculative activities are restricted if they burden interstate commerce; fraudulent practices and activities like cheating, bucketing, wash sales, and cross trades are criminal offenses. The issuance of false crop and market conditions statements to deceive is illegal.

Problems

Modern business and governmental developments and policies have virtually obliterated the commodity exchange's functions in various fields. The prevalence of monopolies or government controls in many areas fixes prices and determines commodity distribution. Trading in commodities is nonexistent in many areas. The government has directed a goodly part of its resources to produce certain essential goods or to curtail inflation. The growth of socialistic, communistic, and fascistic spheres of economic and political influence, the growing animosity between east and west, and the always prevalent danger of industrial mobilization have expanded governmental controls, government price fixing and state sanctioned price fixing. Argentina, Great Britain, Russia, and Brazil are among the countries whose national policies are frequently inimical to the exchange.

> An impossible condition would exist, if organized futures trading were attempted in a market where the supply or price of the commodity is under *effective* control and could be increased or diminished at the will of any government, group, cartel, corporation, or individual. The market would then function, not as an efficient price-making machine, but merely as an adjunct to the arbitrary will of the controller of the supply or price of the commodity.[8]

Can farm crops eligible for price support under the United States Government's farm program enjoy a futures market? An affirmative answer is justified because a good part of the crop is not assumed by the

---

[8] Baer and Saxon, *op. cit.*, p. 112.

government either through purchase or loan; this part of the crop will have a futures market. The price of the crop for any year is set by the parity figure established at the start of the year. Since futures contracts can extend beyond the period when the parity price is effective, a crop can have the advantages of a futures market. No one knows the new parity figure when a new crop matures. Finally, crop prices can decline below the figure at which the government will take them over, depending on the crop eligible for loan, the fear of government dumping, and the unstable supply and demand. Mr. J. H. Mehl, Chief of the Commodity Exchange Administration, speaking before the Chicago Mercantile Exchange in 1941 said:

> I do not believe that the commodity markets ever again will afford the opportunity for speculative adventure that they have in the past. The loan programs, quite aside from the fact that they have operated as minimum price guaranties, have also enabled farmers directly to carry a part of the risk load that formerly had to be assumed by speculators. This means a smaller volume of trading in some commodities at the time these commodities are going under loan. But it does not affect the need for the futures markets for hedging purposes when the commodities again move back into commercial channels.[9]

Suggested Readings

BOOKS

Baer, J. H. and Saxon, O. G., *Commodity Exchange and Futures Trading*. New York: Harper & Brothers, 1949.

Boyle, J. E., *Speculation and the Chicago Board of Trade*. New York: The Macmillan Company, 1921.

Commodity Year Book. New York: Commodity Research Bureau, 1950.

Garside, A. H., *Cotton Goes to Market*. New York: F. A. Stokes & Company, 1935.

Shepherd, G. S., *Marketing Farm Products*. Ames, Iowa: Iowa State College Press, 1946.

PAMPHLETS

Commodity Exchange Inc., *Trading on the Commodity Exchange in New York*, and *History and Operation of The New York Coffee and Sugar Exchange, Inc*. New York: The Exchange, 1947.

Lesar, M. S., *Hedging an Insurance Medium in Marketing Agricultural Commodities*. Chicago: Chicago Board of Trade, 1948.

Marketing Grain Through a Grain Exchange. Chicago: University of Illinois, College of Agriculture—Vocational Agricultural Service in cooperation with The Chicago Board of Trade.

Merrill Lynch, Pierce, Fenner & Beane, *How To Buy and Sell Commodities*. New York, 1949.

---

[9] "The Future of the Futures Market," September 10, 1941. p. 7.

11

Stockbrokers and Dealers

by AUDLEY H. F. STEPHAN

Chairman, Department of Economics
University College, Rutgers University

Historical Development

Stockbrokers and dealers. The first instances of the buying and selling of securities, other than by the principals involved, are unrecorded in history. They probably occurred, in sufficient numbers to be recognized as such, some time early in the seventeenth century. Most likely they took place in connection with one or more of the joint stock companies that were given royal grants for the development of foreign trade, such as the Dutch East India Company and the South Sea Company. In the United States it is quite possible that some of the more prosperous colonists were familiar with "stock jobbers" long before the Revolutionary War. By the time of the founding of our federal republic, the principal securities entering into trading were government and bank securities; public trading took the form of auction, and competition was limited to the buyers of securities. Coincident with such trading, a number of men attended the auctions regularly to engage in the buying and selling of securities. Among these men were our first brokers and dealers. The Buttonwood Tree Agreement, signed May 17, 1792, contains the names of 24 signers. The signers identified themselves as brokers, merchants, insurance broker, auctioneer and broker, stockbrokers and auctioneers, insurance and stockbrokers, and one was warden of the Port of New York. Out of these firms and others not signers to the agreement, the modern brokerage firm has grown. Present-day brokerage firms exist in the form of sole proprietorships, partnerships, and corporations. Combinations and mergers have characterized the development of many of these firms. One prominent firm traces its predecessors to include some

87 firms, with the likelihood that there would be more if records were available; in this case the oldest record goes back 130 years to 1820.

Securities markets. Broadly speaking there are two main classes of markets in which securities are bought and sold: the listed exchanges and the over-the-counter market. The listed exchanges are treated in Chapter 12 on Stock Exchanges and will not be dealt with here, except incidentally. In this chapter the nature and scope of the over-the-counter market will be covered, for this market fits in with the work of stockbrokers and dealers. At this point it is useful to mention the major distinguishing features that make up the differences between the listed exchanges and the over-the-counter markets.

1. On listed exchanges only those securities are traded that are admitted to trading, whereas in the over-the-counter market both listed and unlisted securities are traded.
2. Securities trading is done on the "floor" of the exchanges, only by members of the exchange, under rules laid down by the exchange authorities; the over-the-counter market has no "floors" or places for buyers and sellers to meet personally. Contact in the latter market is most frequently by telephone between the offices of the various brokers and dealers.
3. Trading on the listed exchanges is by the auction or rather double auction method. (The term double auction refers to the fact that competition exists not only among buyers, but also among sellers using the auction method.) In the over-the-counter market, trading is by negotiation. Competition also exists among sellers and among buyers in the over-the-counter market; but in this market a buyer of securities seeks out various sellers, selects the one willing to sell at the lowest price, and then negotiates with that seller; and a seller of securities seeks out various buyers, selects the one willing to pay the highest price, and then negotiates with that buyer—both negotiations are intended to obtain a better price.
4. Primary distribution of securities is limited to the over-the-counter markets. (The term primary distribution of securities refers to the selling of a new securities issue to investors. It is an integral part of the investment banking business involved in the retailing or selling function.) Secondary distribution (the buying and selling of securities among investors), takes place both on the listed exchanges and in the over-the-counter market.

Terms used in the securities business.

1. BROKER. A broker is a person who buys and sells securities for others. He assumes no risk, and he charges a commission for his services. A broker acts as agent for his principal.

2. DEALER. A dealer is a person (or firm) who buys and sells securities for his own account. When he buys he becomes the owner, and when he sells he disposes of securities which he owned by reason of previous purchases. A dealer assumes the risk of ownership, and he derives his compensation or profit from the spread between the price at which he buys and the price at which he sells.

3. TRADER. The term *trader* must not be confused with the term *trading* which refers to the actual buying and selling of securities as a transaction. A trader is one who buys and sells for his own account (rarely for the account of others), and who attempts to lessen the risk of ownership by completing his buying and selling transactions within a short period of time.

4. CREATING AND MAINTAINING A MARKET. A dealer creates a market by standing ready to buy or to sell a security at prices he quotes; he maintains a market by continuing to quote prices at which he will buy or sell a security. The prices do not necessarily remain constant.

5. TAKING A POSITION. A dealer is said to take a position when he accumulates an inventory of a given security. This accumulation of inventory is known as a "long" position, since it indicates that the dealer owns an inventory or number of securities against which he will trade. When a dealer thinks the current market price of a security is low and likely to rise in the future, he increases his inventory or long position in the hope of selling later at a better price. A "short" position refers to a dealer who has not only sold out his own inventory of a security but has continued to sell beyond that point. A dealer holding a short position anticipates that the price will fall and that he can buy the needed securities at a lower price. (The mechanics of short sales are described later in this chapter.)

Types of securities firms.

1. MEMBER FIRMS. These are concerns which hold membership on listed exchanges and trade on those exchanges. Exchange member firms may also trade in the over-the-counter market.

2. OVER-THE-COUNTER HOUSES. These firms are not members of the exchanges, but they deal chiefly in domestic corporate and foreign securities in the over-the-counter market. Such securities may or may not be listed on the exchanges.

3. INVESTMENT BANKING HOUSES. Most investment banking firms also have trading departments dealing in the secondary distribution of securities. These trading departments are called investment banking houses.

4. MUNICIPAL BOND HOUSES. These firms, neither members of an ex-

change nor investment banking houses, specialize in state and local government bond transactions in the over-the-counter market.

5. GOVERNMENT BOND HOUSES. A firm which specializes in United States government obligations is referred to as a government bond house or government house.

6. DEALER BANKS. These are regular banking concerns that are permitted by law to deal in governments and municipals. Trading in such securities is in the over-the-counter market. Should such banks wish to buy or sell other securities, the transaction would be handled by some other securities house.

7. SECURITIES HOUSE. This term is a broad one used to indicate practically all firms (other than dealer banks) that deal in securities.

Functions of Stockbrokers and Dealers

The place of stockbrokers and dealers in the economy. When a clothing manufacturer produces a suit of clothes, it is sold to a consumer who is willing to pay for it, in order to satisfy his want for clothing. The sum total of all producers supplying the wants of all consumers makes up the economy of a nation, and this process of supplying the wants of consumers brings income to producers. A summation of all such income in a country constitutes the national income.

In the process of supplying the wants of consumers, not all producers are engaged in the manufacture of tangible goods; consumers also want services, such as the services of doctors, lawyers, schools, hotels and a host of other services. Among these services are the services of stockbrokers and dealers who supply the wants of buyers and sellers of securities.

The amount of goods and services consumed (the standard of living) in any economy depends primarily on the amount of goods and services produced, since goods and services cannot be consumed if they are not produced. The amount of goods and services produced in a free and private enterprise economy depends on the amount of capital (plants, machinery, tools, and so on) made available to the producers, plus the number of producers employed. Both the amount of capital available to producers and the number of producers that can be employed depend upon the amount of capital that has been saved out of prior production. In a money economy, such as ours, ownership of saved capital takes the form of monetary savings. If the standard of living is to be raised and the number of producers employed is to be increased, the monetary savings and the capital they represent must be made available to potential producers; that is, savings must be invested. It is in the process of investing savings and in the activities related thereto that stockbrokers and dealers render their over-all function.

Stockbrokers and dealers as intermediaries. It is quite obvious that if every corporation or other issuer of securities were required to canvass the general public in order to find purchasers of the corporation's securities, a great deal of time and expense would be involved for each issuer and considerable duplication of effort would result. On the other hand it is equally obvious that if each individual holder of investable funds were required to seek out potential users of such funds, much time and effort would be consumed, and many investments would not be made. It is primarily in this field that stockbrokers and dealers render their major function; that is, stockbrokers and dealers bring together those people desiring to sell securities and those investors desiring to purchase securities.

Aside from the function of serving as an intermediary between issuer and investor, stockbrokers and dealers also act as go-betweens among various investors wishing to sell securities and other investors wishing to buy securities. Stockbrokers and dealers act as intermediaries for the following:

1. Sellers of securities
   a. Issuers
   b. Present holders of securities
2. Investors

There are many ways of identifying the issuers of securities. Reference to Table 3, New Securities Offered for Cash in the United States, on page 313 will find issuers classified as corporate and noncorporate. Within the corporate classification are all the manufacturing and other producing businesses that seek capital funds for their operations. Various levels of government and other nonprofit institutions make up the noncorporate classification, and they also seek monetary savings for the conduct of their operations. These are the issuers of securities, practically every one of whom seeks the services of stockbrokers and dealers in finding investors.

The second class of sellers of securities are the present holders of securities. These holders seek to dispose of their present investments for any one of a multitude of reasons. It may be that circumstances require the consumption of their previous savings; therefore their investments must be sold to meet their consumer needs. It may be that the present holders desire to take their savings out of a particular enterprise and to invest them in a business which shows more promise. This ability of investors to render judgment, as it were, on individual concerns does much to increase the efficiency of production within the economy. It may be that conditions within the present holders' own personal circumstances have altered so that their own needs would be better served

by reinvestment in other securities. It may be that general economic conditions make it advantageous for present holders of securities to dispose of their holdings and invest their savings in some other form. Regardless of the reasons, present holders of securities make use of the services of stockbrokers and dealers when selling their securities.

The second large class of individuals with whom stockbrokers and dealers act as intermediaries is the group of investors—in other words the buyers of securities. Obviously for all sales of securities there must be buyers and these buyers of securities are those individuals and institutions that have accumulated funds that they desire to invest in order to receive some return. Investors may be classed in various ways: institutional and noninstitutional is a convenient classification. Institutional investors may be defined as institutions which invest other people's money; and generally institutional investors are founded primarily for purposes other than investment. Insurance companies (formed primarily to spread risks) rank high among institutional investors; annually they buy billions of dollars' worth of securities. Fiduciary institutions, such as trust companies and banks with trust departments, are large buyers of securities in connection with the estates and trusts that they administer. Commercial banks—by investing their time and demand deposits—held $72,360,000,000 in investments at the close of January 1951, of which $12,330,000,000 were in securities other than United States government obligations. Mutual savings banks, on the same date, held another $13,210,000,000, of which $2,330,000,000 were not Untied States government securities. Another institutional investor is the rapidly growing group of investment trusts and companies. Eleemosynary institutions, about which there may be debate on the point of investing other people's money, are also classed as institutional investors. This group includes colleges, universities, and other educational institutions; churches and various religious groups; benevolent, charitable and similar institutions; hospitals, foundations and endowments of all kinds; and public and private pension and retirement funds. Individually the securities bought by these investors range from millions of dollars to much smaller sums; but in the aggregate the securities lump large; particularly, there has been a notable increase in pension and retirement funds.

Noninstitutional investors include corporations and other business firms having surplus funds to invest, certain estate and trust funds administered by individuals, and the very large group of private individuals who accumulate funds through savings and a desire to "put their money to work."

The question has been asked frequently as to how many stockholders there are in American industry. An accurate answer would indicate

broadly the function of stockbrokers and dealers as intermediaries for buyers of stocks, since relatively few stocks are sold without the services of stockbrokers and dealers. A number of estimates have been made ranging from five to 15 million stockholders. The Federal Reserve System estimated the minimum number at six million stockholders in the early part of 1949.[1] Mr. Robert H. Fetridge, writing in *The New York Times,* estimated the number at 15 million; he based his estimate on a report made by the New York Stock Exchange to the effect that there were 4,432,640 stockholders holding stock in 50 of the 1,043 companies listed on that exchange. Since there are some 530,000 corporations in the United States, Mr. Fetridge's estimate does not appear excessive. Nor does the estimate of 15 million individuals appear excessive when it is realized that this figure represents an average of slightly less than 30 owners of stock per corporation; if the 50 corporations with 4,432,640 stockholders are eliminated, that average number of stockholders for the remaining corporations falls to less than 20 owners per corporation. Common stockholders of the American Telephone and Telegraph Company alone number some 1,000,000 in April 1951. General Motors had 436,000 on the same date, and its number of stockholders will soon reach 500,000, a consequence of its stock split-up in June 1950. Certainly if bondholders are added to stockholders, it is safe to say that stockbrokers and dealers serve, as intermediaries, some 15,000,000 investors.

Maintaining a market for securities. Another highly important function of stockbrokers and dealers is the maintenance of a market for securities. Maintenance of a market for any item means the buying and selling of that item so as to reflect its current dollar value at the time and place of the transaction. The uses to which the current dollar value of specific securities may be put are many. Such data are useful to prospective issuers of like securities, to prospective investors in securities, and to the legions of institutions, organizations, and individuals, who are owners of securities and who desire to compute their current financial position.

It is not within the scope of this chapter to discuss the many factors which bring about the changes in the dollar value of an item of wealth; it is sufficient here to repeat that dollar value is subjective in nature and can best be determined by an actual monetary exchange transaction. Unless an exchange transaction is conditioned by some sort of repurchase agreement or option, a buyer is never certain of the dollar value of the thing he has bought until he sells that thing to another buyer. But this uncertainty regarding the dollar value of the thing he owns can be greatly reduced if others are buying and selling similar items. So in the field of securities, the more buyers and sellers and the more

[1] *Federal Reserve Bulletin,* October 1949, p. 1190.

actual transactions in any given security, the more definitely anyone can determine the dollar value of that security.

A market is said to be "dull" or "thin" when few or no sale transactions are being made; under such conditions the dollar value of the market items involved can only be estimated. The market for real estate has experienced (particularly in the early 1930's) periods of dullness, and during such times the owner of a home has little idea whether or not he could sell his property for as much as, or more, or less, than he paid for it. In the securities market periods of relative dullness may exist, but it is the function of stockbrokers and dealers to find someone to buy or to sell, or to offer to buy or to sell themselves, any given security. In no other market is this obligation to maintain a market fulfilled more completely than in the securities market.

Or perhaps of even greater importance to the investing public is the fact that a purchaser of securities knows before he makes his purchase that should he desire to sell at a later date, the sale can be arranged without too much difficulty. This adds a high degree of "liquidity" (that is, convertibility into cash) to the ownership of securities. The "liquidity" that goes along with the ownership of securities due to the efforts of stockbrokers and dealers in maintaining a market is highly desirable in any economy, since liquidity tends to put idle dollars to work: money is more efficiently used to the benefit of the user, the investor, and the public.

The maintenance of a market for securities is an important function of the registered exchanges (dealt with elsewhere in the text), but it is important to understand that many more securities are bought and sold off the exchanges than on the exchanges. The "over-the-counter" market is by far the largest securities market in the country. As of January 1, 1949, there were 4,123 securities issues admitted for trading on the 24 exchanges in the country; but there are some 135,000 [2] securities issues traded in the over-the-counter market by stockbrokers and dealers. While it is a fact that many of the largest corporations have their securities issues listed for trading on the registered exchanges, this does not mean that the corporations' securities are only bought and sold on the exchanges. A considerable volume, in some cases conceivably greater than the volume traded on the exchanges, of these same listed securities are bought and sold through stockbrokers and dealers operating in the "over-the-counter" market. Unfortunately the difficulties of collecting data on transactions handled by the more than 4,000 stockbrokers and dealers operating in the over-the-counter market are so great that figures

---

[2] Estimated.

are not available. The lack of information also makes estimates of doubtful value.

Other functions of stockbrokers and dealers. An enumeration of all other functions of stockbrokers and dealers would entail a list of all the things that they do. Only the major functions are discussed here, but some of the others will be apparent in the remainder of the chapter. Stockbrokers and dealers, like other financial institutions, are characterized more by their multiplicity of functions and the overlapping of functions (found also in other financial institutions), than by a distinctive nature confined to a single purpose. The wide range of the customers they serve and the attempts to improve the service to the public account for many of their lesser-known functions.

1. Service to the Business Community. The modern business world could not function were it not for the many services rendered to business by stockbrokers and dealers. In planning not only their own financial structure but also their future productive activities, all businesses seek data concerning the operations of stockholders and dealers. Business executives base many of their decisions on indicators that become apparent through the securities markets. Just as many factors and events are reflected in the securities market, so also happenings in that market form the basis in part of activities in other phases of the business world.

More directly, stockbrokers and dealers (as the ultimate retailers of securities) assist the business community in carrying out its financial programs. Being the final link in the investment banking chain, the stockbrokers and dealers bring together the issuer of a security and the investor. In this sense stockbrokers and dealers "find" the money needed by corporations to conduct productive operations. The relationship between stockbrokers and dealers and investment bankers is an intimate one—so much so in fact that many firms of stockbrokers and dealers are also investment bankers. This is especially true of the larger firms of stockbrokers and dealers.

2. Service to Government. Just as stockbrokers and dealers assist the business community, so also do their services extend to federal, state, and local governments. Governmental securities have become relatively so large in the total of all securities that management of the federal debt, for instance, is no small undertaking. Activities in the securities market furnish data used in part to determine governmental debt policies. And in a direct way the brokers and dealers in governments and municipals assist the carrying out of governmental financial programs, as well as play an important role in the maintenance of an orderly market for such securities. An early instance of the service of stockbrokers and dealers utilized by the federal government was the employment of Jay Cooke in the spring of 1863 to sell government securities to finance the Civil War.

Of an issue of $500,000,000 of government bonds authorized on February 25, 1862, only $32,000,000 had been sold by April 1, 1863. Through the services of Cooke, $157,000,000 were sold in the next three months.

3. Services to Other Financial Institutions. The case of a financial institution, no matter what its function, that does not or has not availed itself of the services of stockbrokers and dealers would be rare indeed. Banks and all forms of savings institutions are served by stockbrokers and dealers in the investment of funds in the securities making up banks' investment portfolios. Trust companies and administrators and executors of wills carry out their functions with the active assistance of stockbrokers and dealers. Even the so-called "closed" financial institutions, i.e., those that gather the savings of a specific group and in turn invest these savings within that same group, at times find themselves with funds over and above their own requirements and seek the services of stockbrokers and dealers in making profitable investment of such excess funds. In a similar manner many nonfinancial institutions also avail themselves of the services of stockbrokers and dealers for investment of excess funds.

4. Services to the Public. By far the greatest volume of services rendered by stockbrokers and dealers is included in the relationship with the investing public. To the stockbrokerage firm no question asked concerning the investment field is too trivial to be neglected. Considerable sums are spent each year by stockbrokers and dealer firms in their research activities to compile data in the anticipation of, and in direct answer to, questions asked by the investing public.

In addition, stockbrokers and dealers carry on a banking function for their customers. Many investors deposit their investable funds with a brokerage house where the funds are retained to be invested as directed by the customer. Customers' credit balances, the amount on deposit with the brokerage firm, represent funds deposited by customers and the proceeds of customers' sale of securities left by them with the brokerage firm. Under certain conditions these credit balances earn interest for the customers while the funds are held by the firm. Customers' debit balances represent sums owed by customers to brokerage firms and result chiefly from trading on margin (to be discussed later); in effect debit balances represent loans (similar in some respects to bank loans to bank customers) made by securities firms to customers.

The many and varied services to the public are inherent in the nature of the business of stockbrokers and dealers; in addition, competition for new business, on the part of the firms, makes it advisable to render many services at no charge, for which a direct benefit to the firm may be difficult to identify.

Operations of Stockbrokers and Dealers

Types of brokers and dealers. In addition to the fundamental distinction between brokers and dealers as set forth at the beginning of this chapter, the development of the modern securities business has produced certain specialized services which tend to distinguish the operations of certain brokers and dealers. Some of this specialization results from the nature of operations on the registered security exchanges, and some is the result of meeting the demands for service in the general securities market. While distinctions are made between certain types of brokers and dealers, it is important to realize that individual firms both large and small may act as more than one type; further it should be noted that individuals may at different times act as different types.

1. Floor Broker. A floor broker executes orders to buy or sell securities on the floor of an exchange. He must be a member of the exchange but may or may not be a member of a stockbrokerage house. If he is a member of a firm, he executes orders for his firm which receives a commission for the service rendered. If the floor broker is an independent broker, he may service one or more firms; it is, however, necessary for him to identify the firm he is servicing with each order he executes. Independent brokers are sometimes known as $2 brokers. This designation stems from the time when their share of the commission charged the customer was $2 per hundred shares; nowadays the floor broker's compensation is fixed by a sliding scale running from less than $2 for certain stocks to a much higher figure.

2. Floor Trader. The use of the word "floor" again indicates operations or transactions conducted on an exchange. The floor trader buys and sells securities for his own account or for the account of the firm. The primary function of the floor trader is to minimize a temporary disparity between demand and supply for a given security. He is said to take a position, that is, to buy or to sell the security and thus absorb the temporary excess of demand or supply. In this manner the floor trader adds materially to the liquidity of the market. Because of the potentiality of abuse, the activities of the floor trader are covered by many restrictive rules.

3. Odd-Lot Dealers and Brokers. The registered exchanges have found that it is more efficient and economical to conduct trading in securities by limiting transactions to a certain number of shares, known as a unit of trading, or multiples of that unit. For most listed stocks the unit of trading is 100 shares. However, there is need in meeting the requirements of customers, to buy and sell in less numbers than the "round-lot" or unit of trading. To meet this need a certain few firms buy and sell

listed stocks in amounts from one to 99 shares. (Since certain "inactive stocks" are traded in 10-share units, odd-lot transactions in these securities would be 1 to 9 shares.) Odd-lot dealers are the firms that buy and sell in odd-lot amounts, and odd-lot brokers are the individuals who execute the orders on the floor of the exchange. The operations of odd-lot dealers enable the small investor to trade in the same free and open market as the larger investor trading in round or full lots.

4. The Specialist. The specialist is so designated because of the particular securities in which he deals. He may limit his dealings to the securities issued by a given industry, to a few concerns within a given industry, or to any other limited number of securities. Somewhat like the trader, the specialist operates to minimize disparity between demand and supply for his securities. He may hold orders in his securities that cannot be executed at the time they are received by the broker initially concerned; or he may buy or sell for his own account at prices at which he has no public orders. In the latter case, the specialist does much to reduce the spread between the prices at which public investors are willing to sell and others are willing to buy.

5. The Bond Crowd. More bonds are bought and sold off the exchanges than on the exchanges, but under certain conditions members of exchanges are required to send orders for the purchase or sale of bonds to the floor for execution. Brokers and dealers specializing in bonds are known as the bond crowd. On the exchanges the bond crowd is divided into: (1) the active or free crowd; (2) the inactive, book, or cabinet crowd; (3) the foreign crowd; and (4) the government crowd. Trading by the active crowd is done much the same as is the case for stocks—the unit of bond trading being $1,000 original principal amount. The inactive crowd trade in bonds designated inactive by the exchange, which provides a method of trading unlike that for active bonds. The name of "book" or "cabinet" comes from the method of trading in which bids and offers are placed in a "book" or "cabinet," a file under the jurisdiction of an employee of the exchange. Before a trade is consummated, the brokers involved meet and complete the trade by confirming the price and exchange names. The foreign crowd trade in foreign government and foreign corporation bonds; the members of this crowd are in turn divided into an active and an inactive crowd. The government crowd, as the name indicates, trades in United States government bonds; since the trading is usually in large quantities, the trading is similar to the active crowd.

6. Over-the-counter Market. Brokers and dealers not members of the registered exchanges (and including some who are) trade in securities without the use of facilities provided by the exchanges. The over-the-counter market antedates the exchange markets, and the name refers

to the time when securities trading was actually conducted over the counters of the various securities firms. While it is the largest securities market from the points of view of number of security issues traded, the number of brokers and dealers trading in the market, and the dollar volume of trading, it is much less understood by almost everyone, except experienced brokers and professional traders, than the organized exchanges. Various names have been suggested to indicate more clearly the nature of the over-the-counter market, especially since it no longer involves the actual counters of the firms. Since trading is done by telephone, telegraph, and teletype, it has been suggested that this market be named the "wire" market; but considerable wire communications are used by the organized exchanges, especially in reaching the branch offices of member firms. The "unlisted market" has been suggested, but again many securities listed on the organized exchanges find their broadest market in the over-the-counter market. Another suggestion made is the "off board" market, since trading transactions are not recorded on the boards of the organized exchanges; but this has a weakness similar to the "unlisted market." Until some better name is devised, the term "over-the-counter" probably will be used because of its more general acceptance.

In the absence of a "floor" on which to conduct trading, the over-the-counter market consists of the offices of the securities dealers, each of which has more or less extensive communication facilities to get in touch with other securities dealers. Trading contracts are completed by communication rather than by the methods used on the floor of an exchange. Since there is no board on which trading transactions can be recorded, nor other means of publicizing quotations of bids and offers, a considerable amount of the work performed in the offices of over-the-counter dealers involves the making of quotations to one another. In addition the National Quotation Bureau, a private organization, by arrangement, makes quotations available for a fee. Bureau quotations may cover in excess of 5,000 securities in one day.

The business of the over-the-counter market is carried on, much as is the work of the organized exchanges, by brokers, traders, and dealers with the necessary qualifications inherent in the nature of the over-the-counter market. Nothing would be further from the truth than to label it an unorganized market, since the extensive communication system which serves it enables it to complete transactions in a matter of minutes, even though an order may originate in New Orleans or San Francisco and be completed in New York or Chicago. One house describes the operations as follows: "Feature players in this whole process are the traders themselves. A crackerjack off board (over-the-counter) trader is an alert, aggressive individual who has a nose for news, a flare for

figures, and a knack for 'horse-swapping.' A prime requisite of any trader is know-how which takes years and years to acquire. Another requirement is an ability to remember quotations in a rapidly changing market; he must be able to give up-to-the-minute bids and offers on scores of securities. At another time he must act as confidential agent for a customer. This is especially important in large orders, for if he tipped his hand while trying to buy 1000 shares the sellers would demand a much higher price. On the other side, poor handling of a large sale order might cause bids to vanish like snow in a thaw. And last but not least, a trader must be responsible for large amounts of money since many of them have the power to buy or sell big blocks for the account of their firm." [3]

Popular misconception sometimes identifies the over-the-counter market with highly speculative securities, but the large volume of trading in United States government bonds, obligations of states and municipalities, plus some of the highest grade securities found in railroads and industrial corporations belies any such misconception. In addition mention has already been made of the large volume of listed securities traded in the over-the-counter market. This market has served as a broad seasoning ground for many securities of both old and new companies—securities that later have been listed on a registered exchange.

Later in this chapter the nature of regulation of the over-the-counter markets is discussed.

Types of securities. The various types of securities entering into trading by stockbrokers and dealers are many. This variety is due to the issuance of certain types of securities to meet certain needs. In general the type of a security issue is determined by the needs of the issuer in combination with the needs of the ultimate investor. Only the more general types are discussed here.

1. Common Stocks. Ownership of a corporation is divided among the individuals owning shares of the corporations. These shares are evidenced by stock certificates which state the name of the corporation, the name of the owner of shares, the number of shares, and the class of stock. Common stockholders are basically the owners of the corporation: the assets of the corporation belong to the common stockholders, and they are entitled to share in residual profits in the form of dividends after other obligations are paid. There are various classes of common stocks such as voting and nonvoting, par and no par.

2. Preferred Stocks. Preferred stocks, in addition to being stock that represents ownership, carry some sort of preference. Usually the preference is as to dividends, though it may be as to assets or some other preference. Preferred stock, preferred as to dividends, simply means that

---

[3] *Off Board Securities Market,* a publication by Merrill Lynch, Pierce, Fenner & Beane.

dividends at a certain rate or amount will be paid preferred stockholders prior to payment of other dividends. Many classes of preferred stock may be issued, each designed to meet a certain need; and in effect their provisions for preference run all the way from preference stock that is hardly distinguishable from common stock on one hand to preference stock that is hardly distinguishable from bonds on the other hand.

3. Bonds. Bonds are evidences of debt. The relationship of a bondholder to the issuer organization is in no sense that of ownership, but rather that of creditor. By a bond the issuer obligates himself to pay a fixed sum of money at a stated future date and to pay interest at a specified rate during the life of the bond. Like other securities, bonds are designed to meet various needs. Bonds also run the gamut of varying provisions; some bonds may even include profit-sharing clauses.

4. Convertible Securities. A word should be said concerning convertible securities. These are most frequently some form of a corporation's bond or preferred stock issue which may be converted (exchanged with the issuer for some form of security, generally common stock). By definition there is no reason why convertible stocks could not be issued to provide for conversion into bonds, but the implications about the future financial conditions of the issuer might not be good. Convertible bonds enable bondholders (creditors) of an issuer to become stockholders—that is, owners of the corporation. Conversion is at the option of the investor, but the procedure does have the advantage to the issuer of reducing its bonded debt.

The market price of convertible bonds is influenced by a factor not present in other bonds. In principle the dollar value of a bond should be that amount of dollars which, if invested at the current rate of interest for the period to the maturity of the bond, will produce the same amount of income, assuming all other factors (such as risk, tax status, and so on) are the same. For example, a 5 per cent bond pays interest at $50.00 a year. If the current rate of interest (for like investments) is 4 per cent, the bond is worth $1250 ($50 ÷ 4% = $1,250), and if the current rate of interest is 6 per cent the bond is worth $833.33, ($50 ÷ 6% = $833.33). But if the bond is convertible into 10 shares of stock, the market price of the bond will not go below the market price of 10 shares of stock, since it can be converted into that stock. For this reason if the market price of each share of stock is $100 and the current rate of interest should be 6 per cent, the market price of the bond will not go down to $833.33; it will remain at $1,000, the market price of 10 shares of stock. On the other hand if the market price of 10 shares of stock is $1,000 and the current rate of interest is 4 per cent the market price of the convertible bond will rise to $1250 and no conversion is likely. From this the general principle may be stated that the market

price of a convertible bond will rise and fall with the market price of the stock into which it can be converted, and that the price of a convertible bond may rise independently of the market price (but will not fall below the market price) of the stock.

In the illustration above, the conversion rate was stated as 10 shares of stock, a definite number of shares. Frequently the conversion rate is expressed by stating that the bonds are convertible into stock at 100 or 120 or some other figure. If the figure is given as 80, it simply means that the stock is valued at $80 a share for conversion purposes and that a $1000 bond can be converted into 12½ shares of stock ($1,000 ÷ $80 = 12.5). A 120 figure would mean that one bond can be converted into 8⅓ shares of stock. When the stock is selling in the market at exactly the conversion rate, the bonds are said to be at their conversion point, since conversion can be made at this point without gain or loss.

5. Dividends. Income return to stockholders is paid in the form of dividends; that is, corporations pay dividends to their owner stockholders. Dividends may be paid at any time, subject to certain legal restrictions, that the board of directors may decide. Most corporations have regular dividend paying dates during the year, but many corporations decide the amount and date of payment as circumstances permit. The announcement of a dividend payment on a given stock issue will provide that the stockholder, as of record on a certain future date, will receive the dividend, which will actually be paid after the record date. Since the stock may be bought and sold on the record date, the question arises as to whom the dividend is payable. The decision is regulated by rules of the exchanges for their members and by the National Association of Security Dealers for its members. In general the rule is determined by the method of delivery of the stock to the purchaser. If the transaction is a "cash" transaction, the buyer on the record date receives the dividend, since his name will be recorded as owner of the stock at the close of that day. Where the transaction is not "cash," the principle is that purchasers of stock are not entitled to the dividend, if the stock is purchased within the time period allowed to the seller to deliver the stock to the purchaser. For example, if the rule allows the seller to deliver the stock he sells to the purchaser on the third day following the sale transaction, then purchasers of the stock during the period of two full business days immediately prior to the dividend record date would purchase the stock without being entitled to the dividend. The reason for this rule is that the purchaser's ownership of the stock would not be recorded until the day after the record date. Under such conditions the stock is said to be sold ex-dividend—that is, without the dividend. Obviously all other things being equal, the market price of the stock should fall the amount of the dividend the day the stock becomes

ex-dividend. The term cum-dividend is used to indicate a stock's being sold on which a dividend is payable. The time involved here is the period between the announcement of a dividend payment and the time the stock becomes ex-dividend. Obviously the purchaser is as entitled to the dividend on stocks sold cum-dividend as he is at all other times except during the ex-dividend period.

What has been said regarding dividends refers principally to the payment of dividends in the form of cash. Dividends are also sometimes paid in the form of additional shares of stock, bonds, scrip, and other property. As a matter of fact, within legal requirements and when cash dividends are permissible, there is no reason why any form of wealth owned by a corporation could not be distributed to its stockholders as dividends. Regardless of the form the dividend payment may take, the principles discussed above concerning cum-dividend and ex-dividend stocks are applicable.

6. Rights. Rights are another type of security bought and sold in the securities markets. As in the case of dividends, the terms ex-rights and cum-rights are also found in purchase and sale transactions. A right is a privilege to purchase a stock. If a corporation decides to increase its capital by increasing the amount of capital stock it is authorized to sell, the present stockholders are extended the privilege of purchasing the new stock. This procedure is in accordance with principles of equity, since it enables stockholders to retain their proportionate share of interest in, and control of, the corporation. (This right of stockholders is protected in nearly all states as part of state corporate law.) Under the principle, each share of stock outstanding at the time the new stock is to be issued inherently carries in it a pre-emptive right to purchase some portion of the new capital stock issue. The proportion is determined by the relation between the amount of old stock outstanding and the amount of new stock to be issued. Thus, if there are 100,000 old shares outstanding and 25,000 new shares are to be issued, each old share of stock will contain the privilege to purchase $\frac{1}{4}$ new share, or the rights attached to four old shares will contain the privilege to purchase one new share. As in the case of dividends, the corporation will announce a record date for the distribution of rights; the announcement will contain the number of rights required to purchase new shares, the price at which the new share is to be purchased, and the time period within which the right must be exercised. It should be noted that each old share always carries one right and the number of rights needed to procure a new share is determined by the proportion of old stock to new stock. Thus, if the amount of stock is to be doubled, each right contains the privilege of purchasing one new share, and if the amount of stock is

to be trebled, each right contains the privilege of purchasing two new shares.

The price contained in the announcement at which the new shares can be purchased is called the offering price, and this sum together with the number of rights required will procure a new share of stock. Should one right contain the privilege of purchasing more than one share, then the number of shares the right will procure times the offering price is the sum of money required, not forgetting the right itself. Since the offering price is below the current market price of the old shares, each right has a monetary value; and immediately upon announcement, trading in the rights begins. At this time trading is on a "when, as, and if issued" basis. In principle the monetary value of a right can be computed to be the difference between the current price of the old stock less the offering price of the new stock, divided by one plus the number of rights required to purchase one new share. Thus if four rights are required to buy one new share and if the current market price of the old stock is $90 and the offering price is $80, the value of one right would be $2 $\left(\dfrac{90 - 80}{4 + 1} = \dfrac{10}{5} = 2 \right)$. The one is added to the number of rights required since the market price of the old stock includes the value of one right.

From the date of announcement until the record date (or until the date the stock goes ex-rights under the principles explained above in connection with dividends), the stock is said to sell cum-rights, and the value of a right is computed as illustrated. When the stock is selling ex-rights, the value of a right would be determined in a similar manner, except that the divisor would not include the 1 in addition to the number of rights required to purchase one new share. Assuming that on the day the stock went ex-rights it lost the value of the right it formerly contained, the market price would be $90 − $2 = $88. Then the computation of the value of one right would be $\dfrac{88 - 80}{4} = \dfrac{8}{4} = \$2$, the value of one right. The stock would sell ex-rights from the date it went ex-rights until the expiration date of the privilege of exercising the right. During this period the rights themselves would continue to be traded in the market. After the expiration date, obviously the rights no longer have any value.

While mathematical illustrations are given above, it must not be understood that the market prices of rights and of the stock would follow exactly any such computation. During the period of trading in rights, the market value of the stock would fluctuate in all likelihood. Further, the market value of the rights themselves would be subject to all the influences that go to make market prices. The mathematical

computations are useful to illustrate a principle; and even in a practical way, such computations should be made and the results considered along with other factors if actual investments are being made.

7. Warrants. Somewhat like convertible securities discussed above, warrants are sometimes used to "sweeten" an issue of bonds or preferred stocks. A warrant is an option or privilege given by a corporation to purchase a security of the corporation, usually common stock, at a stated price in a given amount, and within a given time. When a stock purchase warrant is attached to a bond, the warrant gives the bond purchaser the privilege of becoming an owner (and thus a sharer in profits) of the corporation, as well as a receiver of stated interest in his creditor position as bondholder. Since, like rights, the offering price stated in the warrant is less than the current market price, warrants have value and are traded in under conditions similar to rights. Warrants, like other securities, vary greatly in the specific provisions they contain; but warrants are issued in two general forms: detachable and nondetachable. Detachable warrants may be detached from the bond with which they were issued and sold separately, with the privileges accompanying and being extended to the holder of the warrant. In this respect detachable warrants are similar to rights. Nondetachable warrants may not be detached from the bond except when the privilege of sale is being exercised, and then they are detached by an agent of the issuing corporation.

8. Voting Trust Certificates. Under certain conditions the stockholders of a corporation may find it advantageous to pool their voting power. In such cases their stock may be transferred to trustees, and they receive in return a voting trust certificate. All the rights and privileges of the stock except voting are retained by the stockholders, and such rights and privileges are evidenced by the voting trust certificates. These certificates are freely transferable and are traded in the securities market.

9. Equipment Trust Certificates. These securities are among the highest grade obtainable from the point of view of security of principal. They arise mainly out of financing the purchase of railroad equipment. Equipment trust certificates are debt securities which are secured by a lien on the equipment of the issuer. Title to the equipment does not pass to the issuer until the certificates have been redeemed. During the life of the certificates, title rests with a trustee who holds it for the certificate owners.

10. Other Types of Securities. The kinds of securities discussed above are by no means exhaustive but are intended to be representative of the more common types. It should be remembered that financial instruments, such as securities, may contain provisions of varying degrees, each intended to meet a given need or to make a certain appeal. As the financial world becomes more complex, it is to be assumed that addi-

tional and new types of securities will be devised to meet changing conditions. Any of these newer types that are freely transferable will doubtless be traded in the securities markets.

Types of transactions.

1. Cash Transactions. The purchase and sale of securities may be accomplished just as any other purchase and sale—that is, for cash payment at the time of the transaction. But there are other varying types of trading transactions used by stockbrokers and dealers. As a matter of fact the term "cash" transaction is used within the security business to designate a certain type of clearing transaction to be discussed below. At this point the term "cash" is employed to mean the actual payment for securities purchased or sold. It is entirely possible for anyone to walk into a brokerage office, place an order to buy certain securities, and pay for them at the time of purchase. The more usual way, however, is for the investor to open an account with a securities house, much as a bank account is opened, and then place orders to buy and sell securities and have the resultant funds involved charged or credited to the account. Securities bought and sold for cash in this sense will result in the full value of the securities being entered in the account. It should be noted that brokerage commissions charged to the customer also are entered in the account.

2. Margin Transactions. The use of credit is present in all markets in our modern economy, and the securities market is no exception. Securities can be bought and sold under conditions involving the use of credit. Thus an investor desiring to purchase certain securities can arrange to make payment out of his own funds for a certain proportion of the total value of the securities, and he can arrange with his broker or dealer to borrow the remainder. The proportion that the customer must pay out of his own funds has never been entirely at his own discretion. Like any other lender, each broker or dealer has decided what amounts he would lend to his customers as borrowers; and in addition the exchanges have had rules governing the lending operations of their members. Beginning with the Securities Exchange Act of 1934, authority to set the minimum amount which a customer must pay out of his own funds has been given to the Federal Reserve Board. Since that time the Board, under its Regulation T, sets the amount, in percentage, that the customer must pay. Thus if the requirement is stated as 75 per cent, it means the customer must use his own funds up to a minimum of 75 per cent of the market value of the securities on the day of the transaction, and the broker or dealer may not lend the customer more than 25 per cent. Under Regulation T of the Board, the percentage

required has ranged from 20 per cent on certain accounts effective October 1, 1934, to 100 per cent on all accounts effective January 21, 1946. During that period between 1934 and 1946, the percentage was raised in steps; since 1946 the Board has lowered the percentage required, first to 75 per cent on all accounts effective February 1, 1947, then to 50 per cent on all accounts effective March 30, 1949. On January 17, 1951, the percentage went back to 75 per cent.

The effect of margin requirements on profit or loss sustainable in the securities market may be illustrated, as in Table 1. Assume that a purchaser of securities has $1,000 of his own funds to invest, with shares of the desired security selling at $100 per share, and a subsequent change in market value of $5 per share.

TABLE 1

EFFECT OF MARGIN REQUIREMENT

Margin Requirement	Customer's Funds Invested	Amount of Credit Utilized	No. of Shares at $100 Each Purchased	Total Value of Investment	Change in Market Value Per Share	Profit or Loss— Sustainable
10%	$1,000	$9,000	100	$10,000	± $5	± $500
25%	1,000	3,000	40	4,000	± 5	± 200
50%	1,000	1,000	20	2,000	± 5	± 100
75%	1,000	333.33	13.3	1.333.33	± 5	± 66.50
100%	1,000	....	10	1,000	± 5	± 50

From Table 1 it may be stated that the higher the margin requirement, the smaller the profit or loss sustainable on a given investment.

3. Round Lots and Odd-Lot Transactions. As stated above, certain brokers and dealers specialize in handling odd-lot transactions on the exchanges. This does not mean that all customers must contact these few firms. Any firm can handle a customer's order for any number of shares. Firms other than odd-lot dealers simply handle the transaction through the odd-lot firm, which charges a fee for its service. The odd-lot fee, known as differential, is paid by the customer in addition to the broker's commission. Where the round lot is 100 shares (stocks traded on the floor of the exchange in 100-share units) the odd-lot differential is $\frac{1}{8}$ ($12\frac{1}{2}$ cents per share). For 10-share round lots the differential is scaled according to the price of the share from $\frac{1}{4}$ (25 cents) to $\frac{1}{2}$ (50 cents) per share.

4. Short Sales. The adjectives long and short are used as standard terms in the securities markets. In general longs may be said to be those who have, "the haves," whereas shorts are those who need but have not, the "have nots." A long on the market is one who holds certain securities, and a short is one who must eventually buy certain securities. Thus a person may be long on some securities and at the same time short on others.

Applied to sales in the case of the person who owns securities and sells

them, the sale is said to be a long sale. If a customer places an order to sell securities which he does not have, either he or his broker must borrow the securities, with a promise to return at a later date; such a sale is designated a short sale. Short sales are made in anticipation of a decline in the price of a security, so that the seller may be able to buy the security later at a lower price. At the present, margin requirements are equally applicable to both long and short sales.

The requirement to borrow securities involved in a short sale arises out of the need to make delivery of the securities to the purchaser. Securities are borrowed in three different ways: (1) flat; (2) at a rate; and (3) at a premium. Under flat the lender of the securities receives a compensating loan of money equal to the market value of the securities. Neither loan carries a fee or interest. When securities are loaned at a rate, the lender of the securities pays the borrower interest on the funds the latter has advanced to the securities lender. The loan of securities at a premium is the reverse of a loan at a rate, in that the borrower of the securities also pays a premium in addition to advancing the market value of the securities.

Short sales are now under various restrictive rules and practices (including price), so that whereas considerable controversy used to exist concerning the merits and demerits of short sales, restrictions have lessened the effects of such sales.

5. Puts and Calls. Options to buy and to sell are found in the securities markets as they are in many other markets. In the securities markets, two such options are known as "puts" and "calls." A put may be defined as an option to sell a certain number of securities at a set price within a specified time. The seller of the option, usually a securities dealer, receives a stated amount for giving the options. Options are usually written for 100-share units and the price stated in the put is usually below the current market.

A call, on the other hand, is an option to buy a certain number of securities at a set price within a specified time. Again, the seller of the option usually is a securities dealer, and he receives a stated amount for giving the option. Calls are also written for 100-share units, and the price stated in the call is usually above the current market.

6. Clearing Transactions. The purchaser of securities expects to receive the securities he purchases, and the seller expects to receive his funds all within a reasonable period of time. Considering the large volume of securities bought and sold each business day, the work of making delivery is of no small proportions. Delivery is accomplished in a number of ways, the more common of which are: [4]

---

[4] Delivery methods given here are those defined by the Uniform Practice Code of the National Association of Securities Dealers, Inc.

a. "Cash" Transaction. When a transaction is designated as "cash," "delivery shall be made at the office of the purchaser on the day of the transaction."

b. Regular Way. A "regular way" transaction calls for delivery to be made at the office of the purchaser on the third full business day following the date of the transaction. "Regular way" on the registered exchanges sometimes requires delivery on the second full business day following the day of the contract.

c. Delayed Delivery. This type transaction calls for delivery to be made at the office of the purchaser on the seventh calendar day following the date of transaction.

d. Seller's Option. Delivery is required to be made at the office of the purchaser on the date on which the option expires. In this type of transaction, if the seller gives to the purchaser in writing one full business day's notice, the seller may then make delivery any time after the third full business day following the transaction and before the expiration date of the option.

e. Buyer's Option. Delivery shall be made at the office of the purchaser on the date on which the option expires, but a purchaser may accept delivery when tendered by the seller prior to the expiration of the option if the purchaser so elects.

f. "When, As, and If Issued." Securities sold on a "when, as, and if issued" basis are delivered in accordance with: (1) the rules established by the District Uniform Practice Committee of NASD; (2) the written notice of seller to purchaser; (3) the date of settlement of the syndicate or selling group contracts, if securities are being sold by a syndicate or selling group.

In the cases of "delayed delivery," "seller's option," and "buyer's option," if the contracts mature on a Saturday, a holiday, or a half-holiday, the contracts carry over to the next full business day.

7. Bond Transactions. Bonds and similar interest-paying evidences of indebtedness are traded usually on an "and interest" basis. This simply means that interest accrued between interest paying dates is added to the price of the bond sale and paid by the purchaser to the seller. The purchaser recoups his interest payment to the seller on the next interest paying date of the bond. Income bonds (bonds paying interest only if earned), certain adjustment bonds, and bonds in default (including bonds on which notice of default has been made), are traded "flat." Bonds traded "flat" are bought and sold without regard to interest. Bonds are traded "ex-interest" under conditions similar to stocks traded "ex-dividend," except that the interest date in the case of bonds may or may not be publicly announced for each interest date. Clearing transactions described above are applicable to bonds as well as stocks.

Types of orders.

1. Details Contained in an Order. Principally to meet the needs of their customers and to provide for orderly trading, stockbrokers and dealers handle various types of orders. In order for a securities transaction to be effected, it is necessary to know: (1) the security to be traded; (2) whether it is a buy or sell order (in the case of a sell order, it is also necessary to know whether it is a long or short sale); (3) the number of shares or other securities to be traded; (4) customers' limitations as to price; (5) customers' limitations as to time; and (6) any other instructions. The first three are self-explanatory.

2. Customers' Limitations as to Price.

a. Limit Orders. It is obviously a privilege of any purchaser of securities to state what price he is willing to pay for such securities, and it is equally obvious that a seller of securities may state at what price he is willing to sell his securities. When a customer states the price at which the securities are to be bought or sold, the order is known as a "limit" order. Limit orders are stated, "buy at 90" or "sell at 92" and are executed by the broker or trader only if a purchaser or seller can be found to meet the limit orders. Thus in the illustration if no seller could be found willing to sell at 90 or if no purchaser could be found to buy at 92 the transactions would not be completed.

b. At the Market Orders. A customer may not know what price he will have to pay to purchase a security, or a seller may not know at what price he can dispose of his securities. In such a case the customer may instruct that his order be placed "at the market." This phrase means that the broker or dealer handling the order is to get the best price obtainable for his customer. Conditions surrounding the trading on the registered exchanges differ in publicity given to them from the over-the-counter market. Trading on the exchanges is publicized, transaction by transaction, over the ticker tape, and daily transactions are summarized in all leading newspapers, so that a customer whose order is handled on the exchanges may see within rather narrow limits what the market price of a security is from time to time. No such publicity exists in the over-the-counter market. The rules of fair practice of the NASD prohibit any member from making a representation to a customer that his order would be handled "at the market," unless the order is for a listed security (in which case the "market" would be that indicated on the exchange), or unless a reasonable market for the security does exist outside that made or controlled by the member himself. Determination of a fair market price may be difficult in many instances. Generally the following criteria may be used in the order listed:

(1) Sales on exchanges for listed securities traded.

(2) Asked prices for listed securities not traded.

(3) Highest offer for unlisted securities on the professional markets.

(4) A fair and reasonable price for inactive unlisted securities.

Fortunately, due to the relatively few trades made under conditions of (4), and to the general integrity of security brokers and dealers, not many cases arise to cause disputes in this category. For brokers or dealers not members of registered exchanges and not members of NASD, willful violation of the rules above subjects the dealers and brokers to revocation of registration or license by the Securities and Exchange Commission and the state regulatory bodies.

3. Customers' Limitations as to Time. Customers' orders given to brokers and dealers automatically expire at the close of the business day in which the orders were given unless they were: (1) executed that day; (2) cancelled that day; or (3) otherwise indicated. Such orders are known as "day" orders. Other time limitation orders are: (1) "week," that is, they expire on the last trading day of the calendar week; (2) "month," expire on the last trading day of the calendar month; and (3) G.T.C. orders, which mean good till cancelled.

In general the question of limitations as to price or time depends on the factor uppermost in the customer's mind. Orders limited as to price may be subject to considerable delay or even nonexecution; orders limited as to time may result in less attractive prices.

4. Other Customers' Instructions.

a. Stop Order to Sell. An investor holding a certain security, especially one which he has purchased previously at a price below the current market price, may desire to protect himself against any decline in the market price. Under such conditions he would place a "stop loss" or stop order to sell his security if the market price turns down to the price his order indicates. For instance, a security may have been purchased at $30 and subsequently have risen to $40; an investor may wish to protect a part of that gain, so he places a stop loss order with his broker to sell at 38 stop. Should the security decline in price to $38 or below, the order becomes a market order to sell at the best price obtainable.

b. Stop Order to Buy. A prospective investor may think that if a certain security rises a given amount above its present market price, it will eventually rise even higher. Or as is more often the case, a customer who has made a short sale may desire to protect himself against too great a loss if his judgment (that the security would decline in price) proves to be wrong. In such cases, he may place an order to buy at a given price stop. For instance if the current market price of a security is $40 and a customer has made a short sale in anticipation that the price would de-

cline, he may place an order to buy stop at $42. If the security rises instead of declining as he anticipated, this means his loss will be limited to about $2 per share, because at the moment the security rises to $42, his order to buy $42 stop becomes a market order and is executed at the best price obtainable.

5. Special Offerings and Secondary Distributions. As explained earlier, a major function of stockbrokers and dealers is to provide "liquidity" or ready convertibility into cash for securities. So long as securities are traded in relatively small amounts, the effect of each individual transaction on the current market price is small. But there are times when a holder of a relatively large block of securities will desire to dispose of the holding in a relatively short time; still he wishes to obtain a price consistent with the current market price. Perhaps an estate may be required to dispose of a large block of securities for the purpose of meeting tax payments; or a widow may find that holding large blocks of particular securities is unsuited to her purposes. Under such conditions, to offer these securities in the trading market might depress the price considerably, and the return realized could be out of all proportion with the current market value of the securities.

For instance, to use an example of a listed stock, on Tuesday, June 27, 1950, the New York Stock Exchange had its largest volume of trading for any day since 1939; a total of 4,860,000 shares were traded. Included in this total were 14,300 shares of Pennsylvania Railroad selling around $15 a share. The total dollars traded that day in this stock represented about $210,000. If some estate or a large institutional holder had been required on that day to dispose of 25,000 to 50,000 shares—an investment of one-half to three-quarters of a million dollars—trading in the regular way on the exchange, the price would have dropped considerably, and the loss might have been as much as 20 per cent or more in the return realized.

Recognizing such a situation, the rules of the exchanges for listed securities, with the approval of the SEC, provide for what is known as special offerings. For unlisted securities and trading in the over-the-counter market, the term secondary distribution is used. In regard to special offerings SEC states: "Rule X-10B-2 permits special offerings of large blocks of securities to be made on national securities exchanges, provided such offerings are effected pursuant to a plan which has been filed with and approved by the Commission. Briefly stated, a security may be the subject of a special offering when it has been determined that the auction market on the floor of the exchange cannot absorb a particular block of a security within a reasonable period of time without undue disturbance to the current price of the security. A special offering of a security is made at a fixed price consistent with the existing auction

market price of the security, and members acting as brokers for public buyers are paid a special commission by the seller which ordinarily exceeds the regular brokerage commission. Buyers of the security are not charged any commission on their purchases and obtain the security at the net price of the offering." [5]

Secondary distribution takes place in the over-the-counter market and may involve unlisted securities, or a listed security so traded with the approval of the exchange, generally after the close of the exchange trading. In the over-the-counter market an agreement is made between the seller of the securities and the broker or dealer who is to handle the secondary distribution. When the distribution is handled on a dealer basis, the usual procedure is for the seller to sell the securities to the dealer at a price slightly below the current market value. The dealer then resells the securities in small amounts to customers at a price sufficiently above his purchase price to net him his expense and profit in handling the transaction. It is usual for a dealer to arrange with other dealers in selling the securities, such other dealers being permitted to purchase the securities at a price sufficiently below the offering price to customers to provide the spread required by the other dealers.

When the secondary distribution is handled on a broker basis, the broker sells the securities for the seller under conditions laid down by the seller and agreed to by the broker, especially as to price. For his compensation the broker receives a commission. In many cases of secondary distribution, a securities firm may combine the capacity of dealer and broker by agreeing to purchase as dealer a certain proportion of the block of securities to be distributed and to sell the remainder on a commission basis.

Frequently the price at which such securities are offered to the public is the last price at which a sale was made on the exchange, if the security is a listed one, and at the current offering (offer to sell) price in the over-the-counter market. Should an exceptionally quick distribution be desired, or for other reasons to overcome expected difficulties, the price to the public may be somewhat below current prices. A "low limit," or price below which the securities will not be sold, is usually set.

The first special offering was made on the New York Stock Exchange on February 19, 1942. For the year ending June 30, 1949, 25 special offerings were effected on the national securities exchanges; 24 of these were completed. The original offerings involved 266,094 shares, of which 263,-733 shares were sold for a total value of $5,750,000. Of the 24 offerings completed, six were completed within 15 minutes, 15 more within the same day, and the remaining three took more than one day. Secondary distributions of listed stocks were of much greater volume than special

---

[5] Securities and Exchange Commission, *15th Annual Report*, 1949, p. 35.

offerings. Ninety-seven distributions were made of these stocks during the fiscal year ending June 30, 1949, of which 87 were completed. The original distributions involved 4,564,313 shares of which 4,480,953 shares were sold for a value of $129,014,000. Of the 87 secondary distributions completed, 59 were completed the same day, 18 on the following day, and 10 took longer than the following day. Once again the volume of secondary distributions of unlisted securities in the over-the-counter market is not known because of the lack of reported data.

Securities firm internal operations.

1. Organization of a Securities Firm. Figure 1 depicts the internal organization of the firm of Merrill Lynch, Pierce, Fenner & Beane. It can hardly be said that that organization is typical of all securities firms (because of the high degree of specialization found in a great many firms), but one or more of the activities shown in the chart will be found in almost all firms. This firm is selected because of its size and the volume of the securities business that it handles. During the calendar year 1949 it handled 9.3 per cent of all the round-lot transactions, and 13.7 per cent of all the odd-lot transactions on the New York Stock Exchange. The New York Stock Exchange does about 85 per cent of the dollar value of stock transactions taking place on 16 registered exchanges. Notwithstanding the fact that more than 50 per cent of this firm's total income is derived from commissions, the firm has paid out to floor brokers commissions of approximately $12,000,000 during the ten-year period 1940–49.

All firms have what may be called an Executive Division (represented in the chart by the directing and managing partners, since this firm depicted is a partnership). If the firm is a corporation, the Executive Division would be the officers of the corporation, for when a securities firm operates as a corporation, the officers, having invested their own capital in the firm, are also the owners of the corporation.

The Underwriting Division and the Commodity Division need not be discussed in this chapter, since the former is an investment banking function, and the latter relates to the commodities markets, both of which are included elsewhere in the text. The inclusion of an Administrative Division as a separate division depends largely on the size of the firm, but its functions, as depicted on the chart, are the usual administrative procedures of all firms and must be conducted somewhere within the organization. The presence of a Sales Division as a separate division in the typical securities firm depends on the amount of business the firm does directly with investors. Obviously a firm specializing in transactions with other dealers and brokers is not likely to have a sales division. The Sales Division is the contact between the firm and its customers. Its aim is to increase the business of the firm in accordance with general policies

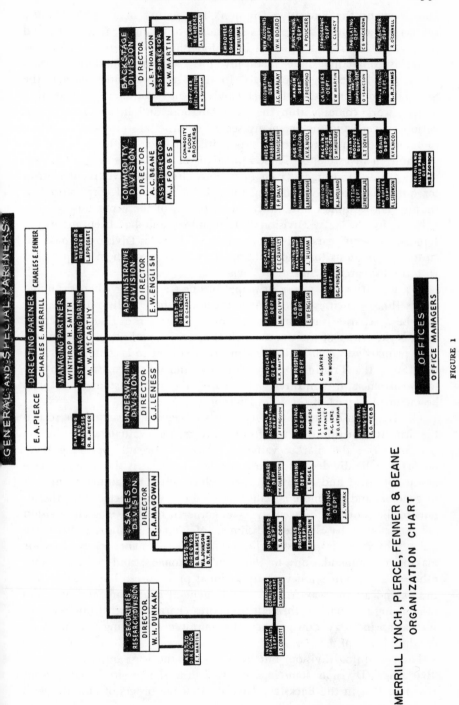

MERRILL LYNCH, PIERCE, FENNER & BEANE
ORGANIZATION CHART

FIGURE 1

laid down by the Executive Division. The nature of a firm's business reflects the activities of the Sales Division. For example, if a substantial portion of the firm's business is in odd-lot share amounts, the Sales Division is contacting more small investors, whereas round-lot business tends to indicate larger investors. In the over-the-counter markets the Sales Division emphasizes the merchandising of retail offerings. Sales promotion work comes within the Sales Division, and in addition to the various advertising media, many securities firms are engaged in active campaigns designed to acquaint potential investors with opportunities available in investments. These campaigns may take the form of investment courses for women given in various cities and investment courses for industrial executives looking toward the increase of corporation accounts. The volume of literature on all phases of the firm's business distributed by the Sales Division is tremendous and has been increasing rapidly in recent years. It is the function of the Sales Division to meet all customers' requests for information, which it does, often in conjunction with the Research or Statistical Division.

In a securities firm whose principal business is trading (that is, buying and selling securities for its own account), the Trading Department may be a separate division. In fact in such firms the Trading Department is the center of the concern's chief activities, and other departments exist primarily to enable the Trading Department to accomplish its mission. Since the Trading Department buys and sells securities from and to its customers, it is in direct contact with the firm's customers and may be included as part of the Sales Division.

The Research or Statistical Division is the eyes and ears of the securities firm. Its function is to recognize, measure, and evaluate all the factors that influence the market value of securities. Broadly speaking these factors may be divided into two fields: general, that is the financial, economic, political and other influences which affect the securities market in general; and the more specific factors directly connected with the affairs of the issuer of the security. Data gathered by the Research Division are used: (a) as bases for establishment of policies by the Executive Division; (b) as guides to assist the Trading Department; (c) as bases for making recommendations to the firm's customers; and (d) as various other aids in connection with operational procedures. The usual activities extend all the way from the more general conditions and attitudes influencing the market, through influences characteristic of one segment such as an industry, down to actual circumstances existing within an individual issuer of securities.

The remaining division, but by no means the least important, is the "Backstage" Division, sometimes referred to as the Service or Operations Division. It is in the Backstage Division that the orders originating with

the customer are actually processed to completion, all records of dealings between customer and firm are kept, and such services as are incidental or required in connection with securities trading are performed. A glance at the chart will make clear many of the activities of the various departments included in the Backstage Division. Some idea may be gained concerning the speed of operations in the Backstage Division of a modern firm from the following:

a. The time required to transmit an order from a branch office anywhere within the United States to the firm's home office is measured in seconds.

b. The time required to execute an order either on the floor of the exchange or in the over-the-counter market is measured in minutes.

c. The time required to record all essential data in connection with an order on the primary books of the firm (including data for delivery and other incidental services) is measured by a period of less than two hours.

In a test case one firm timed the various steps through which an individual order passed with these results: (1) the order was handled by 22 individuals in a net handling time of 9 minutes and 41 seconds; (2) the elapsed time to complete the three operations above was 1 hour and 20 minutes. On a conducted tour, with explanation of each operation, the time required 2 hours and 40 minutes.

2. Over-the-Counter Operations. The operation of trading on the floor of an exchange is covered elsewhere in the text; in the over-the-counter market the trading, conducted largely over telephone, is best illustrated by the account of an over-the-counter transaction.

Assuming a customer has called the OTC firm saying that he is interested in trading in a given security. (He need not at this point indicate whether he wants to buy or sell.) The customer asks for the "market" in American Common.

The OTC firm would then "check the market" by calling those houses which were known to be making a market in American Common. Each such firm would reply stating its bid and offering price. Assume the following market:

1st	Firm	Bid 31½	Offering	33
2nd	Firm	31¼		32¾
3rd	Firm	31		32½
4th	Firm	31⅜		32⅞
5th	Firm	31⅛		32⅝

The OTC firm then tells its customer that it can probably sell American Common for him at 31½ or buy for him at 32½. Assume that the

customer then tells the OTC firm to buy for him 100 shares of American Common at 32½ or better.

In the above market 3rd firm was making the lowest offering to sell, so the OTC firm calls 3rd firm asking for its market in American Common. 3rd firm replies 31–32½, meaning 31 bid, offered at 32½. The OTC firm (wanting to know how many shares the 3rd firm is willing to buy or sell) asks, "What is the size of your market?"

3rd firm states how many shares it stands ready to buy and the number it stands ready to sell. If the number is the same in both cases 3rd firm may answer, "100 shares either way," but as yet 3rd firm does not know whether the OTC firm wishes to buy or sell.

The OTC firm may then attempt to get a better price for its customer's order, in which case the OTC firm may say to 3rd firm, "I will pay 32¼ for 100." 3rd firm (if it is willing to make a concession on its price) may say, "I will sell at 32⅜." Since the customer has authorized the OTC firm to pay as high as 32½, the OTC firm may accept the 3rd firm's new offering at 32⅜ and say, "I will take 100 at 32⅜." 3rd firm then completes the transaction by saying, "I have sold you 100 shares of American Common at 32⅜."

The transaction above takes place in about one minute; had the customer placed an order to sell, the transaction would have been similar except that the OTC firm would probably have dealt with 1st firm, the highest bidder, and might have tried to get a higher price.

In the above example the OTC firm acted as broker for its customer. It may be that the OTC firm is also making a market in American Common, or that it wishes to trade for its own account, in which case it would act as dealer. The Rules of Fair Practice of the NASD provide that the securities firm must notify the customer in what capacity it is acting, either as broker or dealer. In the case of the security firm's acting as broker, the rule provides that a "fair commission or service charge" shall be charged, "taking into consideration all relevant circumstances including market conditions with respect to such security at the time of the transaction, the expense of executing the order and the value of any service he may have rendered by reason of his experience in and knowledge of such security and the market therefor." Should the firm act as dealer, "he [the member of the NASD] shall buy or sell at a price which is fair, taking into consideration all relevant circumstances, including market conditions with respect to such security at the time of the transaction, the expense involved, and the fact that he is entitled to a profit." [6] Members of NASD, in addition to notifying customers of the capacity in which they are handling the transaction, must also notify or stand ready

[6] Paragraph 4, Article III, *Rules of Fair Practice*, National Association of Securities Dealers, Inc.

to notify the customer of the other party to the transaction, and the source and amount of any commission or other remuneration received or to be received in connection with the transaction.

3. Other Internal Operations.

a. Customer's Accounts. A great many laws, orders, and regulations govern the operation of the securities business to cover the activities of representatives of the firm, accounts and records to be kept, and other items. Details of these and of accounting procedures are omitted here. So far as a prospective investor is concerned, the procedure for opening a securities account with a securities firm is quite simple and easy. In some cases it may not involve more than a telephone conversation between the customer investor and the securities firm. Actually the procedure for opening an account is very much like opening an account at a commercial bank.

In opening a cash account (that is, one in which the customer intends to pay in full for securities purchased), the procedure is like opening a deposit account in a bank. Identity must be established, and the funds must be deposited to cover the securities purchased. If the customer is selling securities he must be prepared to deliver the securities and establish the fact that he is the owner of such securities. In case the customer does not wish to pay in full for securities purchased, he may open a margin account, which, in many ways, is similar to receiving a loan from a bank with which to open an account. Trading on margin is subject to regulation by the Federal Reserve Board; since such trading involves borrowing funds or securities, the customer must establish his credit to the satisfaction of the securities firm, and he must comply with certain other requirements, such as signing an agreement which permits the securities firm to pledge the securities held on margin as collateral for a loan from a lender. Once having opened an account a customer may give his orders to the securities firm by telephone, telegraph, cable, mail, in person, or by any means he desires.

b. Customer's Statements. In addition to a confirmation notice sent to the customer for the completion of each order, the securities firm sends monthly statements to its customers on which are recorded the details of each transaction affecting the customer's account. These details include a record of the sale, commission charges, taxes, dividends or interest received, and deposits and withdrawals by the customer. The customer's statement is a copy of the account record kept by the firm on which entries are made each day a transaction occurs.

c. Clearance and Delivery of Securities. In connection with the operation of customers' accounts and the firm's own account, it is necessary to make delivery or to accept receipt of securities involved in trading. Where clearing institutions are employed, the transfer of securities is on

a net basis similar to bank clearing operations. The clearing and delivery of securities is a function of the Cashier's Department within the firm.

d. Brokers' Collateral Loans. In fixing margin requirements the Federal Reserve Board uses two regulations: Regulation T is used for credit involved between brokers and dealers and their customers, and Regulation U is used for loans by banks on listed securities. Assume that the margin requirement under both regulations was fixed at 50 per cent; this means that for a loan of $50,000, there must be pledged $100,000 of securities. In order to reduce the need for invested capital, securities firms may borrow from banks or other legal lenders on loans secured by collateral in the form of securities. It is a function of the Cashier's Department to handle such loans. Loans may be made on the collateral of securities owned by customers, if the customer has so authorized, and on the collateral of securities owned by the firm. The former are known as customers' loans and the latter as firm loans. Customers' loans are used to finance the credit involved between the securities firm and its customers under margin trading.

Brokers' collateral loans may be on a time basis or on a demand or call basis. The former are for a definite period and carry the same interest rate throughout the life of the loan. Call loans may be terminated by the lender at any time, with interest on a day-to-day basis. Call loans not called prior to 12:15 P.M. are automatically renewed for another business day at the call loan rate set for such loans.

e. Taxes, Commissions, and Fees. The transfer of securities has been subject to taxation by the federal government and some of the states. Most of the taxes are stamp taxes, and the tax is paid by buying stamps that are affixed to the securities document involved. The federal tax is fixed at five cents for each $100 of par value or fraction thereof, or if there is no par value, five cents per share for shares selling at less than $20. For shares selling at or above $20 the rate is raised to six cents. The rate on bonds is five cents per $100 of face value or fraction thereof. Since the tax applies to transfers of legal title, it is payable by the seller. In the case of odd-lots, however, the purchaser is required to pay the federal tax. Responsibility for complying with transfer taxes is generally assigned to the Cashier's Department; taxes on listed securities on some exchanges are handled by the clearing house. Securities transfer taxes generate more revenue in those states in which the larger securities markets exist. On this basis New York, Pennsylvania, and Massachusetts levy such taxes. Florida, South Carolina, and Texas also levy securities transfer taxes, but the revenue is slight. Owing to the size of their securities markets, Illinois and California might be expected to levy such a tax, but they do not.

Commissions for trading on the exchanges are fixed and published

for the information of all concerned. On the New York Stock Exchange the commission rate ranges from 6 per cent on a transaction with a value of less than $100, down to $\frac{1}{10}$ of 1 per cent plus $26 on values of $4,000 and above. If the value is less than $15, a minimum commission is fixed as agreed upon by customer and firm. Odd-lots carry the same rates (except minimums) less 10 per cent, but this rate should not be confused with the odd-lot differential previously explained. Commission rates apply both to buying and selling. Commission rates on bonds run from 75 cents on orders of five bonds or more which are selling at less than $10 per $1,000 of principal, to $5 on orders of one or two bonds selling at $100 and above per $1,000 of principal.

In the over-the-counter market commissions are not fixed; it would not be equitable to set fixed rates of commission here since trading conditions are not uniform. Trading is not done on the floor of an exchange; instead it is done between offices, and the expense involved may be little or large for like transactions. Notwithstanding the lack of fixed commission rates in the over-the-counter market, SEC found in a study in the fiscal year ending June 30, 1949, 86.16 per cent of the transactions of over-the-counter dealers analyzed "were made at a mark-up of 5 per cent or less." [7] While this study dealt particularly with dealers' profits, it is reasonable to estimate that brokers' commissions in the over-the-counter market generally compare favorably with commission rates on the exchanges.

The SEC charges a registration fee to each exchange for doing business during the preceding calendar year. The exchanges collect the fee from their members at the rate of one cent for each $500 of transactions, and the members in turn withhold the sum from the amount credited to accounts of customers for whom the transactions are made.

f. Customer Services and Protection. In the business world the law of principal and agent is widely encountered, but in no business perhaps is the law more widely encountered than in the securities business. A primary feature of this law is the protection of a principal from the fraudulent acts of his agent. Where fraud exists the victim has the right to sue; but bankruptcy may make such a right of little value. For this reason various regulations and rules exist for the protection of the customer dealing with a securities firm. (For instance, Rule X-15 C3-1 of the Securities Exchange Commission provides that the aggregate indebtedness of a broker or dealer shall not exceed 20 times his net capital. Similarly NASD requires its members to make available to inspection by any customer information concerning the member's financial condition.) Perhaps the best measure of customer protection is to be found in the solvency record of securities firms. Figures are not available for all

---

[7] Securities and Exchange Commission, *15th Annual Report,* 1949, p. 58.

firms, but the record of member firms of the New York Stock Exchange is impressive. During the first 50 years of this century only $^{27}/_{100}$ of 1 per cent of these firms have become insolvent. During the past 10 years no firms became insolvent. Compared with other financial and commerical institutions the record of solvency for the period 1900–49 is: Stock Exchange members 99.73 per cent; all U.S. banks 98.46 per cent; national banks, 99.13 per cent and commercial houses 99.24 per cent. There is reason to believe that the financial soundness of securities firms in the over-the-counter market is quite similar to that of exchange members. With an average of slightly over 4,000 securities firms registered with SEC during the year ending June 30, 1949, some 772 inspections were made by SEC. In these inspections questions concerning the financial condition of firms arose in 33 cases; of these, only two firms had their registration revoked for unsound financial conditions.

That the securities business is highly competitive is evidenced by the many customer services rendered by securities firms. In no other industry can it be said that "what the customer wants" has greater influence on operations. Not only is extensive research made to obtain data helpful to customers in their investing problems, but considerable expense is incurred in publishing and distributing such information. One prominent firm spent $1,407,000 on combined research, publishing, and advertising activities during 1949; $315,130 of that sum was spent for newspaper and magazine space. The $1,407,000 represented 6.61 per cent of the firm's total operating expenses.

Customer services range all the way from opening branch offices in communities likely to have investors residing there—one firm has 100 branch offices—to free courses in finance and investments. Not all these services can be listed here but a few of the major ones should be indicative of the wide range.

(1) Supplying up-to-the-minute quotations on securities
(2) Providing facilities for the execution of orders within seconds and minutes
(3) Answering inquiries regarding individual investment problems
(4) Recommending securities for inclusion in individual investment portfolios
(5) Furnishing news of, and evaluating developments affecting, the financial world
(6) Conducting industry-wide surveys and publicizing such data
(7) Investigating and appraising financial conditions within individual firms
(8) Providing customers with forms and instructions concerning tax matters

(9) Providing and suggesting procedures for individual handling of investment funds

(10) Issuing and distributing information on the operation of the securities markets

(11) Publishing educational material on the mechanics of making investments

(12) Publishing educational material on the financial structure of corporations

(13) Providing educational instruction on interpretation of financial reports

(14) Issuing regularly, news of general interest in the investment field

(15) Conducting formal educational courses dealing with the whole field of finance.

These are some of the customer services provided by securities firms with a view to extending knowledge about the securities markets and to make it easier for sound investments to be made. All these services are expensive to render, and some of the benefits derived by individual securities firms cannot be measured directly; but the over-all results must be a wider and wiser investing public and a sounder and more profitable securities business.

4. Regulation of Stockbrokers and Dealers. It would be unrealistic to discuss the internal operations of securities firms without making some mention of regulation. Among competitive enterprises none may be said to be more highly regulated than the securities business. (Chapter 23 deals in more detail with the subject of regulation.) Regulation of brokers and dealers stems from two main sources: (1) regulation by private organizations, sometimes spoken of as self-regulation; and (2) regulation by governmental agencies. The origin of self-regulation may be traced back at least to the organization of the first exchanges where members were required to trade with one another. Since then by the adoption of constitutions and rules governing trading, members have been subjected to sanctions for violations. In the exchanges the Governing Committee has absolute power over members and may expel any member for, among other things, inequitable conduct in trading. Members are subject to penalties for violation of rules of the exchange, even though no civil law is violated. It is a primary purpose of the exchanges to safeguard the interest of the public in its dealings with brokers and dealers. Aside from stringent rules regarding securities that can be traded on exchanges, brokers and dealers are regulated by rules of the exchanges covering the conduct of trading, the handling of customers' accounts, the distribution of false and misleading statements, the giving of

required information, the financial requirements for invested capital in the securities firm, and various other practices.

Self-regulation in the over-the-counter market took a long step forward with the passage of the so-called Maloney Act in 1938. Prior to this act self-regulation outside the exchanges was limited largely to voluntary cooperation, and enforcement powers were lacking. (The NIRA Act did provide for the administration and enforcement of self-regulation through a code of fair practices while it was in existence.) The 1938 Act, in the form of an amendment to the Securities Exchange Act of 1934 adding section 15A, permits associations of brokers and dealers to register with SEC and upon the approval of SEC to make and enforce rules and regulations for its members. It is under this act that the National Association of Securities Dealers, Inc., operates. In setting forth its objectives the certificate of incorporation of the NASD in addition to the usual corporate powers includes the following purposes:

(1) To promote through cooperative effort the investment banking and securities business, standardize its principles and practices, to promote therein high standards of commercial honor, and to encourage and promote among members observance of Federal and State securities laws;

(2) To provide a medium through which its membership may be enabled to confer, consult, and cooperate with governmental and other agencies in the solution of problems affecting investors, the public, and the investment banking and securities business;

(3) To adopt, administer and enforce rules of fair practice and rules to prevent fraudulent and manipulative acts and practices, and in general to promote just and equitable principles of trade for the protection of investors;

(4) To promote self-discipline among members, and to investigate and adjust grievances between the public and members and between members.[8]

Pursuant to its powers NASD has published with the approval of SEC its Rules of Fair Practice, and the enforcement activities of the NASD are annually supervised by SEC. Penalties include suspension, expulsion, fines, and censures.

Regulation by governmental agencies began in the United States with the passage of the first "blue-sky" law in Kansas in 1901. Today every state, except Nevada, has a law for the regulation of the securities business. Nearly all state laws require the registration of brokers and dealers and their salesmen, agents, and solicitors; a few states require only the registration of security issues. About half the states require bonds or other satisfactory proof of financial responsibility as a condition of registration. The state laws vary among the states and so do the registration or licensing fees required to be paid; usually such fees are paid on an annual basis. Delaware, Maryland, New Jersey, and New York regulate

---

[8] Certificate of Incorporation, National Association of Securities Dealers, Inc.

the securities business by means of anti-fraud laws. Such laws empower the state to prevent fraud or threatened fraud and to prosecute the commitment of fraud. While the United States Supreme Court early recognized the power of states to regulate the securities business, state powers are limited to state boundary lines.

Beginning with the Securities Act of 1933 and the Securities Exchange Act of 1934, the federal government entered in a major way the field of regulation of the securities business as supplementary to state regulation. The powers of the federal government derive from its powers over interstate commerce. Under the 1934 Act brokers and dealers in the over-the-counter market, with certain exemptions, are required to register with SEC; the same act gives SEC supervisory and regulatory powers over the conduct of trading in that market. In addition to annual financial reports filed by brokers and dealers with SEC, on an average slightly less than 20 per cent of the brokers and dealers are inspected each year by SEC. In the main SEC supervision and regulation cover the following points:

a. Compliance with regulation T (relating to margins) of the Federal Reserve Board

b. Proper hypothecation of customer's securities

c. Compliance with rule X-15 C3-1 of the SEC relating to the capital of securities firms

d. Trading fairly with customers at prices reasonably related to the current market

e. Compliance with rule X-17 A-5 of the SEC requiring the annual filing of the firm's financial conditions

f. Compliance with other rules and regulations and standards of fair practice.

During the five year period from 1945 to 1949, SEC revocations of registration for all purposes has averaged less than $3/10$ of 1 per cent of brokers and dealers registered.

Current Status of Securities Trading

Present size of securities trading business. Any attempt to compile accurate data concerning the over-all operations of the securities business is fraught with difficulties. This problem stems from the nature of the business, its organization, and methods of procedure. For reporting purposes this business is both centralized and decentralized, so that published data suffer from two main weaknesses: partial coverage and/or duplication. Membership in the exchanges, for instance, does not represent the number of persons actively trading on such exchanges, nor does it indicate the number of firms dealing on the exchanges. Registrations

of firms and representatives with the SEC or membership in NASD would not reflect accurately the number of firms or individuals in the securities business, since registration is not required under certain circumstances and membership in NASD is voluntary. For the vast over-the-counter market no centralized agency exists; therefore complete reporting is not available. All this is, in no sense, a plea for such a centralized agency—either governmental or otherwise; in fact, the nature of our federal republic itself practically prevents such an agency. Notwithstanding the difficulty of obtaining information, there are certain data of some help.

As stated earlier trading is done in two general markets, the listed exchanges and the over-the-counter market. Data concerning the listed exchanges are given elsewhere in the text. Brokers and dealers trading on the over-the-counter market, except those who do an exclusive intrastate business or deal exclusively in exempt securities, are required to register with the SEC. Table 2 gives the number of firms registered with the SEC, together with the number of branch offices.

TABLE 2

BROKERS AND DEALERS REGISTERED UNDER SECTION 15 OF THE
SECURITIES EXCHANGE ACT OF 1934,[9] AS OF JUNE 30, 1949

| | | Number of Registrants | | |
| | | Sole | Partner- | |
	Total	Proprietorship	ships	Corporations
New York City	1,200	385	608	207
Outside New York City..	2,755	1,186	677	892
Total United States ...	3,955	1,571	1,285	1,099

| | | Number of Branch Offices Maintained by Registrants | | |
| | | Sole | Partner- | |
	Total	Proprietorship	ships	Corporations
New York City..........	839	17	643	176
Outside New York City..	1,030	26	578	426
Total United States ...	1,869	43	1,221	602

Table 2 indicates the degree of concentration of the industry within New York City. Slightly over 30 per cent of the principal offices of registrants are in New York City, and in addition, a number of firms with principal offices located outside New York City maintain branches within New York City. The total number of registrants does not include the 39 foreign concerns.

The National Association of Securities Dealers, Inc., is the only

[9] Adapted from Securities and Exchange Commission, *15th Annual Report*, 1949, Table 7, p. 222.

securities association registered as such with SEC under section 15A of the 1934 Act. Membership in NASD has shown a net increase of 414 to a total membership on June 30, 1949, of 2,695. Early in 1946 NASD adopted a rule requiring registration with the association as "registered representatives" of all partners, officers, and other employees of broker-dealer firms "who generally do business directly with the public." Since January 15, 1946 (the date the rule became effective), the number registered has increased from 21,351 to 27,249 registered on June 30, 1949. The turnover in this personnel is indicated by the fact that during the year ending June 30, 1949, registrations terminated numbered 3,599; re-registrations and new registrations totaled 4,620.

Another means of measuring the size of the securities trading business is the number of employees. At least two governmental agencies report figures on employees; SEC reported the number of proprietors, partners, and senior executive officers on June 30, 1949 as 12,774 (about one-third in New York City) and the number of employees as 56,128 (about one-half in New York City); this makes a total of 68,902 on that date. The Bureau of Foreign and Domestic Commerce, in its annual national income issue reports the number of "full-time equivalent employees," under an industry heading of "Security and commodity brokers, dealers and exchanges." The classification is not similar to the SEC group, since the Bureau includes commodity traders and employees of exchanges. According to the Bureau's figures the peak employment was reached in 1929 with 128,000 full-time equivalent employees. The number declined to 38,000 in 1943 and has since increased to 53,000 in 1946, falling to 48,000 in 1948.[10] Based on total full-time equivalent employees for all industries, the Bureau reports that $\frac{1}{10}$ of 1 per cent of total number of employees are engaged in the security and commodity brokers, dealers, and exchanges industry.

Each year the Bureau compiles the total national income using a classification of 11 major groups of industries which are subdivided into 69 different industries. One of these subdivisions (as mentioned above) is "Security and commodity brokers, dealers and exchanges," which accounted for $257,000,000 of income in the year 1948 out of a total national income of $226,204,000,000.[11] Measured in this way the in-

---

[10] In reconciliation between the Bureau and SEC, the Bureau Reports for its classification of "Security and Commodity Brokers, Dealers and Exchanges," the number of persons engaged on December 31, 1948, as 63,000, whereas the SEC figure of 68,902 is for officers and employees of registered firms on June 30, 1949. It is evident that many persons employed are not full-time employees.

[11] *Survey of Current Business*, U.S. Department of Commerce, Bureau of Foreign and Domestic Commerce, July 1949, Table 13 (National Income, by Industrial Origin, 1942–48), p. 14.

dustry [12] produced something more than $\frac{1}{10}$ of 1 per cent of the total income for that year, not a large figure. Yet it produced more income than such industries as forestry, fisheries, pipe line transportation, radio broadcasting, and television.

While the number of employees engaged in the industry and the total income originating within the industry are comparatively small when compared with totals, the degree of training and skill required in the industry far overshadows that of any other industry when measured by average annual earnings per full-time employee. Among the 48,165,000 full-time equivalent employees in 1948, the average annual earnings were $2,809; employees in the stockbrokerage industry had average annual earnings of $5,208, ranking number one in the list of 69 industries. Number two on the list was pipeline transportation, with average annual earnings of $4,067.[13]

Volume and nature of securities trading. The total volume of securities traded again is not available, but data are available on the volume of new securities issued, and the volume of trading on the exchanges. By a combination of these data some indication is made of the total.

Table 3 sets forth the details of issuers and the types of securities they issued for the years 1948 and 1949. In explanation of the table the term "offering" is used to describe the process of issuing (that is, offering for sale) a given type of security by a certain issuer. Offerings are classified as public and private. Public offerings are those sold by competitive bidding—whether sold directly to the ultimate investor or through other financial institutions. Private offerings, on the other hand, are those sold without competitive bidding to a restricted number of investors. The services of stockbrokers may or may not be utilized in private offerings. Types of offerings are subdivided further into those registered with the Securities Exchange Commission and those not registered because they are exempt from registration requirements of the law. Slightly less than 15 per cent of securities were registered in 1949 and somewhat less than 16 per cent in 1948. This information should be interpreted in the light of the fact that governmental units are included in the list of exempt issuers, and offerings of governments accounted for 73 per cent of all offerings in 1949.

All offerings are also classified by type of issuer, whether corporate or noncorporate. Corporate issuers embrace those units of business that use the corporate form of organization and are subdivided by type of

---

12 The term "industry" is used here following the terminology of the National Income Statistics of the Department of Commerce to avoid any discussion of whether stockbrokerage is a profession, trade, or other vocation.

13 *Survey of Current Business,* U.S. Department of Commerce, Bureau of Foreign and Domestic Commerce, July 1949, Table 26 (Average Annual Earnings per Full-Time Employee, by Industry, 1942–48), p. 21.

TABLE 3

NEW SECURITIES OFFERED FOR CASH IN THE UNITED STATES
FOR THE YEARS 1948 AND 1949

(In thousands of dollars)

	1948	1949 *
All Offerings	20,284,988	20,492,238
Type of Offering:		
Public	17,013,188	18,611,276
Registered under 1933 Act	3,210,580	3,049,760
Unregistered because of:		
Type of issue or issuer	13,662,416	15,451,520
Size of issue	135,673	107,862
Intrastate	4,519	2,134
Private	3,271,799	1,880,961
Registered under 1933 Act	5,000	0
Unregistered because of:		
Type of issue or issuer	21,780	10,887
Purchase by limited group	3,245,019	1,870,074
Type of Issuer:		
Corporate	7,112,820	5,410,018
Manufacturing	2,225,757	1,291,409
Public Utility	2,187,390	2,275,652
Railroad	623,348	429,981
Other Transportation	152,924	202,847
Communication	901,663	535,368
Real Estate and Financial	593,649	427,045
Commercial and Miscellaneous	428,090	217,715
Noncorporate	13,172,168	15,082,219
United States Government (including		
issues guaranteed)	10,326,937	11,804,320
Federal Agency (issues not guaran-		
teed)	0	215,538
State and Municipal Governments...	2,689,719	2,939,227
Foreign Governments	150,000	116,250
International Bank	————	————
Eleemosynary and other nonprofit...	5,512	6,884
Type of Security:		
Common stock	613,509	735,605
Preferred stock	491,535	418,825
Bonds and notes	19,179.944	19,337,806
Corporate	6,007,776	4.255,587
Noncorporate	13,172,168	15,082,219

* Preliminary.

Source: *Statistical Bulletin*, Securities and Exchange Commission, Vol. 9, No. 4, p. 3, April 1950.

NOTES: Data in Table 3 cover substantially all new issues of securities offered for cash sale in the United States in amounts over $100,000 and with terms to maturity of more than one year. The figures represent offerings, not actual sales, but figures representing actual cash sales do not differ materially.

Figures include only issues offered for cash sale for account of issuers; they do not include securities sold through continuous offering, such as issues of open-end investment companies and employee-purchase plans.

Issues exempt from registration under the Securities Act of 1933 but included in Table 3 are: issues privately placed; intrastate offerings; securities of railroad companies; issues of the federal, state, and local governments, banks, and eleemosynary institutions; and issues between $100,000 and $300,000 in size offered pursuant to amendment of Regulation A of the Securities Act of 1933.

Excluded from the data on new cash offerings are: notes issued exclusively to commercial banks; intercorporate transactions; United States government "Special Series" issues and other sales directly to federal agencies and trust accounts.

industry as shown in the table. Noncorporate issuers are governmental units (domestic and foreign) and charitable and nonprofit organizations.

Types of securities offered for sale are classified as common stocks, preferred stocks, bonds, and notes. Since common and preferred stocks are types of securities characteristic of corporations, noncorporate issuers do not issue them.

Table 3 indicates that some $20,000,000,000 of new securities were being added annually during 1948 and 1949 to the former amount of outstanding securities. At the same time new securities are being issued, some outstanding securities are being retired. This is particularly true of such debt securities as bonds and notes. During the first six months of 1950, for instance, exclusive of United States government bonds, $2,350,-717,000 of new bonds were sold publicly and $663,677,000 were called for redemption. The 1950 offering figure was the largest for a similar period since 1930, and the redemption figure was exceeded during a like period in 1947. Stock issues during the first five months of 1950 totaled $319,912,000. Practically all of these new security issues would be sold on the over-the-counter market. The concentration of bond dealings on the over-the-counter market is clearly indicated when it is considered that the $3,350,717,000 of new bonds sold does not include trading in outstanding issues; yet the total bond transactions on both New York Stock and New York Curb Exchanges for the first six months of 1950 amounted to $586,555,670. Transactions in United States government bonds are rare also on the exchanges. During the month of June 1950 only $10,000 of these bonds were sold on the New York Stock Exchange, out of its total bond dealings of $105,473,900 for that month.

Outstanding securities are being traded each business day, and on the exchanges the dollar value of stocks traded far exceeds that of bonds; but there is a sizeable bond market on the over-the-counter market. The nature of new securities being issued indicates in part the present trends in securities trading. Going back to Table 3, less than 15 per cent of new securities issued in 1949 are of the type that is required to be registered with SEC. In the matter of private business as against government, slightly over 26 per cent of total securities were issued by the former and slightly over 73 per cent by the latter. Debt securities far overshadowed stock securities, for the latter represented less than 6 per cent of the total. Debt securities represented 78.65 per cent of all corporate securities issued and, of course, 100 per cent of government securities. The United States government accounted for 58.6 per cent of all securities issued; states and municipalities added another 14.3 per cent. The trend indicated in 1949 has continued during the first six months of 1950.

Another consideration of new securities being issued relates to whether

the proceeds derived from new securities are used to retire old securities or used to expand the capital of corporations. Of the gross proceeds from the sale of new securities in 1949 of $5,410,018,000, the cost of issuing amounted to $88,117,000; this leaves net proceeds to corporations of $5,321,901,000. Of this $3,500,328,000 was invested in new plant and equipment; $776,817,000 was added to working capital; $744,248,000 was used to retire securities, including $33,886,000 of stock, all preferred; and $300,508,000 went for other purposes.

Characteristic of depression years, the 1930's saw new corporate securities being used primarily to retire old securities. This condition continued during most of the war principally because other funds were used to meet the needs of corporations. In the period 1946–49, however, $18 billion of proceeds from the issuance of new corporate securities has been used to expand capital, against $5 billion for retirement of old securities. Add to this the $9 billion of state and municipal securities issued during that period, the $4 billion issued by federal credit agencies, and the $2 billion for other purposes, and the total securities issued exclusive of the United States government direct obligations amount to $38 billion. During this period the amount of the United States government debt has not changed materially, but refunding operations have far exceeded the total of all other securities issued. For all these securities some $50 to $60 billion of investment dollars annually during that period had to be found, and brokers and dealers—especially on the over-the-counter market—played a large part in finding these investors. Refunding operations of the United States government are currently (July 1950) running in excess of $46 billion annually.

Stock vs. *bond yields.* In general since 1945 the yield on stocks has been rising whereas the yield on bonds has not risen to any marked extent. First, a word in explanation of yield. The investor's return from stocks is paid in the form of a dividend; the investor's return from bonds is paid as interest. If a common stock is selling at $50 a share and it is paying a $3 annual dividend, the yield is 6 per cent. This is derived by dividing $50 into $3 to arrive at the percentage. Bond yields are somewhat more complicated. It is true that if a bond is selling at 100 (meaning $1,000 for a $1,000 bond) and the stated interest rate is 3 per cent, the investor's return is $30 and the yield is 3 per cent. But complications arise if the bond is selling at a discount (below 100) or at a premium (above 100). These complications arise out of the fact that no matter what the selling price of a bond may be, at its maturity the face value of the bond ($1,000 generally) will be paid. Stocks do not provide for repayment of principal at any time. Bonds' yields, then, to be accurate, must take into account the amortization of the premium or the discount. For instance a bond selling at 90 costs $900 but will pay $1,000 at

maturity; or a bond selling at 110 costs $1,100 but will still pay only $1000 at maturity. Therefore each period (year) the difference between the selling price of the bond and its face value must be considered in determining yield. In actual practice an accurate method is used, but the following illustration will approximate the method used to determine bond yield. Assume a 3 per cent bond due in 20 years selling at 90:

Annual interest return   = $30
Amortization (Discount)   =   5 ($1,000 — $900 = 100 ÷ 20 years = 5)

Total return $35
Average cost of bond = $950 ($900 at sale + 1,000 at maturity ÷ 2 = $950 average)
New yield = 3.684% ($35 ÷ $950)

There are many factors beside yield that influence investors to buy bonds or stocks for investment. There is the factor of risk involved. While it is true that not all bonds are free from risk, bonds do establish a debtor relationship on the part of the issuer to the investor; stated interest rates are given (except in rare cases); and the maturity date of the debt is stated. In general bonds are "safer" than stocks. Because bonds do have stated interest rates, they do not pay a higher return than stated; but stocks may do so. In general bond yields ought to be sufficiently below stock yields to compensate for the amount of risk that goes with ownership of stock, all other things being equal.

It might be noted that there have been times when bond yields are higher than stock yields. This was the condition in early 1929 and it caused President Coolidge to remark when asked about it: "Why, I'm not sure. But I do know that when stocks yield 2 per cent and bonds yield 4 per cent either dividends must go up or stocks must go down." [14] Of course there is another possibility: yield on bonds may go down through increased prices for bonds.

The spread between corporate bond yields and stock yields increased from less than one point (100 basis points in bond language or 1 per cent in stock yield) in 1945 rapidly during 1946, 1947, 1948, and it receded slightly in 1949. But the spread is still about 4 per cent.

Various reasons may be cited in explanation of the spread between bond and stock yields; for instance, bond yields have been kept low due to the government's fiscal policy of maintaining low interest rates. Also stock prices were not high throughout the war. (The 1942 low was somewhat lower than the 1938 low, and at no time up to the end of 1945 did prices reach the high of 1936.) Stock prices dropped rapidly about the middle of 1946 and remained in a narrow range from then until the

[14] *Investors Reader*, a Publication of Merrill Lynch, Pierce, Fenner & Beane, January 18, 1950, p. 2.

TABLE 4

COMPARISON OF STOCK AND BOND YIELDS

	Bond Yields in Per Cent						Stock Yields in Per Cent
	U.S. Government		Munici-pal	Corpo-rate	Aaa	Baa	
Year	1 to 9 Years	15 Years or More					
1945	1.60	2.37	1.67	2.87	2.62	3.29	3.6
1946	1.45	2.19	1.64	2.74	2.53	3.05	4.8
1947	1.59	2.25	2.01	2.86	2.61	3.24	6.3
1948	2.00	2.44	2.40	3.08	2.82	3.47	7.8
1949	1.71	2.31	2.21	2.96	2.66	3.42	7.0

Sources: *Federal Reserve Bulletin* for bond yields and *Investment Facts* published by the New York Stock Exchange for stock yields. Ultimate source of municipal bond yields is Standard and Poor's Corporation; of Corporate, Aaa, and Baa, Moody's Investors Service.

middle of 1949 when a gradual rise was started. This rise has continued until the present (January 1951). The fact that stock prices were not unduly high, at least up to June 1949, coupled with the increasing dividends paid in cash by corporations, tended to increase stock yields. Corporate cash dividends rose from $4.7 billion in 1945 to $8.4 billion in 1949.

The increasing spread may be a partial reason for the relatively large bond issues by corporations during the period. With low bond yields, corporations can raise capital funds more cheaply with bonds. To the extent that the increased fixed charges can be met during any period of falling profits, there is no need for corporate financial worries. But indebtedness capital contains more risk than sale of ownership.

On the other hand there has been a great demand for investments in funds accumulated by insurance companies, pension and retirement funds, and the like, to all of whom bond investments are desirable provided the yield is high enough. Rising stock yields tend to favor the smaller businesses that find it difficult to borrow money at low bond yields. So long as the government is committed to low interest rates, bond yields should not advance substantially, and bond capital will be in demand by larger corporations. This means that securities trading will probably involve considerable bonds for some time, and most of the trading in bonds will occur in the over-the-counter market.

Yield vs. *appreciation.* Another form of return to investors other than yield is that derived from the buying and selling of securities at different prices. Securities that are sold at a price higher than the price at which they were purchased yield a return to the investor, and this return is known as appreciation. Whereas yield involves both price and dividend or interest return, appreciation involves only price. Using corporate high grade bond prices (Standard and Poor's Corporation, quoted in *Federal*

Reserve Bulletin), bond prices rose during 1945 over 1944. During the first eight months of 1946, prices moved within a narrow range but began to decline in September 1946. Some recovery was made early in 1947, but a gradual decline beginning in June 1947 gained momentum as the close of the year approached. From a low in December 1947, bond prices recovered until June 1948 when a further decline reached its low in October 1948. From this date, except for slight recessions in June and October 1949, prices rose until March 1950. Rising prices in 1949 are consistent with the lowered yield shown in Table 4.

Buying when prices are low and selling when prices are high constitutes income from appreciation. This is known as "timing," and as can be seen from the movement of stock prices and bond prices, timing is all important for appreciation. Fluctuations in prices, once a security has been purchased, have no effect on yield to the individual investor.

Men and women stockholders. The title of this section might better be "women and men stockholders," for there is substantial evidence that women either now are, or are rapidly becoming, more numerous than men as owners of American industry. Statistics are not available for all corporate shareholders, but one reliable estimate gives the composition of company shareholders at the close of 1949 as: women 44 per cent; men 35 per cent; charitable institutions, trusts and estates, private corporations, and foundations, 21 per cent.[15] In many large corporations (duPont, General Motors, American Telephone and Telegraph), women far outnumber men in the total of individual stockholders. In the United States Steel Corporation women come within .7 of 1 per cent of equaling the number of men.

Certain facts of interest to the future of the investment field can be seen in the growing number of women shareholders. In general women are heavy investors in stocks with long dividend records; women show some preference for utility shares and the basic industries. It cannot be stated that women are more or less willing than men to undertake risks, but from the data available, the conclusion is evident that women tend to be more conservative than men as investors. To the extent that this generalization is true, large corporations will tend to become larger, and small businesses will find it more difficult to raise capital through sale of ownership.

Another interesting fact concerning stockholders is that, in the case of some large corporations, stockholders outnumber employees. Also it is interesting to note that a number of such corporations have a high percentage of their stockholders living in the vicinity of the corporations' plants. The latter observation seems to indicate the need for greater

---

[15] *The Exchange,* a publication of The New York Stock Exchange, April 1950, p. 7.

efforts to spread knowledge about a company's operations for the information of investors.

Contemporary Problems of the Securities Business

Lack of public knowledge concerning investments. Notwithstanding publicity efforts by government agencies, by securities associations, by the exchanges, by firms, and by brokers and dealers, the misconceptions and fallacies that characterize the general public concerning securities remain many and varied. Tons and tons of literature are published, and daily invitations appear in the press to encourage people to send for free booklets and other literature. Magazines carry articles, lectures and courses are given, radio programs are broadcast, and movies are produced and distributed—all because a number of individuals connected with the securities business are conscious of the need for a better understanding of investment on the part of the public.

Without investment, an economy must stagnate, and the tremendous investment that has taken place throughout the history of this country needs to be reconciled with the general lack of knowledge. The problem arises in part out of the nature of the securities business itself. At the foundation of the business is money; while many recognize money when it is seen, few understand its proper uses and limitations. All securities involve risk, and unless there is a pioneering spirit among people, interest in securities cannot be general. Investments involve savings, and unless the hope for gain in the future far overshadows the pleasure of current spending, possibilities of making investments dwindle. Then too the actual transaction of making an investment decreases in cost as the size of the investment increases, with the result that many small investment transactions are so costly that they cannot be efficiently made.

For this problem of the lack of public knowledge concerning investments, solutions have been attempted along two main lines: first, to educate the public; and second, to alter the conduct of the investment business so as to restrict the need for more widely extending knowledge. To date the education has been undertaken pretty much by the securities business itself, and to some extent by certain firms within the business. There is an evident need for more widespread efforts in this educational process throughout the business; and perhaps even more important, the users of capital, the issuers themselves of securities, would find this part of their financial operations much less costly if they too invested in the creation of a well-informed, investing public.

The answer to the problem along the lines of altering the conduct of securities transactions has taken the form of the creation of financial institutions to gather the savings of the general public and thus con-

centrate the investment of these savings in fewer hands; and the second form is the issuance of securities which are themselves claims on a wide variety of other securities. The former needs no explanation for they are the familiar banks and savings institutions; the latter are the various investment trusts and counseling concerns which in essence attempt to "sell" investment knowledge to make it possible for investors to invest without knowing how to invest.

Although altering the business to meet present conditions may be a most practical solution, in the long run a much wider public understanding of securities cannot help but be in the best interest of the nation, the economy, the securities business, and the individual himself, whether he be an investor or not.

Internal conditions within the securities business. No attempt is made here to include a complete discussion or even listing of the current problems arising within the securities business. This is not to say that the business is all problems, for it is not; but if no problems existed it could only mean that no business existed.

1. Attitude Toward Regulation. As has been stated earlier, the securities business is perhaps the most regulated of all competitive enterprises. Considerable debate within the securities business has been occasioned with each new major flood of regulations. By and large, however, some regulation has been desired by those within the business; in fact, the establishment of the exchanges themselves was the result of a desire for regulation. Regulation is not so much the result of the need for regulation within the securities business as it is an effort to prevent an erring few from taking advantage of an uninformed public. Considering the thousands of individuals and firms engaged in the securities business and the intimate personal relations with their customers, the total number of improper dealings found is relatively insignificant. Merciless publicity is given, and should be given, to those few cases when they arise; unfortunately the attitude of the business toward regulation is too often judged solely on the basis of the publicity given to a few cases of improper dealings. One prominent brokerage firm, and in this case it is typical, in adopting basic policies for the guidance of its employees included these: "We heartily endorse the laws designed to protect investors"; "We will disclose the interest of our firm in securities mentioned in our printed literature"; "When we sell a security owned by the firm we will disclose this fact to the customer before the transaction"; "Our capital will always substantially exceed the requirements of law." [16] Regulation is not a general problem, but rather it is a problem confined to a minute minority.

2. Competitive Situation Between Firms. Competition within the se-

[16] *Annual Report,* Merrill Lynch, Pierce, Fenner & Beane, 1949, p. 5.

curities business has been mentioned several times. The very nature of securities trading makes it highly competitive, whether competition be by "double" auction or by negotiation. Membership in the exchanges and in NASD together with regulation might be presumed to be factors tending to eliminate competition; but the universal policy underlying such membership and all regulation is that prices must be free, that services to the customer must be wide open, but that commissions and charges must be reasonable. Under such circumstances one firm prospers over another only to the extent that it can: (1) obtain a better price; (2) render a greater service; (3) keep its individual charges at a minimum. Healthy competition is the natural result, and health is evidenced by the large amount of free services rendered by firms in the securities business. One glance at the financial page of any metropolitan newspaper will give substantial proof of the existence of competition. Competition in the securities business between firms is not a problem; it is a way of doing business.

3. Availability of Facilities for Conduct of Business. An inspection tour of the communication facilities in the exchanges and of the offices of brokerage firms might produce the impression that further facilities were impossible. Yet the ticker tape does get behind under the rush of orders, and in the over-the-counter market the almost complete lack of publicity on transactions has some disadvantages. At present orders from all over the country can be completed in a surprisingly short time, and it is doubtful that great reductions in time could be made even if additional facilities were added. But technological progress may bring facilities to do the work better or quicker, and perhaps some means will be provided to make up for the lack of publicity where it exists. Certainly if the improvements made in the past are to be characteristic of the future, many additional facilities will be provided.

4. Stabilization and Manipulation. By stabilization is generally meant the buying of a security to prevent a decline in its price. Stabilization can also mean the selling of a security to prevent a rise in price. Manipulation on the other hand is an attempt artificially to induce a change in price. There still remain many arguments both for and against stabilization. As a device it prevents the free flow of market influences from affecting the price of a security. Generally stabilization is sanctioned during the period a new security issue is being sold to the public. Without stabilization during such a period, many difficulties might arise to prevent the flotation of the issue, yet it may be that at the end of the stabilization period the price of the securities may drop. In answer to the problem, issues sold under stabilization agreements must be fully advertised as such for the information of investors. That stabilization has merits is evidenced by the fact that the Federal Reserve Banks

(through their Open Market Committee) have stabilized the price of United States government issues over various periods of time.

The SEC is empowered to define and regulate manipulative and other fraudulent devices. This it has done through promulgating a set of rules, generally known as "the over-the-counter rules." In general these rules require brokers and dealers to make known to their customers prior to any transaction the details concerning the transaction that, if unknown, might permit manipulation. In its 1949 annual report SEC states: "As a result of the act [Securities Exchange Act of 1934] and its administration manipulation is no longer an appreciable factor in our markets." [17]

General problems affecting the securities business. Again there are listed here certain current problems that affect the securities business. The list is not intended to be complete nor is the order intended to reflect the relative depth of the problem.

1. General Economic Conditions. The securities business is affected by and in turn affects general economic conditions, a circumstance not confined to the securities business. When times are good (or thought to be becoming good), trading in securities increases, and the flotation of new issues is in order. Savings are increasing and funds are available for investment. During depressed times the situation is reversed and securities trading is "thin" or "dull." Bad as depressed times may be on the securities business, they are not as devastating as the so-called "panic" times that are characterized by large declines in prices. The outbreak of war or the imminence of war may set off a large volume of selling and consequent price declines. World War I and II produced such results.

General economic conditions affect the securities markets in two matters—namely, price and volume of trading. Changes in price affect the profits and losses of dealers and investors. A broker makes his commission so long as the transaction is made, regardless of whether the price is up or down.

2. Economic Stability and Risk Taking. To repeat, without risk there can be no investment, yet the presence of risk accompanies economic instability. Progress requires a certain form of economic instability, for to remain stable means to remain without change. As a cure for many evils during recent years the goal of economic stability has been set high. But to the extent that such a goal is realized, the securities business and economic progress must suffer. In the securities business, as in other businesses, changes in prices induce activity, and activity is an integral part of production. Economic stability and stagnation may well be synonymous.

---

[17] Securities and Exchange Commission, *15th Annual Report,* 1949, p. 43.

3. Federal Fiscal Policy. Government fiscal policy does affect the securities business to a marked degree. The existence of a large volume of government debt not only absorbs tremendous savings that might have been invested in securities of productive enterprises, but also the influence of government bond yields tends to set the pattern for corporate bond yields. Since the war the federal government has used a fiscal debt policy of low interest rates; this policy has prevented the yield on corporate bond from rising to any appreciable amount. Taxation, which has remained at war levels, since the war has also tended to absorb funds that otherwise might have found their way into securities. Corporate taxation, to the extent that it reduces corporate profits, also reduces funds available for dividends; and stocks without dividends have no yield. Since dividends themselves are the object of taxes, income yields to investors in stocks are further curtailed. The economic effects of government expenditures is much too broad a subject to be included here, but government expenditures, insofar as they are made to private industries, tend to direct activity to those industries. Private industries may appear prosperous, but the increased demand in such industries cannot help but affect adversely other industries. The net result in the securities business is to make it necessary to follow in detail the nature of government expenditures in determining future trends in the market.

4. Corporate Dividend Policies. Some profits realized by business corporations are used to meet tax payments, some are paid out in dividends, and some are retained in the business for capital expansion purposes. In principle, profits retained in the business should increase the value of stock proportionately, but whereas the book value of stock on the corporation's books may be increased, the market value or price of the stock on the market may or may not be changed accordingly. To the average investor the market price of stock is of more direct interest, for unless retained profits are reflected in market price, the investor can derive no additional income.

The dividends paid by corporations constitute the corporations' dividend policy, and dividend policy plus current market price determine stock yields. And stock yields determine investor income (other than from appreciation which is not always realized by the investor, since to realize income from appreciation the stock must be sold). Corporations with long records of high dividend payments offer most appeal to investors interested in yield.

During the war cash dividends paid by corporations did not fluctuate widely. According to the Department of Commerce estimates, the low was $4.3 billion and the high $4.7 billion annually, during the period from 1941 to 1945 inclusive. Each year since 1945 cash dividend payments

have increased up to a total of $8.4 billion in 1949. Table 5 indicates taxes, dividends, and retained profits for the years 1940–49.

TABLE 5

CORPORATE PROFITS, TAXES, DIVIDENDS, RETAINED PROFITS, AND
YEAR END STOCK PRICES

1940–49

(In billions of dollars, except year end stock prices)

Year	Profits before Taxes	Taxes	Dividends	Retained Profits	Year End Stock Prices
1940	9.3	2.9	4.0	2.4	$ 93.82
1941	17.2	7.8	4.5	4.9	78.13
1942	21.1	11.7	4.3	5.1	82.30
1943	25.1	14.4	4.5	6.2	92.48
1944	24.3	13.5	4.7	6.1	106.41
1945	19.7	11.2	4.7	3.8	134.18
1946	23.6	9.6	5.8	8.1	119.61
1947	31.6	12.5	7.0	12.1	118.36
1948	34.8	13.6	7.9	13.2	114.69
1949	28.8	11.4	8.4	8.9	133.78

(Source: *Federal Reserve Bulletin.* Year end stock prices, *The New York Times*, Closing Prices of 50 combined stocks.)

Reference to Table 4 indicates the correlation between dividends paid, year end stock prices and stock yields. The increase in stock yield in 1946 was due to an increase in dividend payments and a drop in price. (During May 1946 stock prices reached a high above 1945 but dropped rapidly during the third quarter of the year.) The 1947 and 1948 increase in yield reflects chiefly the increased dividend payments, since prices were off only moderately during those years. During 1949 the increased dividend payments were not sufficient to affect the increased prices with the result that yield fell.

Stock prices are not determined solely by dividend payments, so no direct correlation would be expected between the two for any extended period. Rumors on the unexpected announcement of an extra dividend payment will send stock prices up, if there are no other influences to counteract the movement. The influence of dividends on investors is seen from their inclusion in "sound" securities of common stocks having long dividend records. By 1950, 26 corporations whose stock is listed on the New York Stock Exchange had been paying dividends consecutively for 65 to 102 years; and if the period is extended from 20 to 102 years, the number of corporations paying dividends consecutively increases to 285.

Because of higher yields on stocks over bonds due to dividend payments, 1949 saw some shift in investment portfolios of insurance funds, trust funds, savings funds and the like, that in part increased return.

Adoption of "prudent man" laws extended common stocks to former legal lists. So long as yields on debt securities are held down, this movement to common stocks probably will be maintained.

Regardless of future turns in the market, however, so long as there is a need to finance business capital requirements, stockbrokers and dealers will play a prominent part in that operation.

Suggested Readings

BOOKS

Atkins, Willard E.; Edwards, George W.; Moulton, Harold G., *The Regulation of the Securities Markets.* Washington, D.C.: The Brookings Institution, 1946. Complete text.

Badger, Ralph Eastman and Guthman, Harry G., *Investment, Principles and Practice,* Third ed. New York: Prentice-Hall, Inc., 1941. Parts II and IV.

Bogen, Jules I., (Editor), *Financial Handbook.* New York: Ronald Press Company, 1948. Sections I and II.

Bonneville, Joseph Howard and Dewey, Lloyd Ellis, *Organizing and Financing Business,* Third ed. New York: Prentice-Hall, Inc., 1946. Chapters VII, VIII, XII through XVI.

Investment Bankers Association of America, *Fundamentals of Investment Banking.* New York: Prentice-Hall, Inc., 1949. Chapters I to IV inclusive, Part III.

Jordan, David F., *Jordan on Investments,* Fourth rev. ed. New York: Prentice-Hall, Inc., 1946. Part I.

Losser, John C., *The Over-the-Counter Securities Market—What It Is and How It Operates.* New York: National Quotation Bureau, Inc., 1940. Complete text.

McCormick, Edward T., *Understanding the Securities Act and the SEC.* New York: American Book Company, 1948. Complete text.

Prime, John H., *Investment Analysis.* New York: Prentice-Hall, Inc., 1946. Chapters I to VIII inclusive.

Shultz, Birl E., *The Securities Market and How It Works.* New York: Harper & Bros., 1946. Complete text.

GOVERNMENT AGENCY PUBLICATIONS

Department of Commerce, *Survey of Current Business* and other reports.

Federal Reserve Board, *Annual Reports, Federal Reserve Bulletin, Chart Book,* and other publications.

Securities and Exchange Commission, *Annual Reports, Statistical Bulletin,* and other publications.

PRIVATE AGENCY PUBLICATIONS

Association of Stock Exchange Firms, *Understanding the Modern Securities Market,* and other publications.

National Association of Securities Dealers, Inc., various publications.

New York Stock Exchange, *Annual Year Book, The Exchange,* and various other publications.

Various securities houses' reports, digests, surveys, and other publications intended to assist the investor.

12

Stock Exchanges

---

by HERBERT SPERO

Associate Professor of Economics, the City College of New York

Corporate Growth and Security Marketability

SECURITIES MARKETS are vital organs of a highly industrialized society. Before the development of the railroad and other modern inventions businessmen were small entrepreneurs. They accumulated capital through the arduous process of saving, with little reliance upon other people's money to finance their organizations. The modern industrial age brought great changes. It frequently requires the funds of not one man but the savings of many men to develop large business corporations. If investments offered are to be considered desirable, the investors must believe that their security holdings will yield a satisfactory return and be salable if conditions so warrant.

A stock market, formal or informal, must be created to provide a market for security owners anxious to shift their holdings to other investors or speculators. The development of corporate industry and the growth of the stock exchanges are closely intertwined economic phenomena. Their interdependence was succinctly expressed by Francis Truslow Adams in a 1947 address before the First Hemispheric Stock Exchange Conference:

> One hundred years ago stock exchanges were of negligible significance in our economy. Today they are an essential element. The rise of stock exchanges in the United States during the past hundred years has coincided with the rise of corporations. The phenomena are mutually dependent and neither could have occurred without the other. The contributor to the latter required the services of the former as a major inducement to contribution. The position in our economy of stock exchanges as the central market places for the pur-

chase and sale of corporate ownership and debt thus increases in importance. . . .[1]

A stock exchange is an organized market for the purchase and sale of securities. Brokers, acting for their clients and charging reasonable commissions, discharge their clients' orders to buy or sell. An exchange can be likened to a free and open auction market where security prices are determined by the supply of and the demand for stocks and bonds. The exchange does not fix prices. It only offers trading facilities. All security buyers and sellers are not located in the city housing the exchange. But they are in contact with one another through such rapid means of communication as the financial ticker, private wire services connecting brokerage branch offices in the many sections of the United States with their main big city office, and the business and financial sections of leading newspapers. A national market for corporate and government securities is created through the publicity afforded by these channels of communication. In brief, a stock exchange offers the securities dealt in by its member brokers not only an organized but a broad market. A local, perhaps even a nation-wide or international community of buyers and sellers trades in securities on this organized market.

Importance of Marketability

Marketability benefits all segments of society. A large army of potential investors, cognizant of security market developments, assures a greater number of bids for securities in such central markets as New York, Chicago, or Los Angeles. At the same time, securities owners following stock market quotations closely offer their holdings for sale when they believe prices justify liquidation. This centralization of potential buyers and sellers reduces price changes, for bids are largely balanced by offers.

Marketability aids people in special circumstances. Inheritance taxes frequently necessitate sale of security holdings to meet the imposts; personal emergencies in the life of the medium and small income receiver and security owner often call for ready cash.

Marketability and Investment Banking

Broad marketability of new and seasoned issues stimulates the investment of liquid funds in long and short-term capital commitments. A growing volume of capital investment is vital to business development, full employment, and progress. A declining new capital issues market

---

[1] Record of Proceedings, First Hemispheric Stock Exchange Conference, New York, 1947, p. 20.

is an ominous indicator of contracting business activity, smaller returns to security holders, and mounting unemployment. A flourishing and active new issues market depends on both the business trend and the ability of investors to market their holdings whenever they desire. The investment banker's business of selling new issues to the investing public is thus closely related to the stock market function of providing an open competitive area for trading in these issues following their flotation. The tie-up between marketability and investment was well expressed by Charles R. Gay, former president of the New York Stock Exchange, who in 1937 said:

> Funds are invested irrevocably by the people as a whole in the creation of real wealth, a one-way process by which higher living standards and the public welfare are promoted. But the welfare of the individual requires the two-way process of investment and subsequent withdrawal by the only available means—resale of the security to another who has available funds for the purpose. Only to the extent that this process of withdrawal is readily available to the individual investor is his welfare reconciled with that of the nation to the degree necessary to promote essential investment in the development of national wealth. Ready and prompt convertibility of securities into cash is fundamental requisite of the basic investment process.[2]

Security Prices as a Guide to Security Values; "Seasoning"

The purchase and sale in the open market of new issues will suggest whether a security was over or underpriced or correctly evaluated by the issuer and its bankers. The levels at which issues are traded will determine the prices at which additional emissions of the issues can be marketed and the cost of capital to them. The exchanges provide a "seasoning" ground for a new issue. The process of seasoning continues until the security shows its real worth as an investment. During the "seasoning" process it is traded in principally by speculators—people who purchase it in anticipation of a rise in price or greatly increased dividends. If the issue does not meet their expectations, they sell it. Eventually the issue may establish its investment merit and be closely held by a large body of conservative investors who are confident of the security's steady return and capital protection value. However, if their beliefs are dashed by an adverse turn in the issuer's fortunes (with unhappy effects upon the price of the security), the issue will again be considered a speculation.

The administration of an exchange should create public confidence in security trading. It can encourage the flow of idle capital into industry by insuring the establishment of prices in a fair and orderly manner.

---

[2] New York Stock Exchange, *Annual Report of President Charles R. Gay*, May 1937, "Security Markets and National Welfare," pp. 38-39.

Fraudulent practices must be prevented and artificial influences ruled out as determinants of security prices.

Security Prices as a Business Yardstick

People attempt to judge the effects of good or bad business developments on the securities market and attempt to accumulate or liquidate securities accordingly. Analysis of the trend of stock prices has thus come to be considered as a business forecasting device. However, the forecasting capacity of the stock market is no longer held in high regard:

> Whether those dealing in stocks forecast general business or not, they have all of the vital information about the individual companies in which they typically make large investments. This information may indicate a change in profit prospects before the change actually takes place in the rate of production of the individual company.[3]

Business Services of Security Markets

Security market operations have fostered the growth of valuable business services. Banks lend on marketable securities because the securities enjoy a market and a collateral value protecting bank loans. An investor can retain legal ownership of his security holdings while borrowing on them. The uses to which loans can be put may yield an income sufficient to pay them off. Corporate reports issued to stockholders and available to would-be investors serve as a guide to investment policy. Daily newspaper and ticker reports on financial affairs in general and the past record and future prospects of listed investments provide additional business guideposts. The broad marketability afforded by securities markets and the wide public knowledge of the securities market have stimulated the growth of research and statistical organizations to advise both investment and speculative clients. Stock market officials have increasingly realized their responsibility to safeguard member firm clients in their dealings with their brokers. Stock market officials examine their members' financial statements and business practices; the officials also require an independent audit of the members' financial statements to assure adherence to minimum financial requirements and fair business practices.

Types of Securities Markets

Organized securities markets like the New York Stock Exchange and the New York Curb Exchange are auction markets where bids and offers

---

[3] Elmer C. Bratt, *Business Cycles and Forecasting*. Chicago: Business Publications, Inc., 1937, p. 420.

are coordinated through a well-developed trading technique. The bids and offers do not assure a perfect auction center; their volume even on the New York Stock Exchange is not large enough to guarantee a perfect balancing of bids and offers. Only infrequently is there a constant equilibrium of bids and offers at a fixed point for any length of time. Lack of a balance causes price variations in the securities handled. Some stocks are inactive because they are closely held or because would-be buyers and sellers have widely differing ideas of security values.

The over-the-counter or off board securities market deals in unlisted issues whose value is fixed through bargaining among sellers and securities dealers on the one hand or among securities dealers acting for their own account. The participants in over-the-counter trading shop around for the best price and engage in considerable negotiation before a deal is finally agreed upon. Unlike traders on organized exchanges, these participants do not enjoy the advantages of a central market place, nor are sales prices on all deals available to them. Only the bid and asked quotations enjoy a limited amount of publicity.

The New York Stock Exchange

Listing. When a stock is listed on the New York Stock Exchange, the Exchange's Stock List Department admits it to active trading. Principally seasoned issues of large and financially powerful corporations are given a place on the Big Board although some small (in assets and security issues) but strong companies are also listed. Speculative issues are discouraged until they have proved their worth on other exchanges. The stock issues seeking admission must be those of established enterprises enjoying a broad market for widely distributed issues. Common stocks must have voting power, whereas new preferred stocks can be listed only if they enjoy specified minimum voting rights or the privilege of electing at least two directors upon default of a maximum of six quarterly dividends. Relatively small issues could not secure listing privileges prior to 1934, for exchange authorities feared that such issues would lend themselves to manipulation. Since the passage of the Securities Exchange Act of 1934, this fear has been dissipated, for the legislation prohibits or regulates manipulation. Bonds of domestic and foreign corporations and governments are also dealt in on the Exchange when they meet its listing requirements.

Listed securities enjoy better and broader trading facilities. The widespread public knowledge of these stocks and bonds smoothes the way for new issues and the exchange of shares in company mergers. The danger of minority control through concentrated holdings is lessened. But listing is not always desirable. An issue may be well known in a

smaller community or region and its securities traded actively on local or regional exchanges. Listing on the New York Stock Exchange would be superfluous. Trading confined to out-of-town or regional exchanges would minimize speculative activity. If an issue is handled over-the-counter, Securities and Exchange Commission stock exchange registration, reporting requirements, and statutory legal liabilities could be avoided.

The Stock Exchange's Department of Stock List prescribes the rules governing listing. These rules require that securities be registered with the Securities and Exchange Commission and comply with the Securities Exchange Act of 1934. The applicant must advise the Department of Stock List of the nature of his business, provide financial statements for the preceding five years, describe his capitalization, and establish a transfer agency and registrar in the Borough of Manhattan, New York City. A security is considered listed 30 days after receipt by the Securities and Exchange Commission of the stock exchange's certification (or sooner if the government agency issues an accelerating order). The listing procedure provides the security buying public with such information as the listing or registration statements include. These statements are available either at the offices of the Exchange or the Securities and Exchange Commission and are summarized in the financial press and in investment statistical manuals. The investing public is afforded a firm basis to judge the merits of the security accorded active trading privileges. The authorities of the exchange can also judge the desirability of the security as a member of its trading family.

Trading. Trading takes place in the board room on the main floor of the Stock Exchange Building. Member firm floor brokers in direct telephone contact with their offices receive security orders and other messages. The flashing of a broker's number on the two black annunciator boards on opposite walls of the board room call him to his telephone. Trading in stocks takes place at 18 posts, the focal points for dealing in a number of listed equity issues. Trading in other listed stocks occurs in an adjoining wing; in yet another room, bond transactions are arranged. Security price quotations and sales in both the United States and Canada are reported over the stock exchange ticker system to assure a broad public knowledge of quotations. The Stock Clearing Corporation located in the basement below the trading floor clears security sales. Similarly situated are members' safe deposit vaults.

Nonmembers of the Exchange can see its trading activities from a visitor's gallery on each side of the Exchange floor.

Methods of Trading. Stocks are traded in full lots of 100 shares, except for a few inactive issues. Stock brokers at each trading post bid for or offer 100 share blocks or any multiple thereof. Prices on the

Exchange are quoted in terms of $\frac{1}{8}$ of a point (as, 10, $10\frac{1}{8}$, $10\frac{1}{4}$, $10\frac{3}{8}$, although buying demand for a stock can increase a quotation from 10 to 11. A few low priced issues are permitted to vary less than $\frac{1}{8}$ of a point. U.S. Government bonds are quoted in $\frac{1}{32}$ of a point.

Buyers and sellers may order purchases or sales at the market for the most advantageous prices at which securities can be bought or sold. There is no limitation on the prices at which these orders may be executed. Buyers and sellers can limit their broker's power to execute their orders as to prices and the time during which they may be effected. Day orders are good only for the trading day when the broker receives them. G.T.W. (good this week only) and G.T.M. (good this month only) orders limit the time during which they may be carried through. G.T.C. (good till cancelled) orders remain on the broker's books until executed or cancelled. Stop-loss orders are placed with brokers to limit customers' losses or preserve their profits. The stop-loss orders become market orders when stock holdings decline to customer designated prices. If a customer's broker cannot sell the stock at the specified quotation, he is under instructions to sell it at the best price obtainable. Stop-loss orders are also intended to limit the risks of short sellers due to rising prices. All these types of orders make a security market.

Brokerage firms that buy and sell for people and investing institutions help create this trading area. Along with the security markets these firms enable long-term bondholders and preferred and common stockowners to sell their claims on and interests in corporate and government securities to other security minded investors. Stock and bond markets make a reality of shiftability.

Marketability depends on: (1) The closeness of bid and asked prices; stock exchanges are not perfect auction markets for the volume of bids and offers on even the largest exchanges and in the very active securities do not guarantee a perfect meeting of the minds of buyers and sellers; (2) the capacity of the market to absorb large offerings without a sharp price decline. (Whether prices are unsteady will hinge on the distribution of the security, the size of the issue, general security market conditions and the issuer's credit standing. If prices change drastically between sales, the marketability of the issue deteriorates. The borrower on the security and his creditor will be upset, hesitate to handle the issue, and cause a drying up of the market); (3) whether the issue's market price really reflects changing basic economic and political conditions and industrial progress or whether it responds merely to passing situations, such as the changing technical position of the market reflecting only temporarily large bids and a meager volume of offerings.

Members of the exchange.—Stock and Bond Brokers and Dealers.

Purchases and sales of stocks and bonds are made through several types of New York Stock Exchange members. Stock brokerage commission houses execute the buying or selling public's orders for equities. These houses maintain branches in different cities; the main office may even be located outside New York City. Branches are in constant touch with the main office through leased telegraph and telephone facilities. Such firms are called wire houses. A full lot trade between buyer and seller in different cities is thus described by the New York Stock Exchange:

Mr. R. L. Stoddard, a druggist in New Haven, Conn., owns 100 shares of General Motors stock. However, when he suddenly finds that he needs additional funds for running his business, he decides to sell them. Fortunately, listed securities are readily convertible into cash so Mr. Stoddard merely stops in at the New Haven office of a member firm of the New York Stock Exchange and consults with a partner or a customers' broker.

Looking at the "board" in the office, Mr. Stoddard sees that the latest sale that day in General Motors was at 57. But since the "board" doesn't show the time at which the sale occurred, which may have taken place several minutes ago, Mr. Stoddard asks for a "quote"—in other words, for the current best bid to buy and lowest offer to sell in General Motors shares on the Exchange's "floor."

Calling over a direct private wire connected with his firm's New York office, a clerk asks for a "quote" on General Motors. The request is instantly relayed by a second clerk in the New York office who telephones the quotation department of the New York Stock Exchange, again over a direct wire.

Located in the same building with the Exchange's trading floor, this department is in continuous contact with quotation clerks stationed at the trading posts on the "floor." These clerks promptly notify the "quote" room, over special telephones, of changes in the bid and asked prices throughout the trading day.

To answer Mr. Stoddard's request, therefore, one of the quotation girls has only to look at the current report for General Motors and say, "General Motors 57⅜." This means that someone wants to buy at 57 and someone else desires to sell at 57⅜.

Scarcely sixty seconds after he asked for it, Mr. Stoddard gets his "quote"—it has taken no longer than if he had been sitting in a New York City brokerage office. Satisfied with the quotation, he instructs his broker to sell 100 General Motors "at the market."

The order is immediately sent over a direct wire to the firm's New York office, where it is relayed over a second private wire to the firm's telephone clerk on the trading floor. As the clerk writes out the order to sell 100 General Motors "at the market," he "puts up" the number of the floor member of his firm on the large wall annunciator boards. Seeing his number, the member comes immediately to his telephone booth, gets the order, and hurries to Post 4 on the trading floor, where the stock of the General Motors Corporation is traded.

Many securities—about 70 on the average—are assigned to each post. Each stock has one definite location at the outer edge of the horseshoe-shaped post where all trading in its shares take place.

Arriving at Post 4, the broker with Mr. Stoddard's sell order asks "How's

General Motors?" A member replies, "57⅜." In other words, the highest bid to buy is 57, and the lowest offer to sell is 57⅜.

In the meantime, a doctor in Seattle who has some funds to invest has decided that he wants to acquire some General Motors stock. He, likewise, has gone into the local office of a Stock Exchange firm and has entered an order to buy 100 shares of General Motors "at the market."

Received almost simultaneously in New York, his order has been written out and telephoned to the clerk of this other firm who hands it to his floor member. This member arrived at Post 4 just a few moments after the broker with Mr. Stoddard's order had entered the group and offered to sell at 57¼.

The broker with the Seattle buy order bids 57⅛ for 100 shares. Mr. Stoddard's broker says "sold."

The two brokers have made a contract in this stock which is thereupon printed on the ticker tape for all to see and, within three days, 100 shares of General Motors stock are delivered by the first broker to the second for transmittal to the doctor in Seattle.[4]

Many people do not buy or sell stocks in full lots; sometimes odd lots of less than 100 shares are bought and sold. If an odd lot dealer whose sole business is the execution of odd lot orders in all listed shares receives an order from a commission house to buy five shares of General Motors common, he purchases the stock at the next quoted ticker tape figure or bid price, adding ⅛ of a point to the price since his chief interest in the transaction is the ⅛ commission differential. Orders to sell odd lots are effected at prices ⅛ under the next quoted ticker tape or asked price. To secure the five shares ordered by the buyer, the dealer had to purchase a full lot of 100 shares. He must dispose of the excess 95 shares to avoid an overloaded portfolio of General Motors stock. Since this dealer is seeking to maintain a balanced market position in General Motors and other securities that he handles on an odd lot basis, he employs numerous odd lot brokers at various trading posts to even out his position. The odd lot dealer renders an economic service to the stock market; since he is willing to take a position and make a market in a security, the compensation for his service is the price differential of ⅛ of a point.

Floor (or "two-dollar") brokers and specialists act for other brokers. Commission house brokers occasionally are too overloaded with business to handle all orders that come their way. The two-dollar broker carries out an order and receives a part of the commission paid the commission house. But his present nickname is no longer descriptive of his rate of compensation. It only reflects the fixed commission of two dollars per 100 shares that he once earned. Specialists are brokers and dealers centering their operation on one or a number of "assigned" stocks at a

---

[4] *The Nation's Market Place.* New York: New York Stock Exchange.

single trading post. They carry out the orders received at commission rates identical to those paid two-dollar brokers. As a broker the specialist handles customer orders to be fulfilled in the future or at a price away from the market. He keeps a close eye on market quotations and fills the orders as conditions warrant. Naturally, the principle of "first come first served" is followed in the discharge of his functions. When a specialist acts as a dealer, he trades for his own account in issues that are of particular interest to him. Both the Securities and Exchange Commission and the stock exchange authorities control his activities as a specialist to protect the stock market public from a broker who may take advantage of inside knowledge of a stock (provided by his book of orders) to enrich himself personally. Only the officers of the Exchange are allowed to examine a specialist's book of unfilled buying and selling orders.

A floor trader, expecting to gain from price changes, buys and sells on the Exchange floor for his own account. Since floor traders are on the floor, they have an excellent opportunity to evaluate the movement of security prices and the breadth of the trading volume. Inasmuch as they are Exchange members, they do not pay commission charges but are subject to federal and state taxes. Floor brokers make for a broad market and provide bids and offers for many securities in an inactive market, so assuring greater price stability.

Bond broker and dealer services are also available in the bond room. These brokers and dealers carry out customers' orders for the purchase of listed bonds, and the brokers also trade in them for their own account in the "bond crowd."

But over-the-counter bond dealings are more important than trading on the floor, even though Exchange bond prices largely determine over-the-counter quotations. Interest paying bonds are quoted at prices including interest charges from the last coupon paying date to the date of purchase and "flat" when in default. Bond trading originating at points distant from New York may be arranged with delivery deferred up to seven days. This practice developed out of a wide national interest in fixed interest-bearing obligations which could not be borrowed freely for delivery. An effort to stimulate floor dealings in listed bonds has been incorporated in the rule that orders to buy or sell less than $15,000 par value of a listed bond must be executed on the floor, unless a more attractive price is obtainable in over-the-counter trading.

Tradition and the unlimited liability carried by each member of a stock exchange firm has established the principle that cooperation among member firms is essential for their prosperity.

NEW YORK STOCK EXCHANGE
MINIMUM NON-MEMBER COMMISSION RATES
ON STOCKS
SELLING AT 50¢ PER SHARE AND ABOVE

(As Revised October 31, 1947)

On single transactions not exceeding 100 shares based upon the amount of money involved, the following rates apply:

Round Lots

(A unit of trading, a combination of units of trading, or a combination of a unit or units of trading plus an odd lot, amounting to 100 shares or less). Commission charges are: 6% on the first $100; 1% on the next $900; ½% on the next $3,000 and 1/10% over $4,000.

To facilitate computation, it is stated as follows:

Money Value	Commission
If less than $ 100.00	6%
$ 100.00 to 999.99	1% plus $ 5.00
$1,000.00 to 3,999.99	½% plus 10.00
$4,000.00 and above	1/10% plus 26.00

Odd Lots
(Less than a unit of trading)
Same rates as above, less 10%

Minimum Commissions
(Notwithstanding above, each transaction is subject to following minimum charges)

Money Value	Commission
Under $15	As mutually agreed
$15 or more but less than $100	6% of money value
$100 or more	Minimum not to exceed 50¢ per share, but not less than $6 per transaction.

These minimum charges are not subject to the 10% deduction.

To determine the commission charges to be made on a transaction involving multiples of 100 shares, e.g., 200, 300, 400, etc., shares, multiply the applicable 100-share commission by 2, 3, 4, etc., respectively, as the case may be.

The commission rate for buying is the same, as for selling. In addition to commissions, New York State and Federal Transfer taxes are applicable to securities transactions.

Commission rates for bonds are shown in the following table.

NONMEMBER MINIMUM COMMISSION ON BONDS
(Excepting Government, Short Term or Called Bonds)

Price per $1000 of Principal Bond	Minimum Commission Rate per $1000 (of Principal) Bond			
	On orders of 1 or 2 bonds	On orders of 3 bonds	On orders of 4 bonds	On orders of 5 bonds or more
Selling at less than $10 (1%)........	$1.50	$1.20	$0.90	$0.75
Selling at $10 (1%) and above but under $100 (10%)	2.50	2.00	1.50	1.25
Selling at $100 (10%) and above ...	5.00	4.00	3.00	2.50

Taxes

Stocks—Federal and New York State taxes are payable on all sales. In the case of odd lots, the purchaser is required to pay the Federal Tax.

Stocks selling under $20 par value are subject to a Federal Tax of 5 cents for each $100 of par value or fraction thereof, or 5 cents a share for stock of no par value.

Stocks selling at $20 or more per share are subject to a Federal Tax of 6 cents for each $100 or par value or fraction thereof, or 6 cents a share for stock of no par value.

The New York State Tax is as follows:

On stocks selling	The tax is
Under $5 a share	1 cent a share
At $5 a share but not less than $10 a share	2 cents a share
At $10 a share but less than $20 a share	3 cents a share
At $20 a share and above	4 cents a share

Bonds—The Federal Tax on sales of corporate bonds, debentures or certificates of indebtedness is at the rate of 5 cents on each $100 of face value or fraction thereof (50 cents per $1,000 bond). There is no tax on obligations of governments or municipalities. There is no New York State tax on bonds.

SEC Fees—Under the Securities Exchange Act of 1934, each national securities exchange pays to the Securities and Exchange Commission a registration fee for doing business during the preceding calendar year. This fee is collected by the exchange from its members at the rate of 1¢ for each $500 represented by their transactions. These sums are withheld by member firms from the amount credited to accounts of principals for whom the transactions are made.

Source: Commodity Research Bureau Inc., Securities Division, *Understanding the Modern Securities Market*, New York, 1949, pp. 17-18.

The value of a "seat." Members of the Exchange own "seats"—the right to act as brokers and dealers on the floor of the Exchange. Persons seeking a seat must be sponsored by two Exchange members and approved by a two-thirds vote of the members of the board of governors at a regular meeting. The determinants of approval are the candidate's business and personal record. Any person lending a candidate money to buy a seat subordinates his claim and does not enjoy a lien on the seat. If a member forms a firm, his partners become "allied members of the Exchange" and are subject to its constitution and rules. If the Exchange seat owner is a general partner of a firm, the latter is known as a "member firm" of the Exchange.

As of January 1, 1950, 1,375 seats affording trading privileges on the floor of the Exchange were outstanding. New York members of the Exchange totaled 1,174, and out-of-town memberships numbered 164 Thirty-seven memberships were held in the names of deceased persons.

Membership prices vary with the volume of trading. A high volume of trading yields large commissions to seat owners and increases the value of their membership right. During the prosperity year of 1929 when the total volume of trading in stocks reached 1,124,800,410 shares, the price of a seat hit a record high of $625,000. But during the following years of sluggish trading, the price of a seat plunged to a new modern low of $17,000 in 1942, when only 125,685,298 shares were turned over.[5]

The Stock Clearing Corporation. The Stock Clearing Corporation, a subsidiary of the New York Stock Exchange, settles the net balances between buying and selling member brokerage firms daily. Where differences in money or number of shares of securities exist between the listings of the Stock Clearing Corporation and the records of selling and buying member firms, the net balance is resolved. The settlement price is the mean closing bid offer to the nearest dollar.

Organization. The organization of the New York Stock Exchange is as simple as trading conditions permit. Originally, its rules were set by the entire membership, while only a president and a secretary were needed to meet the needs of the small group of brokers trading in a limited number of securities for people located within communicable distance of New York. The Exchange established the committee form of government in 1869, when the industrial growth of the United States outmoded the initial form of internal supervision. A governing committee of 40 members vested with administrative and executive powers was the final authority in all matters. When the working load on the governing committee became too burdensome, a permanent staff of employees was hired to do the spade work. But the governors were still overly tied up in administrative work; therefore, a committee was appointed to recommend a simpler organization. The Conway Committee's report of 1938 urged a salaried president, a chairman of the board chosen from its members, a smaller governing board and a reduced number of standing committees. Its recommendations were approved and incorporated into the Exchange's constitution. The standing committees were replaced in 1941 by departments within the Exchange. A chart of the current organization of the New York Stock Exchange is presented on page 339.

The Board of Governors is the over-all ruling body, regulating the business conduct of its members and assuring fair trading practices. Its chairman is a member of the Exchange elected by the membership, while the president, also a member of the Board of Governors, is its chief executive officer responsible for the management of affairs. To

---

[5] *New York Stock Exchange Year Book, 1950*, pp. 7 and 34.

ORGANIZATION OF THE NEW YORK STOCK EXCHANGE

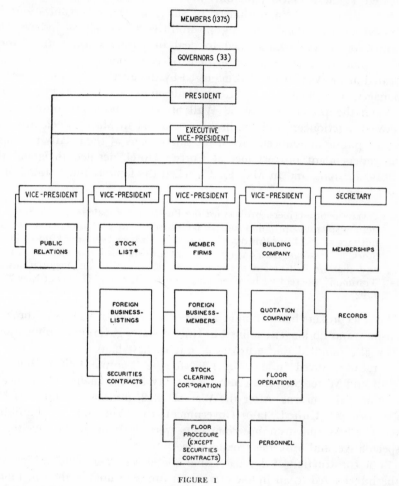

FIGURE 1

* Applications for listings must be approved by the Board of Governors; additional shares are subject to approval of the president.

assure a consistent governing policy, only one-third of the Board is elected each year.

History. When the United States Government redeemed its own and the individual states' depreciated securities after the Revolutionary War, it did more than rehabilitate its finances; it also created a market for United States government securities, termed public stock.

Trading in securities first took place at the foot of Wall Street where trading in merchandise and produce also was prevalent. The first trades were made daily at noon by five auction brokers selling government

obligations in rotation. This procedure proved unsatisfactory since it created a sellers' market, for bids were received only from buyers. The net result was the establishment of small brokerage organizations intrigued by the money making possibilities in acting as independent agents for people who wished to deal in public stock. Out of these developments came the creation of two rival stock exchanges: one was located at 22 Wall Street and managed by the auctioneers; the other was managed by independents who met daily under the famous buttonwood tree on the present site of 68 Wall Street. A more pronounced split between auctioneers and the brokers occurred in March 1792. Annoyed by the public announcements of the auctioneers at their daily meetings, the independent brokers met at Corre's Hotel, decided to ignore the public auctions, and in May 1792 reached the famous Buttonwood Tree Agreement:

> We the Subscribers, Brokers for the Purchase and Sale of Public Stock, do hereby solemnly promise and pledge ourselves to each other, that we will not buy or sell from this day for any person whatsoever, any kind of Public Stock, at a less rate than one quarter per cent Commission on the Specie value and that we will give a preference to each other in our Negotiations. In Testimony whereof we have set our hands this 17th day of May at New York, 1792.

The stockbrokers had triumphed over the auctioneers. The stockbrokers' business was no longer confined to United States government obligations; they also handled the securities of our earliest banks.

Trading moved indoors in 1793 to the Tontine Coffee House at Wall and Water Street, a center of activity for merchants, bankers, and commercial concerns. After the War of 1812, trading expanded as new issues of the United States Government, the road and canal building states, banks and insurance companies were dealt in by the investment, speculative, and brokerage community.

The construction of the Erie Canal and closer trade relationships with the interior led to an inflow of western funds to finance the call money market. Stock exchange operators primarily in New York City were the bidders for the call funds while the banks provided the financial means. The stock exchange was an integral part of the money market.

So active was the trading on the New York exchange that need was felt for a more formal organization. Copying the example set by the Philadelphia Stock Exchange, organized in 1800, a similar constitution was drawn up for the New York Stock and Exchange Board. The Board's president was authorized to call the stocks in rotation, reading off the names of stocks and awaiting bids. Membership in the Stock and Exchange Board was determined by the constituent brokers; three negative votes could exclude a candidate who must have engaged in the

brokerage business (either as a broker or an apprentice) for one or more years immediately prior to his election.

When the entire list of stocks had been called, trading officially ended for the day; but it continued to some extent on the "Curb."

The volume of trading was still small and continued so until dealings in railroad stocks began in 1830. But it slumped with the depression of 1837.

The Panic of 1837 put the nonrailroad securities (state and bank obligations which had suffered heavily from default) into disfavor. Carrier issues were strongly preferred by the security buying public. But the size of this public dwindled in the depression following the panic. So sharply had the volume of trading declined that the Stock and Exchange Board voted to divide its surplus among its 80 members. Fortunately, the desire of the Board was not fulfilled, and a greater public interest in securities guaranteed the continued life of the Exchange.

The extension of the Atlantic Cable and commercial telegraph created the beginnings of a national market for securities traded on the New York Exchange. Its growth was fostered by railroad development and the gold bonanza in California. Speculation was rife but the depression of 1857 readjusted values downward. The Exchange then proved its social value by offering a market for listed securities as against the unlisted securities lacking a ready market and sold at auction at heavy sacrifice to the sellers.

The trading area of the Exchange was expanded by the opening of Goodwin's room adjoining the Exchange. This room was the center of trading among brokers not members of the Exchange. The prices quoted on the Exchange served as the basis of trading in Goodwin's room.

The securities market adopted the name New York Stock Exchange in 1863. Two years later it moved to a building situated where the present main stock exchange building is located.

An open Board of Stock Brokers, established in 1864, initiated continuous trading or trading between calls. The payment of an annual fee admitted both members and nonmembers of the Stock Exchange to trading privileges, The regular and open boards subsequently joined forces, and brokers chose particular locations on the floor to deal in active stocks.

The New York Stock Exchange Board attributed no monetary value to the privileges enjoyed by the brokers. The latter made up a private club in essence, and a new member required an existent member's sponsorship. If a member decided to withdraw from the select circle he merely resigned. Since his withdrawal did not involve the loss of material values to the Stock and Exchange Board, the departed member was merely replaced. Not until 1861 was any recognition given the

value of the Stock Exchange as a meeting ground for investors. The seats of deceased members were then auctioned off to the highest bidder, and in 1868 stock exchange seats were made salable.

The New York Stock Exchange's government bond department was added to the New York Stock Exchange's membership in 1869, and the Exchange government was entrusted to a general governing committee and seven standing committees. The Open Board of Brokers of 354 members was combined with the New York Stock Exchange in the same year. The New York Stock Exchange in 1871 enjoyed its first real continuous market accommodations in its new remodeled quarters. Stock calls were discontinued in 1882 and bond calls in 1902. Trading hours of 10 a.m. to 3 p.m. were initiated in 1873.

Since the Civil War numerous aids to expedite trading have been introduced: the stock ticker in 1867, telephones in 1878, and the electric annunciator board in 1881. The Exchange acquired controlling interest in the New York Quotation Company in 1890. The organization of a clearing house in 1892 facilitated the security clearance procedure.

Industrial issues were first heavily traded in the early 1900's. They diverted some investor and speculator interest from railroad, government, state, and municipal securities. Once financed by small entrepreneur capital, big business ultimately required the investment banker, investment public, and security market interest. During these years the Committee on Stock List secured the compliance of listed companies to issue annual reports and abide by accounting and corporate practices developed in the stockholder's interest.

General public participation in the stock market developed government interest in security market operations. Governor Hughes of New York State arranged for an investigation into commodity and security speculation in 1909. The committee concluded that speculation is a concomitant of productive activity that tends to steady prices. Under no legal compulsion the Exchange voluntarily effected certain reforms such as the elimination of its unlisted trading department in 1910 and the prohibition of member houses' dealing with bucket shops. The federal government's famous Pujo investigation of 1913 approved the regulation of the security market through stock exchange incorporation, margin requirements, and full corporate reports by those enterprises seeking security market listing. But these recommendations were forgotten in the turmoil of World War I.

The New York Stock Exchange organized the Stock Clearing Corporation in 1920 to effect a daily money settlement among members and to clear trades in active stocks. The Stock Clearing Corporation set up a system of central delivery among its members as well as among members and large New York City banks.

During the early months of World War I, trading was suspended to prevent sharp deflationary trends due to heavy European liquidation. Upon America's entry into the war in 1917, the increase of the federal debt boomed trading in United States bonds. But a sharp reaction developed in 1920.

Following the business decline of 1920, a new speculative surge gripped the American community. Security prices attained new highs, and new issues skyrocketed while the number of Exchange seats increased from 1,100 to 1,375 to care for the larger volume of trading.

The great depression of the 1930's and the public distrust of stock market speculation and investment banking activity led to an investigation of stock exchange practices and investment banking. These investigations gave rise to the Securities Act of 1933 and the Securities Exchange Act of 1934.

Speculation in Securities

Margin trading. The security market transaction described on pages 333 and 334 is an outright purchase and sale. The buyer did not use broker or banker credit to finance the transaction. Were such credit employed, the buyer would ordinarily do so in the hope of reaping an attractive reward in a relatively short time through security appreciation of a larger number of shares than he could buy with his own money. He is speculating on this chance rather than counting (as an investor would) on a steady, attractive dividend rate or an expected price rise.

Margin trading is a technique of speculation. The buying customer pays only a part of the market price of the security purchased. The remainder is provided by his broker or banker protected by the pledge of the purchased stock. Both brokers and bankers lend only against listed issues. The margin trader must keep his margin good by adding cash or acceptable securities to bulwark his bank or broker loan if security prices decline. If the margin is insufficient, the customer is advised of the inadequacy and is requested to bring his account up to the required margin. The New York Stock Exchange requires a maintenance margin of 25 per cent of all securities purchased on margin account. However, the Security Exchange Act of 1934 vested the Board of Governors of the Federal Reserve System with broad power to set initial maximum loan values for margin trading on National Security Exchanges—exchanges complying with all Securities and Exchange Commission rules and regulations with respect to listing requirements and operations to protect the public interest and investors. Transactions on unregistered exchanges are prohibited. Some small exchanges are exempted from registration because their small volume of trading does not

make it practical, necessary, or appropriate in the public interest, or for the protection of investors.[6]

The Board of Governors also regulates the withdrawal of securities and funds from margin accounts, the substitution of securities in margin accounts, and related matters. If a customer's account is more than adequately margined by a security market price advance, the customer is privileged to withdraw cash or securities from his account.[7]

Short selling. The short seller is another type of speculator who either sells a security he does not own or sells a security which he does own but does not plan to deliver. The latter sale is called a sale "against the box." The short seller anticipates a security price decline which will permit him to cover his sale by a purchase at a lower price. The difference between the higher selling quotation and the lower purchase price will yield a profit. Since the short seller must deliver the stock on the third day following the sale under the settlement rules of the New York Stock Exchange, he borrows the security from a broker in the "loan crowd" who is carrying it in a long account—an account consisting of securities purchased for the rise or for its investment merit. The broker lending the stock is protected by a pledge of money equal to the market price of the security lent. The "loan crowd" broker pays an interest rate which fluctuates with the short demand for stocks and the supply of stock available for lending purposes. If the demand for the stock is heavy, the interest rate on the pledged money will move downward. (In fact the stock could lend "flat," with no interest rate being paid by the broker lending the stock.) A situation might arise where the demand for stock from the "loan crowd" is so great that a borrowing broker may even have to pay a premium which the lending broker splits with the customer who owns the borrowed stock. If the stock fluctuates in price, the money pledged with the lending broker will be increased or decreased in line with market prices. Loans of stock are callable on 24 hours' notice at the option of either party. Margin requirements were first imposed on short sales in 1937. Short selling has been strongly attacked because of its adverse effect on security prices. Critics claim short selling drives prices down unduly and below their real value when buying orders are meager, and then it exaggerates the volume of security purchases and the upward price trend when shorts cover. Floor traders and specialists "on the inside" can take advantage of their knowledge and profit thereby. The defenders of short selling maintain that it broadens the market for securities. Short

---

[6] Securities Exchange Act of 1934, Sections 5 and 6.

[7] Regulation T of the Board of Governors of the Federal Reserve System, effective 1934, governs the extension and maintenance of credit by brokers, dealers, and members of National Securities Exchanges. Regulation U of the Board covers loans by banks for the purpose of purchasing or carrying stocks registered on a National Securities Exchange, effective 1936.

sellers hold up a sagging market when they cover as prices decline, while they offer stocks for sale on the rise and so minimize price advances. The short sellers' stabilizing and broadening influence is supplemented by the specialists, odd lot dealers, and floor traders whose functions could not be successfully executed without taking the short side of the market as conditions warrant.

The Securities Exchange Act of 1934 has ruled out short sales on a National Securities Exchange if they violate Securities and Exchange Commission rules or regulations deemed essential to the public interest or for investor protection.[8] A short sale must occur at the last preceding sales price, providing that price exceeded the last different sales price.

Corners. A corner develops when short sellers are unable to cover their obligations. The technical position of the market may be such that stocks can be borrowed only at high interest rates, or it may be such that the required stocks are being bought for control, thus reducing the market's floating supply and raising the stocks' value or making them unavailable. A technically sound short position depends upon an adequate floating supply of the short issue. The New York Stock Exchange is empowered to act against corners: it can postpone deliveries of the stock; and it can require that all outstanding contracts be closed at a fixed price to prevent a skyrocketing and disturbing price level. The Stock Exchange requires its members to report their short position in a stock, and the Exchange will investigate the adequacy of the floating supply of stock. The Exchange can also strike an issue from its trading list to guarantee the maintenance of its outstanding function as a free and open market. The Securities and Exchange Commission can also use its powers to prevent the use of manipulative and deceptive devices.

Options or privileges. Dealings in options or privileges including "puts," "calls," and "spreads" or "straddles" foster speculation. A "put" is a negotiable contract requiring the seller to deliver a specified number of shares not yet owned to the buyer at a specified price and time, in the expectation that a price decline will enable the seller to profit on the transaction. In a "call" contract the buyer has the privilege to purchase a specified number of shares at an agreed upon price at a specific time. The seller purchases shares for delivery when the price may have moved up to a quotation yielding a profit. A "spread" or "straddle" gives the bearer of the contract the privilege of either buying or selling a particular stock at a specified time for an agreed upon price. He acquires the stock if the market is bullish and moves up above the specified figure, and he expects to sell ultimately at a profitable price. Only a sudden and sharp change in the market trend endangers the buyer. He sells if the market is bearish, moving down below the specified price, for he fears a con-

---

[8] Securities Exchange Act of 1934, Section 10 (a).

tinued price drop. This speculative operation permits speculators to participate in the market at a small risk and with a relatively small capital investment.

Economic effects of speculation. Speculation has often been condemned for its uneconomic by-products. Margin trading has forced excessive security price advances unjustified by the business situation, whereas short selling has intensified business gloom and trade decline. Business psychology in some part is a result of security price developments. Again, sometimes periods of prosperity and security price advances have attracted far too much of the savings of the small man intrigued by apparent get-rich-quick opportunities. The losses of this uninformed speculator wipe out his savings when stock prices collapse and discourage his personal initiative. In another point of criticism, the United States still remembers its unfortunate 1929 stock market experience involving billions of dollars of credit diverted from legitimate trade channels. The giddy times built partly on a weak structure of bank credit financing were followed by a sharp credit deflation and the economic prostration of the 1930's.

But speculation has contributed to the growth of the American economy. Speculators have provided the funds for nascent and growing industries when investors have preferred to put their money into well-established and safer enterprises. The old model T Ford and its successors might never have existed if it had not been for the courage of speculative capital. Especially since 1934, when large margins were imposed, margin trading has encouraged the movement of adequately protected bank funds into relatively untried companies.

Speculation is inherent in and essential to a growing free enterprise economy dependent upon broad and active security markets to assure buyers and sellers new issues.

The New York Curb Exchange

Functions. The growth of America's industries, prior to the Civil War, the financing of new techniques, and the development of new territories required new capital investment. This capital was obtained through the sale of corporate shares, only some of which were traded on established exchanges. Outdoor brokers provided a market for the other issues and thus stimulated the flow of capital into new and untried enterprises. During the country's economic expansion, the curb market has served as a:

> ... seasoning ground for the stock issues of new organizations which later took their places as leaders in our economy. Here, through an authentic kind of

public auction, corporations of every category obtained new capital for their development and expansion.[9]

In addition to its "seasoning" function the present day Curb Exchange assures a free auction market for security issues of leading industries both in the United States and abroad. Annual Curb Exchange transactions now exceed the total of all other National Security Exchanges other than the New York Stock Exchange.

Trading. The Curb Exchange moved indoors in 1921 to a six story building offering services far superior to the crude and improvised type of trading typical of the outdoor curb. Broad public participation in security trading and a greatly increased number of new issues in the 1920's necessitated an expansion of the Curb Exchange to 14 stories on September 14, 1931.

Fully listed issues as well as securities admitted to unlisted trading privileges are dealt in. Unlisted trading takes place when an issuer does not seek to list, but an adequate trading interest creates a market for his security. Since the passage of the Securities Exchange Act of 1934 that favored trading in listed securities, few securities have been admitted to unlisted trading privileges.[10] However, unlisted securities purchases and sales are still a substantial proportion of Curb Market activity.

Trading is conducted at 24 stock trading posts and three bond trading posts. The brokers at each post can determine almost immediately from three projection screens, visible from every part of the room, stock and bond Curb quotations and New York Stock Exchange stock prices. Each stock post is a center for dealings in the securities of designated corporations, and each post permits the essential paperwork by standees both inside and outside the stock posts. When a broker is wanted at his phone desk or booth ranged along the east and west sides of the trading floor, his telephone clerk lights up his number on one of the two large annunciator boards placed on the north and south walls of the trading room. Thus brokerage houses in any part of the United States can contact floor brokers.

The Curb Exchange handles both full lot and odd lot orders. The full lot orders are executed as on the New York Stock Exchange; the odd lot orders and limit orders are dispatched to their proper trading posts and there executed by floor specialists. The trading posts advise the ticker transmitting station of security price quotations to speed the information to the trading public. Brokerage houses report the quotations to their customers on teleregister boards in their offices. When a broker wishes to secure the latest quotation on an issue, he dials its

---

[9] The New York Curb Exchange, *Silver Anniversary*. New York: The New York Curb Exchange, 1946.

[10] Securities Exchange Act of 1934, and Amendments, Section 12 (f).

designated code number on a telephone connected by private wire with the central quotation department. The operator receiving the call determines the quotation from a huge quotation board and reports it to a broker.

The graduated Commission rates for brokerage services, effective February 14, 1949, follow:

NEW COMMISSION RATES

New York Curb Exchange

Effective February 14, 1949

MINIMUM NONMEMBER COMMISSION RATES ON STOCKS, RIGHTS AND WARRANTS

Selling at	Commission
1/256 of $1	0.1c per share
1/128 of $1	0.15c per share
1/64 of $1 and under 2/32 of $1	0.5c per share
2/32 of $1	0.5c per share
Over 2/32 of $1 and under 8/32 of $1	1.0c per share
8/32 of $1 and under 1/2 of $1	2.0c per share
1/2 of $1 and under $1	5.0c per share
$1 and under $2	7.0c per share
$2 and under $3	8.0c per share
$3 and under $4	9.0c per share
$4 and under $5	10.0c per share
$5 and under $6	11.5c per share
$6 and under $7	12.5c per share
$7 and under $8	13.5c per share
$8 and under $9	15.0c per share
$9 and under $10	16.0c per share
$10	17.0c per share
Over $10 and under $142	14.5c per share
plus 1/4 of 1% of the total amount involved in the transaction	
$142 and above	50.0c per share

NOTE: To compute the minimum commission on a transaction of 100 shares selling at over $10 and up to and including $142 per share, add $58 to the price per share and divide the result by 4. An amount in the final figure of less than 5 mills should be disregarded; for 5 or more mills add 1c. To compute the commission charge on a transaction of 200, 300, 400, etc., shares, multiply the applicable 100 share commission by 2, 3, 4, etc., respectively, as the case may be.

To compute the minimum commission on a transaction in less than 100 shares, selling at over $10 and up to and including $142 per share, multiply the applicable 100 share commission by the number of shares in the transaction and divide by 100. An amount in the final figure less than five mills should be disregarded; for 5 or more mills add 1c.

Notwithstanding the foregoing rates, when the amount involved in a transaction is less than $15, the commission shall be as mutually agreed; when the amount involved is $15 or more but less than $100, the minimum commission shall be not less than 6% of such amount or the prescribed rate, whichever is greater; and when the amount involved is $100 or more, the minimum commission shall be not less than $6 or the prescribed rate, whichever is greater.

Prior to 1923, buying and selling brokerage houses sent messengers to pick up certified checks in payment for delivered securities. This system was so clumsy that in 1923 the Clearing House night division was organized to handle 21 of the most actively traded stocks. Trades were paired and grouped on a balance sheet markedly reducing the numbers of securities and checks interchanged. The Stock Clearing Corporation of

the Exchange took over the work of the night division in 1931 and established a day branch and central delivery department which serves as agent for the actual delivery of securities between clearing members. The day branch of this Corporation operates as a money settlement department. A central comparison department of the Corporation was inaugurated in 1946 to compare trades between member firms. Comparison slips for a day's transactions are examined for accuracy, they are matched against one another, and the matched slips are then reissued to the respective firms.

Membership. The Curb Exchange's constitution permits a maximum of 499 regular members acting as specialists or commission brokers, or where inactive, operating through floor commission brokers. Associate members, unlimited in number, are chiefly members of the New York Stock Exchange and are privileged to trade through regular members at reduced commission rates. All members must pay initiation fees based on the going price for a regular seat on the Exchange. The fees vary from $500 to $2,500 for regular members and from $250 to $2,500 for associates. As in the case of the New York Stock Exchange, the prices of seats fluctuated violently between 1921 and 1950. Membership cost only $8,000 when the Exchange moved indoors; and in 1929 the price advanced sharply to a high of $254,000. During the dog days of low volume trading in 1942, the privilege of membership could be purchased for as little as $650.

Organization. A Board of Governors consisting of 32 members is charged with the duty of providing trading facilities and promoting high standards of business conduct. Fifteen governing committees operating under the Board's jurisdiction are charged with the task of investigating membership applicants and formulating new policies and procedures to protect and benefit the investing and trading public.

Three principal internal divisions—the division of transactions, the division of securities, and the division of administration—were set up in 1948 to discharge administrative responsibilities.

Unique nature. The Curb's high listing standards are laudable, but they do not equal the requirements of the New York Stock Exchange insofar as corporate size, national prominence, public distribution of securities, and listing fees are concerned. The Curb imposes only an initial listing cost, unless additional securities of an outstanding issue are listed or an entirely new stock or bond is traded on this National Securities Exchange. The less stringent listing requirements facilitate the use of the Curb for "seasoning" purposes.

This market is noted also as an international securities trading center. Foreign corporate shares are dealt in through the use of American depository receipts. An approved New York bank or trust company puts out these receipts against the deposit abroad of the original foreign shares

with the European branch of the New York organization. When transactions are effected, depository receipts (not the stock certificates) change hands. Thus the stock certificates need not shuttle back and forth between the United States and foreign countries. Arbitrage transactions in securities traded on foreign stock exchanges are simplified.

Over-the-counter market.—Nature and Services. The over-the-counter market brings together buyers and sellers of securities not actively bought and sold on organized exchanges, although they may be listed thereon. It is the broadest securities market in the United States. More issues are handled in this trading mart than on all United States stock exchanges combined, and its business volume exceeds the turnover on organized security markets.

Over-the-counter trading flourished as the country's developing communication facilities enabled securities buyers and sellers to contact one another through security dealers rather than through stock exchange brokerage firms. For many years the term "over-the-counter" has been archaic: ". . . since the term originated in Colonial Days when securities trading was a face-to-face affair over the counters of brokerage establishments. Today, however, virtually all trading is done over a vast filigree of communication systems and personal contact is rare indeed." [11]

This ever ready securities market and the marketability it affords helps dealers and security underwriters to sell billions of dollars of new issues prior to exchange listing. As business and financial information on the securities spreads, credit standing is established and a demand for the issue spreads. Eventually an over-the-counter issue may be listed on a National Securities Exchange.

Dealers. There are two types of securities dealers: (1) Securities houses; and (2) dealer banks which carry on regular banking activities and handle exclusively United States government and municipal issues. The law prohibits each from dealing in any other type of security. The National Association of Securities Dealers, an organization authorized by Section 15A of the Securities Exchange Act of 1934 (the Maloney Act) supervises dealing on the over-the-counter market to protect and further investor interests.

Trading. Dealers trade in unlisted stocks such as bank and trust company issues whose sponsors do not care to have their price fluctuations widely reported. Insurance company stocks are usually unlisted as are the common stocks of smaller industrials and investment trusts and the preferred issues of public utility companies. United States, state, and municipal government bonds are actively dealt in on the over-the-counter

---

[11] *Off Board Securities Market,* a Merrill, Lynch, Pierce, Fenner & Beane publication. New York, 1941, p. 1.

market although some are listed on organized exchanges. New issues as yet without listing privileges also enjoy the facilities of this market.

A customer purchasing an over-the-counter issue buys directly from a dealer, or his broker negotiates a purchase through an over-the-counter dealer. If a dealer does not wish to trade his own portfolio, he contacts other dealers by telephone and teletype. To assure fair business practices a dealer must indicate whether he is acting as a dealer or for customers. A dealer, such as an underwriter or distributor, specializing in an issue is always prepared to buy or sell the security—that is, to make a market for it. He provides bid and asked prices. A quotation is good only for the moment and lapses if not accepted at once. Firm quotations are usually good for 10 to 20 minutes to permit checking with a customer to determine whether the quotation is satisfactory.

A security buyer can determine a fair price for inactive issues by contacting several dealers. The National Quotation Bureau Incorporated reports bids and offers filed with the Bureau along with the name in each case. These reports are distributed to the Bureau's subscribers and can be consulted at brokerage offices. But the prices at which transactions take place are not available as in organized markets.

Comparisons of over-the-counter trades are made by sending reports of purchases and sales from one house to another. Stock certificates are delivered against certified checks. This procedure freezes up a larger volume of funds than comparable transactions on organized exchanges.

There are several ways of clearing security transactions. The regular way, used by firms in the same city, requires delivery of the sold securities to the purchasing dealer by 12:30 p.m. of the third full business day following the transaction. Delayed delivery calls for delivery on or before the seventh full business day. However if more time is required, the seller must deliver and receive payment within an agreed upon time after giving one day's notice—a seller's option sale. If the seller cannot deliver as agreed, the buyer's broker may buy in the securities and charge any difference to the seller. Sales can be for cash, but delivery and payment must be effected the same day or early the following day.

National Association of Securities Dealers

Section 15A of the Securities Exchange Act of 1934 legalizes and encourages securities dealers associations. Almost all investment banking houses and over-the-counter dealers are members of the National Association of Securities Dealers.

The National Association of Securities Dealers establishes standards of business conduct among its members and in their relations with the investing public; this association also disciplines through censure, fine,

suspension, or expulsion a member violating a standard. Loss of membership requires the expelled broker or dealer to deal with members only at the same prices, the same commissions or fees, and the same terms as accorded the general public. Misunderstandings and disputes have been minimized by the development of a uniform practices code to guide members. District business conduct committees hear all complaints and requests for arbitration of a National Association of Securities Dealers member or the public. However, this committee's decisions are subject to review by the Securities Dealers Board of Governors and finally by the Securities and Exchange Commission, except in arbitration cases where the decision is final by agreement of the involved parties.

The off board market is a seasoning ground for practically all securities as well as a market for unlisted issues. The greater number of new issues are initially traded on the over-the-counter market, and the investing public is familiarized with the issuing company's management and financial status. Thus, a corporation's securities establish a reputation which may lead to listing on National Stock Exchanges.

Regional Stock Exchanges

A regional exchange combines the trading facilities of two or more formerly independent exchanges and is situated at an important business or trading center within its financial community. The exchange's brokers handle orders to buy or sell the stocks and bonds of local corporations and also carry out customer orders for securities listed on the Big Board.

Purposes. A regional exchange offers a wide range of sectional investment opportunities, thereby freeing local security purchasers from complete investment dependence on the country's leading money and security markets. In fact, a regional exchange can become a focal trading point for national as well as community enterprises. To illustrate:

> Ever alert to the needs of the Pacific Coast, the San Francisco Stock Exchange has provided markets for local securities as well as those of national corporations, the Hawaiian Islands and the Philippines. Surveys have shown that stockholder lists of the 11 western states are increasing at a much faster rate than elsewhere in the country. Years ago a trend developed whereby Western corporations which became nationally known would list on the Big Board. This trend is now reversing itself; several of the large eastern corporations are now listing here to provide a regional market for investment-minded Westerners.[12]

The regional exchange broadens the public's knowledge of sectional business activities and organizations when local companies list their securities or increase the number of shares outstanding. Both the com-

---

[12] *The Investment Dealers Digest,* December 12, 1949, pp. 95-96.

panies with securities on such an exchange and the exchange cooperate to increase public knowledge of its affairs to attract greater financial activity in the area served.

The Salt Lake Stock Exchange is the only true regional exchange, since its list is composed virtually of only regional enterprises. The location of Salt Lake City stimulates the localized character of the Exchange, for it is cut off from the Midwest and the Pacific coast. It is the epitome of the original concept of a regional exchange: "The essence is summed up in the word isolation. Nowadays, except for Salt Lake, the regional exchanges are no longer isolated." [13]

Trading. Regional exchanges use several different methods of trading. The Washington Stock Exchange employs the call system of trading. The presiding officer determines the bid and asked prices from the member brokers, and security deals are arranged at the quoted prices in predetermined stock units or numbers of bonds. In most cases 10 shares of stock or one bond may change hands. When the call is completed trading continues among the members. But neither the price nor the number of shares of bonds involved in each trade need comply with the rule governing operations during the call.

The Boston Stock Exchange trades in fully listed regional stocks and permits trading in about 250 listed New York Stock Exchange equities with unlisted trading privileges on the Boston Stock Exchange. About 75 per cent of the markets purchases and sales are in the latter securities. If their book condition permits, brokers are permitted to engage in odd lot and round lot trading. All odd lot orders for the New York stocks must be executed. The fully listed securities are traded in a special section of the floor in "open auction." Exchange members seated at odd lot tables secure the New York quotations from the New York ticker tape and trade odd and round lots of the New York stocks. This "Boston System" assures the investing public of purchase or sale of a stock at the same figure it was quoted in New York when the broker received the order. Other regional exchanges also "trade off the tape" on dually traded stocks while handling regional securities deals on a bid and asked basis.

The Midwest Stock Exchange located in Chicago is a consolidation of the Cleveland, Minneapolis-St. Paul, St. Louis and Chicago exchanges. It employs a communication system and stock exchange procedure affording the members in the Twin Cities, Cleveland, St. Louis and other locations the same advantages as a Chicago broker. A direct wire system between St. Louis and Cleveland brokers and their Chicago offices enables them to place orders and to receive quotations and confirmations by telephone. Transactions are cleared by a St. Louis or Cleveland bank

---

[13] *Ibid.*, p. 4.

named as clearing agent. Members in the Midwest Stock Exchange range from huge national organizations to "one-man shops" in small towns. Each organization can retain full commission on purchases and sales. Each can render the same fast efficient service.

Advantages. The regional exchange provides a local trading center for regional securities. It offers the investor an opportunity to diversify the uses of his investable funds. Regional industry will benefit from this financial institution serving a growing community need. On the West Coast the Los Angeles Stock Exchange is valuable to heavily populated Los Angeles County, a vital national production, marketing, and consuming area.

Problems. Officials of the Midwest Stock Exchange want corporations with listed stocks to inform their stockholders better of their business condition and to issue more frequent financial reports. A greater public knowledge of securities market activities can be afforded by broader reporting of daily transactions. Further, the proximity of Eastern regional exchanges to the national New York market hampers their development. Security buyers are interested in buying directly through New York brokers rather than in "trading off the tape."

Problems of Securities Markets

Ever since the 1929 stock market crash, securities exchanges have suffered a small volume of trading that hardly justifies the existence of many brokerage firms. Stock market transactions must average about 2,000,000 shares per day to warrant the stockbrokers' business investment. Failure to measure up to this mark has forced many organizations to close up or to combine with other houses in an effort to cut down overhead and pool resources and abilities to earn a satisfactory return. Although the daily average volume of trading in 1929 amounted to more than 4,000,000 shares, it then slumped drastically and reached a low point of slightly more than 455,000 shares in 1942. Speculative and investor interest picked up thereafter, but in the years following World War II the trading volume was still only slightly above 1,000,000 shares daily.

Stock exchange officials are highly critical of the federal government's tax policy, for they believe it discourages individuals from venturing their savings in productive enterprises and retards the nation's economy. The New York Stock Exchange has urged modification of the heavy tax burden of recent years through these recommendations:

> 1. Make a start in eliminating the unjust double taxation of dividend income by allowing individuals to take a credit equal to 10 per cent of their dividends on common stocks when computing their income tax liability.

2. Revise the treatment of capital gains and losses by reducing the tax rate on long-term gains to 10 per cent, increasing to $5,000 the amount by which capital losses can be offset against ordinary income each year, and shortening the holding period to three months.

In proposing the above tax revisions designed to give individuals increased incentive to venture their savings in productive enterprise, we have not lost sight of the present revenue needs of the Federal Government. We believe that by encouraging increased dividend distributions, reducing the impediments to the sale of capital assets, and stimulating enterprise generally the measures we advocate would have the net effect of increasing tax receipts.

. . . one of the ironical consequences of government policies that result in shutting off the flow of equity funds is to make it appear that the government itself is the only source of capital, jobs, and the spirit of enterprise.[14]

Other factors have also deterred stock purchases and the work of the securities exchanges. The failure of equity prices to respond to increased business earnings during World War II and the years following discouraged their accumulation. If stocks had appreciated in line with larger corporate profits, as in earlier prosperity periods, the stock markets would have been stimulated. Perhaps the fear of a sharp postwar depression may have been responsible for the low level of prices and trading.

The changing political and economic complexion of the United States since the boom days of the 1920's also contributed to the depressed state of affairs on the securities markets. The growing role of the government in industry and the work of its financial agencies like the Reconstruction Finance Corporation [15] adversely influenced prospective investors: "The government through its various agencies, of course, has not furnished

---

[14] *Jobs and Taxes*, A Tax Study Submitted by the New York Stock Exchange, August 1949, p. 54.

[15] When the Reconstruction Finance Corporation was established by an act of Congress on January 22, 1932, it was intended to combat the deflationary depression forces of the times. Its counter-cycle influence was exerted through loans to banks and other financial organizations, railroads, insurance companies, and farm credit agencies. The improvement of business conditions following the darkest days of the 1930's was accompanied by an expansion of the loan organization's civilian powers and the execution of war and defense responsibilities assigned to it by the federal government.

Currently the RFC can lend alone or in conjunction with banks to business enterprises; it can assist financial institutions, purchase the securities of or lend to states and municipalities and their agencies to finance public projects and to aid financially catastrophe stricken localities. Loan purchases and commitments for these purposes cannot at any one time exceed $3,500,000,000. The lending power of the RFC is derived from the sale of $100,000,000 capital stock to the Treasury of the United States, the retention of a $250,000,000 surplus fund, and borrowings from the U.S. Treasury as needed.

A subsidiary of the RFC, the Federal National Mortgage Association, can purchase FHA insured mortgages or Veterans Administration guaranteed mortgages. The Alaska Housing Act permits it to finance real estate operations in Alaska if the real estate is insured by the FHA. This subsidiary may commit itself on these operations for a maximum of $2,500,000,000 at any one time.

The Housing Act of 1948 authorizes the RFC to lend to and purchase the obliga-

equity capital in the strict sense in which we use the term, but the loans made by such agencies as the Reconstruction Finance Corporation and the Federal Reserve Banks have served the same general purpose in most instances as equity capital. Here again the future would seem to me to hold an expansion of this type of activity rather than a contraction or merely a continuance of the present role." [16]

The securities market picture also has its bright side. Upper income bracket stockholders have lost some of their appetite for stocks, but middle and lower income bracket investors have expanded their security market undertakings. Odd lot purchases have persistently exceeded odd lot sales. The small security owner has been attracted to pen-end investment trust issues and has liquidated his corporate bond holdings. The possibility of broader equity purchases by insurance companies and savings banks may increase stock exchange activity.

Suggested Readings

BOOKS

Badger, R. E. and Guthmann, H. G., *Investment Principles and Practices*. Third Edition. New York: Prentice-Hall, Inc., 1941.

Bogen, Jules I. (Editor), *Financial Handbook,* Third Edition. New York: The Ronald Press Company, 1948, Section 2.

Dice, C. A. and Eitmann, W. J., *The Stock Market.* New York: McGraw-Hill Book Company, 1941.

Guthmann, H. G. and Dougall, H. E., *Corporate Financial Policy*, 2nd Edition. New York: Prentice-Hall, Inc., 1948, Chapters 14-17.

Investment Bankers Association of America, *Fundamentals of Investment, Investment Banking*. Chicago: Investment Bankers Association of America, 1947, Section 1, Part II; Section 8, Parts 1-2; Section 10, Part 1; Section 11, Part III.

Lesser, J. C., *The Over-the-Counter Securities Market. What it is and How it Operates,* New York: National Quotation Bureau, 1940.

Lettler, G. L., *The Stock Market*. New York: The Ronald Press Company, 1951.

Schultz, B. E., *The Securities Market and How it Works*. New York: Harper & Brothers, 1946.

Stabler, C. N., *How to Read the Financial Section of a Newspaper*. New York: *New York Herald Tribune*, 1948.

The New York Curb Exchange, *The New York Curb Exchange Silver Anniversary*, New York: The New York Curb Exchange, 1946.

---

tions of any business engaged in prefabricated housing activities or large scale modernized site constructions to a total of $50,000,000 at any one time.

The Rubber Act of 1948 authorizes the depression-born agency to participate in the manufacture and sale of synthetic rubber, while a Joint Resolution of 1947 directs it to engage in tin refining, stockpiling, and sale of the metal to private industry.

[16] *The Journal of Finance,* Louis A. Froman, "Can Individual Investors Be Induced to Furnish More Capital?" The American Finance Association, June 1950, p. 196.

PAMPHLETS

First Hemispheric Stock Exchange Conference. 1947.

Jobs and Taxes—A Tax Study Submitted by the New York Stock Exchange, New York, August 1949.

Merrill Lynch, Pierce, Fenner & Beane, New York:
How to Invest, 1948.
How to Read a Financial Report, 1947.
The Off Board Securities Market, 1946.

Understanding the Modern Security Market, Commodity Research Bureau, New York, 1949. *1950 Yearbook*, New York Stock Exchange, New York.

13

The Corporation and Its Securities as Financial Institutions

---

by MERWIN H. WATERMAN

Professor of Finance, University of Michigan

A SURVEY of the corporation as a financial institution can fairly start with the concept that it is a being without a soul; this concept leads logically to the conclusion that neither the corporation nor its instrumentalities are ends in themselves. Any justification of the corporation must recognize that it is but a means to an end and that it has no excuse for being in and of itself. It is certain that no one has ever seen a corporation enjoying itself, hating, fearing, loving, or taking a day off to go to the ball game. Even though modern laws and procedures may provide for the marriage of corporations (through merger) and for the conception and birth of corporate children (through the creation of subsidiary corporations), it still remains that all these creations are but means to an end, and it is in this light that the instrument will be examined.

As a tool or instrument for use in the business field, the corporation may have a number of potentialities; it may provide a handy means of organization; it may permit the formation of business entities to parallel regulatory jurisdictions or to accomplish other ends which in the strict sense would not be considered "financial." The scope of this discussion, however, will be confined to the discovery and development of the financial contributions that the corporation has made and can make to our private business enterprise. The corporation as a financial tool can be used or abused. It has both its possibilities and limitations, and it may be that a careful examination of the financial problems of business will make more intelligible the inevitable confusion surrounding the use of the corporate form of organization as a financial medium.

Can it be more than a coincidence that since the early days of our

358

country's existence there has been a parallel between the development of the American business corporation and the contribution of business to the wealth of our community? Between 1825 and 1860 the estimated wealth in the United States increased nearly $13 billion from an estimated $3,273 million to an estimated $16,160 million; but during the next 20 years the increase amounted to more than $27 billion as the estimated wealth reached $43,300 million in 1880.[1] Trade statistics reveal similar movements in the United States economy when we find that "Realized Private Production Income," excluding agriculture, jumped from $618 million in 1829 to $2,813 million in 1859, and then in the 20 years to 1879 it went up $2,442 million to $5,276 million.[2] Data for the comparable earlier periods are not available, but during the 20 years from 1859 to 1879 we find reported manufacturing establishments increasing but 76 per cent (from 140,433 to 253,852), and number of wage earners increasing only 108 per cent (from 1.3 million to 2.7 million), whereas "Value of Product" increased 185 per cent (from $1.9 billion to $5.4 billion per year) and "Value Added by Manufacture" increased 131 per cent (from $.85 billion to $1.97 billion). This is the beginning of the evidence which wound up in 1939 with only 184,230 establishments (then excluding home manufacturers), with wage earners numbering 7.9 million but with "Value of Product" totaling $57 billion and "Value Added" reaching $25 billion.[3] This evolution of "Value Added by Manufacture" from $650 per wage earner in 1859 to $720 in 1879 and to $3,160 in 1939 is ample proof of the increasing contribution of capital as a factor in production. Again, is it merely a coincidence that (as Evans points out) there was recorded the most substantial increase in the number of new manufacturing corporations beginning in 1860 in those states whose records are available?[4]

The corporation had answered the call as a financial instrument before the demands of the Civil War and post-Civil War period for industrial capital developed, although not on as large a scale as in the post-Civil War years. Incorporations of turnpike companies coincided with the capital requirements of that specialized business in the 1840's in Ohio, Pennsylvania and New Jersey.[5] Still earlier, as far back as 1800 in New York State the public utilities—such as turnpikes, canals, and ferries—had used this business device, and railroad corporations were formed to assist in the accumulation of capital funds for that phase of

[1] U.S. Bureau of Census, *Historical Statistics of the United States, 1789–1945*. Washington, D.C., 1949, Series A2, p. 9.
[2] *Ibid.*, Series A154-155, p. 14.
[3] *Ibid.*, Series J1 and 10, p. 179.
[4] G. H. Evans, Jr., *Business Incorporations in the United States, 1800–1943*. New York: National Bureau of Economic Research, Inc., 1948. See Chart 3, p. 23.
[5] *Ibid.*, Chart 2, p. 22.

transportation development.[6] This device was nothing new even then, because the form of the corporation was well-established in the colonies before the Revolution where it had developed as soon as the stigma of English precedent was wiped out by independence.[7] Throughout the history of our country's economy, the growing demands for business capital have led to the further use of the corporate device; in 1929 it was estimated that 92 per cent of the "Value of Products" manufactured in the United States came from firms operating under the corporate form.[8] Diligent research might turn up a railroad, a gas pipe line or distributor, or an electric power business that today is not operated by a corporation, and one could find a few small personally-owned telephone exchanges; but it is safe to say that practically 100 per cent of the tremendous investments in all those fields commonly classified as public utilities are corporately owned and operated.

As the capital requirements of our economy grew over the years—stimulated by the development of mechanized production, necessitated by large scale exploitation of natural resources, and required by the growth of distribution systems and the large totals of funds involved in public service enterprises—one wonders how the job of capital accumulation would have been accomplished without the use of the corporate form. Of course, it is possible that some ingenious person might have devised some other technique for bringing together from the four corners of the earth the investment savings of individuals and for making those savings available as usable capital to such an organization as the American Telephone and Telegraph Company. It is possible that some other medium might have been created whereby John Doe in New York City would have been willing to supply his capital along with that of hundreds or thousands of other investors to finance the development of a manufacturing enterprise conceived, originated and gotten under way by Richard Roe in San Francisco. We don't know what might have happened without the corporation, but we do know what has happened in recent decades through the use of this investment medium. The recent history of corporate capital raising according to the *Commercial and Financial Chronical*[9] compilation of new capital issues by domestic

[6] *Ibid.*, Table 9, p. 17.

[7] J. S. Davis, *Essays in the Earlier History of American Corporations.* (2 Vols.) Cambridge: Harvard University Press, 1917. Davis concludes this interesting and documented history with "By the end of the eighteenth century, the business corporation, in one form or another, was a familiar figure in all the large towns and through much of the country, notably so in thrifty, enterprising New England."

[8] Twentieth Century Fund, Inc., *Big Business, Its Growth and Its Place.* New York: Twentieth Century Fund, Inc., 1937.

[9] Reported in composite form in *Banking and Monetary Statistics*, Table 187, p. 487 and *Federal Reserve Bulletin*, May 1950, p. 555; both are publications of the Board of Governors of the Federal Reserve System.

corporations shows that the amount of new capital attracted to American industry from investors by use of corporate media in 30 years was 1⅔ times the total national wealth in the United States in 1880; while the yearly accumulations had their ups and downs paralleling the cyclical changes in fund requirements, the total was $72 billion of new capital during the years 1920–49.

One can only conclude that the net contribution of the corporation to the development and advancement of American industry has been considerable. Criticisms of the use of the corporation have been many and varied; the corporate form has been cited as a tool for over-concentration of economic power,[10] it has been indicted as a means of minority control,[11] and pilloried as the holding company hijacker of the public utility industry.[12] Whoever invented the hammer not only provided mankind with a valuable tool but also made available an instrument of murder, and whosoever has pounded his thumb has maligned the instrument as a weapon of pain. The common sense conclusion with respect both to the corporation and the hammer is, of course, that in the hands of evil or unskilled persons either tool may accomplish more harm than good.[13]

How the Corporation Works

In 1946 workers in all manufacturing enterprises in the United States were using an average of $7,113 of capital investment per worker to carry on the activities of various industries, and that average ranged from $24,515 per worker in the chemical business to a minimum slightly less than $3,000 per worker in the leather goods industry.[14] It is the ability to maintain and increase the availability of capital per worker that will spell our chances for increased productivity and increased standard of living. The raising and management of capital thus assumes important proportions in our scheme of private enterprise; true, financing may be called incidental to production, but it is so important an incident that we cannot possibly run our system without it. How then

[10] See Berle and Means, *The Modern Corporation and Private Property*. New York: Commerce Clearing House, 1932, and U.S. Temporary National Economic Committee, *Bureaucracy & Trusteeship in Large Corporations*, Monograph Number 11, Washington, D.C., 1940.

[11] W. Z. Ripley, *Main Street & Wall Street*. Boston: Little, Brown & Co., 1927.

[12] U.S. Federal Trade Commission, *Utility Corporations*, Senate Document 92, Part 72A, 70th Congress, 1st Session (Washington, D.C.)

[13] For a balanced consideration of the social benefits and detriments of the corporate form, see Purdy, Lindahl and Carter, *Corporate Concentration and Public Policy*, Second Edition. New York: Prentice-Hall, Inc., 1950.

[14] National Industrial Conference Board, *The Economic Almanac of 1950*. New York: The Conference Board, 1950, p. 376.

can the corporation best be used to tackle this fundamental job of (1) providing the means of concentrating sufficient amounts of capital in business enterprises to carry on effectively our production and distribution processes, and (2) providing the environment that will at once encourage savings to take the form of capital investment and set up the machinery for investor participation in business enterprise?

Capital will be invested in a business enterprise only in hope and anticipation of a profit, and such profit in turn can come only as a participation in the profits of the enterprise. The chief attribute of the corporation is that it does provide a means for that participation and does so in a variety of forms. First, let us consider some of the legal characteristics of the corporation and then see how they can be adapted to this problem of investment participation. There are different legal theories with respect to the nature of the corporation; but whether, according to Marshall, it owes its separate existence to contract,[15] or whether it exists merely as an association of indiviudals joined to achieve a common goal,[16] the fact remains that in practice today appropriate and careful legal procedure can bring about the creation of a business corporation which will have the following characteristics:

1. Except as a defense against fraud, the business enterprise will have its own separate entity distinct from its owners, and important corollaries of this feature will be
   (a) an identity independent of the life or even continued ownership of specific individuals, and
   (b) transferability of ownership in the enterprise.
2. Separation of management from ownership and control, in the sense of power to speak for or to bind the enterprise.
   (a) This is in important contrast to partnerships or other personal forms of business organization where the power of mutual agency tends to run throughout the personnel of ownership.
   (b) Delegation of power to manage to directors and officers of a corporation permits ownership participation by all comers whether interested in or capable of managerial direction of a business.
3. Limited liability probably constitutes the most important feature of the corporate form because, again under proper safeguards and procedures, the owners are not responsible for the debts or acts of the incorporated business. This characteristic means
   (a) that owners can limit their potential losses to the amount of their investment, and
   (b) that maximum risks of participation in a corporation can always be known, whereas the risks of investment in personal forms of business may absorb one's personal as well as business wealth.

---

[15] Trustees of Dartmouth College vs. Woodward, 4 Wheaton 518 (U.S. 1819), wherein Chief Justice Marshall of the Supreme Court said, "It appears to me, upon the whole, . . . incontrovertibly, that a charter of incorporation is a contract."

[16] A good, brief discussion of basic legal concepts is found in C. C. Bosland, Corporation Finance and Regulation. New Pork: The Ronald Press Company, 1949.

Characteristics of Investment Participation

Let us consider now the combination of these corporate characteristics with the characteristics of the business problem of capital raising and management. The problem is simply that of providing a satisfactory means of investment participation in business by those persons or institutions with investable funds. Investment participation inevitably carries with it certain implications: (1) there are bound to be risks inherent in every investment, be it ownership or creditorship participation; (2) the universal expectation of investment is income or profit, and without such an expectation there would be no motivation to create the savings for investment; (3) ability to exercise control is a third factor common to all investment, since the saver who invests does not relish the idea of waiving all opportunity to maintain future control over his invested savings. These, then, are what might be called the essential characteristics of investment participation, and no form of investment can be evaluated or criticized except in terms of these inherent characteristics.[17]

The fact that the corporate form achieves a degree of immortality for a business affects the characteristics of investment participation on all three counts—risk, income, and control. Investment in any business dependent on one or a few personalities is obviously more risky than investment in a situation where organization or group management is predominant. Use of the corporate form will not guarantee, but it will at least make possible a degree of continuance if not perpetuity in the management force. Individual owners and individual managers may come and go, but the machinery is there to carry forward the business without regard to change. Today many investments represent commitments of funds for periods beyond any one generation; we see many such long-lived investments in the assets of the so-called "heavy industries" such as steel and in the railroads and public utilities. By incorporation the life of the business unit can be made more in accord with the life of the business itself or its assets. Particularly for businesses large enough to need capital from the investing public, the risk of business life is significantly affected by this corporate feature of independent existence.

By the same token the income potentialities of the future of a busi-

---

[17] Hastings Lyon, *Corporation Finance*. New York: Houghton Mifflin Company, 1916. In this his earliest treatment of corporations as financial tools, Lyon developed the idea of "Incidents of Ownership," (Chapter 1), a concept of investment characteristics applied to ownership-management, income, and risk. The clear logic of this approach was not repeated in his subsequent and more elaborate *Corporations and Their Financing*, but it sets the pattern for this analysis of the characteristics of investment participation.

ness are related to corporate longevity. While the administration and distribution of profits are, by the nature of the corporate form, delegated to the managers, nevertheless the distinction between capital and income is maintained by law; a degree of certainty is therefore maintained as to procedure in distribution if not as to the amount. Also, whatever control is exercisable by investment participants in a particular corporate setup is firmly set by provisions of law and contract, and the rights of control are not dependent on the whims of individuals, nor are they changeable with time.

The transferability of corporate investment participations also bears on risk and the control thereof. In the field of investment management an important method of controlling risk is through shifting investment —that is, withdrawing capital from one business and investing it in another as judgment dictates such moves in response to the stimulus of economic and investment analysis. A commitment is not frozen in a corporation when that investment can be sold, and saleability is facilitated by the fact that participations can be transferred from one investor to another.

The limited liability characteristic of the corporate form is, of course, aimed directly at the risk element of investment participation, and there it registers a bull's-eye. Inherent in the separation of the corporation from its constituents is the fence it builds between claims against the business and the investors in the business. The risk of the participant is not eliminated, but it is limited, and normally that limit is set at the dollar amount of the investor's original contribution. The problem of sending money away to work in business is therefore simplified by the fact that no call can be made on the investor for mistakes or losses engendered through the use of his funds—a situation quite different from one where you or I as individuals or partners might finance a business and thus become responsible for its debts and financial mistakes to the limit of our total resources.

Beyond the risk-limiting potentialities of the corporation there are possibilities of creating different degrees of risk based on participations in the same business situation, and these possibilities will be the subject for later discussion in considerable detail. Likewise varying degrees of control can be achieved, but for summary it is sufficient to repeat that it is the essence of the corporate form that it takes the control characteristic of investment participation and concentrates it in the hands of paid managers who themselves may or may not be investors in the situation. The raising of large amounts of capital and the subsequent management of substantial accumulations of wealth in business assets require as much organization and specialization to be effective as are necessary to produce the efficiencies of specialization of production processes in large

scale enterprises. As the techniques of production, marketing, and financing become more complex in an ever increasingly complex economy, professionalism in management assumes greater and greater importance. Direct, individual participation in management by individual investors, even though democratic in form, becomes ineffective and inefficient in practice. An investor's delegation of administrative authority to corporate officials while he exercises a degree of control by the choice of those officials through elected directors makes it possible for a corporation to handle large business resources effectively.

The contribution of the separate legal entity and the features of unlimited liability and delegation of management would not alone in their bareness have made the corporation the effective instrument that it is for raising and managing business capital. It is within the framework of these basic features, however, that it has been possible to evolve varieties of combinations in the characteristics of investment participation which at once are able to meet the needs of particular business enterprises and the desires of those who commit their capital. The over-all view of the possibilities in this respect may be observed by considering that the corporate securities which are used to represent investment participations in that form of business are essentially contracts—contracts between the issuing corporations and the purchasing investors. When you take the basic characteristics of investment participation—risk, income, and control—and recognize that by contract these characteristics can be divided into varying degrees and various combinations, you sense the almost limitless permutations and combinations that are available.

There are, of course, some basic limitations on these combinations; the limitations exist in the laws of the 48 states upon whose sovereignty the existence of corporations depends. Long ago the practice of granting charters (rights to do business as corporations) by specific legislative enactment ceased, and today all states have their corporation statutes [18] which in effect set the broad pattern of corporate powers, purposes, and procedures; and by so doing, the statutes set the scope and limits on the ways and means of dividing up the characteristics of investment participation. A corporate charter or certificate of incorporation is at once a contract between the state and the incorporators and a contract between and among the owners of the corporation. The ownership represented by shares of stock has its characteristics defined in the charter, and possession of one or more shares of stock carries with it assent to the terms of that contract. The rights, duties, privileges, and obligations of stockholders, albeit important, will not be discussed here in detail; suffice it to say these provisions are dependent on the several statutes and the

---

[18] Lindahl, Purdy and Carter, *op. cit.*, pp. 44-46.

charters issued thereunder with the interpretive backing of the common law.[19]

In practice, of course, owners are not the only investment participants in a corporate enterprise; in sharp legal contrast to owner-participants are the creditors. Legally, the creditors are not the part of the corporation that the owner-stockholders are; only the former have claims *against* the corporation according to the law; the latter have claims *within* the corporation.[20] Laws to the contrary notwithstanding, corporate creditors are participating investors in corporate business; while their rights may have peculiar legalistic status, the creditors nevertheless depend upon the corporation, its assets and earning power for satisfaction of their claims. Because of the limited liability characteristic of the corporation, creditors cannot look beyond its bounds either for specific performance of promises to pay interest and principal nor for settlements in lieu of performance. For the purposes of this discussion of the corporation as a financial instrument, and for reasons that will be developed further, corporate owners (stockholders) and creditors (bondholders, noteholders, etc.) will be considered as one class, i.e., investment participants in corporate enterprise.[21]

In front of this undetailed backdrop of the corporation as a form of business organization, with sketches of the legal characteristics and indications of general economic significance, it is proposed now to bring on to the stage characters in the way of corporate security contracts that will portray the strengths and weaknesses of the various media of investment participation. Just as in the drama it is never possible to depict all of a character's emotions, reactions, thoughts, and intentions, just so here it will be impossible to recreate in all detail the purposiveness of any security contract representing the mixture of motives in the "character" of investment participation. It should be possible, however, to show by example the possibilities and limitations of some combinations of characteristics and to reason from there to some principles appropriate to various scenes and business environments.

These character analyses will be carried forward primarily in terms of those inherent characteristics of investment participation that have already been developed, i.e., risk, income, and control. Each situation will be analysed from two points of view: (1) the appropriateness of security contract to the business situation, and (2) its adaptability to the security market environment. The real test of a capital raising con-

[19] A. S. Dewing, *The Financial Policy of Corporations,* Fourth Edition. New York: The Ronald Press Company, 1941. Vol. I, Chap. 5.

[20] C. W. Gerstenberg, *Financial Organization and Management,* 2nd Revised Edition. New York: Prentice-Hall, Inc., 1939. Chap. X.

[21] Individual and institutional investors consider creditor claims just as much a form of "investment" as they do stocks.

tract lies in those two areas. Is the contract one with which the business can live in reasonable comfort? Is it one that will efficiently and effectively attract capital from the investors for the business purposes of the enterprise?

Common Stock Participations

The first actor to appear on the stage of corporate financing and the last one to leave is common stock, unless perchance the whole business is a failure, in which case this common stock will be the first to leave and will do so with mourning which befits the demise of the chief risk taker. Common stock in its part represents the residual participation in all the characteristics of investment; it has all of the risk, income, and control characteristics which by contract have not been passed on to some other participant. If common stock is the sole participant—that is, there is no other class of owners or creditors—the risk of such owners would be practically synonymous with the business risks of the enterprise itself. The common stock profits would be the profits of the business, and control would rest exclusively with the owners of the common stock except for such restrictions as might be imposed by law.[22] The term "equity capital" is often applied to this common stock participant in capital accumulation, i.e., equity in the sense of ownership embodying risk. If investors are to become owners—common stockholders—there must be balancing profit (income) and control features to compensate for the risks. Thus this type of investment participation (if it is to be effectively used as a capital raiser) must be sold on the basis that such a balance exists; profit on the one side, risk on the other, with the element of control being available to affect both elements of the equation.

Creditor-stockholder relations. The complete coloration of common stock cannot be portrayed as long as it is alone on the stage. We need the contrast of other investment participations to develop by interplay the relationships that exist in practice. It is unrealistic to think of a modern corporate enterprise, large or small, whose entire working assets are furnished by the owner-stockholders. In the normal course of events creditors soon appear on the scene; if in no other form, they will appear as "Accounts payable" or "Wages payable" when materials and supplies are purchased and labor is applied thereto. In its simplest form, therefore, we have the emergence of creditor participations in the enterprise. An account payable is in essence a contract whereby the corporation agrees to pay its bills according to terms of purchase, perhaps in 10

---

[22] For instance, a manufacturing corporation's assets could not be invested in the commercial banking business by vote of common stockholders; they would have to reincorporate under appropriate banking statutes.

days, perhaps in 30 or 60 days, but definitely and unconditionally. Likewise labor contracts, written or oral, carry an obligation to pay in accordance with service rendered.[23] What happens the minute these creditors share the corporate stage with the common stockholders? There is no direct relationship between the two groups, because it is the corporation that has incurred the obligations; but the obligatory nature of the credit claims causes them to stand ahead of the stockholders in all of the characteristics of investment participation.

With respect to risk, for instance, the fact that the corporation has *promised to pay* the creditors (whereas the stockholder-owners have a residual position) now takes on real significance in terms of priority; the promises come first, and only after they are fulfilled can the owners have any participation. This priority minimizes the risk of the creditors and maximizes that of the owners. In simple balance sheet terms, for example, let us assume assets, liabilities, and equity as follows:

Assets		*Liabilities and Equity*	
Fixed assets	$10,000	Accounts payable	$15,000
Currents assets	20,000	Common stock equity	15,000
Total	$30,000	Total	$30,000

If this business should so operate that when it becomes necessary to meet the $15,000 of accounts payable it is found that the value of its total assets are only $20,000, the full loss of $10,000 would rest upon the owner-stockholders; a loss of $\frac{1}{3}$ of total assets would be magnified into a loss of $\frac{2}{3}$ of the equity. This results from the fact that the creditors do not share the average risk of the total investment (the $\frac{1}{3}$ loss); rather they have a priority of claim the significance of which depends on the thickness or amount of equity behind them. The thicker that equity the less the risk of the creditor; in the example above the values could decline 50 per cent (to $15,000) before the risk would begin to bite into the creditor participation, whereas if the equity had been $10,000 and the liability $20,000, a loss of only $33\frac{1}{3}$ per cent could be absorbed without sacrifice by the creditors. Those creditors do participate as investors by furnishing capital, probably capital in the form of goods, and their risks may come home to roost. It should be clear that in spite of their priority, the creditors are not "riskless" investors even though they "risk less" than the owners. Assume that the assets in the example above shrink to $10,000; under those circumstances the stockholders would lose 100 per cent of their investment (and no more, because of corporate limited liability), whereas the creditors could recover $\frac{2}{3}$ of their investment on this hypothesis. Here we have the simplest example of the crea-

---

[23] Further, labor claims are usually given the added support of statutes governing wage payments which are designed to give more than normal protection to labor.

tion of qualitative differences in risk by the use of capital contracts. The risk exposure of the creditor participation is reduced to less than the average exposure of the business as a whole; inevitably the risk of the owner participants is raised above the average. In this situation that attracts creditor capital to a business, the supplier of goods does not ordinarily wish to take an owner's risk (or the average business risk) when he sells on credit to a customer. He will, however, furnish capital under the less than average risks created by a cushion of ownership equity.

In the simplified situation described so far, the income element of investment participation seldom enters explicity. Only occasionally do normal credit terms call for payment of interest, although quite often terms of sale call for such payments on overdue accounts, while cash or prepayment discounts—as well as being a collection device—contain at least an element of interest. The primary motivation for credit sales may lie with the sales department competing for custom; nevertheless there are evidences of the income characteristic of investment even in this medium of capital accumulation.

Beyond a shadow of doubt the creditors assume a significant degree of control over the operations of the enterprise, because the credit terms require specific performance in terms of payment of a specific amount at a specific time. This control may be carried even further; for example, a supplier of brass told a manufacturer of castings that he would "go along" and let his account run to a certain limit as long as the financial affairs of the manufacturer were kept in order and as long as the manufacturer's finances were not depleted by payments of profits to stockholders. In this case the supplier wanted monthly financial statements from the manufacturer as a guide to his control of the manufacturer's credit.

Endless examples could be cited of supplier-creditors who exercise varying degrees of control by agreement with business in their desire to minimize the risks of their "investments." They may go so far as to legalize their priority of claim against specific assets of the borrowers: this they do by asking that their loan be secured by a mortgage, usually a chattel mortgage placing a lien against some of the corporation's personal property such as inventories, receivables or equipment. This modification of contract introduces a device the effectiveness of which depends on the value of the pledged assets independent of the operations of the borrowing business. A pledge of $25,000 worth of wheat to secure the payment of a $20,000 account payable would render the risk of such a contribution rather nominal, regardless of the equity of the debtor; if the corporation should fail to pay, the creditor would become the owner of assets "as good as the wheat" as the saying goes. This points

to the technique in business financing of furnishing capital on a secured basis. The limitations on this method of risk reduction are suggested by consideration of a proposal to pledge $10,000 worth of eggs in the incubator stage to secure a hatchery's promise to pay for same. A brief failure in the mechanical incubator might well reduce the value of the collateral inventory to less than zero, and if the hatchery corporation could not pay, the supplier would become the proud possessor of a lot of eggs! The ultimate in contingent control—namely, ownership—is then accomplished, but one wonders whether the oft-mentioned "pride of ownership" would suffice to satisfy the creditor's claim in such an instance.

From the account payable it takes no more than a change in make-up to represent "Notes payable" as contractual evidences of investor participation in a business. Either on an unsecured or secured basis creditors may put capital into a corporate enterprise in return for a promissory note which is no more than a formal representation of the same type of relationship achieved by an account payable. The risk and control elements involved also will run along the same lines as exist in the case of open-book accounts payable. The note is more apt to be a promise to pay not only the principal amount but also interest at a contractual rate, and it is easier to see the relationships between the characteristics of such participations.

The explicit interest payable to creditors in such a contract must be large enough to compensate for the risks involved. When a representative of a corporation goes with a blank note in hand to seek capital from a bank, finance company, insurance company, or individual, the bargaining process in that capital procurement process will center about the following basic variables. If the corporate debtor-to-be has sufficient equity to back up its promise, the risk will be minimized; the risks may run practically to zero so that the interest rate will be no higher than "pure interest." But let there be any doubt of ability to pay, and up will go the rate commensurate with the risk. A more complete classification of possible risk elements will be discussed later in connection with bond issues, and it should then be recalled that the risk elements apply equally to notes payable as capital raising instruments.

One of the limitations on the corporate form might well be emphasized at this point. The limited liability feature of corporate ownership was mentioned earlier as a means of facilitating the attraction of equity or ownership capital. By the same token, however, when the owner's liability is limited so is the cushion protecting the potential creditor. The combined personal wealth of corporate owners might far exceed the ability to pay of the corporation itself, but this would be of no avail in protection or satisfaction of creditors' claims against the corporation. It occa-

sionally happens in connection with corporate borrowings that when the corporation seeks to borrow more than its equity will support and when the resulting risks are considered excessive, the creditor may ask to have his note endorsed by one or more of the corporate stockholders. This process breaks through the corporate line and supplements the corporate promise with the unlimited liability of the endorsers; the endorsers in effect promise to pay if the corporation fails to do so, and they thus assume the risk that the creditors are unwilling and the corporation is unable to assume.

Bond Contracts

(The plot thickens. A myriad of security characters appears on the scene, all of the genus "creditor," but with endless variety of make-up and costume. Lurking in the background hundreds of lawyers may be seen ready at a moment's notice to come center and soliloquize on terms of bond indentures. All is very confusing.)

In the midst of all the confusion surrounding bond indentures and their uses as corporate instruments of capital raising, it will help to remember first that "indenture" is nothing but a $5 word for "contract" and second, that a "bond" is always basically a promise which, exactly like the note and account payable, involves the corporation in (usually) an unconditional obligation or a series of obligations. The purpose of all of the obligations and accompanying impediments is to effect divisions and combinations of the inherent characteristics of investment participation so as to attract capital on an efficient basis. In an attempt to demonstrate the workings of various combinations of risk, income and control, the subsequent pages will present an analysis of a series of "characters" in the way of specific bond contracts, and each analysis will afford the writer the opportunity to show how the characteristics can be made to fit (or not to fit) the business situation involved.

Security. In April 1950, Georgia Power Company issued and sold for new capital-raising purposes $15 million of bonds which were part of an issue of one billion dollars (authorized by the stockholders) to be issued from time to time as a means of borrowing money. After the sale of this issue there were approximately $138 million outstanding as corporate promises to pay, and those promises are secured by a mortgage which is "a direct first lien on substantially all the fixed property and franchises owned by the Company." [24] The "property" referred to consists of generating stations (hydraulic and steam), transmission system (4,700 miles), distribution system (14,000 miles), and 864 substations. Also included are nine miles of steam mains and such of the company's

---

[24] Prospectus, dated April 5, 1950, p. 25.

transportation properties (busses and garages) as are actually owned and not leased from others. The franchises comprise the company's right (nonexclusive) to carry on its electric, steam and transportation business in various areas in Georgia.[25] All told, the company, as of 1950, was promising to pay annual interest in an amount exceeding $4,700,000 in addition to repayment of principal. The effect of the morgage is to permit these creditors legally to become the owners of the property and franchises in case of default on the corporation's obligations to pay. You may well ask, "What are the conditions under which Georgia Power Company will fail to pay its interest and principal?" Obviously, the corporation in the interests of its owner-stockholders will not permit the creditors to take over if such action can possibly be avoided. The only imaginable conditions under which payment could not be made would be those which would render the company unable to earn any profits from rendering its services in the area prescribed. Then, under those conditions, the creditors could, under the terms of the mortgage, become the proud possessors of generators, transmission and distribution systems, substations and rights to do an unprofitable business. If these assets couldn't make money in Georgia, it would be foolish to try to move them elsewhere; any value they might have would be largely consumed in costs of destruction and reconstruction.

Compare this contract with that of New Jersey Bell Telephone Company [26] which, as of 1950, had $70 million of "promises to pay" outstanding with annual charges for interest in excess of $2,000,000, but which had no asset security behind these promises. Although this promise stands alone, the promise of New Jersey Bell Telephone Company is just as firm as the promise of Georgia Power Company, and in case of default the creditors of New Jersey could legally demand satisfaction before owners could participate in any sale or liquidation. In both cases, therefore, the risk of creditors is minimized by the companies' "promises" —their unconditional obligations to pay interest and principal; in both cases there is adequate motivation to live up to the promises to avoid loss to the owner-stockholders; in both cases the creditors have priority over the owners. This emphasizes the chief accomplishment of creditor contracts over ownership; the creditor contracts achieve priority and exert pressure to pay, and do so whether the contracts are secured or unsecured.

This raises a question of the usefulness of the corporate mortgage as an effective capital-raising device; this is a basic question because a

[25] For an excellent discussion of the form and substance of mortgage liens, see William Lilly, *Individual and Corporate Mortgages*. New York: Doubleday, Page and Co., 1921.

[26] See Prospectus dated March 14, 1950.

mortgage is expensive to use in terms of lawyers' fees, recording expenses and trustees' expenses, let alone expense of the red tape involved when pieces of mortgaged property are sold, retired or exchanged. The theory of the mortgage was developed in the days when businesses were less complicated and when, as a matter of fact, the lien security was usually attached to a piece of real property whose value was apt to be quite independent of the earning capacity of the borrower. In today's usage the relative significance of the corporate mortgage lien may be pictured by contrasting it with a home mortgage. The latter is used to secure a personal loan, and it is usually fairly certain that the value of a piece of residential property in almost any normal community will be determined not by what the mortgagor (borrower) may be earning in salary and other personal income, but rather by a ready resale market for real estate. On the other hand, there is no market for telephone company property such as that of New Jersey Bell Telephone Company or for utility assets such as those of Georgia Power Company. The only values, other than scrap, that exist in such assets are the values rooted in the earning power of the borrower, and these earning values are just as effectively behind and supporting an unsecured debenture bond [27] as they are behind a secured mortgage issue.

The minimal significance of mortgage liens on immovable specialized assets suggested above is based on the assumption that all creditors are to share the same degree of risk and that they all have the same priority over owners. There is the possibility, however, of creating qualitative differences among creditors by establishing varying levels of priority. In the case of New York Telephone Company in June 1947, the corporation sought permission from the New York Public Service Commission to issue $125 million of unsecured debentures.[28] At that time the company already had outstanding $75 million of 3 per cent mortgage bonds, and the Commission refused permission for an unsecured issue. One of the grounds for the refusal was that the already outstanding mortgage bonds would be improved in their risk characteristics by having a priority to all assets ahead of those financed by the debentures, and that the latter, in turn, would be more risky and thus more costly as the result of their secondary position. The debenture creditors would still be ahead of owner-stockholders with their claims, but the debenture creditors would be behind the morgage creditors by virtue of the fact that any values that might remain in the business in case of default would attach

---

[27] Largely under the influence of the Securities and Exchange Commission, terminology has tended to become standardized, and the term "debenture" usually refers to an unsecured bond issue. This does not mean, however, that you might not find "secured debentures"; it would be a question of fact, since "debenture" is a generic term for debt.

[28] Case Number 13020, June 11, 1947. (New York Public Service Commission.)

necessarily to the assets and thus go first to the satisfaction of mortgage claims. Only in case all values should disappear would the risks of these two classes of creditors be equated by participation in zero. There is no doubt that a qualitative difference among creditors would have been achieved by the proposed combination, although the Commission's denial of the request to issue the bonds prevented a test of whether the added risk would have been sufficient to have increased the cost.

The coexistence of mortgage and debenture bonds is not the only way of achieving qualitative differences in the risk of creditor investment participations. In 1950 there appeared on the general investment market for the first time "subordinated debentures" [29] which accomplished the same result. Lit Brothers (a Philadelphia department store) raised $6,000,000 by the sale of their obligations [30] which were "unsecured obligations of the Company and are expressly subordinated . . . to other obligations of the Company with respect to the payment of principal, interest and sinking fund requirements." On January 31, 1949, the "other obligations" of Lit Brothers totaled over $5,800,000 and could, according to this debenture contract, run as far as other creditors would allow with the understanding that the claims of the debentures would always remain in a subordinate position. Again, these subordinated creditors would have priority over owners in settlement of claims, but only after settlement with other creditors. We see in this arrangement the same effective scale of priority that would have existed in New York Telephone Company had it been permitted to have outstanding simultaneously mortgage bonds, debentures and stock.

The State Loan and Finance Corporation similarly raised $4,000,000 [31] with a contract which stated that "the payment of the principal of and interest on the debentures is subordinated in the event of any receivership, insolvency, bankruptcy . . ., reorganization . . ., dissolution, or liquidation . . . to the payment of any indebtedness of the Company at the time outstanding . . . on unsecured bank loans or on commercial paper . . . which shall mature not more than twelve months from the date of their original issue . . ., and on funds obtained by the Company and evidenced by unsecured obligations . . . having a maturity of more than twelve months. . . ." Thus State Loan and Finance Company borrowed $4,000,000 without disturbing—in fact by improving—its general unsecured credit. Commercial bankers increased their lines

---

[29] The same effects had been produced by "subordinated loans" made from private sources previous to 1950 and had been quite a common occurrence, particularly among finance companies.

[30] Prospectus, dated April 4, 1950.

[31] Prospectus, dated April 11, 1950.

of credit after this financing on the basis of the additional "secondary priority" money which was added to the company's assets.

Examples of the adaptability of credit contracts to affect the risk quality of such participations could go on endlessly, because there are never two contracts exactly alike. But enough has been said to suggest both the possibilities and limitations of "security" as a variable. Particularly with respect to corporations having assets of independent value, it is interesting to note the extent to which corporations do go to use that independence in minimizing the risks of their creditors and thus their own capital costs. Equipment trust obligations are the prime example, and in that instance corporations actually go so far as to create a lease agreement with a trustee-owner—an arrangement designed to insulate ownership of equipment against any possible joining of claims by other creditors of railroads or bus companies—and then to mortgage the equipment to secure the carriers' promise to pay "rent." Here the alternative use value of the equipment is practically assured by the movability and ready resale value of standard equipment; in contrast to an electric generating station, a bus or standard gauge railroad car or prime mover can be shunted from an unprofitable to a profitable situation, and thus its value and earning power can be preserved without recourse or reference to the ability to pay of any particular borrower.[32]

One step further has been taken over the line from the owner-creditor to the user-landlord relationship in the now common arrangements for corporations to get their usable capital by leasing stores, warehouses and the like from owning investors such as insurance companies. Renting property is certainly not a new means of acquiring the use of capital by business enterprise nor is the method confined to the corporate form, but no consideration of capital raising instruments would be complete without mention of the leasing possibilities. Except perhaps in the case of equipment trust obligations, the ability of the user to pay is tested as accurately by a potential landlord as it is by a potential creditor, in spite of the fact that the property such as a store or warehouse may have value independent of that user. Such properties do not have the feature of mobility that will preserve value in case of a declining community.

Maturity. When a corporation draws a credit contract, where shall the maturity date be placed and how shall the principal be repaid? Generally, short-term loans are at lower cost than long-term loans in the money market; there is the temptation, therefore, for corporations to seek the lowest cost. The clearest example of the influence of maturity can be found in equipment trust certificates which are typically sold with a series of maturities, all other features of the contract being equal.

---

[32] Dewing, *op. cit.,* Vol. I, pp. 205-210.

On March 2, 1950, Pennsylvania Railroad Company, 2¼ per cent Equipment Trust Certificates were offered to the public at prices to yield as follows: [33]

Maturity	Price to Yield	Maturity	Price to Yield	Maturity	Price to Yield
1951	1.40%	1956	2.00%	1961	2.40%
1952	1.55	1957	2.10	1962	2.45
1953	1.70	1958	2.20	1963	2.50
1954	1.80	1959	2.30	1964	2.525
1955	1.90	1960	2.35	1965	2.55

This spread in yields indicates the market's preferences which discriminate most widely in the first three years and least in the last three maturities which run up to 15 years. This is in part a reflection of the different markets available for different maturities; bank investment funds are seldom available beyond the five year mark, and those investors who commit their funds for longer periods run more risk of increasing money rates even though the credit of the borrower may be unquestioned. This risk of changing money rates, particularly in days of generally low yields when future changes seemingly can be only in an upward direction, together with the risks inherent in the borrowers' operations find definite market reactions. The maturities for industrial bonds tend to run shorter, for instance, than for public utilities. State Loan & Finance Company debentures [34] not only had a final maturity of 10 years but also called for periodic retirement; $200,000 per annum for the first three years, $250,000 for the next four, $400,000 for the eighth and $500,000 for the ninth year, thus leaving only $1,500,000 of the original $4,000,000 for the final payment at maturity. In this instance a long-term commitment to a small concern in the competitive finance business probably looked a bit risky. However, the character of the company's assets (receivables) gave the issuing corporation the ability to meet the schedule of maturities more or less in spite of its earnings. If business turned good, earnings would provide the funds; if it turned bad, receivables would liquidate and funds would become excess for the declining volume and could be devoted to fulfillment of the retirement schedule. From both the market and user points of view the contract made sense.

What appears to be a fairly long term contract for Hallingsworth & Whitney Company [35] (pulp paper manufacturer) in its $8,500,000 of debentures (issued in 1949 and due in 1969) turns out to be not so long when one considers the fact that the company in its "sinking fund" [36]

---

[33] Announcement from *The Wall Street Journal,* March 2, 1950.

[34] Prospectus, *op. cit.*

[35] Prospectus, dated March 21, 1949.

[36] One might suspect that, in line with the general confusion in financial terminology, the chief reason for designating periodic debt retirement provisions as "sinking fund"

agreement provides for annual retirements of from $200,000 to $375,000 per year, leaving only $2,125,000 to be paid at the end of the 20 year period. From the standpoint of the issuing corporation there isn't much difference in the financial burden of such a contract and that of a contract like the one which American Light and Traction Company sold in November 1948; this was an issue of $15,000,000 of serial bonds with actual piecemeal maturity. Individual notes were drawn with $500,000 of maturity per year from 1949 to 1953, $1,000,000 each year from 1954 to 1957 and $8,500,000 in 1958. The interest rate on the 1949–53 notes was 2¾ per cent; 1954–55, 3 per cent; 1956, 3½ per cent; 1957, 3¾ per cent; and 1958, 4 per cent, or an average (weighted by amount only) of 3.6 per cent. Whether this benefit of average rate effected by the low-cost short maturity would have been achieved with a sinking fund requirement of equal annual amounts is a serious question. The investor in this type of issue could never tell whether his bond would be short or long; it would depend on the draw or on the bonds purchased in the market. As a matter of fact this American issue was sold privately to institutional investors, and it is probable that each took maturities that would fit its portfolio requirements; thus the corporation was able, by tailoring its maturities, to average down the annual cost of its borrowings.

Among the public utilities substantial sinking funds are seldom used, and the maturity dates tend to be longer. For such corporations the investment is longer lived and the need for capital is correspondingly longer. The market, in turn, seems willing to accept the premise that the future earnings and values of utilities are less subject to potential ravages of time and tide than are those of competitive industrial concerns. Typical utility maturities range from 25 to 35 years with occasional extensions to 40 years particularly among the operating subsidiaries of American Telephone and Telegraph Company. In further reaction to the permanence of the need for capital, sinking funds, if any, tend to be nominal. Retirement of 1 to 1½ per cent of an issue is often called for on these 25-30 year issues, and obviously such retirement makes little contribution to ultimate payment at maturity. The effect market-wise of a small sinking fund purchase, however, may be considerable; when 80 to 90 per cent of an issue is in the hands of institutions intending to hold until

---

provisions is that there is no "fund" involved, and there is no "sinking" except by the issuer in attempting to meet the terms of the contract. This bit of terminology, as a matter of fact, is a hang-over from the days when corporations actually did accumulate funds in their treasury or in the hands of a trustee in anticipation of payment of the full amount of a debt at maturity date. No modern contracts provide for a "fund"; all contractual amounts are almost immediately spent to retire bonds either by market purchase or by call. A more descriptive if less euphonious title for such contracts might be "amortizable bonds."

maturity, an annual purchase of 1 per cent of the total issue would be an annual pickup of 5 to 10 per cent of the floating supply; and this could, in turn, have a significant influence in holding up the quoted market prices for the benefit of all concerned.[37]

Conversion. By the same token that a typical bond contract creates priority by a corporation's promise to pay specific sums, the contract also sets a limit on the creditors' participation in the business. It's a "no more, no less" proposition; the risk may be limited, but there is a ceiling on income. There are times when in face of all the environmental and business risks involved, the market prefers not to have a specific ceiling on its investments and expresses that preference by being willing to lend money more cheaply, if it can taste the flavor of unlimited profits which characterize a common stockholder's participation. Convertible bonds comprise the technique for combining priority and the chance for residual participation. When Connecticut Light and Power Company wanted to raise upwards of $8,000,000 in 1949, the corporation gave potential investors a choice; they could buy either common stock at $50 per share or 3 per cent bonds which were convertible at the option of the bondholder into common stock, the terms being:

> 1. If such conversion is on or before January 1, 1952, at the conversion price of $52.50 per share; i.e., at the rate of one share of Common Stock for each $50 principal amount of Debentures plus $2.50 in cash.
> 2. If such conversion is after January 1, 1952, at the conversion price of $54 per share; i.e., at the rate of one share of Common Stock for each $50 principal amount of Debentures plus $4.00 in cash.[38]

By this means the corporation was able to appeal at once to those who wanted to minimize their risk (they could hang on to their bonds) and to those who wanted to take a chance. The chance-takers could become stockholders, and they would do so when and if the bonds as rights to stock become worth more than they would be just as limited priority income participations.

Thus we see a contract which has really a dual appeal to the capital supplier, while to the corporation needing capital the contract represents a means of acquiring funds first in debt form but with the opportunity of getting out of debt through a shift to ownership at some future date. Variations in terms of conversion can add to or detract from the contract's appeal as a capital raising device; and in reciprocal fashion the contract can detract from or add to its cost to the issuer, since what constitutes a favorable conversion ratio (i.e., a large number of common

---

[37] For an analysis of public utility security contracts in 1946–48, see *Financing Utility Capital Requirements,* a joint report of committees of the American Gas Association and Edison Electric Institute, (New York, 1949), Chapter VI.
[38] Prospectus, dated February 18, 1949.

shares for each bond) requires that common stockholders share their residual position with an increased number of owner participants. It is an exceedingly complex device, and the problems of balancing risk and income potentialities in this type of contract require careful consideration.

The one contractual feature of modern credit contracts of corporations which could probably be labelled "universal" is the call or redemption feature. The drawing of such a contract maturing even as near in the future as 10 years involves controls and commitments on the part of the corporation which are set as of the date of issue. No management can have sufficient foresight to know positively that all the terms of the contract with respect to interest rate, sinking funds, liens, and the like are going to continue to meet economically the needs of the business until maturity date; the business may change and the economic environment in which it operates may change; interest rates may go down or limits to borrowing set in original contracts may cease to be realistic. Hence, no present day security contract of nonresidual character running more than two or three years is ever written without provision for optional redemption. The corporation always reserves the right to call its bonds either in whole or in part, and since it will obviously be motivated to do so by advantages accruing to it, the corporation can reasonably be expected to pay for the privilege. The most common occasion for call is when money rates decline or a corporation's credit improves so that it becomes entitled to cheaper money from the market. Under the same circumstances, of course, the creditor-bondholder finds his investment improved, and he will not take the chance of being deprived of such appreciation without compensation. Payment for the sacrifice of giving up a favorable investment participation is reflected in the call premium (that is, the price above contractual maturity value) that the corporation agrees to pay for the right to withdraw from the contract. Ordinarily this premium is on a sliding scale starting out at about one year's interest above the price originally paid by the investor; if a 3 per cent bond is sold at 102, the starting call price will probably be about 105. From that point it often declines year by year to maturity value during the last year of the contract life. The logic of such a scale lies in the reasoning that to call an issue just after it is sold would require the greatest inconvenience, lost interest, and expense of reinvestment on the part of the investor. As time marches on toward maturity date, the extent of sacrifice will decline; finally comes the day when the investor would by contract be required to surrender his participation. Hence we see the declining scale of call premiums.

Miscellaneous. Of all the possible classifications of credit contract characteristics, "miscellaneous" would undoubtedly be the largest. When

one considers the process of fabrication of such contracts and recognizes that the purpose of the various provisions is to fit individual situations, it is easy to understand why provisions are unlike; they are as unlike as the businesses and market conditions for which they are designed.

Early in 1948, East Tennessee Natural Gas Company had a problem. This corporation had been organized in 1947 for the purpose of constructing and operating a natural gas pipe line system for the transportation of natural gas from a connection with the Texas line of Tennessee Gas Transmission Company to the area of East Tennessee. Upwards of $10,000,000 was needed for the first stage of construction, and it was going to be a year or two before deliveries (and thus revenues and earnings) could begin. The corporation sold mortgage bonds for $7,-700,000 of the required capital but was confronted with the fact that no stock, either preferred or common, could be sold on the basis of early dividend possibilities. In fact, it would not be legally possible to pay any kind of dividends until earnings developed at some time in the future. The corporation's answer was the sale of $1,860,000 of 5 per cent Interim Notes, Series A and $440,000 of 5 per cent Interim Notes, Series B to round out the required $10,000,000.[39] The interim notes were promises to pay interest at 5 per cent per annum until maturity in 1950 when, at the option of the company, the A notes could be paid off with 5 per cent preferred stock dollar for dollar; the B notes were similarly payable in common stock at 1 share for each $4 principal amount of notes. If there ever was a hybrid security, that is one: a promise to pay notes at maturity with ownership participations. There was definite purpose in the contract, however; it enabled the investor participants legally to receive immediate payment of interest, and at the same time the contract eliminated any cash burden for meeting the $2,300,000 maturity. The A noteholders agreed to become preferred stockholders, but not until the corporation was expecting to be earning enough money to be in a position to declare dividends. The B noteholders obviously took more risk because they were to become residual common owners, but again not until there was at least a chance that dividends could be paid.

This contract of East Tennessee is cited merely as an example and to emphasize the possibilities of using the variables of risk, income, and control participation in business under the corporate form to accomplish by combination that type of credit contract which will meet the needs of a specific situation. Within the scope of the powers of a corporation set by statute and charter, there are no limits to the ingenious devices that may be used (or misused) in the processes of capital raising. The real problem lies in achieving the proper combination of contractual

---

[39] A prospectus, dated March 3, 1950, relates to a refinancing of these "A" and "B" notes but contains description of the 1948 issues.

provisions: the combination that will really meet the needs of a situation and honestly reflect the circumstances of the particular business. Promises that knowingly can't be fulfilled constitute fraud; promises that obligate a business to make payments of interest, sinking fund or principal at maturity when future circumstances are uncertain, promise only trouble —for both the borrowing corporation and the investor.[40]

Ownership Variations

A long process of evolution involving application of the Darwinian theory of "the survival of the fittest" has brought about some degree of standardization in the use of ownership capital contracts as the media of owner participation in corporate enterprise. There still remains plenty of room for variation, and after consideration of some generalities a few examples and adaptations to special situations will be examined.

Just as creditor participations in business were previously characterized as appearing on the corporate financial stage as universally garbed in promises and obligations, so we may envision all owner participants made up to act as characters who take what is left; they may wax fat or lean depending on the particular business situation and on the extent of obligatory priorities that may have been put into the act with them. Fundamentally the owner participants must be regarded as residual interests with all of the risk, income, and control features that have not otherwise been contracted away in creditor form. Among the owner-stockholders all of the incidents of ownership may be regarded as running pro rata to these owners, if nothing in the charter as the basic contract is said to the contrary. On the stage each owner would look exactly like every other one except that there would be variations in size. Such would be the scene for a corporation that used nothing but common stock to attract capital and represent its ownership.

Preferences. Mutations among owner-stockholders can be accomplished, however, in much the same way that variety is achieved among creditor participations—namely, by contract. According to the articles of incorporation under the laws of the State of Maine, certain stockholders of American Cyanamid Company are "entitled to receive, in preference to the holders of the Common Stock, when and as declared by the Board of Directors out of the surplus or net earnings of the Company, cumulative dividends . . . at the annual rate of $3\frac{1}{2}$ per share. . . ." [41] The par value of the stock in this instance is $100 so the $3\frac{1}{2}$ per cent equals

---

[40] For a thorough analysis of security contracts (up to date of publication), see A. S. Dewing, *A Study of Corporation Securities.* New York: The Ronald Press Company, 1934.

[41] Prospectus, dated May 18, 1950.

$3.50 per share. The preference also runs to this group in case of liquidation of the business—in the amount of $100 plus accumulated dividends if the liquidation should be involuntary and $106 should it be voluntary.

The effect of such a provision is to create a priority group without the form of obligation; it can't be obligatory because of the "ifs" involved. In the contract above, which is reasonably typical of modern provisions, the dividends must be paid before anything is paid to common stockholders—but only "when, as and if" declared by the directors, and then not only according to contract but also according to statutory requirements, the payments must be limited to "net income." [42] This is in contrast to creditors who are entitled to receive their interest and principal without any "ifs" or "buts." This method of putting one group of owners ahead of another does shift some of the risk of the investors' participation from the priority holders to those who stand in line behind them. It is particularly effective with respect to dividends, since the agreement contains motivation to pay within the framework of the priority; the common stockholders cannot receive any distribution until the preferred dividends have been paid. The typical preference concerning assets in liquidation probably has less to be said for it; seldom do corporations liquidate voluntarily; when the occasion is involuntary it is apt to be characterized by insolvency. If the corporation is really insolvent, then by definition there are no values left for any of the owners, and a priority is a first chance at nothing. In corporate reorganizations that may not require all of the values to settle creditors' claims, the priority feature of this type will achieve a preference over common stock participation.[43]

With respect to the income characteristic of preferred stock participation, the payment or balance for the risk reduction feature appears in the form of limited income. In the American Cyanamid Company contract above, it was $3.50 per share—no more. This was a means of attracting capital by reducing the risk and limiting the profit participation of one group, while leaving the residual owners to take the greater risk with no ceiling on what might be their participation.

The cumulative feature is a universal accompaniment of priority in present day preferred stock contracts designed to raise new capital. Only a year-by-year priority such as characterizes noncumulative dividend

---

[42] Although the various state statutes differ widely in details of terminology, their universal effect is to limit dividend distributions to profits; some states approach the problem negatively by saying that dividends cannot be paid out of capital, which by elimination leaves profits as the limiting figure.

[43] The "fair and equitable" requirements of the Federal Bankruptcy Law (Chapter X) have been interpreted to assure this priority. See Case vs. Los Angeles Lumber Products Co., 308 U.S. (1939) and Consolidated Rock Products vs. du Bois, 312 U.S. 510 (1940).

participations could not achieve the desired end of giving assurance of an annual rate of income. The mere fact that in one year a set dividend must be paid prior to a common dividend distribution would not assure that the basic discretionary characteristic of all dividend payments might not be misused. Directors might skip all dividends for a time until sufficient funds were available to satisfy a single year's priority and still leave a balance for common stock. Attempts to stop this gap and at the same time to remove the pressure of cumulation by making dividends "cumulative, if earned" have never been satisfactory, except possibly to lawyers and accountants who might get in on disputed problems of income determination.[44]

Control. Variations in the control characteristic as it may be divided among the groups of owners run the gamut. A few contracts may still be found which by agreement deny practically all voting and control rights to some groups—usually to those with priority as to dividends. This is not the modern trend, however, which tends more to recognize the fact that, priority or not, stockholders are owners, have the risks of owners, and thus should as a matter of balance have the same opportunity to control the enterprise as do their fellow owners.[45] We still find as in Virginia Electric and Power Company [46] where "The Preferred Stock has no voting rights except . . . ," but the exceptions cover consent by two-thirds majority of the preferred stock as a class to change adversely the relative position of this prior security with respect to common stock. Most importantly, in case of default in payment of dividends for one year, the stock as a class has the right to elect a majority of the company's board of directors. Whether this power would enable the company to cure the default is a question, but at least the interests of the group would be adequately represented in the policy chambers. The preferred shareholders of American Cyanamid Company can elect only one-third of the directors in case of default, and otherwise have no voice in the election of directors,[47] whereas their counterparts in California Water and Telephone Company [48] have one vote per share on all corporate matters along with common shares. Some states, such as Illinois, have in their statutes the requirement that all shareholders regardless of class or priority must have one vote per share, and wherever the influence of the Securities and Exchange Commission has been felt through

---

[44] W. H. S. Stevens, "Rights of Non-Cumulative Preferred Stockholders," *Columbia Law Review,* 34 (1934), 1439.

[45] W. H. S. Stevens, "Stockholders' Voting Rights and the Centralization of Voting Control," *American Journal of Economics,* 40 (1926), 353; and "Voting Rights of Capital Stock and Shareholders," *Journal of Business,* University of Chicago, 11 (1938), 311.

[46] Prospectus, dated March 7, 1950.

[47] *Ibid.,* p. 21.

[48] Prospectus, dated March 15, 1950.

regulation, the policy has been to insist on such an arrangement. There is much to be said for leaving with the stockholders, whether they have priority rights to dividends or not, the natural prerogative of owners in the form of such control as shareholders can exercise through election of directors and voting on corporate affairs.

Retirement. In the natural order of things one would expect the ownership participation in a corporate enterprise to last as long as the enterprise itself; in other words, it is not natural to have a maturity date attached to any stock contract. Most corporations do have the charter right to purchase corporate stock under conditions prescribed by law which are designed to prevent the siphoning off of assets without recognition of contractual priorities. These rights, however, are optional to the corporation.

The fact that priority contracts are necessarily initiated by the common shareholders, (for they are the ones who grant the priorities) permits the inclusion of redemption provisions similar to those included in debt contracts. Southern California Edison Company has one old preferred stock which is not redeemable; it bears a 5 per cent dividend rate with provision for participating equally with any other priority issue which may carry a rate higher than 5 per cent and with common if common dividends go above 5 per cent.[49] Those owners have an unusual degree of protection, and by today's standards an unusually high dividend rate. But since the stock is not callable it stands as a perpetual contract, and the only way out of it—the expensive way—would be for the corporation to buy the stock in the open market. Viewed today, one might say that it was a mistake for the company to have arranged such a contract, and probably no one would more like to be out of it than the company. The record shows, however, that the stock or its predecessor contract has been outstanding at least since 1902. The circumstances of its issue may have demanded that investors be offered not only priority but also the right of unlimited profit (dividend) participation along with owners in subsequent positions. It is from lessons such as this, however, that corporations have learned to include redemption provisions in specialized and priority stock contracts; to the issuer such an option is even more important in ownership than in creditorship relations. Creditorship at least has an ultimate end at maturity date whereas ownership is by nature perpetual. Other Southern California Edison Company priority issues are all redeemable, in each case at a premium, the most recent 4.08 per cent issue (par $25) at prices scaling down from $26.25 per share down to the original sale price of $25.50 per share after 1965.

---

[49] Prospectus, dated May 17, 1950.

For the same reasons that bond contracts are occasionally made convertible into common ownership, preferred shares are also sweetened with this provision when the situation makes it feasible. It should be remembered that in no case does priority eliminate risk; it merely serves to make risk less than it might otherwise be in relation to a given business situation. If either general market conditions or the circumstances of a particular business indicate that even with priority there is considerable risk, there must be compensation for that risk to attract capital. One method of compensation would be to raise the dividend rate high enough to cover the risk. Another possibility is to provide compensation in the way of a conversion feature. In 1947 Dow Chemical Company needed additional ownership money. It had already outstanding 4 per cent preferred stock which was then selling on a 3.56 per cent yield basis (price approximately $112 per share) which gave some indication of what the cost of further priority participation might be. Rather than sell more of that class of stock, the company chose to issue a secondary priority issue (behind the 4 per cent preferred, but ahead of common stock in dividend and liquidation claims) and then to make it convertible into common. By so doing the company was able to put a 3.25 per cent dividend rate in the contract and to sell it at $102, a yield basis of 3.23 per cent.[50] It is obvious that this stock attracted capital not alone (if at all) because of its priority; rather it was the purchasers' chance to become a common stock holder that brought the price of $102 per share. Without that right such a secondary priority would necessarily have carried a yield higher than the 3.56 per cent attaching in the market to the first priority, perhaps as high as 4 per cent. This would have put the nonconvertible value of a 3.25 per cent dividend at approximately $81 per share. On this assumption it was the right to convert that brought in $21 of the $102 per share on the sale price. This was not "free" capital, however, since the conversion of this priority issue into common would ultimately require that the company's residual common stock participation be so increased to permit this group to own 842,106 out of 5,836,930 shares, or over 14 per cent of the common [51]— this at the contractual conversion price of $47.50 per share. During most of the period from July 1947 to July 1950, the common stock could have been sold on the market at prices in the 50's and 60's, thus indicating the dilution effect of conversion at $47.50 per share.

Another modification of ownership contracts used to simulate the maturity features of debt has come with the introduction of so-called sinking fund provisions into these specialized ownership agreements.

[50] Prospectus, dated July 23, 1947.

[51] As of May 31, 1950, only 160,000 shares remained outstanding, indicating conversion of roughly 80 per cent of the issue.

Retirement of ownership by definite contractual arrangements sounds like an anomaly, but we find, for instance, that when Household Finance Corporation sold its 4 per cent preferred stock it agreed "each year, beginning in 1951 . . ., to set aside as a sinking fund . . . an amount sufficient to retire . . . 2,000 shares . . ." (of the total 100,000 shares) which would result in retiring the entire issue in 50 years.[52] Other contracts permit the amount devoted to retirement to vary with earnings, as in the case of Keyes Fibre Company, which agreed to retire $75,000 annually of its $2,500,000 issue, a 33 year retirement program. The Keyes Company's expenditure need only average $75,000 and might drop below that figure if net income should drop below in particular years.[53] The wording of these contracts may suggest an obligation: the Keyes Fibre Company "is required to pay," and Household Finance Company "will be required to set aside" according to their respective prospectuses; but in spite of this wording it is impossible to put these agreements into the tone of an obligation on a par with agreements made with creditors; these are agreements with owners—as if I were to promise to pay me— and such an agreement certainly cannot be used to jeopardize the position of creditors.

The purpose of such sinking fund provisions, which probably will be effective although not enforceable, is in some instances to provide a definite retirement program; often the provisions aim at retirement in 25 to 35 years, and thus they do simulate a long-term bond maturity. This motive loses force when the annual sinking fund is 2 per cent as in the case of the Household Finance issue described above, since 50 years is too long a period to plan or program for in most businesses. The answer to this nominal annual retirement, just as in the case of bonds, is to lend market support. As long as life insurance companies and other institutional investors are large buyers of such issues, they will be particularly interested in market price. The insurance company portfolios of stock (both common and preferred) are valued for regulatory purposes at the market; in 1947 their preferred stock investment values suffered quite severely as prices went down in accompaniment to an increase of over $\frac{1}{2}$ per cent yield in high grade preferreds. Under such conditions a $3\frac{1}{2}$ per cent preferred stock going from a $3\frac{1}{2}$ to a 4 per cent yield basis would drop the price from $100 to $87.50. In the hope that even a 2 per cent annual retirement would absorb a much larger percentage of the floating supply on the market and thus hold up the price, these institutions ask for and get such provisions in the stocks they purchase. The fact that market price influence rather than real retirement was the motivating influence is demonstrated by the contract drawn by

---

[52] Prospectus, dated May 15, 1950.
[53] Prospectus, dated April 18, 1950.

Consumers Power Company, wherein this company agreed that it ". . . will endeavor to purchase, annually commencing with the year 1949, on a national securities exchange or in the open market, at prices not exceeding . . . the proposed purchase price to the public . . . ($102.725) . . . 2 per cent . . ." of the issue.[54] No shares of this stock had been purchased as of February 1950, because the price per share on the market to that date had never been as low as $103, so the company's "endeavors" would have been in vain. This use of a "purchase fund agreement" is a frank admission of the desire on the part of purchasers for a degree of market price support when they buy fixed income stocks whose prices react inversely to changes in yield rates for such investments. At the same time the agreement recognizes the coincidence of a company's long term or perpetual need for capital and its perpetual capital contracts in stock form by keeping the retirement program at nominal levels or by making retirements contingent on falling prices for the stock.

Conclusions

There has been neither the space nor the occasion here to delve into all of the details of contractual security agreements that are essential to complete bond or stock agreements. This has been only an attempt to stimulate consideration of the possibilities and limitations in the adaptation of the corporate tool and its security fixtures to the task of raising business capital. Emphasis has been placed on the fact that all securities bear the common elements of investment participation—risk, income, and control. Security contracts are but ways and means of creating appropriate combinations and qualities with respect to these participations.

While no word has been said about whether a corporation should issue bonds or how many (or if preferred stock, how much), it should be obvious that this is really the basic problem of financial management. Mortgages, liens, priorities, sinking funds, and all of the other gadgets combined cannot by contract produce quality of investment participation where none exists in enterprise itself. The risks of a business and its income potentialities, if it has any, can be divided and parcelled out among creditors and various classes of owners by judicious combinations of contractual provisions. Control over and rights to the assets of a corporation can be divided and priorities established. That is all; one shouldn't expect to be able to make something out of nothing.

In the final analysis judgment and experience must dictate how the contracts are to be drawn. In the acquisition of the requisite judgment and experience, it may be helpful to have in mind the essentials of se-

---

[54] Prospectus, dated June 23, 1948.

curity contracts and the part which the corporation can play in reaching solutions to the capital raising problems of business.

Suggested Readings

Bosland, C. C., *Corporate Finance and Regulation*. New York: The Ronald Press Co., 1949.

Buchanan, N. S., *The Economics of Corporate Enterprise*. New York: Henry Holt and Co., 1940.

Dewing, A. S., *A Study of Corporation Securities*. New York: The Ronald Press Co., 1934.

Dice, C. A., and Eiteman, W. J., *The Stock Market*. New York: McGraw-Hill Book Co., Inc., 1941.

———, *Financial Policy of Corporations*, 4th Revised Edition. New York: The Ronald Press Co., 1941.

Gerstenberg, C. W., *Financial Organization and Management*, 2nd Revised Edition. New York: Prentice-Hall, Inc., 1939.

Lyon, Hastings, *Corporations and Their Financing*. Boston: D. C. Heath and Co., 1938.

Masson, R. L., and Stratton, S. S., *Financial Instruments and Institutions—A Case Book*. New York: McGraw-Hill Book Co., Inc., 1938.

Purdy, H. L., Lindahl, M. L., and Carter, W. A., *Corporate Concentration and Economic Policy*, second edition. New York: Prentice-Hall, Inc., 1950.

Stevens, W. H. S., "Voting Rights of Capital Stock and Shareholders," *Journal of Business of the University of Chicago*, October 1938, pp. 311-348.

14

Investment Banking—History and Regulation

by ROGER W. VALENTINE

Halsey, Stuart & Co. Inc.

INVESTMENT BANKING, which is concerned primarily with the merchandising of securities, is frequently interpreted in terms of the activities of Wall Street and La Salle Street without a clear differentiation between the basic functions of the investment banker and the functions of other types of financial institutions whose activities are centered in, or related to, the securities market. A clear conception of the differences in function of these various institutions is essential to an understanding not only of investment banking but also of the place it occupies in the American economy. This is particularly true with regard to the functional differences between commercial banking, investment banking, and the operations of organized security exchanges.

The distinction between these three can best be brought out, perhaps, by reference to their relationship in the process of providing the capital funds business enterprises normally require for regular operations, or for expansion and development purposes. These funds are usually divided into two categories. The first is long-term, or fixed capital—funds which are expended to acquire assets such as land, buildings, machinery or other equipment. The second is short-term, or working capital—funds used to purchase inventories, finance accounts receivable, pay salaries and wages, and meet other operating expenses. Both types of funds, in the final analysis, are obtained primarily from: (a) the investment of personal savings by individual owners or stockholders of the business; (b) from earnings retained in the business; (c) from various kinds of loans or credit advances, and (d) from the issuance and sale of securities.

The generally accepted functions of commercial banking in theory center in supplying short-term working capital to business enterprises to

finance the production, distribution, and sale of goods or services. Funds for these purposes are made available by the commercial banks through such mediums as direct loans of short maturity or the purchase of bills of exchange. On the other hand, providing long-term or fixed capital funds for business enterprises is the function of investment banking. Here the method of making such funds available is largely through the sale of stocks, bonds, notes or other instruments to various types of investors. It is in the character of the funds made available and the means of doing so that the primary distinction in theory exists between commercial and investment banking. And it is in the matter of providing capital funds to business enterprises that the functions of these institutions are to be distinguished from those of organized security exchanges. Security transactions on organized exchanges are not a means for directly providing capital funds to business enterprises. The primary function of the organized exchanges is to provide a mechanism through which the ownership of securities already outstanding can be readily transferred. This is done through brokerage firms that execute orders, on a commission basis, for customers in the purchase and sale of securities.

This broad distinction between the functions of commercial banking, investment banking and organized security exchanges is important if confusion is to be avoided in observing or interpreting the organization and operation of the capital market. In the day-to-day conduct of business activity a wide variety of financial transactions are carried out, and the individual institutions through which they are handled do not always confine their business activities to a single field of endeavor. Consequently, one finds an overlapping of functions in the types of business conducted by many banks, investment houses, and brokerage firms. It is not uncommon for commercial banks to engage in investment banking activities in the purchase and sale of government and municipal obligations. And many security houses do both an investment banking and a brokerage business. For this reason it is necessary, as pointed out above, to have a clear conception of the functions of investment banking in order to understand its operation in the capital market.

Nature of the Capital Market

The term "market" carries the connotation in the minds of most people of a place where buyers and sellers of a commodity come together and transact business. This is exemplified in a tangible manner by the local fish or produce markets, and in another but somewhat less tangible way, by the grain markets on the Chicago Board of Trade, or the stock market on the New York Stock Exchange. The term "capital market," however, is more intangible, for it does not involve a specific place of meeting in

the ordinary sense of the word. It does imply, nevertheless, a group of buyers and a group of sellers of what, in this case, are known as capital funds. On the demand side of the market are the many and various types of business enterprises such as public utility, industrial, and railroad companies which are in need of funds for the construction of new plants, the improvement of existing facilities, the purchase of new equipment, or the payment of maturing debt. There are also the federal, state, and local municipal bodies which need funds for various purposes. They express their demand for funds by issuing and offering for sale their securities in the form of stocks, bonds, notes, or other instruments. On the supply side of the market are millions of individuals who, as investors, are seeking an outlet for their savings either directly or indirectly through institutions such as insurance companies, savings banks, trust companies, or other investment channels. And the prices at which these funds are purchased and sold are expressed in the yields on bonds and notes or the yields available on preferred and common stocks. This market is nation-wide in scope, and the mechanism through which funds flow from their sources on the supply side to their users on the demand side of the market is what is known as the investment banking system in this country. It comprises the investment banking firms, large and small, doing business throughout the country, either locally or on a nation-wide basis. The investment banking firms stand as the intermediary linking together the two sides of the capital market, and it is largely through their activities that the flow of funds in this market takes place. Although volume varies from year to year, the total amount of this flow during the 30 years from 1920–50 (as represented by new securities issued for various purposes, excluding United States government obligations) has been more than 175 billion dollars.

Nature of Investment Banking

In performing the function of an intermediary in the capital market, the investment banker does so in the capacity of a merchant. Usually, he does this by purchasing outright—either directly from issuers such as business enterprises and governmental units, or through other investment bankers—new securities which are made available to the market. In certain instances an entire issue will be acquired by a single investment banker. In other instances a group of bankers will join together for the purpose of handling a given issue of securities. Inventory thus obtained is then offered for sale to various types of investors.

In these and many other respects, investment banking is similar to other forms of merchandising activity. As business entities, investment banking is conducted as individual proprietorships, as partnerships, and

as incorporated firms. In addition to the equity capital employed in the business, temporary working capital is also utilized through borrowing from commercial banks for the purpose of carrying inventory until sold. There is specialization in the business based upon the type and quality of securities handled, although the degree of specialization is less today than formerly. A number of factors have produced this tendency toward a more general security business among investment bankers. Among these factors have been the effects of a lower level of interest rates, a broadening of the scope of the investment market particularly from an institutional standpoint, the effects of a higher income and estate tax structure, and more intensive competition in the business.

In certain other respects, however, investment banking has some characteristics that make it noticeably different from other merchandising businesses. It will be noted that the average unit transaction is large in dollar amount and therefore requires large sums of capital. The business also operates on a relatively low margin of gross profit, which makes the risk factor in carrying inventories extraordinarily large. This risk factor is enhanced by the high degree of sensitivity in the securities market to changes and developments in other segments of the economy, as well as by the psychological influences arising out of political factors, both local and national. And in recent years the business has been subject to a far greater degree of public regulation than most other forms of merchandising activity. Finally, the business is highly technical in character, and it makes possible the rendering of special services by the investment banker in connection with the merchandising function being performed.

History of Investment Banking

Our present-day investment banking mechanism is the product largely of a development which is often considered as having its beginning shortly before the year 1900. Its origins, however, extend back into the early days of the republic, and it is in this era that the evolution of investment banking in America really started. This evolution historically is one of a slow and gradual beginning during the years prior to the Civil War, followed in turn by a period of growth and adaption to an expanding capital market during the next half century, and finally emerging in full stature immediately after World War I to experience its greatest expansion and most dynamic performance during the period from 1919 to 1931. The following decade was one of contraction and readjustment under federal regulation during a period of world-wide economic depression. Then came World War II, and with it came basic changes in the capital market, followed by a revival in investment banking activity in the postwar years. During the course of this long period of years the nature and character

of investment banking have undergone various changes which reflect the impact of the many dynamic forces that exerted themselves on the economic and social development of the nation. Some of these changes have historical significance as a basis for understanding many aspects of the problems related to investment banking in this country at the present time.

Period Prior to Civil War

Although the issuance and sale of securities in this country dates back to colonial days, most businesses during this early period were conducted largely as individual or partnership enterprises, with funds provided directly by those identified with them. It was not long, however, after Alexander Hamilton had given the debt of the federal government an investment status (through his providing for the assumption of the state debts in 1790) that earmarks were evident of a capital market beginning to take form in a small way. Government bonds and a few bank stocks were being bought and sold. Long-term municipal bonds made their first appearance when Philadelphia in 1799, New York in 1812, and Baltimore in 1817, created small amounts of this type of debt.[1] Later corporate bonds were utilized in financing the construction of railroads. The Philadelphia Stock Exchange was organized in 1800 and The New York Stock Exchange in 1817.

The demand for capital during this period, particularly after the opening of the Erie Canal, was primarily in connection with the development of turnpikes, canals, railroads, and banking and insurance enterprises. The financing of these undertakings was accomplished partly through bank loans, partly by the issuance and sale of securities to private investors, but in large part through the assistance of the states which issued bonds for this purpose.

The investment banking mechanism through which these securities were sold was relatively simple. In the case of state and municipal bonds, the state governments generally appointed commissioners, who acted as agents and sold the securities either by solicitation or by contract to bankers and wealthy merchants. New York, Philadelphia, and Boston were the centers for such transactions, but a large number of the bonds sold in these cities were for English and Dutch bankers such as Baring Brothers & Company in London and Hope & Company in Amsterdam. In 1836, after the charter of the Second Bank of the United States had expired, Nicholas Biddle, the bank's President, opened a London agency to distribute American securities to British investors, and about this time

---

[1] L. A. Shattuck, *Municipal Indebtedness*. Baltimore: Johns Hopkins Press, 1940. The Johns Hopkins University Studies in Historical and Political Science, Series 58, No. 2, p. 14.

the Rothschilds sent August Belmont to New York as their personal representative.[2] Other foreign firms also had American branches, and many Americans went abroad to negotiate loans directly with foreign bankers. The Panic of 1837 and the defaults by many of the states on their obligations were a severe setback to this development. After 1845, however, negotiations were renewed, but the interest of foreign investors was centered largely in railroad securities. The establishment of these relationships between American and European capital markets during this period was a development of historical significance. After the Civil War, this link between these two capital markets was a major element in our investment banking mechanism for over 60 years.

Another development of similar significance during this period was the rise of a large group of private banks, exchange dealers, and brokers—many of whom were originally importers and merchants—and their gradual transformation into dealers in new securities. Having accumulated wealth in shipping and mercantile activities particularly during the Napoleonic wars, they gradually developed a commercial banking and brokerage business as an offshoot to their trading operations. Thus they became natural mediums to be used as an aid in finding an outlet for securities by those who were seeking new long-term capital. And the same was true with regard to those who were desirous of investing money. In this way a kind of investment banking business on an agency basis developed as a side line to the private commercial banking and brokerage business of this period. This dual function of private bankers continued to exist until the passage of the Banking Act of 1934, but the investment banking phase in the course of the intervening period had become in most instances the predominant activity. The passage of the National Banking Act in 1863, providing for the chartering of commercial banks under federal government supervision, made for strong competition in the commercial banking field. On the other hand, an expanding capital market after the war provided more attractive outlets in investment banking for the private bankers and brokers. This transformation in the major role of private bankers from commercial banking to investment banking in the United States is an interesting phase of the development of our financial mechanism in this country.

Civil War to World War I

During this period in the evolution of investment banking, four significant developments are to be noted. They are: (1) the rapid growth of

---

[2] H. P. Willis, and J. I. Bogen, *Investment Banking*, Revised Edition. New York: Harper & Brothers, 1936. Chap. VIII gives a more detailed account of these developments.

the capital market under the impetus of a great industrial expansion; (2) the rise of international banking houses to a predominant position in investment banking activities; (3) the development of retail distribution of securities on a broad scale; and (4) a high degree of specialization in the business of certain individual houses or firms.

The period between the Civil War and World War I for the most part was one of tremendous economic expansion. Except for short periods following the panics of 1873, 1893, and 1907, there was little interruption in the industrial development of the country. Railroad mileage, for instance, increased nearly 150,000 miles between 1865 and 1895, and another 70,000 by 1915. Manufacturing and trade multiplied rapidly, and in the latter part of the century a wave of new inventions (including the telephone, the electric dynamo and the internal combustion engine) were all factors promoting the development of new enterprises. The demand for capital was prodigious.

During the first part of the period between the Civil War and World War I, it again was necessary to resort to the European capital market for funds. The investment banking houses which had established connections abroad with bankers in England, Holland, and Germany,—to whom Americans could sell the securities they sponsored—were in a commanding position to direct the flotation of new issues. The pre-eminence of this group was soon established, and they became the main channel through which new capital was obtained from abroad. The magnitude of the amount of such funds raised in this way in Europe is shown in estimates to the effect that the total holdings of leading foreign countries in American securities of all kinds in 1899 were in excess of three billions of dollars, most of which were railway stocks and bonds acquired after the Civil War.[3] This was about 30 per cent of the total capitalization of the railroads at that time. By the turn of the century the great consolidation movement in American industry was well under way and, except for a short period following the panic of 1907, the demand for large amounts of capital continued unabated. Up until this time bankers had been concerned primarily with the flotation of government and municipal bonds, railroad securities, and bank and insurance stocks. After 1901, however, public utility and industrial securities became the predominant element in the market. International banking houses continued to maintain the pre-eminence of their position by active management of new flotations of these securities in the American market, as well as beginning the introduction of offerings of securities from European, Far Eastern and Latin American areas, a project that was a little later to assume large proportions.

---

[3] W. Z. Ripley, *Railroads Finance and Organization*. New York: Longmans, Green & Co., Inc., 1920, p. 6.

A third development of this period was the retail distribution of securities on a broad scale. It had its beginning during the Civil War when the Treasury experienced great difficulty in raising funds through the sale of bonds. Jay Cooke, a Philadelphia banker, was appointed as a special agent by Salmon P. Chase, Secretary of the Treasury, to promote their sale. He organized a country-wide advertising and distributing organization and launched a campaign based on a patriotic appeal to save the Union.[4] He chose as associates in promoting the bond selling program a number of firms of high standing and is said to have employed over 4,000 salesmen at one time in his campaign to sell bonds in small amounts to individual investors. He was highly successful in telling the country that the generation fighting the war should not be called upon to pay for it and in portraying a national debt as a national blessing.[5] The popular interest thus enlisted made the campaign a success. He has been called, therefore, the originator of the retail distribution of sound securities among small investors.[6] Cooke undertook to sell railroad bonds in the same manner after the Civil War. As an investment banker in that connection, he also introduced the principle of purchasing securities outright and forming an underwriting group to take up any unsold bonds. However, Cooke's firm failed in 1873 and this procedure was cast aside for the time being. Later the principle of retail selling through salesmen was again introduced by N. W. Harris in Chicago, who organized in 1882 the firm of N. W. Harris & Company; and this organization began the distribution of well secured bonds through the medium of widespread personal solicitation and organized sales campaigns. Similar policies were later adopted by other firms including Harris, Forbes & Co., N. W. Halsey & Co., and Halsey, Stuart & Co. Inc. The latter, as successor firm to N. W. Halsey & Co., is today the only large house of its kind which has confined its activities entirely to the bond business. The principle of retail distribution by solicitation thus became an established part of the mechanism for distributing negotiable securities in this country and has been widely used in all phases of the investment banking business.

Another development which characterized this period was the rise of specialization in the business. The growth of large scale corporate industry and the extension of investment banking to include public utility, railroad and industrial securities of every description, along with government and municipal obligations, produced a relatively high degree of

---

[4] For an interesting account of Cooke's activities, see E. P. Oberholtzer, *Jay Cooke, Financier of the Civil War*. Philadelphia: G. W. Jacobs and Company, 1907.

[5] D. R. Dewey, *Financial History of the United States,* 9th Ed. New York: Longmans, Green & Co., Inc., 1924, p. 311.

[6] A S. Dewing, *Financial Policy of Corporations,* 4th Ed., Vol. II. New York: The Ronald Press Company, 1941, p. 1097.

specialization. Some houses specialized in bonds, others in stocks. In some cases in both fields certain houses, being concerned only with railroad or public utility financing, limited themselves to a given industry, sometimes even in only gas or electric companies. In bonds, some firms specialized in governments; others confined themselves to municipals (often on a geographical basis). This element of specialization also developed somewhat on a functional basis. Some of the larger firms confined their efforts primarily to originating and wholesaling new issues. Others engaged only in retail distribution. And still a third group did both a wholesale and a retail business. After the war, however, this tendency toward specialization was reversed. A broader interest in and knowledge of securities by various classes of investors tended to reduce the opportunity or need for specialization. Competition in the business also became a factor in bringing about the change. It was with great reluctance that many of the older firms broadened their activities, but most of them made the adjustment to the changed conditions in the business as time passed.

World War I and After

The outbreak of hostilities in Europe in the summer of 1914 and the entrance of the United States into the War in the spring of 1917 had a tremendous impact upon both the American capital market and the investment banking business. There suddenly developed a demand for what were then huge sums of money with which to finance, first, the purchase of war supplies by European countries, and later, the American war effort. This demand was exemplified by the absorption in the American market of approximately $2,250,000,000 of American securities transferred from foreign to domestic ownership, and about $2,000,000,000 of securities issued by foreign governments between the beginning of the war and the end of 1916.[7] The Liberty Loans of 1917 and 1918 followed in turn. One of the important results of this war financing was a vast increase in the popular ownership of securities. This is shown by the fact that there were over 4,000,000 subscribers to the First Liberty Loan, over 9,400,000 for the Second Loan, 18,300,000 for the Third Loan, and 22,770,000 for the Fourth Loan.[8] Only a very small percentage of these subscribers were institutions. It has been estimated that there were 200,000 holders of securities in this country before the war and 20,000,000 afterward.[9] The American people thus were initiated to security ownership, but for many of them the period was brief; it has been estimated that nearly 18,000,000

---

[7] *Annual Report Federal Reserve Board 1916*, p. 1.
[8] *Annual Report of the Secretary of the Treasury, 1917–1919*.
[9] Paul M. Warburg in an address delivered before the Bond Club of New York on May 23, 1919.

original purchasers of Liberty Bonds sold out their holdings within two years to some 4,000,000 investment buyers.[10] Nevertheless, the vast potentiality of the private investor as a market for the distribution of other securities had been indicated, and it was intensively cultivated during the next decade.

Another effect of the war was to change the United States from the position of a debtor nation to that of a creditor nation and, for the first time, an international investor on a large scale. The significance of this development is evident in the demand for funds that was made upon the American capital market from abroad in a relatively short period of time as is shown in Table 1. It will be noted that in the 16-year period 1915–30,

TABLE 1

FOREIGN SECURITY ISSUES OFFERED IN THE UNITED STATES [11]

(In millions of dollars)

Year	Number of Issues	New Capital	Refunding	Total
1915–16	182	$ 1,959	$ 18	$ 1,977
1917–18	93	703	40	743
1919–30	1,782	10,032	2,077	12,109
Totals	2,057	$12,694	$2,135	$14,829

inclusive, a total of over 2,000 foreign capital issues were publicly offered in the United States amounting to $14,829,000,000, of which $12,694,-000,000 was new capital and $2,135,000,000 was refunding. Later experience was to show that neither the American investors nor the investment bankers in this country were fully prepared to assume the role of international investors and bankers on the scale that they did during the decade following the war. As one large underwriter of foreign bonds, in commenting favorably upon America's becoming an international investor, stated so prophetically but unwittingly in a brochure in 1929, "It is doubtful if people generally have realized some of the consequences that have and will result therefrom." How unexpectedly, but, unfortunately, true in a different sense did this observation prove to be two years later when a long series of defaults on interest and principal payments began following the Hoover moratorium and the international banking crisis which forced England off the gold standard.

The demand from domestic sources upon the American capital market for funds also increased tremendously after the war. State and municipal governments along with the railroads continued to be borrowers, and vast

---

[10] C. F. Childs, *Concerning U.S. Government Securities.* Chicago: Lakeside Press, 1947, p. 138.

[11] *Statistical Abstract of the U.S. (1939),* p. 307.

sums were required to finance the expansion and development of electric light and power companies and various industrial enterprises. Real estate and financial securities likewise represented another important element of demand in the market. As a consequence, there was a big increase in the number of issues offered and the volume of funds raised through the investment banking mechanism during this period. In the 13 years, 1919–31 inclusive, new capital flotations for domestic purposes totaled over 63 billion dollars and those for refunding exceeded 11 billion dollars. To handle this enormous volume of financing required a substantial expansion in investment banking facilities. Established organizations expanded their activities and new institutions were formed to engage in the business. It was during the latter part of this period that the investment banking mechanism in this country reached its pinnacle from the standpoint of size, capital employed, distributive capacity and volume of activity.

One of the most important elements in this expansion centered in the assumption of investment banking functions on the part of many commercial banks chartered under either state or federal statutes. Although there is no comprehensive data available regarding the exact nature or the extent of the early participation in investment banking activities on the part of individual commercial banks, there is evidence that they were beginning to play an important part in the capital market near the turn of the century, even though the number of banks doing so was relatively small.[12]

There were several reasons why commercial banks began doing an investment banking business about this time. Among them were: (1) many banks did not have a sufficient loan demand to absorb all of their available funds, and investment banking activities afforded a way to employ these funds profitably; (2) banks were engaging in other activities such as operating savings departments, managing safe-deposit vaults, acting as corporate trustees, doing fiscal agency work, acting as mortgage loan agents, and other similar work—it was an easy step to add another department; (3) the larger city banks had a good clientele from which to originate securities to sell, and their correspondent banks and individual depositors offered a good potential outlet for the sale of securities; and (4) investment banking was a means of obtaining securities for the commercial banks' own portfolio at a lower cost than through regular investment channels.

---

[12] F. C. James, *The Growth of Chicago Banks*. New York: Harper & Brothers, 1938. James gives an interesting account of the growing security operations of a few of the large commercial banks in Chicago toward the end of the eighties. A pioneer in this field was the First National Bank of Chicago which in 1891 sold more than "seven million dollars' worth of bonds at an aggregate profit of eighty thousand dollars." (Page 564.)

It was the larger banks for the most part which engaged in merchandising securities, and they usually did so either directly through a department set up as a unit within the bank or through an affiliated company. A department within the bank was the medium most generally used because it could be more fully coordinated with the other activities of the bank, particularly those related to making loans on securities and the management of the investment portfolio. The affiliated company was employed in some instances because it afforded a wider opportunity for operation, but in other instances it was used primarily because there was a question as to whether commercial banks could legally engage in the business of buying and selling certain securities. This was particularly true in the case of national banks prior to World War I, for the Comptroller of the Currency had raised the point of legality in connection with the activities of certain institutions in New York. And in another connection the counsel to the Federal Reserve Board cited in a ruling that national banks had no explicit power to buy and sell securities.[13] Later, however, after the war a substantial number of national banks directly engaged in the business under an interpretation of their general powers, and the Comptroller "raised no objection because this type of business had become a recognized service which a bank must render." [14] In 1927, national banks were given by act of Congress the power to buy and sell without recourse marketable obligations in the form of bonds, notes or debentures, commonly known as investment securities under such further definition of the term as made by regulation by the Comptroller of the Currency.[15] This did not include the power to buy and sell stocks.

Although commercial banks were an element in the capital market for a number of years before World War I, it was during the years from 1920 to 1931 that they played their most important role. Some idea of the increase in their significance is evident in the tabulation given in Table 2 showing the number of banks engaged in the securities business either directly or through operating affiliates.

While the number of bank affiliates engaged in the securities business was substantially smaller than the number of banks operating directly, the affiliates, nevertheless, became a more important constituent in the origination and distribution of new issues. The banks' relative position in the origination of bond issues, for instance, is indicated in Table 3. The rapid rise in the relative importance of commercial banks and their affiliates to that of other investment banking institutions in this respect during this period is also indicated in these tabulations. Further evidence

---

[13] *Commercial and Financial Chronicle*, February 12, 1916, pp. 550-551.
[14] *Annual Report of the Comptroller of the Currency, 1924,* p. 12.
[15] *Ibid.*, 1927, p. 11.

TABLE 2

NUMBER OF NATIONAL BANKS, STATE BANKS, AND THE AFFILIATES OF
NATIONAL AND STATE BANKS ENGAGED IN THE SECURITIES BUSINESS [16]

| | National Banks | | State Banks | | |
Year	Operating Directly	Operating Affiliates	Operating Directly	Operating Affiliates	Total
1922	62	10	197	8	277
1925	112	33	254	14	413
1929	151	84	308	48	591
1930	126	105	260	75	566
1933	102	76	169	32	379

TABLE 3

PERCENTAGE ORIGINATION OF BOND ISSUES BY ALL HOUSES [17]

(Handling 20 million dollars or more per annum)

	1927	1928	1929	1930
National Bank Affiliates	10.1	15.6	24.6	27.6
Other Bank Affiliates	2.7	7.7	16.9	11.6
Commercial Banks and Trust Companies	9.2	6.2	4.0	5.4
Total Commercial Banks and Affiliates	22.0	29.5	45.5	44.6
Other Investment Bankers	78.0	70.5	54.5	55.4
Total	100.0	100.0	100.0	100.0

of the importance of commercial banks and their affiliates in originating
bond issues is found in the fact that of the 15 houses which headed new
bond issues totaling $300,000,000, or more, during the five year period
1927–31, six of them were bank affiliates and one a commercial bank.
During these years certain banks and bank affiliates were active distributors of stock issues as well. Generally speaking it may be said that by
1929 in the field of long-term financing the commercial banks and their
security affiliates occupied a position comparable to that of private investment bankers from the standpoint of physical facilities, capital employed,
and the volume of securities underwritten and distributed. This situation
changed quickly, however, a short time afterward as the Banking Act of
1933 compelled the commercial banks to sever connections with their
security affiliates and refrain from engaging in investment banking activities except those related to the purchase and sale of certain state and
municipal obligations and United States government securities.

---

[16] W. N. Peach, *Security Affiliates of National Banks*. Baltimore: Johns Hopkins
Press, 1941, Johns Hopkins University Studies in Historical and Political Science, Series
58, No. 3, 1941, p. 83.
[17] Peach, *op. cit.*, p. 109. Also Senate Banking and Currency Committee: *Hearings on
Senate Resolution No. 71* (February 1931), p. 299.

Another aspect of the expansion of the investment banking business during the years immediately after World War I is to be noted in certain developments which were reflected within the business itself. The enormous increase in the volume of security flotations focused attention to a greater degree upon the problems of distribution. This in turn tended to place a primary emphasis upon salesmanship and the development of large distributing organizations, some nation-wide in scope. Because of the large commitments involved in many instances, speed in distribution became increasingly significant as a means of reducing the financial risk inherent in adverse changes in market conditions. The private investor and country bank market attained a position comparable with the eastern institutional market as a major investment outlet for new security issues, and the investment banking machinery was geared largely during this period to service this new market. The aggressive activity on the part of various firms in both the origination and distribution of new issues tended to narrow the profit margin in the business. During much of this period a high level of industrial prosperity and an abundance of funds available for investment generated a rise in security prices. With it, the individual investor's interest in stocks increased rapidly relative to that in bonds as a medium of investment. Potential appreciation, as compared with security and income, became more and more a factor in determining attitudes and decisions relative to the purchase of securities on the part of many people. This made for an overemphasis of the element of speculation and an undue consciousness of the profit possibilities in the distribution of securities. Too frequently the orderly process of analysis and investigation gave way to the promotion of marginal undertakings in the flotation of new issues. This was especially true in connection with financing an organization and with consolidating various investment company and holding company pyramids among industrial, public utility, and railroad enterprises. Something of the extent to which this was the case is shown in the estimate that out of a total of approximately $9,400,-000,000 of public issues by domestic corporations in 1929, less than $2,000,000,000 was for the purpose of providing real "productive" capital.[18]

The wild speculative mania which developed during this era came to a climax in October 1929, and the highly inflated structure of security prices which had been built up suddenly collapsed. The violent decline in values which ensued left an enormous financial wreckage throughout the country. Almost immediately both commercial and investment bankers became the target of political attack and investigations, some of which

---

[18] J. A. Schumpeter, *Business Cycles*. New York: McGraw-Hill Book Company, Inc., 1939, Vol. II, p. 879. Also G. A. Eddy, "Security Issues & Real Investment in 1929," *Review of Econ. Stat.*, May 1937, Cambridge, Mass.: Harvard University Press.

have continued with varying degrees of intensity throughout the intervening years to date. Particularly significant, in this connection, was the hearing before the Senate Committee on Banking and Currency in 1932, which revealed a number of practices in certain phases of the securities business that were open to abuse and not in accord with high standards of business conduct. Among them were the formation and operation of pools, the giving of preferential treatment to certain individuals in the distribution of securities, manipulation of markets for the benefit of special groups, the furnishing of inadequate information regarding new security issues, handling reorganizations in a manner to control the future financing of the reorganized company, and the use by commercial banks of their investment affiliates for the disposal of slow or poor loans. Many instances were uncovered where the interests of investors had been grossly disregarded and abused in a manner that in reality was a betrayal of public trust and confidence. In the wave of popular indignation which followed these revelations, the investment banking business as a whole was put under a cloud of disrepute and suspicion. Little, if any, distinction at the time, however, was made between these abuses and the basic mechanism of investment banking and the effectiveness with which its principal functions were performed.

Considering the nature and character of the abuses which had occurred and the state of public opinion at the time, federal regulatory legislation perhaps was inevitable, for existing state laws had been ineffective in preventing the conditions which had arisen. In dealing with the problems involved, Congress passed several acts affecting either directly or indirectly the investment banking business: the Securities Act of 1933 (as amended), the Securities Exchange Act of 1934, the Public Utility Holding Company Act of 1935, the Banking Act of 1933, the Trust Indenture Act of 1939, the Investment Company Act of 1940, the Chandler Act and the National Bankruptcy Act (as amended). In this legislation the Securities and Exchange Commission was established and endowed with broad powers for the supervision of the securities business. Through its rules and regulations the Commission has exercised this supervision in minute detail with far reaching effects upon many aspects of the conduct of investment banking activities.

Conditions in the investment banking business changed rapidly after the collapse of the boom in 1929. Both the demand for and the supply of funds in the capital market largely disappeared with the advent of the depression and the bank holiday. The devaluation of the dollar and cancellation of the gold clause undermined for a time public confidence in long-term investment commitments. Domestic corporate new capital issues totaled only $161,000,000 in 1933 and $177,000,000 in 1934, compared with over $8,000,000,000 in 1929. Total new capital issues of all

kinds during the entire decade 1931–40 amounted to about 30 per cent, of that of the preceding decade. The decline in interest rates made possible the refunding of a substantial amount of corporate bond issues in the institutional market after 1934 (but at a much narrower profit margin than had previously prevailed on new issues).

During the depression a broad realignment took place among investment banking firms. Consolidations, changes in name or shifts in personnel and control, retirements from the field, and the appearance of many new but mostly small concerns characterized these years. Heavy capital losses and contraction of activity contributed substantially to this development. The Banking Act of 1933 forced the commercial banks to limit their investment banking activities to government and municipal bonds and to divorce their security affiliates. It also compelled private bankers to choose between remaining in the security business or commercial banking. All told there was a tremendous contraction in physical facilities as well as a substantial reduction in the number of strong underwriting houses. Indicative of the changes which took place among the larger concerns, the fact may be cited that of 36 houses which in the five-year period 1927–31, headed $100,000,000 or more of new issues, 11 were banks and bank affiliates which came under the provisions of the Banking Act of 1933, 10 combined with other organizations, reorganized or ceased to function, leaving only 15 survivals without change of name or function. It was in this period of terrific economic upheaval that federal regulation of the investment banking business was inaugurated. To the problems of economic adjustment, therefore, the strain of adjustment to rigid control and supervision was added. Many problems created by this development are still unsolved.

Regulation of Investment Banking

The subjection of investment banking to public regulation under both state and federal legislation is a relatively recent development in this country. Until shortly before World War I, the sale of securities for the most part was conducted with freedom of action and was virtually unrestricted by restraining legislation. To be sure, legal recourse was available in case of fraud and false representation, but the rule of caveat emptor— let the buyer beware—was a generally accepted basis upon which the risk of investment was assumed in security transactions. Under such conditions, unsophisticated investors, often gullible in their desire to obtain large returns upon their investments, were vulnerable to fraud and deceit in the promotion of fantastic schemes and contrivances by swindlers. These investors likewise were vulnerable to the highly speculative potentialities of purchasing securities of gold mines, oil wells and real estate

developments. As the market for securities broadened and the number of investors steadily increased after the turn of the century, overzealous and unscrupulous promoters, as well as the stock swindlers, found this field a fertile one in which to operate—with telling effects upon an ever growing number of victims. It was the demand for protection on the part of these victims of fraud and speculation which ultimately brought about the passage of the various "blue sky" laws enacted by most of the states either shortly before or after the war. And it was the political reaction to a similar demand on the part of a mass of disillusioned and bewildered speculators after the market crash in 1929 which gave impetus to and made possible the passage of the Securities Act of 1933, the Securities Exchange Act of 1934, and other federal regulatory legislation.

Kansas in 1911 enacted the first so-called "blue sky" law (thus named from a legislator's remark that some companies sought to "capitalize the blue skies") relating to the sale of securities, and similar laws were passed by a number of other states shortly afterward. These statutes were immediately attacked and tested in the courts, largely on the question of their constitutionality. This point was settled in 1917, when the Supreme Court of the United States in a series of decisions held that such laws were a constitutional and proper exercise of the police powers of the states to legislate for the general welfare of the people.[19] Today every state except Nevada has some type of regulatory statute covering the sale, or offer for sale, of securities within the state.

Although these statutes vary widely both in structure and scope, they are usually classified under the headings of fraud laws, licensing laws, registration laws, or a combination of these. The fraud type of law exists today in New York, New Jersey, Delaware and Maryland. For the most part, it merely prescribes penalties for fraudulent actions and makes provisions whereby investigations and injunctive proceedings to protect the public from fraud may be instituted by some state official, such as the Attorney General. Neither the licensing of dealers nor the registration of securities is required by these laws on the theory that they unduly hamper security distribution and trading, whereas ample protection can be afforded the investor through aggressive prosecution of fraud.

In the case of licensing laws, primary emphasis is placed upon exercising control over the distribution of securities through the registration or licensing of brokers and dealers by an administrative agency of the state. A general requirement in this connection is the submission of proper evidence of personal integrity and financial responsibility as a condition to registration. Failure to comply with the law is usually subject to penalties, including the refusal, suspension or revocation of registration.

---

[19] Hall *vs.* Geiger-Jones Co., 242 U.S. 539 (1917); Caldwell *vs.* Sioux Falls Stock Yards Co., 242 U.S. 559 (1917); Merrick *vs.* N. W. Halsey & Co., 242 U.S. 568 (1917).

In registration laws, control over the securities themselves is the basis of regulation. It is exercised by providing for the registration of issues to be sold in the state. Such registration may be accomplished either by notification or by qualification as set forth in the statutes. Registration by notification is usually confined to certain classes of securities that are not exempt, as described below, but concerning which, because of their quality, a minimum amount of information is required. The filing of these data with the administrative agency along with the proper fee constitutes registration, and sale of the security is allowed without formal action or issuance of a permit unless the regulatory agency issues an order prohibiting the sale. Registration by qualification becomes necessary for all issues not exempt or entitled to registration by notification, and certain additional specified data must be filed for examination and the necessary fee paid. Sometimes special hearings are required to complete registration. Usually the securities cannot be sold until an order has been issued by the regulatory authority declaring them qualified for sale.

In most instances, certain classes of securities and certain types of transactions are exempt from the statutory requirements of blue sky laws where the character of the security or the nature of the transaction requires no regulation, either because they are already regulated by other agencies, or because they are normally less susceptible to fraudulent operations. Included in these categories are the securities of the United States government, states, cities and other political subdivisions; certain public utility and railroad companies, banks, trust companies, and, frequently, securities listed on recognized stock exchanges or qualified as legal investments for savings banks and trust funds. Exempt transactions include, for example, sales to dealers, banks, insurance companies, trust companies and similar institutions.

Although the basic techniques of regulation incorporated in state blue sky laws can be classified in the above manner, in a great majority of the statutes today a combination of these techniques is utilized. However, the regulations are far from being uniform in general construction, and wide variations exist between statutes with respect to the type and kind of information required in the administrative procedures set up, and in the general applicability of the laws. From an investment banking standpoint, this lack of uniformity in existing blue sky legislation is particularly significant because it imposes at the present time a heavy burden upon the legitimate issuers and distributors of securities operating on a nation-wide basis.

By and large these blue sky laws have been beneficial in certain respects to the individual investor in most states. But they proved to be entirely inadequate for stopping the flow of worthless securities. In a large measure this ineffectiveness was due to the fact that the states had no jurisdic-

tion over transactions in interstate commerce. But poor administration in some instances and public indifference at times were also contributing factors. In any event these laws had little restraining effect upon the forces which operated in the security markets in the latter half of the decade of the 1920's. But when the crash came the demands for corrective legislation re-echoed again—this time for a federal program on a much broader basis.

Federal Regulation

The Securities Act of 1933, as amended, is designed to prevent fraud in the sale of securities through the full and fair disclosure of the character of securities offered for sale in interstate and foreign commerce and through the mails. The fundamental premise upon which the act is based is that disclosure and publicity of all the facts essential to an intelligent appraisal of the value of a security is the best means of protecting investors against fraud. There is also embodied in the philosophy underlying this legislation the theory that full disclosure (placing adequate and true information before the investor) and publicity in connection with the sale of securities are strong deterrents to the inception of fraud, dishonesty and unethical conduct in corporate financial management.[20]

The Act requires that issuers of securities subject to the act must file with the Securities and Exchange Commission registration statements setting forth prescribed information about the securities; and it further provides that investors must be furnished, either at or before delivery of the security purchased, a copy of a required prospectus containing the more important items of such information.[21] These requirements are designed to provide the investor with sufficient facts about the security to enable an informed judgment of the merits of the issue to be made by him before purchasing the security being offered.

The information which is required to be incorporated in the registration statement is quite comprehensive and includes data under some 34 topical headings and certain special items as well as a substantial number of exhibits. It is designed to provide a clear picture of the character, size, and profitableness of the business, its capital structure, its ownership and control, and the application to be made of the funds realized from the sale of the securities. Details are given relative to the remuneration of officers and directors, bonus, profit sharing, pension and retirement

---

[20] D. Saperstein, "Governmental Regulation of Investment Banking," in *Fundamentals of Investment Banking*, published by Investment Bankers Assoc. (1947), p. 356. Also E. T. McCormick, *Understanding the Securities Act and the SEC.* New York: American Book Company, 1948.

[21] *Annual Report of the Securities & Exchange Commission, 1949*, p. 1.

plans; options, warrants and rights outstanding; management contracts, underwriting agreements, and pending or threatened legal proceedings. There must also be included in the registration statement certified financial statements, the interest of management and others in recent transactions, and the relationship with registrant of experts named in the registration statement. As exhibits there are included, among other things, a copy of the charter, existing by-laws, franchises, a specimen or copy of each security being registered, the indenture if there is one, and a copy of material contracts not made in the ordinary course of business. The registration statement must be signed by the registrant, its principal executive officer or officers, its principal financial officer, its controller or principal accounting officer, and by at least the majority of the board of directors or persons performing similar functions.

The effective date of a registration statement is the 20th day after filing or such earlier date as the Commission may determine. In some cases when an amendment is filed, the date of the filing of the registration statement is deemed to be the date of the filing of the amendment. Immediately after the filing of a registration statement it is made available for public inspection at the office of the Commission. At the same time the Commission proceeds with an examination of the material submitted, and if there are any deficiencies in the statement the registrants are informally advised of the fact in a "letter of comment" and afforded an opportunity to file correcting amendments before the statement becomes effective. On the other hand, if the registration statement, in the opinion of the Commission, includes an untrue statement of a material fact or omits an essential material fact necessary to make the statements therein not misleading, or fails to make adequate disclosure, the Commission can refuse to permit the statement to become effective; or, if the statement is already effective, the Commission, after proper notice and opportunity for hearing, can issue a "stop order" suspending the effectiveness of the registration statement. In this way control can be exercised over the adequacy of disclosure required under the law.

In this connection it is important to note that the elimination of risk in the purchase of securities is not an objective of the act—the primary purpose is the disclosure of sufficient information to enable the investor to make an intelligent appraisal of the risk involved. The Commission, therefore, in enforcing the act, neither approves or disapproves an issue, nor does it pass upon the investment merits or the value of any security.[22] The making of any representation to the contrary is a criminal offense under the law.

The public offering of a security subject to the act cannot legally be

---

[22] Under the Securities Act, speculative issues can be registered and sold provided full disclosure is made regarding the issue.

made unless a registration statement is in effect at the time of offering. To assure that the disclosure provided in the registration statement is made readily available to the investor, the act requires that the essential elements of these data be incorporated in a prescribed prospectus, a copy of which in final form must be given to the investor either at or before the time of the delivery of the security purchased. For this purpose it is unlawful to use any form of a prospectus which does not meet the requirements of the act. It was the intent of Congress, however, that the 20-day period between the date of filing the registration statement and its effective date would permit widespread dissemination among investors of the information contained in the registration statement. To this end, therefore, the Commission has approved the use of a preliminary or "red herring" prospectus if it contains substantially the same information as the final prospectus with certain specified omissions. In this connection, however, it should be emphasized that it is unlawful for anyone to offer for sale, or to solicit an offer to purchase, the security prior to the effective date of the registration statement. The "red herring" prospectus, therefore, must not be used in a manner which might be interpreted as constituting an offer to sell or a solicitation of an offer to buy. Some highly technical problems arise here in actual day-to-day business operation. It has been difficult for the Commission to resolve these problems in a manner making for the most effective utilization of the "red herring" prospectus for disseminating information during the waiting period.

Not only does the act aim at full disclosure of important information in the issuance of securities, it also makes the sponsors of these securities accountable for the representations they have made. This is done by making them subject to civil liabilities in case "any part of the registration statement, when such part became effective, contained an untrue statement of a material fact or omitted to state a material fact required to be stated therein or necessary to make the statement therein not misleading." Persons subject to being sued are (1) every person who signed the registration statement; (2) all directors and partners of the issuer; (3) accountants, engineers, appraisers and other professional persons who consented to being named as having prepared or certified any part of the registration statement or any report or valuation used in connection with the registration statement; and (4) underwriters. Civil liabilities may also arise in the case of any person who sells a security in violation of certain sections of the act relating to a registration statement being effective and to the requirements regarding a prospectus or oral communication. In addition, the act makes it unlawful for anyone to engage in any fraudulent scheme or misrepresentation in the sale of securities by the use of the mails or any other means in interstate commerce.

Broad regulatory powers over certain phases of investment banking

are also invested in the Securities and Exchange Commission by the Securities Exchange Act of 1934. The purpose of this act is to eliminate fraud, manipulation and other abuses in the trading of securities, both on the organized exchanges and in the over-the-counter markets. Manipulation is specifically prohibited by the act and the Commission is empowered to adopt rules and regulations to define and prohibit manipulative practices. This statute is closely related to the Securities Act of 1933 and brings under federal regulation the trading of securities after their original issuance. In this connection it requires that brokers and dealers in securities on over-the-counter markets be registered with the Securities and Exchange Commission unless their business is entirely intrastate or exclusively in exempt securities. As of June 30, 1950, a total of 4,000 brokers and dealers were registered with the Commission. In 1938, the Maloney Act, an amendment to the Securities Exchange Act, established the mechanism by which brokers and dealers can organize "national securities associations," to be registered with the Securities and Exchange Commission, for the purpose of self-regulation by agreeing upon and enforcing fair trade practices among the members. To date only one such association has been organized, the National Association of Securities Dealers, with a membership of 2,798 as of August 31, 1950. Membership in the Association at this time is necessary in order to engage in underwriting activities with other members of the Association and to be able to purchase securities from any member at a discount below the price at which they are made available to the public in general.

Investment banking activities have been affected in one way or another by other federal legislation such as the Public Utility Holding Company Act of 1935, the Trust Indenture Act of 1939, the Investment Company Act of 1940 and the Investment Advisers Act of 1940.

In view of the fact that the primary purpose of the Securities Act of 1933 and the Securities Exchange Act of 1934 is the prevention of fraud and manipulation in connection with the issuance and sale of securities, an evaluation of the effectiveness of these acts should be made from that standpoint. This is difficult to do, however, as there is no way of determining the amount of fraudulent securities that would have been issued or the extent to which manipulation would have occurred had these statutes not been operative. Nevertheless, it is interesting to note the extent to which criminal proceedings have been instituted as provided for in these two acts during the 16-fiscal-year-period, 1934–49, and the results thereof as shown in the tabulation on page 411.

The cases covered in these proceedings varied widely in nature and involved fraud in the promotion of new businesses, inventions, and fraternal organizations; fraudulent schemes in connection with the sale of oil and gas interests and mining ventures; fraud perpetrated by brokers

SUMMARY OF CRIMINAL CASES DEVELOPED BY THE COMMISSION [23]

	1934–41	1942–49	Total
Number of cases referred to Department of Justice ..	296	206	532
Number of cases in which indictments were obtained by U.S. attorneys	259	173	432
Number of defendants in indicted cases	1,464	584	2,048
Number of defendants convicted	807	289	1,096
Number of defendants acquitted	182	66	248
Number of defendants as to whom proceedings were dismissed by U.S. attorneys	470	121	591 *
Number of defendants as to whom cases are pending	5	108	113 †
Total	3,483	1,547	5,060

* Includes 41 defendants who died after indictment.
† About half of these are residents of Canada and cannot be extradited.

and dealers in securities and their representatives; frauds in whiskey warehouse receipt transactions; and fraudulent purchases and sales of securities by corporate "insiders." [24] Most of these cases represented operations on the fringe rather than within the central area of investment banking. Generally these frauds were accompanied by the willful avoidance of the registration provisions of the Securities Act of 1933. Other violations presented included the manipulation of the price of stock registered on a national securities exchange, the filing of false reports by a corporation whose securities were registered on such an exchange, and failure to keep required books and records and the filing of false financial statements by registered broker-dealers. By and large, however, these violations involved only a very small percentage of the number and the volume of security issues handled through the investment banking mechanism. When considered in their proper perspective, the number and character of these proceedings over this 16-year period emphasize the fact that the standards of business conduct in the field of investment banking in general are high. Undoubtedly, this legislation and the work of the Securities and Exchange Commission have contributed to making this true.

Suggested Readings

Atkins, W. E., Edwards, G. W., and Moulton, H. G., *The Regulation of the Security Market*. Washington, D.C.: The Brookings Institution, 1946.
Bogen, J. I., "Investment Banking," *Encyclopedia of the Social Sciences*. New York: The Macmillan Company, 1937. Vol. VIII, pp. 268-277.
Burtchett, F. F., and Hicks, C. M., *Corporation Finance*, Revised Edition. New York: Harper & Brothers, 1948. Part IV, Chap. 21 and 24.

---

[23] *Annual Report of the SEC, 1949*, p. 269.
[24] *Ibid.*, p. 163.

Cherrington, H. V., *The Investor and the Securities Act*. Washington, D.C.: American Council on Public Affairs, 1942.

Dewing, A. S., *Financial Policy of Corporations*, 4th Ed. New York: The Ronald Press Company, 1941. Vol. II, Book IV, Chap. 7 and 8.

Dowrie, G. W., and Fuller, D. R., *Investments*. New York: John Wiley & Sons, Inc., 1950. 2nd Ed. Chap. 4 and 5.

Edelman, J. M., *Securities Regulation in the Forty-Eight States*. Chicago: Council of State Governments, 1942.

Fundamentals of Investment Banking. Chicago: Investment Bankers Association of America, 1947.

Guthmann, H. G., and Dougall, H. E., *Corporate Financial Policy*, 2nd Ed. New York: Prentice-Hall, Inc., 1948. Chap. 14.

Hoagland, H. E., *Corporation Finance*, 3rd Ed. New York: McGraw-Hill Book Company, Inc., 1947. Chap. 21 and 23.

Husband, W. H., and Dockeray, J. C., *Modern Corporation Finance*. Chicago: Richard D. Irwin, Inc., 1947. Chap. 20 and 21.

Jome, H. L., *Corporation Finance*. New York: Henry Holt & Company, Inc., 1948. Chap. 22.

McCormick, E. T., *Understanding the Securities Act and the S.E.C.* New York: American Book Company, 1948.

Taylor, W. B., *Financial Policies of Business Enterprise*. New York: D. Appleton-Century Company, Inc., 1942. Chap. 28.

Willis, H. P., and Bogan, J. I., *Investment Banking*, Revised Edition. New York: Harper & Brothers, 1936. Chap. 2, 8, 16, and 22.

15

Investment Banking—Distinctive Features and Recent Developments

by ROGER W. VALENTINE

Halsey, Stuart & Co. Inc.

INVESTMENT BANKING is fundamentally a merchandising business. The primary objective in its structural organization and operation is the purchase and sale of securities. The basic conception upon which the business is conducted, however, is that the investment banker acts as a principal rather than as an agent. In doing so he takes title to the securities he buys and passes title to them when he sells. A clear distinction between acting as a principal and acting as an agent in the purchase or sale of securities is important because a dealer in securities must handle his transactions in keeping with the instructions and understanding of his customer. It is true that in the regular course of business, many strictly investment banking firms frequently handle certain transactions on an agency basis; but generally speaking, these transactions are either incidental or secondary to doing business as a principal. There are firms, however, which regularly do both an investment banking business and a brokerage business. Where this is the case, the distinction between these two types of business needs to be clearly understood. The basic approach to the investment banking business, therefore, rests upon the principle of buying and selling securities for and out of inventory.

As a usual thing, the securities which investment bankers or dealers have available for sale can be divided into two groups: (a) those representing the initial offering of new issues, and (b) those already outstanding that are not a part of an initial offering. There are several sources through which dealers ordinarily can acquire inventory for sale. In the case of new issues, other than United States government obligations, at the time of original offering the primary sources are (1) through partici-

pation as an underwriter in the purchase of the securities direct from the issuer or its fiscal agent; or (2) through purchase from the underwriting group, as a selected dealer; or, (3) as is sometimes possible, the purchase as a dealer direct from a member of the underwriting group or from another dealer. In the case of securities already outstanding, or of new issues after the dissolution of the underwriting group, the primary sources are either other security dealers or various investors offering the securities for sale. The relative importance of these sources of inventory varies as between different firms. Some organizations depend largely upon new issues and the participation in underwriting activities as the primary sources of supply for the securities they buy. On the other hand many dealers rely almost entirely upon being able to purchase securities from other firms or from various investors interested in selling certain holdings.

In general, securities are purchased by investment bankers through the following methods: (1) by subscription to an offering made directly by the issuer or its fiscal agent; (2) by private negotiation between the purchaser and the seller of securities, either directly or through the medium of an agent; (3) by competitive bidding through either sealed bids or auction sales; and (4) through the conversion of warrants or rights which have been acquired. The subscription method is commonly used by the United States government and certain of its instrumentalities in the public offering of securities. Competitive bidding is widely used in the issuance of state and municipal obligations and public utility and railroad securities. In most other instances private negotiation is employed.

The organization of investment banking for the distribution of securities is such as to make it difficult to classify firms on a strictly functional basis. A very small number of houses do largely a wholesale business; they act as syndicate manager and handle the distribution of new issues to a few large institutions and to other dealers in the business. They originate new issues and participate to some extent in other underwriting groups. A larger yet still a limited number of firms do the same type of business, but in addition this group of firms engage in general retail distribution through their own sales representatives. A still larger group participate in the underwriting of new issues but devote their major effort to retail selling. There are a few houses with substantial capital which participate in new underwritings but which do practically no retail selling. They assume the risk in underwriting but depend upon the syndicate manager or dealers who do a retail business to distribute the securities. And there is a very substantial number of small dealers whose capital is inadequate to permit them to originate or participate in the flotation of new issues, but who buy securities from other dealers and from underwriting groups in small blocks for retail distribution.

In addition, there are a limited number of large commercial banks which underwrite and distribute state and municipal obligations.

There is also a wide variation in the kind of securities handled by different firms. Some specialize in stock issues, others in bonds, and a third group distributes both stocks and bonds. Some firms deal only in high grade general market issues while others concentrate on the lesser known types of securities. There are those who distribute securities on a nation-wide basis, and there are the small dealers whose market is in a local area. Much of the same type of variation exists in the capital of various firms. Some operate almost on a shoe string, while others have large capital resources amounting to several millions of dollars for a single firm. The combined capital funds of investment banking firms today probably are in excess of 500 million dollars, a sum which is currently adequate for the needs of the business at the moment but might not be under other circumstances. All told this network of distributing organizations constitutes a highly developed mechanism through which the flow of investment capital is maintained.

In this connection several other distinctive features of the investment banking business are to be noted which distinguish it from most other forms of merchandising activity. For instance, the character of the merchandise is entirely different from that generally handled in other kinds of business. Most commodities, for example, possess certain tangible qualities which have much to do with the determination of their value. This is not true, however, of securities. Here the element of value rests upon a group of intangible qualities largely in the form of various rights which have evolved from custom, tradition, laws, court decisions, and the actions of corporate and governmental officials or directors.[1] It is these rights embodied in such instruments as stocks, bonds, notes, and debentures which constitute the merchandise that is bought and sold by the investment banker. It is entirely different from that of other commodities. Another feature is that these instruments for the most part are readily negotiable, and many of them are in bearer form. Also the unit value in each transaction is usually larger than in most other types of business, and the transaction is generally handled on a cash rather than a credit basis. And particularly important is the extent to which state and federal regulations are controlling factors in determining the nature and character of the form of merchandising activity employed in the investment banking business. As a consequence of various regulatory requirements, a relatively high degree of standardization in procedure has become a

---

[1] A. S. Dewing, *Financial Policy of Corporations*, 4th Ed., Vol. II. New York: The Ronald Press Company, 1941, p. 1164.

significant element in the purchase and sale of securities. A final feature to be noted is the extent to which the purchase and sale of security issues, particularly at the time of issuance, are undertaken by investment bankers in association or cooperation with one another through formal agreements relating to matters of common action. These agreements, frequently referred to as underwriting or syndicate agreements, are a form of contract (a) as between the several purchasers or underwriters covering the purchase of an issue of securities, and (b) as between the purchasers or underwriters and the selling dealers covering the sale of an issue. They are drawn in each instance to cover an undertaking relating to a single or separate issue of securities and vary in detail so as to meet the specific requirements of each particular situation. To a large measure, these agreements set forth the conditions which control the actual purchase and offering for sale of an issue of securities when acquired by more than a single underwriter, or when offered for sale through a selling group. They are a means of providing for a closely defined form of cooperation in a highly competitive undertaking. They are a distinctive feature of the investment banking business characteristic of no other type of merchandising activity.

Several factors have contributed to the development of this method of operation. The most significant, perhaps, are the size of many issues offered in the market and the need for diversifying the risk element entailed on the part of individual firms in the underwriting and merchandising of securities. A great many issues which come into the market are larger than a single firm in most instances can handle. The assistance of other firms in the undertaking, therefore, is necessary. Furthermore, too heavy a concentration of risk in any single issue is dangerous. Only by keeping the investment in any single issue within a reasonable relationship to the capital of a firm and then participating in a' broad list of issues can the risk factor in merchandising securities be kept at a minimum. It has been primarily with this objective in view that the practice of syndicating security issues has developed.

In the years prior to the passage of the Securities Act of 1933, a wide variety of arrangements prevailed in connection with the practice of investment bankers of purchasing and selling securities in conjunction with one another. Some of these arrangements were simple in form and involved very few firms; others were more complex and included a large number of houses. In its simplest form two or more firms together would purchase an issue and sell it. In other instances one group would purchase the issue, but a much larger group would be organized in connection with the sale of the issue. It frequently was the practice to have one or more larger groups set up in between the small original group of pur-

chasers and the final selling group.[2] Often included in these intermediate groups were large commercial banks having bond departments or affiliates and investment houses with large sales organizations. Each group would purchase the issue from the preceding group at a step up in price. From the standpoint of the original purchase group, these intermediate groups provided a means of spreading the financial risk involved.

The profit margin involved was sufficient to permit this type of arrangement, and the number of members of the usual original underwriting group was small. But since the enactment of the Securities Act of 1933, the formation of these intermediate groups has practically disappeared, largely because securities subject to the act cannot be sold legally before the effective date of the registration statement. A public offering immediately after the effective date of the registration statement tends to eliminate the need or advantage of an intermediate group. The increased size of underwriting groups as original purchasers of securities is also a factor, for the risk spreading function of the intermediate group is provided in this manner. Another reason is the smaller margin of profit, especially on bond issues. The margin that would be available to an intermediate group is an insufficient inducement for assuming the liabilities of an underwriter under the Securities Act. Under another set of conditions, however, this type of group might appear more often.

The importance of the types of agreements used in the purchase and sale of securities by investment bankers today warrants a more detailed consideration of them. Before doing so, however, reference should be made to the confusion of terminology which permeates this subject, particularly in the use of the terms "syndicate," "group," "joint account," and "account." All these terms carry a variety of connotations and have been used in different ways. Sometimes the terms are used interchangeably and other times with a fine degree of technical meaning. Efforts at standardization of meaning, however, have never been very successful and "street" usage generally has been to employ the broader rather than the more technical interpretation of these terms. Since the early 1930's, however, the use of the terms "group" and "account" has increased somewhat, in the belief that the element of severalty is more clearly indicated than is the case with the term "syndicate" when employed in connection with the purchase and sale of securities. But the terms are still used interchangeably in many instances, and no clear line of distinction is made between them. Custom and inertia, perhaps, largely account for this. But another reason is that the legal aspects of the matter have never been fully tested or clearly defined in court decisions.

[2] For a detailed description of the organization and operation of these groups, see Arthur Galston, *Security Syndicate Operations*. New York: The Ronald Press Company, 1928.

Agreement Among Underwriters

As a result of the standardization of syndicate procedure which has occurred in recent years, the primary groups organized today in connection with the purchase and sale of securities are the underwriting group and the selling group. The agreement drawn relating to the underwriting group is usually called the agreement among underwriters or the agreement among purchasers. It is an agreement in form between each purchaser and every other purchaser in the account, and between each purchaser and the manger or representative of the group covering the points of common action in connection with the purchase of a given issue of securities. In some instances the agreement is simple and concise; in other instances it is more involved and in greater detail, depending upon the nature and character of the transaction covered by it. Among the items usually covered in the agreement are the amount of participation of each member; the nature of the liability assumed; the good faith deposit required and the manner in which it is to be provided; the allocation of expenses; the manner and form of payment and delivery of the securities; the effective date and termination of the agreement; the authority given the manager or representative in acting for the members of the group and the compensation to be paid for such services; the matter of legal opinions where they are involved; provisions relative to price stabilization operations if authorized; and several other essential details.

Because of the wide variety of securities which are issued by corporate and governmental units, special provisions will be found in the agreements to cover conditions that are peculiar to a given type of security or are applicable only to some unusual feature related to the issuance of the security being purchased. For instance, agreements relating to the purchase of municipal obligations or equipment trust certificates having serial maturities will differ in detail from those covering single maturity issues. The same is true as regards corporate securities that must be registered under the Securities Act as compared with those not subject to registration. Agreements covering the purchase of securities at competitive bidding will differ somewhat from those acquired through private negotiation.

An interesting development in recent years in connection with the formation of underwriting groups has been the emphasis which has been placed upon the element of severalty in the agreement. Prior to the passage of the Securities Act of 1933, somewhat the opposite situation existed. Syndicate accounts frequently were organized and operated on a joint and several basis with the element of joint liability recognized. Since 1933, however, underwriting accounts covering corporate issues

have been set up for the most part on the basis that each member of the account participates separately and not jointly in the purchase and sale of the issue and that no joint liability exists as between them. This is shown in the fact that the purchase agreement with the issuer is drawn as between each participating member severally and the issuer; the agreement among purchasers is drawn as between each member severally and the manager or representative of the several purchasers. By acting severally in the purchase and sale of the securities, certain financial liabilities can be limited to the amount of participation in the account; whereas, in acting jointly, the liability assumed by each member would be the total amount of the issue. To some degree at least, the drawing of underwriting agreements on a several basis is a recognition of the practical limitations of joint liability in large issues on the part of participants with limited capital resources. There are other reasons for the several account that are more concrete: they are the elimination of dual transfer taxes and the limiting of liabilities under the Securities Act.

There is one point, however, which is common to practically all underwriting group agreements. Each participant has a definite or determinable commitment in the account. As to the matter of liability, under the commitment there are two basic types. One is the unlimited liability account, frequently called an undivided account, and the other is the limited liability, or divided account. The distinction between them is fundamentally important. In the unlimited liability account, the liability is not extinguished until the account is entirely closed out. In other words each member has a continuing liability, on a proportionate basis, in the unsold balance in the account so long as it is open. On the other hand, in the limited liability account each member can discharge his liability at any time by taking down from the account the remaining amount of his commitment. This feature of the divided account is particularly attractive to underwriters who have the facilities to distribute securities effectively, for they can discharge their liability through their selling efforts. But the divided account does not appeal to underwriters who do not have well established facilities for selling securities. The divided account is generally employed in the sale of corporate securities with a single maturity. The undivided account, however, has certain definite advantages in connection with issues having serial maturities, particularly when some maturities may be more attractive marketwise than others, as is generally the case. The undivided account prevents some members from being able to discharge their liabilities by readily selling or taking down the attractive maturities and leaving the less attractive maturities to the other members of the account, for each member has a continuing liability in the unsold portion of each maturity at all times. With an issue having serial maturities there are times when

the advantages of both the divided and the undivided account can be utilized. The result is an agreement providing for undivided liability in some respects and divided liability in other respects. The undivided liability account is widely used in the municipal field and with certain corporate securities having serial maturities, such as railroad equipment trust certificates.

Selling Group Agreement

As has been indicated in the above discussion, the members of an underwriting group may sell the securities purchased without forming another group of dealers to assist in distributing the issue. This is the usual practice in the municipal business and occasionally so in the corporate field when the demand for an issue is quite strong, or the size of the issue is small. But as a rule in the distribution of corporate securities, a selling group is utilized. When a selling group is organized an agreement is drawn between the members of the underwriting group as the purchasers and the selected dealers constituting the selling group. Part or all of the members of the underwriting group may become members of the selling group as well. This agreement covers the terms of the public offering, the concession to be allowed to dealers, and the reallowance, if any, which can be made to other dealers or brokers. The terms and conditions of payment will also be included as well as a provision for supplying copies of the prospectus in reasonable quantities, if one is required. Likewise, provisions relative to the termination of the agreement, the relationship of the selected dealers to the purchasers, and the right to reject or allot all subscriptions received will be included. In the case of registered issues a copy of the prospectus usually accompanies the invitation to join the selling group. Two types of invitations are extended to the selected dealers. One type offers the dealer an allotment of a specific amount of the securities subject to acceptance by a certain specified time. Acceptance of the allotment is equivalent to purchase and becomes a definite commitment by the dealer. In the other type the dealer is merely offered the privilege of subscribing for and purchasing a part of the issue, but the subscription is subject to rejection in whole or in part or to allotment at the discretion of the representative of the several underwriters.

Purchase Agreement

Besides the agreements already mentioned there is a third one to which attention should be directed. It is the purchase contract or purchase agreement as between the members of the underwriting group and the issuer of the securities. In the case of corporate issues subject to regis-

tration, this agreement is a carefully drawn and detailed legal document dealing with all aspects of the purchase and delivery of the securities. It sets forth among other things the time, place, and method of payment and delivery of the securities along with an enumeration of certain conditions that must be fulfilled by the company prior to the time of actual purchase. Also included are various covenants of the company to supply specified information and data necessary to meet the requirements of the Securities Act in connection with the sale of any of the securities after issuance. Certain warranties and representations by all parties to the contract that information furnished by them for use in the registration statement or prospectus is not untrue or misleading are likewise included, as well as indemnity agreements connected therewith. The agreement also contains provisions relating to the conditions under which the contract might be terminated and provisions covering any unusual aspects of the issue.

Prior to the enactment of the Securities Act of 1933, most purchase agreements once signed were positive commitments as far as market conditions were concerned. It was customary procedure in those days to sign an underwriting contract with the issuing corporation sometime in advance of the public offering. Experiences after the market crash in 1929 and with the 20-day waiting period provision under the Securities Act, brought into vogue the practice of including in the purchase agreement a "market out" clause providing that the agreement could be terminated by the underwriting group prior to public offering of the securities in case certain unfavorable conditions developed. The purpose of such a clause is to protect the underwriters from having to assume certain risks beyond their control and of such a nature to impair seriously the market for the issue. Risks coming under this category would include the development of adverse market conditions from some such cause as a declaration of war, the closing of the stock exchanges, or a general bank moratorium. Other "out" clauses running generally until the delivery date are based on important and adverse changes in the affairs of the company. In only a very few instances, however, has any underwriting group ever made use of such clauses.

Contracts covering the purchase of railroad securities are usually less involved, for the securities do not have to be registered under the Securities Act. Furthermore, the Interstate Commerce Commission has regulatory authority over the issuance of securities by the railroads. Contracts covering the purchase of new issues of railroad securities, therefore, normally are based upon the company's obtaining approval of the Commission to issue the securities.

State and municipal obligations generally are purchased subject to the legal opinion of certain recognized attorneys who make a specialty of

this type of work. The essential details relating to the legality of an issue are covered in a legal opinion, and these obligations generally are not accepted as good delivery unless accompanied by such an opinion in final and unqualified form. In a published invitation for bids on an issue of securities, the conditions of sale usually are set forth and bids submitted in accordance with them. In some instances, however, the offer to purchase will be based upon certain conditions stated in the bid. The acceptance of a bid (either by a financial officer having such authority or by formal action of the governing body) results in a contractual agreement. A good faith deposit generally must accompany a bid and it tends to strengthen the status of the contract when a bid is accepted.

TABLE 1

METHOD OF DISTRIBUTION OF SECURITIES FOR CASH SALE
FOR ACCOUNT OF ISSUERS [3]

September 1, 1934–June 30, 1949

Method of Distribution *	1935–39	Five Fiscal Years, Inclusive 1940–44 (In thousands of dollars)	1945–49
Through invest. bankers	$10,826,739	$6,008,008	$18,981,176
By purchase and resale	8,899,612	5,108,852	15,742,378
On best-effort basis	1,927,126	899,156	3,238,799
By issuers	798,899	803,655	3,267,542
Total	$11,625,637	$6,811,664	$22,248,717

* Based on registrations fully effective under the Securities Act of 1933.

The character of the contract involved in a purchase agreement depends upon the type of commitment assumed by the underwriters. As a rule, they come under one of three general types commonly designated as a firm, a stand-by, or a best-effort commitment. In what is known as a firm commitment the underwriters agree to purchase an entire issue of securities outright. A stand-by commitment is one in which the underwriters agree to purchase any portion of an issue not otherwise absorbed. Such an issue is offered first to the present security holders, usually through subscription or exchange rights. So far as the potential liability of the underwriters is concerned, this is a firm commitment. But whether or not an actual purchase of the securities will ensue depends upon there being an unsubscribed balance of the issue on a specified date. If there is such a balance, the underwriters take it up. In the best-effort commitment the underwriters agree to use their best efforts to sell the securities but the underwriters assume no risk or liability in connection with any unsold portion of the issue. Here the issuer carries the risk that the se-

[3] *Annual Report of the Securities and Exchange Commission, 1949,* p. 204.

curities are not satisfactorily marketed. In reality, this type of commitment is a form of agency agreement. Occasionally the firm and the best-effort commitments are combined in an underwriting agreement.

The relative importance of the firm commitment as compared with the best-effort method of distributing securities is indicated in Table 1. The use of the best-effort method has been primarily in connection with the issuance and sale of common stocks and various types of certificates of participation.

Management of Underwriting Accounts

Diversification of risk and enlistment of selling strength by joint action through the medium of an underwriting account in the purchase and sale of securities are the keystones of the investment banking business as it is conducted today. The successful functioning of this system of underwriting and distributing securities centers in the effective coordination and direction of the work which is involved in the management of an underwriting account. This work is exacting and frequently extends over a protracted period of time. Every phase of it requires the exercise of seasoned judgment as well as a prodigious amount of routine activity. Far from being a perfunctory job, as those unfamiliar with its numerous ramifications might think, the management of an underwriting account is a highly technical operation which only a well trained and experienced organization can properly discharge. Consequently, a relatively small number of firms which have specialized over the years in originating new issues, organizing underwriting accounts, and directing the public offering of securities regularly act in this capacity in connection with the larger issues. To a large degree, the work these firms do in this connection constitutes what might be called a hub around which the investment banking business revolves. Included in this group are a few large metropolitan banks whose activities by law are limited to handling certain state and municipal obligations.

One important phase of the work of these investment banking firms precedes the actual issuance of securities and is more or less advisory in character. It is common practice for the management of a corporation or officials of a municipality to obtain the ideas and advice of investment bankers regarding a proposed piece of financing. Being in close touch with the market and having had a broad experience in handling different types of issues, these firms are in a position to assist an issuer on many important questions of policy and procedure relative to the issuance of securities. Consultations of this kind, therefore, are a very important aspect of their activities in this business. When an issue is being set up and prepared for public offering, there are many technical points

in connection with it which must be settled and agreed upon by the issuer and the representative of the underwriters. Matters such as the type of issue, the protective provisions to be incorporated in a bond or preferred stock, the call price or the basis for determining it, conversion privileges, sinking fund provisions, the maturity, and the dividend or coupon rate are typical items of this kind. Here again consultations and negotiations in connection with such matters are a regular part of the work of a firm which manages underwriting accounts. In some instances, where special problems are involved, firms of this kind are retained by an issuer as financial adviser on such matters.

Another important phase of the work of these investment banking houses is the formation of underwriting groups which they in turn manage. Their activities in this respect are particularly significant in connection with the flotation of large issues of securities which they either acquire through private negotiation or bid for in competitive sales. Although it is not always clearly defined or rigidly drawn, there is a fairly definite degree of specialization in the type and kinds of securities which these various firms handle. As a consequence a high degree of technical proficiency in the organization and management of underwriting accounts of this type is evident. This is brought out in the manner in which such accounts are formed. A careful effort is always made to bring together in an account a group of houses capable of carrying the financial risk involved and at the same time able to accomplish an effective distribution of the securities. The choice of members, therefore, involves serious and careful consideration of all who have expressed an interest in participating in the account, as well as the selection of other dealers who are known through past performance to be interested in such issues and whose participation will give strength to the account. To choose effectively from a large number who may aspire to positions in an attractive account, or to build up a strong representative group in a dubious or desultory market, calls for an intimate familiarity with the financial position and distributing ability of a large number of firms in all sections of the country. Experience in evaluating matters of this kind is a very important element in building up a properly balanced underwriting account. This is true with small accounts, as well as large ones, and with municipal as much as with corporate accounts.

A third phase of the work done by these investment banking firms is related to the management of an underwriting account. It is the firm's duty as a manager to act as the representative of the members of the account in all matters pertaining to the preparation and public offering of an issue. This duty often involves a large amount of detailed work. Among other things, for instance, it is necessary as a rule for the manager of an account to: (1) examine carefully all documents and papers relat-

ing to the issue and, in some cases, to assist in preparing them; (2) supply each member with copies of the essential papers; (3) keep members advised of any important changes or developments regarding the issue and to answer inquiries concerning them; (4) make, at times, an examination of the physical properties of the issuer; (5) request qualification of the securities, where necessary, under the laws of various states in which members of the account are registered dealers; (6) prepare a statistical comparison of the issue with other similar issues for use in price meetings; (7) obtain, in the case of registered issues, certain data from all underwriters in the account concerning their relationship, if any, with the issuer or trustee; (8) obtain from counsel, if needed, an opinion regarding the legality of the issue for purchase by savings banks, trust funds, and life insurance companies; (9) negotiate the purchase price with the issuer in a privately negotiated issue; (10) attend price meetings and assume leadership in determining both the bid price and the public offering price on issues sold competitively; (11) make offerings to certain special accounts and selected dealers at the time of public offering; (12) arrange settlement with the issuer and make delivery of securities to underwriters, dealers, and special accounts; and (13) make a final accounting to members of the account after its termination. The volume of work involved in each instance will depend upon the nature of the individual issue, the size of the underwriting account, and many special factors of one kind or another.

In connection with the underwriting and distribution of an issue of securities, a great many matters arise which cannot be anticipated and covered specifically in the agreement among underwriters. In the agreement, therefore, the representative of the underwriters usually is given full authority to take such action as may be deemed necessary or advisable in respect to all matters pertaining to the underwriting agreement, the purchase contract, and all offerings and sale of the securities. As a consequence, the manager of an underwriting account must exercise his discretion on many points which arise during the time the underwriting agreement is in effect. It is in connection with the use of this discretionary authority, as well as other matters of judgment based upon experience in managing underwriting accounts, that the success or failure of the flotation of an issue of securities is sometimes determined.

The manager of an underwriting group may or may not receive specific compensation for the services rendered in managing the account. Prior to the passage of the Securities Act of 1933, it was common practice for the manager of an underwriting group to rely upon the profit margin available as an original underwriter for compensation for management of an account. The prestige of heading an account and the value of the publicity it afforded were added compensation for the work

of management. To a large degree this is still true today as regards the management of municipal accounts. But with corporate securities, for the most part, this is no longer the case; it is now a common practice for the manager of an underwriting account to receive compensation in the form of a management fee. On bond issues, the fee is usually established either as a fixed percentage of the par value of the issue or as a percentage of the gross spread between the purchase price and the public offering price. Either system may be used on a negotiated issue, whereas the percentage of gross method is customary on competitive issues. Currently it may run ⅛ or ¼ of 1 per cent of the par value, or up to 10 per cent of the gross spread, on negotiated issues, as against 5 per cent of the gross on competitive issues. On stock issues the management fee is usually a stated amount per share; this amount depends upon the price and the margin of profit per share.

Recent Developments in Investment Banking

As was pointed out in the preceding chapter, conditions in the investment banking business changed rapidly after the collapse of the speculative boom in 1929. The entire economic and social structure of the country was disrupted by the depression which followed. Doubt and uncertainty regarding the future quickly replaced the excessive optimism that had prevailed during the years prior to the 1929 crash. As a consequence a tremendous decline in the demand for new capital on the part of business enterprises set in at once. The extent of this decline and its significance from an investment banking standpoint are evident from the fact that the total volume of corporate new capital issues brought out during the four-year period 1932–35 inclusive, amounted to only a little more than one billion dollars. This was less than 5 per cent of the amount of such securities issued during the years 1926–29 inclusive. Although conditions improved somewhat during the next few years, it was not until after the end of World War II in 1945 that a substantial revival of new capital financing occurred. During the four years, 1946–49, as shown in Table 2, the total volume of corporate new capital issues was more than 19 billion dollars, an amount almost as large as for the four years 1926–29.

During the depression a combination of factors such as the existence of idle capital funds, the rise of large excess bank reserves and the premium investors placed upon security and liquidity brought about a general downward movement in interest rates. This in turn made possible the refunding of a large volume of securities on a lower yield basis prior to World War II. Governmental control of the money market and the fiscal policies of the Treasury during and immediately after the war

caused a further easing of interest rates and more refunding operations. As a result, during the period 1932–49, a total of 27.5 billion dollars of corporate securities were issued for refunding purposes, as compared to 28.5 billion dollars of corporate new capital issues. This large volume of refunding was a very significant factor in keeping many investment banking firms in business during the years 1935–45.

TABLE 2

CORPORATE, STATE AND MUNICIPAL ISSUES, 1932–49 [4]

(Millions of dollars)

Year	New Capital Issues		Refunding Issues	
	Corporate	State and Municipal	Corporate	State and Municipal
1932	326	762	318	87
1933	161	483	218	37
1934	177	836	311	106
1935	403	854	1,863	365
1936	1,192	734	3,385	382
1937	1,224	711	1,208	191
1938	872	971	1,266	129
1939	383	938	1,727	189
1940	736	751	2,026	482
1941	1,062	518	1,555	434
1942	624	342	416	181
1943	375	175	685	259
1944	651	235	2,468	404
1945	1,263	471	4,937	324
1946	3,556	952	2,952	208
1947	4,795	2,228	1,480	44
1948	5,929	2,604	284	82
1949	4,843	2,803	414	104
Totals	28,572	17,368	27,513	4,008

Somewhat the same pattern also applies to the issuance of state and municipal obligations since 1932 (see Table 2). During the depression years, the volume of new capital issues was sustained to a considerable degree because of the financing of unemployment relief. But in the postwar years, revenue bonds and soldier bonus issues have been important factors in the large increase in volume of new capital issues. For the four years following the war, new capital issues totaled about 8.6 billion dollars. This was approximately one-half of the total for the entire period 1932–49. The volume of refunding issues for the most part has been relatively small.

A comparative summary of the total capital flotations in this country during the 13-year period 1919–31 and the 18-year period 1932–49 is

---

[4] Compiled from figures published by *The Commercial and Financial Chronicle.*

TABLE 3

CAPITAL FLOTATIONS IN THE U.S.[5]

(Millions of dollars)

Type	1919–31		1932–49	
	New Capital	Refunding	New Capital	Refunding
Domestic Corporate				
Bonds	26,612	8,284	21,448	24,363
Preferred Stock	7,373	954	3,466	2,766
Common Stock	11,795	1,272	3,658	384
Total ·	45,780	10,510	28,572	27,513
State and Municipal Obligations.	15,652	327	17,368	4,008
Farm Loan and Government Agencies Obligations	1,863	300	5,145 *	10,466 *
Foreign Obligations †	10,293	1,911	890	1,411
Total	73,588	13,048	51,975	43,398

* Includes certain government guaranteed obligations.
† Includes Canadian securities.

shown in Table 3. The relative importance of new capital issues in comparison with refunding issues in the two periods is evident, as well as the relative significance of corporate financing in relation to the other types shown. These figures give some indication of the general character of the investment banking business during the two periods. Corporate preferred and common stock issues represented about 26 per cent of the total volume of new capital issues in the 1919–31 period and about 14 per cent in the 1932–49 period.

Expansion of the Institutional Market

One very significant development in the investment banking business since 1933 has been the change which has occurred in the relative importance of the major investment outlets for new security issues. In the preceding chapter reference was made to the fact that one of the direct results of the Liberty Loan campaigns in connection with the financing of World War I was a vast increase in the individual ownership of securities. During the decade following that war, the private investor and country bank market were cultivated intensively and attained a position comparable with the eastern institutional market as sources of investment funds. But the devastating effects of the market crash in 1929 and the years of depression which followed, together with high taxes, a decline in interest rates, and the financing of huge Treasury deficits through the sale of government securities, practically eliminated the private investor,

---

[5] Compiled from figures published by *The Commercial and Financial Chronicle.*

the commercial banks, and the savings banks as active factors in the market for corporate securities until after World War II. Some restoration of the private investor market has been attained in stocks since the war, but the low yields available on most corporate bonds have prevented any broadening of this phase of the market among individual investors.

In contrast to this decline of the private investor as an outlet for corporate bonds has been the increased significance of certain institutional outlets such as insurance companies, pension funds, trust accounts, and, to some extent since the war, commercial banks and savings banks. Particularly important in this respect has been the phenomenal growth of the financial resources of the life insurance companies since 1933. For instance, the combined resources of these institutions increased from $20,896,000,000 on December 31, 1933, to $59,280,000,000 on December 31, 1949. This is a gain of over $38,000,000,000 in 16 years. This increase is shown in Table 4 concerning the type of assets and the change in holdings during the prewar years 1934–41, the war years 1942–45, and the postwar years 1946–49. It will be noted that the increase in the holdings of securities of business and industrial enterprises during the three periods combined totaled over $17,000,000,000. This amount is equivalent to approximately 60 per cent of the total of corporate new capital issues during this period. Most of this increase was in the securities of public utility, commercial and industrial enterprises. Stocks represent a little more than 5 per cent of the amount, and bonds represent the remaining portion.

TABLE 4

CHANGES IN ASSETS OF U.S. LIFE INSURANCE COMPANIES [6]

(In millions of dollars)

	1934–41	1942–45	1946–49	Net Increase 1934–49
U.S. Government Securities	5,816	13,889	− 5,391	14,314
Foreign Government, State, Provincial, and Local Bonds	1,259	− 742	1,143	1,660
Securities of Business and Industry	4,862	963	11,404	17,226
Mortgages	− 254	208	6,256	6,210
Real Estate, Policy Loans, and Miscellaneous Assets	152	− 2,252	1,071	− 1,029
Total Net Increase	11,835	12,066	14,483	38,384

Not available are similar figures covering pension funds, trust estates, and other institutional outlets. Estimates of the increase in corporate security holdings of such outlets, however, indicate that perhaps as much

[6] Based upon data published by Institute of Life Insurance.

as 90 per cent or more of the new issues of corporate bonds issued since 1933 ultimately became a part of the portfolio of institutional investors. The large supply of funds from institutional sources seeking investment in such media has been an important factor in reducing the rate of interest during these years. At the same time, the decline in interest rates was a significant element in the withdrawal of the individual investor from the corporate bond market and in channeling vast quantities of corporate obligations into institutional portfolios.

Private Placements

During this period another development that is highly significant from an investment banking standpoint has been the growth of the private placement of bond issues with a single purchaser or with a small group of purchasers. For the most part, these placements have been with insurance companies—sometimes with the assistance of an investment banker, in other instances without it. In both cases, however, the procedure involves a purchase of the securities by the buyer directly from the issuer and either eliminates all of the functions of investment banking or embodies only certain services by a single firm.

The direct private placement of securities was relatively unimportant prior to 1933. It has been estimated, for instance, that only about 3 per cent of all corporate bonds distributed between 1900 and 1933 were sold in this manner.[7] Following the passage of the Securities Act of 1933, however, both the number and the volume of corporate bond issues placed privately with insurance companies or other institutions rapidly increased. Between July 1, 1934, and June 30, 1949, a total of about $15 billion of new corporate securities offered for cash sale were placed privately, of which approximately 98 per cent were bonds and 2 per cent were stocks. Almost $9 billion of this amount, or nearly 60 per cent, were issued during the last four years of this period. Private placement of corporate bonds since 1933 has amounted to about 35 per cent of the combined total of new capital and refunding bond issues. As shown in Table 5, industrial securities have constituted the largest percentage of private placements.

There are several reasons for this growth of private placements. From the standpoint of the issuer, the most widely expressed reason is the opportunity afforded to save the effort and expense incident to registering an issue under the Securities Act and to making a public offering. Also important, in many instances, is the 20-day waiting period normally required before the registration statement becomes effective. Another rea-

---

[7] H. G. Fraine, "Direct Sale of Security Issues," *Journal of the American Association of University Teachers of Insurance*, Vol. XVI, No. 1, p. 40.

TABLE 5

PRIVATE PLACEMENTS OF CORPORATE SECURITIES [8]

(Estimated gross proceeds in thousands of dollars)

Type of Issue	June 30 1934–45 Amount	Per Cent	June 30 1946–49 Amount	Per Cent	Total Amount	Per Cent
Industrial	2,735	44.6	6,033	67,1	8,768	58.0
Public Utility	2,796	45.7	1,967	21.9	4,763	31.5
Railroad	234	3.8	61	.7	295	2.0
Real Estate and Financial	361	5.9	927	10.3	1,288	8.5
Totals	6,126	100.0	8,988	100.0	15,114	100.0

son undoubtedly is a desire to avoid the liabilities the Act imposes on the issuer and its directors and principal officers for untrue or misleading or incomplete statements in a registration statement. A fourth reason centers in the position of the institutional purchaser during these years. The tremendous increase in the volume of funds which these institutions have to invest has induced considerable competition among them in the search for investment outlets. The initiative they have taken in negotiating for the purchase of whole issues of securities has been a very important factor in promoting the growth of private placements.[9] The personal considerations involved and the exemption from registration make the procedure an easy one to carry out.

The advantages of private placement to the issuer in many respects may be more apparent than real, and temporary rather than long term. For example, some of the expense and effort incident to the preparation of an issue for public offering is also necessary in preparing an issue for private placement. The expense to the purchaser of negotiating and acquiring an issue by private placement usually is passed back to the issuer in one way or another and will absorb a part of the indicated savings of the costs of a public offering. The purchaser generally tries to obtain a buying advantage at least equal to a part of the savings resulting from an avoidance of registration. Savings at the time of issuance may be more than offset later, because of the inability of the issuer to take advantage of changes in market conditions in acquiring securities for sinking fund or other purposes. (As a practical matter, the actual savings that may be derived in the private placement of an issue of securities compared with a public offering cannot be definitely determined at the

[8] Annual Report of the Securities and Exchange Commission 1949, p. 212.

[9] For a discussion from the viewpoint of the purchaser, see: Rogers Churchill, "Purchase By Life Insurance Companies of Securities Privately Offered," Harvard Law Review, Vol. 52 (March 1939), p. 773; S. C. Badger, "Private Placements—A New Medium of Financing," Com. & Fin. Chronicle, Oct. 14, 1948, p. 15.

time of issuance. The intangible elements involved often are the determining factor.)

Although the advantages of private placement to the issuer may appear to be greater than will ultimately prove to be the case, the fact remains, nevertheless, that such advantages have seemed sufficiently important in recent years to cause this method of issuance to be used extensively. The advantages of private placement, however, accrue primarily to the issuer and to the purchaser. To the investment banker and other institutional investors, private placement on a large scale is a distinct disadvantage in that it reduces the number and volume of issues publicly offered. Over a period of time this reduction can result in the concentration of a large volume of the better grade issues in the portfolios of a very limited number of institutions. A trend of this kind can have widespread implications as regards the adequacy of proper diversification in the investment portfolios of smaller financial institutions.[10] The strength and permanency of our system of private financial enterprise rest upon maintaining a reasonable balance in the competitive position of these institutions. This is true relative to investment outlets as well as other phases of operation.

Since the advantages of private placement to the issuer center primarily in the exemption from registration under the Securities Act, the question has been raised whether this exemption should be continued, since it discriminates against the public offering of securities. In the case of small issues no serious problem is involved. But in the case of large general market issues, the situation is quite different. Making private placements of this type of issue subject to the registration provisions of the Securities Act, the same as issues publicly offered, would help to equalize the competitive aspects of this problem. Fundamentally, this is the most important phase of the subject, for the whole question of exemption goes much beyond the matter of certain savings in cost and effort to the issuer.

Competitive Bidding

Next to the inauguration of federal regulation of the securities business, the most important development in recent years in investment banking has been the extension and growth of competitive bidding in the sale of new security issues. In this method of sale it is customary to advertise in advance the time, date and place at which bids will be received for an issue of securities and to state the conditions of sale. Upon receipt of bids at the designated time, the issue is sold to the bidder offering the most advantageous bid in keeping with the terms of sale. Usually, the issuer reserves the right to reject all bids if those submitted are not con-

---

[10] Some of these institutions have already expressed complaints to this effect.

sidered satisfactory. This method of sale is in contrast to the privately negotiated method in which an issue is sold by direct negotiation between the issuer and the purchaser, to the exclusion, in most instances, of other possible purchasers.

Competitive bidding has been utilized in the sale of state and municipal securities for many years and is the commonly accepted practice today. In the case of corporate securities, however, competitive bidding on an extensive scale is a comparatively recent development, although there are instances of its use dating back many years. The statutes of Massachusetts, for example, since 1870 have provided that, with certain exceptions, capital stock of gas and electric companies not taken by shareholders pursuant to their pre-emptive rights shall be sold through competitive bidding.[11] In 1919 Massachusetts also enacted a statute to the effect that such companies in issuing bonds shall invite proposals for the purchase thereof by advertisement in certain newspapers.[12] In 1918 and 1928 the Indiana Public Service Commission required certain public utility companies to sell their securities through competitive bidding.[13] Since 1926 the Interstate Commerce Commission has generally insisted upon competitive bidding in the sale of railroad equipment trust certificates.[14] In 1935 the District of Columbia Public Utilities Commission and the New Hampshire Public Service Commission adopted orders requiring competitive bidding.[15] And in 1939 the Federal Power Commission applied a rule to the few public utility companies under its jurisdiction.[16]

Up to this point competitive bidding on corporate securities, other than equipment trust certificates, was distinctly limited in scope and still in an experimental stage of development. This procedure was greatly extended, however, in 1941 when the Securities and Exchange Commission adopted what is known as Rule U-50 requiring, with certain exceptions, competitive bidding in the sale of securities by corporations subject to the Public Utility Holding Company Act of 1935.[17] A further extension of this procedure occurred in 1944, when the Interstate Commerce Commission, after a hearing on the matter, took the position that competitive bidding, with certain exceptions, should be required as a

---

[11] Mass. Public Acts 1870, Chap. 179 (cited in Dewing, *op. cit.*, Vol. II, p. 1108).

[12] Mass. G. L. (Ter. Ed.) Chap. 164, Sec. 15. This law was amended by Chap. 393, of the Acts of 1950, to include notes and debentures as well as bonds.

[13] Re Hydro Electric Light & Power, P.U.R. 1918 A. 325; Re Citizens Gas Co., P.U.R. 1928 C. 354. Competitive bidding was also required in 1946, Indianapolis Power & Light Co., Decision No. 18106 of the Public Service Commission of Indiana, March 29, 1946.

[14] Western Maryland Equipment Trust, Series D, 111 I.C.C. 434, June 23, 1926.

[15] Re Issuance and Sale of Securities, 12 P.U.R. (N.S.) 9. Re Public Service Company of New Hampshire, 12 P.U.R. (N.S.) 408.

[16] Federal Power Commission Order No. 62, (1939).

[17] Securities and Exchange Commission, Holding Company Act, Release No. 2676, April 7, 1941.

condition to its approval of the sale of railroad securities, and that railroads applying for authority to issue securities would be expected to observe these findings.[18] In 1946 the then California Railroad Commission, which has jurisdiction in California with respect to the issuance of public utility securities, adopted a competitive bidding rule.[19] The New York Public Service Commission in recent years, as a matter of policy, has required competitive bidding in the sale of most of the securities of public utilities under its jurisdiction.

In addition to companies subject to these regulatory requirements, competitive bidding has been used in recent years by certain telephone, electric, and gas companies which were under no legal or regulatory compulsion to do so in making public offerings of securities—the outstanding example being the American Telephone and Telegraph Company. As a result of these developments most of the railroad and public utility debt securities publicly offered since 1941 have been sold by the issuer at competitive bidding. On the other hand, very few issues of industrial securities have been offered in this manner. Comparative figures covering competitive and negotiated public utility, railroad, and industrial debt issues of $2,000,000 par value and over for the period 1941–49, inclusive, are given in Table 6.

TABLE 6

PUBLIC UTILITY, RAILROAD AND INDUSTRIAL DEBT ISSUES
PUBLICLY OFFERED, 1941–49 [20]

(In millions of dollars)

	Competitive Sale			Negotiated Sale		
	Number of Issues	Amount	Per Cent	Number of Issues	Amount	Per Cent
Public Utility	374	$ 8,826	88.9	54	$1,098	11.1
Railroad	451	4,375	98.2	9	81	1.8
Industrial	2	28	.9	181	3,250	99.1
Total	827	$13,229	74.9	244	$4,429	25.1

During this period (1941–49) approximately one billion dollars of preferred and common stocks of public utility companies were sold at competitive sale. This was about 38 per cent of the total amount of such

---

[18] Interstate Commerce Commission, Ex Parte 158, In the Matter of Competitive Bidding in the Sale of Securities Issued Under Section 20a of the Interstate Commerce Act, 257 I.C.C. 129.

[19] California Railroad Commission, Case No. 4761, Decision No. 38614, Jan. 15, 1946.

[20] Based upon additions made to data published by R. S. Peterson, "Negotiated vs. Competitive Debt Financing," *Vanderbilt Law Review*. Nashville, Tenn.: Vanderbilt University School of Law. Vol. I, No. 4, June 1948.

securities issued. No issues of railroad or industrial stocks were sold at competitive sale during these years.

The competitive bidding requirements as prescribed by the Securities and Exchange Commission, the Interstate Commerce Commission, and various state commissions evolved largely from the regulatory function of these bodies. In this connection, two factors have been particularly significant in the adoption and application of these requirements. One centers in the relative absence of competition in the underwriting of security issues under the traditional relationships which developed over the years between certain investment banking houses and the more important issuers of securities. The second factor is the relationship which exists between the price received by the issuer for securities sold to an underwriter and the cost of capital. Since these bodies have placed great emphasis upon the cost of capital as an element in the determination of rates, the matter of the price received in the issuance of new securities becomes a matter of primary consideration. It was on the premise, therefore, that competition rather than private negotiation generally would afford the most satisfactory means of obtaining the best price in the issuance of securities, that competitive bidding was instituted by these regulatory commissions.

Considering the fact that competitive bidding was instituted as a regulatory procedure, it is not possible to distinguish fully between the effects of competitive bidding upon the investment banking business and the over-all effects of regulation and the large volume of funds available for investment during these years. This lack of any definite means of measuring effects has contributed to the widespread differences of opinion regarding competitive bidding which have existed from its inception. A vigorous support of these divergent points of view relative to the merits of competition, as against private negotiation, in the underwriting of corporate security issues has characterized all discussions and actions on the subject. Some of these points of view are based upon personal or vested interests. Other opinions are influenced by a disinclination to make adjustments to new and changed conditions. Still other issues more fundamental in character, center in the basic functions of investment banking. Space does not permit a presentation, or an evalution, here of all the issues involved.[21] Some general observations, however, may be noted. From a regulatory standpoint, the experience to date with competitive bidding, on the whole, has been satisfactory. The same is true of its use by a number of utility companies which were not required to

---

[21] For more detailed presentations, see: J. F. Weston, "The Economics of Competitive Bidding in the Sale of Securities," *Studies in Business Administration*, Vol. XIII, No. 1, Univ. of Chicago Press, 1943. S. M. Robbins, "Competitive Bidding in Sale of Securities," *Harvard Business Review*, Vol. 27, Sept., 1949, p. 646. J. L. Weiner, "The Problem of Maintaining Arm's Length Bargaining and Competitive Conditions in the

do so by regulatory compulsion. From a merchandising standpoint, competitive bidding has created a greater degree of equalization in underwriting opportunities and has expanded widely the process of evaluating security issues at the time of issuance. And from the position of the investment banker the issues involved, in the final analysis, basically are not so much a matter of whether competitive bidding will work, but a question of whether issuers and underwriters want it to work. The answer that is ultimately given to this question probably will determine the future of the private capital market in this country.

* * *

Within the narrow span of a 20-year period, the investment banking business has been subjected to the impact of several years of economic depression, the development of federal regulation, basic changes in market outlets, the growth of private placements, the establishment of competitive bidding, the direct competition of government agencies, and the many forces generated by the war. A continuous process of adjustment to rapidly changing conditions has been necessary during all these years. The scope and character of these adjustments, however, have tended to obscure the fact that the basic functions of investment banking still remain to be performed. In this connection, therefore, it is important that by and large the changes and adjustments which have occurred in the business during these years have strengthened rather than weakened the capacity of the industry to perform these functions effectively. Evidence of this is found in the proficiency with which the large volume of new security issues since the war has been handled. But the complexities of this highly specialized field of merchandising keep this fact from being readily discernible to the average citizen. With the government encroaching more and more upon the private capital market, the need for a proper public understanding of the role of the investment banker in our economic life is more essential than ever before if private enterprise is to continue to be the foundation of the American economy.

Suggested Readings

Bogen, J. I., Editor, *The Financial Handbook*. New York: The Ronald Press Company, 1948. Section I.

Bosland, C. C., *Corporate Finance & Regulation*. New York: The Ronald Press Company, 1949. Chapter 10.

Sale and Distribution of Securities of Registered Public Utility Holding Companies and Their Subsidiaries," S. E. C. (Public Utilities Division), Dec. 18, 1940.

S. E. C. Holding Company Act Release No. 2676, April 7, 1941.

I. C. C., Ex Parte 158 cited above, 257 I. C. C. 129.

McClintock, F. T., "Competitive Bidding in the Origination of Securities." *Fundamentals of Investment Banking*, Investment Bankers Assoc. of America, 1947.

Burtchett, F. F., and Hicks, C. M., *Corporation Finance,* Revised Edition. New York: Harper & Brothers, 1948. Part IV, Chapters 22 and 23.

Cherrington, H. V., *Business Organization and Finance.* New York: The Ronald Press Company, 1948. Chapter 9.

Dewing, A. S., *Financial Policy of Corporations,* 4th Ed. New York: The Ronald Press Company, 1941. Vol. II, Book IV, Chapters 8 and 9.

Fundamentals of Investment Banking. Chicago: Investment Bankers Association of America, 1947.

Haven, T. K., "Investment Banking Under the Securities and Exchange Commission," *Michigan Business Studies.* Ann Arbor: The Univ. of Mich., Press, 1940. Vol. IX, No. 3.

Hoagland, H. E., *Corporation Finance,* 3rd Ed. New York: McGraw-Hill Book Company, Inc., 1947. Chapters 20 and 21.

Koch, A. R., *The Financing of Large Corporations 1920–39.* New York: National Bureau of Economic Research, Inc., 1943. Chapter 6.

Prime, John H., *Investment Analysis.* New York: Prentice-Hall, Inc., 1946. Chapter 7.

Weston, J. F., "The Economics of Competitive Bidding in the Sale of Securities," *Studies in Business Admnistration.* Chicago: The Univ. of Chicago Press, 1943. Vol. XIII, No. 1.

Willis, H. P., and Bogen, J. I., *Investment Banking,* Revised Edition. New York: Harper & Brothers, 1936. Chapters 17, 18, and 19.

16

Investment Companies

by DOUGLAS H. BELLEMORE

*Chairman, Economics Department, College of Business Administration,
and Investment Economist, American Institute of Finance*

INVESTMENT companies are cooperative financial institutions whose purpose is to bring together the savings of many individuals and to invest them in a diversified group of securities—either common stock, preferred stock, bonds, or a combination of these types of securities—which have been selected by the management of the investment companies. The stockholders of the investment company have the advantages of the distribution of risks and expert management of their funds, which most of them could obtain in no other way; in addition the stockholders receive a higher income derived from equity shares than can be obtained in savings institutions or from savings bonds.

The term "Investment Companies" for some of the companies using the title is a misnomer and is as misleading as the title "Investment Trusts" which preceded it. The generally accepted goal of an "Investor" is first, the protection of principal; second, the maintenance of income; and third, gain or appreciation in principal. A number of corporations using the name "Investment Company" do not consider conservation of principal to be their primary objective. Probably, therefore, a better all-inclusive title for "Investment Companies" would be "Cooperative Financial Enterprises," since the assets of each company consist of a pool of funds obtained from many investors. After management expenses are deducted, any income from either dividends or interest received, or from capital gains, belongs to the stockholders and is usually distributed to them.

Investment companies, as do individuals, have different investment objectives ranging from highly speculative commitments in untried innovations (such as the American Research and Development Corpora-

tion) to companies which deal in special situations (such as the Atlas Corporation) to other companies (such as the Keystone Custodian Funds) which offer a number of completely separate funds. The investor can purchase securities in funds providing diversification according to the type of security which the investor may wish to purchase, for example, high-grade bond funds, speculative preferred stock funds, blue chip common stock funds, speculative common stock funds, and the balanced type fund, a combination stock and bond fund such as the Scudder, Stevens, and Clark Fund. Some companies emphasize conservation of principal first; the other extreme places high income or capital appreciation first.

Characteristics of Investment Companies Common to Ordinary Corporations

The investment company receives its capital, as do other corporations, by selling common stock and in some cases preferred stock and bonds. Before 1940 the investment company was much more likely to sell bonds than is the case today, because the fastest growing investment companies are open-end companies which have not been permitted to sell bonds since the passing of the Federal Investment Company Act of 1940.

Unique Characteristics of Investment Companies

The investment company obtains its capital from thousands of investors who generally purchase securities in the investment company because they believe that the diversification offered reduces their risk of capital loss considerably, compared to the general run of investment securities, and because the yield will be higher than that they can receive elsewhere, given the same amount of security. In the case of open-end investment companies, the company stands ready to sell (or buy back) its stock at all times, so that its capital is constantly changing. The investor is always able to sell his stock at any time.

The main purpose of the investment company (with some exceptions) is to invest in a large variety of enterprises and thereby take advantage of the principle of diversification to reduce investment risk. For example, the company may invest in securities of major industries such as the utility, railroad, chemical, oil, merchandising, and food industries.

Except in the case of fixed trusts, which are not popular today, the management exercises constant supervision of the investments, making changes, switches, additions, and reductions in the portfolio as the individual situations or market conditions are interpreted by the management. The British type of investment company has always given the

management quite a large amount of freedom in the selection of securities. After the 1929–30 stock market debacle in this country, the tendency in the United States was to favor limiting management considerably in its selection of securities. Temporarily, the fixed type of trust became popular. However, since 1940 the trend has been again toward open-end companies in which the management may have some restrictions but in which the management may still exercise considerably its own discretion in the selection of securities. Today the fixed type of trust is essentially out of the picture. Some cynics have commented a little harshly that management, to be safe from criticism, seems to purchase just about what the other big investment companies are buying and in turn selling what and when others are selling. Of course, such a comment could apply with equal force to the investment committees of most large life insurance companies. Only in the case of a fixed trust is the management limited to a definite fixed list of investments.

The investment company purchases securities for investment and not for the purpose of controlling the companies whose securities are owned. Its diversified portfolio generally means that it does not own enough of any one security to exercise control (by law, less than 10 per cent). But even where a small percentage of stock might give the management of the investment company control, it generally does not choose to exercise that control. In this regard, its attitude toward the management of the company whose security it owns is little different from that of the average investor who takes no part in management other than sending in his proxy.

The management has two sources of income: first, the interest and dividends received on securities owned; second, the profits obtained from selling securities above their cost price. Historical precedent and our tax laws and the desires of many investors encourage many of the managements to attempt to secure capital appreciation by buying securities which they believe can be sold later at a profit; and managements also attempt to pay these profits as capital dividends rather than to retain them as reserves against possible future capital losses.

In the case of investment companies which have preferred stock and bonds outstanding as well as common stock, the principal of leverage is introduced. If the management can earn a higher return on its over-all capital than it must pay on its preferred stocks and bonds, the surplus earnings represent additional earnings to the common stockholders. The so-called leverage companies resemble the British type of funds in offering preferred stock and bonds to the public as well as common stock. The common stock and especially the warrants of such leverage companies may be highly speculative. The stocks and warrants of leverage companies will rise faster than the stock market averages in a bull or rising

market but will fall faster than the market in a bear or falling market. Leverage is most clearly indicated by the percentage that the common stock capitalization bears to the total assets. The smaller the percentage, the higher the leverage. With the exception of two or three open-end companies, only one of which is very important, leverage companies are all closed-end companies. These companies may secure leverage by bank loans, and sometimes these loans may be completely paid off.

Classification of Investment Companies

Depending on the purpose of classification, there are a number of ways of classifying investment companies. The most common classification used today is (a) closed-end investment companies and (b) open-end investment companies.

Closed-end investment companies. Closed-end investment companies have a relatively fixed capital structure. They issue a certain amount of authorized stock at a particular time, and then for a certain period of time at least, they do not issue any additional stock. The procedure followed in a stock offering is similar to that used by a business corporation; and at some later date the outstanding capital stock may be increased by another stock issue. Investors who wish to purchase issued stock of such investment companies must, therefore, buy it from existing stockholders on the security exchanges where it is listed or on the over-the-counter market. Most closed-end companies have senior securities, bonds and preferred stock, outstanding as well as common stock.

In practice there is another major difference between open-end and closed-end companies. With a very few exceptions, none of the open-end companies is of the leverage type—that is, none of them has outstanding any senior securities, either bonds or preferred stocks or bank loans, which give its funds leverage. On the other hand, the majority of the large closed-end companies do have senior securities outstanding in varying amounts, and accordingly the companies have varying degrees of leverage. The important facts in leverage are the ratio of senior securities to the total capitalization of the corporation and the relationship of the rate of interest paid on senior securities to the rate of return earned on the assets of the corporation. If the ratio of senior securities to the total capitalization is high and the investment company pays a low rate of interest on these borrowed funds but earns a higher rate of return on its over-all assets, there is considerable leverage. This leverage magnifies the rate of return to the common stockholder; it gives the common stockholder a considerably higher rate of return on his investment than he would earn if the entire capitalization was in stock.

The possibility of greater profit must also obviously be balanced against the possibility of greater loss. More risk is involved in such an investment than in the case of non-leverage companies. Assume that a company is capitalized with 100 shares of capital stock having a par value of $100, and the fund is invested 100 per cent in earning assets which yield 5 per cent. Then assume that the corporation borrows $2,000,000 from a bank at 2 per cent interest and invests it in similar securities also bringing 5 per cent. The effect of leverage is to raise the earnings per share due to the spread received between income on the borrowed $2,000,000 ($100,000) and the interest charge of only $40,000. On the other hand, debentures and preferred stocks on which 5 per cent and 6 per cent interest must be paid exert practically no income leverage on the market, unless income earned on over-all assets is significantly above 5 per cent or 6 per cent.

During a period in which the stock market fluctuates a significant amount, such as in 1949, the assets of some common stock companies may fluctuate twice as much as the Dow-Jones Industrial averages. Some straight "bond" funds may fluctuate only one-tenth as much. This illustrates the fundamental difference between bond funds and common stock funds. Among the so-called specialized bond funds during the 1948 and 1949 stock market decline, there were several which showed no depreciation at all. Naturally these funds showed a correspondingly lower yield than the common stock fund. For example, Keystone B-1, which fluctuated less than one-tenth as much as the industrial averages, yielded about 3.1 per cent at the time.

Open-end investment companies. Open-end investment companies, often called mutual investment funds or Boston-type funds, stand ready at all times to issue additional shares of stock or to repurchase stock which they have issued previously. The characteristics of this type of company have been well summarized by Alec Brock Stevenson:

1. The two principal distinguishing characteristics of the mutual investment funds are: (a) the continuous offering of securities at prices which will net the fund an amount equivalent to the net asset value of each outstanding share at the time of sale, and (b) the obligation of the investment company to redeem or repurchase its outstanding shares by paying the equivalent of the net asset value per share (in some cases less a small redemption fee). Of the two the second is potentially the most significant; in fact, (a) is really a corollary of (b).

2. So long as the mutual investment fund maintains its readiness to redeem or repurchase its shares upon demand, it must certainly maintain a sales force to offer the shares continuously so as to prevent too fast a shrinkage of the fund in the normal course of redemptions over a period of time. Essentially this does not differ from the practice of life insurance companies whose assets would eventually be similarly depleted by the

maturity of policies upon death of the insured if new policies were not continuously sold.[1]

By far the largest growth in investment companies since 1940 has been in the open-end or mutual funds. The closed-end type of fund had its great growth in the early days of the investment companies, but after 1944 the total assets of open-end funds exceeded those of closed-end companies. In 1950 there were some 100 mutual funds or "open-end" investment companies operating in this country having combined assets estimated in excess of $2,000,000,000 represented by approximately 1,000,000 shareholders.[2]

Fixed Trusts

Fixed trusts are unimportant today, for most trusts are of the management type. Investment company management generally has wide latitude in the selection of securities, but in some cases the management is strictly limited under a fixed trust agreement. A fixed trust is established under a contract between three parties: the corporation itself; the trustee, usually a bank or trust company; and the investors who receive certificates of beneficial interest in the trust. The trust invests in a specified fixed list of securities which are deposited with the trustee and against which are issued the certificates of beneficial interest. The term of the trust is definitely set and is commonly 25 years. The shares or certificates of beneficial interest are issued in either a registered or bearer form. A given number of these shares is equivalent to a unit of underlying securities and usually may be converted into these underlying securities or their current market value at the option of the owner at any time.

The management is strictly limited to the list of specific securities it may purchase. In the case of the semifixed trust, a supplemental list of securities may be used by management. Except during the early '30's, when investors had been disillusioned by the poor record of management, fixed trusts have not been popular in the United States. Most investors realize it is much better to look for good management and then give the managers flexibility in the selection of securities. The overwhelming majority of investment companies today are of the management rather than the fixed type.

The Securities and Exchange Commission has two additional classifications: (a) companies whose securities are sold on the installment plan, "periodic payment plans," and (b) companies issuing face amount in-

[1] Alec B. Stevenson, "Shares in Mutual Investment Funds," *Investment Company Shares.* New York: Fiduciary Publishers, Inc., 1949, p. 47.

[2] Thomas P. Swift, "Investment Trust Faces S.E.C. Curb," *The New York Times,* Financial Section, p. 1F, Col. 5, Aug. 20, 1950.

stallment certificates which promise to pay a stated amount at maturity (providing all periodic payments have been made) or promising a specified cash surrender value if turned in before maturity.

The range of investment companies is from extremely speculative to extremely conservative. The prospective investor is, therefore, offered a chance to select the type of management and security which will best suit his needs. Despite the great range of management policies, most investment companies in the period from 1936 to 1950 showed a slightly greater percentage increase in their capital assets than the equivalent rise in the stock market averages. The slight extra percentage of increase of the average fund over the Standard and Poor's Stock Index is worthy of notice, for the average investor in the market during these years would not have done nearly so well as the market averages. Furthermore, the investors of small or moderate means would have had to pay a considerable amount of brokerage fees if they had purchased the stocks in the averages. In buying the securities of an investment company, only one brokerage fee is paid—the selling or loading charge— and the investor is thus able to own fractional shares in many companies which are diversified by industry, type of security, and in other ways.

Investment companies originated in England, Scotland, and Holland. The early companies had conservative management and emphasized safety of principal and reasonable income in their investment policies. Profits from the sale of investments were placed in a reserve fund and were not considered as earnings to be paid out as dividends. Later almost all of these funds became leverage funds.

In the United States, investment companies of the management type and then generally of the closed-end variety had a phenomenal growth during the 1920's; but their management was on the whole poor and their record was no better than that of the average buyer of stocks during this period, which was a pretty poor record. They were part and parcel of the speculative fever of the '20's. Items in the overhead of investment companies (such as salaries, advertising expenses, and selling commissions) were frequently exhorbitant. These companies attempted to secure profits primarily from the market appreciation of the securities in their portfolios; and when profits were made from the sale of securities, they were paid out as dividends. Reserves were not provided against possible losses, and the absence of reserves ultimately caused many of these companies to fail.

While many persons who purchased stocks in these companies in the 1920's were consciously speculating, others buying securities of an "investment trust" thought they were placing their savings in investment companies where a high degree of safety for their capital was a primary concern of management. Actually some of the investment companies

became the recipients of securities which affiliated investment and banking firms could not sell elsewhere, and these transactions contributed to the severe losses suffered by these companies during the early '30's. Most of the companies invested in common stocks at the very high levels prevailing in the late '20's, and many of the stocks were extremely speculative issues.

Regulation of Investment Companies

Traditionally investment companies have secured most of their capital from individuals in the middle-income group, although the companies also have sold a considerable amount of securities to wealthy investors. Because of this, investment companies came to be regarded as public institutions in need of strict regulation. The blue sky laws of the various states and the requirements laid down in 1929 and 1931 by the New York Stock Exchange proved quite inadequate to regulate companies which had such a public character. A very complete investigation started in 1935 at the request of Congress and made by the Securities and Exchange Commission resulted in the passage of the Investment Company Act of 1940. The purpose of the Act was (1) full disclosure and (2) the prevention of the speculative abuses and management manipulation characteristic of the late '20's. The abuses and the severe losses suffered during the early '30's by investors explained their reluctance to invest again in such a medium to any great extent until five or ten years later. When they did invest in investment company securities, they favored the fixed type of company. The fact that during the '30's most closed-end securities sold at a very considerable discount under their book value was another indication of public distrust of management.

Public faith in investment companies gradually returned, particularly after the passage of the Investment Company Act of 1940; since that time their growth has been phenomenal. It was reported in 1949 that there were 1,000,000 shareholders of 124 investment companies having net assets of over $2,250,000,000. These totals compared with 750,000 shareholders eight years before in funds having total assets of only approximately $1,000,000,000. Giving public recognition to the trend, the Chairman of the Board of the Federal Reserve System, Thomas B. McCabe, stated, "Investment trusts have diversified holdings of preferred and common stock and other securities, and these can offer the small saver diversification of risk together with the higher income to be derived from equity shares."

Investment Company Act of 1940 [3]

The elimination by law of many malpractices that investment company management perpetrated upon the public in the late 1920's has encouraged the public to invest again in the securities of such companies. Fly-by-night companies are discouraged, for the Act requires a minimum capital of $100,000 before the stock of an investment company may be offered publicly; the management itself earns little money for its supervisors if the fund is below one or two million dollars. The full-disclosure provisions of the Act give the investor adequate knowledge of management operations and also inspire investor confidence. The Act regulates companies which are not generally subject to the rules and regulations of the Securities Act of 1933 and of the Security Exchange Act of 1934; and, furthermore, the Act of 1940 goes much farther than do the Acts of 1933 and 1934, for the latter rely mainly on full disclosure to prevent malpractices. Management is held legally responsible under this 1940 Act for violations of its provisions. Management is prohibited from inequitable self-aggrandizement. Congress felt that prior to 1940 investment companies were too often the tool and stepchild of investment banking interests; the Act of 1940 specifically attempts to prevent domination of boards of directors by such interests. A majority of the directors must not be connected with investment banking firms or connected with the sales distributing organization of the investment company; and at least 40 per cent of the directors may not be officers of the company or outside investment advisers to the company. The distribution of the securities of these companies is also controlled by the Act to prevent a recurrence of the malpractices of earlier periods. In 1949, one of the largest of the investment companies was cited by the S.E.C. and ordered to desist from making certain statements in the marketing of its securities.

Investors must be provided with complete and accurate financial reports. Such reports are required by the Act to be submitted quarterly to the Securities and Exchange Commission and semiannually to the stockholders, but many investment companies issue the statement quar-

---

[3] "The provisions of the Investment Company Act are directed on the one hand ·toward elimination or at least restriction of any control which might be exercised by investment companies over other companies and over industry in general; and, on the other hand, toward improvement in various operating matters, with particular attention to investment influence such as relation with brokers, investment bankers and banks, dealing with insiders, restrictions in investments. . . .

"Broad objectives of the measure were the restoration of a general feeling of confidence in investment trusts as investment institutions and the establishment of the industry on a basis where the primary emphasis might be placed on the management of other people's money rather than on the distribution of securities." (Stevenson, *op. cit.*, p. 38.)

terly to their stockholders as well as to the S.E.C. More information is now available concerning the financial status, assets, liabilities, capital, and financial operations and earnings of investment companies than almost any other type of corporation. The investor, if he wants to read, can find out exactly what he is buying. He can examine the past performance of the company, the present portfolio holdings, and determine what the present management's particular problems are by using the annual book *Investment Companies*[4] by Arthur Wiesenberger. This book makes comparisons of records of the various investment companies.

The Act of 1940 did not require a change in the capital structure of existing companies, but the Securities and Exchange Commission issued rules regarding the subsequent issue of senior securities after that. Open-end or mutual investment companies incorporated after 1940 may issue only common stock. They may secure a slight amount of leverage, however, by borrowing limited amounts from banks. Closed-end companies are restricted in issuing senior securities, except for refunding purposes. Section 18 of the Act provides that funded debt (or bank loans) created by a closed-end company after 1940 must be covered at least three times by assets. Preferred stocks must be backed by twice the amount of assets. For example, an issue of $15 million of preferred stock must be covered after issuance by total assets of $30 million.

The Act requires that the investment companies express their investment policies in clear and specific language. Having made such a statement, they cannot change their policies without the consent of the stockholders.

Most investment companies belong to the National Association of Investment Companies. This trade association has worked closely with the S.E.C. to improve standards in the field, especially in the distribution end of the business. It has improved considerably the public relations of the industry.

Effect of Income Shifts on Investment Companies

The rapid growth of investment companies can be traced in part to the gradual shift of income that has taken place in this country. The lower- and middle-income groups are receiving a larger share of the national income each year. The major market for securities of investment companies is in these groups. Investors in the middle-income groups seek safety of principal and sound management of their securities. While they desire a higher yield from their savings than the 2 to 3 per cent they can obtain today on funds placed in savings banks, other savings institutions,

---

[4] Arthur Wiesenberger, *Investment Companies*. New York: Arthur Wiesenberger & Company, 1950 Edition.

or government bonds, many of them are not interested in high-yielding speculative securities. Prior to 1930 they could place their funds in savings banks at 4 or 5 per cent or perhaps in mortgages at 6 per cent. When interest rates were reduced, many investors decided to take somewhat greater risks with their money in order to earn higher yields.

A large portion of the savings in the middle-income group will go into United States Savings bonds, savings banks, and life insurance companies. Such companies invest primarily in bonds and mortgages rather than in equity securities. As a result, many individuals feel that there will be an insufficiency of funds going into equity securities. What is needed is a satisfactory medium for diverting these savings into the equity market. The record of aggressive salesmanship by the merchandizers of investment company securities since 1940 (and especially since 1945) gives some assurance that the investment company will provide this medium.

President Roosevelt in 1935 [5] and President Truman in 1949 recognized that investment companies might provide a satisfactory medium to achieve this end. Their statements indicated that the expansion of such companies, properly regulated, should be encouraged in order to tap the resources of the middle-income group and make the funds available for equity investment. The Economic Report of the President, transmitted to Congress January, 1949, stated:

> Economic policy should recognize that the bulk of savings will come from people in the middle-income brackets, which are rightly more concerned with the safety of their investment than with gains that involve high risks. This calls for financial institutions that transform their savings into venture capital. Study should be made of the experience of nationwide or local investment companies which can extend venture capital with diversification of risk.

As Arthur Wiesenberger points out, "Main Street has been using the investment company movement to bring its dollars to Wall Street. In the three years, 1946–48, 69 per cent of the $898,913,000 of investment company shares sold originated in areas accounting for only 31 per cent of the volume of trading in the New York Stock Exchange." [6]

Investment Companies and the Small Investor

Individuals in the lower- and middle-income groups cannot afford to pay the fees charged by high-grade investment counselors for the management of their small accounts. These accounts are also too small to be

---

[5] "Bona fida investment trusts that submit to public regulation and perform the function of permitting small investors to obtain the benefit of diversification of risk, may well be exempt from tax." (From *The Economic Report of the President,* June 10, 1935.)

[6] Wiesenberger, *op. cit.,* p. 10.

handled as trust funds by banks except as part of the so-called "common trust funds." Some investment counsel fees, for example, range upward from a minimum of $500 annually per account. Professional investment advice available from disinterested parties (that is, not from brokers or investment bankers who have a direct interest in selling securities and obtaining commission thereby) has therefore for the most part only been available to wealthy investors. The fees for investment counsel service may be a small percentum charge ($\frac{1}{2}$ of 1 per cent to 1 per cent on accounts over $50,000), but the minimum fees are prohibitive on small accounts.

By placing their funds in investment companies, individuals with small accounts may secure both wide diversification of risk and investment management equal in quality to that obtained by wealthy investors.

As a matter of fact, some investment counsel firms manage an open-end investment company catering to small investors in addition to performing their main function of investment counseling for wealthy investors. The Lehman family has always managed and has also had considerable personal investment in the Lehman Corporation, a closed-end investment company. Investors buying shares in such an investment company find the following three problems at least partly solved for them.

1. *The problem of proper selection.* Our economy is consistantly changing and the tempo of change is faster now than ever before. Uncertainty and change increase the difficulty of investment decisions. The problem of selection is more difficult now than it has been in the past. Proper analysis takes time, requires access to specialized statistical information, and requires the ability to interpret this information. This can best be done by an experienced analyst trained in economics, finance, and accounting as well as in practical experience. With the best of tools and training and good judgment, proper security selection is still no easy task; without them it is virtually impossible.

2. *The problem of diversification.* Most investors realize the need for diversification in their security holdings. They are aware that wealthy investors and financial institutions place their funds in a wide variety of securities. The small investors cannot secure adequate diversification at reasonable cost, for it is prohibitively expensive to buy one share in each of a large number of enterprises. Attempts at adequate diversification also make the problem of selection more difficult. If the small investor is not able to analyze properly a few securities, how can he hope to cope with a large list? The investment company attempts to solve this problem for him. If the small investor purchases stock in an investment company which, in turn, reinvests his funds in a wide variety of other

companies, the investor secures adequate diversification and careful selection if the investment company is well managed. For example, in 1950 the Lehman Corporation, a closed-end fund, had a substantial investment in over 70 corporations and lesser investments in many others. Most investment companies offer more diversification than the average small- or medium-income investor can possibly hope to secure otherwise. This diversification, ranging in different trusts from 30 to 150 different issues, should enable the investment company to do at least as well as the over-all average of security prices, given sound policy.

3. *The problem of timing.* It is nearly impossible, if the past record of the average investor serves as any criterion, for individual investors to time their securities transactions properly and profitably. In the vast majority of cases investors lose money because of bad timing, and only a few investors experience over-all net capital gains for any long period of time. Investment companies enable the investor to solve the problem in two ways. In the first place he can purchase securities regularly under a dollar averaging plan. The investment company, because of its wide diversification, offers the best medium for following a program of this type—that is, the investor must purchase a certain amount of securities regardless of whether the securities markets are rising or falling. In the second place, regardless of whether or not an investor is following a dollar averaging plan, the investor who believes the timing problem cannot be solved by forecasting may secure the advantage of automatic formula timing by purchasing the securities of an investment company whose management publicly states that it is following an automatic formula timing plan. Investors may question their own ability to time their purchases properly, but they may be willing to have the skilled management of an investment company time their security purchases and sales.

Legal Recognition of Investment Company Securities for Trust Accounts

An interesting recent development has been the recognition of investment company securities by trustees and by courts as satisfactory investment outlets for trust funds. In states that require all investments to be chosen from a "legal list," the trustees can invest beneficiaries' funds in investment company securities only if such securities appear on the legal list. In states (such as Massachusetts) which follow the prudent-man rule, the trustees may legally invest in the securities of investment companies. If trustees decide that they must invest in common stocks to maintain income, investment company shares may prove a sound medium for such

investments. After the Annual Meeting of the Probate Judges of Massachusetts in 1948, Judge Dillon reported,

> It was the unanimous feeling that the Probate Judges of this state, to keep abreast of the times, should recognize the fact that such purchases [shares of investment companies] are not such a delegation of authority on the part of the trustee as would warrant an objection on that score alone. The judges reserve the right, however, to apply the prudent-man rule in every case, and the trustee will be held to the same rigid standard in the purchase of those securities as he would be in making other investments.

In the state of Ohio, it was held in 1947 that in cases where trustees are not restricted to statutory investments and can invest in stocks, they can purchase the shares of investment companies. A New York court handed down a similar decision in 1947. This legal recognition indicates the widening area of investment company investment.

Specialized Services of Investment Companies

In the past decade investment companies have offered specialized types of funds which are aimed at fulfilling specific economic needs, or in some cases simply designed to meet the demand by investors for securities that are fashionable at the time (such as Television Fund, Inc., in 1949). Certain funds offer a means to hedge against inflation or deflation. Other funds offer a substitute for margin trading, and still others serve as a replacement for tax sales.

The stock of certain investment companies is a speculative investment, but now this fact must be stated publicly in sales and other literature so that those buying the security will be aware of the fact. Such companies offer the real speculator opportunity to purchase individually, through his purchase of the investment company shares, a widely diversified list of speculative securities which should enhance his opportunity to profit relative to what his position would be as a small investor speculating in a few stocks. It is even more important for the speculator to diversify widely than it is for the conservative investor, although it must be emphasized that diversification is important for both.

Trading Fees

When an investor purchases the securities of an open-end company, he pays a "selling charge" over and above the net asset value of the shares. With most funds when the security is redeemed by the company, the investor receives the liquidating or break-up value at that date with no deductions. At least once a day and usually twice a day, the investment company calculates the break-up value of its stock. There is no redemp-

tion charge in most companies. The investor simply pays the "selling charge" of 6 to 9 per cent at the time he purchases his security, but usually there is no charge when the stock is sold back to the company.

In trading in the stock of a closed-end investment company, the investor pays two brokers' commissions: one when he purchases the stock and one when he sells the stock, just as he does in buying or selling stock of other corporations such as General Motors or American Telephone and Telegraph Company. On the other hand, he may at times be able to purchase closed-end investment company shares at a liberal discount. Historically the shares of closed-end investment companies have generally sold at a discount below their current book value. By purchasing the shares of a closed-end company at a liberal discount, the investor may more than make up for the commission paid if he can later sell at a smaller discount or at no discount at all. Thus a profit is possible on such a transaction.

The following table shows the discount from asset value for selected stocks of closed-end companies.

TABLE 1

DISCOUNT FROM ASSET VALUE [7]

	Year End Discounts						
	1948	1947	1946	1945	1944	1941	1936
Adams Express	31%	35%	39%	32%	31%	32%	33%
General American	21	25	27	13	16	42	27
Lehman	3	0	14	7	14	24	13
National Aviation	27	25	19	11	28	52	13
Newmont Mining	29	40	37	21	26	35	9
U.S. and Foreign	36	41	47	34	22	*	37

* Premium above asset value.

A high discount can operate to the benefit of the shareholders of investment companies because it means that the company has more than one dollar's worth of earning assets for each dollar of market price of the stock when purchased at a discount. For example, if the investor buys $100 worth of Niagara Share "B," he might be buying the earnings of roughly $170 worth of assets. If these assets earn at the rate of 4 per cent, a conservative figure, there will be $7 worth of earnings available for the $100 investment. As this company has followed the policy of paying out roughly $4 in the form of dividends and using the balance to pay off bonds and preferred stocks and to purchase its own shares in

[7] Wiesenberger, op. cit., 1948 Edition, Table, p. 22.
"The only exceptions to these discounts in closed-end issues have been some of the low priced, high leverage stocks and warrants which characteristically sell at a premium." (Wiesenberger, op. cit., 1949 Edition, p. 182.)

the open market, it has been increasing the asset value of the remaining shares.

Because of the multiplier effect, investment companies selling at high discounts may offer a higher yield than other companies, excluding dividends paid on capital gains. In 1948, the average yield, based on income alone, of four typical companies selling at discounts of 4 per cent to 16 per cent was 4.4 per cent while that of four other companies selling at discounts of 35 per cent to 42 per cent averaged 5.4 per cent.

It is interesting to note in connection with dividends and discounts that "registered" companies—the ones which have elected to pay out 90 per cent of their earnings (including capital gains) in return for certain concessions—generally sell for lower discounts than nonregistered companies. The median discount of a group of nonregistered companies as of December 31, 1948, was 33 per cent, compared with a median discount of registered companies of 23 per cent.

Leverage and Volatility

In a changing market, shares in an investment company having leverage will always move faster (up or down) than the general market because the company's fixed indebtedness does not change. The advantages of leverage do not necessarily accrue to the stockholder but may be absorbed by management in the form of higher overhead expenses. In 1947, for example, Affiliated Fund, then operating as a leverage company, showed a return of 4.9 per cent and an expense ratio of 0.84 per cent. On the other hand, Massachusetts Investors Trust, a nonleverage company, showed an identical return with an expense ratio of only 0.37 per cent. On the liability side of the leverage picture, we find that the asset value, expressed as a percentage of the low, varied about 220 per cent for Affiliated Fund in the decade ending January 1, 1948, against only 89 per cent for the Massachusetts Investors Trust.

Practically speaking, in dealing with investment companies, the effect of leverage on income is not as important as the volatility which it gives to the market price of the shares. Volatility, which is not considered to be a favorable attribute from an investment point of view, can be very useful for hedging or speculative purposes. High leverage can be achieved not only through the medium of senior securities but also through the investment portfolio. For example, Tri-Continental Corporation common shares rose from a low of 3/4 in 1942 to 12 5/8 in 1946 not only because of the leverage of the company's capital structure, but also because of the fact that 17 per cent of the assets were invested in high-leverage shares of other investment companies.

If a company purchases assets of a very volatile nature, these assets

will rise rapidly in market value in a bull market and will fall rapidly in a bear market. Therefore, two leverage companies may have exactly the same type of capitalization—that is, the same percentage in bank loans, bonds, or preferred stocks—but if one company invests in securities of a volatile nature while the other invests in securities which follow the market averages, the leverage factor of the first company will be considerably magnified.

If the objective of an investor is to make a conservative investment in closed-end shares, he will put his funds in a nonleverage or a low-leverage company that invests in conservative—not volatile—assets. If, however, he wishes to speculate, he will look for a high-leverage company holding volatile assets.

Leverage categories. Wiesenberger divides leverage shares into four broad categories.[8]

Category	% in Senior Securities	Typical Example
Conservative or low leverage	20	General American Investors, Common
Moderate leverage	30	U.S. and Foreign Securities, Common
High leverage	40-70	Selected Industries $1.50 Preferred
Extreme leverage	....	Central States Electric 6% Preferred

Leverage and margin accounts. As Wiesenberger points out, the speculator can use leverage investment company shares to secure the same effect that he would get operating on a margin account but with less risk, for his chances of losing all are not so great with the leverage company shares. The investor cannot be sold out with investment shares, but he may be completely wiped out if he is operating a margin account. Speculation is always risky, and leverage shares are certainly speculative. The more leverage, the more speculative they are.

Marketability

In addition to discounts and leverage, a third factor exists which differentiates closed-end and open-end companies. This factor is the marketability of the securities. It has already been pointed out that open-end shares possess almost complete marketability because of the fact that, practically without exception, companies of the open-end type stand ready to redeem any shares offered to them at their current book value. The cash to redeem the shares has in the past been supplied by the sale of new securities to other purchasers with a considerable surplus to spare.

---

[8] Wiesenberger, *op. cit.*, 1948 Edition, p. 37.

In each year since 1940, gross sales of new shares for all open-end companies have exceeded repurchases by very large amounts. What would happen if the reverse ever occurs and new sales are not sufficient to counteract repurchases? The assets of most of these funds are invested in highly marketable securities so that redemptions up to a point could be made by selling these assets. However, such action by investment companies, if on a major scale by many companies, would act to depress the stock market and thus reduce the asset value of the shares of the remaining shareholders. This is particularly true since so many of the "best securities" are held by many of the companies, and they would all then be selling the same securities. In fact, conceivably a very serious situation might arise if wholesale redemption is ever requested by the owners of these shares.

Shares of many closed-end funds have high marketability because they are very actively traded on one of the large security exchanges. Some typical funds which are listed on the New York Stock Exchange are Adams Express, Chicago Corporation, General American Investors, Insurance Shares, Ctfs., Lehman Corporation, Tri-Continental Corporation, and United Corporation.

On the New York Curb Exchange we find American Superpower Corporation, Equity Corporation, and Pennroad. A volume of 1,000 shares per day is common for some of these issues, which assures the purchaser of a relatively good market under normal conditions. Besides aiding marketability, listing furnishes a certain standard of quality which is accepted by many banks as a significant feature in determining whether a stock certificate is eligible as collateral for a bank loan.

Thus we can conclude that good marketability of shares is not restricted to the open-end type, although there we find it universally. Certain listed shares of closed-end companies also have an extremely good market.

Investment Policy

Investment companies may be classified according to the investment policies they pursue. This classification temporarily groups open-end and closed-end companies together. However, all investment companies (closed-end or open-end) may be reclassified according to the degree of conservativeness or speculativeness of their management and their investment policies. In other words, there are very conservative open-end and very conservative closed-end companies, very speculative open-end and very speculative closed-end companies, and all gradations of each. This is one reason why in the beginning of the chapter it was suggested that these funds be called "cooperative financial institutions" rather than in-

vestment companies, which implies that they are all of an investment caliber. The great preference of investors since 1940 for the open-end companies has been mentioned, and of the open-end group balanced funds and common stock funds have been the most popular. Purchases of closed-end companies have also favored the balanced funds or the pure common stock funds.

Effect of Increased Size of Investment Companies

Certain dangers may arise if the individual investment companies and investment companies in the aggregate continue to grow at the rate experienced in the past 10 years. One danger is that investment company action may have an important market influence on either side of the market. An officer in one of the largest of the open-end companies stated in 1950 that it was not worth while or efficient for his company to make a purchase of a block of stock in a corporation unless it could accumulate at least one-half million dollars' worth of the stock of that company. Otherwise the result of the purchase would have no appreciable effect on the over-all assets or earning power of the investment company and, therefore, it would not have justified the time and expense involved in deciding on this selection and investment. This statement might hold for all the large investment companies. When purchases are made in such an amount, the price of the security purchased would have some tendency to rise.[9]

When an investment company decides that a security is a good buy, it may not be able to accumulate a sizable block of the stock without bidding the price to a level higher than the investment company is willing to pay. If the investment company is able to purchase only a small amount at the desired price, it will have a problem to solve. Shall the company sell what it purchased because it is too small an amount of one issue to justify its holding? Or shall the company wait to accumulate more stock when and if the stock declines in price at a later date?

Selling by investment companies will present a similar problem. When the investment company wishes to sell a block of a particular security, either because it does not like a particular security or because it is selling some of its stock in order to repurchase bonds (say under a formula timing plan, or because it expects the general market to go lower), it may not be able to unload the stock without depressing the price significantly. This would be especially true in periods of thin markets such as pre-

---

[9] In 1949 the S.E.C. preferred charges against an employee of a large investment company and certain other outside individuals who worked with him for securing profits because they had advance information as to which securities the investment company planned to purchase. The individuals concerned were convicted, fined and sentenced to jail. (See Wiesenberger, *op. cit.*, 1948 Edition, p. 37.)

vailed during most of the 1940's. This is a serious problem if the management has definitely decided that a particular security should be sold.

If a large number of investment companies decide to sell at the same time, the problem becomes more acute, and as more of all securities are controlled and owned by the investment companies, the dilemma will become greater. However, in the market break in 1950 which occurred with the outbreak of the Korean War (when more shares were traded in one day than at any time since the invasion of Poland), the open-end companies were net buyers of stock, for they continued to sell more new shares than they were redeeming.

The net effect of the buying of investment companies which follow formula timing should have a stabilizing effect on the market. These companies follow a policy of buying stocks when they are comparatively cheap, so it is conceivable that when the Dow-Jones average is falling these companies may act to stabilize the market on the down side. Conversely, when it is rising, the companies may act to stabilize the market on the up side.

In the case of the open-end investment companies, there is a loading charge or selling charge in the neighborhood of 6 per cent to 9 per cent which must be paid when securities are purchased. It may take almost two years before the return in income will take care of the loading charge. This loading charge reduces the advantages of short-term trading in these shares. Short-term movements of asset value of open-end companies are generally narrower than 7 per cent. The principle is that investors will purchase the securities of these companies with the intention of holding them over some period of time.

Speculators favor either closed-end companies with high leverage or the open-end ones which are invested largely in highly volatile issues. The shares of companies which invest largely in highly speculative securities will obviously fluctuate more in both directions with changes in market conditions than do the Dow-Jones averages. The speculator who believes that he can forecast accurately the long-term market swings has the greatest speculative opportunity if he deals in the option warrants of certain high-leverage companies. The greatest speculation would be in the warrants of closed-end companies having high leverage and having invested in volatile assets.

Taxation of Investment Companies

It should be quite obvious that if the investment company were taxed as any other corporation, we would not only have the double taxation of which we hear so much, but we would actually have triple taxation. The corporation whose securities the investment company owns would

pay a tax before distributing dividends to the investment company. The investment company would pay a tax on the investment received before distributing the income to its stockholders; and finally the stockholders would pay a tax on income received. President Roosevelt favored elimination of this triple taxation, and the Internal Revenue Code has enabled the investment companies to avoid this problem. The tax exemption provided under the code is obtained by an investment company if it agrees irrevocably to be registered as a regulated investment company, and if it further agrees to distribute at least 90 per cent of its net income received from interest and dividends of securities owned. The investment company must pay the regular corporate tax on any of such income retained in the company. It enjoys the same exemption on capital gains which are distributed to security holders in the same year; but it must pay a flat 25 per cent on any long-term capital gains retained in the business. Finally, the investment company, as with individuals, can deduct capital losses from capital gains, including those losses carried over from previous years. The obvious defect of present tax legislation is that it strongly encourages investment companies to be regulated companies under the code, and to pay out most of their income received either in the form of interest and dividends or capital gains. The pressure to pay out capital gain as well as income should be severely criticized, because it does not enable investment companies to build up reserves unless they want to have funds so retained taxed at the rate of 25 per cent.

Suggested Readings

Investment Companies, 1948, 1949, 1950 editions. New York: Arthur Wiesenberger and Co.

Investment Dealers Mutual Fund Director.

Investment Fund Directory. New York: Investment Dealer's Digest.

Investment Trusts and Investment Companies, Report of the Securities and Exchange Commission Pursuant to Section 30 of the Public Utility Holding Company Act of 1935. Washington: Government Printing Office.

Stevenson, Alec B., *Investment Company Shares.* New York: Fiduciary Publishers, Inc., 1949.

Stevenson, Alec B., *Shares in Mutual Investment Funds.* New York: Vanderbilt University Press, 1946.

The Economic Report of the President, 1935.

Tomlinson, Lucile, *Successful Investment Formulas.* New York: Barron's Publishing Company, 1947.

Various statistics, surveys, and other material prepared or released by the National Association of Investment Companies, New York.

17

Trust Companies and Trust Departments of Banks

by JAMES B. TRANT

Dean, College of Commerce, Louisiana State University and Agricultural and Mechanical College

Introduction

THE WORK of trust companies and of trust departments of commercial banks covers all fields of fiduciary business. Trust companies and trust departments have developed appropriate fiduciary services to meet a fourfold need in our social and economic life. These are: [1]

1. The provision of care for those who, by reason of infancy, infirmity, or other incapacity, are unable to care for themselves.

2. The conservation and management of property for those who can not manage their own affairs or for those who want to be free from the responsibility of management.

3. The liquidation and settlement of estates or the distribution of the property to the rightful heirs or owners.

4. The performing of agency services which can be done best by fiduciary institutions.

The development of fiduciary services or trust business may be traced back to the dawn of civilization where the idea of personal guardianships and trusteeships had been firmly embedded in religious philosophy.[2] We see Adam and Eve in charge of the Garden of Eden; we see Joseph as the custodian, conservator, or trustee of the Egyptian food supply; we see Moses as the guardian of the children of Israel in their march to the Promised Land; we see Joshua as executor or administrator parceling out to the various tribes proper portions of the Land of Canaan.

---

[1] James G. Smith, *Trust Companies in the United States.* New York: Henry Holt & Company, 1928, p. 24.

[2] James B. Trant, *Bank Administration.* New York: McGraw-Hill Book Company, Inc., 1931, p. 304.

In this early development, we see an individual serving as guardian or trustee. This arrangement has continued through modern times largely because of the personal nature of guardianship and trusteeship.

Historical Statement

Specialized institutions for handling trust business were slow in development. Guardianship and trusteeship did not exist in the growth of common law throughout the English-speaking world. Care and protection for the orphan child or the incompetent became the responsibility of the King.[3] But the details of such a responsibility were too great for the King to handle. As a result the responsibility for caring for his wards was shifted to the shoulders of the Chancellor. It was impossible, of course, for the Chancellor to serve as the personal guardian of all the infants and incompetents who were theoretically his wards. Since he could not do it, and since he was not an expert at bureaucratic organization, it became necessary to approach the guardianship and trusteeship problem from a local point of view. As a consequence, local courts of equity were developed for the purpose of determining the need for a guardian and the appointment of the guardian to take over the necessary responsibility for caring for the infant or incompetent who, thereby, became the ward of the court.

After the United States became an independent nation, it was assumed that the various states to a great extent had taken over the responsibility for the infant or incompetent who needed a guardian. Following the English system, the responsibility for selecting and appointing a guardian or trustee was left to the local courts of equity, sometimes known as "Orphan's Courts" or "Chancery Courts." The State of Louisiana is an exception in that it does not have an equity court, nor does it make provision for the appointment of guardians. Instead this state's district courts have authority for the appointment of a tutor for infants or a curator for incompetents or interdicts.[4] Act No. 199, approved by the Governor of Louisiana on July 3, 1950, provides for the courts of law to make interpretations for trustees in making investments for estates, thus fulfilling a part of the need for equity courts.

The first institution in the United States to engage in the trust business was the Massachusetts Hospital Life Insurance Company, which was given a charter by special act of the legislature of Massachusetts on February 24, 1818.[5] It immediately engaged in the trust business but its charter did not provide for that until 1823. On February 22, 1822, the

---

[3] Smith, *op. cit.*, p. 46.
[4] Louisiana Trust Estates Act of 1938, p. 2.
[5] American Institute of Banking, *Trust Business, Trusts*, Vol. I, p. 486.

Farmers Fire Insurance and Loan Company was chartered and on April 16 of the same year, it was given trust powers. This company has become the City Bank Farmers Trust Company of New York.

In 1831 the New York Life Insurance and Trust Company was appointed guardian of the property of a minor. This is believed to be the first instance of an institution serving as a guardian in this country. This company was organized in 1830 and is the first to have "Trust Company" in its title.

Following 1830, several insurance companies, or insurance and trust companies, were either organized or obtained permission to carry on trust business. For some time their business was primarily that of serving as trustee under corporate mortgages or for a corporate deed of trust. These instruments were used as the security for bonds sold for the purpose of providing funds for the building of railroads.

Toward the end of the first half of the last century, a number of states passed laws authorizing state banks to enter the field or to organize as state banks and trust companies. There were probably not more than 100 institutions doing a trust business by the end of the century. Most of the trust companies and all of the state banks that were also doing a trust business were competing with national banks for the regular banking business, and national banks could not compete with them for trust business. Agitation, therefore, developed early in the twentieth century for granting permission for national banks to carry on a trust business. This agitation culminated in the provisions of Section 11(K) of the Federal Reserve Act. This act authorized the Federal Reserve Board to grant authority upon application to national banks whose capital and surplus should be equal to or greater than that required of state banks for doing a trust business in the respective states. Regulation F of the Federal Reserve Board contains the requirements with which national banks must comply. There are approximately 1,800 national banks and 800 to 1,000 state banks holding permits to operate a trust department. There are probably not more than 50 or 75 trust companies, as such, in the field.

A great deal of the personal trust business is still handled by individuals, particularly lawyers and relatives. Most of the corporate trust business, however, is handled by the banks and trust companies.

Advantages of Trust Departments and Trust Companies

The advantages of trust companies and trust departments of commercial banks over individuals as trustees vary greatly with the circumstances involved and the particular services to be rendered. A great many small trusts and a great many trusts of a very personal nature lend themselves

to the use of an individual as trustee. On the other hand, many trusts can be handled best by an institution. But in the case of large trusts, great institutional endowments, and the larger financial undertakings of corporations, the trust departments of commercial banks have very great advantages. The ones most widely recognized are as follows: [6]

1. Accessibility. Trust companies and trust departments of commercial banks are conveniently located within the business district of the community. They never travel abroad or to another section of the country. They keep regular business hours every day in the week except holidays and Sundays. As a consequence, they are always available for business and consultation.

2. Continuity of Life. Trust departments and trust companies usually operate under the charter provisions of a general statute, providing for the extension of privileges by complying with the law. This assures renewal of charter and therefore an indeterminate life. This gives assurance that the trustee will continue to exist for the full life of the trust agreement, whether for 10 or 99 years.

3. Economy. Trust departments and trust companies become more efficient than individuals because of the wide and intensive experience they gain from their daily work as trustees. Managers of trust departments and trust companies are frequently not only trained in trust business but also as lawyers and, for that reason, specialized counsel is provided without extra fees. The trust departments or trust companies may be able to deposit securities with the State Banking Department and thereby avoid the expense of a surety bond. All of these factors together make for economy.

4. Experience. Skill and experience are essential in the trust business. The individual serves only a few times in his life as a trustee; therefore he cannot get wide experience in such business. The trust departments and trust companies, on the other hand, through serving as trustees for many at the same time, gain very wide and extensive experience. It is through this experience that trust companies become skilled in a highly technical field.

5. Financial Responsibility. Trust companies and trust departments of commercial banks have large financial resources and are, therefore, capable of meeting their financial obligations. The officers and directors of trust departments are usually men who have demonstrated their financial ability and can give assurance of wisdom in management.

6. Expert Investment Council. With all matters pertaining to the investment of trust funds being handled not only by the trust officers but also requiring the approval of a committee of the Board of Directors, the trust companies and trust departments of commercial banks are actu-

---

[6] Trant, *op. cit.*, p. 304 ff.

ally providing the wisdom of a group of experienced experts on all phases of trust business and, particularly, that of investments.

7. Impartial Service. Trust departments and trust companies offer an impartial service, since as a corporation they are free from personal and family prejudices to which the individual may be subjected. The employees of the trust departments become highly trained in carrying out the provisions of the agreement.

8. Government Supervision. Trust companies and trust departments of commercial banks are chartered and supervised by either the State Department of Banking, by the Federal Reserve Board, by the Comptroller of the Currency, or by all of these. The individual trustee is neither licensed nor supervised except to the extent of accounting to the courts every year or at the termination of the trust.

9. The Use of a Common Trust Fund. Following the stock market panic of 1929, several large trust companies began commingling or pooling small trusts into a common fund for investment purposes. This practice (legalized in the Revenue Act of 1936) gave to the small trusts the same advantages of diversification and large scale operation that the larger trusts had. Individual trustees do not have this privilege.

Terminology

Trust business is shrouded in technical terminology and, for that reason, it appears desirable at this point to include a reasonable amount of definition as a guide to further discussion: [7]

1. Guardian. A guardian is responsible under court appointment, or approval, for taking care of a minor or an incompetent because of his inability to take care of himself. In many instances, it is necessary for the guardian to take care of and manage the property as well as the person of the minor or incompetent. The guardian gets his authority from the court order and the statutes governing the particular situation. He may be designated by the maker of a will, but this action must have court approval. In Louisiana the guardian of a minor has the official title of "tutor," and the guardian of an interdict (incompetent) has the official title of "curator."

2. Trustee. A trustee may be appointed either by a court or by the creator of the trust. His authority rests on the terms of the trust agreement and the general provisions of the law. He holds temporary title to the property for a beneficiary.

3. Trust Institutions and Trust Business. In a statement of principles of trust institutions, the Executive Committee of the Trust Division (American Bankers Association, on April 10, 1933, and approved by the

---

[7] *Ibid.*, p. 307 ff.

Executive Council of the American Bankers Association on April 11, 1933) defined trust institutions and trust business as follows: [8]

> *a.* Trust Institutions. Trust institutions are corporations engaged in trust business under authority of law. They embrace not only trust companies that are engaged in trust business exclusively but also trust departments of other corporations.
>
> *b.* Trust Business. Trust business is the business of settling estates, administering trusts and performing agencies in all appropriate cases for individuals; partnerships; associations; business corporations; public, educational, social, recreational, and charitable institutions; and units of government. It is advisable that a trust institution should limit the functions of its trust department to such services.

4. Testator-trix. A testator-trix is a person who makes a will.

5. Intestate. An intestate is a person who dies without making a will.

6. Executor-trix. An institution or person named by the maker of a will to execute its provisions, which usually provide for the settlement of the estate, is known as the executor-trix.

7. Administrator-trix. An administrator-trix is appointed by a court to make settlement of an estate of a deceased person who failed to appoint an executor by will.

8. Inter Vivos. Inter vivos means a living trust: that is, a person making a trust for his own benefit during his life, or for the benefit of someone else during life.

9. Devisee. A devisee is a person who becomes the owner of real estate through legal descent or by the provisions of a will.

10. Legatee. A legatee is a person who becomes the owner of personal property in the same manner that the devisee becomes the owner of real property.

11. Receiver in Bankruptcy. This is a person or institution appointed by a court to take possession of the property of the bankrupt, pending settlement or reorganization or the election of a trustee.

12. Trustee in Bankruptcy. This is a person or institution elected by the creditors at a meeting called for that purpose to take over the business and either reorganize it or liquidate it for the benefit of the creditors.

13. Trustee Under Corporate Mortgage. A trustee under corporate mortgage is the institution selected by a corporation to hold a mortgage against a part, or all, of its property for the benefit of holders of notes and bond issues against the mortgage and sold through investment houses to the public.

14. Escrow. This is a written instrument deposited with a trustee or agent for safekeeping, pending the accomplishment of a specified event. The escrow may be a deed to be held until payment is made. Stocks or

---

[8] Board of Governors of the Federal Reserve System, Regulation F, June 1, 1940, p. 30 ff.

bonds may be deposited awaiting reorganization. The trustee or agent is obligated to hold the document until the event has been consummated, then to deliver the escrow to the proper person or agent.

Trust Authority

One may well ask, "By what authority may an individual, a trust company, or a trust department of a commercial bank engage in trust business?" Since authority for each one comes from a different source, each will be treated separately as follows: [9]

1. Individual. At one time individuals performed all the trust services then in use, and it was assumed that each individual had the right to do so by virtue of his citizenship. Individuals performed only a few of the functions now covered by trusts, and the right to them was patent under the privilege of citizenship. These individuals usually had to make bond under court appointment.

2. Trust Companies. Trust companies, organized by special acts of the legislature, were given specific authority in the provisions of their charters. Those companies organized under a general statute received authority from the statute and from the regulations of the State Banking Department, or the governing authority.

3. Trust Departments of State Banks. Trust departments of state banks receive their authority from the general statute providing for the organization of banks and trust companies and from the regulations of the State Banking Department. State banks which become members of the Federal Reserve System before organizing a trust department obtain authority from the Federal Reserve Board for carrying on whatever trust business is allowed by state law.

4. Trust Departments of National Banks. Section 11(K) of the Federal Reserve Act of 1913 authorized national banks to engage in trust business upon the approval of the Federal Reserve Board. This law was passed as a means of enabling national banks to compete for trust business on equal terms with state banks and trust companies. As a consequence, national banks will be authorized to do a trust business only when their capital and surplus is equal to or greater than that required for state banks to carry on a trust business. Regulation F of the Federal Reserve Board outlines specific provisions for organizing and operating trust departments of national banks.

Trust departments of national banks are not allowed to receive deposits of current funds nor items for collection. Trust funds awaiting investment must be kept in a separate account but may be used by the

[9] Gilbert Thomas Stephenson, *Estates and Trusts*. New York: Appleton-Century-Crofts, Inc., 1949, pp. 366 ff.

bank for current purposes, provided it first sets aside in the trust department adequate securities approved by the Federal Reserve Board. The assets of the trust department in the national bank must be kept separate from the general assets of the bank, and the records must be kept in a separate set of books. This is true in most trust departments of state banks.

Trust Powers

Individual trustees exercise trust powers as a common right of citizenship. Trust companies and trust departments of state banks have whatever trust powers are allowed to them by their charter or by the statutes giving them authority, and by the State Banking Department.

Trust departments of national banks may by application obtain permission from the Federal Reserve Board to exercise any or all of the fiduciary powers exercised by trust companies, trust departments of state banks, or any other corporation performing trust services. At the end of 1949, the Federal Reserve Board had authorized trust departments of national banks to exercise one or more of the following fiduciary powers: [10]

1. Trustee
2. Executor
3. Administrator
4. Registrar of stocks
5. Guardian of estates
6. Assignee
7. Receiver
8. Committee on estates
9. Any other fiduciary capacity in which state banks, trust companies, or other corporations which come into competition with national banks are permitted to act under the laws of the state in which the national bank is located.

The list does not cover the agency and custodian services performed by fiduciaries, unless it is intended that they should come under No. 9.

Any national bank desiring to organize a trust department and to perform any of the above functions should make application to the Federal Reserve Board through the district Federal Reserve Bank on Form 61. The Federal Reserve Board will give careful consideration to the following factors before making its decision:

a. Whether or not the capital and surplus of the bank are equal to that required by state law for state banks.

b. Whether or not there is a need within the community for the services proposed.

---

[10] Board of Governors of the Federal Reserve System, *List of National Banks Authorized to Exercise Fiduciary Powers*, Dec. 31, 1949, p. 1.

c. Whether or not the capital and surplus are adequate in relation to the assets and liabilities of the bank and proposed new services.

d. The character and ability of the management of the bank.

e. The relation of the training and experience of the investment committee of the proposed trust department to the nature of the supervision to be given the particular trust activity.

f. The character, experience, and qualifications of the proposed executive officer or officers of the trust department.

g. The availability of competent legal counsel to advise and pass upon trust business when necessary.

h. Any other factors which may appear desirable to consider.

State Laws Govern Trust Business

The authority given in Section 11(K) of the Federal Reserve Act was intended to enable national banks to organize and to operate trust departments on an equal basis with state banks and trust companies. Congress had no intention of setting up a separate legal system for the trust business. The organization and operation of national banks are under national laws, except for the trust department. Trust departments of national banks are organized under national law but in conformity with state law requirements. The operations of this department are almost wholly under state law. When state laws require corporations organized under state law to deposit securities with the State Banking Department for the protection of beneficiaries, the trust departments of national banks will likewise have to deposit securities. The requirement of a surety bond is also applicable to national banks. When state banks and trust companies are not required to deposit securities or give a surety bond, national banks are likewise free from such requirements. An individual trustee, however, is required to deposit securities or give a surety bond. National banks are required to conform to state law in taking of oaths and giving of affidavits. The president, vice-president, cashier, or trust officer in a national bank are usually permitted to take oath and give affidavits when required. (In practice, the trust officer is usually the one who performs this service.) Assistant trust officers are not allowed this privilege, and the restriction works a hardship on large trust departments where there are several assistant trust officers. The limitation may be avoided by the appointment of all assistant trust officers to the title of "trust officer"; thereby, any of the assistants could accept the responsibility of giving affidavits and taking oaths.

State laws governing fees, securities eligible for investment, and the methods of handling trust investments are applicable to national banks.

Management of Trust Departments

Under Regulation F of the Federal Reserve Board, before performing any trust service, a national bank must set up a separate trust department which shall be completely free of any other department. This is for the purpose of keeping trust funds separate from any other funds of the bank. Responsibility for managing and supervising the trust department, however, rests with the board of directors of the bank. The board of directors is made responsible for the investment of trust funds, for the supervision of the trust department, for determining the policy of the department, and for the review of actions of the committees appointed by the Board for the trust department.

No trust can be accepted by the department without first having the approval of the board of directors or a committee of the board appointed for that purpose. This requirement makes it necessary for the trust department of a national bank to open new trust accounts and to receive new trusts subject to the approval of the board. Likewise, the closing or relinquishing of any trust must be approved by the board. Records of such approval must be kept in the minutes of the board. As direct aids to the board, the following arrangements are made:

1. Trust Investment Committee. Before accepting any trust business, the board of directors must appoint an investment committee of at least three members who shall be experienced and capable officers or directors of the bank. The investment or liquidation of any trust fund must have the approval of the investment committee. This committee must keep minutes of all the business handled. At least once each year, the investment committee must review all of the assets of the department and of each trust to determine the advisability of making changes. It is sometimes required by law that this be done every three months.

2. Executive Officers. Before using any fiduciary function, the trust department must be placed under the management of an executive officer who is qualified to administer trusts. His duties in general will be prescribed by the board of directors in the bylaws for the department.

3. Competent Legal Counsel. The trust department is required to appoint or employ competent legal counsel not for the practice of law but to be available for advice to the bank and the department.

4. Principles of Trust Institutions. It is required that every national bank conform to sound principles in the operation of a trust department. Such principles were prescribed by the Executive Council of the American Bankers Association on April 11, 1933, and are included in the appendix to Regulation F of the Federal Reserve Board. These principles may be summarized as follows:

a. In the acceptance of personal trust business, the determining factors should be:

(1) Is trust service needed?

(2) Can the services be rendered properly?

b. It is the duty of the bank in the care of a personal trust to administer the trust solely in the interest of the beneficiary.

c. In the case of a corporate trust, the bank should be satisfied that the company is in good state and that the business is of a proper nature for the bank to accept the responsibility. It is the duty of the trustee of a corporate trust to render prompt and accurate service.

d. In the investment of trust funds, it must be borne in mind that the account must be kept separately and that care and management of property—rather than speculation or safekeeping—is the important thing.

e. It is expected that fees shall be reasonable and in accordance with state laws. It is the duty of the trust department to maintain friendly relations with the public, with the bar, and with life underwriters.

Kinds of Trusts

Earlier in this chapter, we listed the services rendered by fiduciaries. That listing included both the care of individuals and of property. It was pointed out that the care of individuals was delegated to a guardian, tutor, or curator.

A trust, however, involves the holding, handling, or managing of property for a beneficiary. A trustee, upon appointment, becomes the temporary titleholder of the property for the beneficiary, who may be a person, institution, community, or corporation. It appears desirable, therefore, to separate the kinds of trusts on the basis of beneficiaries. This may be done as follows: [11]

1. Personal Trust. A personal trust is one which is created for the benefit of one or more persons.

2. Institutional Trust. An institutional trust is one created for the benefit of eleemosynary institutions, such as hospitals and colleges.

3. Community Trust. A community trust is one created for the benefit of the community, whether it be a community playground, a city or a state project, or a national or an international organization.

4. Corporate Trust. A corporate trust is one created by a corporation for its own benefit through providing a mortgage as security for its bond or note issues.

In this chapter, further attention will be devoted to personal trusts and corporate trusts.

---

[11] American Institute of Banking, *Trust Business, Trusts,* Vol. I, pp. 7 ff.

Personal Trusts

A personal trust gets its name from the fact that a beneficiary is a natural person or persons. Humanity's affections for its own members and the family's desire to care for its own are the springboards back of the creation of personal trusts.

The principal personal trusts are created (1) by will, (2) by contract, usually life insurance trusts, (3) by declaration, usually living trusts, and (4) by court appointment.

1. Under will. The creation of a trust under will enables a testate to determine in his own lifetime the manner in which his property will be used for the protection not only of his family as a group but also as individuals in the family. It may be desirable for the mother to maintain the property as a unit until the children are grown. Or the children may be grown and need a distribution of the property, except for a home for the mother. Through the use of a will, the creator is able to make proper provisions to meet the need.

2. By contract, usually life insurance trusts. Life insurance trusts are created by a person having his insurance policies made payable to a trustee for the benefit of some person. Personal insurance trusts may be funded or unfunded. Under an unfunded insurance trust, the creator continues to pay the premium. A funded insurance trust is one in which securities or income-producing property are turned over to the trustee who will use the income to pay the premium on the insurance.

3. By declaration, usually living trusts. Living trusts are created both by declaration and agreement. Such trusts are primarily for the benefit of a settlor or grantor or his family, or for the benefit of a third person. The settlor may create a living trust for the purpose of following a systematic plan of saving without having the responsibility of investing and managing his own property. He usually does this for a given period while he accumulates a competence, or he may do it permanently as a means of creating an independent estate.

On the other hand, the settlor may create a living trust for the benefit of various members of his family, such as his son or daughter or his wife. Again, it may be desirable to create a living trust for some outsider whom he desires to help without appearing to be engaged in charity. Living trusts may be revocable or irrevocable.

4. By court appointment. When the owner of property dies intestate, the courts will appoint an administrator to take over the property and manage it for the benefit of the rightful heirs, pending their reaching majority and obtaining final settlement. The beneficiary must be someone other than the trustee.

Length of a Trust

The duration of a trust is a matter of law.[12] The rule against perpetuities as interpreted in the various states leads to variation in the length of a trust from one state to another. Community trusts and institutional trusts are exempt from the rule against perpetuities and, therefore, may continue indefinitely. Corporate trusts are capable also of being extended over the life of a contract which necessitates the trust.

Personal trusts, however, are subject to the rule against perpetuities and, therefore, vary from one state to another. The rule in general is that the duration of the trust must not be longer than a life or lives in being and 21 years thereafter. This enables a person or persons to make trusts for the remainder of his or their lives and 21 years thereafter. This would assure the maker of a trust care for his youngest child until maturity. In Louisiana, a testamentary or an inter vivos trust can continue for 10 years after the death of the settlor, provided the beneficiary is of age. If the beneficiary is not of age when the settlor dies, the trust is allowed to continue for 10 years after the beneficiary becomes of age.

Upon the expiration of the time limit established by the rule against perpetuities, both the trust department and the beneficiary, because of a need for continuous management of a business, may find it desirable to transfer a trust from a regular account to an agency or custodian account.

The Investment of Trust Funds

The parable of the Ten Talents provides an excellent philosophy for the handling of trusts and investing of trust funds. In "A Statement of Principles of Trust Institutions," adopted by the Executive Committee of the Trust Division, American Bankers Association, April 10, 1933, and approved by the Executive Council of the American Bankers Association on April 11, 1933, this instrument declares that, "The investment function of a trustee is care and management of property, not mere safekeeping at one extreme or speculation at the other."

In the case of trust departments of commercial banks, all investments are made, kept, or sold, usually with the approval of an investment committee which may be composed of the president, a vice-president, and the trust officer.

Much of the time, however, the trust officer and investment committee have no choice in making investments. When the trust instrument makes specific provision for investments or as to the powers of the trust officers,

---

[12] *Prentice-Hall Trust Course.* New York: Prentice-Hall, Inc., 1950, p. 1301.

the terms of the instrument must be followed. If such provisions are against public policy, the courts should be asked to give instructions. If the trust instruments allow discretion in the investment of funds, the guiding principle should be safety of principal and dependability of income.

The ethical principle found in most regulations is that a trustee cannot have a personal interest in the trust investments which it makes as trustee, and that it should not purchase any security from any of its trust accounts.

In general, rules for the investment of trust funds were very rigid and restricted until the last 25 years. It was required that funds be invested in accordance with the provisions of the trust instrument (which might name the type of securities or might allow a choice). If the instrument did not provide for discretion in the investment, the trustee was expected to invest in the list of legal investments provided by the law of the state. Any variation from these rules would make a trustee liable. In more recent years, two types of variation have been allowed either by law or by regulation. These are as follows: [13]

1. The Prudent-Man Rule. The prudent-man rule simply requires that where a trustee has a choice in making investments, he must follow the same policy a prudent man would follow in investing his own funds. This was allowed in Massachusetts by court decision as early as 1830. Three other states had followed the Massachusetts rule by 1900. But the big trend to the prudent-man rule has come out of World War II and includes restricted trust funds. This has come about as a result of the decline in bond yields, the increase in taxes, and the increased costs in trust administration. These things have brought to focus the need for increased income on the one hand and the desirability of protecting the principal from depreciation through inflation. As a consequence of all these factors, the prudent-man rule is rapidly gaining ground. In 1946, there were 18 states which had adopted it by statute or by judicial decision. New York became the 25th state on the prudent-man rule list by the statute which became effective July 1, 1950. This statute allows fiduciaries to invest up to 35 per cent of restricted trust funds "in such securities as would be acquired by prudent men of discretion, using intelligence in such matters, who are seeking a reasonable income and the preservation of their capital."

2. Common Trust Funds. Investing small trust funds which have to be kept separate from one another was expensive and difficult. Trustees had little choice but to invest small trust funds in the so-called "legals" and let it go at that. Following the financial difficulties of 1929, several

---

[13] Board of Governors of the Federal Reserve System, Regulation F, *United Investment Report,* May 22, 1950, p. 207.

large trust companies and trust departments of banks began commingling or pooling small trust funds for investment purposes. This arrangement provided an opportunity for handling small trusts on the same basis as larger ones.

Federal income tax authorities, however, decided that not only income from these funds but also the funds themselves should be taxed. As a result of this double taxation on small trusts when pooled, Congress amended the Revenue Act of 1936 to allow banks to operate common trust funds under the regulation of the Federal Reserve Board when not in conflict with state law, and without being subject to an income tax on the fund itself. Twenty-eight states now permit the use of common trust funds.

Trust departments of banks and trust companies operating a common trust fund follow the prudent-man rule in making investments because it enables larger yields.

The trust department of a national bank or of any bank holding membership in the Federal Reserve System may operate a common trust fund only after obtaining approval of the Federal Reserve Board. A trust department must obtain approval of its own trust investment committee before applying for approval of the Federal Reserve Board. Regulation F of the Federal Reserve Board has placed a number of restrictions on the participation in and operation of the common trust fund. These are as follows:

a. Such funds can be operated only for the benefit of trust funds in the pool. For that reason, certificates of ownership are neither issued nor allowed to be bought and sold.

b. No trust can invest in more than 10 per cent of the fund and, even then, not more than $50,000 in the fund. Any trust which invests in more than one fund cannot have a total invested of more than $50,000 or 10 per cent of the total of both funds, whichever is smaller.

c. In the case of mortgage investment funds which are provided in the same manner and under the same regulations, the restriction for each mortgage fund is $1200, or 2 per cent of the total mortgage fund, whichever is smaller.

It is required that common trust funds be audited annually and reports made to the participants. It is further required that the value of the assets be determined every three months by the trust investment committee for the purpose of determining changes that should be made in the fund.

A recent Supreme Court ruling on proper notice of accounting is worthy of mention. On April 24, 1950, the Supreme Court nullified that part of the New York law of 1937 which had provided that newspaper notice to interested persons is enough notice when a court accounting of

a common trust fund is about to be held. The Supreme Court ruling, therefore, requires that when such an accounting is to be made, it is necessary for the trustee to give a written notice to interested persons. This case was Docket No. 378, Mulane *vs.* Central Hanover Bank and Trust Company. The decision was on the ground that the provision of the New York law on the method of notice was incompatible with the Fourteenth Amendment of the Constitution.

The Settlement of an Estate

Among the most important services rendered by trust companies and trust departments of commercial banks is that of executor or administrator. The first step in the settlement of an estate of a testator is that, upon his death, of going before a probate court and having the will proved or probated and an executor appointed.[14] The executor is frequently nominated in the will. If there is no will, the court should be called upon to appoint an administrator of the estate. Upon receiving appointment either as executor or administrator, it becomes the duty of such appointee to take charge of the estate, have the property assembled, inventoried, and appraised. The estate and inheritance taxes should be determined.

The inventory with the appraised value of the property is an essential record of the court and is the basis for a check on the final accounting.

It is of equal importance to determine the liabilities of the estate. Public notice should be given to the creditors to submit their claims. These claims should be checked and listed in the order of priority.

In general, personal property should be liquidated immediately and the proceeds used to pay the estate and inheritance taxes and the other liabilities. If this does not provide sufficient funds, it will be necessary to liquidate some or all of the real estate. If the real estate does not have to be liquidated to pay obligations, then it is distributed in accordance with the will or in accordance with the devisee laws.

The executor or administrator may find it necessary to operate the business for a considerable time while the estate is in the process of liquidation and settlement. Likewise, it may be necessary to make new investments and liquidate other ones. In such a case it is the duty of the executor or administrator to keep all property and funds separate from any other trusts. In making investments, he must follow the legal requirements in his state.

When the estate and inheritance taxes have been settled and the debts of the estate paid, it becomes the duty of the executor or administrator to distribute the remainder of the estate in accordance with the provisions

---

14 Trant, *op. cit.*, p. 308.

of the will or in accordance with the law and court decisions if the owner died intestate.

When all the property and funds of the estate have been distributed, the executor or administrator must make a final accounting to the court. This final accounting starts with the inventory and appraisal of the property, gives details of each transaction, and records the results. This record is filed with the court so that not only the court but all parties concerned may have the complete history of the trusteeship and, thereby, know that the executor or administrator has performed his duties as required by the will or by the laws of the state.

Some estates may require several years before liquidation and others, only a few weeks. On the average, settlement of an estate will take about a year or a little more. In most states, the bulk of the business done by trust companies and trust departments of commercial banks lies in the work of the executor or administrator.

Corporate Trusts

A corporate trust is one which has been created for the benefit of a corporation. At the same time, the corporate trust may be for the benefit of purchasers of corporate securities. Corporate trusts also include a variety of services rendered for corporations. The trustee for a corporate trust is almost always a trust company or trust department of a commercial bank. Because of the advantages of the services rendered by trust departments and trust companies under the corporate trust, it appears desirable to examine these services in some detail.[15]

1. Trustee Under Corporate Mortgage or Deed of Trust. Providing capital funds for long periods of time for financing the building of railroads, huge industrial plants, expansion of plants, and the buying of new property by means of bond issues secured by a mortgage or deed of trust had its heyday in the 100 years prior to 1930. Great internal improvement programs were carried out in the early 1830's. Some of these were financed by various states issuing their bonds or guaranteeing the bonds of approved companies engaged in improvement. Railroads and other approved businesses which began their expansion programs around 1830 obtained money by borrowing on long-term bonds. As protection to the buyer of the bonds, the railroads and industrial concerns gave a mortgage on a part, or all, of their property, and this mortgage frequently included any property that might be acquired at a later time. A deed of trust is probably used more often than a mortgage, but the two serve very much the same purpose: that of protecting the bondholder with title to the property. The trust department of a bank or trust com-

---

[15] Smith, *op. cit.,* p. 272 ff.

pany is appointed trustee under the terms of the mortgage or deed of trust. The trust department of the bank is then responsible to bond-holders to see that the terms of the mortgage or deed are carried out.

Such responsibility makes it necessary for the trust officer of the bank to exercise care and judgment. This he can do successfully only by know-ing the business. He must determine the provisions of the mortgage or trust deed protecting the bondholders. The conditions or terms of ap-pointment of the bank as trustee should indicate the corporation's finan-cial position, its future plans and needs. From this the trustee should be able to determine whether the bond issue is adequate to finance the project and whether provision has been made for later expansion of the company. The trust department should determine whether provisions have been made for taxes, the payment of interest, the payment of prop-erty insurance, and the fee to have the mortgage recorded. Provision should be made in the mortgage for the substitution of property when-ever necessary changes are made.

The use of an open-end mortgage takes care of the need for additional funds. Sinking fund arrangements must be checked and every phase of the requirements of the mortgage or deed must be known to the trustee and must be such as to protect the bondholders.

The trust department of the bank must see to it that the company lives up to every obligation in the mortgage. If the company fails to do so, the trustee must ask the court for the appointment of a receiver.

2. Receiver. A receiver is appointed on a temporary basis to take over property of the company and make an inventory of it, take over the books and records, and operate the business pending reorganization or the appointment of a trustee or liquidator. In many cases, the receiver is appointed with the view to operating it until it is again on a going basis. The business is then returned to its original owners. If the receiver finds that it cannot be rehabilitated, he will ask the court to appoint a liquida-tor. The receiver, however, has a better opportunity than anyone else to bring the company back to a paying basis. He is operating under orders of the court and, therefore, can make changes, such as reducing costs through making new rent contracts and through reorganizing the capital structure. He may obtain additional funds through the issuance of receivers' certificates which take precedence over all other obligations. He must be careful to follow court instructions and the bankruptcy laws of the state.

A so-called involuntary receivership results from the trustee's or credi-tors' asking the court to appoint a receiver because of the failure of the company to fulfill its obligations under the corporate mortgage. A volun-tary receivership is created when the company itself asks for the appoint-ment of a receiver. The trust company which held the title to the prop-

erty under the mortgage or deed may be appointed the receiver and, thereby, become the holder and manager of the property.

3. Registrar and Transfer Agent. It is a logical thing for large corporations to employ trust companies and trust departments of commercial banks to act as registrar or transfer agent for their stocks. This practice has been in existence for more than a century and a quarter. Some corporations serve as their own transfer agent but most of them use a bank. The stock exchanges require all corporations whose securities are listed to employ a trust company or trust department as registrar. Most states require corporations to keep their stock books within the state of incorporation. The law usually requires the names and addresses of all stockholders and the dates when they became stockholders. The duties of registrar and transfer agent will be discussed separately.

a. Registrar of Stocks. The stock exchanges require corporations whose stocks are listed to employ an approved trust company or trust department of a commercial bank to serve as registrar of their stock. The duty of the registrar is primarily to the public. It has the specific duties of preventing an overissuance of stock. The registrar must, therefore, never sign new stock certificates in excess of the old ones cancelled.

b. Transfer Agent. A corporation may transfer its own stock but, in general, it has been found to be more desirable for the company to employ a bank or trust company as transfer agent. The same bank or trust company cannot serve as registrar and transfer agent of the same corporation. The transfer agent works for the corporation. It is the agent of the corporation and must look to the corporation for instructions, but it must know the rights of stockholders. It must keep complete and accurate records and must be informed on the laws relating to bankruptcy, receiverships, and trusteeships. It must be sure that the stock presented for transfer is in the hands of its rightful owner.

4. Agency Accounts. Banks and trust companies perform many agency services for corporations. The bank or trust company may act as custodian for income-bearing personal property or in an agency capacity for other property. Agency accounts are the result of agreements, and the trust department is paid for the services it renders. The details of the work to be done are prescribed by the agreement. In general, it covers the safekeeping of securities. The trust department keeps a complete record of securities called for redemption, maturities, dividends, and interest payments. It notifies the owners of stocks and bonds of conversion privileges, pays out money in accordance with the agreement, and makes a final accounting to the beneficiaries. The trust department must take the same kind of care that it would in handling its own business unless it specifies some other kind of care in the agreement.

The various corporate trust services rendered by trust companies and

trust departments of commercial banks were studied by the Securities and Exchange Commission in 1936. The report given by the Securities and Exchange Commission recommended improvements which would require greater responsibility and care by trust companies and trust departments engaging in corporate trust business. That statement was particularly applicable to the provisions of a corporate mortgage and in enforcing the requirements protecting purchasers of the original issue of securities and also the new ones in a reorganization.

The result of the report was the passage of the Trust Indenture Act of 1939.[16] The requirements were enacted into law and the Securities and Exchange Commission was given the power to approve the indentures used.

Fees for Trust Services

The fees to be charged for trust services vary somewhat from one state to another, or even from one community to another. In many states, the fees for personal trusts have been fixed by law or by court order. Sometimes, upper and lower limits are fixed. The rate may be worked out on a percentage basis in some cases and on a flat rate for other services. For serving as executor or administrator, it is frequently fixed at $2\frac{1}{2}$ per cent on the inventory value of the entire estate. For service as guardian, tutor, or curator, a minimum charge of 5 per cent on the income is not unusual.

Fees tend to uniformity on various services. Furthermore, regulatory authorities frown on any unreasonable rate.

The Economics of the Trust Business

For many years there has been considerable discussion of the question of whether trust business has any influence on our economic life and whether that influence is good or bad.

It is recognized, of course, that the major tasks of trusteeship are those of preserving and managing economic goods for the life of the trust. Furthermore, the least that can be expected in the management of the goods is that it be done on a prudent-man basis. This should provide productive operation and the creation of new wealth as well as preservation of the old. This would certainly place trust business on the good side of our economic and social system because trust funds would, thereby, be productive.

---

[16] Ray B. Westerfield, *Money, Credit and Banking*. New York: The Ronald Press Company, 1947, p. 976.

From an individual point of view, the prudent-man attitude of the trust business means a great deal:

1. It assures the testator that his accumulations will be safeguarded and, at the proper time, distributed to the various members of his family in accordance with his wishes, or that the property will be liquidated in an orderly manner and settlement made with proper owners.

2. It assures the testator that his wealth will be used for the protection of his widow and children.

3. It assures the creator of the estate that it will be managed by competent agents until settled.

4. In the case of corporate trusts, it aids in the bringing to them of sufficient funds for development and expansion of huge or small undertakings. It is by this means that the railroads and large industrial plants have been built. It has enabled a man of small means to buy some of the capital of large corporations.

On the other hand, there are those who feel that the trust business is constantly accumulating trust funds and that the investment of these funds gives trust institutions a controlling power in our economic life. In theory, that could happen. In practice, however, it appears remote. A great deal of the trust business is handled for only a short period of time. Executorships and administratorships cover the most important trust business for banks and trust companies. Some of the executorships run for a number of years, but the average time for settling all of them is slightly more than one year. In addition to that, the income from trusts, as reported by the income tax returns, is not great. These income tax returns, covering about 21,000 trusts, were made to the Internal Revenue Department in 1947 for a total of only $4.5 billion. That figure is small compared to the total income of the United States or even to the tax revenue of the federal government.

One may say that the question really arises as to the influence trust funds may have in the control of corporations. That question brings up the fact that trust institutions are engaged more in the marketing of securities than in their purchase. In recent years, there has been a trend toward purchasing corporate securities—stocks and bonds. Even under the prudent-man rule, which has somewhat settled on the figure of 35 per cent of restricted funds to be used on that basis, it is hardly possible to think of more than half of the trust funds available being put into corporate securities. That again should be compared to the national debt or the national income to see that the total is really small and that there cannot be much control at the present time. It must be recognized, on the other hand, that trust institutions may exert a strong influence on the individual corporation as to the kind of securities it may issue. Here the Indenture Act of 1939 comes in to protect the public. On the whole,

trust company services are valuable adjuncts to our economic and social life and in no way jeopardize it.

Suggested Readings

BOOKS

American Institute of Banking, *Trust Business*. New York: The Institute, 1934 and 1935. Vols. I and II.

Prentice-Hall Trust Course. New York: Prentice-Hall, Inc., 1950.

Smith, James G., *Trust Companies in the United States*. New York: Henry Holt & Company, 1928.

Stephenson, Gilbert Thomas, *Estates and Trusts*. New York: Appleton-Century-Crofts, Inc., 1949.

Thomas, Rollin G., *Our Modern Banking and Monetary System*. 2nd Ed. New York: Prentice-Hall, Inc., 1950. Chapter 25.

Trant, James B., *Bank Administration*. New York: McGraw-Hill Book Company, Inc., 1931. Chapter 18.

Westerfield, Ray B., *Money, Credit and Banking*, Revised Edition. New York: The Ronald Press Company, 1947. Chapter 33.

Whitney National Bank, *Lawyer's Desk Book*. New Orleans: The Bank, 1950.

UNITED STATES GOVERNMENT DOCUMENTS

Comptroller of the Currency, *Federal Laws Affecting National Banks*. Washington, D.C.: Government Printing Office, 1950.

Board of Governors of the Federal Reserve System, *Annual Report*. Washington, D.C.: Government Printing Office, 1948.

———, *Banking Studies*, third reprint, 1949.

———, *Trust Powers of National Banks*, Regulation F, June 1, 1940.

———, *Membership of State Banking Institutions in the Federal Reserve System*, Regulation H, Sept. 1, 1948.

———, *List of National Banks Authorized to Exercise Fiduciary Powers*, Dec. 31, 1949.

PERIODICALS

The Banking Law Journal (Cambridge), May and June, 1950, Vol. 67, Nos. 5 and 6.

The Burroughs Clearing House, Burroughs Adding Machine Company (Detroit), July 1950.

The Trust Bulletin, Trust Division, American Bankers Association, May, 1950.

United Investment Report, "Common Stocks Under the Prudent-Man Rule," United Business Service Company. Boston, May 22, 1950.

PAMPHLETS

Rules of the Clearing House Association of New Orleans, Rule 20, "Trust Department Fees." New Orleans, The Association, 1940.

The National Bank of Commerce of Louisiana, *Trust Estates Act*. New Orleans, The Bank, 1938.

Trust Company of Georgia, *As Agent for the Safekeeping and Management of Your Securities*. Atlanta: The Company, n.d.

———, *Behind the Scenes in the Trust Company*. Atlanta: The Company, n.d.

———, *A More Complete Service for Trust Customers*. Atlanta: The Company, n.d.

————, *What Every Family Knows or Should Learn.* Atlanta: The Company, n.d.

Whitney National Bank, *Your Executor and Trustee.* New Orleans: The Bank, n.d.

NEWSPAPERS

The American Banker, New York, "Supreme Court Nullifies New York State Law on Notice of Common Trust Accounting," April 25, 1950.

————, "High Court Ruling Poses Common Trust Problems," April 27, 1950.

————, "Sullivan Advises Liberal Investment in Common Stocks for Trustees," May 19, 1950.

————, "Trust Business Must Be Sold," June 19, 1950.

18

International Financial Institutions and the Foreign Investment Outlook

by ARTHUR R. UPGREN
Professor of Economics

and JOHN A. STOVEL
Assistant Professor of Economics

School of Business Administration
University of Minnesota

AFTER A CENTURY featured by the successful world use of the international gold standard (centered upon Great Britain) in settling short-term balances and in maintaining stability in exchange rates, and after a most remarkably successful century of international long-term investment and lending to promote world economic development, the world has been so torn asunder by two wars and a great depression that economic development and stability of the exchanges have been imperiled. The purpose of this chapter is to review briefly the setting of the interwar period and the policies in the United States which in that period frustrated extensive cooperation on our part in the world economy. The reversal of United States policies in the latter part of that period are briefly noted. The errors and failures of this period lead into a discussion of how two new United Nations world financial institutions came into being. These are The International Monetary Fund (more briefly "The Fund"), and The International Bank for Reconstruction and Development (or "The Bank"). The central portion of this chapter deals with The Fund and is followed by a brief discussion of The Bank. There is also a discussion of how U.S. policy developed into a program for European postwar recovery. The chapter concludes with an examination of the future role of United States foreign lending in world economic development.

Stability in the world economy and mutually acceptable processes of promoting both the long-term lending and investment so vital to world economic development and adjustment of exchange rates are inter-

related problems. Currency depreciation can influence another nation's tariff policies and hence the balance of its economy and development. Foreign lending and investment can contribute to economic development. Economic development can favorably influence stability in exchange rates. Thus are these economic processes interlocked and related. Judged by the nineteenth century, the leading, dynamic role is played by international investment. We consider first the more recent background of foreign lending policies by the United States. From this review there can be grasped how the Reciprocal Trade Agreements Act of 1934 and the formation a decade later of The Bank and The Fund have fundamentally altered the economically isolationist policies of the United States.

Strongly based foreign investment never got a fresh start after 1914, though sporadic lending did take place in the 1920's after considerable recovery from the immediate postwar depression. By 1931 a sustained period of net *imports* of capital into the United States was under way. Demands of creditors in the newer, lending countries, notably the United States, were for so rapid a rate of repayment as to contribute notably to the depression in such countries as Germany. Though exchange stability was achieved by the end of the 1920's, competitive currency depreciation was rampant in the early 1930's. Some countries such as Japan and Australia had barely re-established the gold standard in time to see it collapse within a year or two. The United States possessed the economic strength of a creditor nation and a lending creditor, but she pursued policies of high tariffs which made difficult the repayment of loans. As a result, all students of foreign financing and investment reflected upon the impossibility of expecting investments to thrive in the teeth of heavily increased tariffs by the country which now had an enlarged stake in successful foreign lending.

In the period following World War I, the United States increased its tariffs three times. So hasty was its action that the first increases were contained in what was called "The Emergency Tariff Act of 1921." The source of power behind that tariff boost was the threat of large imports of European goods which then could be laid down at low cost in the United States because the currencies had fallen so much in value. Thus fear of being swamped with new imports at the war's end produced higher tariffs. That there were few supplies of goods available for such job-destroying importation was generally overlooked. Similarly overlooked was the inexorable need for increased imports if foreign lending was to have a successful outcome.

The lessons to be drawn from the conflicting policies of the United States were not avoided by the people of the United States. After World War I currencies had depreciated, tariffs had been boosted,

sporadic foreign lending attempted, repayment was hastily demanded or repatriation attempted, and complete international economic demoralization followed. The turnabout in the international economic policies of the United States came before changes were made in political policies of an international character. First, there was the Reciprocal Trade Agreements Act approved June 12, 1934. Under the terms of this act our tariffs could be lowered in bilateral agreement. Tariffs could be lowered by an amount up to 50 per cent of rates in the Smoot-Hawley tariff act of 1930. Later extensions of the act have authorized a repeated reduction by 50 per cent from levels to which tariff rates may have been reduced in the years following 1934. Thus a total reduction of 75 per cent in the 1930 high-water mark rates is possible provided the earlier and the later reductions had each been for the legal maximum. Many rates have been reduced by smaller proportions, but the great rise in values of many imported goods upon which "specific rates" are levied has contributed to tariff reduction expressed in "ad valorem equivalents." In fact, rates which averaged about 48 per cent on all dutiable commodities in 1930 have been reduced to an average placed at about 15 per cent a year or two ago. This estimate of the effective tariff reduction by the United States has been made by Professor Clair Wilcox of Swarthmore College, head of the United States delegation on the International Trade Organization (ITO). The war and postwar inflations and successive tariff reductions emanating from a series of international trade conferences may well place the United States in the ranks of low tariff nations, though rates against many manufactured goods are still high by any standard which may be applied.

In the 1930's there was established the Export-Import Bank of Washington.[1] The intent was to promote United States exports, particularly of machinery to Latin American neighbors. This was a part of the Good Neighbor policy and helped turn attention to constructive policies in international economic affairs, though political policies were still isolationist.

[1] The Export-Import Bank was established in 1934 as a banking corporation organized under the laws of the District of Columbia. The bank was continued as an agency of the United States by acts of Congress in 1935, 1937, 1939 and 1940, and was made a permanent independent agency of the government by the Export-Import Bank Act of 1945. The object and purpose of the Bank, as stated in the Charter, is "to aid in financing and to facilitate exports and imports and the exchange of commodities between the United States and other nations." However, the underlying or long-run purposes of the bank have been largely shaped by two emergencies: the depression and the war. In addition to its capital stock of $1,000,000,000, subscribed by the United States, the Bank is authorized to borrow from the Secretary of the Treasury, not in excess of two and one-half times the authorized capital stock. The Export-Import Bank has grown since its creation in 1934, both in size and in range of activities. Today the Bank is empowered to use its $3,500,000,000 of lending capacity without limitation as to the total amount of obligations thereto of any borrower, endorser,

As a result, it was not surprising that discussions developed during the war years which were oriented to establishing, *in detail,* policies and institutions which would promote a more cooperative world. Early drafts of such policies were designed to provide institutions for international lending, long and short term. These emerged in the form of charters, developed at the International Monetary Conference held at Bretton Woods, New Hampshire, in July 1944. One charter was for The International Monetary Fund (IMF) and the second for The International Bank for Reconstruction and Development (IBRD). The United States had now changed its thinking entirely. With these institutions available to meet the needs of embarrassed countries, loans could be made to secure economic advance and to stabilize currencies. In fact, a prerequisite for a country's joining the International Monetary Fund is that it shall name a rate of exchange for its currency that will be adhered to and that can, upon the promise of advances, be maintained. Thus currency depreciation is made subject to cooperative control and mutual consultation, and a truce is made with competitive, "cutthroat" currency depreciations. The enormous advantage is now that the United States can be relatively free of the fear of currency depreciation, which immediately following World War I had been partly the basis for high tariffs as a means of defense. Add to that the case of the special loan of $3,750,-000,000 to Britain as a special currency "assist" and the removal of fear was believed to be nearly complete.

The International Monetary Fund

Charters for the International Monetary Fund and the International Bank for Reconstruction and Development were drawn up at the United Nations Monetary and Financial Conference held at Bretton Woods, New Hampshire, in July 1944. The United States, sponsor of the conference, ratified the agreements in July 1945, and the inaugural meeting of the Board of Governors of the Fund took place in March 1946. By September 1949, all but four of the 44 nations represented at the Bretton Woods Conference (one exception was the U.S.S.R.) had become members. Later eight additional countries, not represented at the original conference, also joined.

---

etc., at any time outstanding. Moreover, it is empowered to make almost any kind of loan to any borrower as long as the transaction is connected with the trade of the United States.

Résumé of Activities	*Feb. 12, 1934 to June 30, 1950*
Total credits authorized	$4,657,642
Balances outstanding as of June 30, 1950:	
Undisbursed authorizations	560,105
Outstanding loans	2,226,285

Each member country has one representative on the Board of Governors. The Board has appointed a Managing Director, Mr. Camille Gutt, who, with the staff he has selected, performs the research and administrative tasks of The Fund at the principal offices in Washington, D. C. The structure of The Fund further includes the Executive Directors, their present membership being 14, of whom five are appointed by the five members of the largest quotas.

One fundamental issue was whether the lending and other operations of The Fund would be largely automatic or carried on by The Fund's managing director and staff (international civil servants with no loyalty to any other authority), or whether such operations would be managed actively by the executive directors responsible to the particular member governments they represent.[2] The latter was the American position and is the one which has been accepted for reasons that will be discussed in connection with The Fund's policy on lending.

Decisions of The Fund are made by the Board of Governors. These decisions are made usually by a majority of the votes cast. Each member has (a basic) 250 votes plus an additional vote for each paid-in share. Each share has a par value of $100,000 (U.S. dollar equivalent). The United States has 30 per cent of the total voting power, and the United Kingdom has 14 per cent. Either the American or British voting power being greater than 10 per cent, is sufficient to provide an effective veto in the exceptional case of uniform changes in par values—that is, changes in the price of gold in all member countries. Generally, however, decision is by a straight majority of voting power, and no veto applies.

The Fund consists of a pool of gold and foreign exchange of more than $8 billion. Each country has a quota equal to its subscription. For example that of the United States quota is $2,750 million, France's is $525 million, and the United Kingdom's is $1,300 million. Twenty-five per cent of the subscription is paid up in gold (or 10 per cent of the country's holdings of gold plus U.S. dollars, if this is the smaller of the two). The remainder of the subscription is paid in the member country's currency. From this pool of currencies each member country is entitled to draw 25 per cent of its quota in any one year, provided that such action is consistent with the purposes of The Fund. The drawing consists of paying to The Fund the member's own currency in exchange for the foreign currency required. When such drawing results in The Fund's acquiring more than 75 per cent of the member's quota, the member country is technically a debtor to The Fund. However, until The Fund's holdings have exceeded 100 per cent, there has been in effect merely an

---

[2] See R. F. Mikesell, "The International Monetary Fund, 1944–1949," *International Conciliation,* November 1949, where an excellent discussion of this question and others related to the Fund is to be found.

exchange of the member country's original gold contribution for the foreign currency which the member country is obtaining from The Fund. *Net borrowing* does not truly begin until The Fund holdings exceed 100 per cent.

The major purposes of The Fund are: (1) to promote exchange rate stability and to secure orderly adjustments of exchange rates with a view to avoiding the competitive beggar-my-neighbor type of depreciation which was prevalent in the 1930's; (2) to provide short-term financial aid to members in order that *temporary* balance of payments maladjustments may be corrected without resort to undesirable restrictions upon imports; (3) to eliminate foreign exchange restrictions on current as distinct from capital account, or in other words to make foreign exchange received for visible and invisible exports freely convertible into any other currency; (4) to provide machinery for consultation and collaboration on international monetary problems; and (5) to facilitate through constructive international policy the balanced expansion of world trade.

A member country must agree with The Fund on a satisfactory par value for its currency in terms of gold or the U.S. dollar. The agreed upon exchange rate may then be varied by no more than 10 per cent without the approval of The Fund. A change in the par value of the currency is sanctioned only when such a change might serve as a corrective to a "fundamental disequilibrium." This was not defined in the articles of agreement, but subsequent discussion indicates that fundamental disequilibrium exists if there is disequilibrium in the balance of payments in the sense of continued non-offsetting gold and short-term capital movements. Even in the absence of gold and short-term capital movements, fundamental disequilibrium may be present where the avoidance of a balance of payments deficit is at the cost of persistent unemployment in the member country.[3]

Members of The Fund undertake not to impose restrictions on payments for current international transactions, and they seek to avoid multiple currency practices which involve different rates for different types of transactions where, for example, luxury imports are deterred by exchange rates which are higher in terms of the domestic currency. Such obligations have, however, been generally postponed until March 1952, the end of a five-year transitional period following the commencement of The Fund's actual operations. Following the end of the transitional period, members must consult with The Fund with a view to the removal of any remaining restrictions. Failure to comply with the requests of

---

[3] See the discussion by G. Haberler, A. H. Hansen, *et al.* in the *Review of Economic Statistics*, November 1944. Also see *The New York Times*, March 19, 1946, for a clarification elicited from the Executive Directors by Lord Keynes.

The Fund in this matter may lead to ineligibility to use the resources of The Fund or to expulsion from The Fund. However, restrictions and discrimination in the post-transitional period are to be permitted in the case where a particular currency—the U.S. dollar, for example—becomes *generally* scarce, and a formal declaration of scarcity is made by The Fund.

The lending operations of The Fund involve contentious matters of policy. Interest becomes payable to The Fund at one-half of 1 per cent on average daily balances of a member's currency up to 25 per cent in excess of the member's quota, when these excess balances have been held by The Fund for more than three months. The rate of interest increases by one-half of 1 per cent with each subsequent year. Also for each additional bracket of 25 per cent in excess of the member's quota, an additional one-half of 1 per cent is charged. The limits to borrowing are 25 per cent of the quota in a 12-month period, and total borrowings must not cause The Fund's holdings of the member's currency (which is paid to The Fund in exchange for, for example, U.S. dollars purchased from The Fund) to exceed 200 per cent of its quota. In effect, then, *net borrowing* may not exceed the member's quota. The Fund would have to hold in excess of 75 per cent of the quota for four years for the marginal interest rate to reach 4 per cent. When the interest rate reaches this level, The Fund and the member will consider means whereby The Fund's holding of the currency can be reduced. When the interest rate reaches 5 per cent, The Fund may then impose such charges as it deems appropriate.

The loans to a member (technically purchases of foreign currency by a member), have no specific term for repayment, so that the lending policy of The Fund becomes extremely vital. Let us consider the problem in the context of recent world economic conditions. Until 1950, demand for U.S. dollars exceeded the supply, and there is a possibility that without U.S. foreign assistance for defense and other purposes, this dollar shortage may recur in the future. One measure of this dollar shortage of the last 35 years is $100 billion. This includes U.S. gold imports, the unstable, private long-term lending of the 1920's, Lend-lease, and post World War II aid through UNRRA and ERP, for example. Provision of dollars to foreigners by such means amounted to 4 per cent of our national income and 40 per cent of our exports of goods and services over the period.[4] ERP assistance commenced at the rate of $5 billion per year; the credit of $3.75 billion to Great Britain in late 1945 was drawn upon to the extent of $3.25 billion in a year and a half; the Export-Import Bank loaned $2½ billion abroad in the three and one-half

---

[4] See S. Harris. *The European Recovery Program*. Cambridge, Mass.: Harvard University Press, 1948.

years following January 1946. Large loans and grants were required to finance our tremendous export surplus of goods and services which rose to an annual rate of $12 billion in early 1947, and which averaged over $6 billion annually during 1948 and 1949. The total resources of the international institutions could not possibly cope with such huge demands. The Fund's total supply of gold and U.S. dollars amounts to only $3.75 billion, $2.75 billion of which is provided by the U.S. contribution. The remainder of the $8 billion pool of foreign exchange consists largely of currencies which were in excess supply anyway, and which accumulate in The Fund as members purchase U.S. dollars.

The founders of The Fund recognized that the huge demands of the transitional period following the war could not and should not be met by a Fund designed to assist countries in temporary, not fundamental, disequilibrium (see Article XIV, Section 1). However, during the first two years of The Fund's operations following March 1947, approximately $725 million in credits were extended to members. This was less than the gold and dollar contribution to The Fund made by countries other than the U.S. Most of these credits (of which $708 million represent sales of U.S. dollars) were extended to European countries before ERP assistance became available in 1948. Since then the policy of The Fund like that of the International Bank has been to decline assistance to ERP countries for the duration of the recovery program. Despite the fact that The Fund primarily filled in a gap between different types of U.S. aid, the assistance rendered could be criticized on the ground that the deficits of the recipient countries could not reasonably be considered of a short-term nature and capable of correction without considerable passage of time.

The question arises as to whether in our time there is likely to emerge from the transitional period a world in which balance of payments equilibrium is brought about by automatic forces operating in relatively free international markets. It may be more reasonable to anticipate a succession of changing emergencies during which countries will continue to plan their balances of payments through trade and exchange controls, inhibiting the price and income changes which would make for an automatic adjustment. The type of International Monetary Fund (which the United States has opposed) that would mechanically provide credits without satisfactory conditions being insisted upon for repayment might operate in a world in which there were strong automatic tendencies to equilibrium; but it would not operate in a world where disequilibrium as well as equilibrium in a nation's balance of payment could be manufactured.[5]

---

[5] See R. Mikesell, "Role of International Monetary Agreements in a World of Planned Economies," *Journal of Political Economy*, December 1947.

There is a structural weakness of The Fund which would lead one to expect a drain of dollars independent of the current disequilibrium in world balances of payments. This weakness was pointed up by Professor J. H. Williams in his often maligned and frequently misunderstood "key currency" approach to the international monetary problem.[6] The problem here is that The Fund in principle accords equal treatment to all currencies, whereas international payments are generally made in dollars and sterling. Secondary currencies are without significance in the great foreign exchange markets of the world, and such currencies are traded against dollars and sterling only in the local markets concerned. There is no need for a key country like the U.S. to pay dollars into The Fund in order to obtain foreign exchange. As a well-established practice, dollar balances here may be used to effect payment. Other countries would tend to buy U.S. dollars from The Fund in order to pay us, and this would constitute a drain from The Fund even in the absence of any world balance of payments deficit vis-a-vis the U.S.

The repurchase provisions in The Fund agreement were introduced to cope with this problem. Repurchases are required of a member when its currency is held by The Fund, when the member's monetary reserves are higher than its quota, when The Fund's holdings of the member's currency are above 75 per cent of its quota, and when The Fund's holdings of any wanted currency are below 75 per cent of the quota of the member concerned. These repurchase provisions prevent a member from going into debt to The Fund in order to build up its monetary reserves; the latter must be drawn upon to the same extent as The Fund's resources. A member, whose holdings of U.S. dollars or gold acquired from another member have increased, is required to use the increase to repurchase its own currency from The Fund and so repay its debt to The Fund with such increase in its monetary reserves. These provisions would inhibit rather than prevent weak currency countries from drawing dollars out of The Fund. They would prevent an internationally strong country from becoming a debtor to The Fund, but they could not force it to sell U.S. dollars into The Fund beyond this point. Certainly the danger of a dollar drain which Williams pointed to is not removed by the repurchase provisions.

The second special report of the National Advisory Council on the operations and policies of the International Monetary Fund and the International Bank concluded:

---

[6] J. H. Williams, "International Monetary Plans: After Bretton Woods," *Foreign Affairs*, October 1944. This and other relevant articles from the same journal have been reprinted in J. H. Williams, *Post-War Monetary Plans and Other Essays*. New York: Alfred A. Knopf, Inc., 1947; also, see H. C. Wallich, "The Path from Bretton Woods," *Economic Reconstruction* (S. Harris, Editor). New York: McGraw-Hill Book Co., 1945, pp. 370-377.

In the present state of world affairs, characterised by currency inconvertibility, disequilibrium in international accounts and the maintenance of exchange and trade restrictions, the resources of the Fund can be used effectively only to a limited extent to promote the basic objectives for which the Fund was established and which are part of the United States international economic program, i.e., the achievement and maintenance of multilateral non-discriminatory international payments with a minimum of restriction on current account exchange transactions . . . the Council favors only moderate and prudent use of the Fund's resources to assist member countries in meeting genuinely temporary deficits.

In the interim, nevertheless, the Fund has an important role as an international consultative body and as a forum for dealing with important questions relating to foreign exchange. In the long-run this may prove to be the Fund's greatest contribution to the solution of the international economic problems of our times.

It is unlikely that the goal of multilateralism will be reached, as a number of authorities have observed,[7] without the restoration of sterling convertibility, and the confidence that Britain can maintain convertibility at a stable value of sterling over an extended period of time. The role of The Fund in achieving this objective (towards which great progress was made during 1950) is certainly limited. To protect its resources, borrowing members could legitimately be required to demonstrate ability to repay over three or four years, to commit themselves to such repayment, and to take steps to improve their balance of payments positions. It has been suggested that further to increase The Fund's current usefulness, its non-dollar resources might be utilized to stimulate trade among soft-currency countries.[8] One danger here would be that a soft-currency country whose currency was drawn by another would acquire additional drawing rights on The Fund which could be used to obtain dollars. The Fund might do well to limit the use of drawing rights obtained in this way. The potential of The Fund's operations in the soft-currency sphere has been very much reduced since the formation of the European Payments Union, discussed below.

The Fund, based as it is upon principles of nondiscrimination, equal treatment of currencies, and abstinence from trade and exchange controls was not designed to perform important operations in the immediate postwar years, nor during years when defense needs press very heavily upon the economies of member countries. It must be content with its role, a very significant one, as a consultative organ, and husband its limited resources against the day of a less tempestuous world economy. This is not to imply that an economy of relatively flexible prices and incomes similar to that of the nineteenth century or even the interwar

---

[7] E.g., R. Mikesell, *The International Monetary Fund*. Washington, D.C.: Carnegie Endowment for International Peace, 1949, p. 873.

[8] *Ibid.*, p. 865.

period is likely to reappear. A more reasonable hope would be a satisfactory coordination of national policies with the object of achieving a workable system of multilateral trade.[9] Once such coordination were achieved The Fund could play an important operational role, although its extension of credit should not under such conditions be automatic or unconditional. In the meantime, The Fund is capable of playing an important part in influencing member countries in the direction of the requisite coordination.

The European Recovery Program and the European Payments Union

The European Recovery Program was legislated into the Economic Cooperation Act as Title I of the Foreign Assistance Act of April 3, 1948. The program is otherwise known as the Marshall Plan, because it became widely popularized following the Harvard Commencement address of General George C. Marshall, then Secretary of State, on June 6, 1947. First official recognition was given the problem one month earlier by Secretary of State Acheson in a speech in Mississippi. The program is administered by the Economic Cooperation Administration (ECA) initially headed by Paul Hoffman, and now by William C. Foster. All countries west of the Iron Curtain with the exception of Spain but including Western Germany and Trieste participate in the program. They are members in the Organization for European Economic Cooperation (OEEC) through which national programs for recovery are coordinated in Europe and submitted to ECA in Washington for approval.

The program is relatively short-run, being designed to end in June 1952. The United Kingdom has already terminated its dependence upon ECA for aid (as of January 1, 1951). The aid (20 per cent in loans and the rest in grants) will be less than $15 billion. The reasons for the program are economic *and* political. Economic recovery is regarded as a prerequisite to successful resistance to internal and external communist pressure. Thus, the purpose of the program is a purpose vital to the national interests of the U.S., and it is not a "give away" program for its own sake. The economic problems of Europe have their most immediate basis in the war, the direct devastation, the running down of capital equipment, and the shift of resources away from regular peacetime employment. As in the U.S. there was in Europe a tremendous backlog of demand for consumption goods and capital equipment; this demand was due not only to the war but also to the depression preceding the war. These factors operated to increase the demand for imports and to de-

---

[9] *Ibid.*, p. 872.

crease the resources available for exports, thus leading to an acute balance of payments deficit, particularly with the major source of supply, North America. The deficit on merchandise account, partly a result of the great economic strides of the U.S. relative to Europe, was in evidence before the war. It had been largely offset by net earnings on non-merchandise account. Losses of shipping and of foreign investments during the war very adversely affected these earnings. Structural changes in world trade resulting from economic chaos in Germany, the barrier between Eastern and Western European countries, and the decline in dollar earnings by colonial areas (in the Far East, for example), all combined to put European nations in very great need of dollars to finance imports from North America.

The aims of ECA have been: (1) foremost, to stave off economic collapse and to make good the dislocation of the war; thus its purpose has been to complete the winning of the war by our side; (2) to restore the balance in world trade and to establish conditions for a return to international currency convertibility and to multilateral trade; and (3) to work towards political and economic integration of Europe. Judged in terms of realistic possibilities, economic progress has been even more than extraordinary. The primary objective of economic recovery has been achieved and advanced beyond original goals to an extent few optimists would have envisioned; much progress has also been made towards the second objective, balance of payments adjustment, progress that became astoundingly rapid during 1950; the third objective, European integration, was not specified in the original Marshall Plan and is much longer-run than the plan itself.

In addition to providing grants and loans to ECA countries, currency convertibility has been guaranteed where such action would encourage U.S. concerns to establish plants in European countries. Such plants would enable ECA countries to reduce dollar imports. More important has been the encouragement which ECA has given projects for the re-establishment of interconvertibility of European currencies. In the first months of ECA operation, an inducement to intra-European trade was provided in the form of supplemental allotments of dollars that could be used for financing imports from other European countries. Approximately 9 per cent of ECA assistance in 1948 was of this nature. In October of 1948 this technique was replaced by the Intra-European Payments and Compensation Agreement among OEEC members. The object of both schemes was to reduce the necessity for narrow two-way balancing and discrimination which was the result of the host of bilateral trade and payments agreements entered into by European countries. The October agreement permitted debtor countries such as France, the Netherlands, and Greece to draw on special accounts to finance their deficits with

European creditor countries, the principal ones being the United Kingdom and Belgium. These credits or drawing rights, analogous to those in the International Monetary Fund, were established in the Bank for International Settlements. This institution, established in Basle, Switzerland, in 1930, for the purpose of handling payments in connection with German reparations, has served a useful purpose in connection with this and subsequent European payments agreements.

The 1948 agreement suffered from lack of flexibility in that the drawing rights normally could be utilized only for payments to the country making the grant, and could not be transferred for use in another country. On July 1, 1949, when the agreement expired, a new plan was ready. It provided that 25 per cent of the drawing rights could be transferred and so used freely by the debtor against any participating country after bilateral drawing rights had been exhausted. By 1950 there had been great progress. Not only had intra-European trade increased by 50 per cent, but the total of surpluses and deficits which had to be financed had fallen, and fewer countries showed abnormal surpluses or deficits. Time was ripe for a further step to avoid the payments difficulties that so handicap the adoption of measures for liberalizing trade.

This further step took the form of the establishment of the European Payments Union, which came into force July 1, 1950, although the formal convention was not signed until August. Its objective is the complete transferability of European currencies earned on current account. Parallel steps towards the liberalization of trade were taken, the aim being to raise the present 50 per cent of European trade freed of import quotas to 75 per cent by the end of 1950. Discrimination related to both nonmerchandise and merchandise trade among EPU members was to cease at the same time, although discrimination against non-European countries is permitted. In line with the insistence of the United Kingdom, the operations of the EPU will be entirely automatic, and there will be no new regional institution with powers similar to those of the International Monetary Fund. Within Europe there is now a relatively balanced state of trade, and there is no shortage of any one currency which approximates the dollar shortage.[10] Further, there is the OEEC available to coordinate policies. For these reasons, a new authority may not be needed. The Bank for International Settlements will continue to act as the agent through which payment deficits and surpluses will be channeled.

The EPU quotas, which form the basis for the members' borrowing

---

[10] The principle debtors of EPU in the first several months of operation have been Germany and the Netherlands, while Britain and France have been the chief creditors. The OEEC has granted special additional credits to Germany as the result of her acute balance of payments difficulties.

and lending operations, are in general equal to 15 per cent of all visible and nonvisible transactions which took place in 1949 between the country assigned the quota and the other OEEC members plus the sterling area. Total quotas are about $4 billion, of which the United Kingdom on behalf of the entire sterling area has $1,062 million, and France $520 million. The ECA has played a most important role in the establishment of the scheme and has arranged a provisional allotment of $350 million to the EPU working capital fund, a *sine qua non*. Thus, structural debtors suffering from fundamental disequilibrium vis-a-vis other members can be financed without creditor nations suffering indirect losses of gold and hard currencies. The initial contribution of the United Kingdom is $150 million (in an extreme case she could be called upon to contribute $636 million), that of Belgium-Luxembourg is $55 million, while another creditor country, Sweden, will initially contribute an amount equal to her 1950–51 ECA allotment.

A member's deficit up to 20 per cent of its quota will be financed entirely by credit. In excess of that amount deficits will be settled by an increasing gold payment and by a diminishing proportion in credit, so that by the time a debtor country exhausts its quota it will have borrowed 60 per cent of its quota and made gold payments to EPU for the remaining 40 per cent. A creditor country receives payment in gold for 50 per cent of surpluses incurred when these exceed 20 per cent of its quota. ECA assistance is, of course, essential to the gold payments and to the mutual European self-help provided in the plan. EPU will pay 2 per cent interest to creditors and will receive interest from debtors at a rate of 2 per cent on debts outstanding for less than a year, $2\frac{1}{4}$ per cent on debts outstanding for between one and two years, and $2\frac{1}{2}$ per cent on those outstanding for more than two years.

The EPU has not taken the form of an extension of the sterling area as some observers anticipated, but one of the major accomplishments has been the reconciliation of EPU and sterling area arrangements so that deterrents to the entry of the United Kingdom into EPU could be overcome. Creditor countries are permitted to hold sterling rather than EPU credits if they wish to do so. The United Kingdom on her part has conceded that members may use sterling balances, even though the balances were acquired before the formation of the EPU, in order to finance their deficits vis-a-vis EPU. These balances have been estimated by *The Economist* at £150 million.

The Economist, July 15, 1950, reports the EPU as "the first major instance in which the nations in their postwar economic reconstruction (exception being always made for rescue operations such as the Marshall Plan), have based themselves upon the real facts of the world as it is."

Despite the discrimination that will be sanctioned against the hard currencies insofar as they remain scarce, the fact is that:

> . . . EPU is being born with the blessing, almost at the instance and certainly with the effective help, of the United States Government—or at least of a majority of its agencies. Here is a revolution of thought, indeed. It results from the inexorable pressure of the facts. The famine of dollars is a fact. If the European countries are to get on, after the demise of the Marshall Plan, without free gifts of dollars, they must very seriously cut down their dollar expenditures; and if in so doing they are to avoid discrimination, they must treat their imports from all other sources with equal severity. If all currencies are to be convertible by those who hold them into dollars, then every country must take care that nobody holds a single unit of its currency more than he needs. In short, these sacred principles, when combined with the fact of a dollar shortage, become instruments not of expansion but of the most cruel compression of all trade.

The acceptance of the dollar shortage as a virtually unchangeable fact would, of course, not go unchallenged, and the development of an import surplus by the United States during portions of 1950 at least temporarily did away with the problem. How important it is to be in the future may depend primarily upon whether prices of U.S. raw material imports remain relatively high, upon the relative intensity of U.S. and European defense efforts, and upon the extent of U.S. mutual defense financial aid to foreign countries. However that may be, the principles of the new area payments arrangements offer much food for thought. It is too early to judge the significance of EPU, but it might be noted that increased military expenditures and the associated demands for increased controls have jeopardized the movement in the direction of increased liberalization of intra-European trade and payments.

The International Bank for Reconstruction and Development

The articles of agreement, drafted at Bretton Woods in July 1944, are remarkable. They have fashioned an institution which certainly meets the needs of its creditors for lending upon a basis of which they approve. For a while it was feared there might be no eligible borrowers to meet The Bank's requirements of debtors. That was because of the destructiveness of the war and the fact that relief, not loans, had to be the primary vehicle for carrying recovery forward. Because that period of relief is rapidly coming to an end, because political security in much of the free world is being achieved, and because of a remarkable new change in the terms of trade which has every promise to be abiding for many years, The Bank is on the threshold of a period of activity which should promote world development as has not occurred for 35 years.

In the World Bank was created an institution of which the financial

world should be proud. It retains the time-honored role for balance sheet and income statement in the selection of those who are to be able to command resources, at least those resources needed and obtainable from overseas to any borrower. In The Bank is retained the control of the creditor, as a private person or institution, over the reins of those who shall do the lending.

This outcome was not originally expected. In the early stages "in the battle of the plans" what was conceived by some was an institution into which member governments might pour funds for lending. On that basis the managing bureaucracy, not creditors, would be in control and the sum of $10 billion irretrievably committed would go a long way to assure perpetuation of that control, as well as possible ultimate loss of the money committed to the institution.

What has emerged has been an institution whose very formation and personnel has had to meet the acid test of approval by creditors. It has had to meet that test, and it will have to continue to meet that test as long as it continues in business. The test comes constantly to The Bank because by and large The Bank has loaned the funds under its own control and now secures additional funds by floating its own issues in the open financial markets. If it is not approved, if its investments are not approved by the cautious security buyers in those markets, then it does not obtain funds for international lending. Meeting that approval and building a record for usefulness should give The Bank a long life and an important role in expanding the volume of private and governmental investment that should produce an economic development at a rate to match the best that was accomplished in the amazing nineteenth century.

The Bank may best be defined as an institution of subscription and guaranty. To its authorized capital of $10,000,000,000 member nations have now subscribed $8,338,500,000. Of this sum, the United States Government subscribed $3,175,000,000. The paid-in proportion has been 20 per cent, or $1,667,700,000, of which 2 per cent was paid in gold (or U.S. dollars) and 18 per cent in currencies of members. Because "gold dollars" and "United States dollars" are identical, The Bank has received about $730,000,000 in gold or dollars (greatly in demand as a hard or universal currency). The remainder, $930,000,000 of the paid-in portion of its capital, is less loanable for the present, for this sum consists of subscriptions of members in national currencies as yet not in substantial loan demand. Beyond these total paid-in subscriptions of more than one and one-half billion dollars are subscriptions *which it is not intended shall be paid-in.* These subscriptions totaling $6,670,000,000 are subject to call. That call may be made for a special purpose only. They may be called only when required to meet obligations of The Bank *for funds borrowed or loans guaranteed by it.* Now if The Bank is to

come into a position to call all or a part of this subscribed capital (80 per cent) to meet obligations for "funds borrowed" or for loans "guaranteed by it," such funds must have been borrowed or guaranties given *at some prior time*. That requires that The Bank shall have been able *first* to borrow (meet the tests of private creditors) or similarly *first* to give guaranties (which requires that the recipient of the guaranty shall have been able to sell the guaranteed securities in the markets). It is this priority to the tests of private creditors and to private market sale of guaranteed securities which has preserved The Bank as an institution as truly representative of private finance as is any commercial bank, savings bank, insurance company or building and loan association.

By December 31, 1950, The Bank had made loans to member governments and private enterprise of $838,000,000. At the same time it had floated in financial markets $260,000,000 of its own bonds to obtain funds to supplement its near-depleted paid-in funds in the currencies most in demand. The Bank has guaranteed $26,000,000 of securities it has sold. In early March 1951 The Bank sold an additional $50,000,000 of its 25-year 3 per cent debentures. The Bank has substantial loan commitments on which funds have not yet been advanced.

The Outlook for United States Foreign Lending

Many persons who have been concerned with the seeming intransigence of the world "dollar shortage" have modified their views as the result of recent developments. The upswing of the U.S. business cycle from mid-1949 had imposed upon it the tremendous inflationary impetus of the Korean outbreak in June 1950, and U.S. demands for imports at ever increasing prices have swollen the supply of dollars flowing to foreigners. The growing requirements for defense and war purposes superimposed upon peacetime needs have given much weight to forecasts of tendencies towards continued full employment and inflationary conditions in the United States. As a result it now appears that there may be as great a likelihood for a decade, if not for the remainder of the present century, of as good a basis for the solvency of American lending as there was for Western European lending from 1814 to 1914. That indeed would be a welcome change from the sporadic and fraught with default dangers of world lending in the interwar period and the dismal record of the doleful 1930's.

A glance back at the century following the Napoleonic Wars reveals that its two outstanding economic features were the greatest mobility of labor and capital the world has ever known, coupled with a vital complementary relationship between European industry and developing raw material and foodstuff producers overseas. There has never been

anything to equal the trans-Atlantic migration of peoples, mostly at the working ages, during the nineteenth century, when the entire population of the world much more than doubled. The U.S. was peopled by many of these migrants. At the same time, because of rising economic productivity and associated population increases, there was no net loss of population in the lands from which they came. In fact there was gain both in numbers of people and in net output. The city of Berlin grew as fast as the city of Chicago.

The United States in these years adopted a policy of high tariffs to assist in its economic development. In the sense of promoting *national* strength and well-being, that tariff policy was "good," the anti-tariff arguments of any principles of economics textbook to the contrary notwithstanding. Desirable tariff policy in England (from whence most economic thought was imported by the literati and book publishing houses) was one thing; desirable tariff policy was a wholly different thing in the United States. The world was ready to get up and move; capital was eager for outlets; we gave legal and contractual security to capital; we gave a hearty free welcome to all, radical, rich or indigent alike, provided that each was willing to work for a living.

The economy of the United States grew to great power, though we did not become aware of that most important fact of the first half of the twentieth century until the last decade of those 50 years. We grew to great power partly because we had the benefit of much capital, perhaps all told $25 billion of it from abroad, not even counting the very considerable amount of it immigrants brought with themselves. Every person in America has been subsidized in part to his present high standard of living by the rapid advances our borrowing of that large amount of capital made possible. It is fitting to record that practically all of that capital came from precisely those nations which have now for three years been the chief beneficiaries of the grants and loans of the Marshall Plan.

But that lending was not all. What probably was a larger sum was loaned by the same countries to all other new lands. And for what purpose? To get new raw material and food production flowing back to Europe to create industrial strength there. That return flow serviced the advances which made the flow possible at all. The return flow and the outward investment pictured the advancing world.

Soon, however, the giant industrial strength of the United States came to demand the lion's share of all these raw materials. We imported far more rubber than any other country. Its supplies from its original home, Brazil, were utterly inadequate just at the time our automobile industry leapt forward to great size. As a result Englishmen stole its seed

and transplanted it to the Far East amid fertile soil and abundant labor capable of hard work in the tropical climate in which rubber must grow.

By 1917 we were buying $200 million a year of it to make liquid in dollars (if desirable) a vast amount of European lending to grow rubber in the Far East, where soon 99 per cent of all natural rubber was produced. In a similar way, by 1917 we imported and extended no less than one billion dollars for hides and skins, fruits and nuts, vegetable oils, coffee, sugar, burlaps, wool and mohair, copper, tin and fertilizer materials. Here was the source of reward to newer areas for their economic development by older world areas.

Then came a short period of revival in the 1920's followed by long and deep depression and another great war. As a result the development in newer areas which had taken place at so rapid a rate through most of the nineteenth century was cut off. But the United States experienced great growth in the early 1940's. Then finally at long last came a substantial recovery in the countries of Western Europe. Our production in real terms is now 75 per cent above 1929 and Western Europe's production is probably a like amount, for its gain from 1938 is more than 40 per cent.

But no appreciable lending on foreign development had taken place in the same score of years—in fact almost two score years. Partly as a result, in the most recent years, particularly in 1950, the price of raw materials has risen phenomenally to testify to the shortage of raw materials. Tin has doubled in price, natural rubber has more than tripled (though our rapidly growing supplies of synthetic rubber should eventually cut this high price back very sharply). Jute burlap has doubled, sugar is firm, coffee (green) has thrice tripled in price since 1940, though a decade ago coffee was burned instead of roasted, or sunk in the sea instead of brewed for stimulation.

As a result we have seen a period of extraordinary inelasticity of supply and rapidly expanding demand as incomes have risen and total industrial production has grown here and in Europe. The typical consequences of these changes in demand and supply are pictured in the diagram on page 501.

In this diagram we see how the rising demand has boosted price almost perpendicularly. It should be the foremost aim of foreign lending of the United States to bring the prices down. The result becomes a huge, twofold gain: First, we can make a good return on the invested capital; second, that investment will lower prices of the raw materials which that investment expands in supply enough to earn a great profit for the American people, great enough indeed to return to them far more than the possible cost (via taxes) of those governmental arrangements which assist businessmen to make such investments. The foreign country profits

too by enlarging its investment processes, enlarging its employment in expanding industries, and by enlarging particularly the share of its total output which can be sold overseas. That sale overseas then can enable the country to carry on a high standard of living or investment for the purpose of expanding its other industrial processes.

Given today's conditions with respect to demand and supply, their elasticities and shifts, it is more likely that newer and backward world

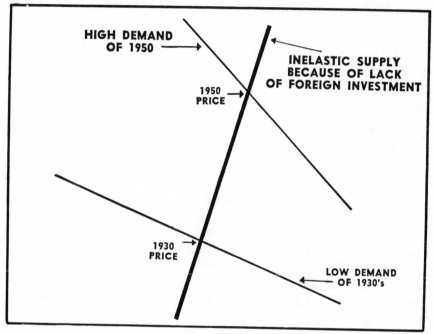

FIGURE 1

When demand rises, as it did from 1930 to 1950, the price goes almost "straight up" because supply is inelastic. Foreign lending of the United States should have as its purpose pushing supply curves over to the right; i.e., making the historical supply curve elastic.

areas can enlarge their standard of life more rapidly by expanding their production of the wanted raw materials and foodstuffs than by directly undertaking domestic industrialization. Domestic industrialization in addition creates a demand for foreign exchange but no supply thereof, although it might assist indirectly by reducing the demand for foreign exchange, for the resultant products are substituted for imports. Advancing the output of needed, wanted, and high priced raw materials creates the desirable supplies of foreign exchange which can service the interest, dividends, and amortization of the foreign investment in these newer world areas. A balance between the two types of industrialization

is no doubt wanted. Such a balance can, by the "industrial" industrialization, reduce the newer country's subsequent demand for imports, whereas "raw-material" industrialization can enlarge supplies of foreign exchange. Usually efficiency, low cost, and optimum size are created more by the latter expansion than by the former contraction.

That carefully planned foreign investment can yield a double profit cannot be doubted. The most striking illustration of the *profit* is afforded by a case where the investment was made at home to expand a needed raw material.

In the early 1940's a subsidiary of the RFC, under the leadership of W. M. Jeffers, formerly chief of the Union Pacific Railroad, completed a program for the production of about one million tons of synthetic rubber as the consequence of the severance of our means of access to Far East rubber supplies. That synthetic rubber capacity cost us $755 million. After the war such production was cut back materially and we once again imported 600,000 tons of natural rubber. Paul Litchfield, chairman of the Goodyear Tire & Rubber Company, has said that had it not been for our synthetic rubber supplies, the price of natural rubber would most certainly have gone to $1 a pound from 1946 to 1950. That is a modest appraisal of a potential price rise, considering not what this expansion of demand but the contraction of supplies had done to price on at least two earlier occasions. But taking the price saved as the difference between $1 a pound and about 20 cents a pound, the price of these years, the saving to the people of the United States has proved to be almost one billion dollars a year since the end of the war ($0.80 saved per pound; $1,600 per ton; total $960 million on 600,000 tons of natural rubber). That saving was made possible by the investment of $755 million. The result is pictured graphically in the diagram on page 503.

How the enlargement of supply by enlarging investment can reduce a high price is revealed in the diagram explaining the method whereby the price of natural rubber was kept from rising after the war. In contrast the price of imported green coffee has risen from less than 10 cents a pound in 1946 to more than 50 cents a pound last year. As a result *we have not saved 80 per cent of the cost of green coffee imports.* In consequence our imports of coffee cost us $796 million in 1949 and perhaps $1,200,000,000 last year instead of the more normal annual cost of $400,000,000 each year. Not having the knowledge of how to make a synthetic coffee that would be satisfactory and not having the foresight to expand our loans for coffee growing, we are now paying far more for this single import than any other. Is it any surprise, therefore, that foreign countries refuse to allow exchange for the importation of a

commodity whose cost has risen so largely because of "investment failures"?

These illustrations taken from our investment experience with rubber (and lack of it with coffee) throw light on needed foreign investment policies to maintain our economic strength. They provide a sound basis for knitting the raw material areas to the side of free countries. We can invest in those countries, and they can sell all they produce to free countries. In contrast Russia's ability to invest is far more limited ($60,000,000

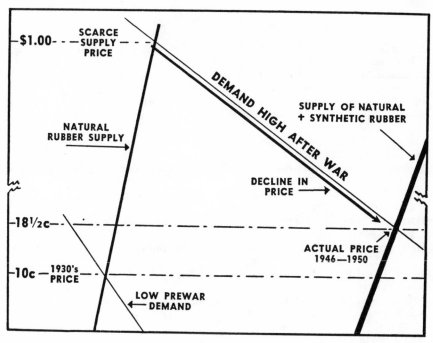

FIGURE 2

When demand for rubber rose after the war, the price was still low because we augmented the supply of natural rubber with an increased supply of synthetic rubber. As a result, the price was not greatly increased.

a year in the Chinese–Russian agreement of 1949 as opposed to our ability to lend, were it proved desirable, 10 or more times than that sum per year). In addition, Russia probably cannot take the entire raw material production of any single large raw-material producing country against the free world's ability, demonstrated, to take the full output of all such countries.

Thus is the need for revived foreign investment clearly indicated. The field for the International Bank and other foreign lending is indicated as being upon an economically sound basis. In the last year there has been

a reversal of more than four billion dollars in the U.S. international current account considered as "a flow" or annual rate. It was running strongly in our favor from 1946 to 1949. In 1950 the reversal was so great as to lead to a two billion dollar outflow of gold and perhaps a like rate of outflow of dollars in all other forms. In fact, the U.S. balance of payments position has become rather weak at least temporarily and possibly permanently. A lending program to bring scarce raw materials back to reasonable levels can restore strength at home and abroad.

Suggested Readings

American Economic Association, *Readings in the Theory of International Trade*. Philadelphia: The Blakiston Company, 1949.

Economic Cooperation Administration, *Report to Congress of the Economic Cooperation Administration*. 1948 to date.

Ellis, H. S., *The Economics of Freedom*. New York: Harper & Brothers, 1950.

Ellsworth, P. T., *The International Economy*. New York: The Macmillan Company, 1950.

Enke, S., and Salera, V., *International Economics*, 2nd Edition. New York: Prentice-Hall, Inc., 1951.

Hansen, A. H., *America's Role in the World Economy*. New York: W. W. Norton & Company, Inc., 1947.

Harris, S., (Editor), *Economic Reconstruction*. New York: McGraw-Hill Book Company, Inc., 1945.

Harris, S., *European Recovery Program*. Cambridge, Mass.: Harvard University Press, 1948.

Harris, S. (Editor), *Foreign Economic Policy for the United States*. Cambridge, Mass.: Harvard University Press, 1948.

International Bank for Reconstruction and Development, *Annual Report*. 1946 to date.

International Monetary Fund, *Annual Report*. 1945/46 to date.

Kindleberger, C. P., *The Dollar Shortage*. New York: John Wiley & Sons, Inc., 1950.

The London Economist.

League of Nations, *Industrialization and Foreign Trade*. Geneva, 1945.

March, D. B., *World Trade and Investment*. New York: Harcourt, Brace and Company, 1951.

Mikesell, R. F., "The International Monetary Fund, 1944–1949," *International Conciliation*, November 1949.

Organization for European Economic Cooperation, *Second Report of the O.E.E.C.* Paris, 1950.

U.S. Department of Commerce, *The United States in the World Economy*. Washington, D.C.: Government Printing Office, 1943.

U.S. Department of State, *Point Four*. Washington, D.C.: Government Printing Office, 1950.

Williams, J. H., *Postwar Monetary Plans and Other Essays*. New York: Alfred A. Knopf, Inc., 1947.

19

United States Treasury Operations and Functions

by NORRIS O. JOHNSON

Assistant Vice President
The National City Bank of New York;
formerly Manager, Research Department, Federal
Reserve Bank of New York; Treasurer-General,
Government of Iran

Introduction

SINCE EVERY government needs a custodian of the public funds, a collector of revenues, a borrower of money, and a payer of bills and debts, a Treasury Department was one of the first departments to be set up when the Executive branch of the federal government was organized in 1789. Today, the U.S. Treasury is the largest financial institution in the country by at least three important criteria of size: (1) indebtedness, which runs beyond $250 billion; (2) annual revenues, which exceed $40 billion a year; and (3) number of employees, which comes to 88,000.

The Treasury also carries on the greatest conglomeration of activities of any of our financial institutions. Indeed, it would be impossible, within the space limits of this chapter, to go beyond the principal functions, and those of greatest public concern. *The United States Government Organization Manual* gives an authoritative condensed description of the Department that is suggestive of the range of activities, which runs from guarding the person of the President (Secret Service), and warehousing the national gold reserves (at Fort Knox, Kentucky), to operating a miniature Navy (Coast Guard), and printing paper currency (Bureau of Engraving and Printing). The following is abstracted from the 1950–51 edition of the *Manual:* [1]

---

[1] Statutory citations, and some of the lesser responsibilities of the Secretary of the Treasury, are omitted. Words supplied are bracketed [ ].

PURPOSE: The original act established the Department to superintend and manage the national finances. This act charged the Secretary of the Treasury with the preparation of plans for the improvement and management of the revenue and the support of the public credit. It further provided that he should prescribe the forms for keeping and rendering all manner of public accounts and for the making of returns. He was empowered to grant, subject to the limitations of the amended act, all warrants for moneys to be issued from the Treasury pursuant to legal appropriations, and to furnish information, upon request, to either or both branches of Congress on any matter referred to him or pertaining to his office. The act further stated it to be the duty of the Secretary "generally to perform all such services relative to the finances as he shall be directed to perform."

With the expansion of the country and its financial structure, frequent revisions and amendments to the act have so broadened the scope of the Treasury Department that it now embraces a score or more of diversified bureaus, divisions, and offices, and many new duties have been delegated to its charge. Besides managing the financial affairs of the Nation, the Department now controls the coinage and printing of money. The Coast Guard, the Bureau of Narcotics, and the Secret Service have been placed under the supervision and jurisdiction of the Department.

The Secretary of the Treasury is required by law to submit an annual report to Congress upon the condition of the finances, and to make public the first of each month the last preceding weekly statement of the Treasury.[2]

The Secretary of the Treasury is Chairman, National Advisory Council on International Monetary and Financial Problems; U.S. Governor of the International Monetary Fund and the International Bank for Reconstruction and Development; and managing trustee of the Federal Old-Age and Survivors Insurance Trust Fund. He is a member of the Board of Trustees of the Postal Savings System, the National Munitions Control Board, the National Security Resources Board, the Board of Directors [of the] Federal Farm Mortgage Corporation, the Advisory Board [of the] Export-Import Bank of Washington, [and] the Joint Committee on Reduction of Nonessential Federal Expenditures.

ORGANIZATION: Affairs of the Treasury Department are generally supervised by the Secretary of the Treasury. He is assisted in the management and direction of the Department's numerous and varied branches by the Under Secretary of the Treasury, two Assistant Secretaries of the Treasury, the Fiscal Assistant Secretary of the Treasury, the General Counsel, and a staff of administrative, special, and technical assistants who supervise and correlate the activities of the different bureaus, offices, and divisions. Each bureau is under the general direction of a chief, who reports to the Secretary and his immediate assistants.

The principal branches of the Department are as follows:

Office of the Secretary
  Office of Administrative Assistant
    to the Secretary
  Office of International Finance
  Office of the Technical Staff
  Legal Division
  Tax Advisory Staff

Office of the Comptroller of the
  Currency
Bureau of Customs
Bureau of Engraving and Printing
Bureau of Internal Revenue
Bureau of the Mint
Bureau of Narcotics

---

[2] In actual practice a Treasury statement is published for every business day.

Committee on Practice
Fiscal Service
  Office of the Fiscal Assistant Secretary
  Bureau of Accounts
  Bureau of the Public Debt

Office of the Treasurer of the United States
United States Savings Bonds Division
United States Secret Service
United States Coast Guard

Secretary's Authority

While Congress, under the Constitution, is charged with the powers "to levy and collect" taxes, "to borrow money on the credit of the United States," and to authorize expenditures of public funds, the Secretary of the Treasury has been granted by the Congress large operational responsibility. The widest grants of discretionary authority to the Secretary are in managing the cash balances of the government; in handling the public debt; and in protecting and maintaining the value of the dollar in the foreign exchange market. As principal financial officer of the government, as well as the second-ranking member of the President's cabinet, the Secretary's views enter into many important government decisions, most notably those relating to the federal budget, financial problems and proposals, and general economic policy of the government.

Influence on the Federal Reserve System

The Treasury's views and wishes always have carried weight with the Federal Reserve, and quite naturally, since both agencies operate in the money market and it is not in the public interest that the two should pursue conflicting policies. By the original Federal Reserve Act of 1913, the Secretary was *ex officio* a member of the Federal Reserve Board and its presiding officer. He was dropped from membership when the Board was reconstituted in 1935, because it was felt to be too subservient to his wishes. Yet the Treasury's influence with the Federal Reserve, exerted to keep interest rates low and government security prices stable, has perhaps been greater in the past nine years than ever before.

Most Essential Responsibilities

The three most essential responsibilities of the Secretary of the Treasury are:
1. To see that there is money on hand to meet current bills and other lawful claims on the government;
2. To borrow as needed to replenish cash balances;
3. To maintain the value of the paper dollar at its gold parity in international markets.

To observe how these operations are carried out, it is necessary first to acquire some knowledge of Treasury reports and of the budget-making process. It is also desirable to have an acquaintanceship with the difference between the "budget" and "cash" methods of accounting for Treasury transactions; to know how federal trust funds, which are outside the regular budget, are handled; and to see how the Treasury's operations impinge upon the banking system, including the Federal Reserve. With this background, understanding becomes easier of Treasury cash management, public debt management, and operations and responsibilities in the field of international finance. The scope of the present chapter is the Treasury function of administering government finances.[3]

Daily Treasury Statement

The four-page *Daily Statement of the United States Treasury* is the basic source of current information on financial operations by or through the U.S. Treasury. Selected items from the Statement are published regularly in newspapers such as *The New York Times* and *New York Herald Tribune*. The first page of the Statement gives a condensed summary of daily receipts, expenditures, and public debt operations; a breakdown of the "general fund" assets and liabilities; and the official reserves of gold and silver together with the obligations outstanding against those reserves. The second page gives a breakdown of budget receipts by major categories and expenditures by major departments and agencies. The third page is devoted to trust account operations and a reconciliation of all transactions with the public debt. The fourth page gives the details on public debt transactions, receipts from securities sold, exchanges of new obligations for those falling due, and expenditures for the retirement of debt.

The Daily Statement for the first business day of each month is enlarged to include a full and detailed "Statement of the Public Debt" outstanding at the close of the preceding month. The Daily Statement for the fifteenth of each month is enlarged to include detailed monthly figures on receipts, expenditures, and trust account operations. The United States is almost without a rival in the world in the wealth of information made promptly available to the legislature and to the citizen on the financial operations of the national government.

Besides the Daily Statement, which is made available with only a two- or three-day lag, the Treasury Department also publishes an *Annual Report* and a monthly *Treasury Bulletin*. These publications contain textual and factual data not available through the Daily Statement, as

---

[3] For authoritative information on ancillary activities, the *Annual Reports* of the Secretary constitute the prime source.

well as summaries of data for months and years. Though invaluable for research workers, their usefulness for keeping abreast of current developments is lessened by long time-lags in preparation and distribution.

Public announcements issued by the Secretary of the Treasury are essential current sources of information on Treasury problems and policies. Speeches by Treasury officials and newspaper reports based on the Secretary's press conferences are frequently illuminating.

Budget-Making Process

The Daily Statement is set up primarily on a so-called "budget basis," to tie in to the annual *Budget of the United States Government.* In the preparation of the budget each department head submits to the Bureau of the Budget detailed analyses of departmental expenditures for the next fiscal year. The Treasury Department, besides figuring its own expenses, has the special task of working up revenue forecasts. The departmental estimates are reviewed by the Bureau of the Budget under the direction of the President, and deletions and additions are made as the President may determine. The President lays these estimates before Congress each January, in a thousand-page document, as his financial program for the new fiscal year to begin the following July 1. It then becomes a matter for Congress to decide how many of the President's proposals to accept, what to add, and what to subtract.[4] Before Congress adjourns, the President may augment his program by supplemental requests for appropriations.

As the table on page 510 suggests, the final results for any fiscal year can be wide of the original plan set out by the President. This may be because of changes in economic conditions (which principally affect revenues), differences of opinion between the President and the Congress on the expenditure or tax programs, or special emergencies requiring the adoption of new spending programs.

Nevertheless, the President's budget is of immense significance. For the Treasury it lays a preliminary basis for projecting ahead plans for the management of the cash balances and the public debt. For the Congress and the public it provides an official appraisal of revenue prospects, and it lays out the financial aspects of the legislative proposals that will have Administration support. The budget becomes a topic of discussion and controversy until the Congress completes its work and adjourns, usually in early summer.[5] The Budget Bureau then prepares for the

[4] The Joint Committee on Internal Revenue Taxation has a small staff which assists Congress in appraising revenue prospects and preparing revenue legislation. The appropriations committees also have staff assistance, but it has not been adequate for thoroughgoing study of expenditure proposals.

[5] Under the Legislative Reorganization Act of 1946, provision was made for the Congress to adopt, after the President's budget recommendations had been received, a

TABLE 1

BUDGET ESTIMATES AND RESULTS

(In billions of dollars)

	1947	1948	1949	1950	1951	1952
			Fiscal Years Ended June 30			
			Net Budget Receipts			
Original budget estimate	$29.9	$35.7	$42.5	$41.0	$37.3	$55.1
Budget review estimate	37.7	39.6	37.9	38.0		
Second budget estimate	38.1	43.2	39.6	37.8	44.5	
Actual result	40.0	42.2	38.2	37.0		
			Total Budget Expenditures			
Original budget estimate	34.3	35.5	37.7	41.9	42.4	71.6
Budget review estimate	39.7	34.9	39.4	43.5		
Second budget estimate	40.4	35.7	40.2	43.3	47.2	
Actual result	39.3	33.8	40.0	40.1		
			Surplus or Deficit			
Original budget estimate	− 4.4	+ 0.2	+ 4.8	− 0.9	− 5.1	− 16.5
Budget review estimate	− 2.0	+ 4.7	− 1.5	− 5.5		
Second budget estimate	− 2.3	+ 7.5	− 0.6	− 5.5	− 2.7	
Actual result	+ 0.7	+ 8.4	− 1.8	− 3.1		

NOTE: Figures for 1947–49 have been adjusted to treat tax refunds as a deduction from receipts rather than as an expenditure in order to correspond with the present practice.

President a "Budget Review" which carries revised forecasts of revenues and expenditures, taking account of Congressional action and other developments since the original budget was presented. In January, further revised estimates for the current year are given in connection with the presentation of the original budget for the following fiscal year. The Daily Statements show how the figures are actually running as the months roll by, and the statement for June 30—the final day of the fiscal year—gives the final result. Meanwhile the cycle of estimates has begun all over again for the next succeeding fiscal year.

"Budget" versus "Cash" Basis

As already stated, the Daily Statement is set up on an accounting basis to tie in to the President's annual budgets. Revenue and expenditure figures on this basis are sometimes identified as on a "budget basis" to distinguish them from figures on a so-called "cash basis." The latter have

formal Legislative Budget for the purpose among others of "fixing the maximum amount to be appropriated for expenditure." Legislative Budgets were developed for the 1948 and 1949 fiscal years and were used by the Congress to demonstrate the feasibility of the reduction in income tax that was put into effect, over the President's objections, in 1948. Partly owing to lack of staff assistance for setting realistic expenditure targets, the idea has never been carried out as originally contemplated.

no legal standing but are officially calculated to measure the cash flow to and from the public resulting from federal government operations.[6]

In the computation on a cash basis, some transactions between government departments which do not involve the public are cancelled out. But the greater difference is in the degree of inclusiveness. The need for adding items onto the budget basis, to get the full picture of government operations, first became important in the '30's when numerous government corporations were set up with government-provided capital, plus the power to borrow from the Treasury. Despite the closeness of these financial relationships, the operations of government corporations at that time were regarded as distinct from the budget itself. The establishment in 1935 of the Federal Old-Age and Survivors Insurance Trust Fund and the Unemployment Trust Fund, both outside the budget proper, provided a further occasion for more comprehensive calculations of government financial operations.

The budget accounting basis, subject to change and improvement from time to time, meanwhile has been broadened. The practice in recent years has been to include the net expenditures of various government agencies and corporations in the budget. The main difference between budget and cash figures now is the inclusion in the latter of trust account operations.

In Congress the figures on the "budget basis" naturally are of dominant importance. They show the cost of running the government during the fiscal year (whether or not obligations incurred are paid in that year) and the revenues available to cover that cost.

Trust Account Operations

The separation of trust accounts from the regular budget figures is justified in their very nature. The resources of the Federal Old-Age and Survivors Insurance Trust Fund, for example, do not become freely usable by the Treasury, except as it sells to them government obligations formally acknowledging repayable indebtedness by the government.

In actual operation, however, the trust funds are as intimately knit into Treasury operations as are those of government agencies and corporations. For the Old-Age Trust Fund—to continue the example—the Secretary of the Treasury is managing trustee. The Treasury, through its

---

[6] As explained in *The Midyear Economic Report of the President* transmitted to the Congress in July, 1950, page 88: Cash payments to and receipts from the public reflect the volume of current cash transactions between government on the one hand, and the public (including business, foreign countries, and international institutions) on the other. All intragovernmental transactions are eliminated. Such data are more useful for assessing the immediate economic impacts of government programs than are the data in the conventional budget. A detailed description of the concepts used is given in the *Budget of the United States Government*, 1950, page 1375.

Bureau of Internal Revenue, has the responsibility for collecting the old-age taxes levied on employers and covered employees. The Treasury also has the responsibility for seeing that there is money on hand to meet benefit payments and administrative expenses. The Old-Age Trust Fund is actually not a fund of cash at all but a fund of claims on the Treasury.

These claims on the Treasury temporarily may be simple deposit credits on Treasury accounts, but the bulk are represented by government securities which the Treasury has sold to the Trust Fund. Some $2 billion of public marketable bonds are held in the Fund, but $11 billion (as of June 30, 1950) are in special issues of Treasury certificates redeemable on demand. When contributions to the Fund come in at a rate in excess of benefit payments, the Treasury keeps the cash and issues more special Treasury certificates. When interest is due on the government securities held in the Fund, the Treasury issues to it more special Treasury certificates; no actual cash transaction is involved. The Old-Age Fund has been an accumulating one. But when the time comes when benefit payments exceed the flow of new contributions, the Treasury will provide the cash and cancel a corresponding amount of the special Treasury certificates.

There are many variations in the way the Treasury operates, under the law or accepted administrative practice, in handling trust funds. The example of the Old-Age Fund is used because it is the largest of all these extra-budgetary operations.

Usefulness of the "Cash" Basis

The usefulness of the government revenue and expenditure figures on the cash basis lies in the fact that they cut around legalisms and provide measures of cash flow into the Treasury from the public and cash outflow from the Treasury to the public. The cash basis, and particularly the "cash surplus" or "cash deficit," are widely used by economists as quantitative measures of global effects of federal government financial operations on the economy. At the same time, a cash surplus measures an accumulation of cash that can be used for retiring debt held by the general public; a cash deficit measures a drain of cash that, beyond limits of available cash resources, will have to be covered by additional borrowing from the public.

While technicians can estimate the cash income and outgo by use of trust account and other supplemental data carried in the Daily Statement, the figures on the cash basis do not directly appear in the Statement. They are published on a monthly basis in the *Treasury Bulletin* and *Federal Reserve Bulletin,* and are projected ahead for each new fiscal

year in the President's annual budget and for the calendar year in the
Annual Economic Report of the President to the Congress.

Increased Scale of Operations

The following table shows the increase in the scale of government
financial operations over the past 35 years. For the later years figures are
given on both the budget basis and the cash basis. For earlier years trust
funds were of minor importance and the cash basis would approximate
the budget basis.

TABLE 2

RECEIPTS, EXPENDITURES, AND PUBLIC DEBT

(In millions of dollars)

Fiscal Years Ended June 30	Net Receipts	Budget Basis Expenditures	Budget Surplus or Deficit	Gross Public Debt, June 30
1914	$ 735	$ 735	$ 0	$ 1,188
1919 (war peak)	5,152	18,515	— 13,363	25,482
1927 (postwar low)	4,129	2,974	+ 1,155	18,512
1939 (depression peak) ..	5,103	8,966	— 3,862	40,440
1945 (war peak)	44,762	98,703	— 53,941	258,682
1948 (postwar low)	42,211	33,791	+ 8,419	252,292
1950	37,045	40,167	— 3,122	257,357

	Cash Income	Cash Basis Cash Outgo	Cash Surplus or Deficit
1929	$ 3,800	$ 2,900	+ $ 900
1939 (depression peak) ..	6,600	9,400	— 2,900
1945 (war peak)	50,240	95,184	— 45,945
1948 (postwar low)	45,400	36,496	+ 8,903
1950	40,970	43,155	— 2,185

NOTE: "Peak" and "low" points are in terms of expenditures. As this is written, the fighting in Korea has led to an acceleration of expenditures, while booming business and income tax increases are enlarging revenues.

The general record—going back to 1789 when the Republic was established—is that government expenditures, the debt, and taxes have risen
during major wars. With the return of peace, expenditures have dropped
sharply, but not so much as they had risen in war, and surpluses have
been achieved for reductions in taxes and in the public debt.[7]

The last 50 years contain some exceptional features. The scale of
government expenditures, and the public debt, have risen far beyond

[7] For a broad perspective on debt policy, see the volume prepared by The Committee
on Public Debt Policy, *Our National Debt*, New York, 1949—especially the first chapter prepared by the late Leonard P. Ayres and entitled, "Our National Debt After
Great Wars."

any previous occasion. Expenditures, from a level of around $750 million before World War I, averaged $3 billion during the prosperous '20's, and were stepped up to a range of $7 to $9 billion from 1935 to 1940 in the effort to recapture prosperity by expanded government outlays financed by higher taxes and borrowing. In World War II expenditures ran up to a peak of $99 billion in the 1945 fiscal year. The postwar minimum of expenditures, in fiscal 1948, was $34 billion.

The public debt rose from $1.2 billion on June 30, 1914, to $25.5 billion at the end of World War I, and was gradually cut down to $16.2 billion on June 30, 1930. A string of 16 big deficits, encompassing the depression and World War II, carried the debt beyond $250 billion.

Tax revenues were raised sharply in World War I, mainly by exploiting the income tax, authorized by a constitutional amendment in 1913. Tax rates were successively eased along with debt reduction in the '20's, and they were successively raised during the depression and World War II. Taxes were eased in 1945 and 1948, but fresh increases designed to cover enlarged military outlays followed in 1950. The annual burden of federal taxes in the years 1944–50 averaged more than $1,000 per family and has amounted to one-fifth of the national income.

The Treasury and the Money Market

The cash flow through the Treasury, including public debt transactions, in recent years has averaged around $300 million a day; but the flow is uneven, with sharp peaks on particular days and lower valleys in between. Tax deadlines and payment deadlines on the sale of government securities bring heavy concentrations of receipts. On the expenditure side, payments rise steeply on days when interest and government securities fall due.

Before the Federal Reserve System was organized, in 1913, the irregularities of Treasury receipts and expenditures led to recurring periods of pressure or ease in the money market since an accumulation of Treasury cash then meant a shift of gold from the banks to the Treasury or vice versa. These operations were carried out through Subtreasuries located in major cities.

Under modern practice, both the Treasury and banks maintain deposits with the Federal Reserve Banks, and shifts of funds which formerly involved the physical movement of gold or other lawful money are carried out by bookkeeping transactions. An accumulation of Treasury funds on deposit at the Federal Reserve Banks (for example, from tax collections) still involves a loss of reserves to the banks. Their reserve accounts carried at the Federal Reserve Bank are debited for tax checks drawn on them by their customers. But such a strain on bank reserves

can be offset by temporary borrowing by the banks from a Federal Reserve Bank, or by Federal Reserve purchases of government securities which put funds into the market. Under the "easy money" era dating back to 1934, the Federal Reserve System has seen to it that bank reserves have been plentifully available to avoid any real scarcity of funds in the money market.

Special Depositaries, Tax-Loan Accounts

Apart from Federal Reserve open-market operations, and the option of banks to borrow from the Federal Reserve to cover a loss of reserves, the Treasury over the years has evolved practices to moderate the drains on bank reserves from Treasury borrowings and, in lesser degree, from tax collections. The current practices have their principal origin in the use, during World War I, of commercial banks as "special depositaries" of the proceeds of War Loan drives. With the enormous increase in the scale of government borrowing and spending, some such device was a practical necessity.

Ever since (including the eight War Loan drives of World War II) the Treasury's general practice has been to allow authorized banks to credit the Treasury on their books for the government securities they and their customers buy, the funds being on call by the Treasury as needed. Treasury bills are excluded from this arrangement; they are settled for in cash immediately. But proceeds from new sales of nonmarketable savings bonds and notes, and marketable Treasury bonds, notes and certificates, are credited to these accounts. The plan is one of mutual advantage to the Treasury and the banks. Without some such arrangement, the payments by subscribers for large issues of government securities would involve serious temporary derangements in the money market.

This machinery has also proved useful in peacetime, and its application has been widened. Since World War II, the Treasury has set up arrangements whereby two types of tax payments may be credited to the War Loan accounts—the old-age pension taxes and the personal income taxes withheld by the employer under the "pay-as-you-go" system. This involves more work for the banks, but they have compensation in having the use of the funds until the Treasury calls for their repayment. The official name of the War Loan accounts has been changed from "Special depositaries account of sales of Government securities" to "Special depositaries, Treasury Tax and Loan Accounts."

Composition and Fluctuations of General Fund Balance

The Daily Statement of the United States Treasury includes each day, in a section headed "Current Assets and Liabilities," an analysis of the

"General Fund" balance, or the Treasury's cash assets. On June 30, 1950, for example, the General Fund balance amounted to $4¾ billion made up principally of $1 billion in so-called "free gold" [8] and $3¼ billion in Tax-Loan accounts. Balances with the Federal Reserve Banks were $438 million of which $161 million represented checks deposited with the Federal Reserve but not yet collected. The General Fund balance also includes, as relatively smaller items, silver coin and bullion, Federal Reserve notes and other paper money held in Treasury offices or vaults, and balances in some special purpose depositary accounts at home and abroad. In calculating the General Fund balance, amounts on deposit with the Treasury by the Post Office and the Postal Savings System, as well as some minor items, are subtracted from the gross available funds.

The deposits at the Federal Reserve Banks are the Treasury's active working balances. The bulk of Treasury checks drawn are payable from these accounts. The Treasury replenishes them by issuing calls for repayment from the Tax-Loan accounts carried with the commercial banks. When tax receipts from quarterly income or other taxes (which are credited directly to the Treasury's deposits with the Federal Reserve Banks) are flush, the Treasury generally suspends Tax-Loan withdrawals and allows Tax-Loan balances to build up. When tax revenues are inadequate to the scale of expenditures, the Tax-Loan accounts are drawn down. Prolonged drafts, of course, can exhaust them. Rarely, however, are they entirely exhausted. Before that happens some new borrowings are arranged.

In the fiscal year ending June 30, 1950, the Treasury maintained its deposits with the Federal Reserve Banks at an average level of $550 million. Most of the time the balances with the Federal Reserve fluctuated between $300 million and $600 million, but in the three heaviest tax collection months—September, March, and June—deposits at the Federal Reserve climbed from less than $100 million on the 15th of the month to around $1 billion on the 30th. The Tax-Loan account balances were maintained at an average level of $2,600 million, with a range from $829 million on July 19 to $3,741 million on April 3. On the entire General Fund balance the average was $4,500 million (the minimum $2,493 million on July 12 and the maximum $6,166 million on March 30).

The over-all General Fund balances seem large but they are not excessive when the scale of financial operations is taken into consideration. The total cash flow through Treasury accounts, including public debt transactions, was around $90 billion in the 1950 fiscal year. The Treasury deposits with the Federal Reserve Banks turned over more than 100 times in that year. The entire General Fund balance turned over 20 times.

---

[8] That is, gold in the General Fund, not obligated.

Cash Management

The perennial task of any treasurer is to see that he is solvent and has enough money to pay his bills. The obligations, current and potential, of the U.S. Treasury are enormous. First there are the payrolls and supply bills, familiar in every business and government body but distinguished in the present instance by the scale. The payrolls, for example, cover more than 2,000,000 employees. The mere business of drawing government checks is a huge, mass production affair. Quite apart from bills for current operating expenses, the Treasury must see that there is money in hand so that government corporations can draw from the Treasury the money they need to lend, buy up commodities, or carry out other authorized purposes. All these operations come under the heading of *budget expenditures.*

In addition the Treasury must see to it that there is money on hand to pay off government securities presented for redemption. When payments by trust funds exceed their current receipts, their cash requirements are met by redemption of special Treasury certificates or notes held by them. The Treasury must also see that there is money in hand to pay off government securities held by the public. These fall into two classes: (1) nonmarketable savings bonds and notes, which are redeemable at the option of the holder; and (2) marketable Treasury bills, certificates of indebtedness, notes and bonds, which are redeemable at maturity (or sometimes on an earlier date when the Treasury has reserved the option to call securities for payment prior to final maturity).[9]

Hovering somewhere in the background, but always demanding recognition, are the possibilities of adverse developments that put a strain on the Treasury—perhaps a foreign armed attack on the United States or on a friendly nation, requiring increased military outlays; or an unexpected contraction in business bringing a drop in revenues; an increase in cash needs of the Unemployment Trust Fund; enlarged benefit payments to farmers, and so on.

Public Debt Management

In any emergency, of course, the Congress can authorize the Treasury to float loans to replenish or increase its available cash balances. The Congress has been doing so, from time to time, since the founding of the nation. Once, during the second term of Andrew Jackson, the national debt was wiped out. Each major war has put the debt up to a new peak. At the onset of World War I in 1914, the national debt amounted to

---

[9] The Treasury commonly reserves this option for issues of longer-term bonds.

$1.2 billion, a figure that now seems insignificant. Two major wars since 1914, and a major depression fought with large-scale government spending and borrowing, have put the public debt up to a current level exceeding $250 billion.

Before World War I, the practice of Congress was to authorize particular loans for particular purposes—such as the refunding of short-term debt, replenishing the gold reserves, or building the Panama Canal. For the second of the five bond-selling campaigns of World War I, the Congress gave the Secretary discretionary powers to borrow as needed but under a statutory limit on the total amount of obligations that could be outstanding at any one time. It is under the Second Liberty Bond Act as amended that the Secretary today holds his authority to manage the public debt. The vast increase in the debt from 1930 to 1945 was accompanied by successive increases in the statutory debt limitation. The legislative action represented an endorsement by the Congress of the purposes for which money was being borrowed.

The absolute debt peak was $279 billion on February 28, 1946. This latter figure was swollen by the fact that the Treasury borrowed much more than was necessary in the eighth and last of the great War Loan drives—the "Victory Loan" drive of October–December 1945. The excess funds raised were used, during 1946, to pay off maturing debt. Budget surpluses in the 1947 and 1948 fiscal years contributed $9 billion to debt retirement, and on June 30, 1948, the debt was $252 billion. Deficits in the 1949 and 1950 fiscal years raised the debt to $257 billion on June 30, 1950. The statutory debt limit now in effect is $275 billion, established by Act of Congress on June 26, 1946.

The public debt is a dominant factor in Treasury administration. The reasons are threefold. First, the debt is huge. Second, the volume of obligations closely approaching maturity is heavy. Third, the proper administration of the public debt has an important bearing on general economic stability.

Size and Composition of Debt

The table on page 519, drawn from the Daily Statement of the U.S. Treasury for July 1, gives the composition of the public debt as of June 30, 1950, with corresponding figures for interest costs.

The distinction between the four classes of public marketable securities requires a word of explanation. The practice is to denominate issues with an original term of five years or more as "bonds," and issues of one to five years as "notes." Certificates and bills are issued for periods up to one year. Treasury bills, first authorized by an Act of June 17, 1929, are distinguished from other classes of government obligations in the manner

TABLE 3

PUBLIC DEBT AS OF JUNE 30, 1950

(Figures rounded to even millions)

	Average Interest Rate	Amount Outstanding
Interest-bearing debt:		
Marketable public issues:		
Treasury bills	1.187%	$ 13,533,000,000
Certificates of indebtedness	1.163	18,418,000,000
Treasury notes	1.344	20,403,000,000
Treasury bonds	2.322	102,795,000,000
Other bonds	2.656	160,000,000
Total marketable public issues	1.958%	$155,309,000,000
Nonmarketable public issues:		
Treasury savings notes	1.383%	$ 8,472,000,000
United States savings bonds	2.748	57,536,000,000
Depositary bonds	2.000	285,000,000
Armed forces leave bonds	2.500	297,000,000
Treasury bonds, investment series	2.500	954,000,000
Total nonmarketable public issues	2.569%	$ 67,544,000,000
Total public issues	2.143%	$222,853,000,000
Special issues to: Federal Old-Age and Survivors Insurance Trust Fund, Unemployment Trust Fund, National Service Life Insurance Fund, and other government investment accounts	2.589%	$ 32,356,000,000
Total interest-bearing debt	2.200%	$255,209,000,000
Matured debt on which interest has ceased		265,000,000
Debt bearing no interest:		
International Bank and Monetary Fund		1,270,000,000
Other ....,...................		613,000,000
Gross public debt		$257,357,000,000

of sale. They are offered (at discounts from face value) on a kind of auction system to the highest bidders.

There is no question but that the public debt is enormous by any standard of past experience in the United States. But it is possible for government policy to be overimpressed with this fact. Taking into account the growth of the nation and the shrinkage in the buying power of the dollar, the present debt is a lesser burden to service than was the debt accumulated in the Civil War. One tendency of public officials faced with a large public debt is to grow tolerant of inflation which reduces the weight of debt at the expense of creditor classes—bondholders, life insurance beneficiaries, pensioners, and holders of money savings. To sustain the credit of the government, in the contractual sense, the Treasury simply needs to see that securities are redeemed and interest paid when due. But there is a moral obligation to protect the buying power of the money

invested in government securities from avoidable depreciation. Inflation can undermine the credit of government just as surely as nonpayment of securities at maturity.

Interest Burden

The interest charge on the public debt, currently $5½ billion a year, is one consideration in management of the public debt. Of this interest, $1 billion goes to Treasury agencies and trust funds, as the following table shows:

TABLE 4

ESTIMATED INTEREST PAYMENTS ON THE PUBLIC DEBT

(In billions of dollars)

Calendar Years	Total Interest	U.S. Govt. Investment Accounts	Federal Reserve Banks	Commercial Banks	Individuals	Other Investors
1940	$1.1	$0.2	$ *	$0.3	$0.3	$0.3
1945	4.1	0.5	0.1	1.3	1.1	1.1
1949	5.5	1.0	0.3	1.1	1.7	1.4

* Less than $50,000,000.
Sources: For 1940 and 1945, U.S. Treasury Department; for 1949, Federal Reserve Bank of New York.

The Treasury Department has taken great satisfaction in the fact that, in terms of interest rates, World War II was financed at about half the cost of World War I. This was partly accident, partly deliberate policy. The cheap money rates prevailing in the depression period were adopted, with minor rectifications, as a fixed pattern for war financing. On marketable public issues the Treasury set the pattern and the Federal Reserve put its buying power behind the maintenance of the pattern, which was scaled from ⅜ per cent on 91-day Treasury bills, and ⅞ per cent on one-year certificates of indebtedness, up to 2½ per cent on 25-year bonds.

With some narrowing in the range of rates, essentially the same strict pattern concept was maintained in the postwar period, 1946–50. The Federal Reserve, when necessary, bought up long-term 2½ per cent bonds to maintain their prices at par or better, and short-term Treasury bills, certificates and notes to assure to the Treasury a ready market for government paper carrying rates of 1¼ per cent or less. With this arrangement, Treasury borrowings strongly favored short-term paper to get the advantage of the cheapest rate.

In August and September 1950, the Federal Reserve authorities, acting on their own responsibility to retard excessive credit expansion, brought sufficient pressure to bear on the money market to raise the rate the

Treasury would have to pay on short-term borrowings from the prevailing 1¼ per cent to 1⅜ per cent.[10] The Treasury attempted to borrow again at 1¼ per cent, but the new issues encountered a poor reception. After considerable public controversy, the two agencies reached an "accord" on March 3, 1951, under which a 2¾ per cent conversion bond was issued and previously outstanding bonds were given freedom to decline as much as two or three points below par. Thus the pattern of rates has been raised and made less rigid.

Large Floating Debt

With short-term securities so heavily favored, the volume of obligations closely approaching maturity—the "floating debt"—is very large. Entirely apart from savings bonds and notes, and special issues redeemable on demand, the Treasury on June 30, 1950, had falling due within one year $13,533 million in 91-day Treasury bills, $26,862 million in Treasury certificates and notes, and $8,760 million in Treasury bonds—a total of $49,155 million.

A floating debt of these proportions has been maintained by persistent use of a "rollover" technique in handling debt maturities. The Treasury has had $1 billion, more or less, of 91-day Treasury bills coming due every week since 1943. These have been rolled over and over, week after week. Though the amount outstanding has been subject to some fluctuation, the standardized practice has been to sell each week enough bills to pay off those maturing. Treasury certificates and notes have been rolled over as they have come due by offering holders new issues in exchange. Bonds, upon reaching maturity or called for payment prior to maturity, have been replaced by certificates or notes. No marketable government securities of more than five years' term have been issued since the Victory Loan drive in 1945.[11]

---

[10] The Federal Reserve action evidently was intended to represent an implementation of a view expressed in conferences between the Secretary of the Treasury and representatives of the Federal Open Market Committee in June 1949, to the effect that "the time had arrived when the Federal Open Market Committee should begin to determine its policies on the basis of the general business and credit situation and orderly conditions in the Government security market, without attempting to maintain a relatively fixed pattern of prices and yields on United States Government securities." See *Annual Report* for 1949, Board of Governors of the Federal Reserve System, pp. 114-115.

[11] Three issues of four or five year notes were put out on exchange offerings in 1949 and 1950. Exchange offers typically have been one-year certificates or 13-month notes.

Federal Reserve Support on Current Financing

On Treasury certificates, notes, and bonds, the rollover technique has involved offering to holders of maturing paper an exchange privilege into a new issue maturing a year or so later. If the terms of the new offering are not attractive, the holders are entitled to decline the exchange and take cash. To avoid a severe cash drain on the Treasury, the Federal Reserve puts in bids for the maturing securities, offering premiums to get them, and makes the exchange. If the Federal Reserve has to buy very many of the securities, this is inflationary. The Treasury, in effect, is borrowing cash from the Federal Reserve to pay off holders of government securities. It was this inflationary process, not less dangerous because it is subtle, which the Federal Reserve acted to retard in a policy change announced August 18, 1950.

The Federal Reserve's action directly affected the results on a Treasury offering, announced the same day, of $13½ billion of 1¼ per cent 13-month notes in exchange for two issues of bonds and two issues of certificates maturing September 15 and October 1. While the Federal Reserve Banks put in bids for the maturing securities and bought enormous quantities, in support of the Treasury, they offered no premiums to induce holders wanting cash at maturity to sell out to them. Moreover, at the same time they sold nearly equivalent amounts of other securities, and on terms more attractive than the Treasury was offering. The proportion of the maturing securities unexchanged, and requiring cash redemption was unusually high, about 17 per cent of the total. Fortunately, the Treasury was in a strong cash position and was easily able to cover this "involuntary" debt retirement out of accumulated balances with commercial bank depositaries.

On every exchange offer that is made, and even under the most favorable circumstances, holders of perhaps 5 or 10 per cent of a maturing issue choose neither to make the exchange nor to sell out in advance of maturity. For reasons of their own they take the option of cash redemption. This involves a need for cash borrowing, in the absence of a surplus, to pay off unexchanged securities. Such borrowings, of course, do not increase the total debt.

The Savings Bond Record

Most widespread among U.S. government securities are nonmarketable obligations, particularly the Series E savings bonds. They pay no interest but increase in value by one-third over a ten-year period. The postwar record on holding of these securities to maturity has been dis-

couraging, despite penalties involved in redemption before maturity. Redemptions averaged above $4 billion a year, 1945–50, and less than half the bonds sold are being carried through to maturity. New sales, however, while falling, provided more than enough funds to cover redemptions. Thus the over-all record has been better than many people had anticipated.

When the ten-year Series E savings bonds began to mature in May, 1951, the Treasury gained Congressional approval for a plan to allow the matured bonds to increase in value by another one-third over a second ten-year span for holders who wished to keep them. Thus, a savings bond bought for $75 in 1941 will be worth $133.33 if kept until 1961.

Dangers in Excessive Floating Debt

At the close of 1945, after the final War Loan drive, the floating debt was at a peak of $68½ billion. In the calendar years 1946–48, $20 billion of excess cash realized from the final drive plus $14 billion of cash surplus were used to pay off maturing obligations. The floating debt, however, still amounted to $42 billion at the end of 1948, since many other obligations, including bond issues coming forward to maturity, were rolled over into one-year paper. No issues of marketable bonds to refund floating debt were attempted. In 1949–50, Treasury bill offerings were increased to raise needed cash. While the rollover technique was modified to include notes of four and five years' term, the floating debt tended to build up.

In periods of emergency governments often borrow at short term; conditions in the bond market may be disturbed and financial needs pressing. But a large floating debt—far in excess of any prospective amount of funds available for retiring debt—can at any time become a source of embarrassment. The handling of maturities time and again has been the object of conflict between Treasury and Federal Reserve authorities. And the volume of nearby Treasury maturities time and again has stayed the Federal Reserve from taking effective action to combat inflation.

Fund Floating Debt?

Following any period of emergency involving a large increase in floating debt, orthodox policy is to "fund" floating debt; that is, to sell long-term bonds to pay off current debt as favorable opportunities arise in the bond market. Such favorable opportunities existed in 1947, 1949, and 1950, but were not used to any significant extent.[12]

Some modern students of public debt have advocated another course—

---

[12] Limited special offerings of Series F and G savings bonds to institutional investors were made in 1948 and 1950. In 1947 a limited sale of "investment series" Treasury bonds, a savings bond type of obligation, was made.

reducing floating debt by funding in a period of boom and increasing the floating debt by borrowing at short term in a period of depression. Sales of long-term bonds in a boom would "mop up" investment funds held by nonbank investors and the proceeds would be used to pay off bank-held debt, including debt held by the Federal Reserve Banks. The Treasury has not followed this policy either; the years 1947, 1948, and 1950 were boom years, but no substantial borrowings were effected to cut down floating debt.[13] Indeed, in 1948, both the Federal Reserve and the Treasury were heavy buyers of long-term bonds for the purpose of supporting their prices. Thus they *added* to the market supply of investment funds, which was precisely the wrong thing to be doing, and neutralized the effectiveness of other anti-inflationary measures taken.[14]

This experience clearly indicates how fixed ideas of the prices at which government securities should be selling, and fixed limits on interest rates that should be paid, are incompatible with efforts to put an effective restraint on inflation, either with the Federal Reserve's open-market powers or the Treasury's debt management powers. It led to a Congressional investigation under the chairmanship of Senator Douglas.

The Douglas Report

Under authority of a concurrent resolution approved in May 1949, the Congressional Joint Committee on the Economic Report appointed a subcommittee to pursue an investigation of "Monetary, Credit, and Fiscal Policies." The subcommittee, headed by Senator Paul H. Douglas of Illinois, solicited information and expressions of viewpoint from the Secretary of the Treasury, officers of the Federal Reserve and other government agencies, as well as private individuals. The following is taken from the final report of the subcommittee: [15]

> We recommend that Federal fiscal policies be such as not only to avoid aggravating economic instability but also to make a positive and important contribution to stabilization, at the same time promoting equity and incentives in taxation and economy in expenditures. A policy based on the principle of an annually balanced budget regardless of fluctuations in the national income does not meet these tests; for, if actually followed, it would require drastic increases of tax rates or drastic reductions of Government

[13] The Treasury in each of these years did improve rates of return offered on short-term paper, for anti-inflationary purposes.

[14] Including redemptions by the Treasury, from surplus revenues, of some maturing securities held by the Federal Reserve Banks, and sales by the Federal Reserve of short-term government obligations from their portfolio.

[15] Senate Document No. 129, 81st Congress, 2nd session, *Report of the Subcommittee on Monetary, Credit, and Fiscal Policies of the Joint Committee on the Economic Report*, Government Printing Office, 1950. The official replies to special questionnaires sent out by the subcommittee vere published in a 443-page joint-committee print entitled *Monetary, Credit and Fiscal Policies*, Government Printing Office, 1949.

expenditures during periods of deflation and unemployment, thereby aggravating the decline, and marked reductions of tax rates or increases of expenditures during periods of inflationary boom, thereby accentuating the inflation. A policy that will contribute to stability must produce a surplus of revenues over expenditures in periods of high prosperity and comparatively full employment and a surplus of expenditures over revenues in periods of deflation and abnormally high unemployment. Such a policy must, however, be based on a recognition that there are limits to the effectiveness of fiscal policy because economic forecasting is highly imperfect at present and tax and expenditure policies under present procedures are very inflexible.[16]

We recommend that an appropriate, flexible, and vigorous monetary policy, employed in coordination with fiscal and other policies, should be one of the principal methods used to achieve the purposes of the Employment Act.[17] Timely flexibility toward easy credit at some times and credit restriction at other times is an essential characteristic of a monetary policy that will promote economic stability rather than instability. The vigorous use of a restrictive monetary policy as an anti-inflation measure has been inhibited since the war by considerations relating to holding down the yields and supporting the prices of United States Government securities. As a long-run matter, we favor interest rates as low as they can be without inducing inflation, for low interest rates stimulate capital investment. But we believe that the advantages of avoiding inflation are so great and that a restrictive monetary policy can contribute so much to this end that the freedom of the Federal Reserve to restrict credit and raise interest rates for general stabilization purposes should be restored even if the cost should prove to be a significant increase in service charges on the Federal debt and a greater inconvenience to the Treasury in its sale of securities for new financing and refunding purposes.

While the subcommittee report failed to receive the endorsement of the full committee, the second paragraph quoted above influenced the Federal Reserve authorities in August 1950, under the inflationary conditions then prevailing, to moderate their cheap money policy, over Treasury objections, and, in March 1951, to allow government bond prices to fall below par.

---

[16] For a spelling out of some of these latter difficulties, see "The Compensatory Budget—Theory vs. Practice," National City Bank of New York, Monthly Letter on Economic Conditions, December 1949.

[17] The Employment Act of 1946 declared: . . . that it is the continuing policy and responsibility of the Federal Government to use all practicable means consistent with its needs and obligations and other essential considerations of national policy, with the assistance and cooperation of industry, agriculture, labor, and State and local governments, to coordinate and utilize all its plans, functions, and resources for the purpose of creating and maintaining, in a manner calculated to foster and promote free competitive enterprise and the general welfare, conditions under which there will be afforded useful employment opportunities, including self-employment, for those able, willing, and seeking to work, and to promote maximum employment, production, and purchasing power.

Management of the Dollar

The Secretary of the Treasury becomes an indirect and unwitting advocate of inflation when he urges the Federal Reserve to peg the prices of government securities at high levels so that he can borrow cheaply. But the Secretary also has vital direct responsibilities for the currency, and most of the time over the nation's history he has been a chief spokesman for sound money. He has been a natural foe of schemes, such as have come up in every age, to finance government expenditures the easy way by straight-out inflation of the currency—printing paper notes carrying a legal tender privilege.

By the Constitution, the right is reserved to the Congress to "coin money" and "regulate the value thereof." The actual work of coinage is carried on in the Bureau of the Mint, to specifications set out in law. Engraving of paper money is carried on in the Bureau of Engraving and Printing, under specific legal authorizations to the Treasury and to the Federal Reserve Banks.[18] Aside from these mechanical jobs, performed by departments of the Treasury, the Secretary has the task of protecting and safeguarding the national gold stock which forms an essential basis for confidence in the dollar. This confidence is vital to economic stability not only in the United States but also in foreign countries that hold dollar deposits in American banks and investments in U.S. government obligations as part of their currency reserves.

The protection of confidence in the dollar historically has required that gold be made available from the national gold stock upon demand. By the Gold Reserve Act in 1934, when the dollar was devalued 41 per cent in terms of gold, it was provided that "no currency of the United States shall be redeemed in gold" except under regulations issued by the Secretary of the Treasury with the approval of the President. Since 1933 private holding of gold coin has been forbidden, but the Secretary has regularly authorized sales to foreign governments or central banks whenever they have wanted to convert dollars into gold.[19] Because of restrictions on convertibility, dollars frequently trade at a discount from their

---

[18] Paper money issued by the Treasury includes gold and silver certificates, which are secured 100 per cent by gold and silver held by the Treasury, and United States notes, which are subject to a specific limit of $347 million and for which $156 million in gold is reserved as cover. A 1933 authorization to issue $3 billion unsecured paper notes, never used, was repealed in 1945.

The Federal Reserve Banks issue Federal Reserve notes for which a minimum cover of 25 per cent in gold certificates is required.

[19] The Gold Reserve Act of 1934 contains a number of provisions that are unnecessary and superseded, or ambiguous and misleading. Proposals to reduce the law to clear and unequivocal terms have been made from time to time but have not been acted upon.

stated gold value in free markets abroad. This has led to the suggestion that the law should be amended to permit circulation of gold coin at par with paper money.

Treasury policy since 1933 has been to oppose recirculation of gold coin and the holding of gold by private individuals as a store of wealth. On the other hand, the necessity for ready sales to foreign governments and central banks to stabilize the value of the dollar in the foreign exchange markets has been recognized. In May 1949 an official statement was made [20] to the effect that:

> . . . the Treasury believes it to be of the highest monetary importance to the United States that it continue to sell gold to foreign governments and central banks at $35 an ounce whenever the balance of international payments turns in their favor and they ask for settlement in gold. To refuse to make such sales at $35 would be equivalent to a devaluation of the dollar and an abandonment of our adherence to a gold standard.

Thus the protection of confidence in the dollar requires the United States to give up gold when gold is requested in international settlements. That is what the gold is for. Protection of the gold stock from dangerous depletion, in turn, demands sound financial policies, prompt and effective action to combat inflationary trends when they develop, and a limitation of governmental financial commitments to what we can afford. A gold outflow serves its traditional function when it reminds responsible officials and people generally of these indispensable elements in a stable and progressive society.

The Secretary of the Treasury is Chairman of the National Advisory Council on International Monetary and Financial Problems, set up in 1945, and Governor for the United States of the two world financial organizations devised at the Bretton Woods Conference of 1944—the International Monetary Fund and the International Bank for Reconstruction and Development. In these capacities he has occupied a position of leadership in postwar monetary reconstruction abroad. During the reconstruction period, the U.S. dollar (of the gold content established on January 31, 1934) has served as a fixed base of reference for other currencies of the world and generally as an international standard of value.

Suggested Readings

Adams, E. Sherman, *Monetary Management*. New York: The Ronald Press Company, 1950. An up-to-date book on monetary management in the environment of the vastly increased public debt. Chapter 7 is specifically concerned with debt management.

Burgess, W. Randolph, *The Reserve Banks and the Money Market*. New York:

---

[20] In a letter from the Acting Secretary of the Treasury to the Chairman of the Senate Banking and Currency Committee.

Harper & Brothers, 1936 and 1946. Chapter VII gives a readable and authoritative account of Federal Reserve activities, prewar, as "Bankers for the Government." Three chapters added in the 1946 edition are concerned with war financing.

Childs, C. F., *Concerning U.S. Government Securities*. Chicago: Privately published, 1947. A 584-page compendium, valuable for reference purposes, written in response to a request for a "brief summary of national financing by the United States Government." The author is president of an old established firm dealing in government securities.

Committee for Economic Development, *Monetary and Fiscal Policy for Greater Economic Stability*. New York: 1948. A pamphlet designed "as an aid to clearer understanding of steps to be taken in reaching and maintaining high levels of productive employment and a steadily rising standard of living."

Committee on Public Debt Policy, *Our National Debt, Its History and Its Meaning Today*. New York: 1949. An intelligent and non-technical appraisal of the national debt, with a practical debt management program. The result of a study financed by the Falk Foundation of Pittsburgh.

Dewey, Davis Rich, *Financial History of the United States*, 12th Edition. New York: Longmans, Green & Co., 1939. An indispensable volume to any research worker in the field. The focal point throughout is government finance and financial policies.

Groves, Harold M., *Financing Government*, 3rd Edition. New York: Henry Holt & Co., 1950. A useful, balanced, and comprehensive text covering the principles, practices, and problems of government finance. The author is a leading expert in his field.

Murphy, Henry C., *National Debt in War and Transition*. New York: McGraw-Hill Book Co., 1950. A reliable, semiofficial history of the financing of World War II which forms the essential backdrop to postwar financial problems and policies. The author was Assistant Director of Research and Statistics in the Treasury Department during most of the war period.

Secretary of the Treasury, *Annual Report on the State of the Finances*. Washington, D.C.: Government Printing Office, annually since 1801. Earlier reports were numerous but irregular. Those prepared by Alexander Hamilton in the first five years of the nation's history, and addressed to the "Public Credit" and other special topics, still stand as monuments to genius.

20

Insurance Companies

by VICTOR V. SWEENEY

Associate Professor of Insurance, University of Florida

Historical Development

THE INSTITUTION of insurance exists because individuals and organizations seek to be relieved of the disagreeable aspects of risk. The uncertainty of risk, that ever present "chance of loss," has long been one of the undesirable features of human existence. Ancient history gives considerable evidence that the peoples of early civilizations sought means of avoiding the full impact of risk by sharing the perils of common dangers, although such history is often vague in the details of the plans used to accomplish these objectives.

While these early schemes used to avoid the undesirable consequences of uncertainty did not take the shape of insurance as we know it today, it is apparent that in the more advanced forms of ancient civilizations there developed "share the risk" plans based on the principle that, if losses were shared by many, the cost to each person in the plan would be relatively small. Five thousand years ago Chinese merchants hit upon the idea of spreading the risks inherent in the shipping of their merchandise on the Yangtze River. It was customary for each merchant, cooperating with the others, to split a shipment into many small units. One boat would then contain a small portion of each merchant's shipment. If two or three of the many boats used were shipwrecked, the resultant loss to any one merchant was therefore not ruinous.[1]

In Greece, in the third century before Christ, "bottomry" and "respondentia" loans also were forerunners of modern insurance. In this

[1] Cf. L. J. Ackerman and R. W. Bugli, *Risks We Face*. New York: Prentice-Hall, Inc., 1944, pp. 9-11, for a more detailed account of this practice as well as other early schemes to spread risk.

case money lenders arranged loans to shipowners or merchants. If the ships and cargoes upon which the loans had been made were lost at sea, the borrower was relieved of his debt; but if the ships reached their destination, the money with interest had to be paid to the lender. Apparently, such a lender made many loans of this nature. Here we see an early form of dependence upon the so-called "law of averages" by professional risk bearers.

In spite of these and other efforts of our forebears to "share the risk," it was not until the end of the Middle Ages that any insurance practices or contracts developed which resembled their modern counterparts. Apparently, risks inherent in maritime ventures of the expanding commerce of the Italian city-states (such as Venice, Florence and Genoa) created a demand for marine insurance and for the use of an insurance contract. One authority on this subject states that the earliest marine insurance policy form known to be in existence was written in Genoa in 1347.[2] From that point the use of the marine insurance contract rapidly spread throughout the Mediterranean area and the maritime cities and states of the Baltic and North Seas. During the last half of the sixteenth century the practice of marine insurance became established in England. By the beginning of the eighteenth century it had become a flourishing business and led to the development of Lloyd's of London as an important insurance institution. In 1779, a uniform Lloyd's marine policy was adopted as standard by all members of Lloyd's.[3] This policy still is the basic ocean marine policy in use today.

The fire of London in 1666, in which most of the city was destroyed, gave considerable impetus to the permanent establishment of fire insurance. Some earlier, scattered uses of this form of protection are recorded, but apparently it was from the London disaster that common recognition of the need of fire insurance developed. Within a year after the fire, one Doctor Nicolas Barbon established himself as an individual insurer to write fire insurance policies. A few years later he acquired a partner in this venture. In 1683 a rival insurance organization known as the Friendly Society entered the field. This was followed by the founding of a third fire insurance concern in 1696 which was eventually known as "The Hand in Hand Mutual Insurance Office."[4]

It was in England also, in 1720, that the first corporate form of insurance enterprise appeared. In that year two fire and marine insurance corporations, known respectively as The London Assurance and The

---

[2] William R. Vance, *Handbook of the Law of Insurance*. St. Paul: West Publishing Co., 1930, p. 11.

[3] *Ibid.*, p. 20. Vance also states that in 1795 the Lloyd's policy was made the standard form by an Act of Parliament.

[4] Cf. Ackerman and Bugli, *op. cit.*, p. 14. These early insurers were not formed as corporations but as sole proprietorships or partnerships.

Royal Exchange Assurance, were chartered. These corporations operate on a large scale today.

About this time life insurance was developing as a business in England. However, it was not until the formation and establishment of the Equitable Assurance Society of London in 1762 that a life insurance organization operated on the underlying principles employed by today's successful life insurance carriers.

Accident and liability insurance did not develop in England until after the middle of the nineteenth century.

The development of the insurance business in the United States. In a general way, the insurance business developed in the United States as in England. There is ample evidence that we copied methods and practices from our English cousins. However, in our later stages of development we have conceived several innovations and variations to adapt insurance specifically to our needs, as explained later in this chapter.

Aside from a few earlier inconsequential and abortive attempts to establish fire insurance in this country, the first fire insurance company was organized in 1752 in Philadelphia on a mutual basis.[5] This company was (and still is) known as "The Philadelphia Contributionship for Insuring Houses from Loss by Fire." Shortly thereafter a rival mutual organization known as "The Green Tree" was formed. The latter company, as well as its earlier competitor, carries on a flourishing business today within a restricted geographical area.

While mutual insurance companies were developed prior to stock insurance corporations, it is the latter that write a major part of the fire insurance business in the United States. The first capital stock insurance company to be founded was The Insurance Company of North America, a Philadelphia concern that is one of today's leading multiple line insurance carriers. This was in 1792. Soon thereafter numerous other mutual and stock fire insurance companies came into being. Naturally, early development was in the eastern part of the United States, in such cities as New York, Hartford, Newark, Baltimore and Boston. Today, while there is still considerable concentration of home offices of fire insurance companies in the East, we find them in all states.

In this country ocean marine insurance has never developed the same relative importance as in England, because, as a nation, we have depended less on foreign trade and more on domestic trade than has Great Britain. Nonetheless, in recent years the premium volume of marine insurance, particularly inland marine, has had a phenomenal increase. Many fire companies were early chartered to write marine insurance, and

---

[5] The meaning of the term "mutual insurance company" is described later in this chapter.

today practically all large fire insurance companies are also in the marine insurance business in some manner or other.

At the outset the life insurance business in the United States developed at a slower pace than did the fire insurance business. It was not until after the Civil War that the life insurance business became of considerable importance, and the great strides toward its present magnitude were made in the twentieth century. Today there are over 193,000,000 life insurance policies in force as compared to approximately 14,000,000 in 1900.[6]

Apparently the first successful effort made to establish life insurance in the United States was the formation of the Presbyterian Ministers' Fund on a mutual benefit basis, in Philadelphia, in 1769.[7] Nevertheless, development of the business was not rapid until the middle of the nineteenth century. Between 1850 and 1860, many life insurance companies were formed, several of which were operated on an unsound basis. With the advent of insurance departments in the several states—the first in Massachusetts in 1858 and the second in New York in 1859—this tendency was soon checked and later suppressed by strict regulations applying to all insurance transactions of companies doing business in the states imposing such regulations.

Casualty insurance, embracing such lines as accident, general liability, automobile liability and material damage, workmen's compensation, boiler and machinery, burglary, and plate glass insurance, was a latecomer in the insurance business. However, it has grown to such proportions that today it is second only to life insurance in total annual premium volume. Corporate suretyship, also of recent origin, while not insurance in its true sense, has always been closely identified with casualty insurance because of similarities in carrier structure, in regulation by state insurance departments, and in the methods used in marketing the product through insurance agents and brokers. Several casualty companies, in addition to companies engaged principally in the surety business, write fidelity and surety bonds.

Accident insurance in the United States is approximately 100 years old. Boiler insurance appeared in 1866, plate glass insurance in 1867, liability insurance in 1886, automobile insurance in 1898 and workmen's compensation insurance in 1910. In 1853, corporate suretyship was approved by the New York Insurance Department but did not become a reality until some 20 years later, when the Fidelity and Casualty Company of New York commenced to write corporate surety bonds.[8] As with fire insurance, the greater part of the premium volume in casualty insurance

[6] *Life Insurance Fact Book*. New York: Institute of Life Insurance, 1950, p. 7.
[7] William R. Vance, *op. cit.*, p. 24.
[8] Edward C. Lunt, *Surety Bonds*. New York: The Ronald Press Company, 1922, p. 4.

goes to capital stock companies. However, the mutual insurance companies play a very important part by writing approximately one-third of the business in this field.

Functions and Operations

The insurance mechanism. While insurance has been built upon the principle of absorbing the economic shock of loss incident with risk, it does not provide a vehicle for the sharing or transferring of all types and kinds of risk.[9] Only risks of a certain nature may be merged or shifted by an insurance plan. One line of division between that which constitutes an insurable risk and that which constitutes a noninsurable risk is the nature of the risk itself. One in which only loss can result if the chance event occurs (such as a hostile fire) is normally insurable; one in which either loss or gain can result (such as a change in the price level) generally is uninsurable. Risks of the latter type, speculative in nature, are sometimes transferred in the commodity markets through a noninsurance device known as "hedging"[10]

Aside from the above limitation, a sound insurance plan requires that an insurable hazard have the following characteristics:

1. The units of risk to be insured must be numerous enough for a workable application of the "law of large numbers" in conjunction with the theory of probability.
2. The units of risk must be "spread." This means that the units must be so diffused that there is practically no likelihood of a single loss or a connected series of losses resulting in a catastrophic loss to the insurance carrier.
3. The units of risk must be homogeneous.
4. The units of risk must be approximately similar in size (measured in terms of monetary units). This result is often achieved through reinsurance.
5. The hazard insured against must be of such a nature that a loss would be fortuitous.[11]

---

[9] As used here, "risk" means the "chance of loss." In actual insurance practice the term "risk" often denotes a business firm or individual exposed to risk (e.g. X Manufacturing Co., or John Doe). Cf. Albert H. Mowbray, *Insurance. Its Theory and Practice in the United States.* New York: McGraw-Hill Book Co., 1946, Chapter I, for an explanation of risk in relation to insurance.

[10] See E. H. Spengler and J. Klein, *Introduction to Business.* New York: McGraw-Hill Book Co., 1948, p. 447 ff., for a simple but effective description of a hedging transaction. See also Chapter 12 of this book.

[11] In addition to the requirements for a sound insurance plan shown here, it is often stated that to be insurable a risk must produce a loss that is definite in time and place. While such a condition is usually considered highly desirable by insurance underwriters, some risks are insured without this requirement. For example, in recent

6. The extent of risk must be measurable. This is necessary so that an adequate and fair rate may be calculated for the risk.

7. The loss insured against must be important enough to constitute a real risk for the insured, i.e., there must be an "insurable interest."

When a risk meets the requirements that have been set forth above, it is said to be insurable. With risks of this nature the basic function of insurance is to furnish protection by replacing uncertainty with certainty. Reduced to its simplest terms, insurance is a social device through which we seek to avoid the uncertainty of a disastrous loss by sharing our risk with others facing the same danger. To accomplish this we substitute a small certain loss (the insurance premium) for the uncertainty connected with the possibility of a large loss (the event insured against).

From a legal point of view, insurance consists of a contract, called the policy, in which the insurer, in consideration of (or the promise of) payment of the premium plus compliance with the policy terms on the part of the insured, agrees to indemnify the insured (as stipulated by the policy provisions) for a loss if the event insured against occurs.

At first thought it might seem that the area of operation of the insurance mechanism would be closely restricted by the requirements for insurable hazard. In actual practice the application of the insurance principle has brought about results that are quite the opposite. The insurance business in the United States is tremendous in both scope and size.

Despite the fact that only certain classes of risk lend themselves to insurance protection, a surprisingly large number of hazards can be so covered. The long list of insurable perils faced by individuals and by business organizations has caused the development of a formidable array of various types of insurance. For example, within the field of casualty insurance alone there are scores of different kinds of coverages in use; in inland marine insurance the list of various policies now utilized is equally long. The so-called "allied lines" of fire insurance present a sizeable number of insurances such as windstorm, hail, water damage, and business interruption. To the uninitiated the nomenclature of many of these insurance "coverages," to say nothing of the protection offered by each, is confusing. On the other hand, to a well-informed insurance man who is familiar with the development of the insurance business, the application of the correct coverage for a given need is apparent.

An understanding of the reason for this division of insurance into numerous classes and types is the first step toward their comprehension. As has been stated above, the extent of the risk must be known, and ratewise must be capable of approximate mathematical calculation. For an insurance carrier to issue a policy with insufficient data as to the

years, many liability policies have been issued to cover liability on a "caused by occurrence" rather than on a "caused by accident" basis.

probable extent of the risk faced and without an approximation of the total amount of losses to expect in a given period of time is to court disaster. Therefore the risk, or risks, to be covered by any particular type of insurance must be confined within a well-defined orbit. These classes of risk tend to define the classes of insurance.

Generally speaking, insurable hazards (perils) fall within three risk groups, which are:

1. The "chance of loss" of earning power by either an individual or an organization.
2. The "chance of loss" through the direct loss of or damage to the property of an individual or an organization.
3. The "chance of loss" to an individual or an organization because of legal liability for injury to the person or damage to the property of another.

If viewed from the vantage point of these three fundamental groupings, any "line" of insurance can be placed in the category in which it belongs, and its purpose becomes clear. For instance, life insurance is used to cover the loss of the earning power of the breadwinner of a family, of a valuable business partner, or of a key man in a corporation due to death. Annuities and old age insurance meet the risk of living beyond the period of earning power—the peril attendant to superannuation. Even business interruption insurance, covering indirect and consequential loss or damage following a fire or windstorm, is a form of insurance that protects a business concern against the loss of earning power.

Fire, riot and civil commotion, automobile collision, water damage, burglary, explosion, and windstorm insurance are examples of indemnity protection against direct loss or damage.

The "chance of loss" because of legal liability for injury to another or damage to his property has developed liability insurance. Examples of such insurance protection are the automobile liability policy, the employers' liability policy, the comprehensive personal liability policy, and the products liability policy. Workmen's compensation insurance is an example of protection against the liability imposed on an employer by statute law.

Classes of insurance. Because of state legislation and long established practices in the insurance industry, its classifications became somewhat artificial and arbitrary. Within the past few years "multiple-line" legislation in many of the states has tended to break down some of these barriers. If this trend continues, it may well be that within a short time all the various classes of insurance will be concentrated into two major groups: life and property insurance. However, for the sake of conformity

with present and past customs, insurance is treated here as consisting of the following five branches:

1. Life insurance
2. Casualty insurance
3. Fire insurance and allied lines
4. Marine insurance
5. Corporate suretyship.

Life insurance. Life insurance is "big business" both in the aggregate and in the size of the individual companies. It is the leading branch of the entire insurance industry, measured in annual premium income and in total assets. The largest life insurance company, which is the second largest American corporation, has over nine billion dollars in assets; the next largest has more than eight billion. In 1949, the premium income of the 609 legal reserve life insurance companies operating in the United States was $7,601,000,000, while the total income of these same companies amounted to $10,257,000,000.[12] The amount of life insurance in force at the end of 1949 was over $214,000,000 distributed among 80 million individual policyholders in approximately 193 million policies. Few other institutions have such far-reaching effect upon the people of this country as does life insurance.

In absolute terms, life insurance has grown rapidly in the past 50 years. For example, in 1900, in contrast to the above 1949 figures, there was only slightly more than seven and one-half billion dollars of life insurance in force, and the total number of policies was about 14 million. In that same year the total assets of life insurance companies was $1,742,-000,000 as compared with $59,555,000,000 at the end of 1949.

Fundamentally, life insurance consists of a contract whereby for a given premium the insurance company agrees to pay the beneficiary a specified sum of money as a lump sum or its equivalent in income upon the death of the insured. In many of these contracts the company agrees to pay this amount (sometimes called the "proceeds" or "benefit") to the insured instead of the beneficiary, if the insured is alive at the "maturity" date of the policy.

To meet the varied needs of purchasers, life insurance companies issue a variety of policy forms. To those unfamiliar with life insurance, the various policies may appear to be a bewildering array. Actually there are but four basic types, which are (1) term insurance, (2) whole life insurance, (3) endowment insurance, and (4) annuities. Due to the fact that policies are often issued which are combinations of these basic types; and because there are several variations in the method of paying premiums, a lack of understanding of these fundamental policies can

---

[12] These and other data given in this and the subsequent paragraph are derived from the *Life Insurance Fact Book, op. cit.*, p. 4 ff.

cause confusion in the mind of the prospective buyer. A brief description of the basic types, together with suggestions about their uses for varying insurance needs, may help to clarify this situation.

Term insurance. A term policy is issued to provide protection for a specific period of time, such as 1, 5, 10, or 15 years. When issued for 15 years or less there is no cash surrender or loan value. A term policy provides benefits only when the death of the insured occurs during the time specified in the policy. The policy can contain a renewable feature, as well as a privilege for conversion to whole life or endowment insurance. Either of these features is considered an advantage to the policyholder, because he may not be insurable as the end of the specified time approaches, and yet he can either convert or renew without a medical examination. The premium charge for the new insurance is, of course, based upon the attained age of the insured at the time of conversion or renewal.

Term insurance is in common use as security for mortgages and other kinds of debt or for some other special need for temporary protection. Occasionally it is used as a temporary means of business life insurance when the long-run status of a firm is in doubt. The general plan in such a case is to convert to a permanent type of policy when the firm's future outlook becomes clear. Term insurance has wide use as group insurance. Its principal personal uses are to provide extra protection during the years when the insured's children are growing up, or to make certain that permanent life insurance can be obtained at a later date.

Whole life insurance. The two typical forms of whole life insurance are ordinary life policies and limited payment policies. Although both provide for payment of the policy proceeds upon the death of the insured, they differ in respect to the premium paying period. In ordinary life, the policyholder agrees to pay his premium annually (or semiannually, quarterly or monthly) as long as he may live,[13] while in limited payment life, the payments of the periodic premiums cease at the end of a specified time, such as 20 years, or at age 60, 65, or some other designated attained age.

The ordinary form is the most widely used of the life policies. It gives permanent protection for the least outlay of premium. However, it has the disadvantage of requiring payment of premiums throughout the life of the insured. Because of this, many insurance purchasers are attracted to the limited payment plan which provides permanent protection but relieves the insured of paying premiums in the later years of his life. This means that, at a given age, the annual premium per thousand

---

[13] Unless the insured outlives the mortality table. He would do so at age 96 under the American Experience Table, at age 100 under the Commissioners Standard Ordinary Table. In such an event the whole life policy would mature as an endowment.

dollars of insurance is higher for limited payment than for ordinary life. The longer the premium paying period in a limited payment policy, the less is the difference between the ordinary life premium and the limited payment premium. If this period is as much as 35 years or longer, the extra premium per year is very little.

Whole life insurance—either ordinary or limited payment life—meets the basic need of life insurance: namely, permanent protection. It is sometimes utilized for old age needs (when protection of beneficiaries is normally no longer necessary), by surrendering it and using its cash value for annuity purposes. Whole life policies, if purchased when the insured is in his 20's or 30's, provide substantial cash values at age 65 (the normal retirement age).

Endowment insurance. An endowment policy is issued for a specific period, such as 20 or 30 years, or to an attained age such as 50 or 60. This is called the endowment period. It provides for the payment of the policy benefit if death occurs during that period, or at the end of the period if the insured is then living. It builds up a cash value comparatively quickly, particularly if it is of the 20 or 25 year variety. In comparison to the other types of policies, the premium is relatively high because the endowment policy is designed as much for savings purposes as it is for protection. When an insured wants as much protection against premature death as he can get for his life insurance premium outlay, the endowment policy is not the policy to buy. However, if the insured is interested in building up a fund for old age protection as well as for premature death protection, the endowment policy is particularly desirable.

An endowment policy is sometimes used as a business insurance policy to serve the double duty of providing typical life insurance protection for a partnership against the death of a partner (or a corporation against the death of an important executive or a "key" man) as well as for building up a fund to retire members of a firm at an advanced age. Occasionally, endowment insurance has been written for the purpose of retiring an outstanding debt of a corporation.

Annuities. Although an important auxiliary function of life insurance policies, other than term insurance, is to build up a cash value for old age, the primary purpose is to furnish to the dependents of the insured protection against the loss of the insured's income. On the other hand, an annuity is for the distinct purpose of providing an income for the annuitant after his productive years have ceased. A life insurance policy is purchased for protection against the risk of dying too soon; an annuity is bought for protection against the risk of living too long (insofar as income producing years are concerned). One is the reciprocal of the other.

The old age benefit provisions of the Social Security Act have helped center interest on the need to provide income for old age. Annuities obtained from private insurance carriers are often purchased as a supplement to annuity benefits to be received under the Social Security Act. Annuities may be classified by method of payment of premium and by type of annuity purchased. There are two classifications of annuities according to method of premium payment, which are:

1. *Immediate Annuities.* These are paid for by a single premium with the annuity beginning within one month, three months, six months or one year (depending upon the regular interval selected by the purchaser for annuity income payments).

2. *Deferred Annuities.* This type calls for annuity income payments to be made to the annuitant (the purchaser) beginning at some specified time in the future. The premium paid by the purchaser may be paid in a single premium or in installments over the period of the deferment.

Both immediate and deferred annuities can be written in the following manner:

1. *Life annuity.*[14] This type of annuity provides for continuous payments for the life of the annuitant, with the annuity income payments ceasing upon the annuitant's death. There is no refund of any part of the premium paid. This is true even though the annuitant should live only a few months or a few years after the purchase of the annuity.

2. *Refund life annuity.* This provides for a refund of the difference between the amount of premium paid for the annuity and the amount of money received as annuity payments by the annuitant before his death. This refund provision has been developed to meet the demand of many persons who prefer that a refund of some kind be made to a beneficiary in the event that only a small portion of the paid premium is returned to the annuitant prior to a comparatively early death.

3. *Annuity certain.* This type of annuity is similar to a refund annuity, except that it will guarantee an annuity income for a given period of time, such as 120 monthly installments, regardless of whether the annuitant dies during this guarantee period. Of course, the annuitant will receive annuity income payments for life (as he will under all types of annuities described above).

Combination Policies. As has been previously stated, combinations of two or more of the basic life insurance forms are often issued as special policies. One of these is the "Retirement Income" policy. This policy is

---

[14] Sometimes referred to as a "straight," "straight life," or "simple" annuity.

principally for the person who is primarily interested in old age protection, and yet who has some need for premature death protection. If the insured dies prior to age 65, the beneficiary is paid the face amount of the policy. If the insured lives beyond that age, he is paid an annuity income of $10 monthly for each $1,000 of face value. Typically, at maturity date, such a policy has a cash value well in excess of its face value (e.g., $1664 in a $1000 policy), which indicates that the savings feature is of paramount importance in this contract.

A popular combination of decreasing term insurance and whole life insurance is the "Family Income" policy. The total premium charged for this contract includes a premium for the whole life insurance and a premium for the term coverage. Essentially this policy provides for the payment of a monthly income to the beneficiary of $10 or $15 per $1,000 of face value, beginning with the death of the insured and ending at a definite time designated in the policy, if the insured's death occurs during a definite specified period (e.g., 15 years from the policy inception date); and it also provides for the payment of the face value to the beneficiary upon termination of the monthly income payments. If death occurs after the period of time specified in the contract, the policy pays only the face value. As an example, if the insured died six years after the effective date of the policy, and if the specified family income period were 15 years, the monthly income would be paid for nine years, and then the face of the policy would be paid. However, if the insured did not die until 15 (or more) years after the policy became effective, there would be no income payments made; only the face value would be paid. Of course, with such a policy the premium rate drops to the whole life level if the insured is alive when the 15-year period comes to an end.

Other methods of classifying life policies. In respect to the manner in which it is sold to the insuring public, life insurance is often classified as "ordinary," "industrial," and "group." Life policies may be further classified as "participating" and "nonparticipating."

When life insurance is sold on the "ordinary" plan, it is usually in units of $500 or $1,000, with $1,000 being the minimum amount for which such a policy will be issued. Normally, premiums are payable (directly to the company) on an annual, semiannual or quarterly basis, although in a few cases premiums are paid in a single payment. All types of policies described are sold through the "ordinary" plan. By far the largest amount of life insurance sold has been via this branch; the total amount of "ordinary" insurance in force in 1949 was $140,500,000,000,[15] and the average policy size was $2,210.[16] It is customary for the prospective

---

[15] *Life Insurance Fact Book, op. cit.,* p. 19.
[16] *Ibid.,* p. 12.

insured to undergo a medical examination, although there are some exceptions to this rule.

"Industrial" insurance is sold to persons who, through necessity or inclination, prefer to pay premiums on a weekly basis. That "industrial" life insurance serves a useful purpose, in making life insurance available to many people who otherwise would not buy it, cannot be ignored as a strong argument in its favor. However, this class of insurance is usually more expensive than either "ordinary" or "group," because of the higher administrative expense (including collection costs), higher mortality costs, and a higher lapse rate. Then, too, the average policy is comparatively low in size ($300 in 1949).[17] Whole life and endowment policies are available, but not term, and the policies may be sold to every member of a family up to age 65 or 70. Medical examinations are rarely required for "industrial" policies. "Industrial" insurance in force in 1949 was approximately $31,800,000,000.[18]

"Group" insurance is the child prodigy of the life insurance business. It came into being in 1911 as a means of insuring a group of persons under one policy. By 1949 this branch of the business had $42,100,000,-000 [19] insurance in force. For the average insured, it is undoubtedly the least expensive form of life insurance protection available. However, not all persons are eligible; only members of qualified groups can participate. In most states the minimum number of persons required in a group is 25; in a few states it is 50. Usually the members of group insurance plans are employees of a common employer, such as a business organization or a governmental body. When such a "group" insurance plan goes into effect, a master policy is issued to the employer, and a certificate of insurance is given to each insured employee. The employer pays the premium monthly, either on an "employer pay all" plan, or on a contributory plan with both employer and employee participating in premium payments. The latter plan is in much wider use than the former. An important tax consideration is that premiums paid by the employer for group life insurance may be considered as a business expense deduction.

A "participating" policy is one for which the premium rate is fixed at an amount slightly higher than the company anticipates will be needed to pay for its cost. On such a policy the policyholder receives a refund, called a "dividend," based upon the actual cost of the insurance. This cost represents the sum of (1) a reserve which is set aside for present and future claims against the policy, (2) reserves for contingencies, and (3) operating expenses. The typical dividend is paid annually, and is

---

[17] *Ibid.*, p. 12.
[18] *Ibid.*, p. 23.
[19] *Ibid.*, p. 20.

usually so paid after the policy has been in force for two or three years.

A "nonparticipating" policy is one for which the premium rate is set at an amount which represents the company's calculated estimate of the cost of providing the insurance. Unlike a "participating" policy, the "nonparticipating" premium rate cannot be adjusted during the life of the policy. It becomes a guaranteed premium rate for the insured. Whether a "participating" or "non-participating" policy will be lower in cost over a period of years cannot be accurately determined in advance, because the amount of the "dividends" which will be paid on a "participating" policy cannot be precisely foretold.

Casualty insurance. The so-called casualty "lines" constitute approximately one-fourth of all insurance written in the United States in terms of annual premium income. Casualty premium volume is currently in excess of three billion dollars per year. In 1940 this figure was approximately one and one-tenth billions. Not only has casualty insurance in the past decade grown tremendously in absolute terms, but also it has grown relatively, both in relation to insurance as a whole and in relation to our general economic development. At the present time casualty insurance is a "dynamic" class of insurance—and its problems, innovations and constant changes reflect this status. A brief description of each of the principal divisions in this field of insurance is given below.

Liability insurance. One of the principal divisions of casualty insurance is that which includes all the liability coverages. It is important in relation to the protection offered a business enterprise and to the protection offered an individual in his private affairs. This type of insurance is designed to protect the insured against financial loss by reason of the liability imposed upon him by law because of bodily injury and damage to property of others which result from an accident for which the insured is held to be responsible. Liability insurance can be written to cover one specific liability hazard, such as the operation of an automobile or the sale of a product; it can be written to cover several such specific hazards under one policy, or it can be written on a comprehensive basis to cover all liability hazards except those specifically excluded by the policy.

What is the nature of the liability that can be imposed on a person by law? It is through the commission of a tort (a civil injury) that a person may find himself in legal difficulty. The consequences of a tort can create a civil action by a private party to recover for damages sustained.

Such civil action for damages usually is based upon the negligence of the defendant. From a legal viewpoint negligence is the failure to observe for the protection of the interests of another person the degree of care, precaution, and vigilance which the circumstances justly demand. While the obligation to exercise care varies under different circumstances,

there always remains the duty to use such reasonable care as should be exercised by a person of ordinary prudence under like circumstances.

The liability so faced by an individual or a firm may be mitigated by such conditions as contributory negligence (negligence on the part of the other party), by the doctrine of comparative negligence (an attempt to measure the negligence of each party involved), or the doctrine of the last clear chance.[20] Nonetheless, the person facing an action instituted by another for damages based on the law of negligence cannot be certain of his liability under the law until the case has been definitely settled in court or by a compromise legal agreement out of court.

A liability insurance policy protects the insured (up to the limit of the policy) for the liability hazard or hazards insured against. It can be used to cover bodily injury liability separately, or it can be used to cover both bodily injury and property damage liability. Experienced insurance advisors almost always advocate that both contingencies be covered.

By sheer weight of number of occurrences and amount of destructive force, the automobile liability hazard is the greatest of liability exposures. This hazard is faced by most business firms and by a large segment of our population. Owing to the general recognition of the automobile liability menace (and to automobile financial responsibility laws in the several states), almost all automobiles used in business and a majority of private automobiles are covered by liability insurance.[21] However, insofar as business organizations are concerned, there can be, and sometimes are, gaps in such protection. To avoid such loopholes the businessman, if he wishes to be adequately insured, makes certain that all motor vehicles for which he might be held liable are covered. This includes such conveyances as motorcycles, motor bikes, and motorscooters. Newly acquired motor vehicles, drive-other-car responsibilities, employees driving their own cars on the employer's business, and hired cars constitute additional automobile liability hazards of many business enterprises.

While automobile liability insurance is the largest of the liability lines measured in terms of premiums paid, many of the other forms of liability coverages have developed into premium producing giants. Among these are business premises and operations, elevator, product, aircraft, and personal liability insurance. In recent years there has developed

---

[20] Briefly, the "doctrine of the last clear chance" means that the plaintiff, even though he had placed himself in a position of peril by his own negligence, has cause for legal action to recover damages from the defendant, if the defendant failed to take advantage of a last clear chance to avoid the accident which resulted in injury to the plaintiff or in damage to his property.

[21] According to a recent survey made by the Hartford Accident and Indemnity Company and their agents, as reported in the *Casualty and Surety Journal*, Nov. 1950, New York: Association of Casualty and Surety Companies.

what is known as the comprehensive liability policy in response to a demand for wider liability protection. A business firm may utilize this form of policy to combine all of its liability insurance protection in one policy. Such a contract is written on the basis that it, in effect, covers all of the firm's legal liability except those hazards definitely excluded. This is in sharp contrast to the older method of purchasing one policy for automobile liability, another for premises liability, and so on. Personal liability is also widely written on a comprehensive basis.

Workmen's compensation and employers' liability insurance. Injuries to employees resulting from occupational accidents are excluded under the types of liability policies which have been discussed above. Business firms are liable under workmen's compensation laws for a majority of the occupational accidents of this nature. In the cases not covered under such laws, the employer faces the hazard of civil action for damages under common law.

To cover these contingencies the employer buys a policy known as "workmen's compensation and employers' liability insurance." If none of his employees come under the workmen's compensation laws of the various states, the employer can protect himself with a policy limited to employers' liability insurance. Even in these cases the purchase of coverage known as voluntary workmen's compensation insurance is not rare.

In general, under a workmen's compensation and employers' liability policy, the insurance company assumes the obligation to pay the compensation and the medical, surgical, and hospital expenses required by the compensation law of the state in which the business of the employer is located. If this business is located in more than one state, a compensation policy (or policies) may be written to cover the obligation of all the compensation acts involved. The amount of insurance is unlimited as respects the payment of compensation and medical benefits, except as these may be limited by the compensation law of a given state; however, the employers' liability provision of the policy is subject to the limits stated in the policy for this provision.

In a great majority of the compensation acts there are provisions for payment of benefits to workers killed and disabled by occupational diseases. In some of these states all occupational diseases are within the scope of compensation laws. In several other jurisdictions only certain specified diseases are considered by the compensation laws to be occupational in origin. Where these specific diseases fall within the scope of the act, the employer can find protection in workmen's compensation insurance. If the disease is not a compensative one under compensation law, the employer can cover the hazard under employers' liability insurance.

It should be noted that the economic theory of workmen's compensation is that the risk of economic loss to workmen due to disabling work

injuries is a cost of production to be borne by industry and, in turn, is passed on to the consumer through the price system.

Insurance covering dishonesty losses. Business concerns and other organizations, as well as individuals, face the risk of loss of money, securities, and other property by burglary, robbery, theft, forgery, and other dishonest acts. Insurance has been available for many years to cover such hazards on a specific cover basis. Recently, however, in keeping with the trend to provide more comprehensive protection, insurance carriers have developed dishonesty policies which are blanket in nature.

In policies designed to cover one or more of these specific dishonesty hazards, the use of terms not precisely synonymous with those of statute and common law, to say nothing of common noninsurance usage, are frequently found. For the purpose of clarity, some of these terms are defined in the policy. Examples of these definitions are:

1. *Burglary.* This term is typically defined in the merchandise cover of the storekeeper's burglary and robbery policy as "the felonious abstraction of such property from within the premises, by any person or persons making felonious entry therein by actual force and violence when the premises are not open for business, of which there shall be visible marks made upon the exterior of the premises at the place of such entry by tools, explosives, electricity or chemicals."

2. *Robbery.* In the same policy the term robbery means "the felonious and forcible taking of insured property (1) by violence inflicted upon a messenger or custodian, (2) by putting him in fear of violence, (3) by any other overt felonious act committed in his presence and of which he was actually cognizant, provided such act was not committed by an officer or employee of the insured, or (4) from the person or direct care and custody of a messenger or custodian, who has been killed or rendered unconscious by injuries inflicted maliciously or sustained accidently."

From these examples it is apparent that certain types of specific cover require a clear meaning of terms which might easily be misunderstood. On the other hand, when the theft hazard is covered there is not the same necessity for an exact definition, for the term "theft" is broader in scope than burglary and robbery, and its meaning is commonly recognized. Usually it means any unlawful taking of a person's property.

These specific covers serve a useful purpose. Nevertheless, the businessman who uses such protection is prudent if he understands definitely just which hazard or hazards are covered. An examination of several of the specific dishonesty insurance policies reveals that a combination of several of these forms of protection is needed to cover the multiple hazards of an active business organization. Some of the widely used coverages are:

1. *Open stock burglary and theft insurance.* This covers loss of and damage to merchandise, furniture, fixtures, and equipment from within stores and other commercial establishments by burglary. For an additional premium, theft may be covered by endorsement.

2. *Safe burglary insurance.* This covers loss of and damage to merchandise, money, and securities in safes within business premises, and damage to the premises, caused by burglary.

3. *Interior and messenger robbery insurance.* This covers loss of money, securities and merchandise by robbery from within the premises and covers similar loss by robbery from a custodian outside the premises. It also covers damage to furniture, fixtures, and other property within the premises caused by robbery or attempted robbery.

4. *Paymaster robbery insurance.* This covers loss by robbery of payroll funds from a custodian inside or outside the premises, and a limited amount of other money or securities not intended for payroll.

5. *Bank burglary and robbery insurance.* This covers loss of or damage to money and securities in safes or vaults by burglary, and similar loss within the premises of the bank by robbery.

6. *Fidelity bonds.* These bonds, when written on a specific hazard basis, cover one or more named individuals, or one or more designated positions.[22]

This partial list of policies for specific business dishonesty hazards could be supplemented by several others, or it could be extended to cover several forms of combination policies which give, in effect, multiple coverage for several specific hazards. Examples of this combination idea are the "storekeepers' burglary and robbery policy" and the "office burglary and robbery policy." These two policies are popular with small business firms, because the policies provide many burglary and robbery coverages in modest amounts for one premium within the reach of the average small business organization.

With the complexity of dishonesty hazards faced by many business establishments, particularly the larger firms and institutions, the selection of specific covers for specific needs may, in itself, be a hazardous undertaking. The danger of a "gap" in such a plan is always present. This situation has led to the development of "blanket" or "all risk" policies. These vary in range as to type of property covered and to the extent of the blanket protection. For instance, a policy known as the "valuable papers" policy insures books, records, drawings, deeds and other valuable papers against loss, destruction or damage. It goes beyond

---

[22] Technically speaking, some writers do not consider fidelity bonding to be insurance in its true sense. G. W. Crist, Jr., *Corporate Suretyship.* New York: McGraw-Hill Book Co., 1950, p. 6 ff., gives a logical explanation of this point of view.

the dishonesty field in its broad cover. The only exclusions are: (1) misplacement or mysterious, unexplained disappearance; (2) wear and tear, gradual deterioration, vermin or inherent vice; (3) war risk. The misplacement and mysterious disappearance exclusion may be eliminated for an additional premium.

Another example of the "blanket" idea is the money and securities "broad form" policy. Practically every kind of peril to money and securities is covered except employee dishonesty, forgery, and war risk. Closely aligned with this policy are the blanket fidelity bonds, known as the primary commercial blanket bond and the blanket position bond. Either one of these bonds will provide blanket cover for employee dishonesty. Forgery cover is available to take up the lack of the forgery exclusion. There is a policy which combines all these features, leaving only the war risk hazard excluded, known as the comprehensive dishonesty, destruction, and disappearance policy.

In the personal insurance field, a very broad form of insurance known as the "residence and outside theft policy" has been developed. This covers the insured's property against loss by theft both at home and away from home. The normal meaning of the word "theft" in this policy is expanded by definition. The policy states "the word 'theft' includes larceny, burglary and robbery. Mysterious disappearance of any insured property, except a precious or semiprecious stone from its setting in any watch or piece of jewelry, shall be presumed to be due to theft."

Boiler and machinery insurance. This is one of the least understood of the casualty insurance lines. Actually there is no good reason why its fundamental principles cannot be grasped as easily as most other covers. The policy agrees to pay: (1) for loss on property of the insured directly damaged by an accident (as defined in the policy) to any insured boiler, pressure vessel, machine or other piece of apparatus; (2) for the reasonable extra cost of temporary repair and of expediting the repair of such damaged property; (3) such amounts as the insured shall become obligated to pay for his liability for the damage to property of others caused by the accident; (4) such amounts as the insured shall become obligated to pay for his liability for bodily injuries, including death, suffered by members of the public because of the accident; and (5) for additional indirect losses, such as business interruption, and consequential loss if provided for by endorsement.

It will be observed that this policy is a combination of direct property insurance and liability insurance. Its primary interest to a businessman who has already secured adequate liability coverage is the direct property protection. As a matter of fact, the bodily injury liability feature of this policy is excess insurance over any other liability insurance, and it can be excluded at a slight saving in premium.

The insurance contract is composed of a basic policy form to which a schedule (or schedules) is attached. The schedule describes the insured objects and gives a definition of the term "accident." An accident to a steel boiler or a pressure vessel, such as an air tank, is basically an explosion; an accident to a cast iron sectional heating boiler, under broad coverage, will also include the cracking of cast iron parts; an accident to an electric motor, under a broad definition of accident, can include the burning out of the motor. Accidents to other types of objects are defined in detail.

The hazards inherent in the use of boilers and machinery are not limited to manufacturers and other industrial firms. Recently a hot water boiler exploded in an apartment house killing one person, injuring another, and causing loss of property valued at approximately $100,000. The newspapers of this country frequently carry accounts of similar accidents. Any business establishment using boilers, pressure vessels, motors, engines, turbines or similar equipment is subject to this hazard in some degree.

An important feature of boiler and machinery insurance is the engineering and inspection service provided under the terms of the policy. Actually a fundamental function of this form of coverage is loss prevention. In the aggregate, more of the premium dollar is expended on this protective service than for the payment of direct losses. Several business firms buy boiler and machinery insurance primarily for engineering advice and periodic inspection.

Accident and health insurance. Financial hardship resulting from inability to earn a living due to disability stemming from accident or illness is a risk faced by most breadwinners. Medical expenses connected with the treatment of such cases are often high and frequently a severe drain on the financial resources of the disabled person or his family. Accident and health insurance is sold to provide protection for such contingencies.

Under the broader forms of accident insurance, an insured may receive weekly payments of a stated amount for total disability, or a fraction of such a stated amount for partial disability. He may also include coverage which will reimburse him for medical care and hospitalization expenses resulting from disability due to an accident. Typically, this policy contains a provision for the payment of a certain sum if death occurs within 90 days of the accident. The scope and amount of protection offered by this contract is geared to the premium the insured is willing to pay within his particular classification. Classifications depend upon the relative hazard presented by the insured's occupation. A college professor is entitled to a lower premium rate than an outside salesman, whereas an outside salesman obtains a lower rate than a carpet layer.

Because the cost is much lower, and because insurance carriers (as a general rule) will more readily issue them, accident policies are within the reach of a larger segment of our population than are health policies. As a result the annual premium volume of accident insurance surpasses that of health insurance. The types of accident policies easily accessible to the insuring public are (1) commercial accident, (2) industrial, (3) limited, and (4) group.

The commercial accident policy, which is the broad form described above, is the most important accident policy with respect to the number of policies issued. With this particular policy, accident insurance companies have tended to concentrate their sales efforts among business and professional men and women because of the purchasing power of these people and their need for substantial amounts of protection. In recent years, several of these companies have broadened their efforts to sell commercial accident policies to housewives and children, with the coverage limited to medical and hospitalization reimbursement, and with some forms containing a stated principal sum for accidental death. Premiums for commercial accident policies are paid on an annual, semiannual or quarterly basis. All state laws require that the policies contain certain statutory provisions designed to protect the policyholders' interests.

A considerable amount of accident insurance business is done among middle and lower income groups (particularly the latter) on a monthly or weekly installment basis, with the insurance representative making a personal call to collect the premium. These policies are lower in price than most policies sold to business and professional people; likewise these policies are narrower in scope of coverage and benefits payable. Policies of this nature are referred to as industrial policies.

The limited accident policy is designed to cover accidental injuries or death resulting from certain specified or designated accidents and none other. Frequently such policies are indeed limited in the extent of the risk assumed by the insurer as compared to the coverage offered by a broad commercial accident policy. As a general rule, a very low rate corresponds to the narrow protection offered by the limited policy.

Group accident insurance is especially written to cover accidents which are nonoccupational in nature. The benefits of workmen's compensation laws apply only to occupational injuries, and, because of this, group accident insurance is primarily designed to cover the cases which workmen's compensation laws do not cover. In addition, the group policy usually covers sickness, except for occupational diseases. Typically the weekly indemnity provided by this policy is determined by the average weekly wage or salary paid to the employee during the three months preceding the disability. A waiting period of a few days before weekly indemnity is payable is the usual custom in this type of insurance. Indemnity benefits

are limited to a certain number of consecutive weeks, such as 13 weeks for any one disability. It must be noted that there is no such thing as a standard group accident and health policy; the terms described here are customary but are by no means in universal use. Group accident and health insurance is often combined with group death and dismemberment and group hospitalization insurance.

Health insurance provides indemnity for loss of time due to sickness as compared to accident insurance, which pays such indemnity for disability due to accident. In addition to covering this loss of earning power, a health policy may be extended to cover certain hospital and medical expenses due to illness. While health policies are offered in several different forms, the two prevailing types are (1) nonconfinement and (2) confinement.

The nonconfinement form normally provides for full policy benefits as long as the insured is prevented by illness from engaging in his occupation, if the illness is contracted during the policy term. There is usually a waiting period before weekly indemnity payments commence, and these payments continue during the disability for a period of not over a certain number of consecutive weeks. Hospitalization expense, nurses fees, and surgical operation fees (within certain limits) may be included in such a nonconfinement form.

The confinement form is similar in its general provisions to the nonconfinement form, but it provides full policy benefits only when sickness confines the insured to his house. Usually the indemnity benefits are reduced by 50 per cent under this policy if the insured is unable to engage in his occupation but is not confined to his home. Because of this limiting provision, this form may be purchased at a premium which is considerably lower than that charged for the nonconfinement form.

The accident and health policies thus far discussed are issued for a period of one year and, at the option of the company, are subject to cancellation. This is due to the fact that the rate charged assumes the coverage of healthy individuals only. Thus, while the insurance company would be justified under these conditions in cancelling the policy of an unhealthy policyholder, such action would leave this individual without insurance when he needs it most. The noncancellable accident and health policy is designed to remedy such a situation. However, despite higher premiums, less coverage, and required medical examinations of applicants, the over-all experience on these types of policies, as a general rule, has not been satisfactory in the eyes of insurance companies. Because of this, relatively few insurance companies will issue noncancellable accident and health policies.

Any survey of accident and health insurance should include a discussion of hospitalization insurance. A newcomer to the field, it has quickly

grown to gigantic proportions. This form of insurance agrees to reimburse for certain hospital expenses and, very recently, has been extended to include reimbursement for certain medical and surgical expenses. Such insurance is written on group, single family and individual bases. Usually a hospitalization policy covers all members of a family, but it can be written to cover one person. There is no standard policy in use, and the various schedules of benefits offered in this field are often confusing to the prospective buyer. A proposed plan of hospitalization insurance usually must be rather carefully compared with schedules offered by other hospitalization insurance carriers to evaluate properly the plan under consideration.

Hospitalization insurance is written by many accident and casualty companies as well as by "Blue Cross Plan" organizations throughout the country. These "Blue Cross" carriers are corporations formed on a nonprofit basis. In the competition for business in this fast growing branch of insurance, all major types of carriers in the field have been able to obtain a sizeable premium volume.

Miscellaneous casualty insurance. It is impossible, in a brief survey such as this, to describe the uses of all casualty insurances. In addition to the covers which have been discussed, there are many others, such as credit insurance, elevator collision insurance, glass insurance, and aircraft insurance. Some lines are written by both casualty and fire companies. Examples of this are the accounts receivable policy, the automobile collision policy, the water damage policy and the sprinkler leakage policy.[23]

With the wide range of insurance coverages attempted by casualty companies, scarcely a year passes in which something new is not developed, even if it is only to broaden an old form of protection. An example of a fairly recent development is the accounts receivable policy. This protects against loss on accounts receivable, if such loss is due to destruction of records from any cause. Another example is the valuable papers policy in its present form.

Fire insurance and allied lines. Among the more common risks insured against is that of direct loss by fire. Residences, apartment houses, hotels, mercantile buildings, factories and almost all other types of structures are generally insured against fire loss. It is also typical for owners of furniture, merchandise, machinery, and other types of physical assets to buy fire insurance protection against the risk of such disaster.

In any one of the United States, purchasers of fire insurance have the protection of a fire insurance policy which is standardized by state law

---

[23] See Robert Riegel and Jerome S. Miller, *Insurance Principles and Practices,* 3rd Edition. New York: Prentice-Hall, Inc., 1947, for a concise but clear description of these miscellaneous insurances.

and which is approved by the state insurance department. A large majority of these states have adopted the 1943 Standard New York Fire Insurance Policy as the required policy. A few states have developed their own particular policies, but these as issued (with customary endorsements) vary only slightly in effect and scope from the New York standard policy. This is in sharp contrast to the situation a century ago, when each insurance company devised and sold its own form of policy. In that era each fire insurance company used its own rate and operated without any noticeable government regulation.

It is significant to note that the first definite steps toward standardization of the fire insurance contract followed closely the establishment of state insurance departments for regulatory purposes. As was earlier stated, it was in Massachusetts that the first of these departments came into being in 1858. Although the initial duty of this department was to regulate life insurance, it was not long thereafter that this department began to regulate the fire insurance business as well. Soon other states followed, and today this practice is carried on in every state.

Prior to 1886 some jurisdictions developed fire insurance policies for use within their own boundaries, but in that year New York put into use a standard policy that was soon adopted by many other states. Judged by conditions existing at that time, it was a liberal contract, and it was extremely important as a means of creating uniformity in a situation which had been confusing and, in certain circumstances, chaotic. This policy was first officially revised as of January 1, 1918. The next revision was effective in 1943, which produced the standard policy now in current use. Each revision tended to clarify and liberalize the contract insofar as the insured was concerned, and to stabilize further the fire insurance business.

The basic standard fire insurance policy is adapted to each individual property risk by forms and endorsements which are attached to the policy with the intent to fit it to the characteristics of that particular risk. For instance, a fire policy covering a private residence and its contents has a dwelling and contents form attached; a policy covering the contents of a store has a stock and fixture form attached, and so on. Endorsements may also be attached which increase the liability of the insurer; others may be attached to decrease this liability.

The standard fire policy with the proper form attached protects the insured against only direct loss or damage caused by fire and lightning. Very frequently an insured will have this coverage extended to include direct loss caused by windstorm, hail, riot, riot attending a strike, civil commotion, explosion, aircraft damage, vehicle damage and smoke, by means of what is known as an "extended coverage" endorsement. In certain sections of the United States the windstorm portion of this coverage is

subject to a deductible amount, such as $50 or $100, particularly in areas where windstorm losses are apt to be frequent or heavy or both. This deductible feature is a tool used in reducing the premium rate because it is the means of relieving the insurance carriers of the expense of handling numerous small claims.

As a general rule fire insurance policies are sold for terms of one, three or five years.[24] The per annum cost is lowered if the insured takes advantage of a three or five year term. Fire insurance premium rates on both building and contents show considerable variation because of type of building construction, use of building, available fire fighting facilities, relative exposure to external fire hazards and, in some instances, to internal protection measures taken. In fire insurance rate-making, a city is graded with consideration of these items as well as of local building laws. Premium rates are expressed in units of $100 of insurance.

The "allied lines" written by fire insurance companies include not only those covers of the extended coverage endorsement but also such insurances as water damage, sprinkler leakage damage, and earthquake. As previously indicated, there is some degree of overlapping in the lines of insurance written by fire and casualty companies such as the valuable papers policy, accounts receivable policy, and automobile collision insurance.

Property destroyed by fire, windstorm, explosion or other causes frequently means that serious consequential losses will follow. A house badly damaged by fire can impose upon the occupants the necessity of seeking shelter elsewhere until the house is again made habitable. This usually entails extra expense in the form of rent. Or a restaurant which is unusable following an explosion means loss of earnings for the proprietor, probably coupled with continued overhead costs. In the former case rental value insurance can be used to pay the rent for temporary quarters; in the latter instance business interruption insurance provides for such loss of earnings and continuing overhead expenses. In recent years, insurance designed to cover such indirect or consequential loss has grown tremendously in annual premium volume. Belatedly it was recognized by the insuring public, particularly businessmen, as an important insurance need.

Very important in premium volume is insurance against direct loss or damage to automobiles. Such insurance includes loss as a result of such causes as fire, theft, windstorm, flood and collision. Traditionally this type of insurance is in the "allied" fire lines; in actual practice it is

---

[24] A recent innovation in some states is the issuance of a fire policy for a one year term, with the insured having the privilege of renewing the policy each year, for the four following years, at a reduced premium. In Florida this practice is already widespread.

closely aligned with automobile liability insurance. For the sake of simplicity and the policyholder's convenience, combination policies have been issued for over 20 years by multiple line carriers, with the direct loss covers in the fire company and the liability insurance in the casualty company. The question of which shall be written by the fire companies, and which by the casualty companies becomes increasingly academic as more and more "multiple line" powers are granted to insurance carriers by legislation.

Until the early 1930's, automobile direct loss or damage insurance was written solely on a specific peril basis such as fire, transportation, theft and so on. At that time, owing to a demand for an "all risk" policy, the comprehensive material damage policy came into being. Today most of the policies issued are of this nature, although the specific peril form still has some use. The comprehensive form, in effect, covers all loss or damage to the automobile except that caused by collision or upset.

Loss resulting from automobile collision or upset may be covered by "collision" insurance, either on a full cover or deductible basis. At the present time full cover policies are seldom written, because of a relatively high premium and a lack of enthusiasm among underwriters for this form. The deductible policy may be written with a $25, $50, $100 or higher deductible amount. This means that the insurance carrier is liable for only that amount of loss which is in excess of the deductible amount. There are some variations of the deductible feature in use. Basically they are all designed to reduce the premium by having the insured bear a certain portion of a collision loss.

Marine insurance. Marine insurance is divided into two general classes, ocean and inland, both of which are related to the transportation of property. Ocean marine insurance is concerned with insurance on a ship, its cargo, expected earnings of the ship, its freight interest, and the liability of the ship owners to third parties. Fundamentally this means insurance on these things in connection with an ocean voyage. Inland marine insurance covers property or liability for property in which the element of land transportation exists.

Ocean marine insurance. As has been stated earlier, marine insurance is old. It is also international in scope, and it flourishes or wanes as international trade rises or falls. Marine insurance exists because it meets a vital need of those engaged in foreign trade; the ocean marine insurance certificate (in lieu of a policy) is considered as necessary a trade document as the bill of lading or the sight draft.

Because of the international character of ocean marine insurance, there is considerably less standardization of forms and practices by statute than in other lines, such as in fire and workmen's compensation insurance. However, the essential terms of the venerable Lloyd's policy are widely

observed in everyday practice as standard. This procedure is due largely to the body of law which has been developed around the Lloyd's policy and the high regard in which these legal interpretations are held by shippers and insurers alike.

In ocean marine insurance it has long been essential to use policy endorsements to fit the individual risk. It has also been necessary to change and expand the perils covered under the old Lloyd's form. Originally the perils covered by the policy were fire, war, and perils of the sea. Particularly in the last 50 years a more comprehensive form of coverage has been necessary to meet the complexities of foreign trade. For an additional premium marine insurance underwriters have extended policies to cover such perils as breakage, leakage, theft and pilferage, fresh water, and machinery. Recently an "all risk" policy has been developed which covers all perils except those specifically excluded.

Ocean marine policies are classified by several methods, which are:
1. By the interest covered such as (a) hull, (b) cargo, (c) freight and profits, (d) protection and indemnity, which, in effect, means liability to third parties.
2. By (a) valued or (b) unvalued policies.
3. By term, such as (a) voyage, (b) time, (c) open policies.
4. By evidence of insurable interest, such as (a) policy proof of interest or (b) interest policies.

Hull policies cover vessels and their equipment. Included in this category is the "builders' risk" policy which covers the risks of construction and "trial runs" of the ship. A cargo policy covers goods which are in transit. Freight charges are covered by a freight policy, and anticipated profits by a profits policy. A protection and indemnity policy covers liability for bodily injury or damage to property of others due to the ownership or operation of a ship or vessel.

A "valued" policy in marine insurance means that a predetermined value of the hull or cargo is decided upon when the policy is issued. If a loss occurs, the value stated in the policy is considered to be the value of the covered property at the time of the loss. In contrast, the "unvalued" policy defers the determination of the value of the property until the time of the loss; at that time the actual loss is considered to be the replacement value of the damaged or destroyed property.

As the name implies, a "voyage" policy covers a definitely described voyage such as "Boston to Southampton" or "New York to Havana and return." "Time" policies give insurance for a specified period of time, often for one year. The "open" policy, on which form over 90 per cent of all insured cargo risks are covered, is a contract under which the insurer agrees to insure all the insured's shipments, and in return the insured agrees to report all shipments and pay a premium on them.

While it is axiomatic in insurance that, to be valid, a policy must be supported by an insurable interest, it occasionally happens in ocean marine insurance that an insured may have an insurable interest in property that would be difficult to establish legally. Under such circumstances, if the insurance underwriters are satisfied that the insurable interest is real, they will clarify the matter by indicating in writing on the policy that the policy is proof of insurable interest. Thus the policy becomes what is known as "policy proof of interest." On the other hand an "interest policy," as is typical of the customary contract of insurance, is one in which the insured has a definitely recognized legal insurable interest.

Inland marine insurance. Ocean marine insurance originally covered a cargo only when it was on board ship. Demand for protection while the goods were on the pier "alongside," or being moved inland to their final destination ultimately brought into being an insurance innovation called the "warehouse to warehouse" clause. While the original clause was more limited, its development to full stature extended the insurance to cover from the point of shipment through the course of transit to its designated destination, or until a certain stipulated period of time had elapsed following the discharge of the cargo from the ship. Under normal conditions, this time limitation was considered ample for the shipment to arrive at its destination. With minor changes this clause is in current use.

From the "warehouse to warehouse" clause, inland marine insurance quickly "grew up." It developed to encompass the inland movement of cargoes of each new means of transportation, such as shipments by rail, motor truck, and air, and even horse and wagon and muleback, to say nothing of all types of inland water craft. From inland transportation the provisions of the clause rapidly branched out to cover bailee liability, certain fixed property, and movable commercial and personal property by means of "floater" policies.

In an effort to define the scope of inland marine insurance, which apparently was making incursions into the fire and casualty domains, the then National Convention of Insurance Commissioners of the United States,[25] in 1933, unanimously adopted what was termed "The Nationwide Definition," which had been drawn up by a group of fire, casualty, and marine executives. Although each state, within its borders, through its insurance department, regulates the extent of the activity of an insurance carrier, the adoption by the commissioners meant that the scope of inland marine insurers would be fairly uniform from state to state. Following this action of the commissioners, most of the states promptly incorporated the "definition" into their statutes. As situations have developed needing clarification since the adoption of the definition,

---

[25] Now known as the National Association of Insurance Commissioners.

interpretive bulletins issued by a joint committee, organized for this specific purpose, have been generally followed by the insurance industry as correct solutions to the problems needing such clarification.

Despite the strides made toward uniformity of action in inland marine insurance matters by the "definition" and the "interpretive bulletins," there has never been a satisfactory definition of inland marine insurance. It, like casualty insurance, for the most part has been what the states have said it is. Nevertheless, by custom, the major inland marine insurance lines, other than transportation insurance, may be classified as follows:

1. *Bailee liability policies.* These include such policies as furriers' customers policies, laundries' policies, and cold storage locker bailees' policies. Basically, these policies protect the insured against financial loss caused by loss or destruction of property of others in their custody.

2. *Fixed property policies.* Such "instrumentalities of transportation" as bridges, tunnels and the like come within the meaning of the "definition" because they are incidental to transportation.

3. *Floaters.* These cover commercial or personal property which may or may not be in the course of transportation, such as the contractors' equipment, theatrical property, salesmen's samples, jewelry and furs, fine arts and personal property.

The personal property floater is worthy of "honorable mention" in recent insurance developments. Despite the fact that it bears several necessary exclusions, such as wear and tear, moths, vermin and inherent vice, and so on, and has limitations such as $250 coverage on unscheduled jewelry and furs, $100 on money, and $500 on securities, the policy is apparently what the public wants—as close to an "all risk" policy on personal property as is currently feasible. Premium volume running into many millions of dollars and increasing by leaps and bounds, gives testimony to the popularity of the contract with the insuring public. This policy will protect an insured's property (and that of his family of the same household) at home or away from home while traveling by any means. Thus, the insured, through one policy, may secure for himself and his family, protection against loss by fire, theft, windstorm, and all other perils not definitely excluded.

Corporate suretyship. As has been pointed out by many authors on the subject of suretyship, the act of a person (or persons) guaranteeing the performance of an obligation or the honesty of another is of ancient origin. Notwithstanding this venerable practice, it was not until well past the middle of the last century that such acts began to be performed by corporate sureties. Today many governmental bodies and business firms require these guarantees to be in the form of surety and fidelity

bonds issued only by surety companies. Thus corporate suretyship has reached mature status.

The business of bonding is generally divided into two classes, (1) fidelity bonds and (2) surety bonds. Essentially a fidelity bond guarantees the honesty of an individual such as a cashier, a city treasurer, or for that matter anyone in a position of trust. A surety bond guarantees that a contract, an act, or an undertaking will be fulfilled. An example of this latter class of guarantee is a contract bond in which the surety is obligated to the extent of the penalty of the bond, if the contractor fails to perform a contract, such as the construction of a building according to stipulated conditions. The penalty of such a bond is expressed as a certain sum of dollars, which may be either for fixed damages or the maximum amount for which the surety can be held liable. Some of the bonds customarily listed in the surety bond category have the characteristics of both fidelity and surety bonds. A public official bond, which covers both the honesty and ability of the official, is such an instrument.

A fidelity bond may be written to guarantee the honesty of one individual, certain designated individuals, specifically designated positions, or all employees of a designated employer. These bonds are known respectively as (1) an individual bond, (2) a name schedule bond, (3) a position bond, and (4) a blanket bond. The blanket bond was developed to provide against loss by the defalcation of any employee, including any employee hired after the effective date, but during the term of the bond. Fidelity bonds pertain to the loss of physical property such as merchandise, furniture and fixtures, as well as to money and securities. Fidelity bond coverage, as mentioned earlier, is often combined with insurance to form the comprehensive dishonesty, destruction, and disappearance policy. The various bankers' and brokers' blanket bonds are also such combinations.

A long list of specific designations comprises the names of the various forms of bonds which are usually classed as surety bonds. Included are appeal bonds, attachment bonds, and replevin bonds—all of which may be grouped as "court bonds." Also included are administrators' bonds, executors' bonds and guardians' bonds, which are known as "fiduciary bonds." Contract bonds pertaining to construction contracts, supply contracts, maintenance contracts, and so on, are other examples of surety bonds. Still others are license and permit bonds, lease bonds, and franchise bonds.

There are three parties to a surety bond: the principal, the obligee, and the surety. The principal is the bonded party; the obligee is the beneficiary, (or as is sometimes said "the party in whose favor the bond runs"); the surety is the party guaranteeing that if the principal fails in

the performance or fulfillment of his obligation, the surety will carry it out, or "make good" through the medium of financial restitution.

Types of carriers and their methods of operation. In the United States there is keen competition between the various types of private insurance carriers, and in some instances there is competition between private and government carriers. No one of these carriers writes every available kind of insurance. Some are in the life business only, others are in life, accident and health, still others engage only in the property and casualty fields; a few specialize in one particular line, paying little or no attention to the others; also two large carriers and their subsidiaries are in the life business and write most forms of property and casualty insurance as well.

Roughly there are two major types of private insurance carriers. One is conducted as a proprietary form of enterprise, known as a stock company, which is in the insurance business for the purpose of earning a profit for its stockholders. The other is a cooperative organization operated on the basis that all residual surplus belongs to the policyholders, and on the theory that the business is being conducted in their interest. The mutual company and the reciprocal exchange are examples of this type. While the two major types are in both the life and the property and casualty business, there are enough distinctions between their operations in these two major fields to discuss each field separately.

In the life insurance business the mutual companies write considerably more than half of all the business written by private carriers. Of the 609 United States legal reserve life insurance companies, the five largest (all mutual companies) hold approximately one-half of the total legal reserve life insurance company assets.[26] Nevertheless, the stock life companies are very important since they write most of the legal reserve life insurance not written by the mutuals. Reciprocal exchanges do not write life insurance.

Other life insurance carriers are the savings bank life insurance organizations (in Massachusetts, Connecticut and New York), the Wisconsin State Life Fund, and the fraternal life insurance orders. The federal government is in the life insurance business through United States Government Life Insurance, which came into being in World War I

---

[26] *Name of Company*	*Admitted Assets (1949)*
Metropolitan Life Insurance Company	$ 9,707,948,000
Prudential Insurance Company	8,325,415,000
Equitable Life Assurance Society	5,269,289,000
New York Life Insurance Company	4,674,991,000
John Hancock Mutual Life Insurance Company	2,696,506,000
Total Assets (5 companies)	$30,674,149,000

(Source: *Moody's Manual,* New York: Moody's Investors Service, *1950*)

for the purpose of making life insurance, up to $10,000, available to any person in the armed forces, and which is still available to veterans of that war. National Service Life Insurance was created in World War II for the same purpose. Moreover, for all practical purposes, the federal government also acts as a life insurance carrier insofar as the old age and survivors benefit provisions of the Social Security Act are concerned.

Mutual life insurance companies issue mainly participating policies. Usually the premium for a participating policy is slightly higher than for the same policy on a nonparticipating basis, but the mutuals point out that the true comparison of cost is the net premium paid by the policyholder after consideration is given to the amount of the dividends paid. A major portion of the policies sold by stock life insurance are on a nonparticipating basis, but a few stock companies issue participating policies as well. When the nonparticipating policies are sold, the stock companies feature the fact that the premium paid is the guaranteed cost of the insurance, and that it is lower than the "going in" premium of a similar participating policy.

In property and casualty insurance (in contrast with the life business), stock companies write a major portion of the business, although the mutual company is an important factor. Also active, although less important in premium volume, are reciprocal exchanges, Lloyd's of London, self-insurers and government carriers.

A reciprocal exchange is organized on the basis that each subscriber to the exchange insures all the other subscribers. While the plan is similar to a mutual company in operation, it is not mutual in the true sense, because each individual is an underwriter who assumes his or her liability as an individual. Each subscriber signs an agreement assuming his or her liability, usually on a "several and not joint" basis. In this agreement the subscriber rests authority in an attorney-in-fact, who manages the affairs of the exchange through this power of attorney. Reciprocal exchanges do not incorporate as do mutual insurance companies.

The insurance policies issued by Lloyd's of London are subscribed to by the members who are all individual underwriters. Each of several underwriters assumes a relatively small portion of the liability on a policy either "on his own" or in a syndicate with fellow underwriters. The Lloyd's of London corporation is therefore not liable on the policy issued. However, the corporation closely supervises the conditions under which the underwriters operate, and by such close control, successfully undertakes the safeguarding of the integrity of each policy. This method of operation has proved to be sound, and within insurance circles, the name Lloyd's of London is symbolic of great financial security. In the

United States insurance market, Lloyd's of London is particularly active in ocean marine insurance and reinsurance.

When a self-insurance plan is adequate, a self-insurer is considered to be a bona fide insurance carrier. It is possible to establish a sound self-insurance plan for a particular organization, such as a large chain grocery or a sizeable railroad, where the number of units subject to a given risk are numerous enough, and the units are so spread that the law of large numbers will operate within the experience of the organization itself. Such a scheme is to be distinguished from "self assumption" of risk. This latter term simply means that an individual or firm has decided to assume risk rather than insure against its consequences.

To determine the soundness of a self-insurance plan, a series of tests should be applied, and if the plan meets these requirements, it is considered as satisfactory insurance. The tests are: (1) Does it have a sufficiently large number of units of risk to permit the operation of the law of large numbers? (2) Are the risks homogeneous? (3) Are the risks of similar size or, if not, have they been made so through the use of excess reinsurance? (4) Are sums similar to premiums transferred periodically to a reserve fund which is calculated on an adequate basis, and is the reserve fund isolated from the general funds of the insured? (5) If there is a risk of catastrophic loss, is there an excess reinsurance provision to absorb such a shock? (6) Is there an internal organization capable of real insurance management?

In the property and casualty field the federal government acts as an insurer in crop insurance, in bank deposits insurance, and in war risk insurance. Certain states and territories act as insurance carriers in such coverages as workmen's compensation insurance, hail insurance, and fire insurance (on property owned by the state). Currently, in all of these, it can be said that only in the field of workmen's compensation insurance is there fullfledged competition between state and private carriers.

The agency system. Both stock and mutual life insurance companies sell their policies through the agency system. This means that the agent solicits the business, and is remunerated for his sales on a commission basis. The agent sends to the company's home office via the branch office or general agency the applications he obtains from prospective buyers. A local medical examiner, designated by the company, similarly forwards a medical report on each applicant. Usually, a confidential report is also obtained on an applicant. The home office appraises the information thus obtained, and if the applicant is found to be acceptable, issues the policy and mails it to the agent for delivery. Agents usually work under the direction of a branch office manager or a general agent. The branch manager or the general agent is given the responsibility of appointing and training agents, and developing business in a certain geographical

area. For example, in Florida several companies have an arrangement whereby the entire state is covered by a branch office or general agency located in one of Florida's cities. In instances where the business of a company has reached large proportions, the state may be divided into two or more territories with a manager or general agent in each territory.

The stock companies also use the agency system in the property and casualty business,[27] while the mutuals do likewise in some instances only. There are several large mutual companies soliciting their business directly through employees of the company, who act as sales representatives. These mutuals are known in the business as "direct writing mutuals" to distinguish them from mutuals using the agency system. Agents in the property and casualty field often write policies in their own offices, a practice which is in sharp contrast to the life business where all policies are issued by the home office.

The agency department of an insurance company, operating from the home office, supervises and directs all agency activities of the company. This department usually is headed by a vice-president in charge of agencies.

Other operations. In addition to the adaptation of policies to fit risk needs and the sale of these policies to the general public, the business of insurance involves the major function of the proper computation of the premiums for its policies, the selection of risks, the settlement of claims, the collection of premiums, the keeping of records, and the investment of its reserves.

The principal differences between insurance carriers, insofar as the accomplishment of these functions is concerned, may again be divided between life insurance carriers on the one hand and property and casualty carriers on the other. In life insurance rate making, a prime consideration is that the event insured against is bound to happen—the only question being when. Contrasted with this, in property and casualty insurance there usually is a better than even chance that the event will not occur at all. Therefore, as a general rule, for a given amount of insurance a life insurance company must build up a larger reserve to pay future losses than a fire or casualty company.

In the selection of risks a life insurance carrier is chiefly concerned with the health status of the prospective insured, whereas in fire and casualty insurance (other than in accident and health insurance), this is one of the lesser considerations. Moreover, when the carrier is called upon to

---

[27] A considerable amount of property and casualty insurance is sold through insurance brokers, particularly in the metropolitan centers. A duly licensed broker is in a position legally to place applications for policies with any company which will accept such business. Many insurance agents are also licensed as brokers in order to have at their disposal a "market" comprised of several insurance companies in addition to the company or companies for which they are licensed agents.

settle a life insurance claim the primary question is, "Is the insured dead?" On the other hand, in fire and casualty insurance the actual cash value of the damaged or destroyed property, or the liability of the insured may well be the paramount question. Even the investment of life insurance reserves presents problems that differ in many ways from the investment problems of fire and casualty reserves.

Rate making. It is customary for insureds to pay for their life policies in annual, semiannual, quarterly or monthly premiums. In lines such as fire, automobile or general liability insurance, it is typical for the insured to pay a single premium for the policy term. If these premiums are expressed as so much per $100 or $1,000 of insurance, they are known as premium rates. Back of these rates are the statistics and computations upon which they are based.

Rate making in its simplest form involves nothing more than arithmetic. However, it can reach highly advanced mathematics in complex instances, particularly in life insurance. The mathematical basis of insurance is known as actuarial science, and the expert mathematician in this field is referred to as an actuary.

The theory of probability is the principal basis of all rate making in insurance. This theory, when applied to large numbers of cases, makes the laws of chance very dependable. The important point to observe is that the number of cases must be large. A simplified explanation of how workmen's compensation insurance rates are made may be used as an example of the use of the theory of probability in rate making. The rates to be charged are determined largely on the combined recent loss experience of many insurance carriers. These rates are made in consultation with the state insurance department, which must approve the rates used in the particular state in question.

The unit of exposure in compensation rates is each $100 of payroll of the insured. Risks are grouped into classifications on the nature of the hazard involved. For example, the classification "Grocery Stores" takes a lower rate than "Tank Erection or Repair" for obvious reasons. For a given classification, loss costs (known as pure premium) are derived by dividing units of exposure into losses. After certain statistical modifications have been made, this figure represents a pure premium rate at so much per $100 of payroll. To this is added a loading for the expense of doing business, and the resulting gross rate is known as the manual rate for the particular classification under consideration. Thus great dependence has been placed upon the theory that the combined loss experience of many insureds (within a given classification) will tend to be repeated in the forthcoming policy period.

In workmen's compensation insurance a small risk does not qualify for any special rate because it is not large enough for any special statistical

meaning to be attached to its experience. But it has been ascertained that, when a given risk reaches a relatively large annual premium volume, it is statistically wise to give some weight to this individual experience in the determination of the individual rate. This has resulted in so-called "merit rating."

Merit rating has resulted in (1) schedule rating, (2) a premium discount plan, (3) experience rating, and (4) retrospective rating. Schedule rating, a method of giving credits or debits for physical aspects of a risk, has largely been discontinued in compensation rating. The premium plan recognizes that certain expense items going into a premium rate do not increase proportionately as the premium increases, and that credit should accordingly be given for this factor. Experience rating allows the rate to reflect the loss experience of a single risk, and the possible applicable variation from the manual rate increases as the premium volume of the risk increases, if the experience of the risk warrants such a variation. Experience rating is prospective, projecting into the next year's rate the variation based on past experience. On the other hand, retrospective rating permits the insured's rate to be influenced by the current year's experience, which is reviewed retrospectively after the current policy year has come to a close. Retrospective rating plans vary to a certain extent between states, but in none is there application of the plan where the annual premium volume of a risk is less than $1,000. A great many states, however, permit application of experience rating where the individual premium volume averages several hundred but less than $1,000 per year.

Workmen's compensation benefits under state laws vary from state to state. Classifications within rating plans also tend to differ. Therefore, when these factors are added to the weight given to the loss experience of a given state, it can readily be seen why compensation rates will differ among states.

In life insurance we also see that the premium rate is based upon the probability or chance of loss occurring during the time covered by the policy. The mortality table (which is, in effect, the recent past mortality experience of a large number of cases modified by statistical considerations) is used to determine the probability that the insured may die while the life insurance policy is in force. The mortality table is also used to ascertain the probability that the insured may survive to collect the maturity value of an endowment policy.

The mortality cost determined by the above method is modified by the interest earnings from invested premium. In life insurance premium rate computations, it is assumed that the portion of the premium needed to cover death claims (or maturity value of an endowment policy) will be invested to earn interest. At 3 per cent interest each dollar would be worth $1.03 at the end of a year. Consequently it is not necessary to

charge full mortality cost when due allowance is made for this interest factor. The figure determined by these two basic factors (the mortality and interest rates) constitutes what is known as the net premium.

It is obvious that there are costs of doing business which must be included in the premium paid by an insured. To the net premium is added the cost of such items as commissions to agents, home and branch office expenses, medical examinations, inspection fees, and taxes. In addition, a life insurance premium rate usually includes a contingency allowance for possible variations from the mortality rate. When such expense and contingency items are added to the net premium, the resulting premium rate is called the gross premium.

It does not follow that insurance rates reflect the exact findings of a perfect mathematical technique. Although the theoretical ideal is probably approached most closely in life insurance rate making, even there perfection has not been attained. In the making of rates for certain insurance lines the judgment factor is still an important consideration. In some instances this is considered necessary because of the likelihood of unexpected variations from past experience, or because these experience figures may not be adequate for the full application of a set statistical method. Then too, insurance is a highly competitive business, and rate making cannot be entirely divorced from this very practical aspect.

Underwriting. The selection of risks is the responsibility of the underwriting department of an insurance carrier. This procedure involves the primary function of selecting risks which will give wide and safe distribution at an underwriting profit. Hence underwriters must be vigilant to avoid selection against the insurer by the insuring public; at the same time underwriters must be reasonable enough in their actions to permit the carrier to insure enough cases to assure the operation of the law of large numbers. In addition, in certain instances, the pressure of competition can influence underwriting decisions. This selection process must also be done on a basis which adheres to a "line limit," either by limiting the amount of insurance accepted on any one risk or by reducing this amount to the "line limit" through the vehicle of reinsurance.

Reinsurance is the ceding of a portion of a risk to another carrier or carriers. Often two carriers reciprocate by obtaining reinsurance from each other. There are a few carriers engaged solely in the business of reinsurance, but the major reinsurance market exists among carriers also engaged in the primary writing of insurance. An underwriter, seeking such a market, may utilize both types of reinsurers at the same time. While considerable reinsurance is done in certain fields on a facultative (reinsurance on a single case) basis, a great amount is done automatically through treaties or jointly through pools.

Methods of underwriting vary according to the type of insurance being

written, as well as the viewpoint of the carrier involved. Underwriting instructions given to branch offices and agents often cite the classes of business considered as (1) unfavorable and (2) dubious. Frequently the highly desirable lines are listed also. These instructions usually give the "line limit" of each type of policy.

Claim settlement. If an insurance company consistently overpays its claims, it will eventually be in an unsound financial position; if it underpays these items, it is cheating claimants out of that which is justly theirs. The responsibility of handling this function properly rests with a carrier's claim department. Its importance to the public and to the institution of insurance can readily be seen. Claim adjusters usually settle claims by following a procedure in which they first make certain that there is a policy in force to cover the claim, and then they ascertain whether the claimant is entitled to payment under that policy. At this point, if everything is in order, the next step is to see if a loss has actually been sustained. If so, the actual amount of the loss sustained must be determined. When this has been done, the insurer generally offers prompt settlement of the claim.

The main source of misunderstanding by the general public in the matter of settlement of property insurance claims stems from the fact that many insurance policies (e.g., fire, theft, auto collision) agree to pay on a basis of the actual cash value of the covered property at the time of the loss. Such a policy does not agree to replace "new for old"; it merely agrees either to pay the actual cash value or to replace with property of like kind and quality.

Collections and accounting. The details of the method of collecting premiums and the keeping of records so vary with the lines of insurance written by a company, that a general statement cannot be made to cover all situations. In property and casualty insurance, local agents collect the major portion of the premiums and, in turn, remit these funds to the company through a branch office or general agent. Other than in the "industrial" field, soliciting life insurance agents seldom act as collectors except for the initial policy premium. It is customary for life insurance policyholders to mail their premium payments to a branch office or general agency.

The accounting department of an insurance company handles a tremendous number of accounts. Such a department is usually headed by a comptroller, with a large staff of cashiers, accountants, clerks, typists, and so on under his direction. Not only must this department keep a record of all money transactions, but also it must keep accurate records of all policy forms as well. Frequent audits of these forms are necessary. Computation of agents' commissions, return premiums, and other disbursement items must be made. The business of insurance is a business

of enormous detail; in no place is this more apparent than in the accounting departments.

Investments of insurance carriers. Every policyholder has an interest in the financial management of an insurance company. The lower the expense ratio and the higher the return on investments (assuming sound underwriting management and a constant loss ratio), the smaller will be the net insurance costs to the policyholder. Of equal importance to the insured is the soundness of these investments.

Since insurance premiums are paid in advance, insurance companies, in effect, serve in a fiduciary capacity. When a company receives a premium, it must put a considerable part of it aside to pay future claims, and in the property and casualty field it must also maintain an unearned premium reserve in the event the policy is cancelled before expiration. These reserves, being earmarked as liabilities, must be safeguarded by a sound investment policy. Good business judgment dictates this action; in addition, the state laws attempt to provide that such a course will be taken. This legal regulation takes the form of restriction as to types and amounts of securities in which insurance funds may be invested. These restrictions differ considerably between life insurance companies on the one hand and property and casualty companies on the other.

Inasmuch as most of the policies of life insurance companies are issued on a long-term basis, as contrasted with fire and casualty policies, which are issued for a comparatively short time, the nature of the liabilities of life companies varies to a great extent from those of companies operating in the other fields. Then, too, the tremendous total sum of assets of life insurance companies (cited earlier) places great significance on the investment activities of these companies.

The objective of life insurance investment portfolio management is common among all companies: to obtain the highest possible yield on funds invested in sound securities within the legal restrictions established by the various states. In attempting to reach this goal, life companies generally follow the principles of safety of principal, adequate yield, diversification, and liquidity. The importance of safety of principal and adequate yield is obvious. Diversification gives "spread of risk" to the entire investment program. It means diversification in type of security, type of enterprise and geographical location, by total numbers, by maturity date and as to time of purchase. A high degree of liquidity to meet claims and maturing policies is not so important as many people believe and as some states indicate by regulatory action. Today life insurance companies receive a steady flow of money from new and renewal premiums, maturing securities, and interest earnings. As a matter of fact, for the past several years this inflow has been considerably greater than the outflow necessary to meet policy obligations; the net result has

been a steady increase in the total amount of available investment funds. Hence the only need for a decided liquid position to meet obligations to policyholders would be an unusual emergency of some sort—which means that extreme liquidity at this time would merely be a precautionary measure far in excess of the requirements of current conditions.

An important aspect of the present situation in certain life insurance investment circles is evidence of a desire on the part of some companies to secure permission to invest a larger percentage of funds in equities (such as common stocks) than is now permitted by state laws. Unless such laws are altered there will be no drastic investment movement in this direction of life companies. Recently, however, sufficient changes have been made in the laws of some states to permit the limited investment of life insurance funds in certain types of real estate, such as multiple housing projects. A few of the larger companies have availed themselves of this opportunity, particularly in New York and California. In no case has a life company invested as much as 5 per cent of its assets in this manner.

A unique current development has been the direct purchase of entire corporate issues by individual companies, or by a combination of two or more companies. Such a transaction, known as a "private deal," is radically different from the orthodox manner of using investment houses as middlemen in the purchase of securities. When such a "private deal" is made, the corporation selling the securities does not have to go to the expense of filing with the SEC.[28] Naturally, this "private deal" practice does not meet with the approval of investment houses. However, the insurance companies involved apparently feel that the practice is warranted by the favorable terms on which they can purchase the securities.

Any discussions of current insurance investments, however brief, should portray the reduced earnings rate problem faced by insurance companies. The assumed interest rate is a factor in the premium rate promulgated for a life insurance policy. With all other considerations being equal, a higher assumed interest rate means a lower quoted premium rate, and vice versa. From 1930 through 1947 the net earnings of life insurance companies dropped steadily from 5.05 per cent to 2.88 per cent. There was some slight improvement in 1948 and 1949, when the earnings rate went to 2.96 per cent and 3.04 per cent respectively. This decline in the earnings rate since 1930 has caused the interest rate assumed by life insurance companies in actuarial calculations to fall from the 3 per cent and $3\frac{1}{2}$ per cent used in the early 1930's to the typical 2 per cent to $2\frac{1}{2}$ per cent used today.[29]

---

[28] Securities and Exchange Commission.
[29] Data in this paragraph were obtained from *Life Insurance Fact Book, op. cit.,* p. 46.

The fire and casualty companies also have their investment problems. They too must follow the principle of seeking investments at the highest possible yield consistent with safety of principal. They likewise are subject to investment regulation by state statutes. However, there are wide differences in the composition of the investment portfolios of these companies as compared with the portfolios of life companies. As a whole, the former companies have a much higher percentage of their assets in stocks and a smaller percentage in bonds than do the latter. The fire companies, for instance, have invested in stocks for certain specific reasons, one of which is for the purpose of liquidity and another is because of a comparatively favorable tax situation. Such a company must have sufficient liquidity to be in a position to meet sizeable loss payments on short notice and to make premium returns on cancellations, if called upon to do so. Stock fire companies receive a sizeable tax credit on most dividend income but none on interest income.

Recently published data show that, in 1949, stock fire insurance companies had stock investments to the extent of 35.9 per cent of their total assets, stock casualty companies had 19.3 per cent so invested, while legal reserve life companies had only 2.9 per cent of all assets in stocks. On the other hand, real estate and mortgage investments combined were only 1.5 per cent of all the assets of the fire companies. The same combination amounted to 1.9 per cent of the casualty companies' assets, while the life companies had 21.7 per cent in mortgages and 2.1 per cent in real estate. The comparative percentages in bonds (government and private combined) were: stock fire companies 46.4 per cent, stock casualty companies 59.2 per cent, legal reserve life companies 65.8 per cent.[30]

Current Aspects and Developments

Services rendered to society. It is quite obvious that insurance has been of considerable assistance to many millions of persons in their quest for security. On the other hand, certain other values of insurance have not been so widely recognized by the public. Nevertheless, most competent insurance observers seem to be in agreement that this institution gives the following services to society. It (1) gives added security to business undertakings, (2) increases business efficiency, (3) serves as a basis of credit, (4) promotes thrift, (5) makes saving possible, (6) assists in the capitalization of earning power, (7) furnishes an investment reservoir, (8) aids in conservation of life and property, (9) tends to create an equitable dis-

[30] Data in this paragraph pertaining to fire and casualty companies were derived from *Best's Insurance News*, Aug. 1950 (New York), p. 15; data pertaining to life companies are from *Life Insurance Fact Book, op. cit.*, pp. 49-52.

tribution of loss costs, and (10) in certain instances, creates emergency funds for policyholders.

The basic function of insurance is to make the uncertain certain. In so doing it cannot help but give added security to business undertakings by relieving the entrepreneur of risks of a certain nature. The costs of these risks being known (in the form of premium) tends to increase efficiency by enabling the businessman to calculate more closely his costs of doing business. The use of credit is necessarily extensive in our complex economy; insurance is often required in the granting of such credit and forms one of the bases of security for it. The use of both life and fire insurance as added measures of security for a mortgage, the use of life insurance as additional security for a commercial loan, and the wide use of marine insurance certificates in foreign trade are examples of utilizing insurance to expedite credit transactions. The purchase of a life insurance policy (other than a term policy) creates a savings fund and develops thrift through the medium of regular periodic payments into this fund. A life insurance policy can also be the means of capitalizing future earning power, particularly if a trust agreement provides for installment payments of the policy proceeds to dependents of the deceased insured. The investments of life insurance companies in United States government securities to the extent of $15\frac{1}{4}$ billion dollars, in securities of business and industry in the amount of $23\frac{1}{5}$ billion, in state, provincial and local bonds of $1\frac{2}{5}$ billion, and in mortages for the sum of $12\frac{9}{10}$ billion, plus similar investments of property and casualty companies, bear testimony to the existence of a huge investment reservoir.[31] Evidences of certain social benefits derived from the institution of insurance are the fact that life insurance companies aid in research projects in public health, give wide publicity to methods available for combating disease, and urge the improvement of accident prevention standards; that casualty companies (through their engineering and inspection departments) constantly work to eliminate causes of industrial and other accidents; and that fire companies, particularly through the National Board of Fire Underwriters (which in turn sponsors the Underwriters' Laboratories) do much to prevent fire waste. Equitable distribution of loss costs is facilitated by insurance carriers in the development of rate making techniques, which tend to give sound mathematical measurement of specific hazards. An emergency loan fund for the insured is made available through the cash value of a life policy. The loan value of a life policy does give assurance of a source of ready cash when a sudden, unexpected need for it arises, although the loan value is not designed primarily for that purpose, and despite the fact that this privilege is sometimes abused.

The services rendered by insurance do not mean that the insurance

---

[31] *Life Insurance Fact Book, op. cit.*, pp. 52 and 56.

industry has always, since its inception, been the "torch" in the movement of the conservation of life and property, or that it has always given all the above mentioned services in plenitude, or to its fullest ability. Nineteenth-century United States insurance history reveals several shortcomings in this respect. But in the twentieth century, particularly since World War I, the work of many insurance companies in life conservation, safety engineering and other loss prevention efforts has been noteworthy.

Intercompany cooperation. One of the interesting aspects of the insurance business is that, despite the intense competition that prevails within it, there exists a degree of cooperation among competitors that is unsurpassed in any other major industry. While this exists in the interest of the insurance carriers, it so happens that it is in the public interest as well. Such cooperation has, by and large, received the approval of state insurance departments on the principle that the prevention of cutthroat competition will tend to strengthen the financial security behind the insurance policies which have been issued. The ability of insurance carriers to meet their financial obligations has long been a prime consideration of conscientious insurance commissioners in their regulation and supervision of the insurance business in their respective states.

This cooperation between carriers has been carried on principally for the purpose of pooling loss experience for sound rate making, for the adoption of standard or uniform insurance contracts, for standard methods of operation, for controlling business expense (particularly acquisition costs), for public relations, for loss prevention efforts, and for educational activities. The danger of the development of monopolistic practices has, of course, been inherent in such close cooperation but, on the whole, such tendencies have been rather quickly checked through regulatory action by government.

Governmental regulation and supervision. This country is getting the most efficient (and the greatest amount of) insurance regulation and supervision by state governments in its history. At the beginning of this century comparatively few state insurance departments were giving suitable regulation and supervision; now practically all these departments are performing in an adequate manner. The possibility of federal regulation has hovered over the insurance industry, in its interstate activities, since 1944. In that year, in the U.S. *vs.* Southeastern Underwriters' case, the United States Supreme Court ruled, in effect, that insurance is interstate commerce when the insurance transaction is carried on beyond the borders of a single state. This was a complete reversal of the philosophy that insurance was not interstate commerce, which had persisted since the Paul *vs.* Virginia decision (in 1868) of the United States Supreme Court. Following the Southeastern Underwriters' decision, through Public Law 15, the insurance industry was given what was, in effect, a mora-

torium to operate under state regulation and supervision in order to avoid confusion and disruption. During this time the various states endeavored to bring their regulatory laws pertaining to insurance into line with federal antitrust laws. This moratorium expired on July 1, 1948.

The powers and duties of a typical state insurance department are administered by an insurance commissioner. The commissioners in many states are empowered to make insurance rulings which have the force of law, unless nullified by legislative or court action. The usual powers and duties of an insurance commissioner include the incorporation, licensing and examination of insurance carriers, the licensing of insurance agents and brokers, the regulation of reserves, investments, expenses, and deposits of insurance carriers, the levying of state taxes to which the carriers are subject, the approval of insurance policies, the regulation of rates, the prevention of discrimination against any segment of the insuring public, and the settlement of differences between carriers and their insureds.

Much progress has been made in the past few years in bringing about uniformity among states in insurance regulatory legislation. This progress has been achieved largely by insurance commissioners working in cooperation with an organization known as the National Association of Insurance Commissioners, and, of course, the impelling force of the U.S. *vs.* Southeastern Underwriters' decision and the provisions of Public Law 15.

Social insurance. In any broad discussion of insurance, mention should be made of social insurance because of its increasing pervasiveness and its economic and political implications. However, the vastness of the subject precludes adequate treatment of it in this short survey. One difficulty lies in the attempt to define social insurance, chiefly because of the difference in opinion as to what constitutes its extent.

A government is generally considered to be engaging in a social insurance scheme when it attempts to apply the principles of insurance by compulsory participation of all members of a group in the plan (with the government acting as the only carrier), for the alleviation of poverty or its prevention. An example of this is workmen's compensation insurance, operating through a monopolistic state insurance fund. The term social insurance can also indicate that a majority of the members of a group are to receive benefits, with the aid of governmental subsidy, in excess of their direct monetary contributions to an insurance fund (again with the government acting as the only carrier), on the theory that such a plan will benefit society as a whole. Apparently this concept includes the old age and survivors' benefit provisions of the Social Security Act. Other social security definitions have gone further to include workmen's compensation insurance in states where only private carriers do the insuring. Some definitions have even included voluntary group life and group

accident and health insurance plans in which there is no participation by the government in any shape or form.

One has only to scan the reports of current controversies over social insurance as they appear in public print to gather the significance of the problem. That certain of these insurance schemes carry the danger of placing upon future generations a heavy burden for benefits to be paid to dependents, to the disabled, and to the aged cannot be denied. On the other hand, the responsibility of society to care for those who, through no individual fault of their own, are economic casualties in one form or another of a complex industrial society cannot be ignored. Thus, the scope and intensiveness of social insurance in this country is far from being determined. To what extent social insurance will minimize, or enlarge, the importance of private insurance is problematical. It does appear, however, that this nation is engaged in a social insurance program, through the Social Security Act, which may result in a portion of the ultimate benefits being subsidized through the federal government.

The dynamics of insurance. The relative importance of any one of its many aspects and problems can change rapidly in the dynamic, complex business of insurance. Certain lines of insurance, such as teams liability can dwindle to a small fraction of its former premium volume, while others, such as group life, automobile, products liability and hospitalization may grow with astounding speed in the course of a few years. Or it is possible that a confused condition will be remedied by cooperation among carriers, or by a combination of cooperation and legislation. The standard automobile policy is an example of the former, the standard fire policy of the latter. In this survey it is impractical to cite more than a few of the many significant situations.

One interesting device that has been developed in the casualty business during the past decade is the "assigned risk plan." A workman's compensation or automobile liability risk, which has been rejected by three or more carriers for underwriting reasons (such as an unusual hazard or adverse loss experience), may secure insurance through such a "plan." For instance, in a given state having a workmen's compensation insurance assigned risk plan, all compensation insurance carriers operating in that state are in the "plan." A risk, seeking coverage through the "plan," is assigned to one of these carriers, which then insures it. Risks are assigned to the member carriers in an equitable manner, so that each carrier receives its proportional share of the risks which seek insurance through the plan. Of course, insurance carriers writing business through an assigned risk plan have protection against the acceptance of risks which do not meet the standards of legality.

Currently many interesting developments are taking place in the insurance industry. Multiple line legislation in practically every state seems

destined to be an accomplished fact. Nonoccupational disability laws, giving benefits to workers for nonoccupational disability and the use of private carriers as insurers of such schemes, are being passed by more and more states. The business uses of life insurance are being applied on a wider scale and on an increasing number of occasions. The trend of state legislation to establish higher qualifications for new insurance agents and brokers is apparent in all sections of the country, and the practices of all insurance agents and brokers are being gradually raised to something of a professional level by those real leaders of the insurance industry who recognize its importance and complexity.

Suggested Readings

Ackerman, S. B., *Insurance*. New York: The Ronald Press Company, 1948.

Ackerman, L. J. and Bugli, R. W., *Risks We Face*. New York: Prentice-Hall, Inc., 1944.

Best's Insurance News, Fire and Casualty Edition. New York: Alfred M. Best Co. Inc., Vol. 51, No. 4, August, 1950.

Casualty and Surety Journal. New York: Association of Casualty and Surety Companies, Nov. 1950.

Company Publications. Hartford: The Travelers Insurance Company.

Crist, G. W. Jr., *Corporate Suretyship*. New York: McGraw-Hill Book Co., 1950.

Education Department Publications. Philadelphia: Insurance Company of North America.

Eutsler, R. B., *Life Insurance Policies*. Economic Leaflets. Gainesville, Florida: University of Florida, April, 1945.

Huebner, S. S., Amrhein, G. L. and Kline, C. A., *Property Insurance*. New York: Appleton-Century Co., 1938.

Investment Bankers Association of America, *Fundamentals of Investment Banking*. New York: Prentice-Hall, Inc., 1949.

Kulp, C. A., *Casualty Insurance*. New York: The Ronald Press Company, 1942.

Life Insurance Fact Book. New York: Institute of Life Insurance, 1950.

Lunt, E. C., *Surety Bonds*. New York: The Ronald Press Company, 1922.

Magee, J. H. *General Insurance*. Chicago: R. D. Irwin, Inc., 1945.

Mehr, R. J. and Osler, R. W., *Modern Life Insurance*. New York: The Macmillan Co., 1949.

Michelbacher, G. F., *Casualty Insurance Principles*. New York: McGraw-Hill Book Co., 1946.

Moody's Manual. New York: Moody's Investor's Service, 1950.

Mowbray, A. H., *Insurance, Its Theory and Practice in the United States*. New York: McGraw-Hill Book Co., 1946.

Pathfinders. Baltimore: United States Fidelity and Guaranty Company, periodically.

Phipps, C. G., *Insurance: Its Mathematical Basis*. Economic Leaflets. Gainesville, Florida: University of Florida, March 1945.

Riegel, R. and Miller, J. S., *Insurance, Principles and Practices*. New York: Prentice-Hall, Inc., 1947.

Rodda, A. B., *Inland Marine and Transportation Insurance*. New York: Prentice-Hall, Inc., 1949.

The Aetna Agency Guide. Hartford: Aetna Casualty and Surety Company, periodically.

Vance, W. R., *Handbook of the Law of Insurance.* St. Paul: West Publishing Co., 1930.

Winter, W. D., *Marine Insurance.* New York: McGraw-Hill Book Co., 1929.

21

Government Regulation of Financial Institutions

by FRANCIS J. CALKINS

Professor of Finance, Marquette University

SINCE THE financial institutions and their practices by which transfers of funds are made from one party to another involve the general national welfare, and often international welfare, there is a need for safeguards around the financial institutions and their practices to protect the savings of individuals and to prevent losses through deception or fraud. These safeguards have been established by federal, state, and even local governments, and by cooperative movements of financial institutions themselves over the period of years. While the protective devices which have been set up are reasonably effective when properly observed and policed, it cannot be said that we have completely eradicated improper practices and the possibility of loss by regulation alone. Nor can it be said that regulation has been extended to all fields in which deception, fraud, or malpractice could occur. Yet, reasonable progress toward these goals has been achieved. The present chapter is devoted to a summary of the federal and state laws which presently regulate the formation and operation of financial institutions and financial practices.

Government regulation of financial institutions and practices may be classed into three categories: those regulations affecting the safety of savings directly; those affecting the use of savings and credit by financial institutions; and those affecting the manner in which financial institutions operate or financial practices of business are carried on. Many laws deal with more than one of these classifications, but a more orderly presentation may be made under these three groupings than by a mere recitation of each set of controlling laws.

Regulations Affecting Safety of Savings

Savings of individuals and of businesses may be placed in financial use in two ways: (1) through deposits in banks and savings and loan institutions for purposes of safekeeping of liquid funds, and (2) through purchases of securities or insurance contracts. The former usually involve temporary or semipermanent transfer of funds; the latter is inherently on a longer-term basis. Each channel has been subject to varied types of regulation or governmental supervision. In addition, safety of savings has been given by loan insurance or guaranties from the federal government.

Savings Account Insurance

Protection for bank deposits became a problem in western states as early as 1907, but lack of effective control over bank practices made early legislation for insurance of bank deposits ineffective. It was not until the wholesale failure of banks caused nation-wide losses to depositors in 1930–33 that political pressure demanded federal action. The Temporary Deposit Insurance Fund was established in 1933; in 1935 this institution was made permanent as the Federal Deposit Insurance Corporation.

. *Federal Deposit Insurance Corporation.* All national banks and members of the Federal Reserve System must become members of the Federal Deposit Insurance Corporation, whereas other state banks may become members if they meet the examination standards established by the F.D.I.C. Originally capitalized by the Treasury and Federal Reserve Banks, this institution in 1948 repaid these advances and in effect became a mutual organization, managed by three directors: the Comptroller of the Currency ex officio, and two appointees of the President of the United States with the advice and consent of the Senate. The Corporation assesses banks at the rate of $\frac{1}{12}$ of 1 per cent per annum on total net deposits as of two designated dates each half-year. In 1950, a revision was made to allow a credit of 60 per cent of net assessments, after payment of expenses and provisions against losses, against the following year's assessment, beginning in 1951. The sizable fund built up has been invested primarily in government securities, except for assets of closed banks being held for liquidation. In addition to these reserves, the Corporation can borrow up to $3,000,000,000 from the Treasury, should emergency needs require.

When an insured bank is unable to pay its depositors and is closed, the F.D.I.C. moves into action as a liquidation agency for national banks

or receiver for state banks, with the consent of state banking authorities. It gives depositors new accounts (up to a maximum of $10,000 a person) in another insured bank or in a new bank which is set up for the purpose, or in any other arrangement deemed appropriate. Each deposit account in an insured bank is insured to a maximum of $10,000, but the maximum payable to a single depositor is $10,000, regardless of the number of accounts held. Approximately 99 per cent of all deposits are thus insured, and about 56.5 per cent of the total amount of deposits as of mid-1949.

The effectiveness of the Federal Deposit Insurance Corporation has not been tested by a severe financial panic, but it doubtless would be able to withstand at least the ordinary run of bank failures in depression periods. Its chief merit appears to lie in the psychological effect made on bank depositors, for they are able to receive their cash or its equivalent immediately upon the closing of a bank.

Federal Savings and Loan Insurance Corporation. When the federal government began to charter savings and loan associations in 1934, these institutions were given the insurance protection of another agency, the Federal Savings and Loan Insurance Corporation. All federal savings and loan associations must (and state-sponsored building and loan associations may) become members of this organization by paying an initial fee of $400 and annual premiums of $\frac{1}{12}$ of 1 per cent on all accounts ($\frac{1}{8}$ of 1 per cent until 1950). The initial capital of the corporation was advanced by the Treasury, but in 1950 it was authorized to begin annual retirements of these funds. The Corporation is authorized to borrow up to $750,000,000 from the Treasury in emergency conditions. It is managed by the Home Loan Bank Board, which also supervises the savings and loan and building and loan associations. Its reserves are invested in government securities, except for such assets as it may take over from closed associations for liquidation.

Should an insured member association be forced to close or be unable to meet depositor withdrawals, holders of accounts are given either (1) equal sized accounts in another insured association, or (2) full cash payment by the Federal Savings and Loan Insurance Corporation, in liquidating the assets of an insured member. The maximum of $10,000 for each person who is a member of a savings and loan association resembles the amount insured by the Federal Deposit Insurance Corporation.

The two federal insurance institutions thus safeguard the savings of individuals and businesses which are placed in banks or associations which are members of either Corporation. Together, they give promise of withstanding at the minimum the first shocks of any great financial panic in the future, at least until other remedial action can be taken by Con-

gress. Perhaps the great growth of time deposits in banks and of accounts in savings and loan and building and loan associations since 1933 reflects the increased public confidence in the potential effectiveness of this type of regulation to safeguard short-term savings.

Some individuals may use savings institutions as media for longer-term investment, but the greater proportion of long-term savings is made available to industry and government through other financial institutions: insurance companies, investment companies, investment banking, and securities markets channels. Insurance against loss in these areas is illogical on various bases: the longer period of time involved increases the risk or probability of loss on the part of the user of the funds; the decisions for direct use of savings are personal and thus subject to the ambitions and abilities of the individual; and the proper investment policy of the saver demands that he build up a liquid reserve before devoting funds to the longer-term capital markets. In spite of this, government guarantees against loss have been given for such longer term loans as F.H.A. mortgages and V.A. loans, even if made directly by individuals to home buyers.

New Security Issues

The ordinary types of long-term investment are made through various contractual devices; protection in this area thus has developed around methods of preventing fraud or deception as to the nature of the contracts. The most prevalent and effective supervision of capital contracts and their offering has been enacted in the fields of new security offerings and in trading in the security markets for outstanding securities. Both state and federal laws regulate the offering for sale to the public of new security issues: that is, any solicitation for purchase of any stock, bond, certificate, warrant, right, or other type of contract normally considered a "security," by any persons not directly named in the resolution of the issuer to offer such security for sale. Only private offerings of new securities to a restricted number of designated persons and of a small amount in value are apparently exempt from most regulation. Some states, however, do require registration of all new security offerings, regardless of size, issuer, or prospective purchaser.

State "Blue Sky Laws." The increase in industrial and business activity in the early years of this century gave rise to many unscrupulous promoters who exploited uninformed people by offering shares of fraudulent or nonexistent companies. Following precedents on the Continent and in Great Britain, various states, beginning with Kansas in 1911, enacted laws requiring registration of security issues offered within their boundaries. The intent was to prevent promoters from selling "a few square

feet of blue sky." [1] Upheld by the United States Supreme Court in 1917, these laws are found in some form today in all states except Nevada.

"Blue sky" laws follow three types, the first two being found in some combination in 43 states: first, registration or licensing of all dealers, brokers, salesmen and agents is required, usually on an annual basis and frequently with a bonding requirement; second, registration or qualification of securities before they may be sold within the state, with certain exceptions, by filing information about the offering firm, the issue, and the conditions or terms of offering. (Should state authorities find fault with the record of a person seeking a license or with the facts concerning the issue being registered, they may withhold such license or registration. A fee is charged in any event.) The third type of state law, found only in Delaware, Maryland, New Jersey, and New York, requires no registration of securities in advance of offering, but this law enjoins threatened fraud and permits quick prosecution of fraud in security sales. This type of law is alleged to be more effective than are registration statutes, but effectiveness depends upon the enforcement measures taken. Variations in details of the laws and in their administration, coupled with inability to deal with out-of-state violators, led to a clamor for federal protection against fraudulent sales of new securities following the 1929 "crash."

Securities Act of 1933. In an effort to control effectively interstate sales of new securities, Congress enacted in 1933 the Securities Act, often called a "truth in securities offerings" statute. This Act provides that a full disclosure of all pertinent information on a proposed security issue be made in advance of the offering, under penalty of civil and criminal actions against violators, should their action result in fraud. The Act is administered by the Securities and Exchange Commission, a five-man board appointed by the President of the United States with the advice and consent of the Senate.[2] It is important to note that the Commission has no power to approve or disapprove any security issue, or to label it "speculative"; it can only require that all material facts on the issue and the offering be disclosed. In this respect the 1933 Act is perhaps of less merit than some state laws for protecting investor savings. On the other hand, it is far more effective in protecting against fraud, once committed, since the penalties are greater and interstate violations can be prosecuted.

The Act requires that all nonexempt offerings be registered by filing the name, location and business of the issuer, details of the issue, offering

---

[1] Shaw Livermore. *Investment Principles and Analysis.* Chicago: Business Publications, Inc., 1938, p. 495.

[2] The Securities Act was administered by the Federal Trade Commission until 1934 when the Securities and Exchange Commission was established under the Securities Exchange Act of 1934.

price, details of the offering, and financial statements. The registration statement must be signed by the principal corporate officials and a majority of the board of directors. All these, together with the other directors, the accountants, engineers, appraisers, or other experts preparing or certifying any part of the statements are liable for sanctions against false or misleading statements or omissions of material facts. All underwriters are also liable, but for only a one-year period instead of the three-year period of liability for the others. It is significant that the law extends to offerings for sale by persons who are controlling stockholders or who are in a position to affect the policies of management through their stock holdings. A filing fee of $25 or .01 per cent of the maximum total offering price to the public, whichever is greater, is required.

Offerings exempt from registration include all issues of government units, banks, religious, charitable or educational institutions, railroads, issues maturing within nine months after issue, those sold by receivers or arising from reorganizations under federal court order, direct security exchanges, and insurance policies and annuity contracts. In addition, all issues which have an aggregate amount of less than $300,000 are exempt from registration. However, the statute provides for no such minimum size exemption for fraud; accordingly, exempt issuers usually file a letter of notification giving all particulars of the issue and issuer, so as to reduce the possibilities of claims of a fraudulent sale.

Registrations become effective 20 days after filing, unless the Commission orders otherwise. After this "waiting period," offerings may be made of registered issues but only upon presentation of a prospectus to the prospective buyer. The prospectus is a slightly abridged form of registration statement, often constituting a bulky document replete with technical and legal verbiage in an effort to reduce the potential liability for any misstatement of fact.

Federal regulation of security offerings has given rise to two definite problems, both affecting the registration statement and use of the prospectus. First, the technical and legal language of this document makes difficult any analysis of the issue by the ordinary investor prior to the time of actual offering. This results in giving the institutional investor an advantage, particularly for the better quality issues. Investment bankers have advocated advance circulation of prospectus information through the "red herring," now in use within investment banking circles, to inform investors of potential issues in which they may deal. The SEC has permitted some reduction of the size of the prospectus, but it has continued to insist on legal language and technical detail. Advance solicitation may eventually be permitted, but it is doubtful that the prospectus can be made more understandable to the ordinary investor. Second, the costs of registration include not only the filing fee but also

the expenses of expert certifications, printing, and legal fees—all borne by the issuer. The aggregate of these costs of floating an issue of $500,000 would approximate 3 to 5 per cent of the total proceeds, to which must be added the underwriting fees and commissions. If the total costs of selling such an issue thus run to 10 or 20 per cent, while the costs for an issue of $5,000,000 are less than 5 per cent, the attractiveness of private placement on the one hand, and the deterrents to equity financing of small and medium-sized firms on the other are emphasized. The dilemma of this effect of federal regulation of new security issues cannot be solved solely by requiring registration of private placements, since they could easily be changed to term loans. It would appear that the exemption amount must either be increased or some relaxation of requirements be made to permit more proper functioning of the investment banker and other financial institutions toward both business and the investing public.

Security Markets

Not only are the initial sales of securities to the public subject to state and federal regulation but so, too, are the institutions and methods of effecting transfer of outstanding securities among individuals, corporations, and financial institutions. State regulation in this field is covered by the "blue sky" laws requiring registration or licensing of all security dealers, brokers, salesmen and agents, and by the various stock transfer acts. More extensive is the federal regulation embodied in the Securities Exchange Act of 1934. This Act arose from a public demand for regulation of the organized exchanges after experience with excessive and deceptive claims by brokers and dealers, frequent cases of price manipulation, and inadequate controls over the use of credit for speculative purposes during the late 1920's.

Securities Exchange Act of 1934. If the Securities Act of 1933 can be called a "truth in securities offerings" law, the Securities Exchange Act of 1934 should be termed a "fair in security dealings" act. It requires registration of all national securities exchanges and their agreement to discipline or expel any members for misconduct or unjust acts toward the public. The Securities and Exchange Commission is given broad powers to regulate the methods of trading, the listing of securities, and other practices in an effort to insure against any deception or manipulation in transactions. The Act also requires registration of all brokers and dealers on exchanges, including all of their representatives, thus affording some protection against entrance of unscrupulous persons into the business. A third phase of the Act requires registration of all securities issues listed on exchanges, and the submission of financial reports to the Commission by all corporations whose issues are listed. For preparation

of these reports, the Commission has established uniform accounting standards in accord with the practices of the American Institute of Accountants.

Because of difficulties of establishing adequate methods of supervising industry practices, the over-the-counter markets were not placed under regulation until 1936 and 1938, when amendments to the 1934 Act required that dealers in unlisted securities form voluntary associations with standards of membership, practices, and regulation similar to those observed by exchanges. One such association was formed, the National Association of Security Dealers. The law requires that all members of this association give no price concessions to nonmembers which are not given to the general public, an effective method of compelling all security dealers to join. Registration of all representatives of N.A.S.D. member firms is required, thus giving the SEC a national control over all security salesmen. Efforts have been made to require public disclosure of financial statements of large companies whose securities are traded in the over-the-counter market, but to date this has not been made effective.

Regulation of the securities markets for new and for outstanding issues is relatively complete. Reports of financial information, of security trading, of responsibility of security dealers and brokers—all are required; unfair practices of price manipulation and "gouging" of less informed investors have effectively been prosecuted under civil and criminal proceedings. Policing is effected directly by the exchanges and the N.A.S.D., with the Securities and Exchange Commission as the supervisor and prosecutor, and with the various Better Business Bureaus in major cities actively cooperating. The most apparent loophole exists in international solicitations of fraudulent securities. This type of activity can only be regulated, however, by international cooperation and by extensive public education.

Investment Counseling

During the 1920's a new financial institution, professional in character, arose as a result of increased investor interest in and need for guidance in the handling of investment portfolios. Many reputable firms were established, but their success attracted others who purported to advise clients for a share in all profits made, a device naturally leading to speculation. Although the security market crash of 1929–32 caused most of the poorer counsels to fail with their clients, the resurgence of security prices after 1933 attracted a new crop of clients and counselors. In addition, security salesmen who could not register under the Securities Exchange Act of 1934 or who could not pass examinations established by the exchanges as a minimum requirement for becoming a broker-

representative turned to investment counseling as a method of controlling the trading of their clients. After a thorough study of the methods of operation in this important segment of the securities industry, Congress passed the Investment Advisers Act of 1940.

Investment Advisers Act of 1940. This Act requires registration of all persons and firms engaged in giving investment advice or supervising investment policies. Exemptions are granted to those advising only investment or insurance companies, and to those who have less than 15 clients and advise only as an incidental part of their professional work in another field. Although the Commission does not pass on the qualifications of registrants, it is significant that the Commission requires a full statement of educational and business experience for 10 years, a requirement not made of security dealers or salesmen.

The law specifically prohibits advisers from contracting for payment on the basis of a percentage of clients' profits and also from assigning contracts without client consent. The former provision tends to reduce any impulse toward speculation, for the adviser has nothing to gain; the latter effectively deters an adviser from borrowing on the basis of contracts that can be canceled for services. Registered advisers may not act to defraud a client, nor act as a broker or principal for a client's trading without his permission. Unregistered and unexempted advisers are prohibited from using any interstate means of transportation or communication.

The effect of this Act has been to close one of the large loopholes for fraud by controlling the "tipster sheet," the adjunct of the "bucket shop" outlawed by the 1934 Act, and its amendments. By placing a definite sense of responsibility for advice given by various investment services and brokerage houses, the Act promotes effectively the professional character of both the investment counsel and the security analyst. Two national groups fostering the growth of investment advisory work by maintenance of high standards of professional competence and conduct are the Investment Counsel Association of America and the National Federation of Security Analysts Societies.

Investment and Insurance Companies

Two major financial institutions through which savings are channeled to productive use are the investment company and the insurance company. No direct protection to the saver is given in either field. But since the investment company issues securities, it is subject to the Securities Act of 1933, as well as to the Investment Companies Act of 1940 supervising its operations. The life insurance company is subjected to regulation of the use made of funds rather than to more direct protection of policy-

holders. Registration of insurance salesmen is required by many states, but no control over their methods of solicitation or advisory procedures other than misstatements concerning companies is exercised. Similarly, there is little regulation in the fields of property and casualty insurance.

Loan Insurance and Guaranties

Protection for lenders of savings, directly or through institutions, has been afforded by the federal government as a direct incentive for expansion in the housing field and as a right to veterans of World War II. The National Housing Act of 1934 established a system of mortgage insurance under the Federal Housing Administration to insure private lending institutions against losses on mortgages on which insurance is obtained. Three major types of loans are insurable: financing of alterations, repairs or improvements or of small new houses, first mortgages up to a maximum of $16,000 on either old or new buildings for one to four families, and mortgage loans for veterans in construction of new houses on the basis of necessary current costs. Loans to builders of single family residences for sale or rent and of multifamily housing for rent are also insurable. A substantial down payment is a general requirement for insurable loans, except as noted above, and payments must be amortized within a period of three years to 25 years depending on the purpose and type of loan. Maximum interest rates on insurable loans are set at 4½ per cent, except to veterans and builders, when the rate may not exceed 4 per cent. The insurance premium is .5 per cent.

Loans to veterans were guaranteed or insured under the Servicemen's Readjustment Act of 1944 if made for one of three purposes: home ownership, farm operation, or business purposes. Home loans may be made under direct loan guaranty by the Veterans Administration to a maximum of $4,000 if amortized monthly within 25 years, or a second mortgage guaranty for the uninsured portion of an F.H.A. insured loan to a maximum of $7,500. Guaranteed loans for farm land purchases are limited only by the appraisal value of land purchased, but added money for farm operation may be had only on a second mortgage for less than $4,000 or 20 per cent of the purchase price of the farm, whichever is lower. Business loans may be used for the purchase of fixed assets or for working capital. The guaranty extends to 50 per cent of the loan or $2,000, whichever is less, amortized within less than 25 years. The interest rate on all guaranteed loans may not exceed 4 per cent, but the Veterans Administration also pays the lender as a gift to the veteran an amount equal to 4 per cent of the guaranty used, applicable to the principal of the loan. If a veteran wishes to insure his loan (instead of having it guaranteed), only 15 per cent of the obligation is charged against the

guaranty privilege, for the lender is then insured to only 15 per cent of the total veteran loans made by the institution. Interest rates on non-real estate loans when insured in this manner may run as high as 5.7 per cent.

Regulation of Institutional Use of Funds

The second large area in which legal control or regulation over the functioning of financial institutions is exercised is the use to which funds placed with institutions are devoted. Since the banking process involves a pyramiding of bank credit upon the funds provided by stockholders and depositors, regulation of commercial bank loans has been a natural development. In addition, the use of funds by various savings institutions and by investment institutions has been subjected to differing forms of supervision and control by state or federal authority, and often by both. In general, the philosophy of regulation in this area has been to require safeguards against unwarranted losses from concentration of risk or unsound, speculative practices.

Commercial Banks

The first and most obvious point of regulation in banking deals with the formation of the institution. Minimum capital requirements are laid down for national banks by the Comptroller of the Currency ($50,000 for towns with less than 6,000 population, plus 20 per cent in surplus; $100,000 plus 20 per cent in surplus for cities with 6,000 to 50,000 population; $200,000 plus 20 per cent surplus thereafter), and by state laws. Only in the states of Iowa, Minnesota, Missouri, Nebraska, North Dakota, Oklahoma, South Carolina, and South Dakota are banks with less than $25,000 capital authorized to operate in small towns and villages.[3] Chartering authorities must also be satisfied that the proposed banking facilities are necessary to the community and that the prospective officials are familiar with the banking business.

The second most obvious point of bank regulation concerns the reserves which are required of banks by statutory provisions or regulatory agencies. Federal Reserve Banks must, by law, keep 25 per cent reserves in gold certificates against deposits. The Federal Reserve Board in turn establishes minimum reserve requirements for all member banks within limits set by law, and these reserves must be kept on deposit with the Reserve Banks. Of all states, only Illinois has no statutory reserve requirements for state banks; only Iowa, Kentucky, and South Carolina require reserves of less than 10 per cent on demand deposits; Connecticut,

[3] Joint Committee on the Economic Report, subcommittee on monetary credit and fiscal policies. *Hearings*, 1949, pp. 79-82.

Louisiana, Massachusetts, and Rhode Island require no reserves against time deposits in savings departments of commercial banks. Reserves for state banks usually include government securities and vault cash as well as bank balances in larger banks.[4]

These primary and all other regulatory measures over commercial banks are effected through a variety of agencies: the Comptroller of the Currency over national banks, the Federal Reserve Board over member banks, the Federal Deposit Insurance Corporation over insured member banks, and state banking commissions over state banks. The overlapping of authority is present, but since the medium of supervision is the bank examination, cooperative measures taken in 1938 to unify procedures have reduced conflicts. Nevertheless, lack of uniformity in legal restrictions and supervisory rulings creates problems for commercial bankers. Control is exercised through direct pressure or action against bank directors who violate laws or continue to practice what in the supervisory agency's view are unsound or unsafe operations.

Bank directors. The courts have long held that the directorship of a bank requires considerably higher personal integrity than does a position in other types of business. Accordingly, supervisory authorities have been given the power to remove from office any bank director who, after warning, continues to violate laws or to conduct bank operations in an unsafe or unsound manner. However, it must be noted that this regulation is negative; it does not require supervisory approval of directors before they may take office. Bank directors generally must be citizens of the United States, residents of the area in which the bank operates, and owners of a substantial amount of bank stock, in addition to having good character and reputation. Bank directors are personally liable for unlawful acts by the bank and are criminally liable for certain specified acts such as receiving a commission for granting a loan, and political contributions.

Bank examinations. Supervision of banks and banking operations began as a part of the charter provisions of individual banks late in the eighteenth century. It was not until general chartering statutes for banks were enacted, beginning about 1850, that minimum capital requirements and specific examinations were required of all banks. The National Banking Act of 1863 provided for regular examinations of all national banks by the Comptroller of the Currency, the chartering agency. By 1914 all states had set up some system of bank examination, but little coordination of efforts or methods was practiced. The formation of the Federal Reserve System in 1913, with the right to examine member banks, began the conflict of interest. As a result, Reserve Banks accepted examination

---

[4] *Ibid.,* pp. 63-66; also pp. 129-130.

reports of state examiners of state member banks until 1920, when the postwar banking crisis made necessary a uniform evaluation of bank conditions. Paralleling these actions by legal authorities were those of clearing house associations, voluntarily set up in most large cities to prevent wholesale financial collapse of large communities because of forced liquidation of banks. By 1933, then, banks were subject to a variety of examinations, the informal examination by the clearing house, legal examinations by either the Comptroller of Currency in the case of national banks or state banking commissions in the case of state banks, and the examination of member banks by the Federal Reserve Banks.

The banking crises of 1931 and 1932–33 revealed that bank supervision had many flaws. Liberal chartering of banks, lack of coordinated techniques, and emphasis on cash realization rather than ultimate recovery values caused a press for liquidation of bank assets during a very depressed period of business activity, with resultant losses to stockholders and depositors. Two agencies set up to assist banks at this time were given the right to examine so as to ascertain the risks involved in the agencies' participation in the banking structure of the nation: the Reconstruction Finance Corporation investigated banks in which it invested through purchase of indebtedness or preferred stock; and the Federal Deposit Insurance Corporation investigated all member banks of the insurance association. The latter agency was also given power to liquidate all closed national banks and to be appointed receiver for all closed state member banks. Since F.D.I.C. was interested primarily in the ultimate recovery values of bank assets, in addition to their immediate liquidity, a new approach to bank examination was fostered. By calling the attention of state banking authorities to unsound practices in insured banks and by being empowered to withdraw deposit insurance if no remedial action were taken, the standards of state bank supervision were raised. Efforts to coordinate the federal agencies were made in 1938, with the National Association of Supervisors of State Banks participating, and an agreement was made whereby the Comptroller of the Currency examines all national banks for all interested agencies; the Federal Reserve Banks examine all state member banks; the Federal Deposit Insurance Corporation and state authorities coordinate examinations of insured state banks; and state authorities examine noninsured state banks. Each supervisory agency makes available to the others the data and results of its examinations; thus duplication of efforts and possibilities of conflict on the examiner level is reduced.

A basic conflict of interests and objectives of bank supervisory authorities exists, nevertheless. The Federal Reserve Board and Banks are interested primarily, and correctly, in measures of monetary control; the Federal Deposit Insurance Corporation is interested in its potential

liability and the ultimate liquidity of bank assets; the chartering authorities, the Comptroller of the Currency and the state banking commissions are interested in bank observance of legal restrictions and in general "soundness," commonly to be interpreted as liquidity; the Reconstruction Finance Corporation is interested in the solvency of the bank for protection of its investment; clearing houses are interested in both liquidity and solvency as they affect local business conditions. Since the R.F.C. has a declining interest in banking due to repayment of loans made and retirement of preferred stock investments, it may be disregarded from long-run analysis of supervisory interests. Similarly, the clearing houses' local interests may be disregarded in any consideration of general supervisory policies.

Bank Loans. Regulation of bank loans extends into four general areas: direct prohibitions, limitations on secured loans, limits on loans to single borrowers, and limitations on interest rates. While no uniformity of restrictions exists among the various types of banks, the following may be taken as representative. In general, banks may not lend to their officers, directors, or employees, nor to any bank examiner; nor may they lend on security of their own stock, except under specified conditions. As to limits on secured loans, national banks may not lend more than 50 per cent of the appraised value of urban or agricultural real estate unless the loan be amortized within 10 years when a 60 per cent limit is permitted. Even these restrictions do not apply to certain types of F.H.A. insured and V.A. guaranteed loans, but an over-all total of real estate loans is set at the total of capital and surplus of the bank or 60 per cent of its time deposits, whichever is greater. Federal Reserve member banks are subject to limits on loans secured by stock or bond collateral as set by the Federal Reserve Board. All loans of banks, brokers, and other lenders made for purposes of purchasing or holding securities are subject to margin regulations of the Federal Reserve Board under specific authority established through the Securities Exchange Act of 1934. Banks are also limited in the amount of loans which may be made to or on the securities of affiliates. In general, a national bank may not lend more than 10 per cent of its capital and surplus at any one time to a single person or business. Exemptions to this limit include drafts, commercial paper, and bankers' acceptances; more liberal limits are permitted for specified types of secured loans.

When state laws set a maximum legal rate of interest, this restriction applies to all banks, regardless of the chartering agency; but if no rate is set, the national banks may charge up to 7 per cent. In addition, such fees as service charges for the preparation of papers and for credit investigations may be levied on borrowers. Any national bank making a

usurious charge may forfeit the entire interest charge if uncollected, or is subject to repayment of double the interest charges collected.

Bank examination is directed not only at investigating the correctness of accounting and at preventing violations of legal restrictions, but also at appraising bank policy and loan practice. The 1938 conference of federal supervisory agencies set up four categories of loans, classed by quality. Class I loans include all those which are unquestionably sound and on which interest payments are current; Class II loans are those on which there is a question of payment when due, but on which ultimate payment appears assured. The latter loans are called to the attention of bank officials for careful watching. Class III loans are those on which ultimate full payment appears doubtful; banks must charge off 50 per cent of these loans. Class IV loans are those believed wholly uncollectible and must be entirely written off by the bank. Ultimate liquidation value is thus the criterion used; this criterion reflects a change from the old banking doctrine of the safety of self-liquidating short-term paper to a newer concept of the shiftability of slower, yet ultimately collectible loans on intrinsic values.[5] To substantiate the character of loans under this newer doctrine banks must collect and maintain adequate credit files on all borrowers, including periodic financial reports.

Bank investments. The supervision of bank investments in securities has gained increasing importance with the shift in emphasis in bank assets from loans to investments. Government securities have always been looked upon as a part of the secondary reserves of commercial banks, even though national banks were not specifically authorized to purchase other types of indebtedness until 1927. Emphasis was placed upon the marketability of securities held and their current prices, a policy consistent with the stress put on short-term liquidity in banks. No standards of quality were set, so banks were free to purchase any bonds deemed suitable by directors. As a result of the drastic decline in bond prices and of interest rates in the 1930–1935 period, the Comptroller of the Currency ruled in 1936 that national banks could not purchase any "speculative" securities, but only those rated favorably by at least two investment rating manuals. Since only large issues are rated, competition for bonds lifted prices as banks sought income from investments to compensate for lack of borrowing by business. This move meant only lower rates of return on these high grade bonds. To relieve the situation, the Federal Reserve Board in 1938 permitted member banks to invest in marketable obligations of indebtedness "salable under ordinary circumstances with reasonable promptness at a fair value," provided the issue was publicly distributed or matured within 10 years with amortization of 75 per cent of

---

[5] Cf. Herbert V. Prochnow, "Bank Liquidity and the New Doctrine of Anticipated Income," *Journal of Finance*, Vol. 4, 1949, pp. 298-312.

the principal before maturity. This broadening of the regulations sur-rounding bank investment portfolios placed the responsibility for safety upon bank directors. But they, in turn, fell back upon the rulings of the Comptroller of the Currency. The impact of this double standard was seen in the policy agreement of supervisory agencies in 1938 for examina-tion of bank portfolios. Four classes of securities were set up for appraisal: Group I comprises all bonds of investment character, rated in the four highest grades by at least two investment rating services, or unrated issues of equal quality, such bonds to be valued at cost, less amortized premium, if any. Group II securities are speculative, rated below the four highest grades, or their unrated equivalent, to be valued at the average market price for the preceding 18 months, and with 50 per cent of the difference from cost to be written off as loss. Group III securities, defaulted bonds, and Group IV, stocks, cannot be carried at value on the bank's books.

Limitations on the amount of securities of a single company which may be held by a bank are similar to those for loans, 10 per cent of unim-paired capital and surplus. Exemptions are granted only for government and state and municipal bonds, issues of the Federal Farm Mortgage Corporation, and all issues made under the Federal Farm Loan Act.

Two problems are raised by the current supervisory practices over bank portfolios. Dependence on ratings established by private investment serv-ices, however well responsibility may be disclaimed by these impartial rating agencies, must be practiced by the smaller banks which lack facili-ties or personnel to make independent analyses. The alternative is reli-ance upon large correspondent banks or investment counsels. Since the ultimate responsibility for bank investment rests on directors, many banks have eschewed diversification and have concentrated their portfolios in low-yield but ever-safe government and municipal securities. Were the supervisory authorities to abandon the permissive use of independent ratings and establish legal lists for bank investment, there is little reason to believe that they would be more successful than have states which use this method of regulating savings bank, trust fund, and other types of fiduciary investment.

Savings bank loans and investments. Legal regulation of the operations of savings banks and of savings departments of commercial banks is, in general, more explicit than is that of commercial banks. It is reasoned that the savings deposited in these institutions are those of lower-income groups and thus must be given more protection. Indeed, New York limits the amount a depositor may have in a single mutual savings bank to $7,500. To prevent speculative investment practices, the amount of inter-est payments which may be made by savings departments of banks is subject to limits set by state banking commissioners or by the Federal

Reserve Board. The limits naturally do not apply to mutual savings banks.

Mutual savings banks, the most important segment in this field, may make first mortgage loans on real estate, usually only within a given distance of the banking office or within the given state, to a usual 60 per cent of appraised value within a limit of 65 per cent of total assets. Banks may join in cooperative housing development ventures up to 5 per cent of each bank's assets or 50 per cent of surplus, whichever is greater. To protect the New York banks, the Institutional Securities Corporation was established as a joint venture to deal in mortgages with member mutual savings banks. The legal restrictions on investments are usually more imposing, particularly in the New England and Middle Atlantic states, where "legal" lists are set by most state banking authorities. Only bonds so listed may be held by the savings banks. Government bonds, state and municipal obligations, railroad and public utility bonds predominate the lists which often must comply with statutory provisions requiring that the issuing corporation be of a minimum size and have demonstrated ability to earn and pay interest charges over a period of years. New York liberalized its restrictions in 1938 by permitting additions to be made to the legal list upon recommendation of at least 20 savings banks in the state. Some other states do not have as rigid formulas for investment selections (some even permit preferred stocks to be held), but reliance is placed on bank examinations to see that conservative practices are observed. New York banks have taken the lead in a new institution, the Savings Bank Trust Company, which can make advances to member banks on the security of bond investments.

Trust investments. The investment of trust accounts is more difficult than that of commercial or savings banks, because each trust fund must be handled separately. Because the usual trust fund is relatively small and the penalties for unwise investment are heavy, many states have enacted regulations which apply whenever specific instructions are not given for investment of a trust account. These laws generally provide for legal lists or set requirements for eligibility which show preferences for government, municipal, railroad, and utility bonds. These legal lists remain purely advisory, however, a condition which has led many states to permit use of a "prudent man" investment principle in which no set regulations are used. In 1950, New York relaxed its former standards to permit trust account investment in marketable common stocks, a step toward full relaxation of legal standards. Should the expected favorable results be realized, legal lists for this type of investment may well disappear in most states.

Life insurance company investments. Laws governing the investment practices of life insurance companies are more flexible than those for

other savings institutions. The most stringent laws are those of New York, but those laws effectively control a major amount of life insurance investment. Eligible securities in New York include government, state and municipal bonds, corporate bonds and preferred stocks of companies which have demonstrated earning power, real estate mortgages to 67 per cent of appraised value unless insured (but only to 40 per cent of total assets), and Canadian government bonds to 10 per cent of total assets. Investment in housing projects is permitted to a maximum of 5 per cent of total assets.

In 1951, New York authorized life insurance companies to invest in common stocks up to 3 per cent of assets, or one-third of surplus, whichever is less. Eligible stocks must have paid dividends for each of the preceding ten years. This step not only recognized the need for higher investment returns but, as in some other states at earlier dates, relaxed the rigidity characteristic of many state laws on legal investments without increasing risk to policyholders.

Property and casualty insurance company investments. Regulation of investments of property, casualty, marine, surety, and similar types of insurance companies is practically negligible. One of the few legal limits applies in New York where prohibitions against holding defaulted bonds or nondividend paying stocks exist. Also, at least 50 per cent of all investments must be made in accord with regulations laid down for life insurance companies.

Investment companies. The principal regulation of the use of funds by investment companies is indirect, extending only to their borrowing power. Before a company may borrow, its assets must equal at least three times the amount of the loan. There is also regulation of concentration of security holdings. A diversified company is one in which at least 75 per cent of all assets are in cash, government securities, and other securities, provided that the holdings in any single company do not exceed 10 per cent of the outstanding issues of that company nor 5 per cent of the total assets of the investment company. These restrictions are made under the Investment Company Act of 1940. Counsel for the investment company must be independent; investment bankers may hold only a minority voice in the management. These provisions, together with a requirement that at least a minority of the board of directors or trustees of the fund be independent of the officers, militate against fraud and deception rather than insure investment safety. Indeed, investors in this type of savings institution must fully realize that gains and losses, as well as income, depend upon the management of the company; that there is no legal safeguarding of savings here such as is present in other cases; that use of this institution involves securities, not contractual obligations to pay back funds to purchasers of investment company or fund securities.

Consumer credit. Protection of borrowers against exorbitant charges for consumer credit has been afforded in most states under the Uniform Small Loan Act which, while exempting personal finance companies from usury laws, does set maximum rates which may be charged by licensed lenders on the unpaid balances of loans.[6] The total amount of a loan made under these laws is strictly regulated. Specific rules of operation are set down in most statutes to insure open dealing and to prevent undue oppression of borrowers. State banking authorities are generally given the right or duty to inspect the affairs of small loan lenders to insure conformance with statutory limitations. Violations may result in forfeiture of license, fine, loss of usurious interest, or even of principal and interest, as well as in civil or criminal prosecution.

Credit unions, chartered by states or by the Federal Deposit Insurance Corporation, are subject to supervision by state banking authorities, the Farm Credit Administration, and the F.D.I.C. Loans may be made only to members at interest usually not in excess of 1 per cent a month on unpaid balances. The maximum unsecured loan is ordinarily $100; secured loans may exceed this limit under certain conditions.

No restrictive legislation has been adopted generally to cover the operations of sales finance companies, discount houses, or other commercial lenders.

Regulation of Corporate Financial Practices

Legal restrictions and regulations in the field of finance extend not only to financial institutions but to the business practices which are purely or often partially financial in character. A summary of the impact of the law on financial operations must give cognizance to legislation affecting the formation of a business, its continuation as an operating entity, the solution of financial difficulties, and the financial relations of the owners and officials to the firm.

All forms of business except the individual proprietorship and the general partnership require that legal procedures be followed in the formation of the business firm. Many of these procedures affect financial matters. In addition, licenses, franchises, and other types of legal permission may be required before an organization may begin to operate. Distinct corporation laws exist in most states to govern the formation and operation of financial institutions. Many of these laws restrict the scope of operations of a financial firm. For example, until 1949, New York restricted an insurance company's operations to a single general field:

---

[6] The highest legal rate in any state under the Uniform Small Loan Act is 3½ per cent a month. The usual limit on loans is $300, but some states have raised this to $1,000.

life, property, casualty, surety, or marine. Other states still continue such restrictions; this practice leads to the formation of groups of companies in allied lines but under common ownership.

Banks. National banks and other Federal Reserve member banks must segregate funds in their trust departments from general banking accounts. All trust departments are specifically subject to examination by state supervisory authorities. The Banking Act of 1933 prohibits banks or their affiliates from participating or dealing in any underwriting, except those of state or municipal securities, and in government issues.

Banking concentration is particularly subject to restriction and supervision. Mergers and consolidations may take place only under strict compliance with federal and state laws. Since 1922, national banks may operate additional offices in the cities in which they are located, unless state laws specifically prohibit, but the combined capital and surplus requirements must equal at least that required for the same number of independent banks. At least 18 states (all of the Pacific Coast and adjacent states most prominently) permit state-wide branch banking, while 9 states (including Colorado, Illinois, Minnesota, and Texas) specifically prohibit any branch banking. All branches established by insured banks must have the prior approval of the Federal Deposit Insurance Corporation. Chain banking is subject to less regulation, but interlocking directorates are outlawed under an application of the Clayton Act that reduced the financial unification in such systems to minority control. The Banking Act of 1933 provides for regulation of bank holding companies, such as Transamerica Corporation and Northwest Bancorporation, if a member bank of the Federal Reserve System is involved. Not only are the member banks in such cases placed under System supervision, but also the holding company itself and all of its affiliates, including state banks, are placed under penalty of expulsion of the affiliates from membership. Voting power over all changes in the holding company banking affiliates is subject to approval of the Federal Reserve Board.

The intent of these control measures over banking practices is to restrict their operations to pure banking and to prevent monopolistic control over credit facilities. Nevertheless, at the present time a holding company is not required to own bank shares only, but it may engage, through other affiliates, in other financial or business lines.

Investment companies. With the exception of banks and possibly of railroads, investment companies are subject to more detailed regulation of financial practices and operations than any other industry in the United States. Although they are also subject to the Securities Act of 1933 and the Securities Exchange Act of 1934, the major supervision is exercised through the Federal Revenue Acts that effectively force compliance with the Investment Company Act of 1940, administered by the

Securities and Exchange Commission. The investment company may limit its federal taxes to apply to only undistributed net income if the company registers as a regulated investment company, annually derives at least 90 per cent of its gross revenues from security income and profits, limits short-term trading of securities to less than 30 per cent of gross income, meets standards of diversification in investment as previously described, and distributes to shareholders at least 90 per cent of its net income and capital gains. If the above conditions are met, the holders of investment company shares may treat "capital gains" dividends as personal long-term gains rather than as ordinary income on their personal federal tax returns. The first of the provisos listed above is the key to supervision of investment companies, since unregistered companies are denied interstate commerce facilities for their operations in addition to having a disadvantage in any offering of shares to the public.

Other of the more important provisions of the Investment Company Act require: a disclosure of general investment policies followed; notification of shareholders and of the SEC of any borrowing incurred or other such financial operations; semiannual financial reports and disclosures of portfolio holdings; selection of independent auditors; disclosure of the source of dividends paid to shareholders, and use of prescribed accounting records. Relations with brokers, investment bankers, and banks are strictly limited; and contracts with investment counsel must be approved by shareholders. Shares of open-end or mutual funds must be priced under rules set by the N.A.S.D.; no officers, directors, trustees, or employees, promoters, or principal underwriters may trade directly with the investment company with which they are connected, except in shares of the company itself and at regulated prices. Direct limitations are set on investment company underwriting of new securities issues.

The intent of these detailed regulations is to protect shareholders through full disclosure of operating results, to guard against "insider dealings," and to facilitate growth of companies by reducing the impact of potential "triple taxation" of corporate income to shareholders who use this method of investing.

Listed corporations. Nonfinancial corporations, except those operating in specific industries in which there is a public interest, generally are unregulated and subject to little supervision in financial matters. States have been unwilling to exercise any control over corporations except to require filing of financial statements of firms chartered. On a national basis, regulations affect only those corporations whose securities are listed on registered exchanges. The Securities Exchange Act of 1934 imposes certain obligations on these corporations in the public interest; these obligations require revelation of "transactions by officers, directors, and principal security holders," and of "appropriate reports . . . to insure the

maintenance of fair and honest markets." The purpose of such regulation is to prohibit price manipulation by "insiders," to cause effective dissemination of financial and other data essential to proper evaluation of investment securities, and to make secure the knowledge essential to shareholders whose votes control the actions of the corporation. Regulation under this heading takes three forms: periodic reports, disclosure of certain transactions, and methods of soliciting proxies.

Periodic reports. Annual financial reports of each listed issuer must be filed within 120 days after the close of each fiscal year in a form prescribed by the Securities and Exchange Commission. This rule applies to all corporations, unincorporated issuers, foreign governments and corporations, bank holding companies, management investment companies, companies in receivership or bankruptcy, insurance companies other than life and title insurance companies, and companies subject to certain provisions of the Interstate Commerce Act, the Motor Carrier Act, or the Communications Act. In addition, interim reports, usually at three month intervals, must be filed giving sales or gross revenue and net income data. Reasonably current reports must also be filed to reveal any changes in the financial structure and nature of the business, the terms and privileges of outstanding or new issues, the lists of directors, officers, underwriters (if any), and of principal stockholders, bonus and profit-sharing arrangements, management contracts, and options existing or to be created. Principal stockholders are defined as those who hold on record or in beneficial interest more than 10 per cent of any class of any stock issue. In addition, the remuneration of officials and directors, together with interests in the issuing corporation or any affiliate, must be disclosed, as must a list of others than officers and directors whose total remuneration from the corporation exceeds $20,000 a year.

Another section of the 1934 Act provides that all directors, officers, and principal stockholders shall file monthly reports of their ownership or beneficial interest in equity securities in a corporation, together with any changes which have occurred in their holdings during the month.

"Insider" transactions. All directors, officers, and principal stockholders are prohibited from making short sales of equity securities in the corporation; in addition, any profits realized by them from a trading transaction within a period of less than six months are recapturable by the corporation. The effect of this and the disclosure of stock holdings is to prevent "insiders" from profiting personally or indirectly from even a temporary withholding of information from the general public.

Proxy solicitation. Solicitation of proxies to vote shares of a listed corporation must be made in accord with rules set by the Securities and Exchange Commission. Preliminary copies of the proxy statement and the solicitation materials must be filed at least 10 days before being sent

to shareholders. Such information must include an annual report (which may be sent at an earlier date), a list of nominees for the directorate with the direct and indirect shareholding of each, their remuneration during the past year, a listing of the three highest-paid officers of the firm, and a specific ballot for approval or disapproval of matters to be acted upon together with a brief statement of the merits of any specific proposals to be considered. Among such specific proposals may be the selection of an independent auditor. While management usually solicits proxies and proposes matters for vote, any qualified security holder may give management reasonable notice of an intention to present a proposal at a stockholder meeting and, with management consent, secure a place on the proxy for balloting. If management opposes such a proposal, it may make a brief statement of the objection, or it may provide the stockholder with a reasonably current list of stockholders to whom he may send solicitations of proxy in accordance with the rules summarized above. A statement of the costs of proxy solicitation and by whom it is borne must be disclosed on the form.

Brokers and security dealers who hold shares in their own name for the account of others must submit proxy materials to the owners of the shares for instruction as to voting on each particular proposal; if no instructions are given, the broker or dealer may vote according to his own wishes. These provisions effectively aid all shareholders by giving them full information on the major questions to be decided at meetings; the provisions permit opposition to be voiced against management, and they allow minorities to be heard. Thus the democratic spirit is furthered in even the largest corporations; even in the most closely controlled firm, attention must be paid to the shareholding owners if continued listing of issues on national exchanges is desired.

Some efforts have been made to extend these provisions to cover reports, trading, and proxies to corporations whose securities are not listed on exchanges; but difficulties of deciding upon the size requirements at which the regulations would become effective, as well as the ancillary question of the relation of listed to unlisted markets, have blocked these moves for the time being.

Bankruptcy. Business firms often become involved in financial difficulties as a result of operations and are unable to pay their debts. The law has provided definite steps to govern the relations of creditors to owners in such cases. If the defaulting firm has insufficient assets to meet its debts, it may be adjudged bankrupt by a court of proper jurisdiction. Usually federal courts make this judgment, although state courts may so act.

Bankruptcy proceedings begin with a petition by either the debtor or by creditors alleging an act of bankruptcy. Such acts include fraud, giving

unfair advantage to one creditor over another with resultant inability to pay the second, attempting to avoid bankruptcy proceedings, or admission of insolvency and a desire for liquidation through bankruptcy. A detailed statement of the assets and liabilities of the firm must be provided in the petition or must be filed in the debtor's reply to the court. The court then takes over the debtor's properties pending proceedings and appoints a receiver or marshall to preserve the assets. After creditors have shown legal evidence of the validity of their claims, the court appoints a trustee to sell the assets at a minimum price set by the court and to distribute the proceeds to creditors in legal order of priority:

1. Expenses of preserving the bankrupt estate.
2. Wages, to a maximum of $600 a person, if earned within three months of the start of proceedings.
3. Costs to creditors of setting aside any other legal steps taken to prevent bankruptcy proceedings.
4. All taxes, federal, state and local.
5. Priority debts, including rent accrued for three months prior to the start of proceedings.
6. Secured creditors are paid from proceeds of the sale of assets underlying such claims, with unsatisfied claims being treated as a general claim.
7. General claims of unsecured creditors.

After a final accounting is made to the court, a release from all unsatisfied debts is given the debtor as he is discharged from bankruptcy.

During the proceedings the court may find that asset values may be increased; or the court may find that debts may be paid off if the business is operated under court jurisdiction for a time and then may order such action to be pursued. Alternatively, the debtor and creditors may cooperate in purchasing the assets of the bankrupt firm by forming a new concern, a procedure often followed in the past when the assets of the firm cannot be sold or operated in a piecemeal manner, as in the case of railroads.

Arrangements. As an alternative to bankruptcy proceedings, if only unsecured trade and bank creditors are involved, an arrangement may be made between the debtor and creditors on a voluntary basis provided complete approval of all creditors is secured. Such an arrangement may include an extension or voluntary postponement of payment, a composition, or agreement to accept partial payment in full discharge of debts; an assignment of assets to trustees for liquidation for benefit of creditors; or a creditors' committee in which management of the debtor is assumed by the creditors for purposes of liquidating their claims. The National Association of Credit Men has operated successfully in the last method to avoid legal expenses to the benefit of creditors. Since approval of all

creditors must be secured, the initiation of an unsuccessful arrangement may become an act of bankruptcy. Thus many firms now prefer the alternative judicial proceedings under Chapter XI of the National Bankruptcy Act.

Chapter XI may be used by debtors who are legally insolvent or who are unable at the moment to meet their debts, but only if there are no secured or publicly held debts. The proceedings resemble those under a bankruptcy procedure, but the proposal resolves into an extension or composition—or combination of both—which if approved by a majority of the creditors in number and amount of debts may be confirmed by the Federal Court and applied to all creditors, including dissenters.

Reorganizations. A reorganization is a more formal change in the capital structure of a corporation, for it involves a change in contractual relations and usually an exchange of securities. These moves may be taken on a voluntary basis with the consent of affected security holders, and the dissenters are paid in cash. Legal reorganizations, however, are effected under Chapter X of the National Bankruptcy Act, administered by federal courts, but must involve some change in debt relations. The petition for reorganization may be filed by the debtor corporation, by three or more creditors, or by an indenture trustee, alleging merely that the firm cannot meet its debts as they come due. Insolvency need not be alleged; insufficient liquidity suffices. If the court accepts the petition, it appoints a trustee who, when the assets involved exceed $250,000, must be a disinterested person, must investigate the causes of the financial difficulty, operate the firm, and formulate a plan of reorganization after consulting with all interested parties. The Securities and Exchange Commission may become a party to the proceedings at the request of or with the consent of the court in an effort to represent the public impartially and to facilitate the reorganization.

The plan of reorganization must provide for some change in the rights of creditors and may involve changes in the rights of stockholders. The plan must set forth in detail the treatment of all claims and shareholdings in accordance with "fair and equitable and feasible" principles. The court may also receive plans from creditors and shareholders. It must then decide on acceptable plans. If the assets involved in the reorganization exceed $3,000,000, the court must, and in other cases may, submit the plans deemed acceptable to the Securities and Exchange Commission for an advisory report on the fairness and feasibility of the plans. When and if the Commission submits its report, the court may then approve a plan and submit it to the creditors and shareholders who are recognized in the plan as having an interest. Those deemed without interest are thus permanently excluded from any further participation in the reorganization. Upon approval of the plan by two-thirds of each class

of creditors and by a majority of each class of stockholders recognized, the court confirms the plan and makes it binding on any and all dissenters. New securities may then be issued in accord with the plan, or cash may be distributed; a final decree is entered after fees and compensation hearings have been determined by the court.

In a plan of reorganization, the Supreme Court has ruled that the wording of the law that the plan be "fair and equitable and feasible" means that a valuation of the firm must be established by capitalizing its potential earning power, that the distribution of the values be made in accord with bankruptcy order of priorities, and that the capital structure of the reorganized firm be so formed as to eliminate potential bankruptcy or reorganization proceedings in the future as a result of the provisions of the plan or the securities issued thereunder.

The intent of bankruptcy and reorganization procedures is to effect a method by which debtors may be relieved of obligations which they cannot pay, and by which creditors may be able to enforce so far as possible their claims according to contractual provisions. Reorganization has made it possible since 1933 to continue the existence of a firm which has economic feasibility but which is unable to meet its current obligations. Reorganization thus facilitates the adjustment of debts without hazarding the potential economic losses of bankruptcy.

Trust indentures. Specific legislation has been provided for more purely financial operations of corporations. Among the more important is the regulation of bond indentures. The controlling legislation, the Trust Indenture Act of 1939, was enacted to protect the investing public from unfair practices of trustees who might be unwilling or unable to take steps for which contractual agreements have been made. The Act provides that no bonds which have not been issued under an indenture registered with the Securities and Exchange Commission or otherwise qualified may be sold in interstate commerce. All bond indentures for issues in excess of $1,000,000 must be registered and provide for specific clauses. The indenture trustee must be a corporation with a net worth in excess of $150,000, may not be a trustee under another indenture of the same debtor, must not be affiliated with the debtor in any manner, and may not own more than stated percentages of the debtor's other securities. Most important, the trustee may not benefit by a preferential collection of his own claims over those of bondholders. The trustee must keep reasonably accurate and current lists of bondholders' names and addresses, supply these upon application of at least three bondholders, or distribute information for such bondholders if they pay all necessary costs. The trustee must make public his relations to the debtor, and must require from it reports of financial condition and of performance under the indenture. The indenture must authorize the trustee to act

on behalf of bondholders in event of default, and he must so act unless stayed by the bondholder votes. Many of the provisions of the trust indenture must be set forth in the prospectus for any new bond issue sold publicly.

Governmental borrowing. More specific legislation has been enacted to control the amount of borrowing which governments may undertake. The federal government operates under a total debt limitation established by Congress. States generally have no debt limits, but many states have limits on the tax rates which can be imposed to pay interest and principal. Such limits can usually be raised or removed by constitutional amendment. Counties, cities, and other governmental units are usually restricted in their borrowing power by state laws which limit either the amount of debt or the tax rate which can be applied to debt servicing. It is customary to require that all municipal bonds be sold under a process of competitive bidding. The intent of all these restrictions is to protect the public confidence in governmental liens through establishing some limit, at least temporarily, after which a reconsideration of debt problems must be made.

Transportation industries. The transportation industries are particularly subject to legislative control on both federal and state levels. Interstate railroad, highway, and marine carriers must submit to federal laws and the Interstate Commerce Commission rules on rates on freight and passenger traffic, standardized accounting methods, approval of all new security issues, supervision of mergers, consolidations, and reorganizations. Similar restrictive measures are applied to intrastate operations by state commissions. Interstate pipelines used for carrying gas and petroleum products are subject to regulation by the Federal Power Commission.

Public utilities. State commissions are the primary media for regulation of electric, gas, water, and telephone companies—a group known as public utilities. Following precedents set in the regulation of railroads, these commissions generally have powers over rates charged and accounting practices; and the commissions must approve the issue of any new securities by a utility operating within the borders of the state. Because of variations in state laws and enforcement measures, large national utility operating corporations have generally not been formed. Instead there are intrastate corporations and interstate holding companies. To regulate the latter effectively and to prevent abuses of power, Congress passed the Public Utilities Holding Company Act of 1935. Precedent for this action has been claimed for the application of the Clayton Act to railroads in 1914; but effective railroad holding company regulation did not appear until 1940, when Interstate Commerce Commission approval for voting power was made a necessary step. Such action is minor com-

pared to the control exercised over utilities by the Securities and Exchange Commission. The first step in holding company regulation was to require that all sales of new securities by holding companies or operating subsidiaries in the utility fields be approved. The most controversial point centered about a requirement that holding companies be integrated into a single geographic utility system and that other holdings be sold or distributed to security holders as soon as practicable. Ancillary to these two basic requirements are: approval of all dividend payments by holding companies or operating subsidiaries; contractual relations with subsidiaries are strictly scrutinized; borrowing from a subsidiary is forbidden; and approval must be secured for purchase or sale of any utility assets or securities. The Federal Power Commission, however, has standardized the accounting systems for all companies engaged in the manufacture or distribution of interstate electric power.

Summary

The national welfare requires that safeguards be placed about the financial institutions and practices which affect the savings of individuals and business firms. Since savings are most important for small income families, protection in the form of insurance of deposits in banks and savings and loan associations was established by the federal government. In addition, the manner in which these institutions may use funds is carefully circumscribed, and observance of legal restrictions is insured by frequent examination by government agencies. Similar restrictions on the use of funds exist for insurance companies, trust companies, and similar investment institutions. In the more direct methods of investment, however, protection for savings cannot be guaranteed because of human frailties. All that can be done is to insure that adequate and accurate knowledge is available to the investor and that serious steps are taken to prevent flagrant defrauding. Supervision and regulation of corporate financial practices and allied matters thus become an integral part of the protective devices afforded by the state and federal governments. While many of these measures may appear to infringe upon individual liberties, the necessity for fair and equitable dealings between debtors and creditors, between the ownership and control interests of business firms, between savers and the users of savings demands that the public interest take precedence. Although the protective devices may have some loopholes and are subject to variations in their application by governmental agencies, the regulations have revealed that definite strides have been made toward increasing the efficient use of savings, a requisite part of industrial progress in the American ecenomy.

Suggested Readings

Atkins, W. E., Edwards, G. W., and Moulton, H. G., *The Regulation of Security Markets*. Washington, D.C.: Brookings Institution, 1946.

Bogen, J. I., Editor, *Financial Handbook*, 3rd Ed. New York: The Ronald Press Company, 1947.

Cherrington, H. V., *The Investor and the Securities Act*. Washington, D.C.: American Council on Public Affairs, 1942.

Federal Reserve Board, *Banking Studies*. Washington, D.C.: Government Printing Office, 1941.

Foster, M. B. and Rogers, R., *Money and Banking*, 3rd Ed. New York: Prentice-Hall, Inc., 1947.

Guthmann, H. G. and Dougall, H. E., *Corporate Financial Policy*, 2nd Ed. New York: Prentice-Hall, Inc., 1948.

Shaw, Edward S., *Money, Income and Monetary Policy*. Chicago: Richard D. Irwin, Inc., 1950.

Westerfield, R. B., *Money, Credit and Banking*, Revised Edition. New York: The Ronald Press Company, 1947.

22

Credit Rating Agencies

by LEONARD RALL

Associate Professor of Economics
Michigan State College

BASIC TO the success of modern industry and commerce has been the development of reliable credit information. The twentieth century businessman need no longer base his decisions involving credit risks on his hunches and good luck omens; he now has at his fingertips such a supply of credit information that much of his procedure has reached a scientific level.

This chapter is concerned with pointing out the chief sources of credit information and showing their relative importance in the financial and business community. It will cover the following credit rating agencies:

1. Dun and Bradstreet, Inc.
2. The Special Mercantile Agencies
3. Security Rating Agencies

Dun and Bradstreet, Inc.[1]

Of all the agencies engaged with providing credit information, only Dun and Bradstreet, Inc., qualifies as a general agency. It alone undertakes to furnish credit information on any businessman or concern anywhere in the world. This agency, which developed as a result of the combination of Bradstreet Company and R. G. Dun and Co., is the largest and the oldest of the mercantile agencies.

To speed and prepare accurately and disseminate the many kinds of reports issued by Dun and Bradstreet, Inc., the United States is divided

---

[1] Special credit should be given to Roy A. Foulke, Vice-President of Dun and Bradstreet, Inc., for supplying much of this basic material.

into 12 regions, similar to those of the Federal Reserve System. These regions are further broken up into districts, suboffices, and reporting stations which are located in the main centers of commerce and industry.

Within the framework of the geographical districts are 10 operational divisions, each of which is engaged in collecting, analyzing, and editing information concerning all types of business and business activity. The distinct methods of operation and a description of the services rendered by these 10 divisions are given in the sections that follow.

The credit report department. This is the primary reporting division which gathers, analyzes, and distributes a continuous flow of credit reports on every business enterprise and its particular activities in the United States. With the trend of commercial and industrial life toward greater complexity, the functions of the credit report department have become highly specialized. As a result it employs different kinds of reporters, each possessing many years of training and experience necessary to meet the demands called for in this meticulous and analytical work.

The chain of events may be followed from the beginning of an inquiry for credit information to the final issuance of the edited statement. The request for credit data originates with a subscriber who sends in an inquiry ticket to any one of the main offices to ask for a credit report on a business firm. If the firm in question is located outside the area of investigation of the receiving office, the ticket is relayed to the office which covers the firm to be checked. If the firm lies within the area of the office, the ticket is checked against the active file. If the available information is current, a report is sent immediately to the subscriber or to the relaying office, which in turn sends it on to the local subscriber. If the available information is over six months old, or if the firm is a new one, the inquiry is turned over for investigation to one of the four types of credit reporters. The methods of investigation and preparation of the credit reports can readily be seen by examining the nature and activity of each of these types of reporters.

The city reporter. Inquiries on large enterprises are turned over to city reporters who are trained and experienced to handle the investigation and analysis of the complex and intricate financial structure of large corporations or companies with subsidiary structures. The work of these reporters is further specialized in that some check only companies engaged in particular fields such as paints, varnishes, and heavy chemicals, while other reporters may specialize in checking department stores and the like. Business concerns of intermediate size, with tangible new investment between $10,000 and $50,000, are turned over to a specialized city reporter. Inquiries coming to the large cities not covered by the above divisions are placed in the hands of another specially

trained city reporter who has been assigned a definite geographical district.

In addition to gathering and organizing all essential data on a business concern, a city reporter also winnows and analyzes the material gathered and prepares a credit report.

Resident reporters. Each office also has what is called a resident reporting staff whose primary purpose is to provide speed in reporting and to keep standing reports currently up to date. The work of the resident reporter is comparable in all respects to that of the city reporter with one general exception. The resident reporter, unlike the city reporter, does not edit the credit report; rather, the resident reporter devotes his full time, on a salary basis, to gathering essential credit information on concerns in the reporter's immediate city. The resident reporter does not specialize in the manner of the city reporter; he handles all kinds of industrial organizations from newsstands to large holding companies. Since the resident reporter concentrates only on the phase of collecting material, his data are edited at the central offices by other specialists.

Local correspondents. There are approximately 30,000 such local correspondents employed throughout the country by Dun and Bradstreet, Inc. Many communities have at least one local correspondent who is employed on a fee basis. He may be a banker or a merchant who is willing to give a portion of his time to outside work of this nature. He handles the investigations that cannot normally be taken care of by the resident reporter, and he also relieves other reporters during certain seasonal peak periods by assuming the excess load. In some small towns and villages all inquiries are forwarded to the local correspondent.

Traveling reporters. In order that each business establishment may automatically be called upon and checked for certain details at least once a year, irrespective of the fact that most of them are also investigated during the year by local correspondents or resident reporters, a traveling reporter is employed. The traveling reporter is given a schedule of cities, towns and villages to cover. For most of the business concerns located in the "semirural sections" of the United States, this process of checking provides an automatically revised investigation. The traveling reporter's job is to revise every name in every community on his route. He does not edit reports but sends the results of his investigations and all financial statements to his home office.

Trade investigations. Simultaneously with the direct contacting and checking by the various reporters and correspondents, each home office sends out thousands of requests for information to be answered by the firms themselves. These requests are sent to manufacturers, wholesalers, and retailers asking for data on their business experience with their customers. Included among the information requested are such items

as the highest credit recently extended, terms of sales, payment of current bills, and general relationships with trade creditors. Through this process Dun and Bradstreet, Inc., obtains a comprehensive list of the names of concerns from whom merchandise is purchased as well as a cross check on data obtained elsewhere.

Additional sources of information.

1. In most county seats a representative is employed to report promptly all deeds, suits, mortgages, and similar legal instruments as they are filed with the county offices.

2. Financial and trade papers are clipped daily in order that no important information bearing on the credit risk of any concern is overlooked.

3. At the beginning of each year every business firm is asked to fill out a financial statement according to prescribed standards. As these financial statements are returned, they are incorporated directly into the reports.

Types of credit reports. As this vast array of information comes into the home offices, it is being constantly examined, condensed, and edited into understandable and meaningful reports. Dun and Bradstreet, Inc., prepares and edits three types of detailed or "narrative" credit reports: the analytical report, the specialized report, and the synopsis report. The analytical report is prepared on large business enterprises who often have complex subsidiary or inter-loan structures. The specialized report is written on medium-sized enterprises, and the standard narrative report is prepared on all other concerns.

The outlined contents of each of the sections of the analytical report are as follows:

Date of the report.

Heading. The legal structure of the organization, whether it is a proprietorship, partnership, or corporation is indicated. The line of business activity, the exact name of the business, and its complete address are shown. The subscriber is asked to note whether the name, business, and street address correspond.

Officers and directors. The names of the members of the board of directors and the officers are listed with their proper titles.

Rating. This indicates in a general way the concern credit standing and the amount of the capital that has been invested in the business.

Summary. This section presents in a forceful manner the strong and the weak points of the risk involved. It is an analytical interpretation of the rating.

Personnel. Here is given in some detail information pertaining to the age, marital status, experience and training, and current and previous business relations of each officer. If some of the directors who are not

officers have important business connections, these connections are pointed out.

History. This section of the report includes the antecedents of the firm. It indicates the date of organization, original authorized and paid-in capital stock, and names of other firms absorbed. It also tells whether or not liabilities have been assumed when companies have been absorbed. All of this is presented in point of time so as to sketch the trend and progress of the firm.

Method of Operation. This portion of the report gives a penetrating view of what the business produces and handles, brand names, the territory in which the product is sold and terms of sale. The physical qualities of the plant and its layout along with a description of the branch offices are also given.

Subsidiaries. This section is one of the most significant in the analytical report. It reveals the intercompany structure. This structure may be built up through various devices such as connecting and underlying units, inter-company merchandise loans, or sales. This information sheds light on the important aspects of financial responsibility of any unit in a group of concerns controlled by the same or allied interests. A company by itself may be weak, but, when bolstered by close relatives, it may change its condition completely.

Financial Statements. Under this heading there are set up comparative balance sheets for the past three years. These sheets reveal the advance or decline in new working capital, liabilities, and other significant financial items.

Analysis. This is an interpretation of what is favorable or unfavorable in the financial data presented above. If there is an upward tendency revealing a progressive trend, this is pointed out; if on the other hand there is reason to believe that other pertinent factors signify disapproval, this likewise is noted.

Trade Investigation. Here is presented the factual trade experience of concerns who have extended credit to the company. The list shows the amounts outstanding, amounts past due—if any, the highest credit recently granted, the manner of payment, and the terms of sale.

Bank Experiences. The recent information obtained from commercial banks indicates whether the company has recently requested loans and whether these applications for loans were granted or refused. If the loans were granted, the legal nature of the notes is indicated—secured or unsecured, endorsed or guaranteed.

Specialized Report. Whereas the analytical report covers several pages, the specialized reports cover only two or three pages. The specialized report is prepared on the middle-sized concerns with capital ranges of

$10,000 to $50,000. Very few of these concerns have affiliations or sub-sidiary organizations.

Synopsis Report. Making its appearance in 1950, this report supplants the well-known standard narrative report. The synopsis report is edited on a far greater number of businesses than any of the other types of reports; and its greater preponderance is due principally to the large number of small enterprises such as grocery stores, restaurants, service stations, and similar business that require a minimum of specialization.

The Insurance Division of the Reporting Department. During recent years insurance companies have become interested in a thorough report upon the integrity of the risks they intend to underwrite. The insurance division serves the needs of fire underwriters in providing the so-called "Fire-Character Report." This report reveals essential antecedent data of the business concern or individual, the physical nature of the property and the immediate neighborhood, the trend of the business, and the fire record, if any. Real estate search reports are made and issued to sub-scribers; these reports give information on mortgages, deeds of trust, judgments, and other liens that may be outstanding. All of this informa-tion aids the underwriter in ascertaining the nature and possible in-crease under strain of the moral hazard of the insured.

Reference books. One of the best known functions of the general mercantile agency is the publication of reference books which give credit information and credit ratings of business establishments. These books, which are issued bimonthly, are regarded as credit dictionaries or en-cyclopedias by the credit profession. The reference book of Dun and Bradstreet, Inc., contains the names of all active commercial and indus-trial business enterprises in every city, town, village, and hamlet in the country. The 1949 editions contained over 2,600,000 names for the United States. Smaller pocket editions for any state or groups of states offer exactly the same information as the larger volume and are used largely as handbooks by firms that sell in a small area and by traveling salesmen who must make credit decisions on the road. Reference books contain the credit ratings of manufacturers and traders in general. With a reference book at his disposal, a subscriber may find the name of any business enterprise in the country and obtain an idea of its credit standing and rating. The reference book is arranged alphabetically by states and communities within the states; the names of the business firms are listed for each locality. The population, post office, and bank-ing facilities of each community are also included. Figure 1 shows a page from such a reference book.

Rating key. Each listed name of a business is preceded by a symbol designating the general kind of business in which the enterprise is en-gaged. To the right of the name are two symbols which comprise the

capital and credit ratings or appraisals. The capital letter indicates the estimated financial strength, while the numerical symbol designates the general credit standing. Where one or both symbols are omitted from the name, sufficient facts have been lacking to base a capital or credit rating.

```
  56 12 Collin's Clothing Store  ...: 2   E 2½
  50 ZJ Delmarvia Oil Corp .......    1   D 2
A 17 11 Diez William E  ......Plbg 0     J 3½
  59 12 Di Francesco Henry  ....Drg 4    E 2½
  54 92 Di Francis Vincent J .....  Del  H 3½
C 17 51 Di Giovanni Gabriel  ....Carptr  K 3½
A 54 22 Di Gregorio Salvatore ....  Mt 0 J 4
  58 32 Dikeman Miss Clara C . Rst 8      D 2
  59 62 Greenley Fred NR..... HayFeed     3
  17 61 Hall E W  ....Roofg 5            K 4
  55 41 Hamilton Raymond E . Sstn 6       J 3½
  50 VB Hammond Charles L . Bldsup 6      D 1½
  52 12 )2
  56 21 Handley & Handley ....Wnwr 7     F 3
  52 51 Halsey Hardware Co ........ 6    E 2½
  20 97 Halsey Ice Co*  .....           F 3
  27 11 Halsey Journal           Pubg
  52 11 Halsey Lumber & Supply Co        C 2
  20 41 Halsey Milling Co Inc RD   FF    E 2
  55 11 Halsey Motor Co  ...... Ats     F 2½
  59x83 Halsey Oil & Coal Co .....       D 2
  54 12 Halsey & Raughley ......   Gr    H 3½
A 56 31 Hawes Grace E  ....Mly 9        J 3
  52 41 Heusser Wm  ...... Elcfix       D+ 2
  55 41 Hobbs Everett J  ...... Sstn    3
C 54 51 Hopkins E Powell  .. Darpdt 6    H 3½
  53 92 Jacobs Wilbur E  .   Dg 6        J 3½
  54 13 Jarrell Rose (Mrs Chas) & Chas
                            GrMt 7      F 3
  59 HA Jerread Charles A ...... Gifts   H 3
  50 VJ Kates J Reynolds ......  Mont    C 2
  20 12 Kirby-Holloway ......MtPkr 4      2
  53 93 Langrell Enos  ........ Gs 2     F 3
  54 12 Langrell Frank        Gr 8      J 3
  72 62 Layton William E . MortFrn 6     D 2½
  57 12 )2
  50 HA Linnecke Harry F .....Nursery    1
  57 23 McAllister Irving N   Radio 8    J 3½
A 59 FA McClain Wilma (Mrs R R)   Pht
                             Sup 8      3
  50 62 McKnatt Reginald .. W&RElcsup    E 2½
  52 41 )2
C 58 12 Marshall Archie  ...... Rst     H 3½
  59 LA Mehan Lewis C `  ... Toys 5      G 3½
A 53 31 Merkley & Hawkins  ... Vs 8      F 3½
  50 42 Moore Benjamin A   Gr            C 2
  50 VC Murphy & Hayes* ... W&RLbr       1 x
  52 11 )2
  42 13 Paddington Express Co*    Trkg  AA 1
        (Br of Cincinnati Ohio)
  75 38 Palmer William   . Atro 3       J 4
  54 13 Potter Wm Arnett  . GrMt 1      F 3
C 20 71 Powers Perry & Violet    Cnf    3
  76 41 Presse Upholstering Studio   6   G 3½
  20 51 Purity French Bakery Inc         E 3
  56 71 Ruze William  ..... Tlr        G 3
  52 41 Satterfield & Ryan  .. Elcsup   E 2½
C 16 11 Savage & Son*  ....RoadCntr     D 2
  50 62 Saviers Electrical Products Corp C 2
  50 28 Saviers H E Paint Store   W&R   * *
  52 31 )2 (See Lammove)

  HARMON—125—Cook (7)
  COOK CO TR CO          .. $48M
  T O Ford Pr L W Hughes Cas

  54 12 Barbier Walter L       Gr    J 3½
  54 13 Bryant Joseph D      GrMt    H 4
  55 11 Davis Gerald Wesley & Mary Ellen
                             Ats 2   D+ 2
  01 41 Enterprise Poultry Co Inc...W&R

  HUTCHINSON (See Edgewater)
  JACKSON—400—Cedar (9)
        Bk town Worcester
  01 31 Ambili Corrado ....    Nursery  H 3½
  56 12 Anderson Don E   ... Cl 8      D 2
  58 13 Buonamici Tomergenito .....Tav   E 2½
  54 13 Central Market & Grocery     3   F 3½
C 55 41 Colmery Lewis W Jr NR Sstn 4     G 3½
  50 72 Desert Hardware Co....W&R 5      E 2½
  52 51 )2
A 54 41 Gilson Harry   ........ Cnf 0   K 3½
```

FIGURE 1

Figure 2, taken from the reference book, shows a picture of the key to ratings. There are 16 classifications for the "estimated financial strength." These range from Aa (showing a tangible net worth in excess of $1,000,000) down to L (which indicates a tangible net worth of less than

$1,000). There are only four classifications of credit worthiness or credit appraisals. These are high, good, fair, and limited; but under these four classifications there are 48 symbols indicating credit rankings. The high

KEY TO RATINGS

ESTIMATED FINANCIAL STRENGTH			COMPOSITE CREDIT APPRAISAL			
			High	Good	Fair	Limited
AA	Over	$1,000,000	A1	1	1½	2
A +	Over	750,000	A1	1	1½	2
A	$500,000 to	750,000	A1	1	1½	2
B +	300,000 to	500,000	1	1½	2	2½
B	200,000 to	300,000	1	1½	2	2½
C +	125,000 to	200,000	1	1½	2	2½
C	75,000 to	125,000	1½	2	2½	3
D +	50,000 to	75,000	1½	2	2½	3
D	35,000 to	50,000	1½	2	2½	3
E	20,000 to	35,000	2	2½	3	3½
F	10,000 to	20,000	2½	3	3½	4
G	5,000 to	10,000	3	3½	4	4½
H	3,000 to	5,000	3	3½	4	4½
J	2,000 to	3,000	3	3½	4	4½
K	1,000 to	2,000	3	3½	4	4½
L	Up to	1,000	3½	4	4½	5

CLASSIFICATION AS TO BOTH
ESTIMATED FINANCIAL STRENGTH AND CREDIT APPRAISAL

INDETERMINATE RATINGS	BRACKET		EXPLANATION
1	$125,000 to $1,000,000 and Over	When only the numeral (1, 2, 3, or 4) appears, it is an indication that the estimated financial strength, while not definitely classified, is presumed to be within the range of the ($) figures in the corresponding bracket and that a condition is believed to exist which warrants credit in keeping with that assumption.
2	20,000 to 125,000	
3	2,000 to 20,000	
4	Up to 2,000	

CLASSIFICATION ONLY AS TO ESTIMATED ANNUAL SALES

	BRACKET		EXPLANATION
1x	$500,000 and Over	If the letter x is combined with the numeral (1, 2, 3, or 4) as (1x, 2x, 3x, or 4x), it is an indication only that the annual sales are presumed to be within the broad range of the ($) figures in the corresponding bracket, and that credit appraisal is neither inferred or not inferred.
2x	75,000 to $500,000	
3x	10,000 to 75,000	
4x	Up to 10,000	

"**Inv.**" in place of the rating is an abbreviation of "**investigating.**" It signifies nothing more than that a pending investigation was incomplete when this book went to press.   NOT CLASSIFIED OR ABSENCE OF RATING
   The absence of a rating, whether as to estimated financial strength, or estimated annual sales, or as to credit appraisal, and whether expressed by the **hyphen** (-), the **dash** (—), or by the (x), or by the omission of any symbol, is not to be construed as unfavorable but signifies circumstances difficult to classify within condensed rating symbols and should suggest to the subscriber the advisability of obtaining additional information.
   The sign (✱✱) is a reminder to look to the other town, or to the other name or style for the rating. It *does not* mean "absence of rating."
   See inside cover of Reference Book for complete key.

Dun & Bradstreet, Inc.
JANUARY, 1951

FIGURE 2

or top rating is open to all concerns whether the estimated financial strength is less than $1,000 or greater than $1,000,000. This "high" rating is reserved to firms that presumably have skillful management and

a strong business organization. It is given to those concerns which have a good record, which discount their bills or anticipate payment, and which are otherwise highly regarded.

A "good" or second grade of credit is open to all businesses regardless of the amount of estimated financial strength. This rating is generally considered to be the normal rating assigned to the average credit risk.

The "fair" or third grade of credit rating, likewise assigned to concerns with any amount of estimated financial strength, usually indicates some weakness; but this rating does not mean that the concern is an unsafe risk. It is generally an indication that the concern is nearer to the border line between a sound and unsound financial condition than is the subject with a good credit rating.

The "limited" or fourth grade of credit indicates a marked degree of financial weakness in most cases. The concern with this rating may continue to operate under these conditions without actually being in financial difficulty. Such a concern, however, can be generally regarded as in a vulnerable position which if not improved will eventually cause trouble.

It should be noted that a given numeral may signify different grades of credit, depending upon the capital rating with which it is connected. For example, the numeral $1\frac{1}{2}$ represents a high general credit when associated with a pecuniary strength rated C. The same numeral represents but a good general credit if it is associated with the capital ratings B +, B, and C +. When connected with capital ratings shown by the symbols Aa, A +, and A, numeral $1\frac{1}{2}$ denotes only a fair general credit. Subjects with a capital rating of E or lower are never assigned a general credit rating as high as $1\frac{1}{2}$. By the same logic those with a business enterprise possessing a net worth of less than $1,000 cannot be assigned a general credit rating higher than fair or a numeral better than $3\frac{1}{2}$.

Credit Clearing Division. In 1928, R. G. Dun and Co. (now Dun and Bradstreet, Inc.) organized a department which is presently called the credit clearing division. The purpose of this department is to serve the apparel trades and their affiliated lines of business with specific advice and recommendations as to whether a given order should be rejected or accepted. It is especially helpful to the individual in a small concern who has responsibility, but who may not have had training or wide experience in this area. He needs, in addition to a credit report from a mercantile agency, advice as to what kind of decision to make regarding the prospective customer in view of the facts in the report. Decisions in the textile trades often must be made without delay. A subscriber to the credit clearing service may, upon receipt of an order, consult the agency either by telephone or by means of a form. A group of credit experts familiar with the selling habits, trade customs, buying seasons,

style hazards, and other pertinent facts surrounding the industry make the decision for the seller with as great speed and accuracy as possible. The headquarters of this department are located in New York City; and 14 other cities (including Chicago, Philadelphia, Los Angeles, and St. Louis) have branch offices.

Every three months this division publishes a specialized reference book known as the *Apparel Trades Book.* This volume contains the names of all retailers of apparel in the United States, their specialty in this merchandising field, and their credit rating based on an appropriate rating key.

Municipal Service Department. This department prepares and issues a survey of any state, county, city, or other borrowing unit when one of these units sells a single issue of general obligation bonds of $400,000 and over, maturing in more than one year. Surveys are kept constantly up-to-date on each of 177 cities of 50,000 population, 73 counties of more than 150,000 population, and the 35 states which enter the investment market as borrowers. In addition the municipal service department makes special investigations of unusually complicated situations for individual institutions and investors.

These surveys are prepared and furnished primarily to commercial banks and trust companies, investment bankers and bond dealers, insurance companies, and individual investors.

The information found in the survey is obtained through personal interviews and comprehensive investigations made by specialists trained in municipal finance. Although the survey contains 10 to 15 pages of detailed information, the "Summary Report" is considered by many subscribers to be the most important page in the entire analysis. Here are found in concise form (a) social and economic background, (b) debt outstanding, (c) management, and (d) current operations, which are classified as either "favorable," "fair," or "unfavorable." The last paragraph of the report provides an evaluation of the future prospects of the community's financial strength. Hence, the "Summary Report" gives a bird's-eye view of the financial standing of the community.

Foreign Department. The functions of the foreign department closely resemble the domestic activities of the reporting department. Data gathered from offices and correspondence maintained in the principal centers of the world are translated, analyzed, and edited into credit reports in the New York City office on practically all foreign names. Reports are designed after the domestic reports. In each report a complete picture is given of the history of the business, lines of merchandise handled, available financial statements, lines of credit recently allowed, and payment records throughout the world. There is included a recent quotation, in dollars, of the foreign currency used in this report. Hence,

the subscriber can see the approximate equivalent in dollars of his client's capital and net worth.

Mercantile Claims Division. This division dates back to before the Civil War and was organized to aid in the collection of past due accounts arising out of mercantile transactions. This department is operated to render a practical collection service at minimum cost. Such activities as receivership adjustments, assignments, and bankruptcies are beyond its scope of operation. As an aid to the collection of delinquent accounts, subscribers to this service are furnished with a "Reminder" sticker in the form of a gummed label. This label, used on past due statements and letters by the subscriber, notifies the debtor that collection of past due accounts is made through Dun and Bradstreet, Inc. If this does not bring results, the claims division requests payment on the account. A very substantial number of accounts are paid at this stage of the proceedings. Accounts which are not settled at this stage are followed by a series of letters in which each letter becomes more pressing. If the account has not been settled by these means, a collector calls upon the debtor personally. Finally, if none of these steps has resulted in payment of the account, it is turned over to an attorney to bring suit for collection.

Business Information Division. This division is primarily a fact finding and research organization for industry and commerce. It is engaged in the preparation of surveys on a wide range of subjects such as the sale and distribution of consumer goods and commodities, product acceptance tests, operating trends of certain lines of business, and other areas of importance to business. The data of these surveys are obtained through personal interviews with the laborer, farmer, housewife, clerk, banker, or business executive, supplemented by other information from available authoritative sources. This work is carried out by a special staff of skilled marketing and economic analysts.

Monthly Magazine Division. Dun's Review, a journal of finance and trade, was published weekly from 1893 to 1933, but is now published monthly. Its circulation is chiefly among the principal commercial and industrial establishments, banks, and insurance companies. This magazine furnishes a summary of business conditions in the United States; particularly covered are the number and aggregate liabilities of business failures. These failure statistics are further broken down by geographical location, types of business, and sizes. Also included are weekly and monthly compilations of bank clearings, building permits and indexes of wholesale prices. The weighted price index of 30 basic commodities which appears later in many newspapers throughout the United States is firsthand information gathered by this agency.

Special Service Department. Although the information available through regular services of Dun and Bradstreet is so complete as to be

practically exhaustive, it was found that occasionally customers had need of a somewhat more intimate type of data than would be of interest to any large number of subscribers. For this reason the special service division was set up in 1943 to handle such individual requests in a way that no relevant detail desired by the subscriber would be overlooked. Payment for such service is arranged on a cost-plus basis. A few of the subjects for which the special service division has been used include furnishing details of unusual financing arrangements, revealing the competitive place that a business concern holds in its industry, studying the background of the management of a business or its owners, and investigating business reputations of contractors and suppliers and even of service organizations. In fact, Dun and Bradstreet's special service division has often been invaluable in furnishing to a prospective purchaser of a business or of a controlling interest in a corporation the specialized financial studies essential to such a venture.

Special Mercantile Agencies

In spite of the size and prestige of Dun and Bradstreet, it does not enjoy a monopoly in supplying credit data, for there are many competitors from the large field of special mercantile agencies. These special mercantile agencies as a rule offer services along different lines from those handled by Dun and Bradstreet, Inc., but in some instances there is a degree of overlapping. These special agencies differ chiefly in confining themselves to one type of service or to a special industry or to a few allied industries. Among the larger of such special agencies are the National Credit Office, Inc., and The Lyon Furniture Mercantile Agency. These agencies receive to a high degree the support of the industries they serve. Many a subscriber finds it advantageous to use both the general agency's services as well as those services of the special agency catering to his own industry.

Advantages and disadvantages. An exhaustive or complete treatment of the advantages or disadvantages of the special agencies cannot be given because of the diversity of functions and many services offered. Nevertheless, a survey of credit services available to subscribers to special agencies and an examination of their general methods of operation may be useful.

One advantage of the general agency is that it gives a wide coverage for the subscriber by including all lines. Hence, only one service may be required. On the other hand, if several different specialized agencies were subscribed to, there would inevitably be some duplication, and even then many lines of business activity in the in-between zone would not necessarily be covered. Furthermore, the general agency claims that

Analytical **REPORT**

D U N & B R A D S T R E E T , ɪ ɴ ᴄ

2071 BRISTOL CANDY CO. (INC.)	(A) CD 4 AUGUST 16 1950 MANUFACTURER	BRISTOL 3 PA. BUCKS COUNTY 100 EDGELY ROAD

Chester G. Hoover, Pres.
Henry T. Conroy, Vice Pres.

Carl S. Freed, Vice Pres.
F. Charles Young, Sec. & Treas.

BOARD OF DIRECTORS: The officers with Mrs. Mary S. Lawrence comprise the Board.

RATING CHANGE: B 1 to B + 1

SUMMARY
THIS BUSINESS WAS FOUNDED IN 1914. A GENERAL PARTNERSHIP FORMED IN 1938, TO CARRY ON THE ORIGINAL BUSINESS, WAS SUCCEEDED BY THE PRESENT CORPORATION ON JUNE 30, 1944. OPERATIONS OF RECENT YEARS HAVE BEEN HIGHLY PROFITABLE. TANGIBLE NET WORTH AT JUNE 30, 1950 WAS $312,817. FINANCES ARE IN A WELL BALANCED CONDITION. TRADE PAYMENTS ARE DISCOUNT AND PROMPT.

PERSONNEL
Chester G. Hoover was born in Connecticut in 1884 and is married. He was employed by the Federal Biscuit Company in Philadelphia, Pa., as General Sales Manager from 1911 to 1921. He resigned to become General Manager of Bristol Confectionery Company Inc. and was General Manager from 1938 to 1944 while the business was conducted as a general partnership. When the business was succeeded by the subject corporation on June 30, 1944, he was elected President, continuing active as General Manager. Hoover owns 15% of the outstanding capital stock. The corporation carries $15,000 insurance on his life.

Henry T. Conroy was born in Maryland in 1901 and is married. From 1922 to 1927 he was employed as cashier of the Union National Bank, Baltimore, resigning to become trust officer of Acme Building & Loan Association, Bristol. That business was liquidated voluntarily in 1929. From 1929 until 1938, Conroy was employed by the Eastern States Grocery Company, Philadelphia, as office manager. In 1938, he resigned to become employed by Bristol Confectionery Co., as credit, collection, and office manager. Late in 1945, Conroy was appointed Assistant Manager in charge of sales. He is now Sales Manager and owns 15% of the capital stock. The corporation carries $15,000 insurance on his life.

Carl S. Freed was born in 1896 in Pennsylvania, and is married. Beginning in 1921, he was employed by the original corporation and in 1928 was promoted to the position of Plant Superintendent. He was a general partner in the predecessor partnership and now is in charge of production. The corporation carries $15,000 insurance on his life.

F. Charles Young was born in 1896 in Michigan and is married. For 15 years he was employed as a cost accountant by the National Candy Corporation, manufacturer, Detroit, resigning in 1936 to become employed by the subject business. He now has charge of finances. Young owns 15% of the capital stock. The corporation carries $15,000 insurance on his life.

Mrs. Mary L. Lawrence is the widow of F. Bradford Lawrence who founded this business in 1914. She owns 40% of the outstanding capital stock.

(CONTINUED)

FIGURE 3

Analytical **REPORT**

D U N & B R A D S T R E E T , I N C .

BRISTOL CANDY CO. (INC.)   BRISTOL 3, PA.
Page 2 (A)   AUGUST 16 1950

__HISTORY__
STARTED: The business was started October 16, 1914 as Bristol Confectionery
Company (Inc.). From 1938 to 1944 operations were conducted as a general partnership, the partners being Chester G. Hoover, Henry T. Conroy, Carl S. Freed,
and Mrs. Mary S. Lawrence.

INCORPORATED: June 29, 1944 under Pennsylvania laws. The corporation acquired
the assets and assumed the liabilities of the predecessor partnership.
Authorized Capital Stock: 250,000 shares with a par value of $1 a share.
Outstanding Capital Stock: 150,000 shares.

__METHOD OF OPERATION__
Products: Manufactures a complete line of packaged confections, including
chocolates, hard candies, and novelty sweets (U. S. Standard Industrial Classification: #2071). 75% of the volume is in chocolates which retail from $1.00
to $2.50 a pound. Brand names used are "Bristols" and "Honey Crunch".

Distribution: To retail candy, (20%), drug (15%), grocery (10%), department (25%),
chain (25%), and variety stores (5%).
Number of Accounts: There are 2,000 active accounts.
Terms of Sale: 2% 15 days net 30.
Territory: The Eastern Seaboard states from Maine to Florida.
Seasons: Approximately 40% of the total volume is handled during October, November,
          and December.
Salesmen: 18 on salary and commission.
Employees: 125.

Production Facilities-Location: The business occupies 40,000 square feet of floor
space. Their equipment includes modern cooking, dipping, wrapping and packaging
machinery. Most of the machinery is automatic. The business is situated in a
three-story brick sprinkler-equipped building. The structure is in excellent
repair and premises are orderly.

(CONTINUED)

FIGURE 3 *(continued)*

DUN & BRADSTREET, INC.

BRISTOL CANDY CO. (INC.)
Page 3 (A)

BRISTOL 3, PA.
AUGUST 16 1950

COMPARATIVE FINANCIAL STATEMENTS

	June 30 1948	June 30 1949	June 30 1950
Cash	$ 78,171	$ 72,913	$ 76,250
U. S. Government Bonds	36,710	50,126	86,235
Accounts Receivable	38,040	29,584	68,640 —
Inventory	58,053	91,874	138,442
TOT. CUR. ASSETS	210,975	244,499	369,569
Fixed Assets	31,232	28,549	28,755
Cash Val. Life Ins.	4,154	5,047	6,416
Prepaid Expense	2,036	1,947	6,496
TOTAL ASSETS	$ 248,398	280,043	411,237
Accounts Payable	$ 20,179	9,802	10,654
Federal Income Taxes	30,395	38,712	79,131
Accruals	18,049	12,816	8,635
TOT. CUR. LIAB'S.	68,624	61,331	98,420
Common Stock	150,000	150,000	150,000
Earned Surplus	29,774	68,712	162,817
TOTAL LIABILITIES	$ 248,398	280,043	411,237
NET WORKING CAPITAL	$ 142,350	183,168	271,148
CURRENT RATIO	3.07	3.98	3.75
TANGIBLE NET WORTH	$ 179,774	218,712	312,817
Net Sales	$ 735,198	771,035	1,106,165
Net Profit	44,774	68,938	124,105
Dividends	15,000	30,000	30,000

CENTS OMITTED. The foregoing figures were prepared from annual financial reports
of the auditors, James Wheaton & Co., C.P.A.'s, Philadelphia, Pa. Statements
were received by mail and accompanied by transmittal letters signed by F. Charles
Young, Treasurer. At June 30, 1950: Accounts Receivable were net after a reserve
for bad debts of $3,106. Fixed Assets were net after reserves for depreciation of
$21,612. Inventory valued at the lower of cost or market. Fire insurance: Mer-
chandise $150,000; Fixtures and Equipment $75,000; the corporation also carries
Use & Occupancy Insurance. Annual Rent: 1% of gross sales under lease to July
1, 1956. No contingent debt reported.

(CONTINUED)

FIGURE 3 *(continued)*

Analytical REPORT

DUN & BRADSTREET, INC.

BRISTOL CANDY CO. (INC.)
Page 4 (A)

BRISTOL 3, PA.
AUGUST 16 1950

ANALYSIS

Operations of this established business were particularly profitable in the three years ended June 30, 1950. Except for dividends totaling $75,000, profits were retained primarily to defray the cost of future construction of a building to provide for the expanded needs of the business, in respect to manufacturing, storage, and distribution facilities. According to the management, sales expansion during the past fiscal year was limited only by the lack of sufficient production capacity. As Net Working Capital was more than adequate, there was no recourse to outside financial assistance during these three years. Surplus funds have been invested in Government bonds.

Financial condition at the close of each year was excellent. At June 30, 1950 inventory represented 45 days average sales. Accounts Receivable are collected well within selling terms and at June 30, 1950 reflected an average collection period of twenty-two days.

Current Investigation: On August 15, 1950, F. Charles Young, Secretary and Treasurer, stated that production continues at capacity. Demand for the company's products continues strong and orders are being booked at the rate of approximately $90,000 a month. July sales were stated to have been 10% higher than sales in July, 1949. He also stated that because of rising costs, no steps have been taken towards construction of the proposed new building.

TRADE INVESTIGATION

Sugar, the basic raw material used, is purchased under annual contract with one broker on a sight draft basis. Such drafts have been honored on presentation. Shipments are scheduled in line with production requirements. Other raw materials such as cocoa, flavorings, nut meats, and packaging materials are purchased from six suppliers. Recent experiences of the seven principal suppliers are included in the following results of a trade clearance completed August 11, 1950:

	HIGH CREDIT	OWE	PAST DUE	TERMS OF SALE	PAYMENTS
1.	$ 30,000	3,450	-0-	2%-10-Net 31	Discount
2.	25,042	---	---	2-10-30	Discount
3.	5,555	-0-	-0-	2-10	Discount
4.	5,399	-0-	-0-	2%-10-31	Discount
5.	5,000	---	---	2-10	Discount
6.	4,939	264	-0-	2-10-30	Discount
7.	3,000	-0-	-0-	2-10-Net 30	Discount
8.	659	---	---	2-10	Discount
9.	Requirements	-0-	-0-	Sight Draft	Prompt

BANKING RELATIONS

Cash balances that average in moderate to high four figures are on deposit with a local bank. Accommodation has not been requested since 1942.
8-16-50 (744   101)

FIGURE 3 *(continued)*

Credit -
MAN'S CONFIDENCE
IN MAN

Dun & Bradstreet, Inc.

MERCANTILE CREDIT REPORTS NECESSARILY DIFFER IN FORM AND IN LENGTH, DEPEND-
ING UPON THE SIZE AND COMPLEXITY OF THE CONCERN REPORTED . . . . THE POLICY
OF THE AGENCY IS TO PRESENT THE ESSENTIAL INFORMATION AS CONCISELY AS POSSIBLE.

RATING
UNCHANGED

5072-5251   (S) CD 8 AUGUST 14 1950
ADAMSON HARDWARE CO.   WHOL. & RET.   LITCHFIELD, ILL.
                                                           MONTGOMERY COUNTY
                                                           294-300 MAIN STREET

Miss Joan M. Adamson, Genl. Partner   Miss Carol T. Adamson, Genl. Partner

RATING: - -

SUMMARY

THIS BUSINESS WAS STARTED IN 1895 BY CARL H. ADAMSON, THE FATHER OF THE PRES-
ENT PARTNERS. HE DIED IN 1945, AND IN 1947, HIS TWO DAUGHTERS ASSUMED OWNERSHIP.
PROFITS HAVE BEEN EARNED IN RECENT YEARS ON A MATERIALLY INCREASED SALES VOLUME.
AT DECEMBER 31, 1949, TANGIBLE NET WORTH WAS $249,540, AND DEBT WAS HEAVY. ASSETS
ARE REPRESENTED LARGELY BY INVENTORIES AND THERE IS GENERAL SLOWNESS IN TRADE PAY-
MENTS. BANK LOANS ARE USED STEADILY.

HISTORY

The business name was registered by the partners on March 15, 1947.
    This enterprise was started in 1895 as a hardware jobbing business by the
late Carl H. Adamson, who subsequently expanded to include both wholesale and retail sales. On February 13, 1945, Adamson died, and his will bequeathed all his
real estate, personal and business assets to his two daughters, Joan M. Adamson
and Carol T. Adamson. The Estate continued the business until 1947, when the
present partners assumed equal ownership. The partners, born in 1891, and 1893,
respectively, are single, and are not active in the management of the business.
    The active management of this enterprise has been left in the hands of Robert
Casey, born 1898, married. He was formerly employed as Sales Manager by Thomas
Hardware & Supply Co., St. Louis, Mo., for a period of twenty years until becoming
employed here in 1946.

METHOD OF OPERATION

PRODUCTS: Wholesales (80% of sales) and retails (20%) hardware, paint, sporting
goods, electrical appliances, linoleum, fire arms, cement and roofing materials.
(U.S. Standard Industrial Classifications: #5072 and #5251). Sales of hardware
alone represent about 65% of the total volume. Merchandise sold is in a medium
priced range.

DISTRIBUTION: At wholesale to dealers (50%), lumber yards (30%), factories (10%),
            and contractors (10%). Retail distribution is to local residents
            and farmers.
Number of Accounts: About 400 active wholesale accounts are sold.
Territory: Surrounding radius of about 80 miles.
Terms: 2%-10th Prox and cash.
Salesmen: Four salaried salesmen.
Seasons: Peak season around March, with low points around January and February,
            and again around July and August.
Employees: In addition to the salesmen, there are fifteen store and office em-
            ployees.

FACILITIES: Store occupies the combined ground floor space of three adjoining
buildings, with warehouse space being utilized in buildings to the rear. Four
trucks are used for delivery purposes, and a siding connects the property with
tracks of the Illinois Central Railroad.

FINANCIAL INFORMATION

	Dec. 31, 1947	Dec. 31, 1948	Dec. 31, 1949
Current Assets	$ 236,967	$ 538,884	$ 494,611
Current Liabilities	31,521	292,808	283,080
Net Working Capital	205,446	246,076	211,531
Tangible Net Worth	206,340	272,629	249,540
Net Sales	250,622	523,408	889,650

(CONTINUED)

FIGURE 3 *(continued)*

Credit -
MAN'S CONFIDENCE
IN MAN

Dun & Bradstreet, Inc.
MERCANTILE CREDIT REPORTS NECESSARILY DIFFER IN FORM AND IN LENGTH, DEPEND-
ING UPON THE SIZE AND COMPLEXITY OF THE CONCERN REPORTED   THE POLICY
OF THE AGENCY IS TO PRESENT THE ESSENTIAL INFORMATION AS CONCISELY AS POSSIBLE.

RATING
UNCHANGED

ADAMSON HARDWARE CO.

(S) CD 8 AUGUST 14 1950
WHOL. & RET.

LITCHFIELD, ILL.
(PAGE #2)

FINANCIAL INFORMATION (Cont'd)
From inventory as of December 31, 1949-cents omitted:

ASSETS		LIABILITIES	
Cash on Hand & in Banks	$ 8,519	Accts. Pay.	$ 148,949
Accts. Rec. (Whol) (A)	46,622	Notes Pay. Bank	125,000
Accts. Rec. (Ret) (B)	14,206	Notes Pay. Trucks	3,365
Merchandise	425,264	Commissions Pay.	3,700
		Accrd. Wages & Tax	2,066
Total Current	494,611	Total Current	283,080
Furn. & Fixts. (C)	7,984		
Real Est. & Bldgs. (D)	22,814	Investment-Joan M.	
Trucks (E)	5,925	Adamson	127,135
Prepaid	1,286	Investment-Carol T.	
		Adamson	122,405
Total Assets	532,620	Total	532,620

(A) Net of reserve for bad debts of $8,516. (B) Net of reserve for bad debts
of $368. (C) Net of reserve for depreciation of $1,398. (D) Net of reserve for
depreciation of $2,358. (E) Net of reserve for depreciation of $2,590.

Operating figures for the year ended December 31, 1949 showed total sales
$889,650; gross profit on sales $179,604; operating profit $39,325; net profit
before income tax $28,615.

Reconciliation of Net Worth figures revealed that as of January 1, 1949, the
Net Worth was $272,629, evenly divided between Miss Joan M. Adamson and Miss
Carol T. Adamson. During 1949, Miss Joan M. Adamson withdrew $23,487, and after
considering that and her one-half of the 1949 net profit, which amounted to
$14,308, her investment in the business was $127,135.

During 1949, Miss Carol T. Adamson withdrew $28,217, so that after consider-
ing her portion of the 1949 net profit, her capital was $122,405.

The foregoing statement was obtained in an interview with the management on
February 10, 1950. It was stated that the statement was based on an audit by
Williams Kearns, C.P.A., Litchfield, Ill. Inventory valued at the lower of cost
or market. No Contingent Debt reported.

-----o-----

For a number of years, sales of this concern were fairly steady, but increased
materially in 1948, and again in 1949, when they reached the highest level in the
history of this business. Sales were built up through intensive promotional
effort following the death of the former owner. In building up sales volume,
however, inventories were considerably increased, a portion of which increase
was financed through bank accommodation. In this respect, the bank loans as of
December 31, 1949 consisted of $55,000 owing to one bank, $45,000 to another bank,
and $25,000 to a third financial institution. The increased inventories also
brought about increases in Accounts Payable, and the partnership became predominantly slow in the meeting of trade obligations.

It was stated on August 11, 1950 by Robert Casey, General Manager, that steps
are being taken to reduce inventories and to put trade payments on a current
basis. Purchasing has been curtailed, prices have been reduced, particularly on
items subject to reduced customer demand, and several employees have been released.
Detailed interim figures were not available, however, it was stated that sales
volume continues to hold even with last year, and that operations have been profitable. Bank debt amounted to $115,000.

Accounts are maintained at three local banks where balances average in high
four to low five figures. Loans have been granted on own paper and borrowings
have been steady since early in 1948.

(CONTINUED)

FIGURE 3 *(continued)*

Dun & Bradstreet, Inc.

MERCANTILE CREDIT REPORTS NECESSARILY DIFFER IN FORM AND IN LENGTH, DEPEND-
ING UPON THE SIZE AND COMPLEXITY OF THE CONCERN REPORTED . . . . THE POLICY
OF THE AGENCY IS TO PRESENT THE ESSENTIAL INFORMATION AS CONCISELY AS POSSIBLE.

RATING
UNCHANGED

(S) CD 8 AUGUST 14 1950

ADAMSON HARDWARE CO.   WHOL. & RET.   LITCHFIELD, ILL.
                                                                (PAGE #3)

HC	OWE	P.DUE	TERMS	PAYMENTS Aug. 12, 1950	
4850			1-10-30	Disc.	Sold 1945 to 1949
2492			2-10-30	Disc.	Sold 1925 to date
7740	2185		2-10-60	Ppt. to	Sold yrs. to 1949
				Slow 160	
14803	10070	5875	1-10-30	Slow 6-7 Mos.	Sold yrs. to date
7550	2650		2-10-60	Slow 30	Sold yrs.
7500	2900	1900	2-10-30	Slow 60-90	Sold yrs. to date
5000	5000	5000	1-10-30	Slow 120	Sold yrs. to date
5000	1588	1588	2-10-30	Slow 150	Sold yrs. to date
5000	1000	1000		Slow 60	Sold yrs.
4475	1642	1642	2-15	Slow 18	Sold 1944 to date
			Prox		
4134	2090	525	2-10-30	Slow 60	Sold yrs.
3839			2-10-30	Slow 30-40	Sold yrs.
2258	330		1-10-30	Slow 30-40	Sold yrs. to date
1738	708	708	1-10-EOM	Slow 120	Sold yrs. to date
1663	596	558	1-10-30	Slow 120	Sold yrs.

In addition to the above, twenty other suppliers also reported selling the
account in amounts as high as $1,600, on various terms. Of these additional sup-
pliers, four reported bills being discounted, five indicated payments prompt, one
showed payments anticipated to discount, eight indicated bills being met slowly;
two reported payments ranging from prompt to slow.
8-14-50 (744-1 29)

FIGURE 3 *(continued)*

Credit-
MAN'S CONFIDENCE
IN MAN . . . .

Dun & Bradstreet, Inc.

MERCANTILE CREDIT REPORTS NECESSARILY DIFFER IN FORM AND IN LENGTH, DEPEND-
ING UPON THE SIZE AND COMPLEXITY OF THE CONCERN REPORTED . . . THE POLICY
OF THE AGENCY IS TO PRESENT THE ESSENTIAL INFORMATION AS CONCISELY AS POSSIBLE

RATING:
UNCHANGED

5912
CITY PHARMACY
    BUTLER, GEORGE S., OWNER

CD 5 FEBRUARY 25 1950

ASHLAND 8 MASS
MIDDLESEX COUNTY
45 MAIN STREET

RATING: G 3

SYNOPSIS

BACKGROUND: A registered pharmacist, owner started here in 1942. Was formerly em-
ployed as a pharmacist.
NET WORTH: $9,901   SALES: $43,927 (1949)
PAYMENTS: Discount and Prompt
CONDITION & TREND: Cash covers small current debt. Operating profitably; sales are
going ahead.

HISTORY

The style, City Pharmacy, was registered by George S. Butler on July 24, 1942.
Butler is 39, married, and was born in Berlin, N.H. He was graduated from the
College of Pharmacy, Temple University, Philadelphia, in 1933 and became employed as
a pharmacist by a Philadelphia drug chain, Sun Ray Stores. On July 27, 1942, Butler
bought this business from Elwin Jones for $5,000 cash which was derived from savings
and a $1,000 loan, since repaid, from his father.

OPERATION-LOCATION

Retails drugs, compounds prescriptions, and operates a soda fountain. About
10% of sales are on 30 day terms; remainder for cash. Prescriptions account for 10%
of sales and the fountain provides 25% of volume. Store occupies space of 15 x 35
feet in the shopping section of this suburban town and is well equipped. Two are employed. This one story frame building, located on a corner, is modern and in good repair.

FINANCIAL INFORMATION

An inventory statement of December 31 1949–cents omitted:

ASSETS			LIABILITIES		
Cash	$	1,181	Accts Pay	$	907
Accts Rec		206	Accruals		116
Mdse		7,659			
Total Current		9,046	Total Current		1,023
Fixts		1,671			
Prepaid & Deferred		207	NET WORTH		9,901
Total Assets		10,924	Total		10,924

Sales for 1949, $43,927; Gross Profit, $13,929; Expenses (including owner's sal-
ary) $11,509; Net Profit, $2,420; Withdrawals, None. Monthly rent, $85; the lease
expires July 1, 1950. Fire insurance: On merchandise, $8,000; on fixtures, $1,500.
Signed February 24, 1950 CITY PHARMACY by George S. Butler, Owner
No public accountant indicated
Received by mail

———O———

This business has been profitable from the beginning and Butler has maintained
his affairs in good shape. A part of the moderate annual earnings have been retained
in the business with the original investment having almost doubled since the business
was started in July, 1942.

HC	OWE	P DUE	TERMS	PAYMENTS Feb 15 1950	
350	225		2-10-60	Disc	Sold yrs
216	150		2-15-N60	Disc	Sold 1942 to date
210			2-10-60	Disc	Sold some time
192	121		Reg	Disc	Sold 1-46 to date
196				Ppt	Sold to date
75			2-10-EOM	Ppt	Sold 1942 to 2-50
2-25-50	(121 88)				

FIGURE 3 *(continued)*

THE HOOPER-HOLMES BUREAU, INC.
CREDIT REPORT - INDIVIDUAL
Form 630-19 (1-46)
CONFIDENTIAL

STAMP RED BALL HERE

File No._____
Bank or Trade References

B—INDIVIDUAL
The purpose of this report is to determine the desirability of the person named below as a credit risk.

VERY IMPORTANT
Is name spelled correctly? If initials only appear, what is first name?

SAMPLE REPORT

Name   T——————: GUS

Residence Address

Occupation   Luncheonette
Business Address   New York City: 930 Tenth Avenue
Name of firm or employer
Age

Date, etc.   7-5-50-B   Co. No.   1452

1. A—Do you personally know the above named person?   B—How long have you or each of your informants known him?
   C—How many informants have been contacted?
   D—Describe them. (Neighbors, employer, business associates, bank, etc.)
   E—If he has been at the present address less than one year, what was former address?

   1. A no   B over 1 to 10 years   CONTACTS
   C 4
   D business trade, associates, neighbors
   E —

2. A—What is his age? (If under 21, give exact age. Minors cannot make a valid contract.)
   B—Of what extraction is he? (Italian, Polish, Greek, etc.) C—Race? (White, Negro, etc.)
   D—Is he married?   E—How many dependents has he?

   2. A 37   STANDING
   B Greek   c white
   D yes   E

3. A—Is his reputation as to habits and morality good? (If not, what is the nature of the reports against him?)
   B—Is he suspected of intemperance in the use of drugs or liquors?
   C—Is his REPUTATION as to business reliability, at all QUESTIONABLE? (If so, explain in detail)

   3. A yes
   B no
   C no

4. A—What is his occupation?
   B—If employed, what is the name of his employer?
   C—How long so employed?   D—Give nature of business.

   4. A —   OCCUPATION
   B —
   C —   D

5. If employed in present position less than one year
   A—Give name of former employer.
   B—Nature of business?   C—Position?

   5. A —
   B —   C

6. A—If in business for himself, how long so engaged?
   B—What is the nature of the business?
   C—How successful is he in business? (State whether very successful, moderately so, or unsuccessful.)

   6. A over 1½ years
   B luncheonette
   C moderately

7. Is he now or has he ever been identified with any unlawful business? If so, explain fully under "Remarks."

   7. no

FIGURE 4

FINANCES

8. A—About how much do you think he earns annually?   8. A $3,600

B—Are there other wage earners in the family?   B no

C—If so, give approximate total income of other wage earners.   C $no

D—Does he pay his bills promptly?   D yes

9. A—About what do you think he is worth?   9. A $4,000

B—What does his worth consist of? (Real estate, savings, etc.)   B savings, business   B $

10. A—Does he own his home?   B—If so, what is its approximate value?   10. A no

C—If not, how much rent does he pay?   C $50 month

11. Is he in financial difficulties or has he had reverses?   11.   no

12. Did you learn of any suits or judgments against him?   12.   no

13. Is the reputation of his family good for meeting obligations?   13.   good

14. REMARKS: Give details of any incomplete or unfavorable answers above. Head your paragraphs under the four titles below and make some comment under each.
   (1) CONTACTS. Show how close informants' contact has been and whether they are in a position to really know about this person's affairs.
   (2) STANDING. Cover habits, associates, home life and reputation.
   (3) OCCUPATION. Cover business record.
   (4) FINANCES. Cover credit reputation.

This report is on ___Mr.___   ___Gus___   _____   ___T_____
Please repeat FULL NAME (Mr.—Mrs.—Miss)   (First name)   (Middle name or initial)   (Last name)
CORRECTLY SPELLED

CONTACTS:

   Business trade associates and neighbors. Known for 1 to 10 years.

STANDING:

   Your subject is a Greek of 37 years of age, white, married, and residing with his wife in this walk-up apartment located in a working-class residential section here at 272 W 25th Street, New York City, where he has so resided for over five years. He came to this country from Greece in 1936 and is a citizen. He has a good general reputation as to habits, morals, and associates, and no criticisms rendered.

H.H.B.
B-Ind.

FILE INFORMATION MUST BE INCLUDED.   (CONTINUE OVER)

FIGURE 4 (continued)

OCCUPATION:

Since coming to this country in 1936, subject has been identified with the restaurant business and was formerly employed in the trade working for various restaurants throughout New York City. For the past 1½ years now, he has been engaged in business as the owner of this counter-type luncheonette here at 930 10th Avenue. This is a small-sized coffee-pot, counter-type restaurant catering to the local factory workers and cab drivers in this section of New York City. Serves no liquor or beer here and only time that he does any business is at noon-time. At any other time of the day, the place is always empty. Section is composed of numerous restaurants here which are cleaner and better organized. Competition is keen here and subject has all to do to stay in business here.

FINANCES:

Worth is estimated at $4,000 consisting of business and savings, and income is estimated at $3,600 per annum which is from business. He has a good financial reputation and pays all bills when due. Learn of no outstanding debts. Carries banking connections at the Bank of Athens at 33rd Street and 7th Avenue. Has a saving account here and no information available on same.

7-7-50 Ken   FULL-TIME INSPECTOR   NEW YORK OFFICE

FIGURE 4 (*continued*)

its greater prestige and the personal call technique give it an entrance where entry would not be accorded the special agency. This method of operation should provide the general agency with pertinent credit data that would not always be available to the special agency. This statement is undoubtedly true where the special agency has not gained a substantial support of the industry, although it would not necessarily apply where the special agency has made itself strong in gaining prestige and support.

The special agency lays claim to superiority through the development of highly trained reporters who possess special know-how. These reporters have the opportunity to become acquainted with the intricacies of the industry, its larger houses, the methods of doing business, and the trends of the industry in general. These reporters soon learn the nature of the personalities and the backgrounds of both the successful and unsuccessful businessmen who operate the individual business enterprises in the industry they cover. This intimacy between management and reporter arises from the narrower industrial or geographical area that the special agency covers. Although these are the factors which are of infinite value to the reporter in the special fields, the same information is also available to the skilled reporter who handles a specialized division of the general agency.

One of the drawbacks to some of the specialized agencies is the lack of speedy and accurate national coverage through the personal call. Since not all of the special agencies use the direct reporting system in every credit investigation, they must rely upon correspondents or local attorneys to obtain information from distant firms or, in some cases, trust to their ability to obtain the information from nearby subscribers. As a result accuracy suffers.

The work of the specialized agencies may be observed on a number of different fronts: some agencies concern themselves with reporting upon individuals; others make investigations of business firms and individuals; and still others concentrate upon business firms alone.

The chief groups that require credit reports upon individuals consist of commercial banks and trust companies, those hiring employees, those underwriting insurance, and those permitting installment purchases. The preparation of credit reports upon individuals for these purposes gives rise to far different problems from the investigation and preparation of credit reports upon commercial and industrial business. Although the technical knowledge of investigation, preparation, and editing may be less rigorous in some respects than that required in reporting on the complex and intricate peculiarities of business firms, this work also demands special experience and training.

The Hooper-Holmes Bureau, Inc. Hooper-Holmes Bureau, Inc., started

business in 1899 as a clearing house for life, accident, and health insurance claims. The main office is in New York City, and 75 branch offices are located throughout the United States and Canada.

The principal function of this business is the collection and preparation of reports upon individuals who are applying for insurance contracts. This activity constitutes about three-fourths of its business. Reports are also made for finance companies and time payment merchandisers; market research is conducted for radio networks, publishers, distributors, and advertising agencies.

The credit reports made by the Hooper-Holmes Bureau, Inc., are characterized as the questionnaire type, in contrast to the narrative and analytical type of the mercantile agencies. In the large cities the reporters are employed on a salary basis, while in the smaller communities they are paid a given sum for each report. The questionnaire report does not provide for a rating; so, of course, the bureau does not publish a rating book.

There are 13 main questions covered in the report. These questions cover such items as the individual's annual salary, other sources of income, his habits of paying bills, his net worth, and his standing in the neighborhood. The report is closed with the reporter's description of the history and occupation of the individual and his financial reputation.

The Retail Credit Company. The other agency of national scope reporting upon consumers is the Retail Credit Company. Headquarters are located in Atlanta, Georgia, and there are over 100 branches in the United States and Canada. Like Hooper-Holmes Bureau, Inc., the chief activity consists of filling the requests for pertinent information about individuals called for by insurance companies. The reports, which consist of the question and answer type, are constructed to meet the particular needs of the subscriber requesting the information. These reports may be divided into six general groups:

1. Credit and character information of farmers.
2. Credit and character information about individuals other than farmers.
3. Character and credit information on proprietorships and firms.
4. Delinquent purchase reports presenting information on which to judge the collectibility of past due accounts.
5. Personal history reports upon individuals being considered for employment.
6. Special investigations not covered in the above reports.

Reporters gather their information by interviewing such sources as bankers, creditors, employers and others. All information is confirmed through records where that is possible. The reports are made up cur-

rently, so that the report gives the status of the individual at the time of editing.

Besides the agencies that provide special investigations upon individuals, there is another group that issues reports of a similar nature, but upon a much wider field of subjects. This group prepares credit reports upon law and accounting firms, investment bankers and counselors, brokers, and thousands of individuals who make a living in the financial world. The reports are of a personal, intimate character and are used largely by the same subscribers of the Hooper-Holmes Bureau, Inc., and the Retail Credit Company.

Bishop's Service, Inc. This agency established in 1897 confines its activity to New York City and its immediate surroundings. Investigations are made both of individuals and concerns of prominence and of questionable integrity. The reports contain antecedent information, opinions of outsiders, and a checking of bank accounts. These reports are prepared in letter form and contain neither summaries nor ratings. The chief subscribers to the service are commercial banks, trust companies, brokers and other financial institutions in New York City.

Proudfoot's Commercial Agency, Inc. This agency was begun in 1900 by Louis Proudfoot, a New York attorney, to provide information for attorneys in the New York City area. As in the case of Bishop's Service, Inc., the reporting is prepared and edited in the form of a special letter. The subjects reported upon consist of corporations, partnerships, proprietorships, and individuals of almost every line of business. While the activities of this service are very broad in scope, most of the reports are upon concerns and individuals employed in the geographical area of New York City.

The information in the reports covers such items as the age, place of birth, kind of education, and business connections of the individual. Judgments, bankruptcies, and law suits, if any, are reported. Also, there is a section on financial responsibility, habits of paying bills, financial integrity, and business reputation.

The last group, composed of special mercantile agencies which prepare credit reports on business firms, will cover selected but representative agencies of this class. These are the National Credit Office, Inc., Lyon Furniture Mercantile Agency, the Produce Reporter Company, the Lumberman's Credit Association, Inc., the Shoe and Leather Mercantile Agency, and The Exchange Bureaus.

The National Credit Office. Organized in 1900 this agency has grown from inconspicuousness to be the largest of the special mercantile agencies. In the textile field it covers manufacturers of clothing and yarns; textile dealers and jobbers; converters, manufacturers, and wholesalers of clothing goods; manufacturers of wearing apparel; and chain stores,

department stores, and other retailers specializing in piece goods. Besides covering the textile field, the National Credit Office has extended into reporting on manufacturing in the following fields: rubber goods, paints and varnishes, leather products, furniture, floor covering and other household furnishings, steel products, automobiles and airplanes, radio and electronics, and household electrical appliances. No retail concerns are covered in these reports except (a) chain stores in the respective industries in which the agency operates, (b) department stores, and (c) large furniture stores.

Also, the National Credit Office has developed a bank service department which issues special reports on concerns selling "commercial paper" on the open market. The notes of the issuing business are classified as to the desirability or lack of desirability. This report is of particular value to the banker who has not had the opportunity to study the affairs of business outside his usual industrial or geographical area.

Reports of the National Credit Office. The reports of this agency are prepared and issued in such a manner that they can be separated into parts. There is an antecedent section which gives the names and history of the directors, a brief history of the company, methods of operation, and the name of the concern's banks. The "current information" part provides summarized financial statements of the past three years, ledger information given by suppliers, and an intense analysis based upon the financial statements and trade reports. The last section of the report consists of a photostatic reproduction of the customer's latest financial statement and the accountant's verification of such statement. The photostatic reproduction has the advantage of eliminating errors of transcription which are bound to occur in dealing with thousands of financial statements.

Certain other features of these reports are distinctive. At the bottom of the "Current Information" section there appears the "line of credit" which is deemed advisable. The amount of the "line of credit" is determined by estimating the seasonal purchase requirements of the firm and dividing this figure by the number of suppliers.

The one fundamental difference in the operation of all departments of the National Credit Office, Inc., is found in the steel industry division, which has found it advantageous to publish two reference books monthly. The ratings included make these reference books valuable sources for sales leads in the steel industry as well as for credit reference desk manuals.

Two other services are provided by the agency. It prepares material for the annual meetings and participates in the discussion at these meetings of the 15 groups of credit men in the textile, rubber, steel, and paint and varnish departments. The agency also provides a sales service

for its subscribers. This service involves the use of a card index on all active concerns in each industry covered by the agency. The card includes such information as the products manufactured, the price range where necessary to indicate the quality of materials used, and an approximate estimate of annual sales.

Lyon Furniture Mercantile Agency. Dating from 1876, the Lyon Furniture Mercantile Agency is one of the older mercantile services. It specializes in credit reporting upon manufacturers, wholesalers and retailers of furniture, floor covering, upholstering, bedding, interior decorating, undertaking, and allied lines of business in the United States. It has a head office located in New York City and six branch offices in key trade centers of the country.

Rating book. The Lyon reference book is known in the trade as the "Red Book." It is issued semiannually in January and July with weekly reports and supplements. The ratings in the "Red Book" follow much the same procedure as those of the general agency ratings of capital and credit, with the exception that in the "Red Book" there is given an additional or third rating called a pay rating. These pay ratings indicate whether the subject takes advantage of discounts and whether he is prompt, medium, slow, or very slow in making payments.

The weekly supplements provide changes in ratings, the names of new firms, dissolutions, successions, removals, assignments, receiverships, trusteeships, failures, bankruptcy petitions, current business changes, and accounts placed for collection. These data provide the semiannual edition with an up-to-date record of all newly assigned ratings and other valuable information to credit men. Available in pocket size are travelers' and salesmen's editions of the "Red Book" covering any state or group of states.

Subscribers may obtain additional credit information by cooperating in weekly interchange of trade experiences. This information is gathered by means of a weekly "tracer sheet." This sheet requests from subscribers their experience with concerns selected because of some unusual circumstances for investigation. When the "tracer sheets" are in, the tabulated results are mailed to those subscribers who have cooperated by submitting their experiences with the various names listed.

In addition to its service in supplying credit information, Lyon also performs a service for subscribers in the collection of delinquent accounts. The collection department thereby becomes a valuable source of information for its credit reporting division.

The Produce Reporter Company. This company was established in 1901 and its first "Blue Book" ratings appeared in 1904. Its headquarters are in Chicago, and it reports on dealers in fruits, vegetables, and other food products in the United States, Canada, and Cuba. The

information is given to subscribers through reports and the rating book. So-called credit sheets are mailed each week and cover important items to the produce industry. These include changes in names, unwarranted rejections of shipments, bankruptcies, and other vital data. Confidential reports supplement the "Blue Book" ratings. Knowledge that a concern pays its bills and possesses sufficient capital is not enough upon which to base a credit decision in the produce business. The owner's reputation for fair dealings is particularly important in this field. More than usual attention is given to fulfillment of agreements under adverse conditions and liberality in the adjustment of disputed matters. Because contracts are often made verbally or by telegram (and also because of the nature of perishability in the food industry), moral responsibility looms high.

The Produce Reporter Company makes available to subscribers business opinions regarding questions of trade practices; it also supplies drafts for collection purposes, offers facilities for collecting past due accounts, and provides a service for establishing the grade and quality of produce when disputes arise over the basis of settlement of contested items.

Lumberman's Credit Association, Inc. This agency began in 1876 and in 1933 combined with its competitor, the Lumberman's Blue Book, Inc., which has been operated as one firm for the Lumberman's Manufacturers Association, a trade association. This association provides a credit information and collection service for all manufacturers, wholesalers, and retailers in the lumber and woodworking trades. The credit reports cover antecedent data, the current financial statement, an analysis of the financial statement, a summary of the credit risk, and finally a rating. The rating system is quite elaborate and comprehensive. A rating book is published twice a year (in spring and fall) with supplements added twice a week. These supplements contain notices of judgments, law suits, creditors' meetings, changes of ownership, changes in ratings, and other current items.

Shoe and Leather Mercantile Agency. The Shoe and Leather Mercantile Agency was established in 1879 at Boston, which has remained the head office. This agency prepares credit reports on all tanners of leather and all retail and wholesale manufacturers of shoes, handbags, luggage, leather belts and leather novelties. Specialists conduct investigations and edit credit reports. The reports contain a brief history of the chief personnel and the business of an organization, comparative summary financial statements for the last four years, a general comment on recent trends in the business, and a credit rating. The rating form is somewhat similar to that of Dun and Bradstreet, Inc., but more comprehensive. The ratings subdivide firms down to $300 of capital while Dun and Bradstreet, Inc., has no division below $1,000.

The "key to code numbers" while not as extensive as that of Lyon Mercantile Agency, does nevertheless allow considerable space for a wide variety of situations. The reporting service is supplemented by a series of four reference books, published in January, April, July and October. They contain ratings on all firms in the shoe, leather, and allied lines of industry and commerce.

The Exchange Bureaus. So far this survey has concerned itself with examining credit information from the point of view of the procedure, practices, and services offered by the general or the special mercantile agency. Historically, direct exchange of credit data among creditors came first, but this method has many drawbacks and inconveniences. To overcome these hindrances incident to the direct exchange of ledger experience, a number of intermediaries developed. Few organizations existed prior to 1900 having as their main objective the collection of complete ledger figures and the ability to make them quickly available to the respective interchanges. A few credit exchange bureaus sprang up after the turn of the century, but it was not until 1912 that a central bureau was opened in St. Louis to enable the various local bureaus to share information. In 1919 the National Association of Credit Men took over the central bureau at St. Louis and has operated it ever since under the Credit Interchange Bureau Department of the National Association of Credit Men.

The Credit Exchange Bureau is an intermediary only for the purpose of assembling and distributing of ledger facts. It has conscientiously avoided the offering of trade and bank opinions, financial interpretation, summaries or ratings. It has left to the individual credit man the task of determining whether each order or risk should be assumed or rejected. It is owned and operated by creditors themselves. The creditor subscribers pay only for the cost of operation.

Fifty-seven bureaus, covering most of the major and minor markets, plus the clearing and coordinating unit at St. Louis constitute the National Association of Credit Men's system. All of the local bureaus are owned and operated under the supervision of local members cooperating with the National Association.

Upon becoming a member of a local bureau each participant supplies the bureau with a list of his accounts and adds to that new accounts as they are opened. This group of listed accounts is then broken down at the bureau and recorded under the names of each customer identified by a code number placed after the customer's name. The name and code of each customer is placed on a card. Thus, when an inquiry is made to the bureau of a customer, the card will show the code numbers of all bureau members who have been or are creditors of the customer. Current checking can be accomplished with ease and speed.

The information is then made available to the central bureau in St. Louis. Through this device the central office has a file which gives a complete picture of all markets in which a firm has purchased merchandise or is attempting to purchase merchandise. The basic responsibility, however, for compiling and writing reports resides with the local bureaus.

The channel of operation proceeds in the following manner: the subscriber inquires at the local bureau about a customer; the card at the local bureau indicates creditors in the immediate locality which can be asked for information; a further check at the central bureau in St. Louis indicates other markets in which the customer buys. The local bureaus of these markets are asked by the central office to report the experience of their subscribers who have dealt with the customer. Upon arrival at the central office, all of this information is assembled and prepared and presented as an analysis of credit standing. When completed, the details are made available to all the bureaus in those areas where the customer has been buying or is expecting to buy.

The report to the subscriber from the local bureau presents a summary under the following headings of actual credit experience of the concerns that have been dealing with the subject under inquiry:

1. Business classification
2. Date of last sale
3. Length of time the customer has been sold
4. Amount owing
5. Highest recent credit
6. Amount past due
7. Unfilled or first orders
8. Terms of sale required of customer
9. Manner of payment
10. Comments.

Other activities of the association. The association publishes a manual on commercial law pertaining to credit and an official monthly magazine. The association maintains a department that investigates and prosecutes perpetrators of commercial fraud. It also sponsors group meetings for the discussion of credit ideas and related matters. In addition, the association has developed a collection department which offers several types of services to its members for hastening the payment and the final collection of past due accounts.

Security Rating Agencies

There has developed a type of service presented in manual form which covers a wide variety of financial and statistical data dealing with corporations. Whereas these manuals are primarily designed as an aid to the

investor, the wide scope of statistical data presented serves many other purposes. Concerns which deal with industrial, public utility and railroad corporations, and fairly large municipalities will find a substantial amount of valuable statistical and financial information in the various manuals.

The first of the four services discussed below deals in the highly specialized field of insurance, whereas the other three cover wider fields of reporting.

Alfred M. Best Company, Inc. Out of the disturbed condition of unusually rapid growth of insurance companies in the late 1890's, the Alfred M. Best Company was organized to investigate integrity, financial standing, management, and benefit paying ability of all classes of insurance companies.

There are about 4,000 stock, mutual, and reciprocal organizations underwriting life, fire, and casualty insurance in the United States today. Each of these companies is thoroughly checked, and the results are compiled and published in manual form by Alfred M. Best Company. The chief subscribers to these manuals are banks, trust companies, brokers, insurance companies, and, in general, any business or individual who is a large purchaser of life, fire, or casualty insurance.

The annual publications consist of the following:

1. *Best's Fire and Marine Insurance Reports*
2. *Best's Casualty and Insurance Reports*
3. *Best's Life Insurance Reports*
4. *Life Charts of Recommended Companies*
5. *Life Underwriters' Guide—Underwriting Practices*
6. *Insurance Guide with Key Ratings*
7. *Recommended Insurance Attorneys with Digest of Insurance Laws*
8. *Directory of Adjusters and Investigators*
9. *Digest of Insurance Stocks*
10. *Aggregates and Averages*
11. *Reproduction of Principal Schedules of Casualty and Surety Insurance Companies.*

In addition to the above annual publications, there are three monthly publications which cover recent developments and news in the fields of life, fire, and casualty insurance, and safety engineering.

Alfred M. Best Company, Inc., obtains its information chiefly from two sources. Financial statements are obtained directly from insurance companies themselves. These statements are analyzed and a general rating is constructed on the basis of this analysis. Each financial statement is carefully examined to determine liquidity, soundness and diversification of assets, yield, and the ratio of investment to resources. Each insurance company in the United States is legally required to file an annual

financial statement with the state insurance department of each state in which the company is licensed to operate. These financial statements are available to Alfred M. Best Company, Inc. They show the assets, liabilities, income and disbursements and various other schedules which reflect the financial standing of the company concerned. This valuable information serves as a confirming check upon the material obtained from other sources.

Most banking houses utilize the annual reports and manuals that cover the fire insurance companies and casualty insurance companies. Besides the annual volumes there is a continuous up-to-date service provided upon request of the bank. Since the mortgage and loan departments of banks are concerned with adequate fire and casualty insurance protection of properties on which they hold mortgage liens, this service is needed by them. Trust companies and administrators handling estate properties are served in the same manner.

Moody's Investors Service, Inc., Standard and Poor's Corporation, and Fitch Publishing Company, Inc., do not specialize in the manner of Alfred M. Best Company, Inc., but cover a much wider variety of corporations and companies.

Moody's Investors Service, Inc. This organization began publishing a railroad manual in 1909 and later extended into the annual publication of manuals on public utilities, industrials, governments and municipals, and banks and financial companies. The names and coverage of the volumes are as follows:

Kind of Corporation Reported	Approximate Number of Firms Covered
Railroads	1,400
Public Utilities	1,700
Industrials	4,400
Governments and Municipals	40,000
Banks, Insurance, Real Estate and Investment Trusts	7,600

The above volumes contain information of value to the investor in the form of financial statements, a list of the directors, the earnings and dividend record, outstanding equity and debt securities, and the high and low market price of the company's securities in recent years.

Standard and Poor's Corporation. This service organization was incorporated to combine Poor's Publishing Service and Standard Statistics Company, Inc. The present concern publishes financial and statistical daily, weekly, and monthly information on corporations with outstanding securities. The information is issued in six volumes in the form of looseleaf binders which make possible the substitution of up-to-date material for that which has become obsolete. These six volumes are classified alphabetically and contain comprehensive facts covering the names of

directors and officers of the business, a history of the business, and comparative balance sheets and income statements.

A seventh loose-leaf volume known as *Daily Corporation News* provides up-to-the-minute news on the concerns listed in the six encyclopedic volumes.

Standard and Poor's Corporation offers a supplementary yearly service which includes a large volume published under the title of *Poor's Register of Directors and Executives, United States and Canada.* This volume contains the names of individuals who serve as officers and directors in the more important corporations in the United States and Canada. If an individual serves more than one corporation as an officer or director, this is indicated. The corporations are further classified both under industry and product; thus it is possible to check on the leading corporations in an industry or in the manufacture of a certain product.

Other services of particular interest to investors include semiweekly dividend reports, daily call service on bonds, an investor's guide to stocks designed for brokerage houses, bond reports, standard trade and industry reports, and unlisted securities reports.

Fitch Publishing Company, Inc. This company publishes a loose-leaf type of service in two volumes known as the stock and bond manual. These volumes are augmented with such services as a trade section, daily news, dividend records, called bonds, and market surveys. Besides the loose-leaf manual the company prepares a special bound volume known as the "Fitch Bond Book." This book has as its chief feature a rating and descriptive service on about 7,000 active industries, public utilities, railroads, and government and real estate corporations.

Suggested Readings

Beckman, T. N., *Credits and Collections* in Theory and Practices, 4th Edition. New York: McGraw-Hill Book Company, Inc., 1939.

Ettinger, R. P., and D. E. Golieb, *Credits and Collections,* 3rd Edition. New York: Prentice-Hall, Inc., 1949.

Foulke, R. A., *The Sinews of American Commerce.* New York: Dun and Bradstreet, Inc., 1941.

Foulke, R. A., and Prochnow, H. V., *Practical Bank Credit,* 2nd Edition. New York: Prentice-Hall Inc., 1950.

Fregoe, J. H., *Credit and Its Management.* New York: Harper & Brothers, 1930.

Olson, E. E., and Hallman, J. W., *Credit Management.* New York: The Ronald Press Company, 1925.

Prendergast, W. A., and Stiener, W. H., *Credit and Its Uses.* New York: D. Appleton-Century Company, 1931.

Shultz, W. J., *Credit and Collection Management.* New York: Prentice-Hall Inc., 1947.

Whitaker, C. L., "Credit Information Sources," *Credit and Financial Management,* March 1939.

Young, R., *Industrial Credits.* New York: Harper & Brothers, 1927.

23

Personal Finance

by ELVIN F. DONALDSON

Professor of Finance, Ohio State University

Establishing a Goal

MANY OF US go through life without stopping to consider what we are after. We are on this earth only a limited amount of time and so should make the best of it. But for what is it that we are striving?

We are told by some philosophers that happiness is one of the goals of life. Regardless of whether or not we aim at this goal, we must admit that most people enjoy being happy. And after all, of what value are material goods if we are not happy? But how many of us plan our lives in such a way that we attain this end?

If it is accepted that happiness is one of the goals of life, then we should consider how to go about attaining this objective. It must be admitted that because of the differences in people, what makes for happiness in one person may not produce the same result in another. Then too, it must be realized that happiness usually does not result from the conscious effort of a person to "go out and have a good time." Rather, it is a by-product of our acts and our state of mind. There are, however, certain qualities that appear requisite for a state of happiness.

One observation that many of us have made is that people who are exceedingly healthy are usually happy. Some of us may not be able to attain perfection in this regard because we chose the wrong grandparents. Be that as it may, most of us can in this day of medical wonders do much in the way of attaining and maintaining good health. Perhaps we should remember the old statement that health is wealth.

Many people have found that their greatest enjoyment has come from helping others. Certainly there is abundant opportunity in this world for us to practice this virtue. Kind words and compliments do much in winning friends, and it appears that many good friends contribute much

toward our happiness. And we should not forget to be friendly with the persons with whom we live, because congenial surroundings are usually a prerequisite of happiness. An optimistic frame of mind can oftentimes do wonders. A great many people find that religion gives them a peace of mind that would otherwise be impossible.

Too many people struggle through life with the hope of starting to enjoy life upon their retirement. This is a serious mistake. The person who has not found happiness during his active years will certainly not find it upon retirement. The ability to enjoy ourselves appears to lessen as we grow older. It is also sometimes true that the more dollars we have, the less is the enjoyment that we get out of spending a dollar. And most of us accumulate more dollars as we get older. It might be inferred from this that we should spend our dollars when we have few of them and while we are young in order to achieve the maximum enjoyment. Such a conclusion, however, is not intended.

Judging from the experiences of most people, it is best to enjoy living every day. A pleasant family life, abundant friends, an optimistic attitude, and congenial work do much toward making us happy. A man's unhappiness or trouble appears in many instances to stem from the fact that he does not have sufficient money. It must be admitted at the outset that money itself brings no enjoyment to anyone but a miser. But it is true that the things that money can buy often do contribute toward our happiness. The worry about inability to meet our bills as they arise does take some of the joy out of living. Most of us perhaps feel that we do not have enough money left after paying our bills.

The solution to such a problem is to increase our income, or to cut down on our expenses—or to do both. There are many ways to increase our income, but it must be admitted that in many instances this would be difficult. Most of us could cut down on certain expenses. The forgoing of certain expenditures today may make for more happiness tomorrow. But sacrificing too much today may produce unhappiness throughout life for a tomorrow which never comes. It is desirable that a person or family strike some happy balance between spending and saving.

Budgeting

Many people owe their financial success in part to the fact that they keep a budget. Most people are poor managers of their personal finances, and most people do not maintain a budget. Many have been able to save for the first time when they started keeping a budget. It takes a little will power to start budgeting. The task appears irksome—one of those things which take the joy out of living. Many people, however, have found that

the maintenance of a budget has enabled them to enjoy more things than would otherwise be possible.

There are two basic objectives of a budget. First, it may enable a person or family to live within their income and still purchase the things that are desired. Second, it may lead to the regular accumulation of savings.

In order not to make too much work, the budget should be as simple as possible. Inexpensive budget forms or books can be secured in book or stationery stores. But such prepared books are not necessary. An ordinary notebook is adequate. The first step in making out a budget is to draw up a record of past expenditures. Checkbook stubs and receipts are of value in this connection. Memory will have to be relied upon for many items. These can be corrected after the budget is put into operation. Using the past expenditures as a guide, the amounts that are contemplated for future expenses are recorded in the budget book. In order to simplify the procedure, only the major expense items should be listed in the budget. The other items can be included under a general heading of "Miscellaneous." Grouping of major items might include the following: Food, Housing, Household Operations, Clothing, Automobile, Medical and Dental, Income and other Taxes, Miscellaneous, Insurance and Savings.

Budgets should be set up to cover the period corresponding to the income receipt. In other words, those receiving their pay every week should set up their budget on a weekly basis; those getting their income once a month should use a monthly basis. Since some expenses such as rent, for example, usually come once a month, however, those receiving their income weekly might find it more convenient to set their budget up on a monthly basis. Although some expenses (such as taxes or insurance) may be paid only once or twice a year, provision for them should be made every month in order to insure that a sufficient amount will be on hand to meet these outlays.

When a person first starts to keep a budget, he will be surprised (and embarrassed) to find that there will be unexpected expenses arising for which no provision had been made. It is therefore advisable at the outset to make liberal allowance for such contingencies.

After a budget has been in operation for some time, it will become apparent that too large an amount of money has gone for certain expenditures. By cutting down on these expenditures, a larger amount may be allocated to savings.

Savings

If a person sets up a budget properly and adheres to it religiously, some savings will result. Some people follow a policy of saving what they do

not spend. This usually results in little or no savings. Others set up a definite amount which they want to save, and then they budget the balance over their various expense items. This latter method is the one which is recommended, and it is the one which will usually result in the largest savings. Many people ask the question, "How much should I save every month?" Naturally the answer would vary according to the income received, the number in the family, and the standard of living desired. If a person wants some goal to shoot at, it is suggested that he try to save 10 per cent of his income. The increase in the cash surrender value of life insurance policies and the amount spent on annuities can be treated as savings.

The importance of regular, systematic savings cannot be overemphasized. Small, regular monthly savings usually result in a larger accumulation over a long period of time than irregular savings of larger amounts. Savings that can be made from payroll deductions are thus recommended. Furthermore, such savings are usually the least painful since the money does not get into the spenders' hands. Payroll deductions for Series E United States Savings bonds are recommended as a practical and convenient way to save. And furthermore, they are good investments for the average person. Where such a provision for purchasing these bonds cannot be made, the individual can (if he maintains a bank account) have the bank purchase the bonds by deductions from his account. No charge is made for this service.

Bank Accounts

The first savings of many persons are deposited in banks. Two different types of accounts may be maintained in a commercial bank: checking accounts and savings accounts. In the case of checking accounts, no interest is paid to the depositor. In many instances, particularly in the larger cities, the bank has a monthly maintenance charge based on the number of deposits made and number of checks written. Some banks have special checking accounts in which the depositor pays the bank from 5 to 10 cents for each check contained in a book of 20, 50, or 100 checks. No further charges are made by the bank for this type of checking account. Checking accounts are maintained primarily for the convenience in paying bills.

The savings account is more important to people who are interested in the regular accumulation of money. Some banks will open a savings account with any amount from $1 up, whereas other banks require a larger amount. Thereafter deposits or withdrawals of any amount may be made. In some instances there is a charge made for withdrawals in excess of a given number per month. According to the contract, banks

may require notice of a stated number of days, commonly 30 days, for withdrawals from savings accounts. During normal times, however, banks do not require this notice; rather they pay out on demand.

The rate of interest paid on savings accounts may sometimes not seem attractive. Many banks are today paying around 1 per cent on these accounts. In other respects savings accounts constitute a good means of saving. They are convenient, liquid, and safe.

Other things being equal, a person should open a checking or savings account in a bank which is a member of the Federal Deposit Insurance Corporation. In such banks accounts up to $10,000 are insured by the Corporation. This insurance offers additional protection to the depositor. In no investment, however, can a person always be assured of 100 per cent safety. Because of the misunderstanding existing relative to the insurance of deposits, an explanation of the true nature of the insurance is in order.

Many people believe that such accounts are guaranteed by the federal government up to $10,000. There are two errors in such reasoning. In the first place, the accounts are *insured,* not guaranteed. In other words, the depositor is not guaranteed that the accounts will be paid up to this amount in case the bank fails. But the Corporation will stand behind the accounts up to the limit of its resources.

The other point is that it is the Federal Deposit Insurance Corporation which does the insuring, not the *federal government.* This Insurance Corporation was formed by the federal government, so it is an instrumentality of the government; but its obligations are not the direct obligation of the federal government. It is possible, however, that should the demands ever become so great against the Insurance Corporation that it could not meet its obligations, the federal government would step in and pour money into the Corporation.

It should also be observed that even the Insurance Corporation is not obligated to pay the depositor cash. It may pay the depositor cash, or it may make available to him a transferred deposit in a new bank in the same community or in another insured bank in an amount equal to the insured deposit. To date, however, the Insurance Corporation has been paying the depositors cash in event of failure of their bank. In order to maintain its credit, it is probable that the federal government would take whatever steps would be necessary in the future to enable the Insurance Corporation to continue to pay cash to the depositors of defunct banks.

Seventeen of the states have mutual savings banks. These are concentrated in the East, particularly in New York and the New England states. The earnings of these banks, after the necessary reserves have been set up, are returned to the depositor in the form of dividends. The dividend,

however, is a more or less fixed amount and varies little from year to year. For all practical purposes the dividends are considered by the depositors as interest. The rate paid by most of the savings banks varies from 1½ to 2½ per cent. In some of the states there are limits on the amount which any one individual may have on deposit. In New York this limit is $7,500.

The savings banks are eligible for membership in the Federal Deposit Insurance Corporation, but to date only a minority of them have become members. In some of the states, however, there are state insurance plans in operation.

According to the laws and regulations, the savings banks may demand from 60 to 90 days notice for withdrawals, but during normal times they pay out on demand. The savings banks have been conservatively operated and are a relatively safe, liquid, and convenient place to deposit savings.

Checks

People who have checking accounts in a bank can write checks against their account to purchase goods and to make payments on debts. It is usually more convenient to pay bills by check; furthermore the cancelled check serves as a receipt.

In making out a check, one should be careful to see that all blank spaces are filled. The name of the person to whom the check is given (called the payee) should always be inserted before the check is delivered or mailed. Ink should be used in order to reduce the chances of alterations.

The account holder should have the bank prepare monthly statements and return the cancelled checks. These cancelled checks should be examined carefully by the depositor; in case of any discrepancies, the bank should be notified immediately.

In certain instances a personal check may not be accepted by another party unless it is certified. Certification will be done by the bank for a slight charge, or sometimes without charge. This adds the bank's liability to that of the depositor and thus makes the check more readily acceptable.

If a person does not have a checking account in a bank and for one reason or another does not want to remit cash, he may for a slight charge secure a cashier's check from the bank. This is a check drawn by the bank on its own account in that bank. Bank money orders are similar to cashier's checks except that in addition to the name of the payee, there is also filled in the name of the person buying the instrument. The person to whom a bank money order is sent thus knows who sent it. The use of this type of instrument eliminates the need of writing a letter.

Furthermore, the remitter has a record of the bank money order, and from this record the bank can produce the cancelled instrument in case proof of payment of the debt is necessary.

People should be careful about taking checks from strangers. Checks should be presented to a bank promptly for deposit or payment. If checks that contain the blank indorsement of the holder are lost or stolen, an innocent purchaser for value would have good title. It is therefore advisable to write above your signature "For deposit only" when checks are to be deposited to your account.

Indorsers of checks are liable to the holders in event that the bank dishonors, provided the checks have been duly presented for payment and due notice of dishonor is given to the indorser. An indorser is liable also in the event that there has been a forgery or material alteration on the check prior to the time that he indorsed it.

Notes

Notes should be distinguished from checks. The latter as we saw above, are orders drawn by an individual on his account in a bank. A note is a promise to pay a sum of money to a designated party on demand or at a fixed time. Notes are similar to bonds, which will be discussed later, but they mature in a shorter time. When a person borrows money he is generally asked to sign a note as written evidence of the amount owed.

In order to preserve the liability of indorsers, a time note should be presented to the maker for payment on the date due. A demand note should be presented within a reasonable length of time after issue—not over from three to six months. In the event that the maker does not pay the note, the holder should notify the indorsers immediately. A person who signs as an accommodation indorser is liable in the same manner as any other indorser.

From the viewpoint of the taker of the note, it is advisable that the note contain a confession of judgment clause, provided such a clause is enforceable in the particular state. Such a clause states in effect that if the note is not paid at its maturity, the holder can take it to an attorney-at-law in the state and the latter will confess that the maker of the note owes the amount stated. A judge will then immediately give judgment against the maker. After this is done the holder may have the sheriff attach the property of the maker. If the maker feels that he does not owe the money, he may take the case to the courts for decision. In the meantime, however, the holder has a lien on the maker's property.

In the absence of this clause, it may take the holder many months to get judgment against the maker through the courts. And by the time judgment is granted, the maker may have no property left to attach.

From what has been said it is obvious that from the standpoint of the maker, it would be better for him to sign a note which does not contain such a clause. It is usually the creditor and not the debtor, however, who has the upper hand when it comes to bargaining.

Savings and Loans

"Savings and loans" is a more modern title for "building and loans," although the latter title is still used in many instances. In Massachusetts these associations are called "cooperative banks," while in Louisiana they are termed "homestead associations." Savings and loan associations are chartered both by the state and by the federal government.

Savings and loan associations are one of the most popular types of savings institutions in the country today, and they are also one of the principal sources for borrowing money for the construction or purchase of a home. Many people do not distinguish between a commercial bank and a savings and loan, so a word of explanation will be given.

When a person deposits money in a bank, he is, strictly speaking, a depositor. He is lending the bank his money. The bank obligates itself to pay him interest on a savings account at a predetermined rate and to repay him his principal on demand. In contrast to this, when a person opens an account in a savings and loan, he is really buying shares. In a legal sense he becomes a part owner of the institution. These shares are evidenced by a passbook, however, rather than a certificate as is the case in ordinary business corporations. Although the savings and loan associations will, in normal times, return the saver's money on demand, if they do not have the necessary cash at hand, they are under no immediate obligation to the saver. The laws vary among the states, but generally speaking the savings and loan associations are compelled to return the money to the saver as it becomes available.

In Ohio the state chartered savings and loans may accept both share accounts and deposit accounts. Although in normal times the institutions pay out on demand on both the share and deposit accounts, in the event of failure of the institution, the deposit accounts would first have to be paid before anything could be paid to the holders of share accounts. In the Pacific and Southwestern sections of the country, the permanent stock savings and loan associations are authorized to issue investment certificates which represent a debt of the association and must, in the event of failure, be paid off in full before anything may be paid to the shareholders. In other states, with the exception of Ohio mentioned above, the state associations are permitted to accept only share accounts. The federal associations are permitted to have only share accounts, regardless of where they operate.

If a person could not get his money back from a savings and loan association in abnormal times, he might conclude that the institution was not safe. This, however, may not be the case. We should distinguish between liquidity and safety. A commercial bank invests its money in short-term government obligations and short-term business loans. This is done because the bank is obligated to meet the claims of its depositors on demand. In contrast, the savings and loan association lends the bulk of its money out to people for the purchase of a home. The loans are to be paid off over a period of 10, 15, 20, or 25 years. A savings and loan may not have the cash on hand or be able to secure it immediately if a large number of savers demand their money at the same time. (The same may, of course, be true of a bank.) But in time the association may get back its money and be able to return all the savers' money. In other words, in times of stress the savings and loan may not be as liquid as a bank, but the savers' money may still be safe.

Today, however, most savings and loans keep an appreciable part of their resources in government bonds, which they could sell if the demands for cash made it necessary. Furthermore, they can borrow up to certain limits from the Federal Home Loan Banks.

There is still another protective feature for the saver. All the federal savings and loan associations are members of the Federal Savings and Loan Insurance Corporation. Some of the state associations are also members. This Insurance Corporation was set up by the federal government to do for savings and loan associations somewhat the same thing as the Federal Deposit Insurance Corporation does for commercial banks. The insurance covers accounts up to $10,000, the same amount as in the case of banks.

What was said about distinguishing between the Federal Deposit Insurance Corporation and the federal government itself applies with equal force to the Federal Savings and Loan Insurance Corporation. And it should be recognized that these two insurance corporations are not connected. In event of default by an insured savings and loan association, the Insurance Corporation will either pay the account holder cash, or it will make available to him a transferred account in a new insured institution in the same community or in another insured institution in an amount equal to the insured account. Since the Insurance Corporation has been set up, it has been paying the savers 100 per cent cash in event of failure of their institution.

Since the return to the saver is in the form of dividends rather than interest (with the exception of deposit accounts in Ohio institutions), the savings and loan association must wait until the end of each six-month period before declaring the dividends for the preceding period.

Where a change from the existing rate is contemplated, however, the association will usually announce this change six months in advance.

Most people having savings and loan accounts look upon them as being the same as a savings account in a bank. In practice that is about the way it works out, but the saver should realize the differences which have been pointed out above.

As is true in the case of bank accounts, it is advisable to select an institution which is large, well-established and which carries insurance of accounts. The majority of the savings and loans are today paying a dividend rate of from 2 to 3 per cent. This is somewhat higher than the percentage banks are paying. These institutions are convenient for the average person and, in the case of the better institutions, offer a relatively safe investment.

Postal Savings

A safe form of investment, but one with which the average person is not acquainted, is postal savings. The postal savings system is operated by the United States Government through the Post Office Department. Accounts may be opened by any competent natural person of 10 years of age or more by depositing any amount from $1 to $2,500. The latter is the largest amount, exclusive of interest, which any one person may have deposited to his credit. Certificates in the same denominations as paper money are issued to cover the deposits.

Deposits and withdrawals may be made at any time. Interest is paid at the rate of 2 per cent per annum. The certificates begin drawing interest on the first day of the month following the month in which the money is deposited. In order to collect any interest, however, the money must have been drawing interest for at least three full months. Thus, if money is deposited on December 15, 1951, for example, interest will start on January 1, 1952. The earliest date on which interest can be collected would be April 1, 1952. If interest is collected, the old certificate is indorsed and turned in. If the depositor wishes to redeposit the principal or the principal and interest, the renewal certificate will begin drawing interest on May 1, 1952. Thus, the depositor really loses one month's interest by cashing in the certificate. Money must be on deposit for even quarters of the year in order to collect interest for the particular quarter or quarters.

If interest has been running on an account for a full year, or a full year and even quarter, the interest can be collected without any loss of interest on the reinvestment of the money. Thus, on money deposited on December 15, 1951, interest starts accumulating on January 1, 1952. If the interest is not collected until January 1, 1953 (really January 2, since

the New Year's Day is a holiday) a full year's interest will be collected, and interest on the renewal certificate will start on January 1, 1953. (This is true if the interest is collected any time during the month of January 1953). In order not to lose any interest it is therefore advisable that a depositor leave his money in at least a full year, or year and even quarter, before collecting the interest.

If a person does not collect his interest at the end of the year, the interest for the second year will be computed only on the principal amount. In other words, the interest does not compound.

In respect to both the principal amount and the interest, postal savings are direct obligations of the United States Government. Since our government is the strongest financially in the world today, it can be said that postal savings, along with United States Government bonds, are the safest investment in the world today. Furthermore, postal savings constitute one of the most liquid investments possible. The rate of return— 2 per cent—is more than is being paid by most commercial banks, and the rate is as high as is being paid by many savings and loan associations. For a short-term investment the rate is higher than that paid by the government on its short-term obligations.

One of the disadvantages of postal savings is that it is often not as convenient as a bank or savings and loan account. Another disadvantage is that the interest is not compounded. And for persons of some means the $2,500 limit on deposits is a drawback.

United States Government Bonds

As mentioned above, since postal savings and United States Government bonds are direct obligations of the government, they are the safest investments in the world today. There are a number of different types of government bonds, but only four types will be discussed here—the Series E, F, and G, Savings bonds, and the Treasury bonds.

The Series E bonds were popular with the American public during World War II, and many persons are continuing to buy them. The bonds are issued in denominations varying from $25 to $1,000 (maturity value). They are called discount bonds because they are sold at discounts from their maturity value. They do not pay current interest, but rather the interest is paid when the bond is redeemed. They mature in 10 years from the first day of the month in which they are purchased.

If the bonds are held for the full 10 years, the rate of interest paid amounts to 2.9 per cent. If they are redeemed before maturity, the rate of return is less than this. Generally speaking, the longer the bonds are held the higher is the rate of return from the issue date to the redemption date. A bond purchased today for $75 can be redeemed in 10 years for

$100. The difference of $25 represents the interest return. This amounts to 33⅓ per cent for the 10 years, or an annual return of 3⅓ per cent. Since the purchaser, however, does not get the use of the interest during the 10 year period, this $25 represents an annual return of 2.9 per cent, interest compounded semiannually.

TABLE 1

REDEMPTION VALUES AND INVESTMENT YIELDS

$100 Series E Savings Bond

Date Period After Issue	Redemption Values	Approximate Investment Yield on Pur- chase Price from Issue Date to Be- ginning of Each Half-year Period	Approximate Investment Yield on Cur- rent Redemp- tion Value from Beginning of Each Half-year Period to Ma- turity
		PER CENT	PER CENT
First ½ year	$ 75.00	0.00	2.90
½ to 1 year	75.00	0.00	3.05
1 to 1½ years	75.50	0.67	3.15
1½ to 2 years	76.00	0.88	3.25
2 to 2½ years	76.50	0.99	3.38
2½ to 3 years	77.00	1.06	3.52
3 to 3½ years	78.00	1.31	3.58
3½ to 4 years	79.00	1.49	3.66
4 to 4½ years	80.00	1.62	3.75
4½ to 5 years	81.00	1.72	3.87
5 to 5½ years	82.00	1.79	4.01
5½ to 6 years	83.00	1.85	4.18
6 to 6½ years	84.00	1.90	4.41
6½ to 7 years	86.00	2.12	4.36
7 to 7½ years	88.00	2.30	4.31
7½ to 8 years	90.00	2.45	4.26
8 to 8½ years	92.00	2.57	4.21
8½ to 9 years	94.00	2.67	4.17
9 to 9½ years	96.00	2.76	4.12
9½ to 10 years	98.00	2.84	4.08
Maturity Value (10 years from issue date)	$100.00	2.90	....

The bonds will be redeemed any time after 60 days from the issue date. If the bonds are redeemed before the end of one year, the purchaser gets back only what he paid for the bond. If one has held the bonds for several years, he should try to hold until maturity, because the rate earned during the later years will be greater. Referring to the table it can be seen that if a $100 bond has been held, for example, five years, interest of $7 will have been earned. This is at an average annual rate

of only 1.79 per cent. But if the bond is held another five years to maturity, it will earn an additional $18, which represents an average annual return of 4.01 per cent for the last five years. The rate for the full 10 years averages 2.9 per cent as stated above. This rate is higher than can be obtained on any other safe investment today. Matured E bonds can now be extended at the option of the holder for another 10 years at 2.9 per cent interest.

These bonds cannot be sold on the market, so they are nonnegotiable and cannot be used as collateral for a loan. Although they may be redeemed at any time after 60 days from the issue date at the option of the holder, the government has no right to call them in until maturity. The investor does not have to depend upon the market in order to determine what price he will get for the bond when he wants to sell it. The redemption prices for bonds held any length of time are clearly stated on the bond. Regardless of how interest rates or bond prices fluctuate in the future, the investor knows at all times just how much he can get for his bonds.

Interest on the bonds is subject to the federal income taxes, but it may be reported in one of two ways. The increase in the redemption price may be reported each year, or the investor may wait until he redeems the bond and then report the total interest earned at that time. The latter method is the easier and is therefore recommended.

The E bonds can be registered in one of three ways: in the name of one individual; in the name of one individual, and payable to a designated beneficiary upon death of the registered holder; and in the name of two persons as co-owners. When registered in the latter way, the bond is payable to either of the named co-owners, and either can upon indorsement cash the bond without the consent of the other. When a beneficiary is named, he has no rights with respect to the bond until the death of the registered owner.

A co-owner more easily can cash the bond upon the death of the other party than can the beneficiary, for the latter must establish proof of death. The co-owner may also have less in inheritance and federal estates taxes to pay than the beneficiary.

The maximum amount of E bonds which may be purchased by any one individual either in his name alone, or with a beneficiary named, is $10,000 (maturity value). If the co-ownership registration is used, the maximum is $20,000 (maturity value). These are double the limits that were established when the bonds were originally issued.

The Series E bonds can be purchased only by natural individuals. Thus corporations, banks, and businesses cannot buy them. Series E bonds are one of the best investments in the world today for the average person. Many people are having their employers deduct a definite amount regu-

larly from their pay to purchase these bonds. Others have the banks buy the bonds for them regularly out of their bank account. Many people are using the E bonds as a retirement or supplement to their retirement plan. For example, $75 invested monthly for the next 10 years will start bringing in $100 a month for a 10-year period. If $50 more is added to this monthly and the money reinvested in the bonds, in 10 years more time the return would provide a monthly income of $200 for the following 10 years.

The Series F Savings bonds are similar to the E bonds with the following exceptions. The F bonds are purchased at 74 per cent of their maturity value, and they mature in 12 years. The yield if held to maturity is 2.53 per cent. They are not redeemable until six months after their issue date; but they have to be held for one year before there is any increase in the redemption value over the purchase price. If the bond is redeemed before maturity, the yield is relatively low, but it increases the longer the bond is held. Series F bonds may be purchased in denominations from $25 to $10,000 (maturity value). They may be purchased by individuals, by corporations, businesses, and organizations. The maximum that may be purchased in any one calendar year is $100,000 (issue price). If the E bonds can be purchased, there is no reason why the F bonds should be bought, since the yield on the latter is lower.

The Series G bonds are similar to the F bonds in that they mature in 12 years and can be redeemed by the holder after they have been held for six months. The yield also increases with the length of time the bonds are held. If the bonds are held to maturity, the yield is 2.50 per cent. The maximum amount of bonds that may be purchased in any one calendar year is also $100,000 (issue price). If both F and G bonds are acquired, the maximum of the combined purchases may not exceed $100,000 (issue price). They may be purchased by individuals, businesses, and corporations, the same as the F bonds.

The distinguishing feature of the G bonds is that they are not sold at a discount. The interest is paid every six months by check at the annual rate of 2.5 per cent. If the bonds are redeemed before their maturity, however, the holder will get less than he paid for them. In this event the yield would be less than 2.5 per cent. The accompanying table shows the redemption values, and yields of a $100, G bond. In event of the death of an owner or co-owner, or if the bond is held by a trustee upon the death of any person which terminates the trust, the full face value of the bond will be paid.

Where current income is needed, the G bonds are recommended instead of the E or F bonds. Because of the fixed schedule of redemption values and higher yield, the G bonds may be preferred by a person over the Treasury bonds.

TABLE 2

REDEMPTION VALUES AND INVESTMENT YIELDS

$100 Series G Savings Bond

Period After Issue Date	Redemption Values	Approximate Investment Yield on Purchase Price from Issue Date to Beginning of Each Half-year Period	Approximate Investment Yield on Current Redemption Value from Beginning of Each Half-year Period to Maturity
		PER CENT	PER CENT
First ½ year	Not redeemable		2.50
½ to 1 year	$ 98.80	0.10	2.62
1 to 1½ years	97.80	0.30	2.73
1½ to 2 years	96.90	0.44	2.84
2 to 2½ years	96.20	0.61	2.94
2½ to 3 years	95.60	0.75	3.04
3 to 3½ years	95.10	0.88	3.13
3½ to 4 years	94.80	1.04	3.20
4 to 4½ years	94.70	1.20	3.26
4½ to 5 years	94.70	1.35	3.30
5 to 5½ years	94.90	1.51	3.32
5½ to 6 years	95.20	1.66	3.33
6 to 6½ years	95.50	1.79	3.33
6½ to 7 years	95.80	1.89	3.34
7 to 7½ years	96.10	1.98	3.35
7½ to 8 years	96.40	2.05	3.37
8 to 8½ years	96.70	2.12	3.39
8½ to 9 years	97.00	2.18	3.42
9 to 9½ years	97.30	2.23	3.46
9½ to 10 years	97.60	2.27	3.51
10 to 10½ years	97.90	2.31	3.60
10½ to 11 years	98.20	2.35	3.75
11 to 11½ years	98.60	2.39	3.94
11½ to 12 years	99.20	2.44	4.13
Maturity Value (12 years from issue date)	$100.00	2.50	....

The Treasury bonds are more similar to ordinary corporate bonds. They can be bought and sold in the general market. They can be purchased by any one without limitation, with some exception in respect to banks. They are issued both in coupon and registered form. The coupon bonds (on which the interest is collected every six months by the holder's clipping the coupon and presenting it to a bank) are recommended for the average purchaser.

The maturity of the Treasury bonds varies from five to 27 years. Most of the issues are callable by the government in from two to five years

before maturity. The holder, however, cannot force the government to redeem Treasury bonds until maturity. He can of course sell the bonds in the market at any time. Naturally the price he will get depends upon the market price at the time of sale.

The rate of interest paid on the longer term Treasury bonds is 2½ per cent. But in order to maintain low interest rates, the government formerly pegged the price of these issues so that they were selling at slight premiums. With the support now off, the bonds are selling at a discount. The yield, based on market prices, is therefore now more than 2½ per cent. If interest rates advance further, the price of the Treasury bonds will go lower. The longer the maturity of the bond, the greater will be the drop in price. This is one of the disadvantages of holding the Treasury bonds. If the purchaser could hold the bonds to maturity, he would be sure of getting the face value of the bonds; but he is never sure that he can do this. The interest on the Treasury bonds issued since 1941 must be reported for federal income tax purposes.

Buying Life Insurance

Life insurance should be one of the first investments made by a man, particularly a married man. The primary purpose of life insurance is to give protection to dependents in event of the death of the insured. A man may be able to save enough money during his lifetime to provide for his dependents, assuming that he lives to be 60 or 65. But there is no assurance that he will live this long. One or several year's savings would not last long if the husband were to die young, but the same amount put into life insurance premiums would increase the size of the estate many fold. The second purpose of buying life insurance (and this applies to most types of policies) is to build up a form of savings account which a man can obtain upon surrender of the policy, or against which the insured can borrow. Some people say that they can save their money and invest it themselves better than can the insurance company, but experience does not always bear this out. People usually find a way to meet their insurance premiums; but if they did not have to pay the premiums, it is doubtful whether they would put aside the same amount of money in a savings account.

It is recommended that life insurance be purchased from a legal reserve company. These are the larger companies, and the amount of the premiums remains the same over the life of the policy. The legal reserve companies comprise both stock and mutual companies. At the beginning of 1950, about 70 per cent of all life insurance in force in the United States was held by mutual companies. The total number of policies in

force with all United States companies as of this date was 193 million. This represented $214.4 billion of life insurance.

The average person is not equipped to determine the best company in which to buy insurance, nor does he know the type policy best suited to him. In regard to the company, it is suggested that he purchase his insurance from one of the larger companies. Generally speaking, they are better established and probably better managed than the smaller companies. Furthermore, the rates may be the same or even lower.

There are a number of different types of life insurance, but the more common forms are as follows:

1. Ordinary insurance
    (a) Whole life
    (b) Limited-payment life
    (c) Endowment
    (d) Term
2. Group insurance
3. Industrial insurance.

Two-thirds of all life insurance in force in the United States is in ordinary insurance. It is made up of the four types of policies outlined above. These are usually bought in units of $1,000. In the case of whole life insurance (which is also called straight life insurance), the purchaser pays the premiums over his lifetime; but as is true in any kind of life insurance, the face value of the policy is paid to his beneficiary upon his death. The annual premiums on this type of policy are the lowest of any of the ordinary insurance policies. After the whole life policy has been in force for several years, there is a loan value and a cash surrender value.

With the limited-payment policy the premiums are paid only over the period of years stated in the policy—such as 20 years, for example—and if the insured is alive at the end of that period, the premiums cease, but the life insurance continues in force for the life of the insured. The premiums paid for this type policy are higher than for the whole life policy, but the loan and cash surrender values are also higher.

The endowment policy runs for a stated number of years—such as 20 years, for example—and if the insured has not died before that time, the full face value of the policy will be paid to him at the end of the stated period. Premiums on this type of policy are higher than for any of the other types of ordinary insurance; but it is likewise true that the loan and cash surrender values are also higher. The table on page 656 shows the annual premium and the loan and cash surrender values for a leading stock company of the three types of policies just discussed. These figures are for a $1,000 policy taken out by a man when he is 25 years old.

Term insurance is written for a designated number of years such as 1, 5, 10, 15, or 20 years. At the end of the stated period the policy is

TABLE 3

LIFE INSURANCE PREMIUMS, LOAN VALUES, AND CASH
SURRENDER VALUES

| Type of Policy | Annual Premium | Loan Value and Cash Surrender Value at End of | | | |
		5th Year	10th Year	15th Year	20th Year
Whole Life	$17.11	$ 39	$109	$185	$ 265
Limited Payment—					
20 Years	28.62	93	229	381	552
Endowment—					
20 Years	46.79	181	417	688	1,000

terminated. If a new policy is then taken out, the insured will have to pay higher rates based on his age at the time. The premiums on term policies are the lowest of the various types of policies discussed, because the total premium goes to pay for the insurance protection—there are no loan or cash surrender values. If one year term policies are taken out, the amount of the premium increases when each new policy is written. Unless provided otherwise in the policy, the insured would have to pass a medical examination each year before the new policy would be granted.

Many people buy a "level premium" term policy. If it is a five year level premium term policy, the amount of the premiums that the insured would have to pay for one year term policies at the various ages is more or less averaged, and the insured then pays the same amount in premiums for each of the five years. It is desirable to have in the term policy a provision that the insured can at any time, without medical examination, convert the term policy into one of the permanent types of insurance.

Term insurance gives the maximum protection for the least cost. It is therefore recommended for the young person who has a small income and a number of dependents. It is also taken out by some to cover the period in which the children will be dependent on the insured. The disadvantages of the term policy are that the policy has no loan or cash surrender value and that the policy terminates at the expiration of the period stated. The table on page 657 shows the annual premiums for the various types of policies discussed above. These figures are for a $1,000 policy written by a leading stock company.

Life insurance premiums are calculated on the basis of the premium being paid once a year. In order not to have to pay out a relatively large amount at one time, many people pay their insurance premiums semi-annually, quarterly, or monthly. This is more expensive than paying the premiums annually, since the insurance company really charges the insured interest for retaining part of the premium money for the period. The rate charged varies among the companies and runs from 8 to 15

TABLE 4

LIFE INSURANCE PREMIUMS

| | Annual Premiums per $1,000 of Life Insurance | | | |
Age	Term: One-Year Renewable	Whole Life	Limited-Payment 20 Years	Endowment 20 Years
20	$ 6.04	$15.19	$26.32	$46.76
25	6.29	17.11	28.62	46.79
30	6.55	19.60	31.35	47.07
35	7.25	22.68	34.42	47.53
40	8.63	27.01	38.42	48.84
45	10.96	32.65	43.27	51.02
50	15.38	40.08	49.35	54.58

per cent. Below are the rates charged by a leading mutual company on a $5,000 whole life policy taken out at age 25. The rate charged by this company is in excess of 12 per cent.

Premium Basis	Total Annual Premiums	Excess Over Annual Basis
Annually	$104.35	....
Semiannually	107.50	$3.15
Quarterly	109.60	5.25
Monthly	110.40	6.05

As the name indicates, group life insurance is that insurance which is taken out on a relatively large number of employees of a particular company. It is a form of term insurance. Because of the smaller selling and administrative costs, and also the absence of a medical examination, this is the cheapest form of insurance. Many group policies provide that if the insured leaves the particular company, he may (by paying a higher premium) convert it into another type of policy. At the beginning of 1950 nearly one-fifth of all life insurance in force in the United States was group insurance.

Life insurance which is written in amounts less than $500 and in which the agent collects the premiums weekly at the home of the insured is called industrial insurance. The average policy is for slightly less than $300. Although the bulk of ordinary life insurance is carried on men, 46 per cent of the industrial life insurance is carried on women; about one-third of all industrial life insurance is on the lives of men, and the rest is on children. Because of the size of the average policy, it is obvious that the primary purpose of industrial life insurance is to cover last illness and burial expenses.

The cost of the protection given by industrial life insurance is the highest of the various forms of insurance. This results from the high administrative and collecting expense and also from the fact that the

face values of the policies are small. It is unfortunate that the lower economic classes, which can afford to pay the least for life insurance, are the ones who buy industrial insurance and thus pay the highest price for the insurance protection they receive. If a person can afford any of the other types of policies, it is recommended that he buy one of these rather than industrial life insurance. Although more industrial life insurance policies are sold than any other kind, only about 15 per cent of the total insurance in force in the United States is industrial insurance.

Thousands of veterans of World War II are carrying the National Service Life Insurance which they took out upon entering the service. This is a form of term insurance and may be continued as such, or it may be converted into one of a number of types of permanent insurance. The government insurance is the cheapest that can be obtained, and furthermore, the policyholders have been receiving dividends from the government which exceed half of the amount they have paid in premiums. The veteran is strongly advised to continue his government insurance. For those who have dropped their policies or cut down the amount of insurance carried, it is recommended that they take the proper steps to have the insurance reinstated. Veterans should consult their nearest Veterans Administration office for any question they have relating to their insurance.

Suggested Readings

See the end of the following chapter.

24

Personal Finance (Continued)

by ELVIN F. DONALDSON

Professor of Finance, Ohio State University

Buying Annuities

ONE OF THE safest ways to provide for security in old age is through the purchase of an annuity. This is a type of contract in which the insurance company agrees to pay to a person a fixed amount of money at stated intervals during his life. The number of annuities sold has increased rapidly in recent years. At the beginning of 1950 there were 85 per cent more annuity contracts than there were in 1941. And this was three times the number in existence in 1935. Group annuities set up under employer-employee programs have accounted for the greater part of this gain.

As people get older they usually worry more about the future. Many are afraid that they will outlive their money. This appears to be the case in many instances regardless of the size of the estate. If the income from the principal amount invested is not adequate, a person hesitates to use any of the principal, for this would reduce the income in subsequent years. Furthermore, he would be afraid of using up all the principal before he died. The annuity offers a solution. By the purchase of an annuity a person can get an annual income which includes in part a return of his principal, but this income will be paid to him for life. He does not have to worry about consuming all his money before he dies.

Annuities may be classified into two groups: (1) immediate annuities and (2) deferred annuities. The immediate annuity is purchased by the payment to the insurance company of a lump sum of money as a single premium; the annuity payments begin immediately and continue for life. This kind of an annuity obviously could be purchased only by a

person who had accumulated a sizable amount of money. A person who is currently earning a living would probably not want an immediate annuity. Thus, an immediate annuity is usually purchased only by an older person.

The deferred annuity is one on which the annuity payments begin at some future time, such as when the purchaser reaches the age of 60 or 65. It can usually be purchased with a single premium or by the payment of annual instalments up until the time the annuity payments begin. The latter is the usual method and, of course, is the only form that could be used by a relatively young person who does not have much money.

Various arrangements can be made relating to the annuity payments. In the case of a life annuity, the annuity payments are made to the purchaser for life; when he dies, the payments stop. This type of annuity gives the purchaser the maximum income possible, but it leaves nothing to his beneficiaries or estate upon his death. Another plan gives the purchaser an income for life, but if he dies before a fixed number of years (such as 10 years, for example), the insurance company will continue the payments to a designated beneficiary for the remaining part of the 10 years. This arrangement results in the purchaser's receiving less per year than under the life annuity, but it does insure that the estate will receive a definite amount in event of an early death.

Deferred annuities usually have loan and cash surrender values up until the time the annuity payments begin. If the purchaser dies before the annuity payments begin, a death benefit will be paid to a designated beneficiary.

The retirement annuity has been the most popular type of annuity sold in recent years. It is a deferred annuity and provides for alternative forms of annuity payments that may be selected before the payments begin. Loan and cash surrender values and death benefits are also provided for in this policy. The contract may also provide for the exchange of the annuity for a life insurance policy.

Many persons buy a policy which is a combination life insurance and annuity. Up to a certain specified age, such as 60 or 65, the policy provides for life insurance of a fixed amount. If the purchaser is still alive at that age, the insurance ceases and the company starts paying him annuity payments for life (or for life with a certain guaranteed number of years). Some persons use the proceeds of an endowment life insurance policy to buy an annuity.

Part of the annuity payments are subject to the federal income tax. A person must report annually that part of the annuity payments which is equivalent to 3 per cent of the cost of the policy. If, for example, a person receives annual annuity payments of $732.50 on a policy which

cost him $10,000, he must report 3 per cent of $10,000, or $300. The balance ($432.50) is considered a return of capital and does not have to be reported.

Social Security

People who qualify for Social Security really have a form of annuity. Those who are employed in factories, shops, stores, offices, and mines, for example, have been covered by Social Security since its inception in 1937. Effective January 1951, the following were included: the self-employed (except owners of farms), agricultural workers, and regularly employed domestics. Employees of nonprofit religious (except clergymen and members of religious orders), charitable, scientific and educational groups and societies may now come under Social Security if the organization and at least two-thirds of the employees want it.

Employees of state and local governments who are not already covered by an existing retirement system may come into Social Security if the particular government accepts coverage for its employees. Some forms of employment by the federal government not covered by other retirement systems have been brought under Social Security. Farm owners and professional people are not covered by Social Security at the present time.

Those that are covered by Social Security have 1½ per cent of their wages up to $3,600 ($3,000 before 1951) deducted from their pay to cover their Social Security payments. Their employers have to pay a similar amount of 1½ per cent. Under present law the amount must be paid by both the employee and the employer and will be increased as follows:

Year	Amount
1954	2 per cent
1960	2½ per cent
1965	3 per cent
1970	3¼ per cent

The self-employed who are covered by Social Security will make their payments at the time they file their federal income tax returns. They will contribute 2¼ per cent of their business income, up to $3,600, beginning in 1951, and continuing through 1953. Under present law the amount of the payments will be increased as follows:

Year	Amount
1954	3 per cent
1960	3¾ per cent
1965	4¼ per cent
1970	4⅞ per cent

As stated before, the rates indicated above for both employees and the self-employed apply to only the first $3,600 of annual income.

To be entitled to the full benefits of Social Security, a person must be "fully insured." To be fully insured a person must have six calendar quarters of Social Security coverage in every case and also either one quarter of coverage for each two calendar quarters after January 1, 1951; or one quarter of coverage for each two calendar quarters after he became 21 years old; or 40 quarters of coverage. A "calendar quarter of coverage" is a period of three months (ending March 31, June 30, September 30, or December 31) in which an individual receives $50 or more in wages, or for which he has been credited with $100 or more of self-employment income.

Upon retirement at 65 or over, a fully insured person will receive a small monthly income for life. This is called the "primary" amount. His wife and unmarried children under 18 likewise are entitled to a fixed amount. The monthly retirement benefit (or "primary" payment) is computed by taking 50 per cent of the first $100 of the average monthly wage, and adding to this 15 per cent of the next $200. (Social Security deductions and payments are based only on the first $300 of monthly wages). If the primary benefit as thus computed comes to less than $20, it will be raised to $20.

Insured persons who are 75 and over can obtain retirement benefits even if they continue to work. The wife of a fully insured person and each unmarried child under 18 will receive monthly an amount equal to one-half of the primary benefit paid to the husband. If the wife is under 65 she will be entitled to the benefits only if she has in her care a child who is entitled to Social Security benefits based on her husband's account. The maximum amount that may be paid to one family, however, is $150.

Social Security not only provides a retirement income, but it also provides for monthly benefits to be paid to the widow and minor children in event of death of the insured person. To receive these benefits, the age of the insured at the time of death is immaterial. The widow is entitled to a monthly amount equal to three-fourths of the husband's "primary" benefit. To be eligible for the benefit the widow must be 65 or over; or, if younger than 65, she must be caring for minor children. The monthly amount paid to dependent children under 18 is equal to one-half the primary benefit of the father.

In addition to the monthly payments to the widow of an insured worker, a lump sum equal to three times the primary benefit will be paid to the widow upon the death of an insured worker.

The Social Security payments described above are for a fully insured person. Some people who do not meet the requirements for a fully insured worker may be able to qualify as a "currently" insured worker. Currently insured workers and their families are not entitled to retire-

ment benefits, but some benefits are provided in the event of the death of the worker. Space will not permit a discussion of the status of currently insured workers.

Some people have worked only a short period of time, and although they have had Social Security deductions taken from their pay, they do not qualify as either a current or a fully insured worker. Many of these individuals are wondering what happens to the amounts that have been taken out of their pay. These amounts go into the general insurance fund set up by the government, and the particular individual gets nothing out of it.

Persons who have Social Security deductions taken from their pay should consult the local Social Security office for definite information relative to their benefits. Even though a person is entitled to Social Security benefits, such payments do not come automatically. It is necessary to file a claim at the local Social Security office. People covered by the insurance should, upon reaching 65, ascertain their rights even if they do not contemplate immediate retirement. Upon the death of an insured worker the family should immediately inquire as to their rights.

Health and Accident Insurance

In order to provide for complete financial security some form of health and accident insurance is desirable. Health and accident insurance can be bought separately, but usually the two are purchased together; or the accident insurance alone is bought. Health and accident insurance policies are usually written for a one-year period. Accident insurance alone is sometimes purchased to cover the period during which a person will be on a particular trip, such as several days or weeks.

The provisions of health and accident insurance vary widely among the different types of companies. Many companies provide for monthly payments in case of illness up to 52 weeks. Some have a waiting period of from 15 to 90 days before the payments begin. Many give lump sum or monthly payments for a limited period of time for loss of hands, feet, eyes, or loss of speech or hearing. In some policies the monthly payments are increased 50 per cent if the insured is taken to a hospital. Surgical benefits ranging from $10 to $200, depending upon the type of operation, are provided in some policies. Doctors' and nurses' fees are sometimes included. Some carry a death benefit in case of accidental death.

Despite its relatively high cost, the noncancellable health and accident policy is recommended. Most policies cannot be cancelled within the year in which the premium has been paid. But if the insured has some accident or illness which may incapacitate him in the future, the insur-

ance company is likely not to renew the policy. Or if it is renewed, the insured may be forced to sign a waiver releasing the company from any liability on the policy for a designated illness or accident. These are the very things for which the person may need the insurance. For this reason the noncancellable policy is desirable.

The term "noncancellable" is sometimes intentionally misused in practice. A true noncancellable policy is one which is not only non-cancellable for the year in which the premium has been paid, but one which must be renewed by the company year after year if the insured pays the premiums. In order to reduce the cost of the noncancellable policy, it is suggested that a waiting period of 90 days be provided for. Many people can stand the cost of a few days or a few weeks of illness, but they need protection against some protracted illness such as heart trouble, cancer, and nervous diseases. Health and accident policies are usually not written on persons 60 years of age or older.

A relatively large number of people in the United States have member-ship in the Blue Cross hospital service plan. This is a form of group insurance which provides for the payment of a designated number of dollars a day while the insured is in the hospital. The amount paid is in most instances sufficient to cover the cost of a semiprivate room. This insurance also covers such incidental expenses as board, special diets, operating room, laboratory, drugs and medicines, vaccines, serum, peni-cillin, sulfa drugs, dressings, and oxygen. In many communities it also covers X-rays and anesthetics. It should be noted that Blue Cross, how-ever, does not cover private physicians' and surgeons' bills, whether or not the services were rendered in or out of the hospital. The Blue Cross policy can be written to cover the individual, or it can cover his entire family. The latter insurance, of course, costs more.

In many sections of the country the Blue Shield group plan for surgical benefits is available. This plan is usually closely allied with the Blue Cross. Payments usually range from $5 to $200, depending on the type of operation. Ordinary doctors' bills in the hospital, in the office, or in the home are generally not covered by this type of policy.

Fire Insurance

For the protection of the property owner, it is highly advisable that fire insurance be carried. The home oftentimes represents lifetime sav-ings, and in many cases the home is the largest single savings.

Fire insurance policies are ordinarily written for one, three, or five-year terms, but the three-year policy is the one commonly purchased by home owners. The cost of the three-year policy is less than three times the cost of an annual policy.

In event of a fire, the policy will pay the actual value of the property destroyed (giving consideration, of course, to the amount of insurance carried), rather than the cost of the property destroyed. Fire insurance is rarely taken out for the total value of the property for several reasons. The value of the lot is not affected by a fire; also, a fire usually does not result in a total loss of the house.

In addition to a fire policy many people take out wind and tornado insurance. The extended coverage policy is here recommended for the home owner. This policy covers loss from fire, windstorm, tornado, cyclone, smoke, and damage from falling airplanes or from automobiles (other than the insured's) hitting the property.

Automobile Insurance

For his own financial security an automobile owner should take out several kinds of automobile insurance. Of great importance to the driver is the public liability and property damage policy. Public liability covers risk incurred as a result of injuries to people. The policy specifies a limit that will be paid to any one person as a result of an accident, and it specifies a higher limit for personal injuries to more than one person as a result of an accident. The minimum coverage usually carried is the so-called "five and ten." This kind of policy will pay up to $5,000 for injuries to one person, and up to $10,000 for injuries to more than one person resulting from the same accident. In recent years judges have been awarding higher claims than formerly, and as a result it is recommended that more insurance be carried. Also, people who have considerable property usually find that the courts are rather liberal in granting claims against them. Many people today carry the "ten and twenty," or "twenty-five and fifty" policy. The latter insures up to $25,000 for injuries to one person, and a total of $50,000 for one accident. The cost of this increased coverage is relatively small.

Property damage insurance covers damage to other people's automobiles or other property. Most companies will not write this policy for less than $5,000, and in most instances this amount is sufficient. The property damage coverage is usually written in the same policy as the public liability insurance.

Collision insurance covers damage done to one's own car as a result of a collision or upset. A person may buy a full coverage policy, but this may not be desirable because of its high cost. A commonly written form of policy is the "deductible" one. In this type of policy the insured stands the first $25, $50, or $100 of the damage, and the insurance company pays the balance. A $25 deductible policy can be bought for about one-third the cost of a full-coverage policy; and a $50 deductible costs

only slightly less than one-fourth as much as the full-coverage policy. Some companies write a policy in which the insured stands a fixed amount of the damage, such as 20 per cent, and the insurance company stands 80 per cent.

The other kind of automobile insurance commonly written is the fire and theft policy. The title is self-descriptive. For the drivers' greatest security the "comprehensive" coverage is recommended. This policy covers loss not only from fire and theft, but also damage resulting from windstorm, tornados, hail, water, riot, and falling airplanes. The cost of comprehensive coverage naturally is greater than fire and theft insurance, but it is generally considered worth the expense.

Owning and Financing a Home

Approximately one-half of the families in the United States own their own homes. To many families a home represents the largest investment made during a lifetime. Usually the investment is justified.

There are advantages and disadvantages in owning your own home, but in most instances the advantages outweigh the disadvantages. The home owner has a feeling of security which is not enjoyed by the average renter. He generally takes a greater interest in the schools, political issues, and civic affairs. Communism is less likely to take hold in a nation of home owners. Most persons buy their homes on the instalment plan. This results in forced savings. If they were not buying their homes, it is doubtful whether they would save an equivalent amount of money.

An individual should try not to buy at the peak of the real estate market. But it is probably at this time that he has more money available. Furthermore, more building is going on then, and there are more new homes on the market. Even though prices may be high at the time, there is always the possibility that they may go still higher, and remain relatively high for some time to come. At times a person is more or less forced to buy in order to secure a place to live.

Many people make the statement that it is just as cheap to own as to rent. One should not be misled by this statement. In buying a house, the monthly payments of principal and interest would usually be larger than the amount that would have to be paid in rent for the same place. The amount that the home buyer pays to reduce the amount of the loan really represents a savings, but it nevertheless calls for a monthly cash outlay. In addition to the payments of principal and interest, the home buyer must also pay his taxes and insurance on the property. Maintenance and repairs are also an item of expense to him. To get the true cost of home ownership, the loss of a return on the money invested in the property should be taken into account. After giving consideration to the

various items, one will oftentimes find that home ownership is actually more expensive than renting. Despite this, most people would be better off in the long run to own their own homes.

In building or buying a home care should be taken to see that the materials and workmanship are satisfactory. The type of neighborhood should be given consideration. Nearness or accessibility of transportation systems, schools, and stores is important. Generally speaking the value of the house should be in line with that of other houses in the same locality.

It is sometimes inadvisable to give too much weight to rules-of-thumb; but if the reader wants a few rules respecting home ownership, here are some that would apply in more or less normal times. The value of the lot should be about one-fifth of the total value of the property. A person should pay not over $2\frac{1}{2}$ times his annual income for a home. He should try to spend not over 25 per cent of his monthly income for housing.

It is of course safer to pay cash for a home, but most people find it necessary to borrow to help pay the purchase price. It is advisable to pay down at least 20 per cent. The loan should run sufficiently long so that the monthly payments are not too large a burden. (Twenty years is suggested.) The loan should be the direct-reduction type. This means that the monthly payments for the retirement of the loan should be applied directly each month toward reducing the principal amount of the loan. This method of payment reduces the base on which the interest is computed and thus minimizes the cost. A person should try to pay not much over 4 per cent interest. At the present time he should not pay over 5 per cent. Included in the contract should be a provision giving the borrower the right to pay the loan off faster than called for in the agreement.

Real estate loans which meet certain standards may be insured by the Federal Housing Administration, an agency of the federal government. The regulations governing FHA (Federal Housing Administration) loans have been changed several times since the law was first enacted, and, of course, subsequent changes may be made. At the present time the maximum loan permitted varies from 90 per cent on homes valued at $5,000 and less, to 50 per cent on valuations of $24,250 and higher.

FHA loans are granted not by the government but by such private lending agencies as savings and loan associations, banks, and insurance companies. The rate of interest charged for FHA loans is $4\frac{1}{4}$ per cent. In addition the borrower must pay an insurance premium of $\frac{1}{2}$ of 1 per cent. Thus the effective rate to the borrower is $4\frac{3}{4}$ per cent. The maximum percentage of valuation which may be lent, and the maximum

maturity of FHA loans will be stated after we briefly consider the GI loan.

Veterans may be able to secure GI (Servicemen's Readjustment Act) loans. These loans are also granted by private lending agencies, but the federal government guarantees 60 per cent of the loan up to a maximum of $7,500. The rate of interest charged cannot exceed 4 per cent.

Effective October 12, 1950, the federal government placed new restrictions on loans granted on one- and two-family homes. These restrictions on the size and maturity of the loans apply to FHA and GI loans on both new and old houses, and they also apply to ordinary conventional loans on new houses on which construction started since noon on August 3, 1950. The maximum maturity of loans on houses valued at $7,000 and less is 25 years. On houses valued at more than $7,000, the maximum maturity is 20 years. The following table shows the minimum down payment necessary under the new restrictions for the various valuations indicated.

TABLE 5

MINIMUM PERCENTAGE DOWN-PAYMENT REQUIRED ON FHA AND GI LOANS ON NEW AND OLD HOMES AND ON CONVENTIONAL LOANS ON NEW HOMES

Valuation	*Minimum Percentage Down-Payment* FHA and Conventional Loans	GI Loans
$ 5,000	10.0%	5.0%
6,000	14.2	4.2
7,000	17.1	7.1
8,000	19.4	9.4
9,000	21.1	11.1
10,000	23.0	13.0
11,000	24.5	14.5
12,000	25.8	15.8
13,000	26.9	18.8
14,000	27.9	21.4
15,000	28.7	23.7
16,000	31.9	26.9
17,000	34.7	29.7
18,000	37.2	32.2
19,000	39.5	34.5
20,000	41.5	36.5
21,000	43.8	38.8
22,000	45.9	40.9
23,000	47.8	42.8
24,000	49.6	44.6
24,250	50.0	45.0
Over 24,250	50.0	45.0

It should be noted that the new regulations do not apply to conventional loans (those other than FHA and GI) granted on old houses (those on which construction started prior to noon, August 3, 1950).

The following table shows the monthly payments necessary to pay a $1,000 direct-reduction loan in from 5 to 25 years with interest rates of from 4 to 6 per cent.

TABLE 6

MONTHLY PAYMENTS TO AMORTIZE A $1,000 LOAN IN FROM 5 TO 25 YEARS
WITH INTEREST AT FROM 4% TO 6%

Length of Loan	Interest Rates				
	4%	4½%	5%	5½%	6%
5 Years	$18.42	$18.62	$18.87	$19.10	$19.33
10 Years	10.12	10.36	10.61	10.85	11.10
15 Years	7.40	7.65	7.91	8.17	8.44
20 Years	6.06	6.33	6.60	6.88	7.16
25 Years	5.28	5.56	5.85	6.14	6.44

The monthly payments necessary to pay a loan of any amount can readily be computed from the above table by multiplying the monthly payments shown in the table by the number of thousands borrowed.

Investing in Securities

The individual should proceed carefully in purchasing corporate bonds and stocks. United States Government bonds are in a class by themselves, and, as stated in the preceding chapter, their purchase is recommended.

Some people have been able to make a considerable amount of money in buying corporate stocks, but some have lost more than they made. Unfortunately many persons do not have a sufficient amount of money for investment to enter the securities field; furthermore, they usually do not devote the necessary amount of time to studying particular securities before buying them.

A person should buy corporate securities only if he is able to stand the loss of part of his principal. Before buying corporate securities he should in most instances perhaps first settle any indebtedness, including any mortgage on his home. His life insurance program should be built up, perhaps an annuity program also, and there should be a sizeable reserve fund in his savings account or in government bonds. It would likewise be advisable that the individual should not be solely dependent upon the anticipated income from the securities for his living.

Diversification is imperative in the purchase of corporate securities. It is impossible to determine definitely whether any particular company will be successful or unsuccessful during future years. Some companies that are enjoying prosperity today may not even be in existence 20 years from now. If purchases are confined to one or two companies, the investment may turn out adversely in the future. In a comparatively large list

of securities that are considered good investments today, the losses that may be experienced in the future on some of them may be offset or more than offset by the profits made on the others. It is recommended that an individual put not over from 5 to 10 per cent of his security investment funds in any one issue.

The most important quality of any investment is the safety of the principal. The promise of a high return or a high anticipated return is no consolation to a person who loses part or all of the principal amount invested. Certainty of income from the investment and a fair income are other qualities sought after in a good investment. Generally speaking, the safer the investment, the lower the return. It is usually unwise for the average person to risk the loss of his principal in the hope of getting a larger return. Many people of limited financial resources feel that they should get a relatively high return on their money, because they have only a small amount to invest. These people are the ones who should be content with a low return, because otherwise they would be subjecting their money to too great a risk. It is impossible to get a consistently high return on a safe investment.

Some people have been able to build up a relatively large estate by the purchase of securities of small, new companies. The majority of the people who buy such securities, however, lose part or all of their money. It is recommended that the average person purchase securities of only the large, well-established companies. Generally speaking, the securities of the larger companies in the leading industries, which are listed on the New York Stock Exchange, will turn out better for the average individual than those of smaller or newer companies.

It probably goes without saying that securities in only those companies which have good management should be purchased. It is difficult for a person to determine the quality of management. But if a company is large, well-established, in a growing industry, and has produced a good record for a long period of years in the past, it will probably do well in the future.

The timing of security purchases is important. A considerable amount of money can be lost by buying good securities high and selling them low. Caution should be exercised in selecting the time of purchase and sale. "Buy low and sell high" is easy to say but difficult to do. What at any one time appears to be a low price, might in the light of future events prove to be a high price. Likewise, what appears to be a high price might later prove to be a relatively low price. No one on earth can determine in advance what the low and high prices for any particular security will be in the future. A person should not expect to be able to buy at the low price. If he is able to buy a security at a reasonably fair price, he should be content.

Past experience has showed us that security prices are lowest in times of business depressions. Likewise they are usually highest in times of prosperity. From this it might appear that all a person has to do to make money in securities is to buy during a depression and sell during prosperity. But it is not this easy. At any time during a depression one never knows whether the bottom has been reached. Also we never know when the peak during prosperity has been reached until after the market has begun to decline. It is oftentimes difficult to determine at a particular time whether we are in a depression or a prosperous period. In addition to these troubles, a person is confronted with the fact that not all securities move in the same direction at the same time.

Security speculation is not advisable for the average person. He should not attempt to make money by trading on the short swings of the market. The only way most people can make money on securities is to buy them at a reasonable price and hold on to them for a long period of time. Naturally care must be taken to select only those securities which give evidence of bearing up well in the future.

Buying Bonds

United States Government bonds were discussed in the preceding chapter. Here we shall be concerned with corporate bonds. When a person buys a bond he is lending the issuing corporation a definite amount of money. The principal amount of the bonds represents a debt of the corporation, and the corporation is obligated to pay to the bondholder a fixed rate of interest. The usual denomination of bonds is $1,000. The rate of interest paid on a bond varies according to the credit of the issuing corporation, the nature of the particular bond, and the prevailing rates of interest at the time the bond is issued.

In contrast to bonds, stock represents ownership in the corporation. The bonds of a particular company are always a safer investment than the stock of the same company. Furthermore, the bondholder is more certain of getting interest than the stockholder is of getting dividends. The bonds of one company, however, may be more speculative than the stock of another company. Since the rate of interest is fixed, the bondholder does not get any larger return when the issuing corporation is enjoying unusual prosperity.

The bondholder may be adversely affected in event of inflation. As prices go up, the purchasing power of money falls. Since the bondholder gets a fixed return on his money, and upon the maturity of the bond he also gets back a fixed amount, the purchasing power of this money may be much less than at the time the bond was purchased. The opposite situation is true in a period of deflation.

Bonds are quoted in terms of a percentage of the face value. Thus a quotation, for example, of 99¼ for a bond which has a face value of $1,000 would indicate a selling price of $992.50. In addition to this price the purchaser would have to pay to the seller the amount of the interest which had accrued from the last interest payment date.

If bonds are bought at a discount from their face value and are held to maturity, the purchaser would be getting back more than he paid for the bond. This is considered as an addition to his return or yield. In the case of premium bonds, the premium lost reduces the yield. In order to compute the yield to maturity of a premium or discount bond, it is necessary to use bond tables which are available to the average person at banks, bond houses, brokerage offices, and libraries.

Most bonds are callable by the issuing corporation before their maturity date. Generally speaking, premium bonds are more likely to be called than discount bonds. If it is contemplated that a bond will be held to call or maturity date, it is recommended that the purchaser compute his yield to call date in the case of a premium bond, and to maturity in the case of a discount bond. In event that the bond is to be held only a comparatively short time, the current yield computation is recommended. This is found by dividing the annual interest paid on the bond by the purchase price.

The market prices of bonds are affected by changes in the prevailing rates of interest. When interest rates fall, the price of existing bonds goes up. Likewise, if interest rates advance in the market, the price of bonds will fall. Changes in interest rates produce a larger change in the price of long-term bonds than in the price of short-term bonds.

When interest rates are relatively low, as they are at the present time, the yield on short-term bonds is less than on long-term bonds. As bonds approach the call or maturity dates, the price tends to approach the face value.

State and municipal bonds are exempt from the federal income tax. Government bonds issued prior to 1941 have certain tax-exempt features. People in the higher income tax brackets bid up the price of such bonds to the point where the yield is relatively low. The person whose income is relatively small would not enjoy the tax-exempt feature to the same extent. Such bonds therefore are not recommended for the average person.

The yields on high-grade corporate bonds at the present time are not much higher than the yield on United States Government bonds. This fact may prompt persons of moderate means to invest primarily in taxable government bonds.

Buying Stocks

Stocks represent ownership in a corporation. The issuing corporation is under no obligation to pay back to the holder the amount which he paid for his share of stock. If the stockholder wants to liquidate his stock, he must sell it in the market and get whatever the market price may be at the time of sale. There is no obligation on the part of the issuing corporation to pay dividends to the shareholder. The law will not permit the corporation to pay any dividends unless there are earnings or surplus accounts sufficient to pay the dividend. When there are earnings, dividends do not have to be paid. It is up to the board of directors to decide whether a dividend is to be paid, and if so, the amount of the dividend.

Since the shareholder is considered a part owner of the corporation, any earnings of the corporation are in a sense his, regardless of whether they are paid out to him in the form of dividends. As a practical matter, however, a consistent policy of not paying dividends affects the stock adversely.

Where only one class of stock is outstanding, it is called common stock. Some corporations also issue preferred stock. The latter is a class of stock which in some way is preferred over the common. The usual preference is in respect to dividends. The dividends on preferred stock for any particular year have to be paid before anything can be paid to the holders of common stock. But there is no legal compulsion to pay the preferred dividend. On some preferred stocks the dividend is cumulative: that is, if the dividends are not paid in any year, they cumulate and must be paid in subsequent years before any dividends may be paid to the common shareholders. As a practical matter if the profits are small or nil, the cumulative feature ordinarily means little. If there are no earnings the directors are not permitted to pay a cumulative dividend. If the profits are small, no dividends may be forthcoming. After dividends have accrued for a number of years, the corporation will usually try to effect some compromise settlement with the preferred stockholders. Oftentimes this settlement takes the form of offering them new stock for their accrued dividends.

Most preferred stocks are nonparticipating. This means that after the preferential dividend has been paid, all the balance, if any, goes to the common stock. Thus the common stockholders stand to gain more if the company is unusually successful. If the company is unsuccessful, both the preferred and common stockholders may lose their money.

Preferred stock is commonly given a preference as to assets and accrued dividends in the event of liquidation of the corporation. Such a right is of little practical value. A corporation usually fails as a result of owing

money which it cannot pay. Creditors come ahead of the shareholders, and in many instances the creditors take all the assets and leave nothing for the shareholders. In other instances the corporation is reorganized, and the shareholders are asked to buy new stock in the reorganized company.

There are a number of good investment preferred stocks in the market, but in many of these instances the common stock of the same company might be as good or even better than the preferred. In general, if a person cannot afford to lose his money, he should perhaps not take a chance on any kind of stock.

When one company guarantees the dividends on the stock issued by another company, then the investment standing of the stock of the latter company is enhanced. In the railroad field there are a number of guaranteed stocks which have risen through lease arrangements.

The investment worth of any corporation's stock depends upon the financial situation existing in the particular company. The stock of one company might be a safer investment than the bonds of another company. Other things being equal, if there are no bonds outstanding, the stock would be in a stronger position.

The price of stocks, particularly common stocks, is subject to wide fluctuations in the market. The price of common stocks generally reflects the public's opinion of the prospective future earnings and dividends of the corporation. Past earnings and the trend of the earnings are commonly used in estimating what the future earnings may be. Sometimes the prospect for favorable future earnings is discounted in the price of the stock to the point where the stock may be overpriced in relation not only to present earnings, but even with regard to future earnings. Then oftentimes the future estimated earnings do not materialize.

The price-earnings ratio is often used to measure the relationship of the price of the stock and the earnings. This ratio is obtained by dividing the price of the stock by the average earnings per share for the past few years. Thus, if a stock whose average earnings have been $8 a share, is selling in the market for $100, it is said to be selling for 12½ times the earnings. It should be noted that "earnings per share" means what the corporation has earned per share of stock outstanding, and not what has been paid in dividends. Dividends paid usually vary according to the earnings of the company. The price that should be paid for a share of stock varies according to a number of different factors. Generally speaking, a person should ordinarily not pay more than from 12 to 20 times the earnings per share.

At times a considerable amount of money may be made by buying the stock of some new company and holding on to it for a number of years. But by the law of averages it is usually inadvisable to buy the stock of a

new company. The average person would perhaps do better to buy the stock of the leading companies in the leading industries.

The timing of purchases and sales is as important or perhaps more important than the decision of what stock to buy. And the determination of when to buy and when to sell is more difficult to decide. It is an old saying that a person should buy stocks when they are relatively low and attempt to sell them when they are relatively high. But no one can accurately predict what the future course of stock prices may be. A person who trades on the short swings of the market will probably lose money. Perhaps the best policy for the stock buyer is to try to buy high grade stocks when they are reasonably priced and hold on to them for a number of years. The dividend return on many stocks may be relatively high over a long period of years if the stocks are prudently bought.

The average person should not try to make money in the stock market. The odds against him are too great. He should be content with savings accounts, government bonds, insurance, annuities, and real estate. The buying of stocks should be left to those who can afford the risk and who will devote the necessary amount of time to the thorough study of the securities.

In the proper instances stocks have their place in an investment program. They afford some hedge against inflation. Furthermore, the return that can be obtained on a diversified list of common stocks may be much higher than can be obtained from other investments.

Many people today are buying shares in the investment companies or funds. The open-end investment funds have been very popular in recent years. How investment in these companies will prosper can be determined better in the future. These companies are discussed in a previous chapter.[1]

Making a Will

Most people intend to make a will; but unfortunately many die before they get around to doing it. It is the privilege of everyone to have his property go to the persons he desires upon his death. But if a will is not made, the property will go to the relatives designated by the statutes of the particular state. In many instances the individual would not want his property to go to some of these relatives. If such is the case, then he should make out a will to make certain that the desired persons get the property.

A will is a legal document, and in order that it will be upheld it must be made out in accordance with the laws of the particular state. It is advisable that a lawyer make out the will. The fee charged for this is usually not large, and probably it would be well worth the cost. Any

[1] See Chapter 16.

competent person, however, may draw up a will without the services of an attorney.

The various states prescribe the minimum age for making a will. This age varies usually from 18 to 21. The person making the will should be of sound mind and know what he is doing when he is making the will. He should sign the will in ink at the end in the presence of two witnesses and before the witnesses sign. The witnesses should be adults, younger than the person making the will, and well known to him. They should not be beneficiaries under the will. The witnesses should watch the particular person making the will sign, and the witnesses should watch each other sign. Their addresses should also be given. Furthermore, it should be stated in the will that all the parties signed in the presence of each other. It is not necessary that the witnesses read the will, but the person making it should tell them that it is his will which they are being asked to witness. The date that the will is signed should be stated.

It is advisable that the will be written on only one page. If it takes more than one, the pages should be numbered consecutively, and the witnesses should initial each page.

An executor should be named in the will. And it should be stated that no bond is required of the executor. Husbands and wives customarily make their spouse the executrix or executor of the will.

The full names and relationships of the beneficiaries should be given. The property concerned should be definitely described. If it is the desire of the person making the will that some relative—such as a child or brother, who would be entitled to part of the property of the deceased according to the laws of the state—be cut off, this stipulation should be specifically mentioned in the will. This is sometimes done by leaving the disinherited person a small sum such as $1. Although a husband can leave all his property to his wife, she is the only person he cannot cut off entirely by means of a will. If he leaves her less than the amount she would be entitled to by the laws of the particular state, such as one-third, she can still claim her one-third share of the estate.

After a will is drawn up it should be reviewed at certain intervals in order to determine whether the property is being divided in the way desired in view of changed conditions. Divorce, remarriage, death of some of the beneficiaries, children born after the will was made out—all may make changes in the will desirable. Wills on which alterations have been made may not be enforced by the court, so it is usually advisable that a completely new will be made, rather than an attempt to change an old one.

After a will has been completed, it should be kept in a safe place where it is accessible to the family in the event of death. The will does not have

to be filed with any state or county official when it is made out. Neither does it have to be signed by a notary public. After the death of the person making the will, it is filed with the probate or surrogate court.

Setting Up a Trust

Trusts have been used to an increasing extent by people of some wealth. A person may set up a trust with a bank or trust company, and he may provide that the income from the trust fund be paid to him during his life, and thereafter to the wife. Upon death of the wife, the trust agreement may state that the estate then passes to the children.

Some persons make their life insurance payable to a trust company and provide that the trust company invest the proceeds and give the earnings to certain designated beneficiaries. Another arrangement is the provision in the will for the setting up of a trust fund from the estate.

Banks and trust companies are better equipped to handle the administration of an estate than is the average individual. In many instances the beneficiaries are wives or children who usually have had no experience in money matters. Trust company officials are trained and have a broad experience in making investments.

Trusts are often set up for the purpose of lessening the inheritance or estate taxes. The state laws vary widely, so we will illustrate the tax savings with reference to the Federal Estate Tax. After an exemption of $60,000, the federal government taxes the estates of a deceased person at rates varying from 3 to 77 per cent. If a man with a large estate leaves his property to his wife, the government gets an appreciable share of it. Then when what is left of the property passes to the children upon the wife's death, the government taxes it again. Thus the estate may have dwindled considerably by the time it reaches the children. To lessen the taxation many a man in the past has left his property in trust to his wife during her lifetime and has specified that it pass to the children upon her death. The Federal Estate Tax would be applied when the wife inherited the property, but the estate would not be taxed when the children got it, since this is looked upon as only one transfer.

Changes were made in the Revenue Act of 1948, however, which make it advisable to modify the arrangements stated above. Under the new law as far as tax purposes are concerned, the wife is considered a half owner of the husband's property (and vice versa). If a husband leaves half of his property to his wife outright, or gives it to her in the form of a trust in which she has the full power to designate who shall get it after her death, then this part of the estate goes to her tax free. Of course the estate tax would have to be paid on this portion of the property when it passes to the children. Many people who set up trust funds of

the kind mentioned in the above paragraph are now changing them to take advantage of the split-property division for husbands and wives. This is being done by setting up two trust funds. In one, half the property is left in trust for the wife during her lifetime, and it is specified that then this half shall go to the children. This half is taxed just as it was before. The other half is put into another trust for the wife, but she is given full power of disposition of the property. This part of the property goes to her tax free as indicated above.

The setting up of trusts is a matter which calls for the expert advice of lawyers and trust company officials. People who expect to leave sizable estates should consult them in connection with the advisability of setting up trust funds.

Suggested Readings

Bogen, Jules I., (Editor), *Financial Handbook* 3rd Ed. New York: The Ronald Press Company, 1948. Sections 6, 7, 10, 11, 12, 14, and 26.

Donaldson, Elvin F., *Personal Finance*. New York: The Ronald Press Company, 1948.

Fowle, Helen, and Harwood, E. C., *How to Make Your Budget Balance*. American Institute for Economic Research, Great Barrington, Mass., 1949.

Giles, Ray., *How to Retire and Enjoy It*. New York: Whittlesey House, 1949.

Jordan, David F., and Willett, Edward F., *Managing Personal Finances*. Rev. Ed., New York: Prentice-Hall, Inc., 1945.

Lasser, L. K., and Porter, Sylvia F., *How to Live Within Your Income*. New York: Simon and Schuster, 1948.

Life Insurance Fact Book. New York: Institute of Life Insurance, 1950.

Managing Your Money. Washington, D.C.: National Education Association, 1947.

Masteller, Kenneth, *How to Avoid Financial Tangles*. Great Barrington, Mass.: American Institute for Economic Research, 1950.

Mennis, Edmund A., and Radcliff, Richard W., *How to Invest Wisely*. Great Barrington, Mass.: American Institute for Economic Research, 1950.

Scott, Louise H., *Income Management for Women*. New York: Harper & Bros., 1940.

Upchurch, Garland R., and Harwood, E. C., *Life Insurance and Annuities from the Buyer's Point of View*. Great Barrington, Mass.: American Institute for Economic Research, 1950.

Washington, Lawrence, *How to Plan Your Financial Security*. New York: Whittlesey House, 1949.

Wormser, Rene, *Personal Estate Planning in a Changing World*. New York: Simon and Schuster, 1942.

25

Consumer Instalment Credit in Commercial Banks

by WALTER B. FRENCH

Deputy Manager, American Bankers Association

Introduction

ALTHOUGH commercial banks as we know them today have been in business for over 150 years, it was only a short time ago that they began to specialize in instalment credit and the credit needs of individuals. Banks always provided credit to individuals and others for business purposes, but borrowing for personal needs was something about which they knew very little. The truth of the matter is that banking philosophy was opposed to personal debt. "Save money" was their advice to the public. However important the reason appeared to be, going into debt was largely discouraged. There were two exceptions to this general rule: (1) the acquisition of real estate because of the substantial amount of credit involved and the reasonably good security it offered, and (2) lending to individuals with substantial means. People who could show a good financial statement found little difficulty in securing whatever credit they needed.

Mortgages to individuals for the purchase of homes have been made by banks for years and today represent the largest outstanding in consumer instalment debt of any single classification—approximately $44 billion.[1] This figure does not include farm dwellings or housing for over four families.

Since this chapter is concerned largely with consumer instalment credit extended by commercial banks to wage earners or people of small means for personal needs or conveniences, mortgages have not been made a part of our study. Before leaving the subject, however, it might be well to note that despite the fact that many opponents of consumer instal-

---

[1] Data from Housing and Home Finance Agency, Washington, D.C., as of December 31, 1950.

ment credit would discourage a person from assuming debt in order to buy, for example, a washing machine that would save many hours of backbreaking labor, or to borrow a couple of hundred dollars for dental work or a needed operation, the same lender would have no hesitancy in advancing thousands of dollars in credit for the purchase of a home. This attitude can be readily understood when it is realized that home buying does represent stability and good effort on the part of the purchaser.

The growth of building and loan associations, and later savings and loan companies, are good examples of lending specialists that developed over the years in order to fill the need for this type of financing. These agencies of credit were found necessary, in addition to others that were supplying a part of this credit, such as individual banks, insurance companies, and mortgage companies. Thinking on this matter began to change when we reached the apartment stage in our housing progress, and many people no longer thought in terms of home buying even though they enjoyed the same income that many home buyers did.

Historical Background

Although consumer instalment buying goes back a good many years, perhaps furniture stores represent the first major industry to enter this credit development in a serious way. As early as 1807 the Cowperthwait & Sons, New York City, furniture house used this instalment system. To illustrate: when a young couple marries, furnishing a home represents a substantial outlay in money; so credit arrangements were made by the furniture store and the debt was paid off over a period of years. This arrangement was considered a good risk because the seller obtained a lien on the furniture, and then, too, it represented the buyer's home.

Pawn shops, too, go back a good many years and represent an early means for the individual to secure cash credit for his personal needs. In the case of pawn shops, as with furniture houses, collateral of value commensurate with the debt was pledged. Pawn shops were found to be operating in this country as early as 1859.

Industrial banks came into existence in the early 1900's. The first Morris Plan Bank was organized in Norfolk, Virginia, in 1910, and from that time on the movement grew. Today they represent a significant factor in this field of lending. The operation in this type of bank is the closest to that adopted by commercial banks. The management of the industrial loan banks was exceedingly helpful to the commercial bankers when they first went into the small loan business.

The industrial banks are a good example of the safety of the consumer credit risk. Out of all the industrial banks operating during the depres-

sion in the early 1930's, not one bank failed or remained closed after the banking holiday. When the fact is taken into consideration that a very high percentage of the resources of these banks is invested in consumer instalment paper, the record is all the more impressive.

As our economy expanded and we entered the machine age and the wonders of mass production, it became more and more apparent that if the goods produced were to be sold and the largest number of people possible were to enjoy owning them, some form of financing was necessary that would permit the purchaser a period of time in which to pay for the goods while benefiting from their use. Over the years consumer instalment buying has developed in practically every consumer field, and today credit is extended by many agencies to fill every consumer need.

Consumer instalment credit is divided into two principal classifications: (1) unsecured or cash lending, and (2) secured or collateral lending. In the case of cash lending, the borrower makes his application for a cash loan; if it is approved, he secures his cash and uses it for the purpose for which it was intended. The lender in this case has only the borrower's note. In the case of secured lending, the lender either extends the borrower credit for the purchase of some durable goods or buys the paper from a dealer who has extended the credit to the borrower. In each case the lender has a chattel mortgage or a conditional bill of sale on the article purchased.

There are four principal reasons why an individual borrows. They are:

1. He needs money for some urgent reason, for example, to pay off debts, to have his home repaired, to have some necessary medical or dental attention, for funeral expenses, or for insurance premiums. Any number of requests are made under this category.

2. It is advantageous for him to borrow, for example, to buy something at a reduced price, to discharge a debt or debts at a reduced figure, or to get a good discount by paying cash.

3. He wants cash in order to buy some article he needs or desires. Here are several possibilities: an automobile, a washing machine, a refrigerator, a radio, a television set, and so on.

4. He wants to borrow because he is an individual of good character and income and feels that he represents a good risk for credit. His reason for borrowing may not be necessitous; he may want to take a vacation or to buy some kind of luxury. In any event, if he is a good risk, the credit is usually extended, if not by one lender then by another.

In order to fill this great need for personal credit, many agencies have developed over the last thirty years. In addition to banks, the most important ones are personal finance companies, sales finance companies. industrial banks, industrial loan companies, and credit unions.

The total consumer instalment credit balances outstanding on January 1951 amounted to $13,255,000,000,[2] and of this amount the agencies mentioned in the preceding paragraph loaned 97 per cent. The outstandings for each type of lender as of the same date are as follows:

Personal loan companies	$1,089,000,000
Sales finance agencies	5,087,000,000 [3]
Industrial banks	387,000,000
Industrial loan companies	225,000,000
Credit unions	518,000,000
Commercial banks	5,611,000,000

One type of lender which should be mentioned is the high-rate, illegal lender. This lender practices his trade outside the law, preying on unfortunate people who need, in most cases, small amounts of money; for these he charges unconscionable rates. Loans made by this group are seldom for more than $25 or $50; and the lender's unethical methods of collecting his principal and interest frequently have him in the courts of law.

Consumer instalment credit has grown to be a major factor in the credit system of our economy over the last thirty years; and commercial banking, despite its hesitancy to accept the business in its early stages, is now playing the major role.

Although there are no reliable statistics available as to how many banks were making consumer instalment loans prior to 1927, it is probable that they numbered less than one hundred. Practically all banks were making some loans to individuals for consumer purchases on the usual one-two-three month discount basis; but the instalment technique as we know it today was not only not in use in banks, it was completely unknown.

In 1928 the National City Bank of New York announced the opening of a department to supply credit for consumer needs. This was the first large bank to enter the business in a formal way. Since it had many bank correspondents, its entry into the small loan field received considerable attention, not only from other agencies doing a small loan business but from banks as well. Another important entry into the consumer instalment business about this time (1929) was the Bank of America in San Francisco, California, with branches serving the entire state of California.

Although these experiments were observed by banks over the country, few did anything about it. There was an understandable hesitancy to enter a field of credit about which they knew nothing. Bank credit men who were usually consulted were aghast at the idea of extending credit to anyone who could not produce a financial statement similar to those they were accustomed to receive from their business accounts. Bankers

---

[2] *Federal Reserve Bulletin*, Washington, D.C., March 1951.
[3] Includes sales finance companies, department stores, mail order houses, etc.

did not realize then that it took a different type of credit man to judge personal credit where character, stability, and earnings were the only factors he had to assist him in passing judgment on a credit application. In other words, character plus ability and willingness to pay equal a good instalment credit risk.

Early operations were cumbersome, in most cases having to do only with personal loans or cash credit. The applications involved cash alone and not the purchase of merchandise or the necessity of taking chattel mortgages or conditional bills of sale. Most of these early operations required co-makers on the note. This requirement discouraged many prospective borrowers; and for this reason more than any other, the business done by banks was limited. Today most of the personal loans made by banks are on a single-name basis.

Again, no reliable figures are available, but by 1934 there were probably less than five hundred banks doing a consumer instalment loan business; and most of these confined themselves to personal loans.

Federal Housing Administration Title I loans. In the great depression of the early 1930's, government leaders began looking for ways and means to stimulate business. Various experiments were tried in an effort to get business going again. These efforts all came under the general heading of "priming the pump." One of the suggestions made to stimulate business for the building trade was in the field of housing. On August 10, 1934, the Federal Housing Administration announced that it would furnish a liberal guaranty to all authorized lenders who would grant credit to borrowers for the repair and modernization of their homes and to lessees whose leases ran six months beyond the term of the loan. This was a fertile field at that time because many properties had changed hands through foreclosures and most of them were badly in need of repairs.

The first guaranty offered by the Federal Housing Administration was 20 per cent on all loans of this type made during the time provided for in the guaranty, a period of twenty months. The maximum maturity for each note was sixty months, and the maximum amount for each note was $2,000, to be paid in equal monthly instalments. The loans were known as F.H.A. Title I, and the guaranty was simple to compute. For example, if a bank made $100,000 of these loans during this period, it would have a guarantee fund of $20,000 against which to charge losses. This was a very liberal guaranty arrangement, and it ran until April 1, 1936. There was no charge for insurance during these first twenty months.

When we take into consideration the fact that the risk was on personal real estate, in most cases representing homes, it offered an excellent credit risk. Because of the nature of the times, which were quite bad, and the lack of experience in the consumer instalment field, a fair percentage of

the banks qualified as lenders under the first twenty months of F.H.A. Title I. These banks actually made few loans, however, and approximately 50 per cent made no loans at all.

When F.H.A. Title I was in the development stage, this government agency called on Roger Steffan, vice president of the National City Bank of New York, for help and advice. This well-informed banker, who was a pioneer in the consumer instalment loan field, did much to formulate and implement the plan.

On April 1, 1936, the F.H.A. announced that the guaranty would be reduced from 20 per cent to 10 per cent of the total volume made by each lender for the period of the guaranty, or about one year. Again, there was no charge for the insurance. Following a lapse of almost one year the guaranty of 10 per cent was extended again to July 1, 1939.

The experience of lenders during the first two and a half years of F.H.A. Title I proved that even a 10 per cent guaranty would be more than ample. Claims filed during the first two and a half years, even with inexperienced bank lenders and poor times, were only 2.359 per cent of the total loans made by all qualified financial institutions. During the first twenty months under the 20 per cent guaranty, 5,822 banks reported loans for a total of $380,685,560. Claims filed by banks amounted to $7,877,775. Although this sum represented a little more than 2 per cent of volume, substantial recoveries were made by the F.H.A.

From April 1, 1936, to April 1, 1937, when the guaranty provision was reduced to 10 per cent, only 3,893 banks reported $52,006,125 loans made. Claims filed under this guaranty by banks amounted to $1,040,123.

During the early operations of F.H.A. Title I, banks were permitted to charge a discount of 5 per cent on the loans, but they were not obliged to pay any part of this discount to the Federal Housing Administration for the guaranty. After July 1, 1939, it was required that an insurance premium of ¾ of 1 per cent for the guaranty be paid by lenders; the rate charged for the loan was still not to exceed a discount of 5 per cent.[4]

Further Development by Banks. Many banks that are important lenders in consumer instalment credit today, can trace their first interest in this credit to F.H.A. Title I loans. As a matter of fact, this operation which began in 1934 had aroused by 1936 sufficient interest on the part of many bankers to investigate other phases of instalment credit lending. From 1934 to 1936 there existed a period of confusion as applied to this credit. There was great reluctance on the part of many responsible bankers to have anything to do with making small loans to individuals. Many bankers believed that goods and services should not be contracted for until a person had the money to pay for them. Some bankers referred to the small loan operation as five-and-ten cent banking, forgetting that

---

[4] Federal Housing Administration, Washington, D.C., *Annual Reports*, 1934–39.

Mr. Woolworth and others did an exceptionally good business for years in the five-and-ten cent field.

The early operations of banks in the small loan field suffered most because of the attitude of many bankers toward the business. In one bank could be found bankers aggressively in favor of the business and bankers violently opposed to it. In spite of some opposition in almost every institution, more and more banks became interested in this new field of credit, and by 1938 almost 4,000 banks were engaged in some form of the business.

As time went on, the desire among bankers to discuss the possibilities of consumer instalment lending increased. They felt that they needed (and they did need) a common meeting ground where ideas and experiences could be exchanged. In 1938 the American Bankers Association, through its Bank Management Commission, made a few studies; but the findings were not thorough enough, perhaps because most bankers were not in the business and knew little or nothing about it. At that time there was no separate department in the Association concerned only with this credit.

In 1938 a small group of bankers, interested in the development of consumer instalment credit in banks, met in Buffalo, New York, to exchange experiences and to talk over common problems. Out of this meeting came the formation of a new bankers group to be known as the Bankers Association for Consumer Credit. After the organization meeting, the banks of the country were invited to take membership, and before many months had passed the association had 150 members. At its first meeting held at Conneaut Lake, Pennsylvania, in the spring of 1939, over 400 bankers attended. The spirit and enthusiasm of all those in attendance encouraged the leaders of this association to renew their efforts to increase membership and to broaden their field of operation.

As a result of the activities of the Bankers Association for Consumer Credit, the American Bankers Association realized the need for information on this subject and announced the formation of a consumer instalment credit department in March 1940. The first meeting was held at Hot Springs, Virginia, on April 21-24, 1940, during the Executive Council meeting of the American Bankers Association. Out of that first meeting came two very important documents for the guidance of banks that were either in the business already or thinking of entering it. Those two documents were a Standards of Practice and a Consumer Credit Creed. They are as follows:

CONSUMER CREDIT STANDARDS OF PRACTICE

The basic principle upon which successful time sales financing is built is that the purchaser will have sufficient down-payment to establish an interest

or equity in the merchandise and will be able to pay regular monthly instalments of sufficient amount to increase that equity faster than the merchandise will depreciate from time and average use.

If a retail instalment sales contract does not so stipulate, a complete statement of the transaction should be provided purchaser to include cash price, down-payment, unpaid balance, insurance cost, principal balance, finance charge, time balance, and the number, amount, and due date of each payment.

Balloon notes on times sales financing should be avoided.

Banks should avoid practices which tend to result in a borrower's or purchaser's becoming involved with obligations beyond his ability to handle.

All banks should determine their actual costs of operation in consumer credit.

All borrowers or purchasers prepaying their obligations should be allowed a refund of the actual unearned interest or finance charge.

Interest or finance charges should be taken into earnings by allocation to the successive periods of time ending on scheduled instalment payment dates in proportions corresponding to the amounts of the successive unpaid portions of the principal amount scheduled to be outstanding.

CONSUMER CREDIT CREED

We believe, That, in order to justify its charter, a bank must serve the reasonable credit requirements of its territory as well as provide a safe depository for funds;

That the extension of credit to salaried or wage-earning individuals on a sound basis is an economically important part of such service;

That, while recognizing the importance of volume in the reduction of loan costs, a bank should endeavor to assist people to get out of debt rather than into it;

That, although a bank must be competitive, it must maintain its practices and policies on a plane which will not bring disrepute to banking, and keep all advertising restrained, truthful, and exact;

That a bank must determine for itself whether it will offer its services directly to the public or through others, but that no bank should uphold or assist such others when they indulge in unfair business practices;

That a bank should determine the costs and hazards inherent in such credit and establish its loan charges accordingly; and, finally,

That any bank which extends credit to individuals under these standards of practice will merit the good will and support of the general public.

In May 1940 the Bankers Association for Consumer Credit merged their activities with the American Bankers Association. The president of the B.A.C.C. was Kenton R. Cravens, at that time vice president of the Cleveland Trust Company, Cleveland, Ohio, and he became the first chairman of the Consumer Credit Council (changed in 1944 to the Committee on Consumer Credit) of the American Bankers Association.

Since its inception, the Committee on Consumer Credit has held annual national conferences, except during World War II years. The conference held in Chicago in March 1951 attracted over 1,000 bankers representing every state of the Union, the District of Columbia, and Canada.

Enabling Legislation

Most states have a legal maximum rate of interest that banks can charge on loans. Although this rate varies in some states, the general maximum is 6 per cent simple interest per annum. But in order for banks to do a small loan business, a rate considerably higher than 6 per cent simple interest is necessary if the amount of the loan, the interview, the credit check that must be made, and the cost of monthly collections are taken into consideration. Therefore, it is necessary for banks to seek enabling legislation in most of the states. Even in the case of F.H.A. Title I loans, it was necessary for most states to pass enabling legislation before banks could make this type of loan. The Committee on Consumer Credit of the American Bankers Association suggested a model bill for the guidance of the banks in the various states. Following is the suggested Model Bill.

MODEL BILL

While the Association hesitates to present a small loan enabling act in the form of a model bill for the reason that it is extremely difficult to prepare model legislation that will be acceptable in every state, the contents of this letter will give you the current thinking of the Consumer Credit Council on the basic philosophy upon which such a bill should be developed.

This philosophy is based on the premise that banks are subject to inspection by and supervision of either state or national departments and that this does or should afford the borrowing public all protection necessary; that discount and instalment loans have long been recognized as normal banking practices; and that the only need for legislation is to remove any possible doubt that such transactions may be usurious. It is our belief that legislation should be passed as an amendment to the existing banking law in the state. The rate of charge permitted should be either the contract or legal rate, whichever is required in the particular state to afford the banks an adequate return.

We believe that the body of the bill should read about as follows:

A Suggested Bank Instalment Loan Statute

AN ACT to regulate instalment loans granted by banks and trust companies.[1]

Be it enacted, etc.:

Sec. 1. Any bank or trust company authorized to do business [2] in this State may contract for a charge [3] for a secured or unsecured loan,

repayable in instalments, not in excess of what the interest would be at the [4] (legal rate) or (highest general contract rate permitted by statute) upon the face amount of the instrument or instruments evidencing the obligation to repay the loan, for the entire period of the loan, and deduct such charge in advance, provided, however, that if the entire unpaid balance outstanding on the loan is paid,[5] the bank shall make a refund or rebate of such charge in an amount computed on the aggregate instalments not due a full instalment period or more under the terms of such instrument or instruments, at the original contract rate of charge, prorated to the period of the loan covered by such unmatured instalments.[6]

Sec. 2. Any bank or trust company making a loan under Section 1 hereof shall set forth the rate used in computing the charge for the loan and the full cost thereof in dollars and cents in the application for the loan, the note, or other instrument evidencing the obligation to repay the loan, or in a written statement delivered to the borrower.

NOTES

1. While it is believed that the suggested title will comply with the constitutional provisions in most, if not all, states, local counsel should be consulted to assure that the title conforms to the constitutional requirements and local practices.

2. This Act is intended as an amendment to the banking law. The term "banks and trust companies" will vary to conform to the statutory description of the institutions intended to be included.

"Authorized to do business in this state" is used in order to specifically recognize the right of national banks to operate under this Act.

3. "Charge" is intended to include all moneys received by the bank for services rendered in connection with the making and handling of the loan and the use of the money but does not include expenses permitted by law to be charged to the borrower. If service charges are permitted by law, they should be specifically mentioned as not prohibited by this Act. This could be accomplished by a provision that "charge" was not intended to include charges for services otherwise permitted by law. If late charges are not specifically authorized by the Act, they should not be imposed unless there are decisions in the state upholding them as liquidated damages.

4. The rate of charge permitted should be either the legal or contract rate, whichever is necessary in a particular state to afford banks a reasonable re turn. Strike out the inapplicable parenthetical provision.

5. "Paid" means by the proceeds of a new loan or otherwise.

6. Illustration: A $1200 loan is discounted January first at 6% per annum and made repayable in 12 monthly instalments. Balance of $500 paid August fifteenth. Therefore, $400 is prepaid a full instalment period or more, and the period covered by such instalments is 4 months. Refund calculated as follows: charge on $400 at 6% rate—$24. Prorate this on ratio of 4 to 12, which is ⅓ of $24 or $8.

In negotiating with the legislative committees on enabling legislation of this kind, it may be necessary for you to set certain limits as to amount and time. Although the act would give greater freedom of operation without such restrictions, if you find that in order to secure passage, you must specifically mention certain limits, it is our suggestion that the maximum amount should be not less than $2,500 and the maximum time should be not less than 15 months, preferably 24 months.

You may also find it necessary, because of competitors' opposition to

your bill, to say something on the matter of advertising, which might be covered by a provision that forbids false or misleading advertising, and the provision might also state that, if the rate of charge is published, it shall include a statement of cost in dollars and cents.

In some cases, it might be insisted that the bill contain a provision penalizing the lending institution for charging more than is authorized under the act. In that event, it might be necessary to insert a provision that, if any bank or trust company fails or refuses to refund excess interest after written demand therefor, it shall be subject to a fine of not more than $500.

There are also some protective provisions which your lawyers would probably want to include, such as a protective clause that, if any provision of the act or application thereof to any person or circumstance is held invalid, such invalidity shall not affect other provisions or applications of the act. They usually insert a provision that all acts or parts of acts inconsistent with this act "are hereby repealed." In this connection, it might be well to consider excepting any statutory provisions in your state that permit service charges, late charges, the charging of examination fees or expenses to the borrower, or minimum charges.

Late charges should either be specifically authorized by the act or not be imposed by the banks. If it is the intention to impose late charges, this may be accomplished by a provision which would read about as follows:

> In case of default in the payment of the principal, or any instalment of the principal of any loan made under Section 1 (a) hereof, such bank or trust company may charge interest on the delinquent instalment at the statutory rate, or in lieu thereof make a late charge in an amount not to exceed five cents (5¢) for each dollar ($1.00) of any instalment that has become due and remained unpaid for a period of five days, provided that no such late charge shall exceed one dollar ($1.00) and only one late charge shall be collected for any delinquent instalment regardless of the period during which such instalment remains unpaid.

Typical of this type of legislation is the following Pennsylvania statute, which is part of that state's banking act.

1. In addition to the general corporate powers granted by this act, and in addition to any powers specifically granted to a bank or a bank and trust company elsewhere in this act, a bank or a bank and trust company shall have the following powers, subject to the limitations and restrictions imposed by this act:

(a) To lend money either upon the security of real or personal property, or otherwise; to charge or to receive in advance interest therefor; to contract for a charge for a secured or unsecured installment loan, which in principal amount shall not exceed thirty-five hundred dollars, and which under its terms shall be repayable in substantially equal installments over a period not exceeding three years, which charge shall be at a rate not exceeding six dollars per one hundred dollars per annum upon the original face amount of the instrument or instruments evidencing the loan for the entire period of the loan, and which such charge may be collected in advance: Provided, That if the entire unpaid balance outstanding on a loan is paid

by cash, renewal, or otherwise at any time prior to maturity, the bank, or bank and trust company shall give a refund or credit of the unearned portion of such charge, which refund or credit shall represent at least as great a proportion of the original charge as the sum of the periodical time balances after the date of prepayment bears to the sum of all the periodical time balances under the schedule of payments in the original instrument or instruments evidencing the loan: Provided, however, That the bank, or bank and trust company, shall not be required to refund or credit any portion of such unearned charge which would result in a net charge on a loan less than the minimum charge provided for herein, nor to make a refund or credit where the amount thereof, computed as herein set forth, would be less than one dollar for each loan paid prior to the maturity date. No additional amount shall be charged or contracted for, directly or indirectly, on or in connection with any such installment loan, except the following: (a) Delinquency charges not to exceed five cents for each dollar of each installment more than fifteen days in arrears: Provided, That the total of delinquency charges on any such installment loan shall not exceed fifteen dollars, and only one delinquency charge shall be made on any one installment; (b) Premiums paid by the bank, or bank and trust company, for insurance required or obtained as security for or by reason of such installment loans; (c) Such amounts as are necessary to reimburse the bank, or bank and trust company, for fees paid to a public officer for filing, recording, or releasing any instrument or lien; and the actual expenditures including reasonable attorneys' fees for legal process or proceedings, to secure or collect any such instalment loan. Any advertising concerning such installment loans which contains a statement of an amount, or rate of charge, shall also contain the percentage rate, either per month or per year, computed on declining balances of the face amount of the loan instrument to which such charge would be equivalent if the loan were repaid according to contract: Provided, That this requirement may be compiled with by stating the equivalent percentage rate which would earn the charge for such a loan repayable in twelve equal consecutive monthly installments, and such state rate may be closely approximate, rather than exact, if the statement so indicates: And provided further, That this requirement shall not apply to an advertisement in which an amount, or rate of charge, is indicated only by a table which contains and is confined to examples of the face amount of the loan instrument, the proceeds to the borrower exclusive of the charge, and the amount, number and intervals of the required payments;

(b) The aggregate amount of unpaid principal due from any one borrower on one or more loans granted pursuant to the provisions of the paragraph shall not at any time exceed thirty-five hundred dollars.

Although rates vary in some states, the rate decided upon in the majority of states that have passed enabling legislation was 6 per cent discount. This amounts to 11.78 per cent simple interest per annum. This discount method appealed to the banks because it was a method with which they were familiar and it made the cost of the loan easily computed by the borrower. For example, a loan of $200 for one year costs $12 at 6 per cent discount. When we take into consideration all the

steps necessary to make and collect a loan for this amount, the cost is moderate. Banks operating on a 6 per cent discount plan are operating as low as any other cash lender and much lower than some, in particular the licensed small loan companies. In actual practice banks charge rates from 3 per cent discount to 10 per cent discount, depending on the amount of the loan and the interest laws governing this type of lending in the particular state.

Opposition to Enabling Legislation. When the banks introduced bills that asked for the right to do a small loan business in their various states, the legislation met with considerable resistance, not from the legislators but from competitive lenders. Most of this opposition came from a few companies that represented one group—the licensed small loan lenders. The Household Finance Corporation began operating as early as 1878, and most of the other companies in this group of licensed small loan lenders have been doing business in some states since 1916 under the Uniform Small Loan Law. Their method of charging interest is on a per cent per month basis. The rates charged vary, but in most states where these lenders are licensed, the rate is from 2 per cent to $3\frac{1}{2}$ per cent per month on the unpaid balance, or, figured on an annual basis, 24 per cent to 42 per cent per annum. The arguments used by this group in their resistance to enabling legislation were that if banks were going to enter the small loan field, they should state their rate on the same basis as the licensed small loan companies. The banks would not agree to this, and in some instances the arguments were long and bitter.

Over the years the licensed small loan lenders had done an excellent job in having their operation accepted by many segments of society as a good operation. They not only proved to the satisfaction of many responsible groups the need for their services but also demonstrated that their method of doing business, including the way they stated their rate, was a good one. These groups include such responsible sources as the Russell Sage Foundation, many of the Better Business bureaus, and educators over the country. Much material has been published over the years, and by diligent effort the companies have made many friends. When the banks met this formidable opposition in some states, it was not easy to overcome. As a matter of fact, the situation is not yet satisfactorily adjusted in some states. In most cases, however, the banks succeeded in getting the bills passed on their basis, and at the present time the opposition to their enabling legislation is, if anything, passive.

Statement of rate. The arguments on the matter of how to state the rate on an instalment loan were many and could be the subject of a book in itself. There was good reason to believe that many competitors of banks in the small instalment loan field feared their entry into the business. It is an actual fact that all lenders have increased their out-

standings during the years the banks have been in the business. How this came about cannot be said for a certainty because banks today are the largest single lender in the small loan field. Some informed sources believe that by going into this field, the banks dignified the borrowing of small amounts of money by individuals for personal needs. Before banks went into the operation, it was not as well understood by the general public as it is today, despite all the time, effort, and money spent by the licensed small loan lenders to accomplish this purpose. As time goes on and people become better educated in the cost of money, the ratio of loans between competing agencies may change; but for the present it would appear that each group of lenders has an appeal to different borrowing groups of our society.

Educating Banks in the Business

The consumer instalment loan business, as indicated earlier in this chapter, is divided into two general classifications:

1. The direct business, where the borrower goes direct to the lender and makes an application for a loan. This is known to the trade as cash lending.

2. The indirect business, where the lender buys consumer instalment paper from dealers and others in one or more pieces. This is known as instalment sales financing.

Each type of business requires a different technique. When banks first entered the field, they were of course without experienced help. Many bank operations secured the services of experienced men from the small loan companies, which do a direct business largely, and men from the sales finance companies, which do an indirect business principally.

The characteristics of the borrower in each case are the same, except that in direct lending the lender does the interviewing and the necessary credit checking, whereas in the indirect operation the interviewing is done by the dealer, who also does some of the credit checking. Many banks trained their own men, and although this took a much longer period of time, it has worked out well over the years. It was for this latter group that some organized effort to publish information was a real necessity. Since the bank-trained group represented by far the greater number, it became apparent in the early days of the business that meetings and manuals of operation were needed to help the bankers in setting up departments so they could expedite loan applications as quickly and as effectively as their competitors who had been in the business for years.

Personal loans were the simplest to process because they offered a procedure with which most banks were familiar. The prospective bor-

LOAN NO.

APPLICATION NO.

Form No. 2 A-G-A

Application for Personal Loan

TO_____ CONSUMER INSTALMENT CREDIT DEPARTMENT
(BANK)
(FILL ALL BLANKS, WRITING "NO" OR "NONE" WHERE NECESSARY TO COMPLETE INFORMATION)

I HEREBY MAKE APPLICATION FOR A LOAN OF_____ DOLLARS ► $ _____   RESIDENCE ADDRESS ☐ BUSINESS ADDRESS ☐   SEND MAIL TO

TO BE USED FOR THE FOLLOWING PURPOSE_____

NAME_____ CITY OF BIRTH_____ DATE OF BIRTH_____
PLEASE PRINT FULL NAME

RESIDENCE ADDRESS_____
PREVIOUS ADDRESS_____
NO. AND STREET   CITY   POSTAL UNIT NO.   STATE   NO. OF YRS. THERE   TELEPHONE NUMBER
DO YOU OWN A MOTOR CAR? YES ☐ NO ☐ YEAR____ MAKE____

SINGLE OR MARRIED_____ NAME OF WIFE OR HUSBAND_____ NUMBER OF DEPENDENTS INCLUDING WIFE_____

SALARY, COMMISSION OR OTHER REGULAR COMPENSATION (PER MONTH)_____ ► $ _____

OTHER INCOME, IF ANY. SOURCE_____ ► $ _____

IS WIFE (OR HUSBAND) EMPLOYED?_____ IF SO, A SEPARATE COMAKER'S STATEMENT SHOULD BE COMPLETED AND SIGNED.

CHECK ✓ WHETHER EMPLOYED ☐   OR IN BUSINESS FOR SELF ☐

NAME OF EMPLOYER OR BUSINESS_____ ADDRESS_____
TEL. No._____ KIND OF BUSINESS_____ YOUR POSITION_____
BADGE OR EMPLOYMENT No._____ HOW LONG WITH THIS EMPLOYER OR BUSINESS_____ NAME AND TITLE OF SUPERIOR_____
IF NOT WITH PRESENT COMPANY TWO YEARS OR MORE STATE NAME OF PREVIOUS EMPLOYER: EMPLOYER_____ ADDRESS_____ YEARS THERE_____

OWE THE FOLLOWING DEBTS AND NO OTHERS: (IF NONE, STATE "NONE")
I LIST BELOW ALL YOUR DEBTS TO BANKS, LOAN OR FINANCE COMPANIES, STORES OR OTHERS, INCLUDING INSTALMENT PURCHASES.

TO WHOM INDEBTED (NAME)	ADDRESS	ACCOUNT NUMBER	ORIGINAL AMOUNT	PRESENT UNPAID BALANCE	AMOUNT DUE EACH MONTH	ARREARS IF ANY

HAVE YOU NOW OR HAVE YOU EVER HAD ANY JUDGMENTS, GARNISHMENTS, SUITS OR OTHER LEGAL PROCEEDINGS AGAINST YOU? (IF NONE, STATE "NONE")
IF SO, GIVE PARTICULARS_____

REAL ESTATE OWNED BY APPLICANT AND/OR WIFE (HUSBAND) (IF NONE, STATE "NONE")_____
ADDRESS - NO. AND STREET   CITY   STATE   PURCHASE PRICE $ MORTGAGE $ ANNUAL EXPENSES $

AMOUNT OF LIFE INSURANCE $_____ COMPANIES_____
BENEFICIARY_____ AMOUNT OF LOANS_____

PERSONAL (OR SPECIAL) CHECKING A/c   NAME OF BANK_____ BRANCH_____
BUSINESS " A/c   NAME OF BANK_____ BRANCH_____
SAVINGS A/c   NAME OF BANK_____ BRANCH_____
ACCOUNT NO._____

IF APPLICATION IS APPROVED. PLEASE ☐ MONTHLY BEGINNING ONE MONTH FROM DAY LOAN IS MADE
HAVE PAYMENTS FALL DUE ☐ MONTHLY ON THE FOLLOWING DATE_____

IN SUBMITTING THE FOREGOING STATEMENT, THE UNDERSIGNED AFFIRMS THAT THE INFORMATION ABOVE SET FORTH IS IN ALL RESPECTS TRUE, ACCURATE, AND COMPLETE, AND IS MADE WITH THE INTENT THAT IT BE RELIED UPON BY THE ABOVE-NAMED BANK IN EXTENDING CREDIT TO THE UNDERSIGNED; THAT IT CORRECTLY REFLECTS THE FINANCIAL CONDITION OF THE UNDERSIGNED ON THE DATE HEREOF; THAT HE HAS NOT KNOWINGLY WITHHELD ANY INFORMATION THAT MIGHT AFFECT THE CREDIT RISK. THE UNDERSIGNED EXPRESSLY AGREES TO NOTIFY IMMEDIATELY SAID BANK IN WRITING OF ANY MATERIAL CHANGE IN HIS FINANCIAL CONDITION, WHETHER APPLICATION FOR FURTHER CREDIT IS MADE OR NOT, AND IN THE ABSENCE OF SUCH WRITTEN NOTICE IT IS EXPRESSLY AGREED THAT SAID BANK, IN GRANTING NEW, OR CONTINUING EXISTING CREDIT, MAY RELY ON THIS STATEMENT AS HAVING THE SAME FORCE AND EFFECT AS IF DELIVERED UPON THE DATE ADDITIONAL CREDIT IS REQUESTED OR EXISTING CREDIT EXTENDED OR CONTINUED. THE UNDERSIGNED EXPRESSLY AUTHORIZES SAID BANK TO OBTAIN FROM HIS EMPLOYER OR FROM ANY OTHER SOURCE SUCH INFORMATION AS MAY BE DESIRED IN CONNECTION WITH THIS APPLICATION, AND EACH SUCH SOURCE IS HEREBY AUTHORIZED TO PROVIDE SAID BANK WITH SUCH INFORMATION AS MAY BE REQUESTED; AND FURTHER AGREES THAT THIS APPLICATION SHALL BE AND REMAIN THE PROPERTY OF SAID BANK WHETHER OR NOT ANY LOAN IS GRANTED TO THE UNDERSIGNED

SIGNED AT_____ THIS___DAY OF___19__ SIGNATURE OF APPLICANT_____
SIGN FULL NAME

THIS SPACE RESERVED FOR USE OF BANK

NO. OF MONTHS [____]
AMOUNT OF NOTE $_____
DISCOUNT CHARGE $_____
PROCEEDS $_____
AMOUNT OF MONTHLY PAYMENT $_____

APPROVED_____ DATE_____ DECLINED_____ DATE_____

FIGURE 1 (front)

rower came to the bank, made his application for a loan, told the interviewer how much he wanted to borrow, what he wanted the money for, how much his income was, how he expected to pay the money back, and so on. Shown in Figure 1 is a simple form of application that is used by many banks.

Major loan classifications. There are four general classifications of the

STATEMENT(S) OF CO-MAKER(S)

TO ______ (BANK) ______ NAME OF APPLICANT

IN SUBMITTING THE FOLLOWING STATEMENT, THE UNDERSIGNED AFFIRM(S) THAT THE INFORMATION SET FORTH BELOW IS IN ALL RESPECTS TRUE, ACCURATE, AND COMPLETE, AND IS MADE WITH THE INTENT THAT IT BE RELIED UPON BY THE ABOVE-NAMED BANK IN EXTENDING CREDIT TO THE APPLICANT; THAT THE UNDERSIGNED HAS/HAVE NOT KNOWINGLY WITHHELD ANY INFORMATION THAT MIGHT AFFECT THE CREDIT RISK. THE UNDERSIGNED EXPRESSLY AGREE(S) TO NOTIFY IMMEDIATELY SAID BANK IN WRITING OF ANY MATERIAL CHANGE IN HIS/THEIR FINANCIAL CONDITION WHETHER APPLICATION FOR FURTHER CREDIT IS MADE OR NOT, AND IN THE ABSENCE OF SUCH WRITTEN NOTICE IT IS EXPRESSLY AGREED THAT SAID BANK, IN GRANTING NEW, OR CONTINUING EXISTING CREDIT, MAY RELY ON THIS STATEMENT AS HAVING THE SAME FORCE AND EFFECT AS IF DELIVERED UPON THE DATE ADDITIONAL CREDIT IS REQUESTED OR EXISTING CREDIT EXTENDED OR CONTINUED. THE UNDERSIGNED AGREE(S) THAT THIS STATEMENT SHALL BE AND REMAIN THE PROPERTY OF SAID BANK WHETHER OR NOT ANY LOAN IS GRANTED AND AFFIRMS THAT HE/THEY CONCURRENTLY SIGNED THE SAME AND THE PROMISSORY NOTE TO EVIDENCE THE LOAN.

NAME ______ PLEASE PRINT FULL NAME
RESIDENCE ADDRESS ______ NO. AND STREET
CITY ______ POSTAL UNIT NO. ______ STATE ______ TELEPHONE NUMBER
YEARS THERE ______ DATE OF BIRTH ______ SINGLE / MARRIED ______ NO. DEPENDENTS INCL. WIFE
LAST PREVIOUS ADDRESS ______ NO. AND STREET ______ CITY ______ STATE
NAME OF EMPLOYER OR OWN BUSINESS ______
ADDRESS ______ NO. AND STREET
CITY ______ POSTAL UNIT NO. ______ STATE ______ TELEPHONE NUMBER
YOUR POSITION ______ BADGE OR EMPLOYMENT NO. ______
NAME AND TITLE OF SUPERIOR ______ KIND OF BUSINESS ______
NO. OF YEARS WITH PRESENT EMPLOYER OR BUSINESS ______ YEARLY SALARY OR WAGES > $
OTHER INCOME, IF ANY. GIVE SOURCE ______ PER YEAR > $

BANK ACCOUNT ______ NAME OF BANK ______ A/C NO. ______ BRANCH
PERSONAL CHECKING A/C ______
SPECIAL CHECKING A/C ______
BUSINESS CHECKING A/C ______
SAVINGS ACCOUNT ______

HAVE YOU ANY JUDGMENTS, GARNISHMENTS, SUITS OR LEGAL PROCEEDINGS AGAINST YOU? (YES OR NO) ______ IF SO,
GIVE PARTICULARS ______
ARE YOU AT PRESENT A BORROWER OR A CO-MAKER ON A PERSONAL LOAN?
(YES OR NO) ______ IF SO, NAME OF LENDING INSTITUTION ______
______ IF CO-MAKER, GIVE BORROWER'S
NAME ______
REAL ESTATE OWNED (IF NONE, STATE "NONE") ______
ADDRESS—NO. AND STREET ______ CITY AND STATE
IS APPLICANT RELATED TO YOU AND IF SO IN WHAT MANNER? ______
HOW LONG HAVE YOU KNOWN APPLICANT? ______
SIGNED AT ______ THIS ______ DAY OF ______ 19 ______
SIGNATURE OF CO-MAKER ______ SIGN FULL NAME

NAME ______ PLEASE PRINT FULL NAME
RESIDENCE ADDRESS ______ NO. AND STREET
CITY ______ POSTAL UNIT NO. ______ STATE ______ TELEPHONE NUMBER
YEARS THERE ______ DATE OF BIRTH ______ SINGLE / MARRIED ______ NO. DEPENDENTS INCL. WIFE
LAST PREVIOUS ADDRESS ______ NO. AND STREET ______ CITY ______ STATE
NAME OF EMPLOYER OR OWN BUSINESS ______
ADDRESS ______ NO. AND STREET
CITY ______ POSTAL UNIT NO. ______ STATE ______ TELEPHONE NUMBER
YOUR POSITION ______ BADGE OR EMPLOYMENT NO. ______
NAME AND TITLE OF SUPERIOR ______ KIND OF BUSINESS ______
NO. OF YEARS WITH PRESENT EMPLOYER OR BUSINESS ______ YEARLY SALARY OR WAGES > $
OTHER INCOME, IF ANY GIVE SOURCE ______ PER YEAR > $
BANK ACCOUNT ______ NAME OF BANK ______ A/C NO. ______ BRANCH
PERSONAL CHECKING A/C ______
SPECIAL CHECKING A/C ______
BUSINESS CHECKING A/C ______
SAVINGS ACCOUNT ______
HAVE YOU ANY JUDGMENTS, GARNISHMENTS, SUITS OR LEGAL PROCEEDINGS AGAINST YOU? (YES OR NO) ______ IF SO,
GIVE PARTICULARS ______
ARE YOU AT PRESENT A BORROWER OR A CO-MAKER ON A PERSONAL LOAN?
(YES OR NO) ______ IF SO, NAME OF LENDING INSTITUTION ______
______ IF CO-MAKER, GIVE BORROWER'S
NAME ______
REAL ESTATE OWNED (IF NONE, STATE "NONE") ______
ADDRESS—NO. AND STREET ______ CITY AND STATE
IS APPLICANT RELATED TO YOU AND IF SO IN WHAT MANNER? ______
HOW LONG HAVE YOU KNOWN APPLICANT? ______
SIGNED AT ______ THIS ______ DAY OF ______ 19 ______
SIGNATURE OF CO-MAKER ______ SIGN FULL NAME

FIGURE 1 (*back*)

consumer instalment loan business, and they were developed by banks in the following order:

1. Federal Housing Administration Title I loans for the modernization of property constituted the first venture into the consumer instalment field for almost half the banks of the country. Also, many banks now have their own modernization loan plan without F.H.A. guaranty.

They have set up their own reserve for losses against which to charge bad debts.

2. Personal loans, which have been described earlier in this chapter, were the second type of loans to be considered by banks. This operation is simple, and banks had little trouble in organizing personal loan departments.

3. The third type of loans for the majority of banks was the automobile loan. This type of loan is divided into two classifications, direct and indirect. In the direct loan the borrower goes to the bank, makes an application for an automobile loan, and, if the loan is approved, gets his money and buys the car. The bank in almost all cases holds a chattel mortgage or conditional bill of sale on the car until all payments have been made.

In the indirect loan the bank buys the consumer instalment paper from the automobile dealer, either in single notes or in a number of notes. This is known as instalment sales financing. In this operation it is necessary to do business with dealers who are careful to see that the car is properly insured and that proper down payments are made, in order that the car purchaser may have a reasonable equity in his purchase. Many banks set up dealers' reserves which in most cases represent a part of the discount fee. This reserve is allowed to accumulate. When it exceeds a certain percentage of the total balances of all notes held for that particular dealer, reserves are paid back to him from time to time.

In recent years in cases in which the bank's experience with a dealer is good, the note is purchased from the dealer at a discount, and the adjustment is made at that time. In most operations of this kind the dealer shares in the discount fee, usually from 1 per cent to 1½ per cent. A fee of 5 per cent discount on new cars and from 6 per cent to 8 per cent discount on used cars is usually made. The down payment on new cars is usually 33⅓ per cent of the purchase price, and on used cars it is anywhere from 33⅓ per cent to 50 per cent, depending on the age and condition of the car.

When banks first developed automobile loans, it was difficult to obtain dealer cooperation. For years the dealers had made their arrangements with finance companies and were well satisfied; in most cases their participation in the discount rate was larger than that offered by banks. This was made possible because of the insurance tie-ups that many finance companies had. In some instances the insurance companies were owned by the finance companies, and therefore their earnings came from two sources on each loan—the discount rate and the insurance premium.

It was this reluctance on the part of automobile dealers to cooperate with the banks that forced many banks into the direct automobile operation. Today insurance is available to banks in many states at rates that

are about 25 per cent off manual or conference rates; thus they can offer a "package" (the combined costs of financing and insurance on an automobile deal) to a car purchaser that costs considerably less than the financing and insurance rates charged by most dealers. The automobile purchaser wants to know what the whole deal is going to cost him—discount and insurance. Dealer opposition to bank plans is fast disappearing.

Inventory financing is a necessary part of indirect dealer financing and is a phase of this operation with which many banks have had difficulty. When dealers have cars on the floor, both new cars and used cars taken as trade-ins, a high inventory value is represented, and most dealers require financing. Sales finance companies, long experienced in this field, were liberal in some of their commitments to finance inventories. As banks gained experience or secured the services of experienced men, they too offered programs that more and more dealers found acceptable. Consequently, dealers today are cooperating with bank financing plans more than they did a few years ago, and as time goes on this cooperation will increase rather than decrease.

The automobile loan represents a fine investment for a small loan department. Not only is the loan made on good value but it is usually in fairly large amounts—from $1,000 to $2,000. The time and effort to make and collect a $2,000 automobile loan is no more than for a loan of $200 for the same period, and the discount of course is much greater.

4. Home equipment loans were the fourth type of loans to be considered by banks. These are loans on washing machines, refrigerators, hot water heaters, and other household equipment, such as radios, television sets, and practically every known durable goods used in or for the home.

The cost of making and collecting loans in this field is very important because the loans are not often large. Any banker who has a good idea of what his costs are soon comes to the conclusion that he cannot make a loan profitably under a certain amount. We find in equipment financing that many banks will not consider loans under a certain amount, say $200, or that they will take smaller amounts at a minimum fee. The fee is usually fixed at an amount that shows some profit or at least permits the bank to break even. This operation requires the same technique as an automobile loan in that the dealer makes the interview and sometimes does a part of the credit checking. Chattel mortgages or conditional bills of sale are retained on the merchandise until the last payment is made.

There is a fifth type of loan that has become important in recent years in the instalment loan operation of banks, and that is the small business loan. Since this type of loan is not a consumer loan, it will not be dis-

cussed here except to say that it is reported in the outstandings of consumer instalment loan departments. Some of these small business volumes are large in particular banks and should not be reported as consumer loans because in doing so the picture becomes confused. This is especially true in periods of governmental regulation when every effort is made to reduce consumer instalment outstandings. The Federal Reserve Board has only the outstandings of reporting banks and other consumer instalment lenders to guide them. Reporting business loans as a part of these figures is building up the consumer credit instalment figure far above what it actually is.

While we are on the subject of Federal Reserve Board figures, it might be well to mention that the *Federal Reserve Bulletin,* published each month by the Board of Governors of the Federal Reserve System, gives figures on consumer credit outstandings not only for each month but also for the years back to 1929. These figures are broken down for the different type of lending institutions and also by loan classifications. Not only are instalment credit figures given but consumer credit figures other than instalment are included, such as charge accounts, single-payment loans, and service credit.

Operating manuals. Educating the banks to do business on a safe, profitable basis in any one or all classes of loans that have been mentioned, has been a major task. It required the effort of some central agency that had direct contact with all banks and an agency in which the banks had confidence. The work was undertaken by the Committee on Consumer Credit of the American Bankers Association. Over the years they have prepared and distributed thirteen publications, including manuals of operation and studies on other technical phases of this business. The manuals cover not only the four general classifications mentioned in this chapter but other phases of the business of small loan lending known as specialties. A list of the publications with a brief description of each follows.

1. *A Bank Manual on Instalment Loans.* Covers credit requirements and operating procedure for banks interested in engaging in the field of instalment credit. It can be used as a manual to train new employees. Various forms used in this department's operation are illustrated.
2. *Direct Automobile Financing.* Presents principles involved in this type of financing, together with some of the methods and procedures used by banks already in this field.
3. *Bank Manual on Automobile Financing—Dealer Plan.* New and used car financing by banks is explained in detail. Retail and wholesale aspects in addition to the credit, collection, insurance, and various dealer plans are discussed.
4. *Home Appliance Financing.* The fundamental considerations necessary in this type of instalment credit are outlined in this manual. A manual of operations for banks interested in purchasing retail instalment paper

on household appliances and in extending the necessary supplementary wholesale floor plan credit.

5. *Streamlining Your Instalment Credit Department.* Coordinates procedures essential to accomplish a uniform and streamlined operation. Study can also be utilized to train new employees. Forms used in this department's operation are illustrated.

6. *Farm Equipment Financing.* The most practical methods and operating procedure for farm implement financing form the basis of this manual. Retail financing and wholesale financing both direct and indirect are explained.

7. *Instalment Loans to Small Business.* This study will assist banks in lending to small business on a broader and more flexible basis. Some of the qualifications for term lending are emphasized and explained in this study.

8. *Aircraft Financing.* Financing the retail sales of new and used private planes, and arranging for floor planning all such planes for dealers, are explained in this manual.

9. *Analyzing the Cost Factors of Instalment Lending.* A knowledge of the costs involved in instalment lending is most important. This study presents a practical procedure that has been developed to assist banks to make a cost study of its consumer and instalment loan department's operation.

10. *Rebate of Instalment Loan Charges.* On prepaid instalment credit obligations a refund of the actual unearned interest or finance charge should be made to the borrower or purchaser. This booklet explains the "78ths" method of rebate and includes a schedule prepared on a percentage basis to help compute the amount of refund.

11. *Know Your Earnings on Instalment Loans.* A number of simple methods of determining monthly earnings on instalment loans are presented in this booklet. A monthly earnings accrual schedule is included, which embraces in percentages the amount of unearned discount to allocate to earnings during a particular period.

12. *Analysis of the Soldiers' and Sailors' Civil Relief Act.* This is a handbook for bank officers who desire quick information to guide them in their decisions on questions relating to the Soldiers' and Sailors' Civil Relief Act. The Relief Act has a direct bearing on bank operations and procedures. In view of the present military situation this analysis will prove helpful to banks confronted with such problems.

13. *Consumer Instalment Lending Directory.* A nationwide reciprocal collection service offered by the commercial banks engaged in the extension of consumer and instalment credit. Includes a listing of over 9,000 banks engaged in this business in addition to the listing of almost 7,000 banks that have agreed to cooperate in this collection service. It is used primarily in the case of "skip" and delinquent accounts which have moved out of the service area of the lending bank.

These publications have been used by thousands of banks. The material was written by one or more authorities on the particular subject. Operating systems for each type of bank had to be developed in order to fit the particular case, whether for small, medium, or large banks. For instance, some operations in small banks required only the part-time

services of one man; in other large operations hundreds of people were employed in the instalment loan department. As many banks developed the business, they also developed their own techniques, which were described in banking magazines and through talks at conferences and meetings. These developments over the years have added considerably to the general knowledge on the subject.

Cost factors. One of the most difficult subjects to handle was the matter of costs. What does it cost to make and collect a loan? Without this knowledge or some careful guidance on the subject, banks were apt to try to do this business on an unprofitable basis. Instalment lending is a costly operation. First there is the interview with the applicant, and then the credit checking. This may take as many as five or six telephone calls and, in some cases, several letters. Next comes the closing of the loan and the necessary ledger cards and payment books to be filled out. If the payments are made by mail, additional steps are necessary. If payments are not made promptly, letters or telephone calls or even personal calls are necessary. Some loans are difficult to collect and become subjects for legal procedure.

The very nature of the operation is one of fast processing. Unlike commercial loans that are for larger amounts, loans in the instalment departments are small, but there are usually many of them as compared with the relatively small number in the commercial loan department. Speed is essential. Too much time cannot be given to each transaction, otherwise the cost of handling each note will be too high. If the operation is to be successful, trained help is needed and fair salaries should be paid. Although the manual on costs, published by the Committee on Consumer Credit of the American Bankers Association, went into the matter very carefully, many banks were under the impression they could do the business cheaper and better than their competitors. When some banks first announced the opening of their departments, they published rates far too low to enable them to do a profitable business. Many country banks arrived at these low rates because of some large operation they had inspected in a city bank where thousands of loans a month were made. Perhaps the city bank's average loan was $400 to $500, whereas the country bank's average loan was $150 to $200. Operating at 6 per cent discount per year, or $6 per $100 per year, the two banks would show quite a difference in income from each note.

Many of the large city operations have discount charges of less than 6 per cent. In New York City, for example, the discount charge is less than 4 per cent. When the country banker accepted this charge as a guide for his own operation, he had an unprofitable operation, and in most cases he did not know it. Much time and effort was spent and is being spent to focus the attention of bankers on this matter of costs. As

they become better acquainted with the business and as the men they have in charge of the departments become better informed, adjustments are being made. One bank, located in upstate New York, makes careful cost studies of its department every two years, offering a breakdown of cost factors. Its average loan costs between $12 and $14 for one year, regardless of the amount or the discount rate. Here is the breakdown.

	Per cent
Salaries and wages	40.0
Advertising	9.0
Credit information	2.5
Cost of money	3.5
Rent	5.0
Losses	11.5
Taxes	11.0
Other expenses	17.5
	100.0

Other expenses of 17.5 per cent are broken down into the following categories:

Stationery and printing
Postage
Legal
Telephone and telegraph
Insurance
Auditing
Automobile and traveling

The cost of each operation will vary from the example used, depending on individual policy. The two items that appear to have the greatest differences are salaries and advertising.

Advertising. How banks advertised was a matter that received considerable attention from the Committee on Consumer Credit of the American Bankers Association. Each bank was urged to be careful and not to adopt the misleading practices of some lenders. Studies indicated that a bank's advertising should be frank and should state that the bank was in the small loan business and interested in taking care of the credit needs of individuals. Some examples of bad advertising are as follows: "We charge legal rates," "We charge bank rates," "Six per cent interest charged here."

Although all of these examples were within the law, the inference was that the bank charged the legal rate for the state, which was 6 per cent simple interest. These examples were taken from a state which has a small loan law for banks that permits a 6 per cent discount rate based on a simple interest yield of almost 12 per cent. This is almost twice the simple interest rate figured at 6 per cent and could be confusing to any person reading the advertising. Examples of good advertising slogans are the following:

"Small borrowers are welcome."

"Small business is big business here."

"Our bank has a loan for every personal need."

"Wise borrowing is a form of thrift."

"Over 94 per cent of personal loan applications granted."

"How much does a personal loan cost? For each $100 for one year, the cost is $6."

On the whole the advertising of banks has been good. It has been directed to the consumer in such a way that he has come to have a better appreciation of credit and of how he himself fits into the credit picture. The use of credit should be an orderly, carefully thought out procedure; and when used in this way by the public, it can be of real benefit. Any high-pressure methods that encourage people to borrow for goods or services they do not need and that force them to carry a debt they can ill afford to carry, does great harm to our economy in good times as well as bad. A lender who uses this method is headed for trouble and will soon find that his operation is costing too much. The collection cost of a department made up of this type of paper is out of all proportion to the amount of money invested. A department with less money invested will make far more profit if it has few troublesome loans.

Rebate on prepaid loans. During the first few years that banks operated in the small loan field, their rebating practices were none too good. Every bank had its own plan. When a borrower paid off his note before maturity, the bank either paid him back too much of the discount or not enough. Many banks felt that if a twelve-month note was paid off at the end of the third month, the bank should receive something over the three-months' discount for the cost of making and processing the loan—a minimum charge to cover acquisition and collection costs.

After some years of practice this idea was discarded by most bank operations because so few of their borrowers anticipated their note maturities. Most banks now follow what is known as the 78ths method of rebate. This takes into consideration the actual use of the money for the period of time it is used and, in addition, the important factor that the largest amount of the loan is used in the early months of the transaction before many payments against principal have been made. Perhaps the best way to explain this method of rebate is to show the 78ths chart itself.

In their enabling legislation for banks, some states require that this system of rebate be used.

Reserve for losses. Losses taken by banks in the fifteen years that the great majority of them have been in the consumer instalment credit business have been small. In their direct operations it has been less than

REBATE SCHEDULE

FOR INSTALMENT LOAN CHARGES

PREPARED BY
CONSUMER CREDIT DEPARTMENT
AMERICAN BANKERS ASSOCIATION
NEW YORK, N. Y.

HOW TO USE THIS SCHEDULE

1. Locate the original term of the loan in months in the vertical column on the left.
2. Locate the number of months the loan **has already run** in either the oblique line at the top or the horizontal line at the bottom.
3. Where the column and the line intersect is the **percentage of the loan charge** to be rebated.

NUMBER OF MONTHS LOAN HAS RUN

TERM OF LOAN	1	2	3	4	5	6	7	8	9	10	11	12	13	14	15	16	17	18	19	20	21	22	23	24	25	26	27	28	29	30	31	32	33	34	35	36	37	38	39	40	41	42	43	44	45	46	47	48
1	0
2	33.33	0
3	50.00	16.67	0
4	60.00	30.00	10.00	0
5	66.67	40.00	20.00	6.67	0
6	71.43	47.62	28.57	14.29	4.76	0
7	75.00	53.57	35.71	21.43	10.71	3.57	0
8	77.78	58.33	41.67	27.78	16.67	8.33	2.78	0
9	80.00	62.22	46.67	33.33	22.22	13.33	6.67	2.22	0
10	81.82	65.45	50.91	38.18	27.27	18.18	10.91	5.45	1.82	0
11	83.33	68.18	54.55	42.42	31.82	22.73	15.15	9.09	4.55	1.52	0
12	84.62	70.51	57.69	46.15	35.90	26.92	19.23	12.82	7.69	3.85	1.28	0
13	85.71	72.53	60.44	49.45	39.56	30.77	23.08	16.48	10.99	6.59	3.30	1.10	0
14	86.67	74.29	62.86	52.38	42.86	34.29	26.67	20.00	14.29	9.52	5.71	2.86	.95	0
15	87.50	75.83	65.00	55.00	45.83	37.50	30.00	23.33	17.50	12.50	8.33	5.00	2.50	.83	0
16	88.24	77.21	66.91	57.35	48.53	40.44	33.09	26.47	20.59	15.44	11.03	7.35	4.41	2.21	.74	0
17	88.89	78.43	68.63	59.48	50.98	43.14	35.95	29.41	23.53	18.30	13.73	9.80	6.54	3.92	1.96	.65	0
18	89.47	79.53	70.18	61.40	53.22	45.61	38.60	32.16	26.32	21.05	16.37	12.28	8.77	5.85	3.51	1.75	.58	0
19	90.00	80.53	71.58	63.16	55.26	47.89	41.05	34.74	28.95	23.68	18.95	14.74	11.05	7.89	5.26	3.16	1.58	.53	0
20	90.48	81.43	72.86	64.76	57.14	50.00	43.33	37.14	31.43	26.19	21.43	17.14	13.33	10.00	7.14	4.76	2.86	1.43	.48	0
21	90.91	82.25	74.03	66.23	58.87	51.95	45.45	39.39	33.77	28.57	23.81	19.48	15.58	12.12	9.09	6.49	4.33	2.60	1.30	.43	0
22	91.30	83.00	75.10	67.59	60.47	53.75	47.43	41.50	35.97	30.83	26.09	21.74	17.79	14.23	11.07	8.30	5.93	3.95	2.37	1.19	.40	0
23	91.67	83.70	76.09	68.84	61.96	55.43	49.28	43.48	38.04	32.97	28.26	23.91	19.93	16.30	13.04	10.14	7.61	5.43	3.62	2.17	1.09	.36	0
24	92.00	84.33	77.00	70.00	63.33	57.00	51.00	45.33	40.00	35.00	30.33	26.00	22.00	18.33	15.00	12.00	9.33	7.00	5.00	3.33	2.00	1.00	.33	0
25	92.31	84.92	77.85	71.08	64.62	58.46	52.62	47.08	41.85	36.92	32.31	28.00	24.00	20.31	16.92	13.85	11.08	8.62	6.46	4.62	3.08	1.85	.92	.31	0
26	92.59	85.47	78.63	72.08	65.81	59.83	54.13	48.72	43.59	38.75	34.19	29.91	25.93	22.22	18.80	15.67	12.82	10.26	7.98	5.98	4.27	2.85	1.71	.85	.28	0
27	92.86	85.98	79.37	73.02	66.93	61.11	55.56	50.26	45.24	40.48	35.98	31.75	27.78	24.07	20.63	17.46	14.55	11.90	9.52	7.41	5.56	3.97	2.65	1.59	.79	.26	0
28	93.10	86.45	80.05	73.89	67.98	62.32	56.90	51.72	46.80	42.12	37.68	33.50	29.56	25.86	22.41	19.21	16.26	13.55	11.08	8.87	6.90	5.17	3.69	2.46	1.48	.74	.25	0
29	93.33	86.90	80.69	74.71	68.97	63.45	58.16	53.10	48.28	43.68	39.31	35.17	31.26	27.59	24.14	20.92	17.93	15.17	12.64	10.34	8.28	6.44	4.83	3.45	2.30	1.38	.69	.23	0
30	93.55	87.31	81.29	75.48	69.89	64.52	59.35	54.41	49.68	45.16	40.86	36.77	32.90	29.25	25.81	22.58	19.57	16.77	14.19	11.83	9.68	7.74	6.02	4.52	3.23	2.15	1.29	.65	.22	0
31	93.75	87.70	81.85	76.21	70.77	65.52	60.48	55.65	51.01	46.57	42.34	38.31	34.48	30.85	27.42	24.19	21.17	18.35	15.73	13.31	11.09	9.07	7.26	5.65	4.23	3.02	2.02	1.21	.60	.20	0
32	93.94	88.07	82.39	76.89	71.59	66.48	61.55	56.82	52.27	47.92	43.75	39.77	35.98	32.39	28.98	25.76	22.73	19.89	17.23	14.77	12.50	10.42	8.52	6.82	5.30	3.98	2.84	1.89	1.14	.57	.19	0
33	94.12	88.41	82.89	77.54	72.37	67.38	62.57	57.93	53.48	49.20	45.10	41.18	37.43	33.87	30.48	27.27	24.24	21.39	18.72	16.22	13.90	11.76	9.80	8.02	6.42	4.99	3.74	2.67	1.78	1.07	.53	.18	0
34	94.29	88.74	83.36	78.15	73.11	68.24	63.53	58.99	54.62	50.42	46.39	42.52	38.82	35.29	31.93	28.74	25.71	22.86	20.17	17.65	15.29	13.11	11.09	9.24	7.56	6.05	4.71	3.53	2.52	1.68	1.01	.50	.17	0
35	94.44	89.05	83.81	78.73	73.81	69.05	64.44	60.00	55.71	51.59	47.62	43.81	40.16	36.67	33.33	30.16	27.14	24.29	21.59	19.05	16.67	14.44	12.38	10.48	8.73	7.14	5.71	4.44	3.33	2.38	1.59	.95	.48	.16	0
36	94.59	89.34	84.23	79.28	74.47	69.82	65.32	60.96	56.76	52.70	48.80	45.05	41.44	37.99	34.68	31.53	28.53	25.68	22.97	20.42	18.02	15.77	13.66	11.71	9.91	8.26	6.76	5.41	4.20	3.15	2.25	1.50	.90	.45	.15	0
37	94.74	89.62	84.64	79.80	75.11	70.55	66.15	61.88	57.75	53.77	49.93	46.23	42.67	39.26	35.99	32.86	29.87	27.03	24.32	21.76	19.35	17.07	14.94	12.94	11.10	9.39	7.82	6.40	5.12	3.98	2.99	2.13	1.42	.85	.43	.14	0
38	94.87	89.88	85.02	80.30	75.71	71.26	66.94	62.75	58.70	54.79	51.01	47.37	43.86	40.49	37.25	34.14	31.17	28.34	25.64	23.08	20.65	18.35	16.19	14.17	12.28	10.53	8.91	7.42	6.07	4.86	3.78	2.83	2.02	1.35	.81	.40	.13	0
39	95.00	90.13	85.38	80.77	76.28	71.92	67.69	63.59	59.62	55.77	52.05	48.46	45.00	41.67	38.46	35.38	32.44	29.62	26.92	24.36	21.92	19.62	17.44	15.38	13.46	11.67	10.00	8.46	7.05	5.77	4.62	3.59	2.69	1.92	1.28	.77	.38	.13	0
40	95.12	90.37	85.73	81.22	76.83	72.56	68.41	64.39	60.49	56.71	53.05	49.51	46.10	42.80	39.63	36.59	33.66	30.85	28.17	25.61	23.17	20.85	18.66	16.59	14.63	12.80	11.10	9.51	8.05	6.71	5.49	4.39	3.41	2.56	1.83	1.22	.73	.37	.12	0
41	95.24	90.59	86.06	81.65	77.35	73.17	69.11	65.16	61.32	57.61	54.01	50.52	47.15	43.90	40.77	37.75	34.84	32.06	29.38	26.83	24.39	22.07	19.86	17.77	15.80	13.94	12.20	10.57	9.06	7.67	6.39	5.23	4.18	3.25	2.44	1.74	1.16	.70	.35	.12	0
42	95.35	90.81	86.38	82.06	77.85	73.75	69.77	65.89	62.13	58.47	54.93	51.50	48.17	44.96	41.86	38.87	35.99	33.22	30.56	28.02	25.58	23.26	21.04	18.94	16.94	15.06	13.29	11.63	10.08	8.64	7.31	6.09	4.98	3.99	3.10	2.33	1.66	1.11	.66	.33	.11	0
43	95.45	91.01	86.68	82.45	78.33	74.31	70.40	66.60	62.90	59.30	55.81	52.43	49.15	45.98	42.92	39.96	37.10	34.36	31.71	29.18	26.74	24.42	22.20	20.08	18.08	16.17	14.38	12.68	11.10	9.62	8.25	6.98	5.81	4.76	3.81	2.96	2.22	1.59	1.06	.63	.32	.11	0
44	95.56	91.21	86.97	82.83	78.79	74.85	71.01	67.27	63.64	60.10	56.67	53.33	50.10	46.97	43.94	41.01	38.18	35.45	32.83	30.30	27.88	25.56	23.33	21.21	19.19	17.27	15.45	13.74	12.12	10.61	9.19	7.88	6.67	5.56	4.55	3.64	2.83	2.12	1.52	1.01	.61	.30	.10	0
45	95.65	91.40	87.25	83.19	79.23	75.36	71.59	67.92	64.35	60.87	57.49	54.20	51.01	47.92	44.93	42.03	39.23	36.52	33.91	31.40	28.99	26.67	24.44	22.32	20.29	18.36	16.52	14.78	13.14	11.59	10.14	8.79	7.54	6.38	5.31	4.35	3.48	2.71	2.03	1.45	.97	.58	.29	.10	0
46	95.74	91.58	87.51	83.53	79.65	75.86	72.16	68.55	65.03	61.61	58.28	55.04	51.90	48.84	45.88	43.02	40.24	37.56	34.97	32.47	30.06	27.75	25.53	23.40	21.37	19.43	17.58	15.82	14.15	12.58	11.10	9.71	8.42	7.22	6.11	5.09	4.16	3.33	2.59	1.94	1.39	.93	.56	.28	.09	0
47	95.83	91.76	87.77	83.87	80.05	76.33	72.70	69.15	65.69	62.32	59.04	55.85	52.75	49.73	46.81	43.97	41.22	38.56	35.99	33.51	31.12	28.81	26.60	24.47	22.43	20.48	18.62	16.84	15.16	13.56	12.06	10.64	9.31	8.07	6.91	5.85	4.88	3.99	3.19	2.48	1.86	1.33	.89	.53	.27	.09	0
48	95.92	91.92	88.01	84.18	80.44	76.79	73.21	69.73	66.33	63.01	59.78	56.63	53.57	50.60	47.70	44.90	42.18	39.54	36.99	34.52	32.14	29.85	27.64	25.51	23.47	21.51	19.64	17.86	16.16	14.54	13.01	11.56	10.20	8.93	7.74	6.63	5.61	4.68	3.83	3.06	2.38	1.79	1.28	.85	.51	.26	.09	0
	1	2	3	4	5	6	7	8	9	10	11	12	13	14	15	16	17	18	19	20	21	22	23	24	25	26	27	28	29	30	31	32	33	34	35	36	37	38	39	40	41	42	43	44	45	46	47	48

NUMBER OF MONTHS LOAN HAS RUN

Copies of this rebate schedule printed on cardboard may be obtained from the Consumer Credit Department of the American Bankers Association at 25 cents for the first copy; 15 cents per copy for additional copies.

FIGURE 2

¼ of 1 per cent for most banks. The indirect operations losses have been higher and have depended to a large extent on the dealers and how careful they have been in checking credits. In most operations where the bankers were experienced in the indirect field, losses were small, probably less than ½ of 1 per cent. One fallacy in all loss figures is the failure to include cost of collection. Before a loan becomes a loss, much time and effort is put forth to try to collect the amount due. This cost really should be added to the actual amount charged off in order to get the true picture. The nature of a bank's bookkeeping does not permit this, however, and cost of collection goes into the general expenses for running the department. It should also be remembered in considering losses, that for the last fifteen years there has been a rising economy with full employment and rising wages. This picture will change when and if an adjustment in the economy occurs because it will affect employment and incomes.

In most cases banks set up a reserve for losses of anywhere from ¼ of 1 per cent to 1 per cent of their volume for most operations. These funds, if not used, are permitted to accumulate until they reach from 3 per cent to 5 per cent of outstandings. Some banks have as much as 10 per cent of outstandings in their reserve for loss accounts. After the desired reserve is accumulated, the reserve percentage is reduced. This policy will be governed chiefly by experience.

The interviewer. The most important person in an instalment loan operation is the interviewer. He has the first contact with the prospective borrower and has the first opportunity to form an impression as to whether the application is good, whether it has some possibilities, or whether it should be declined. After an interviewer has had experience for a number of years, there are certain characteristics he looks for in each loan. Over the years experience has shown that a definite pattern should be followed in judging whether or not a loan should be made.

Dr. John Chapman, of Columbia University, New York City, is the author of a book published in 1940 by the National Bureau of Economic Research under the title *Commercial Banks and Consumer Instalment Credit.* In this study the author describes some of the credit characteristics of borrowers; the present discussion draws heavily on these descriptions. A good interviewer has these points in mind when he interviews a prospective borrower: (1) How much does he want? (2) What for? (3) Can he pay it back? (4) Will he pay it back?

There are five broad credit characteristics that are fairly universal. While a borrower's or purchaser's credit standards of acceptability may vary from lender to lender, these characteristics are generally used in evaluating the credit. In order of importance they are as follows:

1. Character. The borrower must be an excellent moral risk. He must

have a reasonably good record of meeting his obligations and must have the desire and willingness to fulfill a promise.

2. Vocational. The borrower's source of income must be reasonably permanent. In considering this factor the stability and permanence of employment are important. The type of work and type of industry should be given consideration.

3. Financial. The borrower must have sufficient income to repay the loan and maintain his standard of living. What he owns and what he owes are important factors in evaluating ability to pay and to accumulate.

4. Personal. Applicant's age is important. He must be competent and must have the legal capacity to make a binding contract. Number of dependents will indicate his ability to meet his obligations. Stability of residence is also important. A borrower who resides more or less permanently in one community is usually a better risk than one who is continually on the move. Obviously this question must be considered with the employment factor, as sometimes the applicant has found it necessary to shift occasionally to improve his income status.

5. Loan. The amount, purpose, duration, and security offered are the prime loan characteristics. In one case it may be necessary to suggest collateral, whereas in others an unsecured loan for an adjusted period would be the solution. This condition can best be determined after the other characteristics are evaluated.

An applicant should have been employed by the same employer for at least three years. Very low incomes usually are bad risks regardless of the amount to be loaned. Short maturities are only advisable when voluntary. The higher the down payment on a durable goods, the less likelihood of repossession. The down payment is a most important factor in sales financing. More important than income is the borrower's ability to live within his income. The ownership of a bank account, life insurance, or real estate, in addition to financial strength, denotes stability—a willingness to save for the future.

The best of all indices is a good interviewer; he must have experience and intuition. A good interviewer keeps in mind all during the interview the characteristics that have been listed, as well as many others.

Government Law and Regulation

During the defense period before World War II, consumer instalment loan lenders were faced for the first time with two moves on the part of the government that influenced consumer lending. One was a government regulation of credit known then and now as Regulation W, and the other was a law passed by Congress known as the Soldiers' and Sailors' Civil Relief Act.

Regulation W. Regulation W became effective for the first time in September 1941, just three months before Pearl Harbor and the declaration of war. The purpose of the regulation was to fix down payments and terms on all consumer instalment loans. It was used primarily as an anti-inflation measure. Since industry was fast converting from civilian to war production, and it was evident that there would be a shortage of consumer durable goods, the regulation attempted to fix terms that would make these goods more difficult to buy and in that way relieve the market, which would be in short supply, of buying pressure.

As the war continued, down payments were increased and time was reduced on most sales financed items. This regulation, together with rationing and price control, had an influence on the durable goods market. There are some informed students of consumer instalment lending who feel that a consumer regulation similar to Regulation W has very little effect as an anti-inflationary instrument. During a war economy, wages are high and everyone who can work is working. For instance, many families accustomed to one salary now have two salaries coming in—both husband and wife are working at high wages.

If people want goods badly enough, they can either meet the terms or pay cash. In any event a review of the contraction of consumer instalment credit during World War II leaves the impression that most of the contraction took place when no goods were available. In other words, loans went down when there was nothing to buy. In the case of banks, this contraction was sharp, about 70 per cent on the over-all consumer instalment loan outstanding—from $1,700 million to about $500 million.

After World War II attempts were made to have the regulation continued as a permanent control, but following one brief renewal in September 1948 for nine months, it was discontinued. Because of another defense period, the regulation was again reimposed on September 18, 1950. During the first two months of 1951, outstandings dropped—$212 million for the month of January and approximately $200 million for the month of February. Again it must be pointed out that contraction may be due to forces other than Regulation W. To begin with, the consumer has been well supplied with goods, and prices and the cost of living are high. These two factors act as a brake on purchasing, especially of high-priced items. There was evidence in April 1951 that inventories on consumer durable goods were increasing, and loans for inventories for these goods have been on the increase.

During times of strenuous defense effort and war, when an increasing amount of production goes into defense or war effort, the regulation does result in a more orderly market. Competition between lenders to give more liberal terms is eliminated; one lender has no more to offer than the next, except in service and possibly in the cost of financing. There

is some justification for the arguments advanced by some lenders that Regulation W is class legislation and denies the right of purchase to those who cannot meet the terms—down payment and length of time permitted to pay back the amount borrowed. There is also something to be said for the argument that, under a regulation of this type, maximums tend to become minimums. If the government, through a regulation, says that it is all right to take twenty-one months to pay off a used car loan after a down payment of 33⅓ per cent, most borrowers ask for and are granted those terms by the lenders.

Soldiers' and Sailors' Civil Relief Act. Bank consumer instalment lenders during World War II experienced for the first time the operation of these departments under the Soldiers' and Sailors' Civil Relief Act. Briefly, all persons who either enlisted or were drafted into the military forces of our country were granted certain rights and privileges under this act. In the case of intalment loans, they were not obliged to continue payments against the principal amount of their loans; and although the interest did not have to be paid while they were in service, the act did allow the lender to accumulate interest against the unpaid principal at the rate of 6 per cent simple interest for the time no payments were made. At first this appeared to present a real problem because many of the loans were made for the purchase of durable goods which continued to depreciate in value for the time the borrower was in service. Actual experience, however, was excellent in the great majority of cases. The borrowers either disposed of the property through sale before going into the service and the loan was paid in full, or some other party assumed the debt. The great majority of those who continued ownership of the property while they were in service, paid up the loans during this period or after their discharge.

The same experience held true in the case of cash loans. This protection covered the discharged veteran for not only his time in service but in many instances extended beyond the termination of military service. The experience under the Soldiers' and Sailors' Civil Relief Act proved once again what consumer instalment lenders had known for a long time, and that is that most people are honest.

Public Relations Value

Since the development of small loan departments in banks, the public has come to have a better understanding of banks and bankers. The relationship between the people and their community banking institutions has become closer than it ever has been in the history of banking in this country. If the bank and all of its personnel are interested in developing this business and everyone connected with the bank from the

president to the porter knows about the department and what its purpose is, the public will soon know about the credit service the local bank is prepared to offer individuals.

If the interviewer is the right kind of person, he is in a fine position to build up other business for the bank. In many instances a borrower's first experience with a bank is through the services of the small loan department. Paying off a loan by making payments over a period of months often teaches people to manage their incomes better. Many borrowers become good savings accounts after paying off a loan.

Satisfied customers of a bank are its best sales force; and after a department has been operating for a period of time, many loan applicants come to a small loan department because of a good word passed on by some other satisfied borrower.

In developing the small loan business, the bank building often presents a real handicap. In many cases its architecture is severe, with barred windows, and is anything but inviting from the outside. It should be remembered that many people have their first experience with a bank through the small loan department. It is not easy for them to muster up enough courage to come inside. For this reason many small loan departments are not on the main banking floor but are located in other sections of the building or in adjacent properties that are less imposing.

Friendly advertising through the use of newspapers and direct mail has done much to break down the timid feeling on the part of prospective borrowers. After the first experience with a department and the encouragement of other borrowers, consumers accept banks for what they are—service institutions organized for the purpose of advising on all financial problems.

Number of Banks and Scope of Business

If we take 1934 as the year when most banks first considered the possibilities of consumer instalment loan departments, we find that from a small beginning has grown an important bank development. On page 708 are compilations for three different periods showing the outstanding volume of banks engaged in doing a consumer instalment loan business in the four major classifications.

A steady growth is indicated from these figures. They also show that banks are today the largest lenders of any group in the instalment loan field.

There are many large departments connected with city institutions covering wide areas, but the interesting thing to notice is that the large operations in many cases represent only a small percentage of the bank's reserves. Many smaller institutions have outstandings that represent a

OUTSTANDINGS

(In millions of dollars)

As of December 31	Number of banks	Total	Personal instalment cash loans	Repair and moderniza- tion loans	Auto- mobile retail loans	Other retail paper purchased
1950	12,000[5]	$5,645	$1,107	$905	$2,366	$1,267
1940	5,000[6]	$1,450	$ 422	$247	$ 564	$ 217
1935	3,500 (estimated)		$256 (estimated) all types of loans combined			

[5] Committee on Consumer Credit, American Bankers Association, Survey 1950.
[6] Committee on Consumer Credit, American Bankers Association, Survey 1940.

substantial part of a bank's resources. For example, a large bank may have $200 million outstanding in consumer instalment loans, but this amount percentagewise in a $5 billion bank would only be 4 per cent of total resources, whereas many banks of $5 million resources have outstandings of $1 million or more, representing 20 per cent or more of resources.

In many cases the business done by banks is interstate. They may handle all the paper for a manufacturer of consumer durable goods that does business on a nationwide basis, or they may take a district made up of a number of states.

The men who manage the small loan departments in banks, represent a large fraternity of people who are all specialists in the field and who are interested in the development and the refinement of this business. They meet frequently in local areas to talk over mutual problems, and they also hold state meetings and once a year a national meeting.

Reciprocal collection arrangement. Because some consumers move from time to time to different parts of the country, a nationwide collection system has been developed by the Committee on Consumer Credit of the American Bankers Association. By means of this system banks are able to assist one another in collecting notes. For example, a consumer instalment debt is incurred by a New Jersey bank, and before it is paid up, the borrower moves to Texas. If the payments are not continued as originally arranged, the New Jersey bank may consult the Consumer Instalment Lending Directory to locate the bank in Texas nearest to the borrower's residence. The listing of a bank in the directory indicates that the bank is willing to participate in the collection of debts owed other banks. Through this reciprocal collection arrangement, many debts are paid that might otherwise have been charged off. Frequently the borrower renews his payments as soon as the local bank contacts him so that his credit standing in the community will not be jeopardized.

The service provided by the 6,763 banks belonging to this collection system is, in most cases, performed without cost to the originating bank with the exception of out-of-pocket expenses.

Rediscounting. A recent development in the small loan business as it applies to banks is rediscounting of paper by city banks for their country correspondents. A country bank may have a policy whereby it cannot carry more than 25 per cent of its resources in consumer instalment paper. When the ratio of consumer paper to resources exceeds this amount, the country bank sells the paper to a larger bank, usually its own correspondent. The arrangements are not the same in all cases, but the procedure is about as follows: the selling bank will sell the paper to the buying bank but continue to collect the payments. As payments are made, the selling bank remits to the buying bank twice a month. The discount is placed in a separate account by the buying bank, and after all payments have been made, the buying bank takes the amount it agreed upon for rediscounting the paper. The balance goes to the selling bank for originating the loans and collecting the monthly payments.

Another arrangement is for the buying bank to take the paper outright and pay the selling bank a stipulated fee for originating the paper and collecting the monthly payments. In the latter case there is usually some understanding with regard to losses if they should exceed a specified amount.

Future of the Business

Although consumer instalment credit is an important branch of credit today in the commercial banks of the country, we must remember that the development is comparatively recent—only in the last fifteen years for most banks. As the technique of instalment lending is better understood, it will branch out into fields not at first contemplated. Small business loans offer an example. This type of loan lends itself readily to an instalment loan department. The lending officers of this department are better equipped to deal with small business than those bank officers accustomed to dealing with larger accounts. Also, because of the payment plan of instalment notes, the small business obligation is better policed than it would be in the commercial loan department.

Many banks today have a policy that all small business loans not exceeding a certain amount be referred to the small loan department. Some of the large bank operations have trained interviewers who process only small business loans. In some of the larger institutions all loans of $10,000 or under are referred to the small loan department. In the medium-sized and smaller institutions the amount fixed may be $5,000 or as little as $500.

In recent years some banks have gone into other financing specialities, such as accounts receivable and heavy machinery. These latter developments are not consumer instalment lending but are pointed out simply to show how the instalment principle has developed new thinking in banks and opened up new fields for many in the field of credit. Insurance premium financing for industry is another step that is receiving more and more attention from banks. Other fields of instalment lending that are important to some banks include airplane financing, both private and commercial planes; and farm equipment financing is important to country banks.

Although term loans are not new to many banks, for many years they were made by a comparatively few institutions. But this type of loan, too, uses the instalment loan principle. More and more banks are investigating their possibilities. Term loans at one time applied principally to very large credits; today the term loan principle is used for smaller commitments.

The instalment principle may soon become a part of practically every credit, not only because it arranges for fixed payments against the principal of the debt but, of equal importance, because it provides constant policing and reviewing of the obligation. If this principle had been adhered to over the years in the case of mortgages, we would not have had the sorry experience we did have with mortgages in the early 1930's.

Today there are very few banks that do not perform a consumer instalment service of some kind, and most of those that do not cater to a business that does not lend itself to consumer financing. Some large city institutions that do business with large corporations and with other banks would find consumer instalment loans out of line with their general run of business. Many of these large banks do invest in the business, either by making loans to other consumer credit lenders, such as personal finance companies or sales finance companies, or by purchasing consumer instalment paper from their correspondent banks.

Rates. The next step in the development of the instalment loan business will probably come in the field of rates. Most states that have passed enabling legislation for banks to do this business, as well as enabling legislation for other lenders, fix a maximum amount that can be loaned to any one borrower at the rate prescribed under the bill. This amount varies in the different states and may be anywhere from $1,000 to $3,500. In the case of small loan companies the amount is anywhere from $300 to $500, and in two cases it is $1,000. The rates permitted to small loan companies are graduated under most laws because of their relatively high charge. For example, in a state that permits a $500 maximum under the licensed lender law, the act may prescribe a rate of 3 per cent per month on the first $150, $1\frac{1}{2}$ per cent per month on the second $150, and $\frac{1}{2}$ of

1 per cent on the $200 balance. In the case of banks the rate is usually fixed at, say, 6 per cent discount for the full amount permitted.

As the departments continue to develop, the ceilings now fixed by law for banks will probably be increased, and they will also take into consideration a graduated rate, with smaller rates being specified for larger amounts. When loans are large enough, no enabling legislation is needed because the legal interest rate will be high enough to permit a profitable operation. For example, take a state that has a legal rate of 6 per cent or 8 per cent. A loan of $5,000 for one year with twelve monthly payments could be made on a profitable basis on a discount arrangement. A discount of 3 per cent on this loan would give the bank sufficient income to make the loan and still be under the legal rate for the state.

Although people of small means need credit just as badly as those of large incomes, the fact remains that if a small loan operation is to be profitable, a lender needs higher rates on very small loans. The only factor involved is the cost of money, and the cost of money currently is not too important a factor for banks in the present market.

Conclusion

Consumer instalment lending has had its ups and downs over the years. Comedians have found it a good subject for jokes and ridicule. Books have been written by authors of high standing deploring its development and prophesying all kinds of dreadful things for our economy as a result of its use.

But the record of the consumer in handling his debt up to the present time has been excellent, and by going back to the beginning of this type of credit in this country, it can be seen that this same splendid record held true during both good and bad times.

In no other country is consumer credit used in the volume it is in this country, and no other country enjoys the standard of living found in this country. Many people agree that the advance in machines has had much to do with this high standard of living, since machines made possible mass production and mass production in turn made possible the production of goods for less money. But the production of goods en masse is of little value unless the goods can be sold.

How important a part did consumer instalment lending play in developing the consumer durable industry of this country by offering a credit technique that would enable individuals to buy goods and pay for them as they used them? This question has been argued pro and con for years and probably always will be. It would seem evident

that consumer instalment lending has been and is of real benefit not only to the individual but to the economy as a whole.

Bibliography

Cragg, Alliston, *Do You Need Some Money?* New York: Harper & Brothers, 1941.

Gordon, Leland J., *Consumers in Wartime.* New York: Harper & Brothers, 1943.

Lucas, John H., *Consumer Credit.* New York: American Institute of Banking, 1945.

Niefeld, M. R., *Personal Finance Comes of Age.* New York: Harper & Brothers, 1939.

Nugent, Rolf, *Consumer Credit and Economic Stability.* New York: Russell Sage Foundation, 1939.

Seligman, E. R. A., *The Economics of Instalment Selling,* 2 vols. New York: Harper & Brothers, 1927.

PUBLICATIONS OF THE NATIONAL BUREAU OF ECONOMIC RESEARCH, NEW YORK

Bernstein, Blanche, *The Pattern of Consumer Debt, 1935–36.* 1940.

Chapman, John M., and Associates, *Commercial Banks and Consumer Instalment Credit.* 1940.

Coppock, Joseph D., *Government Agencies of Consumer Instalment Credit.* 1940.

Durand, David, *Risk Elements in Consumer Instalment Financing.* c1941.

Haberler, Gottfried, *Consumer Instalment Credit and Economic Fluctuations.* c1942.

Holthausen, Duncan McC., *The Volume of Consumer Instalment Credit, 1929–38.* 1940.

Plummer, Wilbur C. and Ralph A. Young, *Sales Finance Companies and Their Credit Practices.* 1940.

Saulnier, Raymond J., and Neil H. Jacoby, *Accounts Receivable Financing.* c1943.

Saulnier, Raymond J., *Industrial Banking Companies and Their Credit Practices,* 1940.

Young, Ralph A. and Associates, *Personal Finance Companies and Their Credit Practices.* 1940.

26

Consumer Credit Institutions Other Than Commercial Banks

by EDWARD E. EDWARDS

Professor of Finance, Indiana University

AMONG the important types of financial institutions in the United States are several whose principal function is the extension of credit to consumers. These types of financial institutions sometimes are called consumer credit or consumer financing institutions, but they are also referred to frequently as instalment credit institutions, for the reason that, as will shortly be explained, a large part of their business consists either in the making of instalment loans or the financing of instalment sales.

Consumer credit as generally defined includes all credit extended to individuals for nonbusiness purposes, that is, for the purchase of consumer goods and services, and for the payment of bills and other personal debt. Mortgage credit to enable consumers to build or purchase their own homes is excluded, perhaps because the long life of a residence makes the transaction an investment rather than a consumption expenditure. Credit extended for the purchase of other consumer durable goods, however, such as automobiles, washing machines, and radios, and for the repair and improvement of homes, is classified as consumer credit, even though these purposes might also be considered as investment. It is the widespread use of credit for these purposes that has made consumer credit (as defined) and especially instalment credit so important.

Consumer credit frequently is classified into *instalment credit, single payment loans, charge accounts,* and *service credit. Instalment credit* includes (1) loans of money repayable in instalments and (2) sales of goods and services on the instalment plan. Financial institutions are concerned with the latter as well as the former, since merchants who sell on the instalment plan frequently sell their instalment contracts to financial institutions or pledge them as collateral. Financial institutions are also con-

cerned with *single payment loans,* although these are becoming relatively unimportant in the consumer credit field, experience having proved the desirability of repaying personal debt in regular instalments. *Charge accounts,* representing sales of goods by merchants on open account, and *service credit,* representing the performance of services (by doctors, dentists, and many others) on credit, are outside the normal scope of financial institutions. Consumer credit institutions therefore are involved chiefly in the making of instalment loans and in the acquisition of instalment sales contracts from merchants, either by purchase or as collateral.

Both the relative importance of the various types of consumer credit and the trends in consumer credit outstanding are shown in Table 1. Of special significance from the standpoint of financial institutions are (1) the substantial and increasing volume of consumer credit; (2) the increasing relative importance of instalment credit; and (3) the even more rapidly increasing importance of instalment loans. To illustrate the last point, instalment loans outstanding at the end of 1929 amounted to less than single payment loans and to less than 40 per cent of the charge accounts outstanding. Twenty-one years later instalment loans outstanding exceeded charge accounts by a substantial margin and were more than four times as large as outstanding single payment loans. This significant change reflects the growing importance of financial institutions in the consumer credit field.

TABLE 1

TOTAL CONSUMER CREDIT OUTSTANDING, BY TYPE

1929–1950

(Estimates in millions of dollars)

End of Year	Total Consumer Credit	—— Instalment Credit ——			Single Payment Loans	Charge Accounts	Service Credit
		Total	Sale Credit	Loans			
1929	6,252	3,158	2,515	643	749	1,749	596
1933	3,439	1,588	1,122	466	303	1,081	467
1939	7,031	4,424	2,792	1,632	530	1,544	533
1940	8,163	5,417	3,450	1,967	536	1,650	560
1941	8,826	5,887	3,744	2,143	565	1,764	610
1942	5,692	3,048	1,617	1,431	483	1,513	648
1943	4,600	2,001	882	1,119	414	1,498	687
1944	4,976	2,061	891	1,170	428	1,758	729
1945	5,627	2,364	942	1,422	510	1,981	772
1946	8,677	4,000	1,648	2,352	749	3,054	874
1947	11,862	6,434	3,086	3,348	896	3,612	920
1948	14,366	8,600	4,528	4,072	949	3,854	963
1949	16,809	10,890	6,240	4,650	1,018	3,909	992
1950	20,093	13,478	7,923	5,555	1,326	4,227	1,062

Source: *Federal Reserve Bulletin,* February 1951, p. 218.

Financial institutions in the consumer credit field include personal finance companies, sales finance companies, industrial banks, and credit unions. All these types of institutions specialize in financing the consumer, and their additional functions, if any, are subordinated to this main purpose. Financial institutions other than these highly specialized ones also extend credit to consumers and should not be omitted from the list of consumer credit agencies. For example, commercial banks are a major source of consumer credit, yet it could hardly be said that the financing of consumers is the principal function of commercial banking.

It is the purpose of this chapter to describe the nature, scope, historical development, and method of operation of those types of financial institutions whose primary function is to finance the consumer—personal finance companies, sales finance companies, industrial banks, and credit unions. Consumer credit activities of commercial banks, whose other functions have been covered in earlier chapters, were described in Chapter 25.

Personal Finance Companies

Definition. Loosely defined, a personal finance company may be thought of as any person, firm, or corporation other than an industrial bank, credit union, or commercial bank whose business consists in whole or in part of lending small sums of money to individuals or families. Personal finance companies would as thus defined include pawnbrokers and remedial loan societies, institutions which make cash advances secured by the pledge of jewelry, cameras, musical instruments, and other personal property; loan sharks, or persons who make small loans at unlawful rates of interest; and all other persons or businesses which may, even though only occasionally, loan money to individuals.

A narrower but somewhat more useful definition of a personal finance company would exclude loan sharks and other lenders not specifically authorized by law to engage in the business of making small loans. Most of the forty-eight states and the District of Columbia have statutes providing for the regulation of the small loan business and for the licensing of those who engage in it. Licensed lenders under these laws are referred to as licensed lenders, small loan companies, and personal finance companies. Narrowly defined, therefore, personal finance companies are individuals, firms, and corporations that have been licensed to engage in the business of making small loans to individuals.

Reason for licensing. To understand the nature of the personal finance company it is first necessary to realize what the situation might be without licensed lending. Most states have usury laws which prohibit rates of interest in excess of 6, 8, or 10 per cent per annum. Such maximum rates, even in times of very low rates of interest on business loans, are hardly

adequate to pay the costs of making and collecting small loans and to show a reasonable profit for the risks taken. Unless some provision is made for an exception to the usury law, capital will not be invested in the small loan business except by persons who are willing to operate outside the law. While there are always some persons who will risk their capital in unlawful undertakings which promise a high return, the amount of capital that can be obtained is not likely to be enough to make the business sufficiently competitive to protect the public from excessive charges and other abuses.

This analysis of what might happen without licensed lending is not just theoretical. It is based on what did happen prior to the development of licensed lending, and on what is still going on in those few areas of the country where state legislatures have not made adequate provision for lending on a lawful basis.[1] The lending of money to consumers is an economic activity which apparently thrives with or without legal sanction. The only choice is whether such lending is to be done in large part by loan sharks or by legitimate lenders.

The principal reason for licensed lending (and thus for the personal finance company as it now exists) is to prevent people from having to deal with loan sharks. Another way in which this objective might have been attained would have been to repeal or to amend the usury laws so as to permit an adequate rate on small loans. This would have encouraged legitimate capital to enter the small loan business, and would have permitted the personal finance company to develop solely under the forces of competition rather than within the strict confines of a regulated industry. Personal finance companies under such conditions might have been more or less important than they are now, and their methods of operation might have been quite different, but conjecture of this sort is of little practical value in view of the fact that personal finance companies have developed as a highly regulated business.

Nature of regulation. Personal finance companies operate in most states under small loan laws patterned after the so-called Uniform Small Loan Law. Revised many times since, and now in its seventh draft, the original draft of the uniform law was agreed to in 1916 by the American Association of Small Loan Brokers and the Russell Sage Foundation, the latter a philanthropic organization which as early as 1907 and especially after 1910 had interested itself in the elimination of the loan shark. During the years from 1910 to 1916, laws not too unlike the uniform act had been enacted in six states—Massachusetts, Oregon, New Jersey, Ohio, Pennsylvania, and Michigan—so that by 1917, when three states—Indiana,

---

[1] For a good description of unregulated lending, see L. N. Robinson and Rolf Nugent, *Regulation of the Small Loan Business*. New York: Russell Sage Foundation, 1935, Chapter III.

Illinois, and Maine—adopted the uniform act and two others—New Hampshire and Utah—adopted somewhat similar legislation, the development of the personal finance company was well under way. By 1934, one-half of the states had laws conforming in their chief respects to the Uniform Small Loan Law, and by 1950 two-thirds of the states had such laws. (See Table 3.)

The principal features of the typical small loan law are those which provide for the licensing of lenders who wish to charge a rate higher than that permitted by the general usury law; those which recite in detail the terms of lending and the methods of operation for such licensees; and those which provide for the examination of the licensees' business and for the enforcement of the regulatory code by an appropriate agency of the state.

In general, small loan licenses have been available to all who wished to apply, with a minimum of restrictions. Obtaining a small loan license is thus greatly different than obtaining a bank charter, or obtaining permission to operate a branch bank, and this ease of entry into the small loan business has had a profound effect on the structure of personal finance companies. Individuals, partnerships, and corporations operate as personal finance companies, some in a single location, others in several different locations, and a few in regional or nation-wide networks.

Terms of lending and methods of operation, at least insofar as these are controlled by law, are fairly uniform from state to state. Loans must not exceed the maximum amount stated in the law—at one time almost universally $300 but now quite frequently $500 or more. Interest must be stated and computed as a per cent per month of actual unpaid balance,[2] at a rate not to exceed that stated in the law or set by the regulatory agency. Charges other than interest ordinarily are not permitted. The borrower must have the right to repay his loan in full or in part at any time without penalty and without having to pay interest for any period during which he did not have the use of the borrowed funds.

---

[2] The method of computing interest is perhaps the most significant aspect of the legal restrictions affecting operations. Most other types of consumer credit agencies compute interest on the original amount rather than on actual unpaid balances, and hence are able to advertise a rate which in the case of a loan payable in equal installments is only slightly more than one-half the actual rate. For example, interest at $6.00 per year per $100 loaned is about the same as interest at 1 per cent per month on actual loan balance. Lenders who compute interest in this way, however, are more likely to refer to their rate as 6 per cent than as 12.

Owing to the adoption of a $3\frac{1}{2}$ per cent per month rate in the original uniform law, personal finance companies have often been called "42 per centers" and have frequently been thought of as loan sharks. The $3\frac{1}{2}$ per cent rate, however, was far less than the 80, 120, 240 and even 500 per cent per annum charged by the loan sharks. Moreover, the $3\frac{1}{2}$ per cent per month maximum rate has been reduced over the years either by legislative or by regulatory action.

Terms of the loan contract must be fully and accurately stated in writing and a copy thereof given to the borrower.

Small loan laws generally provide for examination of the licensee's books and records by a state examiner. Most states require annual reports and provide that records be maintained in a proper manner to facilitate examination and the preparation of required reports. Violations of the small loan law are declared to be misdemeanors punishable by fine or imprisonment or both and by suspension of the license.

Importance. Personal finance companies at the end of 1950 had outstanding loans in excess of one billion dollars. (See Table 2.) The total of $1,084,000,000 represented about 23 per cent of all consumer instalment loans outstanding other than insured repair and modernization loans.[3] Personal finance companies nevertheless ranked well behind com-

TABLE 2

CONSUMER INSTALMENT LOANS OUTSTANDING

By Type of Loan and Type of Lender

1929–1950

(Estimates in millions of dollars)

End of Year	Insured Repair and Moderni- zation Loans	—All Other Consumer Instalment Loans—				
		Commercial Banks	Personal Finance Companies	Industrial Banks (and Loan Companies)	Credit Unions	Other Lenders
1929	...	43	263	219	23	95
1933	...	29	246	121	20	50
1939	200	523	448	230	135	96
1940	268	692	498	236	174	99
1941	285	784	531	241	200	102
1942	206	426	417	161	130	91
1943	123	316	364	126	104	86
1944	113	357	384	128	100	88
1945	164	477	439	146	103	93
1946	322	956	597	215	153	109
1947	568	1,435	701	300	225	119
1948	739	1,709	817	364	312	131
1949	801	1,951	929	425	402	142
1950	862	2,433	1,084	494	525	157

Source: *Federal Reserve Bulletin*, February 1951, p. 218.

mercial banks, whose outstanding loans (excluding insured repair and modernization loans) were more than double those of personal finance companies.

---

[3] Outstanding balances for insured repair and modernization loans are not reported separately by type of lender, but personal finance companies are not believed to account for very much of this type of credit.

The second-place standing of personal finance companies in the instalment loan field is a marked change from a generation ago. In 1929, personal finance companies accounted for 40 per cent of the amount outstanding and ranked first among the types of lenders. By 1939 commercial banks had gained first place, but they dropped back again during World War II. From 1945 to 1950, however, commercial banks increased their volume by almost two billion dollars while personal finance companies increased theirs by only 600 million.

The importance of personal finance companies should not be measured solely by dollar volume. If numbers of loans outstanding were available for the various types of lenders, personal finance companies would rank relatively higher, since their average loan balance is typically much smaller than in the case of commercial banks. Personal finance companies are of greatest importance in making credit available to the neediest of families, in making loans that no other financial institution would make because of the risk or the relatively high cost of handling.

Number, size, and location. There are probably fewer than 1,000 personal finance companies in the United States, but the total number of locations where these companies do business is nearer 5,000. One of the largest companies, Household Finance Corporation, operated in 1951 a total of 524 branch offices, located in 355 cities in 29 states and 9 Canadian provinces. Many other companies operate offices in several cities, frequently in different states. Such companies sometimes are referred to as "chains" as contrasted with the "independents," or companies which operate from a single office or from two or more locations in a single city.

Small loan offices are found principally in industrial areas and in the larger cities. Some of the larger chains will locate branches only in cities having a population in excess of some minimum which they believe necessary to support an office. Smaller chains and probably most of the independents do business in the smaller cities. In many cases, however, the personal finance business in the smaller cities is combined with sales financing or other types of business activity to provide a total volume adequate to make the venture profitable.

Sources of funds. Personal finance companies obtain their funds from essentially the same sources as nonfinancial corporations. Investment by the owners, as represented by the net worth accounts in individual proprietorships and partnerships and by the common stock in corporations, typically accounts for a substantial share of the total funds. Most companies, both large and small, have been able to obtain bank credit to supplement the owners' funds. The larger corporations, and many of small and medium size, have sold bonds or preferred stock or both to the general public.

The ability of personal finance companies to sell securities publicly

and to borrow readily from commercial banks is ample evidence of the safe and profitable manner in which most companies conduct their operations. With this record of successful operation and with full legal sanction for charging higher rates of interest than permitted by the usury law, personal finance companies can attract the necessary capital to enable them to meet the public demand for small loans. The question might even be asked whether too much rather than too little capital is going into this business.

The large amount of bank credit used by personal finance companies—in some cases more than the amount of capital invested by the owners —raises an interesting question of commercial banking policy. Banks that make personal loans on their own account may find themselves in the position of financing a competitor. Quite often, however, the competition between commercial banks and personal finance companies is more apparent than real, with personal finance companies making loans that, because of their smaller size or poorer credit rating, would not be considered bankable. Moreover, only the small independent operators in the personal finance field are actually forced to borrow from banks with which they are in direct competition in making instalment loans. The larger companies have access to the nation's money markets, and may borrow in New York or Chicago to loan in Fort Wayne or Wilkes-Barre.

Types of loan. Loans made by personal finance companies are essentially character loans, without endorsement and without marketable collateral. Chattel mortgages on household goods are quite commonly taken, but foreclosures are rare, since public opinion would hardly stand for such drastic action. The mortgage probably is taken less for security than to discourage multiple borrowing. Automobile loans are fairly common, but the legal limit for individual loans usually is too low for this type of business except for very old cars. In those states that have raised the loan limit to $500 or higher, the making of automobile loans is more feasible, but it is doubtful whether the increase in maximum loan limits has been as much as the average increase in automobile prices.

Loans generally provide for repayment in monthly instalments over a ten to twenty-four month period. Regulation W of the Board of Governors of the Federal Reserve System has at times limited maturities to as short a period as twelve months. It is believed, however, that a substantial proportion of loans made by personal finance companies are refinanced before maturity, either to provide an advance of more funds or to reduce the monthly payment. Many lenders, without recasting the loan contract, have permitted borrowers to pay less each month than originally agreed upon, thus extending the length of the loan.

Loans range in size from less than $50 to the maximum permitted by law, with the average in most states probably not exceeding $200. There

has been a definite trend over a long period of years toward larger loans, and this trend in recent years has been augmented by the rapid increase in the cost of living. The original maximum loan of $300 has now been increased to $500 or more in eleven states (see Table 3), but rates permitted on the larger loans usually are much less than maximum rates for the smaller loans. Keeping a fairly high maximum rate for small balances encourages personal finance companies to continue to serve the most necessitous borrower and thus to discourage any return of the illegal lender.

Interest rates. Maximum rates permitted by law in most states (see Table 3) are now below the three and one-half per cent per month which was the most common rate a decade or two ago. The recommended maximum in the latest draft (1942) of the Uniform Small Loan Law is 3 per cent per month on the first $100 of loan balance, and 2 per cent per month on any balance in excess of $100. (This draft does not provide for loans in excess of $300.)

Actual rates charged by some companies are less than the maximum rates permitted by law. Competition in the personal finance business has seldom been on an interest rate basis, however, and actual rates are quite close to maximum rates, particularly for loans of average size or less. Borrowers apparently are more interested in getting a loan than in getting the lowest rate, and lenders have been more interested in expanding the total market for loans through advertising and the establishment of new branches than in taking customers away from each other through rate-cutting.

TABLE 3

MAXIMUM RATES OF INTEREST AND MAXIMUM LOANS FOR
PERSONAL FINANCE COMPANIES

A. *States with Laws Similar to Uniform Small Loan Law*

State	Maximum Loan	Maximum Rate of Interest [a]
Arizona	$300	$3\frac{1}{2}\%$
California	No limit	$2\frac{1}{2}$-2% @ $100 to $500 ($2\%$ if security insured), $\frac{5}{6}\%$ @ $500 to $5,000; no maximum above $5,000
Colorado	$300	$3\frac{1}{2}$-$2\frac{1}{2}\%$ @ $100
Connecticut	$500	3-2% @ $100, $\frac{1}{2}\%$ @ $300 to $500; 12% a year after 20 months
Florida	$300	$3\frac{1}{2}\%$
Hawaii	$300	$3\frac{1}{2}$-$2\frac{1}{2}\%$ @ $100
Idaho	$300	3%
Illinois	$500	3-2% @ $150, 1% @ $300 to $500

[a] Monthly rate on actual unpaid principal balances unless otherwise stated. Combination rates (e.g. $2\frac{1}{2}$—2% @ $100) represent plans to permit a higher rate on some minimum part of loan balance, and a lower rate on any excess. In the example indicated, $2\frac{1}{2}$ per cent per month is permitted on the first $100 of loan balance but only 2 per cent on any balance in excess of $100. Combination rates appear to be lower than is actually the case, for as the loan is paid down the effective rate increases.

Source: National Consumer Finance Association, April 1950.

TABLE 3 (*Continued*)

MAXIMUM RATES OF INTEREST AND MAXIMUM LOANS FOR PERSONAL FINANCE COMPANIES

A. *States with Laws Similar to Uniform Small Loan Law (Continued)*

State	Maximum Loan	Maximum Rate of Interest [a]
Indiana	$300	3-1½% @ $150
Iowa	$300	3-2% @ $150
Kentucky	$300	3½-2½% @ $150
Louisiana	$300	3½-2½% @ $150; 8% a year one year after mat.
Maine	$300	3-2½% @ $150; 25 cents min.
Maryland	$300	3%
Massachusetts	$300	2%; 6% a year one year after mat.
Michigan	$500	3-2½% @ $50, ¾% @ $300 to $500
Minnesota	$300	3%
Nebraska	$1,000	3-2½% @ $150, ¾% @ $300 to $1,000
New Hampshire	$300	2% plus $1 or $2 fee
New Jersey	$500	2½-½% @ $300 to $500
New York	$500	2½-2% @ $100, ½% @ $300 to $500
Ohio	$1,000	3-2% @ $150, ⅔% @ $300 to $1,000
Oregon	$300	3%
Pennsylvania	$300	3-2% @ $150; 6% a year after 18 months
Rhode Island	$300	3%
Utah	$300	3%
Vermont	$300	2½-2¼% @ $125
Virginia	$300	2½%; 6% a year after 23 months and in certain other cases
Washington	$500	3-1% @ $300 to $500; $1 min.
West Virginia	$300	3½-2½% @ $150
Wisconsin	$300	2½-2-1% @ $100 and $200

B. *States with Laws Dissimilar to Uniform Small Loan Law*

State	Maximum Loan	Maximum Rate of Interest
Delaware	$300	6% a year discount; 2% service fee; 5% fine; various limitations
Georgia	$300	1½%
Nevada	$300	3½-3% @ $100; $5 year min.; other charges
New Mexico	$500	3-2% @ $150; 1% @ $300 to $500; 5% to $50 step rate; $1 min.; 10% a year one year after mat. and in certain other cases
Oklahoma	$300	10% per year plus service charges not exceeding an initial 5%, and monthly 2% but not more than $2, subject to various limitations
Tennessee	$300	½%; monthly fee not exceeding 1%
Wyoming	$300	3½% on loans to $150 plus $1 fee on loans of $50 or less; $1 recording fee

The real function of the maximum rate is to control the flow of legitimate capital into the small loan business. Too low a rate drives out legitimate lending and encourages the loan shark; too high a rate invites excessive promotion and may result in personal borrowing over and above

actual needs. Present maximum rates in many states probably are on the high side and might be lowered considerably without serious consequences either to the personal finance business or to families in need of emergency credit.

Types of borrowers. Wage earners constitute the majority of borrowers from personal finance companies. Office workers, salespersons and other nonmanual workers in the lower and medium salary ranges are also important borrowers. Business and professional men and farmers account for very little borrowing, chiefly because their credit needs can best be served by financial institutions that typically make larger loans.

Loans sometimes are made to enable borrowers to buy furniture, electrical appliances, and other durable goods, but such loans are relatively unimportant. The purpose of borrowing is more often to pay off other debts or to meet doctor bills or other emergency needs. Failure to save for taxes, coal, winter clothing, and other out-of-the-ordinary expenditures probably accounts for a sizable part of loan demand.

Method of operation. Lending procedures are simple and direct, with a strong emphasis on quick decision and prompt availability of funds for borrowers who meet credit standards. Loan applications are taken by the manager or an assistant. Credit information obtained in the interview is checked by an "outside" man (who may divide his time between credit investigation and making collections), by reference to a local credit bureau, or by telephone calls to employers and other references. Many companies make a minimum of calls, and emphasize in their advertising that loans are arranged in strict confidence.

The interval between application and closing is ordinarily short. Some companies advertise "money available same day," or "telephone your application and your money will be ready for you when you reach the office." Immediate service is practically assured for old customers whose repayment record is at all satisfactory.

Once a loan has been made the operating problems shift to collection. Owing to the type of borrower involved, highly aggressive methods are required to keep payments current and to prevent both loss of interest and loss of principal.

The sum of collection expense and loss of interest and principal constitute a substantial part of personal finance company costs. Some companies stress collections and minimize losses by keeping loans current; others have avoided collection costs (and also the necessity for relending money collected) by allowing borrowers to skip payments or to pay interest only and thus to remain more or less constantly in debt. Such practices, unfortunately, are more or less encouraged by the provisions of the small loan law which permit interest to be computed on actual unpaid balances rather than on balances originally contracted.

Many companies have developed collection methods and personnel which are highly effective in keeping loan portfolios liquid. Whether these methods actually result in borrowers' getting out of debt or merely force them to refinance their indebtedness elsewhere is not exactly clear. Probably a very large percentage of families who borrow from personal finance companies continue in debt to one company or another for a much longer period of time than the turnover of receivables for a given company would indicate.

Sales Finance Companies

Definition. Sales finance companies may be defined as individuals, partnerships, and corporations (other than industrial banks, credit unions, and commercial banks) which finance the sale of automobiles and other consumer durable goods by purchasing from the merchants or dealers who sell the goods the instalment sales contracts or notes which they received from their customers. Sales finance companies become creditors to consumers by taking over the notes or contracts held by instalment sellers, not by lending money to prospective buyers.

Ordinarily when a business firm needs credit in order to make sales to its own customers on credit, it turns to its commercial bank. In fact, the financing of accounts and notes receivable for business concerns is supposedly a major function of commercial banking. Automobile and appliance dealers, however, and to a considerable extent other instalment sellers, have produced a volume of receivables that has warranted the development of highly specialized institutions to finance them. Such specialized institutions are known as sales finance companies.

Some sales finance companies engage in a wide variety of business activities other than the financing of instalments sales to consumers. Most common of these extra activities is the financing of inventories for those merchants and dealers who sell their receivables to the sales finance company. A few of the larger companies write automobile insurance. Some compete with commercial banks in making all types of business loans. Many of the smaller companies do business as personal finance companies, as mentioned earlier in this chapter. The principal function of a sales finance company, however, is the purchase of retail instalment sales contracts or notes.

Reasons for development. The chief reason for the development of sales finance companies has been the rapid increase in instalment selling during the past forty or fifty years. The idea of selling goods for a small down payment, with the remaining balance to be paid in weekly or monthly instalments, dates back to the early nineteenth century, but the total volume of instalment selling was quite small prior to the develop-

ment of the automobile industry. Financing the sale of automobiles has always been a major part of the sales finance business, and despite application of automobile finance methods to the sale of other consumer goods, sales finance companies are still referred to frequently as automobile finance companies.

Whether the automobile manufacturers could have sold the millions of cars they have produced on some basis other than the instalment plan may be a debatable question, but the important fact is that most of the cars that have been produced have been sold in this manner. Similar dependence on instalment selling, although perhaps to a lesser degree, is found in television, refrigerators and other major electrical appliances, furniture, and other consumer durable goods. When consumers can buy goods for a small down payment, the merchants or dealers who sell on such terms must have credit in order to replace their inventories and to make additional sales. The supplying of this needed credit is the chief function of the sales finance company.

Commercial banks also purchase instalment notes or contracts from dealers, or accept them as collateral for business loans. Commercial banks and other consumer finance institutions make personal instalment loans to consumers in order that they may pay cash for the goods that they otherwise would have to buy on the instalment plan. These alternate methods of financing, while important now, did not develop early enough or rapidly enough to keep pace with the steadily increasing output of factories planned for mass production. Sales finance companies were organized, in many cases by automobile and other manufacturers, to do the financing that the banks and other financial institutions either could not or would not do.

Advantages of sales finance companies. Initially, and to a certain extent even yet, sales finance companies enjoyed certain advantages over other types of financial institutions. As compared with banks or other consumer credit institutions that might have solved the problem by loaning money directly to consumers, sales finance companies had the important advantage that they were not subject to the usury law, and hence could charge for financing whatever amount was necessary to cover costs and still yield a satisfactory profit. As compared with personal finance companies, particularly, sales finance companies were not limited to $300 or any other maximum amount that could be owed by a single debtor.

Two special advantages of the sales finance company over commercial banks need to be mentioned. Sales finance companies, by operating largely on invested capital rather than on deposits obtained from the general public, can assume more risk. When instalment selling was first becoming an important way of doing business, many persons believed

that consumer credit was inherently risky and would, in any major depression, result in substantial losses. Not until after the depression of the early thirties were many bankers convinced that consumer credit was sufficiently safe for the investment of depositor funds. Sales finance companies thus enjoyed a period of initial development relatively free from competition.

Sales finance companies enjoy one other advantage over commercial banks, and that is the fact that sales finance companies need not be limited in their operations to a single city or to a single state. In California and a few other states, banks may establish branches in cities throughout the state, but not beyond state-lines. In most states, banks either can have no branches at all or are limited to the city or county in which the bank is located. This type of banking system, whatever may be said of its advantages in other ways, is just not adapted to the quick establishment of new and uniform policies and procedures over a wide area. A sales finance company, however, may operate through branches or subsidiaries in all of the forty-eight states, and may establish uniform practices throughout as wide an area as it wishes. A manufacturer of automobiles or other products sold on the instalment plan throughout the United States might therefore strongly prefer to do business with a finance company rather than to undertake the difficult and tedious job of convincing hundreds of bankers that they should each provide the type of financing service he desires for his dealers.

Importance. Instalment sales credit outstanding at the end of 1950 amounted to almost eight billion dollars and constituted approximately 60 per cent of the total consumer instalment credit then outstanding and about 40 per cent of the total consumer credit outstanding, including single payment loans, charge accounts, and service credit. (See Table 1.) Not all the instalment sales credit was held by sales finance companies, however, since many merchants and dealers finance their own instalment sales and since financial institutions other than sales finance companies also participate in this business.

Sales finance companies probably accounted for around three billion dollars or close to 40 per cent of the outstanding instalment sales credit. This volume gave to sales finance companies the top place among institutions that buy retail instalment sales paper, and a ranking of second to commercial banks in total volume of consumer credit. Outstandings of sales finance companies were roughly three times the total loan volume of personal finance companies, the next most important type of consumer financing institution as measured by total dollars.

The relative importance of sales finance companies as compared with other consumer credit institutions has declined over the past twenty years, chiefly as the result of the steadily increasing importance of com-

mercial banks in the consumer credit field. Commercial banks compete with sales finance companies in two ways: first, by soliciting sales finance business from automobile and appliance dealers and second, by making instalments loans to consumers for the purchase of automobiles and other goods, thus eliminating the dealer from the credit transaction. Bank competition appears to have been most effective outside the automobile field, probably because the finance companies have fought back hardest in this area. As of the present time, sales finance companies are still the principal source of credit for the financing of automobiles.

Number, size, and location. The total resources of sales finance companies are represented by three very large companies which operate throughout the United States; a somewhat larger number of regional companies; and several hundred smaller companies, most of which do business in local areas only. Some of the smaller companies, however, do a nation-wide business in financing sales for a single manufacturer or his dealers.

The three large companies were at one time closely affiliated with important automobile manufacturers, but only one (General Motors Acceptance Corporation) continues to be so. The largest sales finance company (C. I. T. Financial Corporation) is a billion-dollar concern but has other business interests than financing retail instalment sales. Its holdings of retail automobile paper, however, exceeded 500 million dollars at the end of 1949. Commercial Credit Company, the third of the so-called "big three," had total resources at the end of 1949 in excess of 500 million dollars and was approximately double in size the largest of the regional companies (Associates Investment Company).

In contrast to the general practice of personal finance companies, sales finance companies usually try to conduct their business from as few locations as possible. A single office frequently serves a wide territory, transactions with dealers being handled through field men or by telephone and mail, and transactions with instalment buyers being handled chiefly by mail. Millions of persons have had their cars and appliances financed by a sales finance company without ever seeing an employee of the company or setting foot in a company office.

Sources of funds. Sales finance companies, particularly the large companies, rely heavily on commercial banks for their funds. Many have also supplemented their own invested capital by selling long-term bonds. Short-term bank loans give the companies the flexibility they need to meet both seasonal and cyclical demands. Banks consider loans to sales finance companies as prime investments and make them at favorable interest rates, even though the finance companies may be in direct competition with the banks.

During the period of their development, sales finance companies did

not have access to the nation's money markets as they do now and were thus compelled to operate largely on their own capital. One of the important reasons why General Motors and other manufacturers organized their own finance companies was to insure an adequate capital investment and to improve borrowing power. Sales finance companies did not expand their borrowing power beyond rather narrow limits until bankers had reached the conclusion that instalment credit was sufficiently safe for banks to enter the field. By this time the general public as well as investment institutions had also come to regard with favor the securities of sales finance companies, and there are probably few industries today that have available as wide a source of funds as does the finance business.

Method of operation. A buyer of an automobile or other goods on the instalment plan usually enters into a written contract with the seller and frequently signs a promissory note in addition. The terms of the contract usually provide that the buyer will pay a down payment and a series of weekly or monthly payments; that the buyer will have possession of the goods but that title will remain in the seller; and that if the buyer fails to make any payment when due the seller may repossess the goods from the buyer. Contracts frequently require that the buyer keep the car or other goods insured, and quite often the contract provides that the insurance be furnished by the seller and the cost thereof included in the contract.

Contracts should recite clearly the purchase price and terms, including (a) the *cash price*; (b) the *down payment*; (c) the *unpaid balance,* which is the difference between the cash price and the down payment; (d) the *insurance* charge for any insurance to be furnished by the seller to the buyer; (e) the *principal balance,* which is the sum of the unpaid balance and the insurance charge; (f) the *finance charge,* which is the cost to the buyer of buying on instalments; and (g) the *time balance,* which is the amount to be paid in instalments by the buyer and is the sum of the principal balance and the finance charge.

If a note is to be signed by the buyer, the amount of the note will be the time balance of the contract. No interest will be provided in the note except for amounts past due. Contracts and notes should also recite the amount of each instalment payment and the date that each becomes due.

While instalment sellers may draw up their own contract forms, those who plan to sell their contracts to a finance company ordinarily use contract forms furnished by the finance company. The company also furnishes rate cards to enable the seller to compute easily the amount of the finance charge and the insurance, if any. Application blanks or credit information sheets may be furnished by the finance company.

When a sale is about ready to be made, the seller may call the finance company to obtain its approval, since otherwise the finance company might refuse to buy the instalment contract because of the poor credit rating of the instalment buyer. In any case, as soon as the contract and note have been signed the dealer is ready to deliver them to the finance company and thus get his money out of the sale. The finance company will then notify the buyer that it holds the contract and that payments should be made to the finance company. Coupon books frequently are sent the buyer to expedite remittance by mail. If payments are not received, the finance company ordinarily has the responsibility for making collections, although this may depend on the arrangements which have been agreed upon between the dealer and the finance company.

Ordinarily the finance company will pay the dealer an amount at least equal to the unpaid balance plus the cost of any insurance furnished by the dealer. This amount plus the down payment assures the dealer a total receipt at least as great as the stated cash price. Very often the finance company will pay, either at once or at some later date, some amount in excess of the unpaid balance, thus permitting the dealer to participate in the finance charge or to receive a commission on insurance furnished by the finance company.

Arrangements with dealers. The key person in the operation of a sales finance company is the automobile or appliance dealer who originates the instalment sales contracts. The dealer is important not just because he is the one who collects the down payment and obtains the buyer's signature to the contract; he is the one who determines who gets the finance business. The building of volume by the sales finance company thus requires the maximum of cooperation from a maximum number of dealers. Promotion and advertising efforts therefore are aimed at the dealer, although some companies have tried to appeal directly to the consumer and thus bring indirect pressure on the dealer.

Formerly manufacturers that organized their own finance company or developed a financing plan with some one company were in a position to urge or even to force their dealers to use the preferred finance company. For example, it has been claimed that dealers lost their franchises, were unable to get spare parts, received black sedans in the summer and open cars in the winter, and otherwise were discriminated against if they refused to use the finance company of the manufacturer's choice. Such monopolistic practices have now been declared unlawful, and finance companies today must compete for the dealer's business without too much help from the manufacturer.

One of the most common methods of soliciting the dealer's retail paper is to extend credit to the dealer so that he can maintain an inventory of

merchandise. Loans by finance companies to dealers are called "wholesaling" or "floor-planning" and usually are made at very low rates of interest, even though this type of credit frequently is quite risky. When a car or appliance that is covered by a floor-planning loan is sold to a consumer, the finance company must be paid. If the sale is for cash, which would be unusual, the repayment to the finance company is easy. If the sale is on the instalment plan, the dealer has only the down payment with which to pay off the finance company, and this may be in the form of a trade-in. The finance company, however, is more than willing to accept the retail instalment sales contract from the dealer, since getting the retail paper was its reason for doing the floor-planning in the first place.

Another method of interesting the dealer commonly used is to pay him for the business he originates. This may be done by letting him have the agent's commission for any insurance he writes in connection with the instalment sale, or by paying him more for the note or contract than the amount of unpaid balance being financed. This latter practice, which is made possible by permitting or requiring the dealer to write into the contract a higher finance charge than the finance company actually needs, is justifiable to the extent that the dealer ought to participate in the finance charge because of risk he assumes or work that he does in originating the contract. Writing into the contract a finance charge that permits the dealer a "reserve" or "bonus" or "pack" or "kickback" out of all proportion to his risk or services is now unlawful in a few states.

Some companies try to win the dealer's good will by limiting his liability in the event that the buyer fails to keep up his instalment payments. Many of the smaller companies buy paper "without recourse," which means that the dealer has no liability in event the instalment buyer defaults. Other companies limit the dealer's liability through a "repurchase agreement" which provides that the finance company buy paper without recourse but that the dealer must repurchase, usually for the then unpaid balance, any cars or other merchandise which the finance company repossesses.

Regulation. The federal government as well as a number of states have attempted to correct certain abuses in the sales finance business. Federal regulation (except for wartime and mobilization controls of down payments and maturities) has been limited to two areas: misleading advertising and monopoly. Certain sales finance companies that advertised 6 per cent per annum when the finance charge was computed on original unpaid balance, and was thus actually closer to 12 per cent on declining balances, were enjoined from continuing such advertising. Charges of monopolistic practices have been brought against some of the larger finance companies closely affiliated with manufacturers, and in

the cases of two of the largest finance companies a consent decree was agreed upon whereby the affiliations were terminated.

Other abuses have been the grounds for state regulation. Excessive finance charges, excessive participation by dealers in the finance charge, failure to furnish the buyer with a clearly written statement of the contract, failure to furnish agreed-upon insurance, failure to make appropriate refund of finance charge in event of pre-payment, failure to give any accounting to the buyer in event of repossession, and other undesirable practices have been called to the attention of state legislatures. In 1935 Indiana became the first state to enact a comprehensive regulatory code, including provision for the licensing and examination of sales finance companies. Since then, retail instalment financing laws have been enacted in about one-fourth of the states.[4]

Industrial Banks

Definition. An industrial bank is a financial institution that invests its funds chiefly in personal loans which it makes to consumers, and which obtains, or is authorized to obtain, its funds from individual savers, either through the acceptance of deposits or the sale of investment certificates. Industrial banks may operate (1) as ordinary corporations, without specific legal authorization and regulation; (2) under special legislation providing for their organization and operation; or (3) under general banking laws. Those that operate as ordinary corporations, and in some states those that operate under special legislation, are prohibited from using the word *bank* in their corporate title or in their advertising. Some of those that operate under general banking laws have taken on so many of the functions of commercial banks that it is sometimes difficult to determine whether they are industrial banks or commercial banks.

The most widely known industrial banks are the Morris Plan banks and companies. The first industrial bank in this country was established in 1910 by Arthur J. Morris at Norfolk, Virginia, under the title of Fidelity Savings & Trust Company. Under his leadership, many other industrial banks were organized within the next few years. In 1914 the Industrial Finance Corporation was organized to promote the organization of Morris Plan banks and where necessary to provide capital for these institutions. The Industrial Finance Corporation is now the parent body of a complicated corporate system and has control, through a sub-

---

[4] For a discussion of regulation by the various states, see Wallace P. Mors, "State Regulation of Retail Instalment Financing—Progress and Problems," *The Journal of Business of the University of Chicago,* Vol. XXIII, No. 4 (October 1950), and Vol. XXIV, No. 1 (January 1951).

sidiary, of many Morris Plan banks and companies. Many other Morris Plan banks, however, are financially independent of the Morris Plan System but use the Morris Plan name under a sort of licensing arrangement.

Reasons for development. The reasons for the development of industrial banks are similar to those for the development of personal finance companies. The heart of the industrial banking idea was its method of meeting the problem of the usury laws. The industrial bank could make loans to consumers at an effective rate of interest almost double the lawful rate, merely by providing that repayments be credited to a deposit or investment certificate account rather than to the loan. For example, the borrower from an industrial bank might sign a note for $100, to be repaid in twelve monthly instalments of $8.33 each. Since these instalment payments would be credited to a deposit or certificate account, the full amount of $100 would remain as the unpaid balance on the loan for the entire year, and the industrial bank could therefore lawfully make a charge of $8 where the lawful rate of interest was 8 per cent, as was true in most states. Since the bank deducted the $8 at once and began getting the rest of its money back at the end of the first month, the average outstanding balance on the loan would be nearer $50 than $100, and the bank would actually earn about 16 per cent on the money it had invested in loans.

This method of meeting the problem of the usury law was also open to commercial banks, which could easily provide that monthly payments on personal loans be credited to a deposit account rather than to the loans. As has already been pointed out, however, commercial banks were comparatively slow in getting into the consumer credit field for reasons other than rate of return, and it remained for the industrial banks to demonstrate that personal loans could be made safely and profitably on this basis.

To say that industrial banks developed solely as a means of dealing with difficulties growing out of the usury laws would be an exaggeration. In Canada and in many European countries where the usury law was not a factor, specialized banking institutions had developed to serve the needs of consumers. These institutions relied upon the savings of working people for their funds, and they invested their funds chiefly in personal loans. Industrial banks in this country are institutions of this same type, and it is not unlikely that they would have developed even without the special impetus of the usury laws.

Importance. Industrial banks rank behind commercial banks, sales finance companies, and personal finance companies in total volume of consumer credit outstanding. At the end of 1950 they accounted for

approximately 500 million dollars of consumer instalment loans, and less than 200 million dollars of retail instalment sales paper.[5]

The relative importance of industrial banks has declined steadily over the past twenty years. For example, instalment loans outstanding in industrial banks at the end of 1929 were almost five times the total for commercial banks. (See Table 2.) By the end of 1950, industrial bank holdings had doubled, whereas commercial bank outstandings were about fifty times the 1929 total and almost five times the volume currently held by the industrial banks. The relatively slow growth of industrial banks in terms of dollar aggregates results in part from the fact that many industrial banks have merged with or been converted into commercial banks.

Types of loans. Morris Plan and other industrial banks have emphasized character rather than collateral in their lending policies. Comaker loans, for which the borrower had to obtain the signatures of two other persons, made up most of the loans during the years of early development. In recent years lending policy has been broadened to include automobile and other chattel mortgage loans, single name notes, modernization loans, and in some cases real estate mortgage loans. In addition, some industrial banks have entered the sales finance business and buy retail instalment contracts or notes from dealers.

Industrial banks, unlike personal or sales finance companies, must keep their funds invested with some thought to the possible necessity of having to meet withdrawals of deposits or investment certificates. United States government bonds and other liquid or marketable assets usually make up some part of the portfolio. Unless personal loans make up a high proportion of the assets, however, an institution could hardly be called an industrial bank.

A comparison of the loans of an industrial bank with those of a personal finance company would show that the industrial bank makes larger loans and that its borrowers are somewhat better credit risks. There are two reasons for this: one, the fact that industrial banks either have no limit or a much higher limit to the amount they can loan to one borrower; and the other, the fact that the maximum rate of interest that the industrial bank can charge is much lower than the usual rate of interest charged by personal finance companies. The difference in rate not only forces the industrial bank to screen its credit risks more carefully; it also discourages the industrial bank from competing with personal finance companies for the smallest loans, on which costs in terms

---

[5] These estimates, which are taken from the *Federal Reserve Bulletin* for February 1951, include holdings of institutions identified as industrial banks and those identified as industrial loan companies.

of rate per annum are the greatest. The lower rate also appeals to consumers whose credit standing is high and whose needs are substantial.

Sources of funds. Industrial banks are profit-making corporations whose funds are obtained in part from the capital investment of the stockholders. Most industrial banks supplement these funds by soliciting the savings of persons in the communities they serve. Savings may be accepted either as deposits or as payment on investment certificates, which in all practical aspects are the same as deposits but which cannot be called deposits because of some prohibition in the laws of the particular state.

If the state law permits use of the word *bank* in the corporate title and also permits the acceptance of deposits, industrial banks may have their accounts insured by the Federal Deposit Insurance Corporation. Approximately one hundred industrial banks were thus insured in 1947. Most of these institutions appear to be rapidly taking on the characteristics of commercial banks, many of them offering checking account services as well as savings, and providing a wide variety of loan and investment services.[6]

Industrial banks or loan companies that do not have deposit insurance may nevertheless compete effectively for savings. With a long record of safety back of them, and with a rate of return somewhat higher than insured banks can pay, noninsured institutions have been able to supplement their invested capital without too much difficulty. Some companies, however, have not taken advantage of this source of funds at all.

Regulation. Industrial banks as defined herein probably could have been organized in any one of the states as ordinary corporations, without any special legislation. In most states, however, they would not have been permitted to accept deposits or to call themselves banks. Since their operations are essentially banking, approximately one-half the states have enacted special laws designed to protect the funds of savers who make deposits in or buy investment certificates from these institutions. In many states having such legislation, however, the savers are denied the benefit of deposit insurance by provisions against use of the word *bank* and acceptance of deposits.

A few states provide regulation of a type designed to protect the borrower as well as the saver. Industrial banks, however, have established a splendid record of fair dealing with borrowers, free from the abuses that have sometimes been found in other nonregulated lending to consumers and in instalment selling.

---

[6] For a description of insured industrial banks and recent trends in their development, see Ernst A. Dauer, "Radical Changes in Industrial Banks," *Harvard Business Review*, Vol. XXV, No. 4a (Autumn 1947).

Credit Unions

Definition. A credit union is a cooperative association in the consumer credit field, an institution in which the members may place their personal savings and from which they may borrow money.

Credit unions operate under charters granted by a state or by the federal government. Generally, but not universally, credit unions serve persons who constitute a clearly defined group and have a strong common interest apart from their membership in the credit union. For example membership in a credit union may be limited to employees of a single firm, members of a given trade or occupation, members of some other cooperative association, or members of a particular church or lodge. A few credit unions, however, like mutual savings banks and most savings and loan associations, have no such limitations on membership.

One reason for the membership restriction is that credit unions usually are sponsored by an employer for his employees, or by an organization for its members. Office space and equipment and frequently clerical help and other services are provided for the credit union by the employer or the sponsoring organization. For this reason many credit unions seem more like divisions or branches of some other organization than like independent financial institutions.

Importance. At the end of 1950, credit unions had outstanding consumer instalment loans somewhat in excess of 500 million dollars. (See Table 2.) This volume placed them slightly ahead of industrial banks in the instalment lending field; but since credit unions accounted for little or no instalment sales credit, industrial banks ranked ahead in total consumer credit volume. Credit unions thus are the least important of the consumer credit institutions in terms of dollar volume.

Although credit unions have ranked last as far back as figures are available, their importance has increased steadily over the past two decades. For example, credit unions now account for approximately 10 per cent of the outstanding consumer instalment loans, as compared with less than 5 per cent in 1929 and as late as 1933. At their present rates of growth, credit unions will soon pass industrial banks, and may in the not too distant future equal personal finance companies, in loan volume.

The importance of credit unions should not be measured solely by dollar volume. Their large and increasing number, their widespread location, their convenience and low cost, and their rapidly growing membership give them an importance far greater than their aggregate dollar volume would indicate.

Number, Size, and Location. Credit unions exceed in number any other

type of consumer credit institution except commercial banks. At the end of 1949 there were 10,085 credit unions in the United States, of which 9,910 were active. These were widely distributed among the states, with no state having fewer than ten. The largest numbers were found in the industrial states of Illinois, New York, Pennsylvania, Ohio, and Massachusetts, which had, respectively, 882, 767, 640, 616, and 537 active credit unions. State-chartered institutions outnumbered those federally chartered approximately five to four. (See Table 4.)

TABLE 4

CREDIT UNION STATISTICS

Item	1949			1934
	Federal	State	Total	
Number of Credit Unions	4,646	5,439	10,085	2,450
Number Active and Reporting	4,495	5,415	9,910	2,028
Number of Members	1,819,606	2,247,371	4,066,977	427,097
Number of Loans Made during Year	1,339,667	1,667,966	3,007,633	......ᵃ
Amount of Loans Made during Year	$348,912,287	$429,932,234	$778,844,521	$36,200,000
Amount of Loans Outstanding End of Year	$174,647,364	$333,512,888	$508,160,252	......ᵃ
Paid in Share Capital (Savings)	$285,000,934	$415,334,851	$700,335,785	......ᵃ
Total Assets	$316,362,504	$511,603,279	$827,965,783	$40,212,112

ᵃ Not available.
Source: *Monthly Labor Review*, September 1950.

The number of credit unions has increased rapidly since 1934, largely as the result of the active promotion of new credit unions by the Farm Credit Administration following passage of the Federal Credit Union Act in that year. From 1934 to 1941 the number increased from less than 2,500 to more than 10,000, of which almost 5,000 were federally chartered. Many of these newly chartered credit unions—both federal and state— never acquired more than a few hundred dollars of assets and were liquidated during the war years, with the result that the total number of active credit unions dropped to 8,629 by the end of 1945. Since then the number has again been increasing, but not at the high rate of the few years preceding World War II.

Total assets of active credit unions amounted at the end of 1949 to considerably less than one billion dollars. The average assets figure per credit union of slightly in excess of $80,000, however, is quite misleading as a description of a typical credit union. A large part of the total assets is accounted for by a relatively small number of well-established credit unions, and most of the active credit unions have assets well below the $80,000 average.

Sources of Funds. A credit union's chief source of funds is the personal savings of its members. Savings balances ordinarily are represented by credit union shares, which are similar to savings and loan shares in that they are repurchasable by the credit union at the member's option, and in that they receive dividend credits rather than interest. Many credit unions also accept deposits from their members, but federally chartered credit unions and those chartered by some states are prohibited from doing so. Where permitted, deposits usually receive a lower rate of interest than the rate of dividend paid to shareholders, the differential representing the preferred position that depositors, as creditors rather than owners, would have in the event of loss or liquidation.

Types of loans. Unsecured or co-maker loans of less than $300, repayable in weekly or monthly instalments, are the most important type of loan made by credit unions. Except for the very smallest loans, the borrower must obtain the signature of one or more co-makers or provide collateral in the form of a chattel or real estate mortgage, credit union shares, or other security. The maximum loan that can be made without security or without endorsement ranges from $50 to $100 or more.

Loans, in addition to providing for instalment payments of principal, also call for instalment payments of interest, usually at a rate of 1 per cent or less per month on actual unpaid balances. The low interest rate for loans of the size normally made by credit unions gives credit unions the distinction of being the lowest cost consumer credit institution.

Method of operation. The ability of a credit union to pay an attractive return to its members for savings when it charges such a low rate of interest on its loans results largely from the fact that much of the cost of doing business is borne by the sponsoring organization. Few other financial institutions have so few expenses. The low cost of borrowing from a credit union, however, is not entirely due to this absorption of direct and overhead expenses. Credit losses are low and credit investigations and collection procedures are inexpensive.

Responsibility for management of a credit union rests on the directors, who are elected by the members. Actual operation is delegated to committees, of which the credit committee which passes on loan applications is the most important. The treasurer, or clerk-treasurer, is ordinarily the managing officer, but he may not serve on a full-time basis or be paid adequately for his services. Unless the employer or other organization sponsoring the credit union has a genuine interest in its welfare and management, there is every likelihood that the credit union will not amount to much or will get into trouble. On the other hand, with the proper interest on the part of an employer or a well-established sponsoring organization, a credit union can become a most worth-while institution.

Suggested Readings

Clark, Evans, *Financing the Consumer*. New York: Harper & Brothers, 1930.

Cover, John H., *Financing the Consumer*. Chicago: University of Chicago Press, 1937.

Cox, Reavis, *The Economics of Instalment Buying*. New York: Ronald Press, 1948.

Foster, LeBaron R., *Credit for Consumers*. 4th rev. ed. New York: Public Affairs Committee, 1942.

Ham, Arthur H., and L. J. Robinson, *A Credit Union Primer*. 3rd Ed. New York: Russell Sage Foundation, 1930.

Hardy, Charles O., ed., *Consumer Credit and Its Uses*. New York: Prentice-Hall, Inc., 1938.

Haring, Albert, *Instalment Credit Comes of Age*. Chicago: National Retail Furniture Association, 1943.

————, *The Installment Credit Contract*. New York: Consumer Credit Institute of America, 1939.

Neifeld, M. R., *Cooperative Consumer Credit; with Special Reference to Credit Unions*. New York: Harper & Brothers, 1926.

Plummer, Wilbur C., and Ralph A. Young, *Sales Finance Companies and Their Credit Practices*. New York: National Bureau of Economic Research, 1940.

Robinson, L. N., and Rolf Nugent, *Regulation of the Small Loan Business*. New York: Russell Sage Foundation, 1935.

Saulnier, Raymond J., *Industrial Banking Companies and Their Credit Practices*. New York: National Bureau of Economic Research, 1940.

Seligman, Edwin R. A., and others, *The Economics of Instalment Selling*. New York: Harper & Brothers, 1927.

Young, Ralph A., and others, *Personal Finance Companies and Their Credit Practices*. New York: National Bureau of Economic Research, 1940.

27

The American Bankers Association [1]

by HAROLD W. STONIER

Executive Manager, The American Bankers Association

THE American Bankers Association was organized in 1875 at the inception of the development of trade and business associations. Only 14 associations had been formed before that year, and three prior to the Civil War. The need for an organization of bankers had been recognized much earlier in the century, but the difficulty of reconciling different viewpoints of interest prevented positive action. Banking played an important part in the economic development of young America. Banks provided money for the country through the issuance of bank notes. This unique function of banking had such a profound effect upon the public interest that banks could not continue to operate indefinitely without having a clearing house for discussion of their mutual problems, or without having a medium through which their views on banking and related matters could be expressed to the government.

Times of crisis often produce a community of interest. The passing of the First Bank of the United States in 1811 was followed by an attempt to unite the state banks in support of a uniform currency, but the diversity of interest and rivalry among banks proved to be too great an obstacle to success. The expiration of the First Bank's charter eliminated the organization's steadying influence and check upon redemption of notes of state banks. This condition caused new problems, and the banks were unable to agree upon a course of action to remedy them.

A similar development occurred a few years later. The charter of the Second Bank of the United States, which had been organized in 1816, was allowed to expire in 1836. This was followed by the Panic of 1837

---

[1] Other associations in the financial field are described in the following chapter. A separate chapter is given to the American Bankers Association because of its size and because of the great resources its membership represents.

and provided a basis for a meeting of bankers the following year. The issue under consideration was the resumption of specie payments, which had been suspended in the panic.

These incidents of banking history are recounted because they demonstrate two important factors related to the organization and operation of the American Bankers Association during the three-quarters of a century since 1875.

First, the bankers were concerned with the problem of currency. This was a recurring problem. Each wave of prosperity and speculation was followed by a financial crisis of varying degree. Public attention was naturally focused upon the operations of the banks. The establishment of the American Bankers Association was partly the result of an attempt to give broader consideration by banking to the currency problem. It is not coincidence, therefore, that the Association was organized not long after the financial panic of 1873. Bankers came to recognize the need for understanding the nature of such financial panics and the importance of leadership in guarding against such crises. An individual institution, or a limited group, could do little; but an organization to represent the banks collectively would be more effective in dealing with the problem. Since its organization in 1875, therefore, the Association has dealt at length with the question of currency, even though the emphasis has changed from the note-issue of the 1800's to the deposit-credit system of the 1950's.

Secondly, the abortive attempts of bankers in the early days of the century to organize for the purpose of remedying their problems pointed up the importance of resolving sectional, functional or other differences. It could not be expected that there would be unanimity of thinking in all phases of banking, but it was found necessary for the banks to subordinate differences on controversial issues so that they could meet on common ground to further the progress of the American financial system. The founders of the Association recognized at the outset that success could not be achieved unless the differences of viewpoint held by the various classes and types of banks were set aside in order to harmonize interests and weld together a national organization. This principle has been followed in the long history of the Association with remarkable results. The Association's organization finds a close parallel in the American form of government, in which local and sectional interests are joined in a compromise pattern with organization on a national scale.

The First Convention

The first convention of the Association at Saratoga Springs on July 20, 1875, attracted 350 bankers from 32 states and territories in response

to a challenge that "great profit will result from interchange and comparison of ideas and experiences relating to the conduct of our business." These thoughts were formalized and amplified in the constitution adopted the following year, which set forth the objectives as follows:

> . . . to promote the general welfare and usefulness of banks and banking institutions, and to secure uniformity of action, together with the practical benefits to be derived from personal acquaintance, and from the discussion of subjects of importance to the banking and commercial interests of the country; and especially in order to secure the proper consideration of questions regarding the financial and commercial usages, customs and laws which effect the banking interests of the entire country. . . .

It is difficult to classify the Association in the operations directed toward accomplishment of these objectives. It may be considered a trade association from the viewpoint of its assistance to banks in the conduct of strictly business transactions. Nevertheless, many of the functions and relationships in banking are of such a highly specialized character, involving such professional skills as law and economics, that work of the Association oftentimes may be classified as that of a professional association. In some respects it is a service organization performing for its membership a variety of special services which are particularly adaptable to nationwide organization. Finally, the Association may be regarded as an educational organization.

The educational influence of the Association has had a profound effect upon the development of our financial institutions and techniques, and its influence has been felt in such important matters of public policy, as currency reform. It may be stated that almost every activity of the Association is educational in nature. Despite the different forms which educational efforts take, the Association is motivated by the one basic purpose: constant improvement of the banking system in serving the financial and related requirements of the public.

Education of Bank Personnel

One of the foremost undertakings of the Association has been the education of bank personnel. In 1900 the Association organized what is now known as the American Institute of Banking Section. A history of one-half century has established the Institute as an outstanding and the largest unit in the field of adult education. The Institute has made an important contribution to the promotion of better banking by providing educational facilities whereby the employees of banks can secure knowledge of banking and related fields. These facilities have been made flexible in order to serve the requirements of bank employees in locations ranging from metropolitan centers to isolated rural communities.

Under the national organization, chapters of the American Institute of Banking have been organized throughout the country on an independent, self-governing basis for the purpose of arranging lectures and related educational activities. In places where the concentration of personnel is too scant, study groups are developed. There are now approximately 400 chapters and study groups in the Institute. In addition, correspondence courses are provided for individual instruction where attendance in the formal groups is not possible.

The Institute draws upon bankers, lawyers, accountants, and college or university instructors for its faculty in local chapters and groups. Nineteen separate courses are provided. In order to receive a "standard certificate," the student is required to complete satisfactorily, including the passing of final examinations, a total of eight courses, each involving 42 hours of instruction. The Institute also provides a "graduate certificate" for completion of four additional courses. The broad scope of the organization is evidenced by the fact that there are 32,000 standard certificate holders. The Institute has close to 100,000 members, and an annual enrollment of 50,000 students.

A second major field of formal education for bank personnel was added by the American Bankers Association in 1935, with the organization of The Graduate School of Banking under the leadership of Dr. Harold Stonier, Executive Manager of the Association and formerly National Educational Director of the American Institute of Banking. The purpose of the Graduate School is to offer a comprehensive approach to an advanced study of the various administrative problems in banking and trust institutions. The three-year course is conducted at two-week resident sessions at Rutgers University each June, supplemented by extension and thesis work performed by the students during the year. Major courses are offered in commercial banking, investments, savings management, and trusts to bank officers or other bank employees performing duties equivalent in responsibility to those performed by officers. Diplomas are awarded jointly by the Graduate School of Banking and Rutgers University.

The Graduate School has an annual enrollment of about 1,000 men. In the first 15 years of operation, it has granted diplomas to 2,550 graduates. Thus, it has made forward strides in the education of bank-officer personnel for the improvement of banking standards. It has recognized that the future of banking will require a high caliber of management. By providing instruction through a faculty of leading bankers, university professors, the government and the professions, the School molds an important link in the chain of formal education for bankers. Furthermore, it has set the pattern for the establishment of other schools

of banking in various parts of the country to serve the needs of local areas.

Improved Banking Techniques

The educational character of the American Bankers Association is further illustrated by its efforts to improve day-to-day banking techniques and operations by various methods other than the formal courses provided by the American Institute of Banking and the Graduate School of Banking. The Association may be regarded as a research laboratory in which a vast amount of information helpful to bank management flows, is tested and evaluated, and disseminated for broad use in the industry. The pervasiveness of its influence is made possible by reason of the fact that the Association has a membership of 16,600 banking institutions, including 2100 branches. This membership comprises 98 per cent of the number and 99 per cent of the resources of the banks of the country, and membership includes institutions of varying sizes and types. The interest of members in the work of the Association is illustrated by the fact that over 500 banks currently are represented on its roster of committees, commissions, sections, departments, councils, divisions and other units which are actively engaged in carrying out its program.

Public Relations

Another feature of the Association's educational work revolves about the relations of the banks with the public. The criticism directed against the banks during financial crises made it necessary that attempts be made to improve relations with the public. A healthy attitude could only be created by informed public opinion. The Association has been responsible for a major part of the work of the industry along these lines. For many years it has disseminated, among the banking profession and the public at large, knowledge of sound principles of banking, economics and business procedures. Much of the early work of the Association was directed toward the fight for sound money and an adequate banking system. At its very organization, the resumption of specie payments was a major issue. The Association sought to lend the influence of bankers to the solution of such basic problems which so vitally affected the banks' relations with the public; the Association has continued this work as a major part of its operations.

Closely related to public relations work is the public-service function of assisting the federal and state governments in the promulgation of sound banking legislation and the adoption of policies which are considered most favorable to the future welfare of banking and its ability to

serve the needs of a democratic economy. The Association has been frequently called upon to present the viewpoint of organized banking on important legislative matters. It has lent its influence to counteract pending and existing legislation which might endanger the chartered banking system. At the same time, the Association has taken the lead in sponsoring uniform laws in the states relating to instruments of commerce, trust operations, and banking codes. The purpose of these laws is to improve the legislative framework under which the banks operate and to help preserve the dual system of national and state banks.

The history of the Association is replete with instances in which banking assumed a major role in the development of legislation and policy. The Gold Standard Act of 1900 culminated a long struggle by the Association for sound currency. The National Monetary Commission, organized by Congress to study banking and monetary legislation, had been advocated by the Association beginning in 1893. The work of this Commission and further study by the Association laid much of the groundwork for the establishment of the Federal Reserve System in 1913, although differences in viewpoint regarding details of organization arose at the time. In more recent years, the anti-inflation program of the Association provides an example of leadership in banking policy. In 1948 when inflationary forces in the economy were dominant, the bankers of the country, through the Association, embarked on an anti-inflation program which sought to discourage banks from making loans of a speculative nature which would stimulate more inflation; at the same time, the Association encouraged the use of bank credit only for productive purposes to ease the material shortages existing at that time. This represented an attempt of bankers, through their national association, to accept responsibility without government regulation for a sound flow of credit through the economy.

Likewise the Association has been called upon to serve in a liaison capacity between the banks and the government in the conduct of national campaigns, such as the financing of World War I and World War II. Problems of administering sales and redemption of war bonds through the banks, for example, were worked out between the Association, as representative of the banks, and Treasury officials.

The activities of the Association are centered upon the general pattern of predominantly educational and service functions just described. It requires an organizational structure which must be adaptable to the treatment not only of over-all, country-wide banking problems, but which also can stimulate action on local and specialized banking problems. Although counsel of the Association is often sought, as a rule it is not the body's function to advise members on matters pertaining to administrative affairs of the individual banks. The Association merely

serves as a clearing house for the dissemination of banking knowledge and the expression of banking's viewpoint on matters affecting the banking system as a whole or segments thereof. Its organization has grown and become adjusted accordingly.

The national organization might be described as having developed along both vertical and horizontal lines. The unique interests of individual classes of banks with common charter-heritage and problems have provided the basis for organization of the divisions, including the Trust Division, National Bank Division, State Bank Division, and Savings and Mortgage Division. Members of the Association are privileged to enroll as a regular member in one of the four divisions.

However, since an increasing number of banking problems are not peculiar to these divisional groups of institutions but are common to all, the major part of the work is conducted along functional lines by units designed to fill requirements related to specific types of credit, techniques, and operations. This functional approach received its strongest stimulus beginning in 1937, partly as a result of the difficulties of banking during the crisis of 1933. It then became recognized that the challenge to banking was to place its own house in order through better bank management. The development of new departments, committees and councils widely broadened the Association's field of operations to assist banks in understanding operational techniques, principles of credit extension, customer and public relations, and the responsibility for servicing the financial needs of the community.

The integration of Association operations and policies with those of local bankers' associations is another important phase of the work. The Association has a State Association Section whose membership includes representatives of the bankers' associations in all of the states (including the seven mutual savings banking states) and the District of Columbia. The work of these associations at the grassroots is of great importance. They develop local programs to deal with the problems of banking which are peculiar to their own environs. The Association, through its State Association Section, endeavors to coordinate these programs with its own operations. The state associations, having the close ties and personal relationships engendered by neighborly contact, are particularly well suited to implement and advance the national program within their respective organizations.

Administration of the Association

The administration of the Association presents an interesting case study in the coordination of the thousands of members—embracing different types of banking, different economic environments, separate

charter-heritage, and other factors—into a single purposeful unit. The powers of the Association rest in its General Convention of member banks, which lays down the broad policies in annual sessions held in the fall.

These policies are amplified and implemented by an Executive Council which meets twice each year, at the annual fall convention and the spring meeting. This Council has a membership of 125 bankers, including one from each state, 12 chosen at large, and representatives of the various divisions, councils, commissions and committees comprising the specialized working units. The Council administers the affairs of the Association between General Convention sessions, shapes the policies, and reviews the work of the units as transmitted by the Administrative Committee. The latter is responsible for the conduct of operations between meetings of the Executive Council and conventions. The Committee might be described as a "cabinet" of bankers in the various specialized fields. Subject to the Executive Council and General Convention, the Administrative Committee has general supervision over the divisions, committees, sections and other working units.

Membership in the aforementioned working units consists of some 500 bankers who evidence an active interest in a wide range of banking problems and operations, economic and legislative policies, banking education, and the publication of financial knowledge. These bankers serve without compensation. They are assisted by a staff of specialists who administer and help develop the programs set forth by each working unit. This staff works under the supervision of the Executive Manager of the Association. As the operating chief, the Executive Manager administers the affairs of the Association and executes its policies as set forth by the General Convention and the elected officers. He may be described as a liaison officer between the latter and the staff.

The activities of the working units are so broad that only a listing of them is here possible. The units provide groups of bankers with an opportunity to investigate, analyze and report on problems and policies within the scope of their respective organizations. They have resulted in the development of valuable data on various banking and related subjects through their sponsorship of a long list of publications and other media.

Below is a summary of these working units:

Divisions and Sections

Savings and Mortgage Division	State Bank Division
Trust Division	National Bank Division
State Association Section	American Institute of Banking Section

Commissions and Committees

Bank Management Commission
County Bank Operations Commission
Credit Policy Commission
Economic Policy Commission
Small Business Credit Commission
Commerce and Marine Commission
Agricultural Commission

Consumer Credit Committee
Committee on Federal Legislation
Committee on State Legislation
Insurance and Protective Committee
Committee on Public Education
Organization Committee
Committee on Service for War Veterans
Finance Committee
Advisory Committee on Special Activities
Government Borrowing Committee
Treasury Savings Bonds Committee
Committee on Federal Depository Functions and Fiscal Procedures

Councils

Public Relations Council

Research Council

Departments

Advertising Department
Legal Department
News Bureau

Personnel and Customer Relations Department
Office of the Economist

Other Units

Graduate School of Banking
Library

Banking (Magazine)
Foundation for Education in Economics

28

Trade Associations in the Financial Field

by JOSEPH J. SCHROEDER

Executive Secretary, Chicago Chapter, American Institute of Banking
Secretary, Association of Reserve City Bankers

ASSOCIATION is a natural and obvious recourse when two, or many, concerns must deal with a common problem; and even the most violently competitive concerns do have interests in common with their rivals.

Where these interests do not conflict with the interests of the public, association for cooperative effort is encouraged alike by supervisory authority and legislative sanction. Herbert Hoover, when he was Secretary of Commerce, succinctly summed up the legitimate field for the trade association:

> The whole movement toward cooperative action arises from a fundamental need to which we must give heed. Where the objectives of cooperation are to eliminate waste in production and distribution, to increase education as to better methods of doing business, to expand research in processes of production, to take collective action in policing business ethics, to maintain standards of quality, to secure adequate representation of problems before the Government and other economic groups and to improve conditions of labor, to negotiate collectively with highly organized groups of labor, to prevent unemployment, to supply information equally to members and to the public upon which better judgment may be formulated in the conduct of business; then these activities are working in the public interest.[1]

There are other areas, some quite enticing, in which the legitimacy of cooperation is doubtful and the trade association must steer a careful course. Limitation of production, allocation of territory, price-fixing, black lists, boycotts, and the like obviously come within the purview of

---

[1] *Tenth Annual Report of the Secretary of Commerce,* Herbert Hoover (1922), p. 30.

antitrust laws; and it is not always easy to tell when the bounds are overstepped. The field for cooperative action is still large and fruitful.

Trade Association

American Trade Association Executives (executives of trade associations have their own trade association) define the term as follows:

> The term 'trade association' as used in this Constitution and By-Laws, shall include such organizations as are established to perform, upon a mutual basis, an industrial or trade function for the purpose of promoting and protecting the interests of the industry or trade represented by such association, and specifically, associations representing particular manufacturing industries, particular distributing trades and particular service trades, the members of which consist of business organizations. Within this definition are included trade associations which are national, regional, state, or local in their scope.[2]
>
> Today [1949] there are approximately 1,500 national trade associations and an additional 300 national trade associations either consisting of businessmen organized for special purposes or having a large proportion of businessmen as members. The 1,500 trade associations have a paid staff of approximately 16,000 persons and a gross membership of over 1,000,000 business firms.[3]

The trade association is the logical product of the free enterprise system. The more that enterprise is free—not regulated by government— the more incumbent it is upon enterprise to regulate its own processes, to develop standards of ethical conduct, to protect its reputation with the public; thus we have the voluntary association, the annual convention, the regional meeting, and the code of ethics, so familiar to the American scene.

Work of Trade Associations

The core of activity for a trade association, and probably the greatest influence in bringing hardy individualists into the cooperative fold, is the attempt "to secure adequate representation of problems before the Government," as Mr. Hoover puts it.[4]

If an individual does not conform to the canons of social conduct accepted in his community, society provides police to see that his transgressions are prevented or punished. If an industry refuses or fails to act in the public interest, public opinion will eventually force the government to prevent the action or to punish the offender. Thus, to avoid greater ills, industry must have a means of studying the operations of

---

[2] Constitution—Article III, American Trade Association Executives.
[3] National Associations of the United States, U.S. Department of Commerce, 1949.
[4] Tenth Annual Report of the Secretary of Commerce, loc. cit.

individual units, of appraising the broad social consequences of their actions, and if suasion fails, to direct or restrain the government in the measures of compulsion required.

Association efforts are therefore educational, first to study and then to teach. However utilitarian the motive by which this fascinating field is entered, interference may soon demonstrate unsought but desirable by-products. The body of information developed may be used effectively to increase public understanding as well as to influence legislative bodies; it may be used to educate employees, thus providing for successor management, or increased efficiency, or the better morale that accompanies understanding. It may be used to educate the youth in our schools and colleges.

The American Institute of Banking, described in the preceding chapter, is an example of how far a program of employee education may be extended. Founded in 1900, the Institute on its fiftieth birthday, boasted 95,000 members, with class enrollments of nearly 50,000 in some 400 local units. Similar educational offshoots are found in many trade associations in the financial field and will be described in the detailed descriptions which follow.

The Code of Ethics or Fair Trade Practice is another result of self-examination through the association. As every individual has his own code of proper conduct, variety will also be found in the habits and customs of different concerns in the same business; and not all of the customs can be excused. Some practices are to be commended and encouraged; others perhaps merely condoned as a concession to the realities of life; and some, even though within the fringes of law, are obviously not in the best interests of the industry and must be discouraged or forbidden.

Thus the Code of Ethics evolves as a familiar feature of the trade association. Codes tend to acquire weight as evidence in courts of law and often serve as models for statutes.

The Mahoney Act of 1938 even provided a means by which the concerns in a certain industry could enforce the provisions of their voluntarily agreed upon code of ethics, thus actually giving a trade association regulatory power. (See National Association of Security Dealers, page 761.)

Therefore, in the financial association field relations with legislative and supervisory agencies, research and education, and the crystallizing of codes of business conduct may be concluded to be the most significant activities.

Financial Associations

At first glance the number of associations in the financial field may seem to be excessive—there are seven or eight important national associations in the field of commercial banking alone—but examination will show that for the most part they serve distinctive purposes and that the duplication of effort is unimportant. In fact it will be found that a large bank or investment house may belong to a dozen or more associations and take an active part in the affairs of each of them, perhaps through different officials. Cooperation between associations is also the usual thing, and it is not uncommon for several associations to collaborate on a project of mutual interest.

The field of most associations—not all of them—is identified in the title. Thus no one needs to be told that the American Bankers Association represents banking on the national scene, the Investment Bankers Association security dealers and brokers, the Mortgage Bankers Association originators and servicers of mortgage paper, the United States Savings and Loan League savings and loan associations, and the like. Their scope is clear.

Some information of the history and objectives of the better-known associations operating in the financial field will be given in the following pages, along with a discussion of their method of operation, organizational set-up, publications, and other characteristics. For convenience the associations will be grouped into general fields. As a matter of convenience, and because commercial banking has the greatest variety of associations, it will be considered first.

Clearing House and State Bankers Associations

Banking associations may be divided into a number of categories: geographical, functional, special position, and those serving a special purpose or cause.

Of these the most pervasive is naturally the geographical. Starting at the local level there is a clearing house, or at least a clearing arrangement, in every locality in which there is more than one bank. The clearing house has the definite practical purpose of providing a means of exchanging checks, but in many localities it adds some of the features of the trade association by agreements on hours for doing business, holidays, and other similar matters.

In big cities, where not all of the banks belong to the clearing house, this may lead to other associations of nonclearing banks. In some localities local units of the state association are also found, some with quite extensive programs.

In every state and in the District of Columbia, there is an organized association of bankers, and at the national level is the American Bankers Association,[5] which includes a very high percentage of all of the chartered banks of the country, plus some branches, some trust companies which do not do a banking business, bond houses, and other financial institutions.

The American Bankers Association represents banking at the national level in making representations to the Congress and the supervisory agencies, and it may be said that the state associations perform in much the same way at the state level. The American Bankers Association has an extensive research program, and so do the state associations, their programs usually paralleling those of the American Bankers Association to the extent that numbers and resources permit.

Functional Associations

Among the more important of the functional associations in banking (that is, those which devote their attention to some particular function) are the American Safe Deposit Association, the Bankers Association for Foreign Trade, the Financial Public Relations Association, Robert Morris Associates, and the National Association of Bank Auditors and Comptrollers. The fields of all of these are indicated in their titles (except perhaps the Robert Morris Associates, which concerns itself with bank credit policies and practice). Each of these may be considered separately.

The American Safe Deposit Association

The American Safe Deposit Association was founded in 1947 to unite the various safe deposit associations of the country and to develop a program that would promote the general welfare and improvement of the safe deposit business. This Association was designed to succeed The National Safe Deposit Advisory Council, in existence since 1925 but a much more loosely knit organization.

State, city, or district safe deposit groups are eligible for membership. By 1950 the number of members was 17, and the Association is vigorously promoting a campaign for nation-wide membership. The Association is operated by officers elected at an annual meeting, and the organization does not maintain permanent headquarters.

Bankers' Association for Foreign Trade

Founded in 1921, the stated purposes of the Bankers' Association for Foreign Trade are "to promote and foster international banking and

---

[5] See the preceding chapter for a discussion of the American Bankers Association.

foreign trade by doing all things appropriate to the stimulation of public interest therein and to the improvement of existing practices and the development of new techniques thereof." [6]

Regular membership is restricted to domestic banks with established foreign departments. Associate membership is limited to foreign banks which have representatives or agencies in the United States, and to chartered Canadian banks. An individual who has represented his bank in the Association and who has retired may be made a life member. As of 1950 there were 99 regular members, 38 associate members, and 17 life members.

There is no regular publication. The Association holds an annual meeting. Between times its officers and committees keep in touch with developments in its field. Close liaison is maintained with the National Foreign Trade Council, the American Section of the International Chamber of Commerce, and the American Bankers Association, with respect to developments affecting foreign banking operations.

Financial Public Relations Association

Founded in 1916 the Financial Public Relations Association now has about 1,500 members in the United States and Canada. Membership is open to banks and trust companies, investment houses, mutual savings banks, and financial publications, agencies and organizations engaged in financial advertising and business development work.

Members of the Association are pledged to observe the following Standards of Practice:

FIRST   To cling steadfastly to truth in advertising and in all other public relations activities.

SECOND   To seek public confidence on a basis of frankness and fair dealing, and on that basis only.

THIRD   To work unceasingly toward public enlightenment along the lines of economic knowledge, as an aid in advancing the financial welfare of the country, its business structure and its people.

FOURTH   To maintain the highest standards of financial advertising, and to discourage energetically advertising or business promotion methods that do not measure up to these standards.

FIFTH   To study continually methods employed by financial institutions in building business and prestige, and make the results of this study available to its members.

SIXTH   To cooperate to the fullest extent within our membership

---

[6] Article I, Articles of Association.

on all questions of common concern, that the principles and ideals for the Association as herein stated may be advanced.

The Association publishes a monthly bulletin and occasional pamphlets. An annual convention is customary, usually in the fall or early winter. In a number of communities the local members maintain an organization with more frequent meetings, but these meetings are not strictly speaking an Association activity.

In 1948 the Association, with the cooperation of Northwestern University, established the School of Financial Public Relations. The course consists of two summer sessions of two weeks each, plus reading assignments and practical exercises between sessions.

Robert Morris Associates

The national association of bank credit men—named for the Revolutionary hero and financier—has had a great influence on bank credit practices over the past 30 years, particularly in developing techniques for evaluating accounting and statistical material. The stated purpose of the Association is:

"to encourage and protect trade and commerce; to conduct research in credit and related subjects; to improve methods of gathering, compiling, analyzing, and disseminating credit data; to promote friendship and understanding among bank loan officers and credit men; and to promote a closer relationship between mercantile and financial credit men."

A major part of the activities is the development of statement studies, or balance sheet and income data on a number of lines of business, to be used as background in comparing an individual company with the norm for the business. Over 100 such studies have been issued. Many industry studies, pamphlets, and articles have been published over the years. One of the most widely used is a text entitled *The Credit Department—A Training Ground for the Bank Loan Officer*. A monthly bulletin is published.

Robert Morris Associates is an offshoot of the National Association of Credit Men. As early as 1914, bankers attending the annual meeting of the latter started the custom of a meeting for bank men. In 1919 a permanent organization was effected under the current title, and headquarters, now located in Philadelphia, were established.

Membership is corporate and restricted to banks. Banks may, however, enroll additional individual members on payment of a nominal fee. Membership on June 30, 1950, was 1,885, representing about 700 banks. Provision is also made for regional or local chapters, of which there are 21. Chapters may meet as often as monthly. The Association itself meets annually.

The National Association of Bank Auditors and Comptrollers

This Association is concerned with the operating methods and control of expense in commercial banks and with the protection of the bank's assets (that is, physical protection from fraud, embezzlement, and armed assault).

Membership is restricted to banks and trust companies. Founded as a national association in 1924, NABAC, as it is commonly known, started with a nucleus of local groups which had existed for some years in Spokane, Kansas City, New Orleans, Philadelphia, and Chicago, and statewide organizations in California and Ohio. By the middle of 1950 its membership totaled 3,832, operating through 108 Conferences, as local units are called.

Headquarters are maintained in Chicago, where a competent staff co-ordinates the work of 11 standing committees, of which the following are indicative of the scope of the Association's field of interest: Bank Fraud Prevention, Bank Personnel, Direct Verification, Federal Taxes, Research, Cooperation with Regulatory Departments, Savings Banking, Problems of Smaller Banks, and Trust Banking.

Research files are a valuable source of help to members. Facts and ideas that pour into the Department from banks all over the country are carefully sorted, tabulated, and catalogued by subject, and are the most comprehensive files of their kind in banking. Among the 70 files maintained are the following: Defalcations, Analysis of Bank Loans, Auditor's Functions, Audit and Control—Charged Off Assets and Recoveries, Central Files, Director's Duties and Liabilities, Job Evaluation Methods, Pensions and Profit-Sharing Plans, Procedure Manuals, Reserve Method for Bad Debts, and the like.

NABAC sponsors four conventions a year—three regional, in the East, Mid-West and West, and a national convention. Local conferences generally meet once a month. A conference includes all of the banks within traveling distance, but about 1,000 banks are associate members, for they are not close enough to be affiliated with a conference. Meetings are educational in nature, and the members recount experiences or express philosophies evolved therefrom.

A monthly magazine is published under the title *Auditgram*. An average issue of 48 pages contains five full-length articles on various phases of bank audit, control, operation, and related fields. Books and working manuals are also published from time to time.

This is a highly technical and specialized Association, but one to which direct, practical results may be traced.

Other Associations of Bankers

Defying ready classification, but one of the most influential of banking associations, is the Association of Reserve City Bankers. This Association originated as a functional organization concerned with transit and other problems of the correspondent bank business before the Federal Reserve System was organized. In time the Association developed into a group carefully restricted to executive officers of banks in reserve cities.

The Association of Bank Women, obviously, is an association of a special group with some interests of its own as well as a general interest in the fields of other banking associations.

Representative of associations to defend or promote a cause is the Independent Bankers Association, or rather associations, for there are at least four, three operating at local levels.

Association of Reserve City Bankers

The Association of Reserve City Bankers is a small organization of bank executives. It does not maintain a large organization or carry on an extensive program; but because of the vigor and decision with which it has gone into action on occasion, it is regarded as one of the most influential in the field of commercial banking.

Its decisiveness is the result of small numbers and homogeneity. Membership is restricted to executive officers of banks which do a correspondent bank business. This means that, by and large, the banks over which the members preside are large banks and in the money centers of the country. On the other hand, through the correspondent relationship their tie with the smaller banks is close and understanding.

Membership is personal and individual. Moreover, it is limited in both total and the number who may be connected with any one bank. The by-laws are explicit on the executive qualification, reading:

> No candidate shall qualify for active membership who is not an executive officer, active in the administration of the affairs of and in dealing with the general problems and policies of a bank or banking institution located in a designated Reserve or Central Reserve city having deposit accounts with, and/or from other banks or banking institutions and transacting what is commonly known as 'correspondent' business.

The maximum number of members permitted is 450. As a rule not more than four are elected from any one bank. The number of banks with which the members are connected is just over 200, but these 200 carry more than 50 per cent of the bank deposits of the country. The by-laws provide that any member who misses three annual meetings in

succession is automatically dropped from the rolls. Another unusual provision is that two candidates must be nominated for every elective office, including president. The Association is supported by the dues of the members and insists on paying its own way on all occasions.

The Association has had an interesting history. It was founded in 1912 by bank representatives who were active in the solicitation and handling of the reserve accounts of "country" banks. (Under the National Bank Act, banks not located in reserve cities were designated "country" banks.) This was several years before the Federal Reserve Banks were in operation and, except in Central Reserve Cities, banks habitually carried a considerable portion of their legal reserves with other banks. For some years the activities of the Association centered around problems incident to this correspondent banking business, and this is still a major interest of the Association.

However, membership was personal and as members advanced in the profession, their interests widened. In the 1920's the reorganization of failing national concerns and other credit problems became a major interest. In 1933 the Association reached full stature. The Banking Holiday early in the year had made it patent that the banking structure must be strengthened. The compact size of the Association, its homogeneity, and particularly the fact that its members were familiar with large affairs and well-informed on the problems of both large and small banks, made it an effective representative of banking interests. The members accepted the responsibility, adopting the following resolution at the annual meeting in the spring of 1933:

> Recognizing the opportunity and the obligation presented by the present unsettled economic conditions, and the challenge to the bankers of the United States which has come to them from public opinion both informed and uninformed, this Association hereby resolves that it will devote its best energies, in line with its principles of twenty-two years standing, to a new analysis of the business of banking in the light of existing conditions, and to a constructive program of improvement in banking law and practice.

A Commission on Banking Law and Practice was elected to implement this resolution, and the Commission worked hard and effectively during the five years of its existence. Its first efforts were successfully devoted to the task of making practical the harsh provisions for deposit guaranty of the Banking Act of 1933. The Commission was encouraged by the Senate Committee on Banking and Currency to advise with it in the framing of the Banking Act of 1935 and to present the banking viewpoint on the many proposals considered. The Commission also authorized or engaged in other studies dealing with the depression of the '30's.

The Commission disbanded in 1938, and the Association provided standing committees to keep in touch with the various fields of banking

interest. At the present time this task is assigned to the following committees: Committee on Bank Credit Policies, Committee on Correspondent Bank Relations, Committee on Federal Relationships, Committee on Public Relations, and Foreign Committee. Through the war and thereafter, the Association was frequently invited to present the banking viewpoint when Congress was considering financial legislation, or when the regulatory agencies—Comptroller of the Currency, Federal Reserve System, or the Federal Deposit Insurance Corporation—were considering changes in policy or procedure.

As a result of the activities of the Commission on Banking Law and Practice, the Association became conscious of gaps in information on banking and financial practice, particularly the mass or cumulative effect which results when great numbers of independent and competing institutions adopt new lines of reasoning or adjust themselves to changes in the economic structure. In 1937 it encouraged the National Bureau of Economic Research to undertake a program of financial research. Funds were raised by subscription from the banks with which the members are connected, and a Board of Trustees was set up to counsel the National Bureau in the undertaking. The product has been monumental explorations in the fields of consumer instalment financing, business financing, corporate bonds, agricultural financing, and urban real estate financing, besides special studies of war financing in the early '40's.

The Association prints occasional reports and studies, but it has no regular publications except the *Proceedings of the Annual Meeting*, which is distributed to members only. Headquarters are in Chicago.

Association of Bank Women

Founded in 1921, the Association of Bank Women has about 1,000 members. Membership is restricted to women who hold executive positions in national, state, and savings banks, and in trust companies.

The purpose is to bring together women executives engaged in the profession of banking for mutual exchange of ideas and experiences, to forward the interests of women employed in banking, and to uphold their dignity and integrity.

National headquarters are maintained in New York City. An annual meeting is customary. The Association is divided into eight geographical regions, each supervised by a regional vice-president. Group conferences or regional meetings are held at central points. The Association publishes a magazine bimonthly and occasional pamphlets. Studies are made by the members and committees, usually in the field of women's activities in banking. An annual award is made to the woman graduate of the American Institute of Banking "selected as best fitted through the in-

tegrity of her character and efficiency of her work to represent women in banking."

Independent Bankers Association

The Independent Bankers Association was founded in 1930 "to advocate and assist in the enactment of laws, both State and Federal, prohibiting the continuation of branch banking in any form," and "to promote the general welfare and usefulness of the independent unit bank." [7]

The Association has continued a vigorous campaign in the support of these objectives. Membership is corporate and over 3,200 banks are members. Headquarters are in Sauk Centre, Minnesota.

There is also an Independent Bankers Association of the Twelfth Federal Reserve District, with headquarters in Portland, Oregon, and two Independent Bankers Associations in California. The objectives of these three are similar to those of the national Association, but there is no formal connection.

Other Financial Associations

Commercial banks generally do a "department store" business in finance. Savings departments, trust departments, consumer credit departments, bond departments, and the like are common in at least some sections of the country. Banks will therefore be found on the membership rolls of many of the associations which represent more restricted sectors of the financial field.

Among the associations reviewed in the following section, particular attention should be given to the status of the Investment Bankers Association and the National Association of Security Dealers, which operate in the same field. One is a voluntary association, somewhat selective, and the other is a quasi-public institution, the only one so far formed under the Mahoney Act previously referred to.

Included here are brief descriptions of the American Institute of Real Estate Appraisers and the National Institute of Real Estate Brokers, following the review of the Mortgage Bankers Association. The two Institutes are not related in any direct way to the latter, but all three organizations are significant in the real estate field.

There are two associations operating in the savings and loan field. The United States Savings and Loan League is reviewed here because it is the oldest and by far the largest. The National Savings and Loan League (with headquarters in Washington, D.C.) is a splinter group which broke

---

[7] From the Articles of Incorporation.

off in 1943 following disagreement over general policies. The latter claims a membership of 573, of which a considerable number are said also to maintain membership in the original association.

Consumer Bankers Association

As the Consumer Bankers Association restricts its membership to one bank in any community, and it has among its stated objectives to "develop business for its member institutions," it must be classified somewhere between a true trade association and a cooperative agency. It also supplies its members with advertising services of various kinds.

It does, however, have considerable general influence in the field of consumer finance. A monthly bulletin, *Consumer Credit,* is said to have a circulation of 40,000. The Association supplies four publications for distribution to employees of member banks and to the public, publishes a magazine bimonthly, and keeps members informed through a *Confidential News Letter* which is published twice a month.

Founded in 1919, the Association has 85 members, and it operates through four sectional associations. National headquarters are maintained in Washington, D.C., with a full-time, salaried staff. The Association originated with banks organized under the "Morris Plan," but its membership now includes a large percentage of commercial banks. In addition, most of the original Morris Plan banks have since extended their operations into the field of commercial banking.

Investment Bankers Association

The Investment Bankers Association is composed of representatives of all segments of the investment industry. Its purpose is to serve the industry by promoting unity, representing the industry in legislative affairs, and explaining the investment industry to the general public through a coordinated public education program. Established in 1912, the Association has 719 members, operates through 18 groups (of which one is in Canada), and maintains national headquarters in Chicago.

In the field of federal legislation the Association has taken a leading part in concerted action to lighten the tax load carried by the investment field. Close attention is given to all legislation affecting the welfare of the saving-investing community. The State Legislative Committee campaigns for improvement and uniformity of blue sky laws and has prepared model laws to assist members in states where revision is contemplated.

On the local scene the Municipal Securities Committee has developed revenue bond report forms which are not only acceptable to the industry but have received the approval of governmental authorities concerned.

Many other activities are carried on in this field. The Association has sponsored the development of tests for the selection of employees, and it has also sponsored training programs to be offered by local groups or by correspondence.

The Association has 20 active committees, each operating in a particular phase of the investment field. These observers chart the pulse of their assigned divisions and analyze the developments in reports to members.

National Association of Security Dealers

The National Association of Security Dealers is a quasi-public institution. *Any* broker or dealer in securities who meets statutory requirements for membership may belong. Any broker or dealer who expects to operate on a broad scale *must* belong, for the Rules of Fair Practice, to which all must subscribe, provide that "No member shall deal with any nonmember broker or dealer except at the same prices, for the same commission or fees, and on the same terms and conditions as are by such members accorded to the general public." [8]

As nonmembership bars a dealer from the wholesale market, membership is a valuable privilege. The preservation of this privilege gives the Association leverage in compelling adherence to the Rules of Fair Practice and to high standards of commercial honor.

The Association became operative in 1939. It was established under the Mahoney Act of 1938,[9] the broad purpose of which was to encourage self-regulation in various fields of business, and particularly in the "over-the-counter" market in securities. The number of members in July 1950 was 2,784.

Management is vested in a board of governors consisting of 21 members, elected for three-year terms. For administrative purposes the country is divided into 14 districts. In each district there is a local committee of not more than 12 persons elected by vote of the members. Each district committee appoints a district business conduct committee. This committee is empowered to hear charges against members, to bring charges, and to assess penalties, subject to review by the board of governors.

National headquarters are in Washington, D.C., and there are local offices in the principal cities.

Mortgage Bankers Association of America

Mortgage Bankers Association of America was organized to provide an association where the makers of mortgage loans and the investors in

---

[8] Section 25.
[9] Section 15A of Sec. Exch. Act of 1934.

mortgage loans could meet and discuss their problems. It conducts a series of clinic meetings during the year, as well as a national convention, to serve this purpose and to provide forums where both investors and servicing agents can discuss their problems.

Organized in 1914, the Association now has about 1,500 members. Firms organized for the purpose of investing in or servicing mortgage loans, or which do a substantial business of this nature, are eligible for membership. National headquarters are in Chicago. The Association also maintains a Washington office to keep the membership informed on what develops in the nation's capital. The Association issues a monthly publication, a Washington News Letter, and occasional pamphlets on management ideas, advertising, and the like.

The Association is steadily expanding the scope of its educational activities. A three-day conference of senior executives of member organizations has been held every winter since 1946 in connection with the Graduate School of Business Administration, New York University. A mortgage banking seminar for younger men connected with member organizations has been held annually since 1948 in cooperation with Northwestern University. Held on the Chicago campus of the University, five days are devoted to intensive study of mortgage lending history, the effect of interest rates on security prices and the mortgage market, mortgage law, and such practical problems as appraisal of dwelling and business property, loan closing, servicing, and the use of government guarantees. The Association publishes a handbook of *Mortgage Loan Servicing Practices* and is currently engaged in preparing a textbook on mortgage banking.

American Institute of Real Estate Appraisers

The objects of the American Institute of Real Estate Appraisers are: "To award a professional designation to properly qualified real estate appraisers; to formulate rules of professional conduct, including rules of ethics, and to enforce these rules upon and for its members; to establish educational standards for the profession of real estate appraising. . . ." [10]

Membership is limited to individuals holding the professional designation M.A.I. Candidates may attend annual and other open meetings of the Institute. To receive the professional designation, candidates must be 30 years of age, hold some form of membership in the local board or an individual membership in the National Association of Real Estate Boards, must have the equivalent of a high-school education, pass two or more examinations given by the admissions committee, and also secure personal recommendations.

---

[10] From the by-laws.

The Institute has currently 1,365 members and 746 candidates. It operates through chapters in 29 cities in many of which evening courses are given. For 15 years the Institute has conducted intensive two-week demonstration case-study courses in cooperation with universities in various parts of the United States.

A quarterly, the *Appraisers Journal,* is published by the organization. The Institute has published two volumes of *Appraisal Reporting Techniques* and is preparing a third. It has also published several editions of *The Handbook for Appraisers.* Headquarters are in Chicago.

National Institute of Real Estate Brokers of the National Association of Real Estate Boards

Membership is open to any individual or firm who holds any form of membership in The National Association of Real Estate Boards, or is an employee of a local member board. Founded in 1923, the Institute has in the neighborhood of 8,500 members.

The purpose of the Institute is educational, and through its bulletins and meetings it attempts to bring about ever higher standards of ethics and efficiency. Each member receives six or eight bulletins a year dealing with practical experiences and changing conditions. Window displays and other forms of advertising are available through the Institute. The Institute also undertakes to provide panels of members to offer advice on special problems and situations.

The National Association of Mutual Savings Banks

Founded in 1920 The National Association of Mutual Savings Banks is said to have the widest coverage in its industry of any trade association. Member banks carry 99.8 per cent of the approximately $20 billion now deposited in mutual savings banks. The constitution and by-laws state: "It shall have as its purpose the effective cooperation of the mutual savings banks of the United States; to advance the interests of depositors of mutual savings banks; to provide suitable means for the interchange of information and ideas among mutual savings banks; to undertake such studies and research as will be useful in the solution of problems of its members; to keep the member banks constantly advised of developments which may be of interest to them; to make such representations to public authorities and others as may be advisable to protect and promote the interests of savings bank depositors; to encourage thrift and savings among the people of the United States by the extension of the mutual savings bank system and by other means, and through the promulgation of these ideas to serve the interests of its member banks and their depositors.

"Any savings bank, savings fund or savings institution without capital funds may become a member."

The Association operates by direction of a Council of Administration made up of executive officers of savings banks from the various states, from which an executive committee is chosen. In addition, there are a number of standing committees which study problems of federal legislation, mortgage investments, government bonds and the public debt, public relations, savings bank life insurance, railroad investments, insurance, public utilities, federal deposit insurance, methods and services, competition, and the extension of the mutual savings bank system.

In addition to the work of its various committees, the National Association acts as a clearing house of information to its member banks through such means as its monthly publication *Mutual Savings Banking*, monthly statistical bulletins, and press releases. It attempts to keep its member banks informed of new developments through frequent bulletins and other material for distribution to officers, employees and the general public.

Close coordination of activity is maintained between the National Association and the various savings bank state associations, and meetings of the secretaries and executive managers of these groups are held from time to time. In addition to the three-day annual meetings of the National Association, midyear meetings have been held in New York for the last several years. Headquarters are maintained in New York City.

The United States Savings and Loan League

The United States Savings and Loan League was organized in 1892 as a federation of state leagues of savings and loan institutions. In 1925 it became more directly the nation-wide trade organization of these thrift and home financing institutions by a change in its constitution providing for membership on the part of each savings and loan institution in the United States Savings and Loan League. Thus today the United States Savings and Loan League represents the interests of savings and loan associations, cooperative banks, homestead associations, and all institutions of the general savings and loan type, wherever their interests can be advanced more effectively by group action than by individual effort. The number of members is 3,766.

The objectives of the League are:

1. To advance generally the interests of savings and loan associations, which term shall herein include cooperative banks, building and loan associations and other institutions engaged in the encouragement of thrift and the private financing of owner-occupied homes and other improved real estate.

2. To assist in carrying on, by educational means and otherwise, the promotion of thrift and the encouragement of private investment and the purchase of homes upon plans leading to debt-free home ownership.

3. To devise safe and equitable methods of conducting the business of such associations and, through educational means, to endeavor to secure the adoption of such methods.

4. As incidental to the main objectives and purposes of the League stated above, to make studies of statutes, rules, regulations, examination and supervisory procedures affecting the savings and loan business and to devise ways and means of improving the same.

The activities of the League are many and varied and depend largely upon the needs of the member institutions from one year to the next. Basically, the activities center around research, details of operating a savings and home financing business, collection and dissemination of management ideas and operating aids to the entire membership, setting of broad operating and management policies through committees of the League disseminated in a variety of ways, and the promotion of modern practices which contribute to the building of a more useful and sound system of thrift and home financing institutions.

Headquarters are in Chicago. The League also maintains an office in Washington, D.C., where contact with the Washington scene is maintained for the Chicago office.

Through an affiliate organization, the American Savings and Loan Institute, the League conducts an extensive educational program for the officers and employees of member associations, consisting of a curriculum of 20 courses through night school classes in 70 cities, correspondence courses, and a Graduate School of Savings and Loan held for two weeks each summer on the campus of the University of Indiana. It also sponsors a professional appraisal organization, The Society of Residential Appraisers.

The League publishes two monthlies, *Savings and Loan News* and the *Directors Digest,* a quarterly statistical letter, the annual *Savings and Loan Annals,* as well as a *Legal Bulletin,* a *Confidential Bulletin* for managers, and occasional *Management Bulletins.* A news bureau and a library are maintained.

The United States Savings and Loan League is a member of the International Union of Building Societies and Savings and Loan Associations, which comprise the national organizations of all countries where there is an organization of the savings and loan or building society business. It sends delegates to the International Congresses and its leaders hold offices in the International Union.

Other Associations

Descriptions of the Association of Better Business Bureaus, Association of Casualty and Surety Companies, and the National Association of Credit Men are included here although their membership is not made up primarily of financial institutions. Their operations are of interest to the business community, and they do have a financial implication.

Better Business Bureaus cut squarely across industry lines and are united by a single function: that of insisting on truth and candor in advertising and fair dealing generally in business transactions. The casualty companies are risk-bearing, rather than financial institutions, but the line of demarcation is tenuous. The Credit Men's Association is more concerned with trade credit than with business financing, but the commercial banks generally are active in both the national organization and in local units.

The Association of Better Business Bureaus

The Association of Better Business Bureaus, Inc., is an independent, nonprofit corporation which has existed in its present form as a full-time organization with a paid staff since October 1946. Prior to that time it was operated on a part-time basis by the elected officers of the Association. Permanent headquarters are in New York City.

The Association is the service organization of the Better Business Bureau movement. It coordinates the activities of member organizations. It acts in a research, planning, and public relations capacity on behalf of its members. It is comprised of 83 local organizations throughout the United States, the National Better Business Bureau, and six Bureaus in Canada.

The National Better Business Bureau and the local Bureaus enjoy a common relationship with one another through the Association. All Bureaus are independent, nonprofit organizations, directed by elected officers representing a diversity of business firms. Local Bureaus are concerned primarily with advertising and selling standards and practices which are local in nature. The National Bureau is interested in advertising and selling standards which are regional or national. The National Bureau also acts as the operating arm of the Association in that it physically implements many of the projects conceived or planned by the Association. The total number of member firms supporting the Bureaus is approximately 60,000.

Association of Casualty and Surety Companies

This national association is in the happy position that its major operations are as unmistakably in the public interest as they are to the benefit of its members. The business of the 80 stock casualty and surety companies which make up its membership is to carry the risk of accidental injury to persons or property for its policyholders; the policyholders are the direct beneficiaries of the very extensive effort of the Association to reduce accidents, and so are the people who might be killed, or whose property might be destroyed. The national Conservation Bureau—one of the largest departments of the Association—is devoted solely to accident prevention work. More than 350,000 copies of its "Man and the Motor Car," written for drivers' training classes in high schools, are in use in over 4,000 high schools. The Association also financed the founding of America's first advanced school for safety education, the National Center for Safety Education at New York University, and this Association provides the Center's chief financial support.

Founded in 1929 the Association is the successor of the Association of Casualty and Surety Executives, which was created in the early '20's to deal with problems calling for group action in the period of expansion following World War I. Headquarters are in New York City, where a staff of 160 persons handle its extensive program. Branch offices are maintained in Washington, Chicago, and San Francisco.

The National Conservation Bureau, mentioned above, has five major divisions: Industrial Safety, Traffic and Transportation, Education, Special Service, and Library. There are also a number of other departments. The Casualty Department deals with such problems as workmen's compensation insurance, occupational disease, automobile liability insurance, and compulsory health insurance. The Law Department follows legislative, administrative, and judicial developments which affect it and the insuring public. It is said that in one recent four-month period the Department studied and followed no less than 5,800 bills introduced in state legislatures and the Congress for a possible bearing on the casualty and surety business.

The Fidelity and Surety Department studies and analyzes laws and legislative proposals affecting the bonding business. The Claims Bureau labors to improve claim conditions among the member companies and those they serve, to accelerate the just settlement of claims, and to detect and prevent fradulent claims. The Division of Research conducts objective studies of specific problems of the casualty and surety business and seeks to interpret changing conditions in terms of their effect upon the industry. The Library contains 8,000 volumes, and a file of 50,000 clippings, catalogued under 3,000 headings.

Preventing accidents and promoting a safer America, protecting insurance rates against criminal fakers and racketeers, encouraging more equitable workmen's compensation laws, promoting a wider employment of the physically impaired, furnishing principal support for such institutions as the Center for Safety Education, the activities of the Association of Casualty and Surety Companies in reducing losses for its members coincide directly with the public interest.

National Association of Credit Men

Founded in 1896 the National Association of Credit Men now has over 30,000 members cooperating through 134 local associations. National headquarters are maintained in New York City.

The efforts of the Association are directed toward fostering honesty and fair dealing in credit transactions, facilitating the exchange of credit information, combating fraud and crime, and encouraging uniform laws with respect to trade and commerce.

A Credit Interchange Service is operated by national headquarters to provide the members with accurate information on the consolidated obligations of all known creditors. Supplementing this service are over 600 Industry Credit Groups consisting of executives in the same or allied lines of business, which meet to exchange information on their joint problems.

A monthly magazine is published under the title *Credit and Financial Management*. A confidential monthly review of business by the executive manager is another service.

Local associations conduct more or less extensive programs, depending upon the locality. In the larger cities complete organization will be found, with full-time staff members maintaining collection and adjustment bureaus, publishing standardized forms, and conducting courses of education.

Conclusion

Free enterprise imposes upon businessmen responsibility for the good conduct of the industries of which they are a part. Such responsibility for a whole industry can be discharged only by understanding and agreement among the units which compose it. If an industry cannot, in its own self-interest, regulate itself, then it will be regulated by government. To the extent that any industry must be regulated from without, it is that much less a free enterprise.

Thus the trade association is logical, necessary, and in the public interest. To function effectively the association must study and investigate. From its studies emerge rules of good conduct. This is the common

pattern in trade associations, including those which have been reviewed herein.

Suggested Readings

BOOKS

Chapman, Charles C., *The Development of American Business and Banking Thought, 1913–1936*. New York: Longmans, Green & Co., Inc., 1936.

Fainsod, Merle, *Government and the American Economy*. New York: W. W. Norton & Co., Inc., 1941.

Kirsh, Benjamin S. with Shapiro, Harold Roland, *Trade Associations in Law and Business*. New York: Central Book Company, 1938.

Lynch, David, *The Concentration of Economic Power*. New York: Columbia University Press, 1946.

National Industrial Conference Board:
Industrial Standardization. New York: NICB, 1929.
Trade Associations, Their Economic Significance and Legal Status. New York: NICB, 1925.

Naylor, Emmett Hay, *Trade Associations: Their Organization and Management*. New York: The Ronald Press Co., 1921.

Smith, M. A., *Employer-Employee Relations Activities of Trade Associations*. Chamber of Commerce of the United States, Trade Association Department, 1948.

Southern Pine Association, *Trade Associations: Their Development, Value, and Service*. New Orleans: The Association, 1947.

Trade Association Management. Chicago: National Institute for Commercial and Trade Organization Executives.

U.S. Department of Commerce:
National Associations of the United States. Washington: Government Printing Office, 1942.
Trade Associations Activities, prepared by L. E. Warford and Richard May. Washington: Government Printing Office, 1923.
Trade Associations Industrial Research. Washington: Government Printing Office, 1948.
Trade Associations Opportunities in Marketing. Research. Washington: Government Printing Office, 1948.
United States Associations in World Trade and Affairs. Washington: Government Printing Office, 1947.

U.S. Congress, Temporary National Economic Committee:
Monograph #18, *Investigation of Concentration of Economic Power*
Monograph #21, *Competition and Monopoly in American Industry*
Monograph #38, *A Study of the Construction and the Enforcement of the Federal Anti-Trust Laws Made Under the Auspices of the Treasury Department*.

PERIODICALS

Cherrington, Homer V., "National Association of Security Dealers." *Harvard Business Review*, November 1949.

Mitchell, Walter, Jr., "Organization of Industry: British and American Trade Groups Compared." *Dun's Review*, June 1946, pp. 15-17.

Robbins, I. D., "Management Services for Small Business Through Trade Associations." *Harvard Business Review*, September 1948, pp. 627-640.

Smith, M. A., "They Pay Off in Better Bargaining: Got a Labor Problem, See Your Trade Association." *Nation's Business*, July 1948, pp. 35-37.

Sawyer, Charles, "The Place of the Trade Association in the National Economy." *Journal of the American Trade Association Executives*, October 1949, pp. 7-10.

"Trade Associations Influence Grows," *Commerce*, July 1946, pp. 20-22.

Permanent Addresses of
Trade Associations in the Financial Field

American Bankers Association
12 E. 36th St.
New York City 16, N.Y.

American Institute of Banking
12 E. 36th St.
New York City 16, N.Y.

American Institute of Real Estate Appraisers
22 W. Monroe St., Chicago 3, Ill.

Association of Bank Women
60 E. 42nd St., New York City 17, N.Y.

Association of Casualty and Surety Companies
60 John St., New York City 7, N.Y.

Association of Reserve City Bankers
105 W. Adams St., Chicago 3, Ill.

Bankers' Association for Foreign Trade
No permanent address

Consumer Bankers Association
630 Washington Building, Washington 5, D.C.

Financial Public Relations Association
231 So. LaSalle St., Chicago 4, Ill.

Independent Bankers Association
Sauk Centre, Minnesota
(Mr. Ben DuBois, Secretary)

Investment Bankers Association of America
33 So. Clark St., Chicago 3, Ill.

Mortgage Bankers Association of America
111 W. Washington St., Chicago 2, Ill.

National Association of Bank Auditors and Comptrollers
38 So. Dearborn St., Chicago 3, Ill.

National Association of Credit Men
1 Park Avenue, New York City 16, N.Y.

National Association of Mutual Savings Banks
60 E. 42nd St., New York City 17, N.Y.

National Association of Security Dealers
625 K St., N.W., Washington 6, D.C.

National Better Business Bureau, Inc.
Chrysler Building, New York City 17, N.Y.

National Institute of Real Estate Brokers
22 W. Monroe St., Chicago 3, Ill.

National Savings and Loan League
907 Ring Building
18th and M Sts., N.W.
Washington 6, D.C.

Robert Morris Associates
1417 Sansom St.
Philadelphia 2, Penna.

The American Safe Deposit Association
No permanent address

United States Savings and Loan League
221 N. LaSalle St., Chicago 1, Ill.

NOTE: *Rand, McNally Bankers Directory* (published twice a year by Rand, McNally & Company, Chicago 5, Ill.) contains a list of current officers and addresses of banking associations, both national and state, safe deposit associations, chapters of Robert Morris Associates, government agencies operating in the banking field, and other valuable information.

Index

Agricultural financing institutions—*Continued:*
intermediate and short-term credit—*Continued:*
Federal Intermediate Credit Bank System, 238-239
merchants and dealers, 237
private, 236-238
production credit system, 239-240
public and semipublic, 238-242
regional credit corporations, 239
long-term credit, 227-236
commercial banks, 227, 228, 229
Farmers' Home Administration, 235-236
Federal Farm Mortgage Corporation, 234-235
Federal Land Bank System, 231-234
joint stock land banks, 234
life insurance companies, 228, 229-230
private, 227-231
private mortgage companies, 229
public and semi-public, 231-236
Agricultural Marketing Act of 1929, 242
Aircraft Financing, 698
Aircraft insurance, 551
Aldrich, Nelson, 53, 54
Aldrich-Vreeland Act, 53
American Association of Small Loan Brokers, 716
American Bankers Association, 685, 686, 730-747, 751, 752
administration, 745-747
American Institute of Banking, 741, 742, 743
commissions and committees, 747
councils, 747
departments, 747
divisions, 745, 746
education of bank personnel, 741-743
first convention, 740-741
Graduate School of Banking, 742, 743
improved banking techniques, 743
manuals on instalment buying, 697-699
nationwide collection system, 708
objectives, 741
public relations, 743-745
sections, 745, 746
State Association Section, 745
American Cyanamid Company, 381, 382, 383
American Institute of Accountants, 583
American Institute of Banking, 741, 742, 743, 750
American Institute of Real Estate Appraisers, 759, 762-763

American Light and Traction Company, bond contracts, 377
American Research and Development Corporation, 438
American Safe Deposit Association, 752
American Telephone and Telegraph Company, 360
bond maturities, 377
Amortized loan:
defined, 156-157
monthly, tables, 157
Anderson, B. M., 64
Annual report:
filed with proxy solicitation, 598
regulation of, 597
Annuities, 535, 536, 538-540
annuity certain, 539-540
buying, 659-661
combined with life insurance, 660
deferred, 659, 660
group, 659
immediate, 659
life, 539
payments, 660
refund life, 539
retirement, 660
Anti-fraud laws, 309
Apparel Trades Book, 614
Appraisal Reporting Techniques, 763
Appraisers Journal, 763
Appreciation, yield vs., 317-319
Arrangements, alternative to bankruptcy proceedings, 599-600
Assets, earning, 41-42
Associates Investment Company, 727
Association of Bank Women, 758-759
Association of Better Business Bureaus, 766
Association of Casualty and Surety Companies, 766, 767-768
Association of Reserve City Bankers, 756-758
Associations, trade, 748-770
Atlas Corporation, 439
At-the-market orders, 294-295
Auction:
double, defined, 272
trading by, 272
Audit:
annual, of common trust funds, 473
of borrower's accounts, 212
Australia, gold standard in, 483
Automobile:
financing:
instalment plan, 727, 728
loans, 695-696
manuals on, 697

Trader:
defined, 273
floor, 281, 335
Trading:
defined, 273
department, 300
fees, 451-453
margin, 343-344, 346
New York Curb Exchange, 347, 350-351
New York Stock Exchange, 331-332
regional stock exchanges, 353-354
Transactions:
bond, 293
buyer's option, 293
calls, 292
cash, 290, 293
clearing, 292-293
delayed delivery, 293
margin, 290-291
odd-lot, 291
puts, 292
regular way, 293
round lots, 291
sellers option, 293
short sales, 291-292
types of, 290-293
when, as, and if issued, 293
Transfer agent, 37
corporate trusts, 477
Transportation industries, regulation of, 602
Trant, James B., 459
Travelers' checks, sale of, 138, 153
Treasurer of bank, 35
Treasury, United States (see United States Treasury)
Treasury bonds, 652, 653, 654
Treasury Bulletin, 508
Trent affair, 19
Tri-Continental Corporation, 453
Truman, Harry S., 448
Trust:
accounts:
increase in, 429
operations, U.S. Treasury, 511-512
authority, 465-466
business:
defined, 463-464
economics of, 478-479
companies (see also Trusts):
advantages of, 461-463
and trust departments, 459-481
defined, 465
fiduciary services of, 459-460
first, 461
government supervision, 463
history of, 460-461
powers, 466-467

settlement of estates, 474-475
state laws governing, 467
terminology, 463-465
use of common trust funds, 463
deed, 160
trustee under, 475-476
departments, 34 (see also Trust companies):
common trust funds, 473
management of, 468-469
of national banks, 465-466
of state banks, 465
operational management, 36-37
operation of, 42
principles of, 468-469
funds:
common, 449, 463, 472-474
investment of, 471-474
notice of accounting, 473-474
prudent-man rule, 472
indentures, government regulation, 601-602
institutions, defined, 463-464
investments, government regulation, 592
money, fear of, 53-54
powers, 466
Trustee:
defined, 463
for corporate trust, 475
in bankruptcy, 464
trust department as, 36-37
under corporate mortgage, 464, 475-476
under deed of trust, 475-476
Trust Indenture Act of 1939, 403, 410, 479
Trusts:
community, 469
corporate, 469, 475-478 (see also Corporate trusts)
court, 36
fixed, 439, 443-445
institutional, 469
length of, 471
living, 36
personal, 36, 469, 470
setting up, 677-678
Turnpike corporations, 359, 393
Two-dollar broker, 334

Underwriters:
agreements among, 418-420
commitments assumed by, 422
Underwriters' Laboratories, 570
Underwriting:
accounts, management of, 423-426
agreements, 416
division, 298
insurance, 565-566